Essentials of Corporate Finance

Essentials of Corporate Finance

Tenth Edition

Stephen A. Ross

Randolph W. Westerfield
University of Southern California

Bradford D. Jordan
University of Kentucky

Mc
Graw
Hill
Education

ESSENTIALS OF CORPORATE FINANCE

Published by McGraw-Hill Education, 2 Penn Plaza, New York, NY 10121. Copyright © 2020 by McGraw-Hill Education. All rights reserved. Printed in the United States of America. No part of this publication may be reproduced or distributed in any form or by any means, or stored in a database or retrieval system, without the prior written consent of McGraw-Hill Education, including, but not limited to, in any network or other electronic storage or transmission, or broadcast for distance learning.

Some ancillaries, including electronic and print components, may not be available to customers outside the United States.

This book is printed on acid-free paper.

1 2 3 4 5 6 7 8 9 LWI 21 20 19

ISBN 978-1-260-56556-0
MHID 1-260-56556-4

Cover Image: ©vladitto/Shutterstock

mheducation.com/highered

About the Authors

Stephen A. Ross

Stephen A. Ross was the Franco Modigliani Professor of Finance and Economics at the Sloan School of Management, Massachusetts Institute of Technology. One of the most widely published authors in finance and economics, Professor Ross was widely recognized for his work in developing the Arbitrage Pricing Theory and his substantial contributions to the discipline through his research in signaling, agency theory, option pricing, and the theory of the term structure of interest rates, among other topics. A past president of the American Finance Association, he also served as an associate editor of several academic and practitioner journals. He was a trustee of CalTech. He died suddenly in March 2017.

Randolph W. Westerfield
Marshall School of Business, *University of Southern California*

Randolph W. Westerfield is Dean Emeritus of the University of Southern California's Marshall School of Business and is the Charles B. Thornton Professor of Finance Emeritus. Professor Westerfield came to USC from the Wharton School, University of Pennsylvania, where he was the chairman of the finance department and member of the finance faculty for 20 years. He is a member of the Board of Trustees of Oak Tree Capital Mutual Funds. His areas of expertise include corporate financial policy, investment management, and stock market price behavior.

Bradford D. Jordan
Gatton College of Business and Economics, *University of Kentucky*

Bradford D. Jordan is Professor of Finance and holder of the duPont Endowed Chair in Banking and Financial Services. He has a long-standing interest in both applied and theoretical issues in corporate finance and has extensive experience teaching all levels of corporate finance and financial management policy. Professor Jordan has published numerous articles on issues such as cost of capital, capital structure, and the behavior of security prices. He is a past president of the Southern Finance Association and is coauthor of *Fundamentals of Investments: Valuation and Management*, 8th edition, a leading investments text, also published by McGraw-Hill Education.

From the Authors

When we first wrote *Essentials of Corporate Finance*, we thought there might be a small niche for a briefer book that really focused on what students with widely varying backgrounds and interests needed to carry away from an introductory finance course. We were wrong. There was a huge niche! What we learned is that our text closely matches the needs of instructors and faculty at hundreds of schools across the country. As a result, the growth we have experienced through the first nine editions of *Essentials* has far exceeded anything we thought possible.

With the tenth edition of *Essentials of Corporate Finance*, we have continued to refine our focus on our target audience, which is the undergraduate student taking a core course in business or corporate finance. This can be a tough course to teach. One reason is that the class is usually required of all business students, so it is not uncommon for a majority of the students to be nonfinance majors. In fact, this may be the only finance course many of them will ever have. With this in mind, our goal in *Essentials* is to convey the most important concepts and principles at a level that is approachable for the widest possible audience.

To achieve our goal, we have worked to distill the subject down to its bare essentials (hence, the name of this book), while retaining a decidedly modern approach to finance. We always have maintained that the subject of corporate finance can be viewed as the workings of a few very powerful intuitions. We also think that understanding the "why" is just as important, if not more so, than understanding the "how"—especially in an introductory course. Based on the gratifying market feedback we have received from our previous editions, as well as from our other text, *Fundamentals of Corporate Finance* (now in its twelfth edition), many of you agree.

By design, this book is not encyclopedic. As the table of contents indicates, we have a total of 18 chapters. Chapter length is about 30 pages, so the text is aimed squarely at a single-term course, and most of the book can be realistically covered in a typical semester or quarter. Writing a book for a one-term course necessarily means some picking and choosing, with regard to both topics and depth of coverage. Throughout, we strike a balance by introducing and covering the essentials (there's that word again!) while leaving some more specialized topics to follow-up courses.

The other things we always have stressed, and have continued to improve with this edition, are readability and pedagogy. *Essentials* is written in a relaxed, conversational style that invites the students to join in the learning process rather than being a passive information absorber. We have found that this approach dramatically increases students' willingness to read and learn on their own. Between larger and larger class sizes and the ever-growing demands on faculty time, we think this is an essential (!) feature for a text in an introductory course.

Throughout the development of this book, we have continued to take a hard look at what is truly relevant and useful. In doing so, we have worked to downplay purely theoretical issues and minimize the use of extensive and elaborate calculations to illustrate points that are either intuitively obvious or of limited practical use.

As a result of this process, three basic themes emerge as our central focus in writing *Essentials of Corporate Finance*:

An Emphasis on Intuition   We always try to separate and explain the principles at work on a commonsense, intuitive level before launching into any specifics. The underlying ideas are discussed first in very general terms and then by way of examples that illustrate in more concrete terms how a financial manager might proceed in a given situation.

A Unified Valuation Approach   We treat net present value (NPV) as the basic concept underlying corporate finance. Many texts stop well short of consistently integrating this important principle. The most basic and important notion, that NPV represents the excess of market value over cost, often is lost in an overly mechanical approach that emphasizes computation at the expense of comprehension. In contrast, every subject we cover is firmly rooted in valuation, and care is taken throughout to explain how particular decisions have valuation effects.

A Managerial Focus   Students shouldn't lose sight of the fact that financial management concerns management. We emphasize the role of the financial manager as decision maker, and we stress the need for managerial input and judgment. We consciously avoid "black box" approaches to finance, and, where appropriate, the approximate, pragmatic nature of financial analysis is made explicit, possible pitfalls are described, and limitations are discussed.

Today, as we prepare once again to enter the market, our goal is to stick with and build on the principles that have brought us this far. However, based on an enormous amount of feedback we have received from you and your colleagues, we have made this edition and its package even more flexible than previous editions. We offer flexibility in coverage and pedagogy by providing a wide variety of features in the book to help students learn about corporate finance. We also provide flexibility in package options by offering the most extensive collection of teaching, learning, and technology aids of any corporate finance text. Whether you use just the textbook, or the book in conjunction with other products, we believe you will find a combination with this edition that will meet your needs.

Randolph W. Westerfield
Bradford D. Jordan

Organization of the Text

We designed *Essentials of Corporate Finance* to be as flexible and modular as possible. There are a total of nine parts, and, in broad terms, the instructor is free to decide the particular sequence. Further, within each part, the first chapter generally contains an overview and survey. Thus, when time is limited, subsequent chapters can be omitted. Finally, the sections placed early in each chapter are generally the most important, and later sections frequently can be omitted without loss of continuity. For these reasons, the instructor has great control over the topics covered, the sequence in which they are covered, and the depth of coverage.

Just to get an idea of the breadth of coverage in the tenth edition of *Essentials*, the following grid presents for each chapter some of the most significant new features, as well as a few selected chapter highlights. Of course, in every chapter, figures, opening vignettes, boxed features, and in-chapter illustrations and examples using real companies have been thoroughly updated as well. In addition, the end-of-chapter material has been completely revised.

Chapters	Selected Topics	Benefits to Users
PART ONE	**Overview of Financial Management**	
Chapter 1	*New* opener discussing Uber	
	Updated Finance Matters box on corporate ethics	Describes ethical issues in the context of mortgage fraud, offshoring, and tax havens.
	Updated information on executive and celebrity compensation	Highlights important developments regarding the very current question of appropriate executive compensation.
	Updated Work the Web box on stock quotes	
	Goal of the firm and agency problems	Stresses value creation as the most fundamental aspect of management and describes agency issues that can arise.
	Ethics, financial management, and executive compensation	Brings in real-world issues concerning conflicts of interest and current controversies surrounding ethical conduct and management pay.
	New proxy fight example involving Trian Partners and Procter & Gamble	
	New takeover battle discussion involving Verizon and Yahoo!	
PART TWO	**Understanding Financial Statements and Cash Flow**	
Chapter 2	*New* opener discussing the Tax Cuts and Jobs Act of 2017	
	Cash flow vs. earnings	Clearly defines cash flow and spells out the differences between cash flow and earnings.
	Market values vs. book values	Emphasizes the relevance of market values over book values.
	New discussion of corporate taxes in light of the TCJA	

Chapters	Selected Topics	Benefits to Users
Chapter 3	Additional explanation of alternative formulas for sustainable and internal growth rates	Expanded explanation of growth rate formulas clears up a common misunderstanding about these formulas and the circumstances under which alternative formulas are correct.
	Updated opener on PE ratios	
	Updated examples on Amazon vs. Alibaba	
	Updated Work the Web box on financial ratios	Discusses how to find and analyze profitability ratios.
	Updated Finance Matters box on financial ratios	Describes how to interpret ratios.

PART THREE — Valuation of Future Cash Flows

Chapters	Selected Topics	Benefits to Users
Chapter 4	First of two chapters on time value of money	Relatively short chapter introduces just the basic ideas on time value of money to get students started on this traditionally difficult topic.
	Updated Finance Matters box on collectibles	
Chapter 5	Second of two chapters on time value of money	Covers more advanced time value topics with numerous examples, calculator tips, and Excel spreadsheet exhibits. Contains many real-world examples.
	Updated opener on professional athletes' salaries	Provides a real-world example of why it's important to properly understand how to value costs incurred today versus future cash inflows.
	Updated Finance Matters box on lotteries	
	Updated Finance Matters box on student loans	

PART FOUR — Valuing Stocks and Bonds

Chapters	Selected Topics	Benefits to Users
Chapter 6	*New* opener on negative interest on various sovereign bonds	Discusses the importance of interest rates and how they relate to bonds.
	Bond valuation	Thorough coverage of bond price/yield concepts.
	Updated bond features example using Sprint issue	
	Interest rates and inflation	Highly intuitive discussion of inflation, the Fisher effect, and the term structure of interest rates.
	Updated "fallen angels" example using Teva Pharmaceuticals issue	
	"Clean" vs. "dirty" bond prices and accrued interest	Clears up the pricing of bonds between coupon payment dates and also bond market quoting conventions.
	Updated Treasury quotes exhibit and discussion	
	Updated historic interest rates figure	
	FINRA's TRACE system and transparency in the corporate bond market	Up-to-date discussion of new developments in fixed income with regard to price, volume, and transactions reporting.
	"Make-whole" call provisions	Up-to-date discussion of relatively new type of call provision that has become very common.

Chapters	Selected Topics	Benefits to Users
Chapter 7	Stock valuation	Thorough coverage of constant and nonconstant growth models.
	Updated opener on difference in dividend payouts	
	Updated discussion of the NYSE, including its acquisition by ICE and rising role of technology of the floor	Up-to-date description of major stock market operations.
	Updated Finance Matters box on the OTCBB and the Pink Sheets markets	

PART FIVE Capital Budgeting

Chapters	Selected Topics	Benefits to Users
Chapter 8	*Updated* opener on GE's "Ecomagination" program	Illustrates the growing importance of "green" business.
	First of two chapters on capital budgeting	Relatively short chapter introduces key ideas on an intuitive level to help students with this traditionally difficult topic.
	NPV, IRR, MIRR, payback, discounted payback, and accounting rate of return	Consistent, balanced examination of advantages and disadvantages of various criteria.
Chapter 9	Project cash flow	Thorough coverage of project cash flows and the relevant numbers for a project analysis.
	New opener on project failures and successes	Shows the importance of properly evaluating net present value.
	New discussion of bonus depreciation	
	Scenario and sensitivity "what-if" analyses	Illustrates how to actually apply and interpret these tools in a project analysis.

PART SIX Risk and Return

Chapters	Selected Topics	Benefits to Users
Chapter 10	*Updated* opener on stock market performance	Discusses the relationship between risk and return as it relates to personal investing.
	Capital market history	Extensive coverage of historical returns, volatilities, and risk premiums.
	Market efficiency	Efficient markets hypothesis discussed along with common misconceptions.
	Geometric vs. arithmetic returns	Discusses calculation and interpretation of geometric returns. Clarifies common misconceptions regarding appropriate use of arithmetic vs. geometric average returns.
	Updated Finance Matters box on professional fund management and performance	
Chapter 11	Diversification, systematic, and unsystematic risk	Illustrates basics of risk and return in a straightforward fashion.
	Updated opener on stock price reactions to announcements	
	Updated beta coefficients exhibit and associated discussion	Develops the security market line with an intuitive approach that bypasses much of the usual portfolio theory and statistics.
	New discussion of alpha	

PART SEVEN Long-Term Financing

Chapters	Selected Topics	Benefits to Users
Chapter 12	Cost of capital estimation	Intuitive development of the WACC and a complete, web-based illustration of cost of capital for a real company.
	Updated WACC calculations for Eastman	
	Geometric vs. arithmetic growth rates	Both approaches are used in practice. Clears up issues surrounding growth rate estimates.

Chapters	Selected Topics	Benefits to Users
	Updated section on company valuation with the WACC	Explores the difference between valuing a project and valuing a company.
Chapter 13	Basics of financial leverage	Illustrates effect of leverage on risk and return.
	Optimal capital structure	Describes the basic trade-offs leading to an optimal capital structure.
	New chapter opener on Tax Cuts and Jobs Act	
	New discussion of the effects of the TCJA on corporate taxes	
	Financial distress and bankruptcy	Briefly surveys the bankruptcy process.
Chapter 14	*Updated* opener with Apple dividend announcement	Raises questions about why raising dividends and repurchasing stock would please investors.
	Updated figures on aggregate dividends, stock repurchases, and proportion of firms paying dividends	Brings students the latest thinking and evidence on dividend policy.
	Dividends and dividend policy	Describes dividend payments and the factors favoring higher and lower payout policies. Includes recent survey results on setting dividend policy.
	Updated examples and *Finance Matters* box covering buyback activity	Explores the reasons that buybacks are gaining in popularity now, following the recent recession.
Chapter 15	IPO valuation	Extensive, up-to-date discussion of IPOs, including the 1999–2000 period and the recent Alibaba IPO.
	Dutch auctions	Explains uniform price ("Dutch") auctions using Google IPO as an example.
	New subsection on crowdfunding	Discusses the JOBS Act and crowdfunding.
	New subsection on initial coin offerings	
	New discussion of direct listing	
	Updated tables and figures on IPO initial returns and number of offerings	
PART EIGHT	**Short-Term Financial Management**	
Chapter 16	Operating and cash cycles	Stresses the importance of cash flow timing.
	Short-term financial planning	Illustrates the creation of cash budgets and the potential need for financing.
	Updated Finance Matters box discussing operating and cash cycles	Explores how comparing the cash cycles of companies can reveal whether a company is performing well.
Chapter 17	Cash collection and disbursement	Examination of systems used by firms to handle cash inflows and outflows.
	Credit management	Analysis of credit policy and implementation.
	Inventory management	Brief overview of important inventory concepts.
PART NINE	**Topics in Business Finance**	
Chapter 18	*New* opener on corporate cash held in international accounts	Raises questions about how currency appreciation affects the broader economy.
	Foreign exchange	Covers essentials of exchange rates and their determination.
	International capital budgeting	Shows how to adapt the basic DCF approach to handle exchange rates.
	Updated discussion of exchange rates and political risk	Discusses hedging and issues surrounding sovereign risk.
	New discussion of the Tax Cuts and Jobs Act	Discusses how U.S. legislation changes the way that corporations manage their profits to minimize taxes.

Learning Solutions

I n addition to illustrating relevant concepts and presenting up-to-date coverage, *Essentials of Corporate Finance* strives to present the material in a way that makes it engaging and easy to understand. To meet the varied needs of the intended audience, *Essentials of Corporate Finance* is rich in valuable learning tools and support.

Each feature can be categorized by the benefit to the student:

- Real financial decisions
- Application tools
- Study aids

REAL FINANCIAL DECISIONS

We have included two key features that help students connect chapter concepts to how decision makers use this material in the real world.

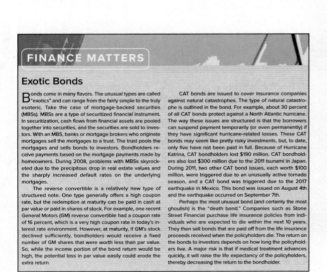

▲ FINANCE MATTERS BOXES

Most chapters include at least one *Finance Matters* box, which takes a chapter issue and shows how it is being used right now in everyday financial decision making.

▼ CHAPTER-OPENING VIGNETTES

Each chapter begins with a contemporary real-world event to introduce students to chapter concepts.

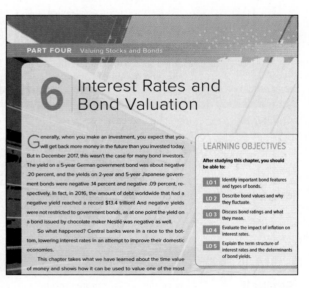

APPLICATION TOOLS

Because there is more than one way to solve problems in corporate finance, we include many sections that encourage students to learn or brush up on different problem-solving methods, including financial calculator and Excel spreadsheet skills.

▼ CHAPTER CASES

Located at the end of most chapters, these cases focus on hypothetical company situations that embody corporate finance topics. Each case presents a new scenario, data, and a dilemma. Several questions at the end of each case require students to analyze and focus on all of the material they learned from the chapters in that part. These are great for homework or in-class exercises and discussions!

▼ WORK THE WEB

These in-chapter boxes show students how to research financial issues using the web and how to use the information they find to make business decisions. All the *Work the Web* boxes also include interactive follow-up questions and exercises.

CHAPTER CASE

Financing S&S Air's Expansion Plans with a Bond Issue

Mark Sexton and Todd Story, the owners of S&S Air, have decided to expand their operations. They instructed their newly hired financial analyst, Chris Guthrie, to enlist an underwriter to help sell $20 million in new 10-year bonds to finance construction. Chris has entered into discussions with Renata Harper, an underwriter from the firm of Crowe & Mallard, about which bond features S&S Air should consider and what coupon rate the issue will likely have.

Although Chris is aware of the bond features, he is uncertain as to the costs and benefits of some features, so he isn't clear on how each feature would affect the coupon rate of the bond issue. You are Renata's assistant, and she has asked you to prepare a memo to Chris describing the effect of each of the following bond features on the coupon rate of the bond. She also would like you to list any advantages or disadvantages of each feature.

QUESTIONS

1. The security of the bond—that is, whether the bond has collateral.
2. The seniority of the bond.
3. The presence of a sinking fund.
4. A call provision with specified call dates and call prices.
5. A deferred call accompanying the preceding call provision.
6. A make-whole call provision.
7. Any positive covenants. Also, discuss several possible positive covenants S&S Air might consider.
8. Any negative covenants. Also, discuss several possible negative covenants S&S Air might consider.
9. A conversion feature (note that S&S Air is not a publicly traded company).
10. A floating rate coupon.

WORK THE WEB

Bond quotes have become more available with the rise of the web. One site where you can find current bond prices (from TRACE) is finra-markets.morningstar.com/BondCenter. We went to the site and entered "AZO" for AutoZone, the well-known auto parts company. We found a total of 10 bond issues outstanding. Here you see the information we pulled up.

Issuer Name	Symbol	Callable	Sub-Product Type	Coupon	Maturity	Ratings Moody's/S&P	Last Sale Price	Yield
AUTOZONE INC	AZO3998669	Yes	Corporate Bond	3.125	07/15/2023	Baa1 BBB	97.584	3.855
AUTOZONE INC	AZO.GI	Yes	Corporate Bond	7.125	08/01/2018	Baa1 BBB	100.829	2.812
AUTOZONE INC	AZO3925874	Yes	Corporate Bond	2.875	01/15/2023	Baa1 BBB	96.504	1.711
AUTOZONE INC	AZO3844612	Yes	Corporate Bond	3.700	04/15/2022	Baa1 BBB	100.733	3.480
AUTOZONE INC	AZO435646	Yes	Corporate Bond	2.500	04/15/2021	Baa1 BBB	97.596	3.402
AUTOZONE INC	AZO4354612	Yes	Corporate Bond	3.125	04/21/2026	Baa1 BBB	92.945	4.205
AUTOZONE INC	AZO4295610	Yes	Corporate Bond	3.250	04/15/2025	Baa1 BBB	95.108	4.078
AUTOZONE INC	AZO.GK	Yes	Corporate Bond	4.000	11/15/2020	Baa1 BBB	101.758	3.152
AUTOZONE INC	AZO4354653	Yes	Corporate Bond	1.625	04/21/2019	Baa1 BBB	99.448	2.280
AUTOZONE INC	AZO4452965	Yes	Corporate Bond	3.750	06/01/2027	Baa1 BBB	96.408	4.238

Most of the information is self-explanatory. The Price and Yield columns show the price and yield to maturity of the issues based on their most recent sales. If you need more information about a particular issue, clicking on it will give you more details such as coupon dates and call dates.

QUESTIONS

1. Go to this website and find the last bond shown in the accompanying table. When was this bond issued? What was the size of the bond issue? What were the yield to maturity and price when the bond was issued?
2. When you search for Chevron bonds (CVX), you will find bonds for several companies listed. Why do you think Chevron has bonds issued with different corporate names?

EXPLANATORY WEB LINKS ▶

These web links are provided in the margins of the text. They are specifically selected to accompany text material and provide students and instructors with a quick way to check for additional information using the internet.

Bond Price Reporting

To learn more about TRACE, visit www.finra .org.

In 2002, transparency in the corporate bond market began to improve dramatically. Under new regulations, corporate bond dealers are now required to report trade information through what is known as the Trade Reporting and Compliance Engine (TRACE). A *Work the Web* box shows how to get TRACE prices.

As we mentioned before, the U.S. Treasury market is the largest securities market in the world. As with bond markets in general, it is an OTC market, so there is limited transparency. However, unlike the situation with bond markets in general, trading in Treasury issues, particularly recently issued ones, is very heavy. Each day, representative prices for outstanding Treasury issues are reported.

To purchase newly issued corporate bonds, go to www.incapital.com.

Figure 6.3 shows a portion of the daily Treasury note and bond listings from *The Wall Street Journal* online. The only difference between a Treasury note and a Treasury bond is that notes have 10 years or less to maturity at the time of issuance. The entry that begins "5/15/2030" is highlighted. Reading from left to right, the "5/15/2030" tells us that the bond's maturity is May 15, 2030. The 6.250 is the bond's coupon rate. Treasury bonds all make semiannual payments

WHAT'S ON THE WEB? ▶

These end-of-chapter activities show students how to use and learn from the vast amount of financial resources available on the internet.

6.1 Bond Quotes You can find current bond prices at finra-markets.morningstar.com/BondCenter. You want to find the bond prices and yields for bonds issued by Pfizer. Enter the ticker symbol "PFE" to do a search. What is the shortest-maturity bond issued by Pfizer that is outstanding? What is the longest-maturity bond? What is the credit rating for Pfizer's bonds? Do all of the bonds have the same credit rating? Why do you think this is?

6.2 Yield Curves You can find information regarding the most current bond yields at

WHAT'S ON THE WEB?

HOW TO CALCULATE BOND PRICES AND YIELDS USING A FINANCIAL CALCULATOR

CALCULATOR HINTS

Many financial calculators have fairly sophisticated built-in bond valuation routines. However, these vary quite a lot in implementation, and not all financial calculators have them. As a result, we will illustrate a simple way to handle bond problems that will work on just about any financial calculator.

To begin, of course, we first remember to clear out the calculator! Next, for Example 6.3, we have two bonds to consider, both with 12 years to maturity. The first one sells for $935.08 and has a 10 percent coupon rate. To find its yield, we can do the following:

Enter	12		100	−935.08	1,000
	N	**I/Y**	**PMT**	**PV**	**FV**
Solve for		11			

Notice that here we have entered both a future value of $1,000, representing the bond's face value, and a payment of 10 percent of $1,000, or $100, per year, representing the bond's annual coupon. Also notice that we have a negative sign on the bond's price, which we have entered as the present value.

◀ CALCULATOR HINTS

Calculator Hints is a self-contained section occurring in various chapters that first introduces students to calculator basics and then illustrates how to solve problems with the calculator. Appendix D goes into more detailed instructions by solving problems with two specific calculators.

EXCEL MASTER ICONS ▶

Topics covered in the comprehensive Excel Master supplement (found in Connect) are indicated by an icon in the margin.

6.1 BONDS AND BOND VALUATION

Excel Master coverage online

When a corporation (or government) wishes to borrow money from the public on a long-term basis, it usually does so by issuing, or selling, debt securities that are generically called bonds. In this section, we describe the various features of corporate bonds and some of the terminology associated with bonds. We then discuss the cash flows associated with a bond and how bonds can be valued using our discounted cash flow procedure.

SPREADSHEET STRATEGIES ▶

The unique *Spreadsheet Strategies* feature is also in a self-contained section, showing students how to set up spreadsheets to solve problems—a vital part of every business student's education.

SPREADSHEET STRATEGIES

HOW TO CALCULATE BOND PRICES AND YIELDS USING A SPREADSHEET

Like financial calculators, most spreadsheets have fairly elaborate routines available for calculating bond values and yields; many of these routines involve details that we have not discussed. However, setting up a simple spreadsheet to calculate prices or yields is straightforward, as our next two spreadsheets show:

	A	B	C	D	E	F	G	H
1								
2	Using a spreadsheet to calculate bond yields							
3								
4	Suppose we have a bond with 22 years to maturity, a coupon rate of 8 percent, and a price of							
5	$960.17. If the bond makes semiannual payments, what is its yield to maturity?							
6								
7	Settlement date:	1/1/00						
8	Maturity date:	1/1/22						
9	Annual coupon rate:	.08						
10	Bond price (% of par):	96.017						
11	Face value (% of par):	100						
12	Coupons per year:	2						
13	Yield to maturity:	.084						
14								

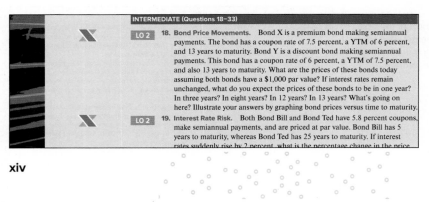

INTERMEDIATE (Questions 18–33)

LO 2 **18. Bond Price Movements.** Bond X is a premium bond making semiannual payments. The bond has a coupon rate of 7.5 percent, a YTM of 6 percent, and 13 years to maturity. Bond Y is a discount bond making semiannual payments. This bond has a coupon rate of 6 percent, a YTM of 7.5 percent, and also 13 years to maturity. What are the prices of these bonds today assuming both bonds have a $1,000 par value? If interest rates remain unchanged, what do you expect the prices of these bonds to be in one year? In three years? In eight years? In 12 years? In 13 years? What's going on here? Illustrate your answers by graphing bond prices versus time to maturity.

LO 2 **19. Interest Rate Risk.** Both Bond Bill and Bond Ted have 5.8 percent coupons, make semiannual payments, and are priced at par value. Bond Bill has 5 years to maturity, whereas Bond Ted has 25 years to maturity. If interest rates suddenly rise by 2 percent, what is the percentage change in the price

◀ EXCEL SIMULATIONS

Indicated by an Excel icon next to applicable end-of-chapter questions and problems, Excel simulation exercises are available for selected problems in Connect. For even more spreadsheet practice, check out Excel Master, also available in Connect.

STUDY AIDS

We want students to get the most from this book and this course, and we realize that students have different learning styles and study needs. We therefore present a number of study features to appeal to a wide range of students.

▼ LEARNING OBJECTIVES

Each chapter begins with a number of learning objectives that are key to the student's understanding of the chapter. Learning objectives also are linked to end-of-chapter problems and test bank questions.

▼ PEDAGOGICAL USE OF COLOR

We continue to use a full-color palette in *Essentials* not only to make the text more inviting, but, more important, as a functional element to help students follow the discussion. In almost every chapter, color plays an important, largely self-evident role.

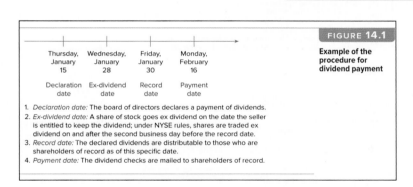

LEARNING OBJECTIVES

After studying this chapter, you should be able to:

LO 1 Determine the future value and present value of investments with multiple cash flows.

LO 2 Calculate loan payments, and find the interest rate on a loan.

LO 3 Describe how loans are amortized or paid off.

LO 4 Explain how interest rates are quoted (and misquoted).

What do professional athletes Alex Avila, Yu Darvish, an Jimmy Garoppolo have in common? All three signed b contracts in 2018. The contract values were reported as $8.25 m lion, $126 million, and $137.5 million, respectively. That's definite major league money, but, even so, reported numbers like these ca be misleading. For example, in January 2018, Avila signed with th Arizona Diamondbacks. His contract called for a salary of $4 milli in 2018 and $4.25 million for 2019. Not bad, especially for someor who makes a living using the "tools of ignorance" (jock jargon fo catcher's equipment).

A closer look at the numbers shows that Alex, Yu, and Jimm did pretty well, but nothing like the quoted figures. Using Yu's contract as an example, although the value was reported to be

---

Thursday, January 15 — Declaration date
Wednesday, January 28 — Ex-dividend date
Friday, January 30 — Record date
Monday, February 16 — Payment date

FIGURE 14.1

Example of the procedure for dividend payment

1. *Declaration date:* The board of directors declares a payment of dividends.
2. *Ex-dividend date:* A share of stock goes ex dividend on the date the seller is entitled to keep the dividend; under NYSE rules, shares are traded ex dividend on and after the second business day before the record date.
3. *Record date:* The declared dividends are distributable to those who are shareholders of record as of this specific date.
4. *Payment date:* The dividend checks are mailed to shareholders of record.

CRITICAL THINKING AND CONCEPTS REVIEW

LO 2 14.1 **Dividend Policy Irrelevance.** How is it possible that dividends are so important, but, at the same time, dividend policy is irrelevant?

LO 4 14.2 **Stock Repurchases.** What is the impact of a stock repurchase on a company's debt ratio? Does this suggest another use for excess cash?

LO 1 14.3 **Life Cycle Theory of Dividends.** Explain the life cycle theory of dividend payments. How does it explain corporate dividend payments that are seen in the stock market?

LO 1 14.4 **Dividend Chronology.** On Friday, December 8, Hometown Power Co.'s board of directors declares a dividend of 75 cents per share payable on Wednesday, January 17, to shareholders of record as of Wednesday, January 3. When is the ex-dividend date? If a shareholder buys stock before that date, who gets the dividends on those shares, the buyer or the seller?

LO 1 14.5 **Alternative Dividends.** Some corporations, like one British company that offers its large shareholders free crematorium use, pay dividends in kind (i.e., offer their services to shareholders at below-market cost). Should mutual funds invest in stocks that pay these dividends in kind? (The fundholders do not receive these services.)

CRITICAL THINKING QUESTIONS ▶

Every chapter ends with a set of critical thinking questions that challenge the students to apply the concepts they learned in the chapter to new situations.

CONCEPT QUESTIONS

6.1a What are the cash flows associated with a bond?

6.1b What is the general expression for the value of a bond?

6.1c Is it true that the only risk associated with owning a bond is that the issuer will no make all the payments? Explain.

◀ CONCEPT QUESTIONS

Chapter sections are intentionally kept short to promote a step-by-step, building-block approach to learning. Each section is then followed by a series of short concept questions that highlight the key ideas just presented. Students use these questions to make sure they can identify and understand the most important concepts as they read.

EXAMPLE 11.4 Portfolio Variance and Standard Deviation

In Example 11.3, what are the standard deviations on the two portfolios? To answer, calculate the portfolio returns in the two states. We will work with the second port 50 percent in Stock A and 25 percent in each of Stocks B and C. The relevant calc summarized as follows:

State of Economy	Probability of State	Returns		
		Stock A	Stock B	Stock C
Boom	.40	10%	15%	20%
Bust	.60	8	4	0

◄ NUMBERED EXAMPLES

Separate numbered and titled examples are extensively integrated into the chapters. These examples provide detailed applications and illustrations of the text material in a step-by-step format. Each example is completely self-contained so that students don't have to search for additional information. Based on our classroom testing, these examples are among the most useful learning aids because they provide both detail and explanation.

SUMMARY TABLES ►

These tables succinctly restate key principles, results, and equations. They appear whenever it is useful to emphasize and summarize a group of related concepts.

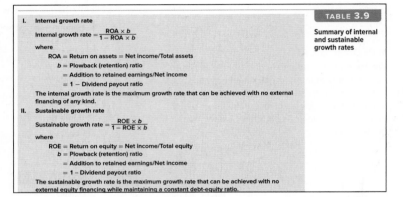

TABLE 3.9

Summary of internal and sustainable growth rates

I. Internal growth rate

$$\text{Internal growth rate} = \frac{\text{ROA} \times b}{1 - \text{ROA} \times b}$$

where

ROA = Return on assets = Net income/Total assets

b = Plowback (retention) ratio

= Addition to retained earnings/Net income

= 1 − Dividend payout ratio

The internal growth rate is the maximum growth rate that can be achieved with no external financing of any kind.

II. Sustainable growth rate

$$\text{Sustainable growth rate} = \frac{\text{ROE} \times b}{1 - \text{ROE} \times b}$$

where

ROE = Return on equity = Net income/Total equity

b = Plowback (retention) ratio

= Addition to retained earnings/Net income

= 1 − Dividend payout ratio

The sustainable growth rate is the maximum growth rate that can be achieved with no external equity financing while maintaining a constant debt-equity ratio.

3.2 RATIO ANALYSIS

Excel Master
coverage online

financial ratios
Relationships determined from a firm's financial

Another way of avoiding the problems involved in comparing companies of different sizes is to calculate and compare financial ratios. Such ratios are ways of comparing and investigating the relationships between different pieces of financial information. We cover some of the more common ratios next, but there are many others that we don't touch on.

One problem with ratios is that different people and different sources frequently don't compute them in exactly the same way, and this leads to much confusion. The specific definitions we use here may or may not be the same as ones you have seen or will see elsewhere.

◄ KEY TERMS

These are printed in blue the first time they appear and are defined within the text and in the margin.

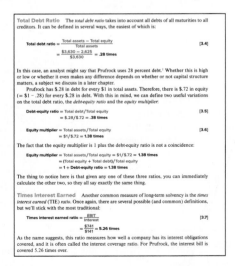

Total Debt Ratio The *total debt ratio* takes into account all debts of all maturities to all creditors. It can be defined in several ways, the easiest of which is:

$$\text{Total debt ratio} = \frac{\text{Total assets} - \text{Total equity}}{\text{Total assets}} \qquad [3.4]$$

$$= \frac{\$3,630 - 2,625}{\$3,630} = .28 \text{ times}$$

In this case, an analyst might say that Prufrock uses 28 percent debt.[1] Whether this is high or low or whether it even makes any difference depends on whether or not capital structure matters, a subject we discuss in a later chapter.

Prufrock has $.28 in debt for every $1 in total assets. Therefore, there is $.72 in equity (= $1 − .28) for every $.28 in debt. With this in mind, we can define two useful variations on the total debt ratio, the *debt-equity ratio* and the *equity multiplier*:

$$\text{Debt-equity ratio} = \text{Total debt/Total equity} \qquad [3.5]$$
$$= \$.28/\$.72 = .38 \text{ times}$$

$$\text{Equity multiplier} = \text{Total assets/Total equity} \qquad [3.6]$$
$$= \$1/\$.72 = 1.38 \text{ times}$$

The fact that the equity multiplier is 1 plus the debt-equity ratio is not a coincidence:

$$\text{Equity multiplier} = \text{Total assets/Total equity} = \$1/\$.72 = 1.38 \text{ times}$$
$$= (\text{Total equity} + \text{Total debt})/\text{Total equity}$$
$$= 1 + \text{Debt-equity ratio} = 1.38 \text{ times}$$

The thing to notice here is that given any one of these three ratios, you can immediately calculate the other two, so they all say exactly the same thing.

Times Interest Earned Another common measure of long-term solvency is the *times interest earned* (TIE) *ratio*. Once again, there are several possible (and common) definitions, but we'll stick with the most traditional:

$$\text{Times interest earned ratio} = \frac{\text{EBIT}}{\text{Interest}} \qquad [3.7]$$
$$= \frac{\$741}{\$141} = 5.26 \text{ times}$$

As the name suggests, this ratio measures how well a company has its interest obligations covered, and it is often called the interest coverage ratio. For Prufrock, the interest bill is covered 5.26 times over.

KEY EQUATIONS ►

These are called out in the text and identified by equation numbers. Appendix B shows the key equations by chapter.

Maximize the market value of the existing owners' equity.

◄ HIGHLIGHTED PHRASES

Throughout the text, important ideas are presented separately and printed in boxes to indicate their importance to the students.

SUMMARY AND CONCLUSIONS

This chapter has described how to go about putting together a discounted cash flow analysis and evaluating the results. In it, we covered:

1. The identification of relevant project cash flows. We discussed project cash flows and described how to handle some issues that often come up, including sunk costs, opportunity costs, financing costs, net working capital, and erosion.

2. Preparing and using pro forma, or projected, financial statements. We showed how pro forma financial statement information is useful in coming up with projected cash flows.

3. The use of scenario and sensitivity analysis. These tools are widely used to evaluate the impact of assumptions made about future cash flows and NPV estimates.

CHAPTER SUMMARY AND CONCLUSIONS ▲

These paragraphs review the chapter's key points and provide closure to the chapter.

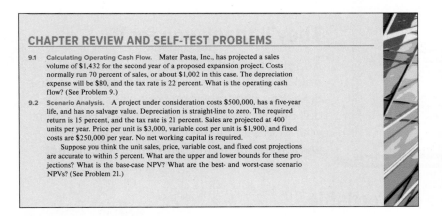

CHAPTER REVIEW AND SELF-TEST PROBLEMS

9.1 Calculating Operating Cash Flow. Mater Pasta, Inc., has projected a sales volume of $1,432 for the second year of a proposed expansion project. Costs normally run 70 percent of sales, or about $1,002 in this case. The depreciation expense will be $80, and the tax rate is 22 percent. What is the operating cash flow? (See Problem 9.)

9.2 Scenario Analysis. A project under consideration costs $500,000, has a five-year life, and has no salvage value. Depreciation is straight-line to zero. The required return is 15 percent, and the tax rate is 21 percent. Sales are projected at 400 units per year. Price per unit is $3,000, variable cost per unit is $1,900, and fixed costs are $250,000 per year. No net working capital is required.

Suppose you think the unit sales, price, variable cost, and fixed cost projections are accurate to within 5 percent. What are the upper and lower bounds for these projections? What is the base-case NPV? What are the best- and worst-case scenario NPVs? (See Problem 21.)

◄ CHAPTER REVIEW AND SELF-TEST PROBLEMS

Review and self-test problems appear after the chapter summaries. Detailed answers to the self-test problems immediately follow. These questions and answers allow students to test their abilities in solving key problems related to the content of the chapter. These problems are mapped to similar problems in the end-of-chapter material. The aim is to help students work through difficult problems using the authors' work as an example.

END-OF-CHAPTER QUESTIONS AND PROBLEMS ▶

We have found that many students learn better when they have plenty of opportunity to practice. We therefore provide extensive end-of-chapter questions and problems linked to Learning Objectives. The questions and problems are generally separated into three levels—Basic, Intermediate, and Challenge. All problems are fully annotated so that students and instructors can readily identify particular types. Throughout the text, we have worked to supply interesting problems that illustrate real-world applications of chapter material. Answers to selected end-of-chapter problems appear in Appendix C.

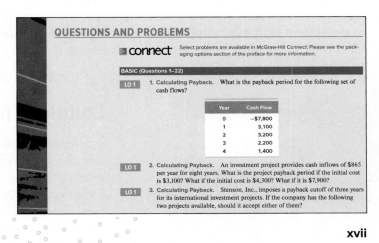

QUESTIONS AND PROBLEMS

≡ connect Select problems are available in McGraw-Hill *Connect*. Please see the packaging options section of the preface for more information.

BASIC (Questions 1–22)

LO 1 1. **Calculating Payback.** What is the payback period for the following set of cash flows?

Year	Cash Flow
0	−$7,800
1	3,100
2	3,200
3	2,200
4	1,400

LO 1 2. **Calculating Payback.** An investment project provides cash inflows of $865 per year for eight years. What is the project payback period if the initial cost is $3,100? What if the initial cost is $4,300? What if it is $7,900?

LO 1 3. **Calculating Payback.** Stenson, Inc., imposes a payback cutoff of three years for its international investment projects. If the company has the following two projects available, should it accept either of them?

 **connect®**

Students—study more efficiently, retain more and achieve better outcomes. Instructors—focus on what you love—teaching.

SUCCESSFUL SEMESTERS INCLUDE CONNECT

FOR INSTRUCTORS

You're in the driver's seat.

Want to build your own course? No problem. Prefer to use our turnkey, prebuilt course? Easy. Want to make changes throughout the semester? Sure. And you'll save time with Connect's auto-grading too.

65%
Less Time Grading

They'll thank you for it.

Adaptive study resources like SmartBook® help your students be better prepared in less time. You can transform your class time from dull definitions to dynamic debates. Hear from your peers about the benefits of Connect at **www.mheducation.com/highered/connect**

Make it simple, make it affordable.

Connect makes it easy with seamless integration using any of the major Learning Management Systems—Blackboard®, Canvas, and D2L, among others—to let you organize your course in one convenient location. Give your students access to digital materials at a discount with our inclusive access program. Ask your McGraw-Hill representative for more information.

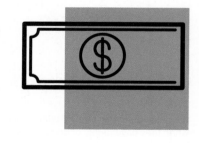

©Hill Street Studios/Tobin Rogers/Blend Images LLC

Solutions for your challenges.

A product isn't a solution. Real solutions are affordable, reliable, and come with training and ongoing support when you need it and how you want it. Our Customer Experience Group can also help you troubleshoot tech problems—although Connect's 99% uptime means you might not need to call them. See for yourself at **status.mheducation.com**

FOR STUDENTS

Effective, efficient studying.

Connect helps you be more productive with your study time and get better grades using tools like SmartBook, which highlights key concepts and creates a personalized study plan. Connect sets you up for success, so you walk into class with confidence and walk out with better grades.

©Shutterstock/wavebreakmedia

❝ I really liked this app—it made it easy to study when you don't have your text-book in front of you.**❞**

- Jordan Cunningham,
Eastern Washington University

Study anytime, anywhere.

Download the free ReadAnywhere app and access your online eBook when it's convenient, even if you're offline. And since the app automatically syncs with your eBook in Connect, all of your notes are available every time you open it. Find out more at **www.mheducation.com/readanywhere**

No surprises.

The Connect Calendar and Reports tools keep you on track with the work you need to get done and your assignment scores. Life gets busy; Connect tools help you keep learning through it all.

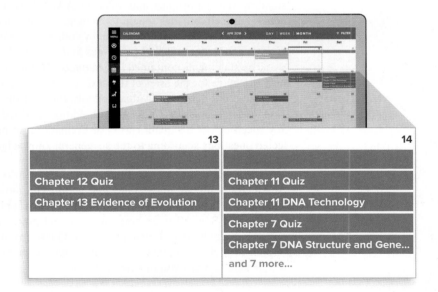

13
Chapter 12 Quiz
Chapter 13 Evidence of Evolution

14
Chapter 11 Quiz
Chapter 11 DNA Technology
Chapter 7 Quiz
Chapter 7 DNA Structure and Gene...
and 7 more...

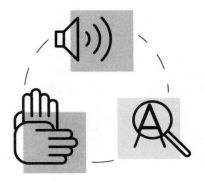

Learning for everyone.

McGraw-Hill works directly with Accessibility Services Departments and faculty to meet the learning needs of all students. Please contact your Accessibility Services office and ask them to email accessibility@mheducation.com, or visit **www.mheducation.com/about/accessibility.html** for more information.

Comprehensive Teaching and Learning Package

This edition of *Essentials* has more options than ever in terms of the textbook, instructor supplements, student supplements, and multimedia products. Mix and match to create a package that is perfect for your course!

Assurance of Learning Ready

Assurance of learning is an important element of many accreditation standards. *Essentials of Corporate Finance*, tenth edition, is designed specifically to support your assurance of learning initiatives. Each chapter in the book begins with a list of numbered learning objectives that appear throughout the end-of-chapter problems and exercises. Every test bank question also is linked to one of these objectives, in addition to level of difficulty, topic area, Bloom's Taxonomy level, and AACSB skill area. Connect, McGraw-Hill's online homework solution, and *EZ Test*, McGraw-Hill's easy-to-use test bank software, can search the test bank by these and other categories, providing an engine for targeted Assurance of Learning analysis and assessment.

AACSB Statement

McGraw-Hill Education is a proud corporate member of AACSB International. Understanding the importance and value of AACSB Accreditation, *Essentials of Corporate Finance*, tenth edition, has sought to recognize the curricula guidelines detailed in the AACSB standards for business accreditation by connecting selected questions in the test bank to the general knowledge and skill guidelines found in the AACSB standards.

The statements contained in *Essentials of Corporate Finance*, tenth edition, are provided only as a guide for the users of this text. The AACSB leaves content coverage and assessment within the purview of individual schools, the mission of the school, and the faculty. While *Essentials of Corporate Finance*, tenth edition, and the teaching package make no claim of any specific AACSB qualification or evaluation, we have, within the test bank, labeled selected questions according to the six general knowledge and skills areas.

McGraw-Hill Customer Care Contact Information

At McGraw-Hill, we understand that getting the most from new technology can be challenging. That's why our services don't stop after you purchase our products. You can e-mail our Product Specialists 24 hours a day to get product training online. Or you can search our knowledge bank of Frequently Asked Questions on our support website. For Customer Support, call **800-331-5094,** or visit **mpss.mhhe.com.** One of our Technical Support Analysts will be able to assist you in a timely fashion.

Instructor Supplements

- **Instructor's Manual (IM)**

  Prepared by LaDoris Baugh, Athens State University

  A great place to find new lecture ideas! This annotated outline for each chapter includes Lecture Tips, Real-World Tips, Ethics Notes, suggested PowerPoint slides, and, when appropriate, a video synopsis.

- **Solutions Manual (SM)**

  Prepared by Joseph Smolira, Belmont University, Bradford D. Jordan, University of Kentucky

  The *Essentials* Solutions Manual provides detailed solutions to the extensive end-of-chapter material, including concept review questions, quantitative problems, and cases. Select chapters also contain calculator solutions.

- **Test Bank**

  Prepared by Joseph Hegger, University of Missouri

  Great format for a better testing process! All questions closely link with the text material, listing section number, Learning Objective, Bloom's Taxonomy Question Type, and AACSB topic when applicable. Each chapter covers a breadth of topics and types of questions, including questions that test the understanding of the key terms; questions patterned after the learning objectives, concept questions, chapter-opening vignettes, boxes, and highlighted phrases; multiple-choice and true/false problems patterned after the end-of-chapter questions, in basic, intermediate, and challenge levels; and essay questions to test problem-solving skills and more advanced understanding of concepts. Each chapter also includes new problems that pick up questions directly from the end-of-chapter material and converts them into parallel test bank questions. For your reference, each test bank question in this part is linked with its corresponding question in the end-of-chapter section.

- **PowerPoint Presentation System**

  Prepared by LaDoris Baugh, Athens State University

  Customize our content for your course! This presentation has been thoroughly revised to include more lecture-oriented slides, as well as exhibits and examples both from the book and from outside sources. Applicable slides have web links that take you directly to specific internet sites or spreadsheet links to show an example in Excel. You also can go to the Notes Page function for more tips in presenting the slides. Additional PowerPoint slides work through example problems for instructors to show in class. If you already have PowerPoint installed on your computer, you have the ability to edit, print, or rearrange the complete presentation to meet your specific needs.

- **Computerized Test Bank**

  TestGen is a complete, state-of-the-art generator and editing application software that allows instructors to quickly and easily select test items from McGraw-Hill's test bank content. The instructors then can organize, edit, and customize questions and answers to rapidly generate tests for paper or online administration. Questions can include stylized text, symbols, graphics, and equations that are inserted directly into questions using built-in mathematical templates. TestGen's random generator provides the option to display different text or calculated number values each time questions are used. With both quick-and-simple test creation and flexible and robust editing tools, TestGen is a complete test generator system for today's educators.

- **Excel Simulations**

  Expanded for this edition! With 180 Excel simulation questions now included in Connect, McGraw-Hill's Ross series is the unparalleled leader in offering students the opportunity to practice using the Excel functions they will use throughout their careers in finance.

- **Corporate Finance Videos**

  New for this edition, brief and engaging conceptual videos (and accompanying questions) help students to master the building blocks of the Corporate Finance course.

■ **Excel Resources**

A great resource for those seeking additional practice, students can access Excel template problems and the Excel Master tutorial designed by Brad Jordan and Joe Smolira.

■ **Narrated Lecture Videos**

Updated for this edition, the Narrated Lecture Videos provide real-world examples accompanied by step-by-step instructions and explanations for solving problems presented in the chapter. The Concept Checks from the text also are integrated into the slides to reinforce the key topics in the chapter. Designed specifically to appeal to different learning styles, the videos provide a visual and audio explanation of topics and problems.

Teaching Support

Along with having access to all of the same material your students can view through Connect, you also have password-protected access to the Instructor's Manual, solutions to end-of-chapter problems and cases, Instructor's Excel Master, PowerPoint, Excel template solutions, video clips, and video projects and questions.

Acknowledgments

Clearly, our greatest debt is to our many colleagues (and their students) around the world who, like us, wanted to try an alternative to what they were using and made the switch to our text. Our plan for developing and improving *Essentials*, tenth edition, revolved around the detailed feedback we received from many of our colleagues over the years who had an interest in the book and regularly teach the introductory course. These dedicated scholars and teachers to whom we are very grateful are:

Vaughn S. Armstrong, *Utah Valley University*

Juan Avendano, *Augsburg College*

R. Brian Balyeat, *Xavier University*

John Barkoulas, *Georgia Southern University*

Laura Beal, *University of Nebraska at Omaha*

Stephen G. Buell, *Lehigh University*

Manfen Chen, *University of Southern Indiana*

Su-Jane Chen, *Metropolitan University College of Denver*

Ingyu Chiou, *Eastern Illinois University*

Paul Chiou, *Northeastern University*

Brandon Cline, *Mississippi State University*

Susan Coleman, *University of Hartford*

Bruce A. Costa, *University of Montana*

Maria E. de Boyrie, *New Mexico State University*

David Dineen, *Seton Hall University*

Alan Eastman, *Indiana University of Pennsylvania*

David Eckmann, *University of Miami*

Dan Ervin, *Salisbury University*

Jocelyn Evans, *College of Charleston*

Ramon T. Franklin, *Clemson University*

Sharon H. Garrison, *University of Arizona*

Victoria Geyfman, *Bloomsburg University of Pennsylvania*

Kimberly R. Goodwin, *University of Southern Mississippi*

Michael Gunderson, *Purdue University*

Karen L. Hamilton, *Lasell College*

Mahfuzul Haque, *Indiana State University*

John J. Harrington Jr., *Seton Hall University*

John Hatem, *Georgia Southern University*

Rodrigo Hernandez, *Radford University*

Keith Jakob, *University of Montana*

Abu Jalal, *Suffolk University*

Marlin Jensen, *Auburn University*

Samuel Kyle Jones, *Stephen F. Austin State University*

Douglas Jordan, *Sonoma State University*

Ashok K. Kapoor, *Augsburg College*

Howard Keen, *Temple University*

Marvin Keene, *Coastal Carolina University*

James D. Keys, *Florida International University*

Ladd Kochman, *Kennesaw State University*

Denise Letterman, *Robert Morris University-Pittsburgh, PA*

Seongyeon (Sonya) Lim, *DePaul University*

Alethea Lindsay, *Grambling State University*

Qingfeng "Wilson" Liu, *James Madison University*

Angelo Luciano, *Columbia College-Chicago*

Suzan Murphy, *University of Tennessee*

Ohanes Paskelian, *University of Houston Downtown*

Milena Petrova, *Syracuse University*

Ted Pilger, *Southern Illinois University-Carbondale*

Alexandros P. Prezas, *Suffolk University*

Charles Reback, *University of South Carolina Upstate*

Thomas A. Rhee, *California State University-Long Beach*

Jong C. Rhim, *University of Southern Indiana*

Clarence C. Rose, *Radford University*

Camelia S. Rotaru, *St. Edward's University*

Andrew Saporoschenko, *St. Louis University*

Michael J. Seiler, *Old Dominion University*

Roger Severns, *Minnesota State University-Mankato*

Gowri Shankar, *University of Washington-Bothell*

Luke Sparvero, *SUNY-Oswego*

Carolyn Spencer, *Dowling College*

Andrew Spieler, *Hofstra University*

Glenn Tanner, *Texas State University*

John Thornton, *Kent State University*

Hiep Tran, *California State University-Sacramento*

Cathyann Tully, *Kean University*

James A. Turner, *Weber State University*

John B. White, *United States Coast Guard Academy*

Susan White, *University of Maryland*

Fred Yeager, *Saint Louis University*

Tarek Saad Zaher, *Indiana State University*

We owe a special debt to our colleagues for their dedicated work on the many supplements that accompany this text: LaDoris Baugh, for her development of the Instructor's Manual and PowerPoint slides, and Joseph Hegger, for his extensive revision and improvement of the Test Bank.

We also thank Joseph C. Smolira, Belmont University, for his work on this edition. Joe worked closely with us to develop the solutions manual, along with many of the vignettes and real-world examples we have added to this edition.

Steve Hailey and Emily Bello did outstanding work on this edition of *Essentials*. To them fell the unenviable task of technical proofreading, and, in particular, careful checking of each and every calculation throughout the text.

Finally, in every phase of this project, we have been privileged to have the complete and unwavering support of a great organization, McGraw-Hill Education. We especially thank the MHE sales organization. The suggestions they provided, their professionalism in assisting potential adopters, and their service to current adopters have been a major factor in our success.

We are deeply grateful to the select group of professionals who served as our development team on this edition: Chuck Synovec, Director; Jennifer Upton, Senior Product Developer; Trina Maurer, Senior Marketing Manager; Jill Eccher and Jamie Koch, Content Project Managers; Matt Diamond, Senior Designer; and Michele Janicek, Lead Product Developer. Others at McGraw-Hill, too numerous to list here, have improved the book in countless ways.

Throughout the development of this edition, we have taken great care to discover and eliminate errors. Our goal is to provide the best textbook available on the subject. To ensure that future editions are error-free, we will gladly offer $10 per arithmetic error to the first individual reporting it as a modest token of our appreciation. More than this, we would like to hear from instructors and students alike. Please send your comments to Dr. Brad Jordan, c/o Editorial—Finance, McGraw-Hill Education, 120 S. Riverside Drive, 12th Floor, Chicago, IL 60606.

Randolph W. Westerfield
Bradford D. Jordan

Brief Contents

Contents

PART THREE VALUATION OF FUTURE CASH FLOWS

PART FOUR   VALUING STOCKS AND BONDS

6   Interest Rates and Bond Valuation   165

7   Equity Markets and Stock Valuation   205

PART FIVE   CAPITAL BUDGETING

8 Net Present Value and Other Investment Criteria 237

9 Making Capital Investment Decisions 275

List of Boxes

1 Introduction to Financial Management

In 2009, Travis Kalanick and Garrett Camp started the ride-sharing app Uber. Uber shot out of the gate, completing more than five billion rides by the middle of 2017. Even though Uber was losing more than $100 million per quarter, its market value reached $70 billion, with Kalanick's personal wealth exceeding $6 billion. Unfortunately, Kalanick was accused of knowing about sexual harassment in the company and doing nothing to resolve the problem. Then, he was videotaped berating an Uber driver. As a result, he was forced to step down as CEO of the company in June 2017, although he remained the chair of the company's board of directors. And, reminiscent of a runaway car, in August 2017, Kalanick was sued by a major shareholder for fraud, breach of contract, and breach of fiduciary responsibility. In 2018, Kalanick became the CEO of start-up City Storage Systems, which focuses on distressed real estate, such as parking lots and abandoned malls, and turning them into spaces for new industries.

Understanding Kalanick's journey from the founder of a ride-sharing app, to corporate executive, to embattled board chair, and finally to CEO takes us into issues involving the corporate form of organization, corporate goals, and corporate control—all of which we discuss in this chapter. And if you are willing to share the ride with us, you're going to learn an uber-lot as you read.

LEARNING OBJECTIVES

After studying this chapter, you should be able to:

LO 1 Discuss the basic types of financial management decisions and the role of the financial manager.

LO 2 Identify the goal of financial management.

LO 3 Compare the financial implications of the different forms of business organizations.

LO 4 Describe the conflicts of interest that can arise between managers and owners.

Please visit us at essentialsofcorporatefinance.blogspot.com for the latest developments in the world of corporate finance.

To begin our study of financial management, we address two central issues. First: What is corporate, or business, finance, and what is the role of the financial manager? Second: What is the goal of financial management?

1.1 FINANCE: A QUICK LOOK

Before we plunge into our study of "corp. fin.," we think a quick overview of the finance field might be a good idea. Our goal is to clue you in on some of the most important areas in finance and some of the career opportunities available in each. We also want to illustrate some of the ways finance fits in with other areas such as marketing, management, and accounting.

The Four Basic Areas

Traditionally, financial topics are grouped into four main areas:

1. Corporate finance
2. Investments
3. Financial institutions
4. International finance

We discuss each of these next.

For job descriptions in finance and other areas, visit www.careers-in-business.com.

Corporate Finance   The first of these four areas, corporate finance, is the main subject of this book. We begin covering this subject in our next section, so we will wait until then to get into any details. One thing we should note is that the term *corporate finance* seems to imply that what we cover is only relevant to corporations, but the truth is that almost all of the topics we consider are much broader than that. Maybe *business finance* would be a little more descriptive, but even this is too narrow because at least half of the subjects we discuss in the pages ahead are really basic financial ideas and principles applicable across all the various areas of finance and beyond.

Investments   Broadly speaking, the investments area deals with financial assets such as stocks and bonds. Some of the more important questions include

1. What determines the price of a financial asset, such as a share of stock?
2. What are the potential risks and rewards associated with investing in financial assets?
3. What is the best mixture of financial assets to hold?

Students who specialize in the investments area have various career opportunities. Being a stockbroker is one of the most common. Stockbrokers often work for large companies such as Merrill Lynch, advising customers on what types of investments to consider and helping them make buy and sell decisions. Financial advisers play a similar role but are not necessarily brokers.

Portfolio management is a second investments-related career path. Portfolio managers, as the name suggests, manage money for investors. For example, individual investors frequently buy into mutual funds. Such funds are a means of pooling money that is then invested by a portfolio manager. Portfolio managers also invest and manage money for pension funds, insurance companies, and many other types of institutions.

Security analysis is a third area. A security analyst researches individual investments, such as stock in a particular company, and makes a determination as to whether the price is right. To do so, an analyst delves deeply into company and industry reports, along with a variety of other information sources. Frequently, brokers and portfolio managers rely on security analysts for information and recommendations.

These investments-related areas, like many areas in finance, share an interesting feature. If they are done well, they can be very rewarding financially (translation: You can make a lot of money). The bad news, of course, is that they can be very demanding and very competitive, so they are definitely not for everybody.

Financial Institutions   Financial institutions are basically businesses that deal primarily in financial matters. Banks and insurance companies would probably be the most familiar to you. Institutions such as these employ people to perform a wide variety of finance-related tasks. For example, a commercial loan officer at a bank would evaluate whether a particular business has a strong enough financial position to warrant extending a loan. At an insurance company, an analyst would decide whether a particular risk was suitable for insuring and what the premium should be.

International Finance   International finance isn't so much an area as it is a specialization within one of the main areas we described earlier. In other words, careers in international finance generally involve international aspects of either corporate finance, investments, or financial institutions. For example, some portfolio managers and security analysts specialize in non-U.S. companies. Similarly, many U.S. businesses have extensive overseas operations and need employees familiar with such international topics as exchange rates and political risk. Banks frequently are asked to make loans across country lines, so international specialists are needed there as well.

Why Study Finance?

Who needs to know finance? In a word, you. In fact, there are many reasons you need a working knowledge of finance even if you are not planning a finance career. We explore some of these reasons next.

Marketing and Finance   If you are interested in marketing, you need to know finance because, for example, marketers constantly work with budgets, and they need to understand how to get the greatest payoff from marketing expenditures and programs. Analyzing costs and benefits of projects of all types is one of the most important aspects of finance, so the tools you learn in finance are vital in marketing research, the design of marketing and distribution channels, and product pricing, to name a few areas.

Financial analysts rely heavily on marketing analysts, and the two frequently work together to evaluate the profitability of proposed projects and products. As we will see in a later chapter, sales projections are a key input in almost every type of new product analysis, and such projections are often developed jointly between marketing and finance.

Beyond this, the finance industry employs marketers to help sell financial products such as bank accounts, insurance policies, and mutual funds. Financial services marketing is one of the most rapidly growing types of marketing, and successful financial services marketers are very well compensated. To work in this area, you obviously need to understand financial products.

Accounting and Finance   For accountants, finance is required reading. In smaller businesses in particular, accountants often are required to make financial decisions as well as perform traditional accounting duties. Further, as the financial world continues to grow more complex, accountants have to know finance to understand the implications of many of the newer types of financial contracts and the impact they have on financial statements. Beyond this, cost accounting and business finance are particularly closely related, sharing many of the same subjects and concerns.

Financial analysts make extensive use of accounting information; they are some of the most important end users. Understanding finance helps accountants recognize what types of information are particularly valuable and, more generally, how accounting information is actually used (and abused) in practice.

Management and Finance One of the most important areas in management is strategy. Thinking about business strategy without simultaneously thinking about financial strategy is an excellent recipe for disaster, and, as a result, management strategists must have a very clear understanding of the financial implications of business plans.

In broader terms, management employees of all types are expected to have a strong understanding of how their jobs affect profitability, and they also are expected to be able to work within their areas to improve profitability. This is precisely what studying finance teaches you: What are the characteristics of activities that create value?

You and Finance Perhaps the most important reason to know finance is that you will have to make financial decisions that will be very important to you personally. Today, for example, when you go to work for almost any type of company, you will be asked to decide how you want to invest your retirement funds. We'll see in a later chapter that what you choose to do can make an enormous difference in your future financial well-being. On a different note, is it your dream to start your own business? Good luck if you don't understand basic finance before you start; you'll end up learning it the hard way. Want to know how big your student loan payments are going to be before you take out that next loan? Maybe not, but we'll show you how to calculate them anyway.

These are just a few of the ways that finance will affect your personal and business lives. Whether you want to or not, you are going to have to examine and understand financial issues, and you are going to have to make financial decisions. We want you to do so wisely, so keep reading.

CONCEPT QUESTIONS

1.1a What are the major areas in finance?

1.1b Besides wanting to pass this class, why do you need to understand finance?

1.2 BUSINESS FINANCE AND THE FINANCIAL MANAGER

Now we proceed to define business finance and the financial manager's job.

What Is Business Finance?

Imagine you were to start your own business. No matter what type of business you started, you would have to answer the following three questions in some form or another:

1. What long-term investments should you take on? That is, what lines of business will you be in, and what sorts of buildings, machinery, and equipment will you need?

2. Where will you get the long-term financing to pay for your investments? Will you bring in other owners, or will you borrow the money?

3. How will you manage your everyday financial activities, such as collecting from customers and paying suppliers?

These are not the only questions, but they are among the most important. Business finance, broadly speaking, is the study of ways to answer these three questions. We'll be looking at each of them in the chapters ahead.

The Financial Manager

The financial management function is usually associated with a top officer of the firm, often called the chief financial officer (CFO) or vice president of finance. Figure 1.1 is a simplified organizational chart that highlights the finance activity in a large firm. As shown, the vice president of finance coordinates the activities of the treasurer and the controller. The controller's office handles cost and financial accounting, tax payments, and management information systems. The treasurer's office is responsible for managing the firm's cash and credit, its financial planning, and its capital expenditures. These treasury activities are all related to the three general questions raised above, and the chapters ahead deal primarily with these issues. Our study thus bears mostly on activities usually associated with the treasurer's office. In a smaller firm, the treasurer and controller might be the same person, and there would be only one office.

For current issues facing CFOs, see www.cfo.com.

Financial Management Decisions

As our preceding discussion suggests, the financial manager must be concerned with three basic types of questions. We consider these in greater detail next.

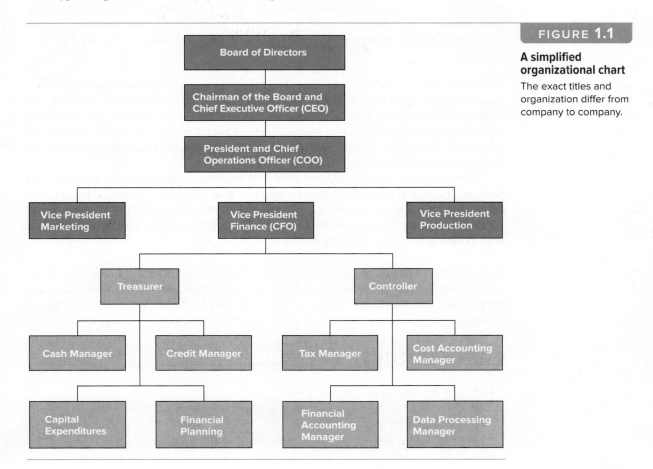

FIGURE 1.1

A simplified organizational chart

The exact titles and organization differ from company to company.

capital budgeting
The process of planning and managing a firm's long-term investments.

Capital Budgeting   The first question concerns the firm's long-term investments. The process of planning and managing a firm's long-term investments is called **capital budgeting**. In capital budgeting, the financial manager tries to identify investment opportunities that are worth more to the firm than they cost to acquire. Loosely speaking, this means that the value of the cash flow generated by an asset exceeds the cost of that asset.

Regardless of the specific investment under consideration, financial managers must be concerned with how much cash they expect to receive, when they expect to receive it, and how likely they are to receive it. Evaluating the *size*, *timing*, and *risk* of future cash flows is the essence of capital budgeting. In fact, whenever we evaluate a business decision, the size, timing, and risk of the cash flows will be, by far, the most important things we will consider.

capital structure
The mixture of debt and equity maintained by a firm.

Capital Structure   The second question for the financial manager concerns how the firm obtains the financing it needs to support its long-term investments. A firm's **capital structure** (or financial structure) refers to the specific mixture of long-term debt and equity the firm uses to finance its operations. The financial manager has two concerns in this area. First: How much should the firm borrow? Second: What are the least expensive sources of funds for the firm?

In addition to deciding on the financing mix, the financial manager has to decide exactly how and where to raise the money. The expenses associated with raising long-term financing can be considerable, so different possibilities must be evaluated carefully. Also, businesses borrow money from a variety of lenders in a number of different ways. Choosing among lenders and among loan types is another job handled by the financial manager.

working capital
A firm's short-term assets and liabilities.

Working Capital Management   The third question concerns **working capital** management. The term *working capital* refers to a firm's short-term assets, such as inventory, and its short-term liabilities, such as money owed to suppliers. Managing the firm's working capital is a day-to-day activity that ensures the firm has sufficient resources to continue its operations and avoid costly interruptions. This involves a number of activities related to the firm's receipt and disbursement of cash.

Some questions about working capital that must be answered are the following: (1) How much cash and inventory should we keep on hand? (2) Should we sell on credit to our customers? (3) How will we obtain any needed short-term financing? (4) If we borrow in the short term, how and where should we do it? This is just a small sample of the issues that arise in managing a firm's working capital.

Conclusion   The three areas of corporate financial management we have described—capital budgeting, capital structure, and working capital management—are very broad categories. Each includes a rich variety of topics, and we have indicated only a few of the questions that arise in the different areas. The chapters ahead contain greater detail.

CONCEPT QUESTIONS

1.2a   What is the capital budgeting decision?

1.2b   What do you call the specific mixture of long-term debt and equity that a firm chooses to use?

1.2c   Into what category of financial management does cash management fall?

1.3 FORMS OF BUSINESS ORGANIZATION

Large firms in the United States, such as IBM and Apple, are almost all organized as corporations. We examine the three different legal forms of business organization—sole proprietorship, partnership, and corporation—to see why this is so.

Sole Proprietorship

A **sole proprietorship** is a business owned by one person. This is the simplest type of business to start and is the least regulated form of organization. For this reason, there are more proprietorships than any other type of business, and many businesses that later become large corporations start out as small proprietorships.

The owner of a sole proprietorship keeps all the profits. That's the good news. The bad news is that the owner has *unlimited liability* for business debts. This means that creditors can look to the proprietor's personal assets for payment. Similarly, there is no distinction between personal and business income, so all business income is taxed as personal income.

The life of a sole proprietorship is limited to the owner's life span, and, importantly, the amount of equity that can be raised is limited to the proprietor's personal wealth. This limitation often means that the business is unable to exploit new opportunities because of insufficient capital. Ownership of a sole proprietorship may be difficult to transfer because this requires the sale of the entire business to a new owner.

sole proprietorship
A business owned by a single individual.

For more information on forms of business organization, visit www .nolo.com.

Partnership

A **partnership** is similar to a proprietorship, except that there are two or more owners (partners). In a *general partnership*, all the partners share in gains or losses, and all have unlimited liability for all partnership debts, not just some particular share. The way partnership gains (and losses) are divided is described in the *partnership agreement*. This agreement can be an informal oral agreement, such as "let's start a lawn mowing business," or a lengthy, formal written document.

In a *limited partnership*, one or more *general partners* will run the business and have unlimited liability, but there will be one or more *limited partners* who do not actively participate in the business. A limited partner's liability for business debts is limited to the amount that partner contributes to the partnership. This form of organization is common in real estate ventures, for example.

The advantages and disadvantages of a partnership are basically the same as those for a proprietorship. Partnerships based on a relatively informal agreement are easy and inexpensive to form. General partners have unlimited liability for partnership debts, and the partnership terminates when a general partner wishes to sell out or dies. All income is taxed as personal income to the partners, and the amount of equity that can be raised is limited to the partners' combined wealth. Ownership by a general partner is not easily transferred because a new partnership must be formed. A limited partner's interest can be sold without dissolving the partnership, but finding a buyer may be difficult.

Because a partner in a general partnership can be held responsible for all partnership debts, having a written agreement is very important. Failure to spell out the rights and duties of the partners frequently leads to misunderstandings later on. Also, if you are a limited partner, you must not become deeply involved in business decisions unless you are willing to assume the obligations of a general partner. The reason is that if things go badly, you may be deemed to be a general partner even though you say you are a limited partner.

partnership
A business formed by two or more individuals or entities.

Based on our discussion, the primary disadvantages of sole proprietorships and partnerships as forms of business organization are (1) unlimited liability for business debts on the part of the owners, (2) limited life of the business, and (3) difficulty of transferring ownership. These three disadvantages add up to a single, central problem: The ability of such businesses to grow can be seriously limited by an inability to raise cash for investment.

Corporation

corporation

A business created as a distinct legal entity owned by one or more individuals or entities.

The **corporation** is the most important form (in terms of size) of business organization in the United States. A corporation is a legal "person" separate and distinct from its owners, and it has many of the rights, duties, and privileges of an actual person. Corporations can borrow money and own property, can sue and be sued, and can enter into contracts. A corporation can even be a general partner or a limited partner in a partnership, and a corporation can own stock in another corporation.

Not surprisingly, starting a corporation is somewhat more complicated than starting the other forms of business organization. Forming a corporation involves preparing *articles of incorporation* (or a charter) and a set of *bylaws*. The articles of incorporation must contain a number of things, including the corporation's name, its intended life (which can be forever), its business purpose, and the number of shares that can be issued. This information must normally be supplied to the state in which the firm will be incorporated. For most legal purposes, the corporation is a "resident" of that state.

The bylaws are rules describing how the corporation regulates its own existence. For example, the bylaws describe how directors are elected. The bylaws may be amended or extended from time to time by the stockholders.

In a large corporation, the stockholders and the managers are usually separate groups. The stockholders elect the board of directors, who then select the managers. Management is charged with running the corporation's affairs in the stockholders' interests. In principle, stockholders control the corporation because they elect the directors.

As a result of the separation of ownership and management, the corporate form has several advantages. Ownership (represented by shares of stock) can be readily transferred, and the life of the corporation is, therefore, not limited. The corporation borrows money in its own name. As a result, the stockholders in a corporation have limited liability for corporate debts. The most they can lose is what they have invested.

The relative ease of transferring ownership, the limited liability for business debts, and the unlimited life of the business are the reasons the corporate form is superior when it comes to raising cash. If a corporation needs new equity, it can sell new shares of stock and attract new investors. The number of owners can be huge; larger corporations have many thousands or even millions of stockholders. For example, the General Electric Company (better known as GE) has about 8.7 billion shares outstanding and 4 million shareholders.

The corporate form has a significant disadvantage. Because a corporation is a legal person, it must pay taxes. Moreover, money paid out to stockholders in the form of dividends is taxed again as income to those stockholders. This is *double taxation*, meaning that corporate profits are taxed twice: at the corporate level when they are earned and again at the personal level when they are paid out.

Today, all 50 states have enacted laws allowing for the creation of a relatively new form of business organization, the limited liability company (LLC). The goal of this entity is to operate and be taxed like a partnership but retain limited liability for owners. Thus, an LLC is essentially a hybrid of a partnership and a corporation. Although states have differing definitions for LLCs, the more important scorekeeper is the Internal Revenue Service

TABLE **1.1**

International
corporations

Company	Country of Origin	Type of Company	Translation
Bayerische Motoren Werke (BMW) AG	Germany	Aktiengesellschaft	Corporation
Montblanc GmbH	Germany	Gesellschaft mit beschränkter Haftung	Company with limited liability
Rolls-Royce PLC	United Kingdom	Public limited company	Public limited company
Shell UK Ltd.	United Kingdom	Limited	Corporation
Unilever NV	Netherlands	Naamloze Vennootschap	Limited liability company
Fiat SpA	Italy	Società per Azioni	Public limited company
Saab AB	Sweden	Aktiebolag	Joint stock company
Peugeot SA	France	Société Anonyme	Joint stock company

(IRS). The IRS will consider an LLC a corporation, thereby subjecting it to double taxation, unless it meets certain specific criteria. In essence, an LLC cannot be too corporation-like, or it will be treated as one by the IRS. LLCs have become common. For example, Goldman Sachs, one of Wall Street's last remaining partnerships, decided to convert from a private partnership to an LLC (it later "went public," becoming a publicly held corporation). Large accounting firms and law firms by the score have converted to LLCs.

A Corporation by Another Name . . .

The corporate form has many variations around the world. Exact laws and regulations differ, of course, but the essential features of public ownership and limited liability remain. These firms are often called *joint stock companies*, *public limited companies*, or *limited liability companies*.

Table 1.1 gives the names of a few well-known international corporations, their country of origin, and a translation of the abbreviation that follows the company name.

You can find the translation for any business type at www.corporate information.com.

CONCEPT QUESTIONS

1.3a What are the three forms of business organization?

1.3b What are the primary advantages and disadvantages of sole proprietorships and partnerships?

1.3c What is the difference between a general and a limited partnership?

1.3d Why is the corporate form superior when it comes to raising cash?

1.4 THE GOAL OF FINANCIAL MANAGEMENT

To study financial decision making, we first need to understand the goal of financial management. Such an understanding is important because it leads to an objective basis for making and evaluating financial decisions.

Profit Maximization

Profit maximization would probably be the most commonly cited business goal, but this is not a very precise objective. Do we mean profits this year? If so, then actions such as deferring maintenance, letting inventories run down, and other short-run, cost-cutting measures will tend to increase profits now, but these activities aren't necessarily desirable.

The goal of maximizing profits may refer to some sort of "long-run" or "average" profits, but it's unclear exactly what this means. First, do we mean something like accounting net income or earnings per share? As we will see, these numbers may have little to do with what is good or bad for the firm. Second, what do we mean by the long run? As a famous economist once remarked: "In the long run, we're all dead!" More to the point, this goal doesn't tell us the appropriate trade-off between current and future profits.

The Goal of Financial Management in a Corporation

The financial manager in a corporation makes decisions for the stockholders of the firm. Given this, instead of listing possible goals for the financial manager, we really need to answer a more fundamental question: From the stockholders' point of view, what is a good financial management decision?

If we assume stockholders buy stock because they seek to gain financially, then the answer is obvious: Good decisions increase the value of the stock, and poor decisions decrease it.

Given our observations, it follows that the financial manager acts in the shareholders' best interests by making decisions that increase the value of the stock. The appropriate goal for the financial manager in a corporation can thus be stated quite easily:

> **The goal of financial management is to maximize the current value per share of the existing stock.**

The goal of maximizing the value of the stock avoids the problems associated with the different goals we discussed earlier. There is no ambiguity in the criterion, and there is no short-run versus long-run issue. We explicitly mean that our goal is to maximize the *current* stock value. Of course, maximizing stock value is the same thing as maximizing the market price per share.

A More General Financial Management Goal

Given our goal as stated earlier (maximize the value of the stock), an obvious question comes up: What is the appropriate goal when the firm has no traded stock? Corporations are certainly not the only type of business, and the stock in many corporations rarely changes hands, so it's difficult to say what the value per share is at any given time.

As long as we are dealing with for-profit businesses, only a slight modification is needed. The total value of the stock in a corporation is equal to the value of the owners' equity. Therefore, a more general way of stating our goal is:

> **Maximize the market value of the existing owners' equity.**

With this goal in mind, it doesn't matter whether the business is a proprietorship, a partnership, or a corporation. For each of these, good financial decisions increase the market value of the owners' equity and poor financial decisions decrease it.

Finally, our goal does not imply that the financial manager should take illegal or unethical actions in the hope of increasing the value of the equity in the firm. What we mean is that the financial manager best serves the owners of the business by identifying goods and services that add value to the firm because they are desired and valued in the free marketplace. Our nearby *Finance Matters* box discusses some recent ethical issues and problems faced by well-known corporations.

Business ethics are considered at www.3 blassociation.com.

Corporate Ethics

Large companies are sometimes guilty of unethical behavior. Often, this unethical behavior takes the form of false or misleading financial statements. In one of the largest corporate fraud cases in history, energy giant Enron Corporation was forced to file for bankruptcy in December 2001 amid allegations that the company's financial statements were deliberately misleading and false. Enron's bankruptcy destroyed not only that company, but its auditor Arthur Andersen as well.

Often, unethical behavior is also illegal and can result in a jail sentence for an individual or fines for a corporation. For example, in March 2018, the investment bank and financial services company Barclays reached a settlement with the U.S. Department of Justice (DOJ). The DOJ claimed that Barclays had misrepresented the quality of the mortgages it packaged and sold to investors. To settle the claim, Barclays agreed to pay $2 billion. Barclays was not the first bank to settle a mortgage-related claim with the DOJ. Banks with particularly large settlements with the DOJ regarding mortgages were Bank of America ($7 billion), JPMorgan ($13 billion), and Citigroup ($16.7 billion).

The difference between ethical and unethical behavior can sometimes be murky. For example, many U.S. companies have relocated to Bermuda for reasons beyond the beautiful pink beaches; namely, Bermuda has no corporate income taxes. With a population of less than 65,000, the island is home to more than 13,000 international companies. Stanley Black & Decker, the well-known maker of Stanley tools, was among the U.S. corporations that considered a move to the island paradise. By doing so, Stanley estimated that it would save $30 million per year in taxes. Stanley ultimately decided against the move, but two of its rivals, Cooper and Ingersoll-Rand, did move to Bermuda. Because the goal of the corporation is to maximize shareholder wealth, this would seem like a good move, and the practice is entirely legal. But is it ethical? What are the issues?

Another corporate activity that has generated much controversy is the practice of outsourcing, or offshoring, jobs to other countries. U.S. corporations engage in this practice when labor costs in another country are substantially lower than they are domestically. Again, this is done to maximize shareholder wealth. But the ethical dilemma in this case is even trickier. Some U.S. workers do lose jobs when offshoring occurs. On the other hand, the Milken Institute estimated that every $1 spent on offshoring a service job to India generated a net value to the United States of $1.13, along with another $.33 to India. And it gets even more complicated: What about foreign companies such as BMW and Toyota that "insource" jobs by building plants in the United States? Is it unethical to outsource U.S. jobs while, at the same time, insourcing jobs from other countries?

Sarbanes-Oxley Act

In response to corporate scandals involving companies such as Enron, WorldCom, Tyco, and Adelphia, Congress enacted the Sarbanes-Oxley Act in 2002. The act, which is better known as "Sarbox," is intended to strengthen protection against corporate accounting fraud and financial malpractice. Key elements of Sarbox took effect on November 15, 2004.

Sarbox contains a number of requirements designed to ensure that companies tell the truth in their financial statements. For example, the officers of a public corporation must review and sign the annual report. They must attest that the annual report does not contain false statements or material omissions and also that the financial statements fairly represent the company's financial results. In essence, Sarbox makes management personally responsible for the accuracy of a company's financial statements.

To find out more about Sarbanes-Oxley, go to www.soxlaw.com.

Because of its extensive requirements, compliance with Sarbox can be very costly, which has led to some unintended results. Since its implementation, hundreds of public firms have chosen to "go dark," meaning that their shares are no longer traded in the major stock markets, in which case Sarbox does not apply. Most of these companies stated that their reason was to avoid the cost of compliance. Ironically, in such cases, the law had the effect of eliminating public disclosure instead of improving it.

Sarbox also probably has affected the number of companies going public in the United States. Recently, many U.S.-based companies have chosen to go public on the London Stock Exchange's Alternative Investment Market (AIM) instead. The cost savings can be enormous, especially for small companies. For example, Protonex Technologies, a fuel cell developer based in Southborough, Massachusetts, estimated that it costs about $1 million per year in compliance costs and mailings to stockholders to be listed on the AIM. In contrast, the annual cost to be listed on the NASDAQ would be about $3 million, with a large part of the increase due to Sarbox compliance costs.

CONCEPT QUESTIONS

1.4a   What is the goal of financial management?

1.4b   What are some shortcomings of the goal of profit maximization?

1.5 THE AGENCY PROBLEM AND CONTROL OF THE CORPORATION

We've seen that the financial manager in a corporation acts in the best interests of the stockholders by taking actions that increase the value of the firm's stock. However, we've also seen that in large corporations, ownership can be spread over a huge number of stockholders. This dispersion of ownership arguably means that management effectively controls the firm. In this case, will management necessarily act in the best interests of the stockholders? Put another way, might not management pursue its own goals at the stockholders' expense? We briefly consider some of the arguments in this section.

Agency Relationships

The relationship between stockholders and management is called an *agency relationship*. Such a relationship exists whenever someone (the principal) hires another (the agent) to represent his or her interest. For example, you might hire someone (an agent) to sell a car that you own while you are away at school. In all such relationships, there is a possibility of conflict of interest between the principal and the agent. Such a conflict is called an **agency problem**.

Suppose you hire someone to sell your car and you agree to pay her a flat fee when she sells the car. The agent's incentive in this case is to make the sale, not necessarily to get you the best price. If you paid a commission of, say, 10 percent of the sales price instead of a flat fee, then this problem might not exist. This example illustrates that the way an agent is compensated is one factor that affects agency problems.

Management Goals

To see how management and stockholder interests might differ, imagine that a corporation is considering a new investment. The new investment is expected to favorably affect the stock price, but it is also a relatively risky venture. The owners of the firm will wish to take the investment (because the share value will rise), but management may not because there is the possibility that things will turn out badly and management jobs will be lost. If management does not take the investment, then the stockholders may lose a valuable opportunity. This is one example of an *agency cost*.

It is sometimes argued that, left to themselves, managers would tend to maximize the amount of resources over which they have control, or, more generally, business power or wealth. This goal could lead to an overemphasis on business size or growth. For example, cases where management is accused of overpaying to buy another company just to increase

agency problem
The possibility of conflict of interest between the owners and management of a firm.

the size of the business or to demonstrate corporate power are not uncommon. Obviously, if overpayment does take place, such a purchase does not benefit the owners of the purchasing company.

Our discussion indicates that management may tend to overemphasize organizational survival to protect job security. Also, management may dislike outside interference, so independence and corporate self-sufficiency may be important goals.

Do Managers Act in the Stockholders' Interests?

Whether managers will, in fact, act in the best interests of stockholders depends on two factors. First, how closely are management goals aligned with stockholder goals? This question relates to the way managers are compensated. Second, can management be replaced if they do not pursue stockholder goals? This issue relates to control of the firm. As we will discuss, there are a number of reasons to think that, even in the largest firms, management has a significant incentive to act in the interests of stockholders.

Managerial Compensation   Management will frequently have a significant economic incentive to increase share value for two reasons. First, managerial compensation, particularly at the top, is usually tied to financial performance in general and oftentimes to share value in particular. For example, managers are frequently given the option to buy stock at a fixed price. The more the stock is worth, the more valuable is this option. The second incentive managers have relates to job prospects. Better performers within the firm will tend to get promoted. More generally, those managers who are successful in pursuing stockholder goals will be in greater demand in the labor market and thus command higher salaries.

In fact, managers who are successful in pursuing stockholder goals can reap enormous rewards. For example, Hock Tan, CEO of Broadcom, received about $103 million in 2017, which is less than Floyd Mayweather ($300 million) and Manny Pacquiao ($160 million). Information on executive compensation, along with a ton of other information, can be easily found on the web for almost any public company. Our nearby *Work the Web* box shows you how to get started.

Control of the Firm   Control of the firm ultimately rests with stockholders. They elect the board of directors, who, in turn, hires and fires management. The mechanism by which unhappy stockholders can act to replace existing management is called a *proxy fight*. A proxy is the authority to vote someone else's stock. A proxy fight develops when a group solicits proxies in order to replace the existing board, and thereby replace existing management.

For example, in July 2017, Trian Partners, headed by activist investor Nelson Peltz, engaged in a proxy fight with Procter & Gamble in an attempt to gain a seat on the board of directors. This was the largest proxy fight in history, with Trian owning $3.3 billion worth of shares in the $223 billion company. Peltz cited disappointing financial results, weak shareholder returns, deteriorating market share, and excessive cost and bureaucracy as reasons for the proxy fight. P&G had fought off a previous proxy fight in 2012 when William Ackman attempted to gain a seat on the board. Ackman ultimately lost his battle and sold the last of his P&G stock in May 2014.

Another way that management can be replaced is by takeover. Firms that are poorly managed are more attractive as acquisitions than well-managed firms because a greater profit potential exists. Thus, avoiding a takeover by another firm gives management another incentive to act in the stockholders' interests. Unhappy prominent shareholders can suggest different business strategies to a firm's top management. For example, in June 2017, Verizon

W🌐RK THE WEB

The web is a great place to learn about individual companies, and there are a slew of sites available to help you. Try pointing your web browser to finance.yahoo.com. Once there, you should see a box with "Quote Lookup." To look up a company, you need its "ticker symbol" (or ticker for short), which is a unique one-to-five-letter identifier. Or you can type in a company's name to find the ticker. For example, we typed in "SIRI," which is the ticker symbol for Sirius XM Holdings, the satellite radio provider. Here is a portion of what we found:

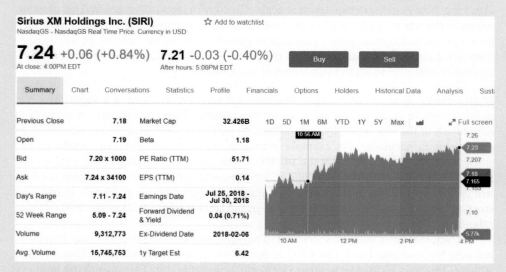

Sirius XM Holdings Inc. (SIRI)
NasdaqGS - NasdaqGS Real Time Price. Currency in USD
☆ Add to watchlist

7.24 +0.06 (+0.84%)   **7.21** -0.03 (-0.40%)
At close: 4:00PM EDT   After hours: 5:06PM EDT

[Buy]   [Sell]

Summary | Chart | Conversations | Statistics | Profile | Financials | Options | Holders | Historical Data | Analysis | Sust

Previous Close	7.18	Market Cap	32.426B
Open	7.19	Beta	1.18
Bid	7.20 x 1000	PE Ratio (TTM)	51.71
Ask	7.24 x 34100	EPS (TTM)	0.14
Day's Range	7.11 - 7.24	Earnings Date	Jul 25, 2018 - Jul 30, 2018
52 Week Range	5.09 - 7.24	Forward Dividend & Yield	0.04 (0.71%)
Volume	9,312,773	Ex-Dividend Date	2018-02-06
Avg. Volume	15,745,753	1y Target Est	6.42

Source: **finance.yahoo.com**

There is a lot of information here and a lot of other links for you to explore, so have at it. By the end of the term, we hope it all makes sense to you!

QUESTIONS

1. Go to finance.yahoo.com and find the current stock prices for Southwest Airlines (LUV), Harley-Davidson (HOG), and Starwood Hotels & Resorts (HOT).
2. Get a quote for American Express (AXP) and follow the "Statistics" link. What information is available on this link? What do "mrq," "ttm," "yoy," and "lfy" mean?

completed its $4.5 billion takeover of Yahoo! The management of Yahoo! had been under fire for several years due to the company's poor performance. Verizon hoped that the combined company could create a third alternative in the digital advertising market to challenge Google and Facebook. Yahoo! CEO Marissa Mayer wasn't part of the plans going forward, although she did receive $127 million when she was let go.

Conclusion   The available theory and evidence are consistent with the view that stockholders control the firm and that stockholder wealth maximization is the relevant goal of the corporation. Even so, there will undoubtedly be times when management goals are pursued at the expense of the stockholders, at least temporarily.

Agency problems are not unique to corporations; they exist whenever there is a separation of ownership and management. This separation is most pronounced in corporations, but it certainly exists in partnerships and proprietorships as well.

Stakeholders

Our discussion thus far implies that management and stockholders are the only parties with an interest in the firm's decisions. This is an oversimplification, of course. Employees, customers, suppliers, and even the government all have a financial interest in the firm.

These various groups are called **stakeholders** in the firm. In general, a stakeholder is someone other than a stockholder or creditor who potentially has a claim on the cash flows of the firm. Such groups also will attempt to exert control over the firm, perhaps to the detriment of the owners.

stakeholder
Someone other than a stockholder or creditor who potentially has a claim on the cash flows of the firm.

CONCEPT QUESTIONS

1.5a   What is an agency relationship?

1.5b   What are agency problems, and how do they arise? What are agency costs?

1.5c   What incentives do managers in large corporations have to maximize share value?

1.6 FINANCIAL MARKETS AND THE CORPORATION

We've seen that the primary advantages of the corporate form of organization are that ownership can be transferred more quickly and easily than with other forms and that money can be raised more readily. Both of these advantages are significantly enhanced by the existence of financial markets, and financial markets play an extremely important role in corporate finance.

Cash Flows to and from the Firm

The interplay between the corporation and the financial markets is illustrated in Figure 1.2. The arrows in Figure 1.2 trace the passage of cash from the financial markets to the firm and from the firm back to the financial markets.

Suppose we start with the firm selling shares of stock and borrowing money to raise cash. Cash flows to the firm from the financial markets (A). The firm invests the cash in current and fixed (or long-term) assets (B). These assets generate some cash (C), some of which goes to pay corporate taxes (D). After taxes are paid, some of this cash flow is reinvested in the firm (E). The rest goes back to the financial markets as cash paid to creditors and shareholders (F).

A financial market, like any market, is a way of bringing buyers and sellers together. In financial markets, it is debt and equity securities that are bought and sold. Financial markets differ in detail, however. The most important differences concern the types of securities that are traded, how trading is conducted, and who the buyers and sellers are. Some of these differences are discussed next.

Primary versus Secondary Markets

Financial markets function as both primary and secondary markets for debt and equity securities. The term *primary market* refers to the original sale of securities by governments

FIGURE **1.2**

Cash flows between
the firm and the
financial markets

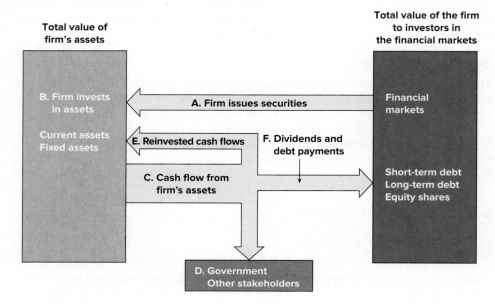

A. Firm issues securities to raise cash.
B. Firm invests in assets.
C. Firm's operations generate cash flow.
D. Cash is paid to government as taxes.
   Other stakeholders may receive cash.

E. Reinvested cash flows are plowed back
   into firm.
F. Cash is paid out to investors in the form
   of interest and dividends.

and corporations. The *secondary markets* are those in which these securities are bought and
sold after the original sale. Equities are, of course, issued solely by corporations. Debt securities are issued by both governments and corporations. In the discussion that follows, we
focus on corporate securities only.

Primary Markets   In a primary market transaction, the corporation is the seller, and
the transaction raises money for the corporation. Corporations engage in two types of primary market transactions: public offerings and private placements. A public offering, as the
name suggests, involves selling securities to the general public, whereas a private placement
is a negotiated sale involving a specific buyer.

To learn more about the
SEC, visit www.sec.gov.

By law, public offerings of debt and equity must be registered with the Securities and
Exchange Commission (SEC). Registration requires the firm to disclose a great deal of information before selling any securities. The accounting, legal, and selling costs of public offerings can be considerable.

Partly to avoid the various regulatory requirements and the expense of public offerings,
debt and equity often are sold privately to large financial institutions such as life insurance
companies or mutual funds. Such private placements do not have to be registered with the
SEC and do not require the involvement of underwriters (investment banks that specialize
in selling securities to the public).

To learn more about stock
exchanges, visit www.nyse
.com and www.nasdaq
.com.

Secondary Markets   A secondary market transaction involves one owner or creditor
selling to another. It is, therefore, the secondary markets that provide the means for transferring ownership of corporate securities. Although a corporation is only directly involved in a
primary market transaction (when it sells securities to raise cash), the secondary markets
are still critical to large corporations. The reason is that investors are much more willing to

purchase securities in a primary market transaction when they know that those securities can be resold later if desired.

Dealer Versus Auction Markets   There are two kinds of secondary markets: *auction* markets and *dealer* markets. Generally speaking, dealers buy and sell for themselves, at their own risk. A car dealer, for example, buys and sells automobiles. In contrast, brokers and agents match buyers and sellers, but they do not actually own the commodity that is bought or sold. A real estate agent, for example, does not normally buy and sell houses.

Dealer markets in stocks and long-term debt are called *over-the-counter* (OTC) markets. Most trading in debt securities takes place over the counter. The expression *over the counter* refers to days of old when securities were literally bought and sold at counters in offices around the country. Today, a significant fraction of the market for stocks and almost all of the market for long-term debt have no central location; the many dealers are connected electronically.

Auction markets differ from dealer markets in two ways. First, an auction market, or exchange, has a physical location (like Wall Street). Second, in a dealer market, most of the buying and selling is done by the dealer. The primary purpose of an auction market, on the other hand, is to match those who wish to sell with those who wish to buy. Dealers play a limited role.

Trading in Corporate Securities   The equity shares of most of the large firms in the United States trade in organized auction markets. The largest such market is the New York Stock Exchange (NYSE), which accounts for more than 85 percent of all the shares traded in auction markets.

In addition to the stock exchanges, there is a large OTC market for stocks. In 1971, the National Association of Securities Dealers (NASD) made available to dealers and brokers an electronic quotation system called NASDAQ (NASD Automated Quotations system, pronounced "naz-dak"). There are more companies listed on NASDAQ than there are on the NYSE, but they tend to be much smaller in size and trade less actively. There are exceptions, of course. Both Microsoft and Intel trade OTC, for example. Nonetheless, the total value of NASDAQ stocks is significantly less than the total value of NYSE stocks.

There are many large and important financial markets outside the United States, of course, and U.S. corporations are increasingly looking to these markets to raise cash. The Tokyo Stock Exchange and the London Stock Exchange (TSE and LSE, respectively) are two well-known examples. The fact that OTC markets have no physical location means that national borders do not present a great barrier, and there is now a huge international OTC debt market. Because of globalization, financial markets have reached the point where trading in many instruments never stops; it just travels around the world.

The Tokyo Stock Exchange in English: www.jpx.co.jp /english/.

Listing   Stocks that trade on an organized exchange (or market) are said to be *listed* on that exchange. In order to be listed, firms must meet certain minimum criteria concerning, for example, asset size and number of shareholders. These criteria differ for different exchanges.

NYSE has the most stringent requirements of the stock markets in the United States. There are minimums on earnings, assets, and number and market value of shares outstanding.

The London Stock Exchange: www.london stockexchange.com.

CONCEPT QUESTIONS

1.6a   What is a dealer market? How do dealer and auction markets differ?

1.6b   What is the largest auction market in the United States?

1.6c   What does OTC stand for? What is the large OTC market for stocks called?

SUMMARY AND CONCLUSIONS

This chapter has introduced you to some of the basic ideas in business finance. In it, we saw that:

1. Business finance has three main areas of concern:
   a. Capital budgeting. What long-term investments should the firm take?
   b. Capital structure. Where will the firm get the long-term financing to pay for its investments? In other words, what mixture of debt and equity should we use to fund our operations?
   c. Working capital management. How should the firm manage its everyday financial activities?
2. The goal of financial management in a for-profit business is to make decisions that increase the value of the stock, or, more generally, increase the market value of the equity.
3. The corporate form of organization is superior to other forms when it comes to raising money and transferring ownership interests, but it has the significant disadvantage of double taxation.
4. There is the possibility of conflicts between stockholders and management in a large corporation. We called these conflicts agency problems and discussed how they might be controlled and reduced.

Of the topics we've discussed thus far, the most important is the goal of financial management. Throughout the text, we will be analyzing many different financial decisions, but we always ask the same question: How does the decision under consideration affect the value of the equity in the firm?

☰ connect POP QUIZ!

Can you answer the following questions? If your class is using *Connect*, log on to SmartBook to see if you know the answers to these and other questions, check out the study tools, and find out what topics require additional practice!

Section 1.2 What are the three main questions to be addressed if you wanted to start your own business?

Section 1.3 What characteristics are important when considering a partnership?

Section 1.4 What does the Sarbanes-Oxley Act require of corporate officers?

Section 1.5 Who are the stakeholders in a firm?

Section 1.6 What are the defining features of a primary market?

CRITICAL THINKING AND CONCEPTS REVIEW

LO 1 **1.1** **The Financial Management Decision Process**   What are the three types of financial management decisions? For each type of decision, give an example of a business transaction that would be relevant.

LO 3 **1.2** **Sole Proprietorships and Partnerships**   What are the four primary disadvantages to the sole proprietorship and partnership forms of business organization? What benefits are there to these types of business organization as opposed to the corporate form?

LO 3   **1.3**   **Corporations**   What is the primary disadvantage of the corporate form of organization? Name at least two of the advantages of corporate organization.

LO 3   **1.4**   **Corporate Finance Organization**   In a large corporation, what are the two distinct groups that report to the chief financial officer? Which group is the focus of corporate finance?

LO 2   **1.5**   **Goal of Financial Management**   What goal should always motivate the actions of the firm's financial manager?

LO 4   **1.6**   **Agency Problems**   Who owns a corporation? Describe the process whereby the owners control the firm's management. What is the main reason that an agency relationship exists in the corporate form of organization? In this context, what kinds of problems can arise?

LO 3   **1.7**   **Primary versus Secondary Markets**   You've probably noticed coverage in the financial press of an initial public offering (IPO) of a company's securities. The social networking company Snapchat is a relatively recent example. Is an IPO a primary market transaction or a secondary market transaction?

LO 3   **1.8**   **Auction versus Dealer Markets**   What does it mean when we say the New York Stock Exchange is an auction market? How are auction markets different from dealer markets? What kind of market is NASDAQ?

LO 2   **1.9**   **Not-for-Profit Firm Goals**   Suppose you were the financial manager of a not-for-profit business (a not-for-profit hospital, perhaps). What kinds of goals do you think would be appropriate?

LO 2   **1.10**   **Ethics and Firm Goals**   Can our goal of maximizing the value of the stock conflict with other goals, such as avoiding unethical or illegal behavior? In particular, do you think subjects such as customer and employee safety, the environment, and the general good of society fit in this framework, or are they essentially ignored? Try to think of some specific scenarios to illustrate your answer.

LO 2   **1.11**   **International Firm Goal**   Would our goal of maximizing the value of the stock be different if we were thinking about financial management in a foreign country? Why or why not?

LO 4   **1.12**   **Agency Problems**   Suppose you own stock in a company. The current price per share is $25. Another company has just announced that it wants to buy your company and will pay $35 per share to acquire all the outstanding stock. Your company's management immediately begins fighting off this hostile bid. Is management acting in the shareholders' best interests? Why or why not?

LO 4   **1.13**   **Agency Problems and Corporate Ownership**   Corporate ownership varies around the world. Historically, individuals have owned the majority of shares in public corporations in the United States. In Germany and Japan, however, banks, other large financial institutions, and other companies own most of the stock in public corporations. Do you think agency problems are likely to be more or less severe in Germany and Japan than in the United States? Why? In recent years, large financial institutions such as mutual funds and pension funds have become the dominant owners of stock in the

United States, and these institutions are becoming more active in corporate affairs. What are the implications of this trend for agency problems and corporate control?

LO 4   **1.14** **Executive Compensation**   Critics have charged that compensation to top management in the United States is too high and should be cut back. For example, focusing on large corporations, in 2017, First Data CEO Frank Bisignano made about $102 million and Live Nation CEO Michael Rapino made about $71 million. Are such amounts excessive? In answering, it might be helpful to recognize that superstar athletes such as LeBron James, top entertainers such as Oprah Winfrey, and many others at the top of their respective fields earn at least as much, if not more.

LO 4   **1.15** **Sarbanes-Oxley**   In response to the Sarbanes-Oxley Act, many small firms in the United States have opted to "go dark" and delist their stock. Why might a company choose this route? What are the costs of "going dark"?

WHAT'S ON THE WEB?

1.1 Listing Requirements   This chapter discussed some of the listing requirements for the NYSE and NASDAQ. Find the complete listing requirements for the NYSE at www.nyse.com and NASDAQ at www.nasdaq.com. Which has more stringent listing requirements? Why don't they have the same listing requirements?

1.2 Business Formation   As you may (or may not) know, many companies incorporate in Delaware for a variety of reasons. Visit BizFilings at www.bizfilings.com to find out why. Which state has the highest fee for incorporation? For an LLC? While at the site, look at the FAQ section regarding corporations and LLCs.

CHAPTER CASE
The McGee Cake Company

In early 2013, Doc and Lyn McGee formed the McGee Cake Company. The company produced a full line of cakes, and its specialties included chess cake,* lemon pound cake, and double-iced, double-chocolate cake. The couple formed the company as an outside interest, and both continued to work at their current jobs. Doc did all the baking, and Lyn handled the marketing and distribution. With good product quality and a sound marketing plan, the company grew rapidly. In early 2018, the company was featured in a widely distributed entrepreneurial magazine. Later that year, the company was featured in *Gourmet Desserts*, a leading specialty food magazine. After the article appeared in *Gourmet Desserts*, sales exploded, and the company began receiving orders from all over the world.

*Chess cake is quite delicious and distinct from cheesecake. The origin of the name is obscure.

Because of the increased sales, Doc left his other job, followed shortly by Lyn. The company hired additional workers to meet demand. Unfortunately, the fast growth experienced by the company led to cash flow and capacity problems. The company is currently producing as many cakes as possible with the assets it owns, but demand for its cakes is still growing. Further, the company has been approached by a national supermarket chain with a proposal to put four of its cakes in all of the chain's stores, and a national restaurant chain has contacted the company about selling McGee cakes in its restaurants. The restaurant would sell the cakes without a brand name.

Doc and Lyn have operated the company as a sole proprietorship. They have approached you to help manage and direct the company's growth. Specifically, they have asked you to answer the following questions:

QUESTIONS

1. What are the advantages and disadvantages of changing the company organization from a sole proprietorship to an LLC?

2. What are the advantages and disadvantages of changing the company organization from a sole proprietorship to a corporation?

3. Ultimately, what action would you recommend the company undertake? Why?

Financial Statements, Taxes, and Cash Flow | 2

In December 2017, the Tax Cuts and Jobs Act was enacted into law beginning in 2018. The new law was a sweeping change to corporate taxes in the United States. For example, rather than depreciating an asset over time for tax purposes, companies are allowed to depreciate the entire purchase price in the first year. Another change was a limit to the tax deductibility of interest expense. However, possibly the biggest change was the switch from a graduated corporate income tax structure, with rates ranging from 15 percent to 39 percent, to a flat 21 percent corporate tax rate.

While the change in the corporate tax rate affects net income, there is a more important impact. Because taxes are a key consideration in making investment decisions, the change in the tax rate could lead to a significant change in corporate investment and financing decisions. Understanding why ultimately leads us to the main subject of this chapter: that all-important substance known as *cash flow*.

Please visit us at underlineessentialsofcorporatefinance.blogspot.com for the latest developments in the world of corporate finance.

In this chapter, we examine financial statements, taxes, and cash flow. Our emphasis is not on preparing financial statements. Instead, we recognize that financial statements are frequently a key source of information for financial decisions, so our goal is to briefly examine such statements and point out some of their more relevant features. We pay special attention to some of the practical details of cash flow.

As you read, pay particular attention to two important differences: (1) the difference between accounting value and market value and (2) the difference between accounting income and cash flow. These distinctions will be important throughout the book.

2.1 THE BALANCE SHEET

The **balance sheet** is a snapshot of the firm. It is a convenient means of organizing and summarizing what a firm owns (its *assets*), what a firm owes (its *liabilities*), and the difference between the two (the firm's *equity*) at a given point in time. Figure 2.1 illustrates how the balance sheet is constructed. As shown, the left-hand side lists the assets of the firm, and the right-hand side lists the liabilities and equity.

Assets: The Left-Hand Side

Assets are classified as either *current* or *fixed*. A fixed asset is one that has a relatively long life. Fixed assets can either be *tangible*, such as a truck or a computer, or *intangible*, such as a trademark or patent. A current asset has a life of less than one year. This means that the asset will normally convert to cash within 12 months. For example, inventory would normally be purchased and sold within a year and is thus classified as a current asset. Obviously, cash itself is a current asset. Accounts receivable (money owed to the firm by its customers) are also a current asset.

Liabilities and Owners' Equity: The Right-Hand Side

The firm's liabilities are the first thing listed on the right-hand side of the balance sheet. These are classified as either *current* or *long term*. Current liabilities, like current assets, have a life of less than one year (meaning they must be paid within the year), and they are listed before long-term liabilities. Accounts payable (money the firm owes to its suppliers) are one example of a current liability.

A debt that is not due in the coming year is classified as a long-term liability. A loan that the firm will pay off in five years is one such long-term debt. Firms borrow over the long term from a variety of sources. We will tend to use the terms *bonds* and *bondholders* generically to refer to long-term debt and long-term creditors, respectively.

Finally, by definition, the difference between the total value of the assets (current and fixed) and the total value of the liabilities (current and long-term) is the *shareholders' equity*, also called *common equity* or *owners' equity*. This feature of the balance sheet is intended to reflect the fact that, if the firm were to sell all of its assets and use the money to pay off its debts, then whatever residual value remained would belong to the shareholders. So, the

Excel Master coverage online

balance sheet
Financial statement showing a firm's accounting value on a particular date.

Two excellent sites for company financial information are finance .yahoo.com and money .cnn.com.

Disney has a good investor site at thewaltdisney company.com.

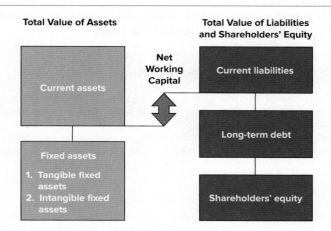

Total Value of Assets

Total Value of Liabilities and Shareholders' Equity

Net Working Capital

Current assets

Current liabilities

Long-term debt

Fixed assets
1. Tangible fixed assets
2. Intangible fixed assets

Shareholders' equity

FIGURE 2.1

The balance sheet
Left side: Total value of assets.
Right side: Total value of liabilities and shareholders' equity.

TABLE 2.1

Balance sheets for U.S. Corporation

				U.S. CORPORATION Balance Sheets as of December 31, 2018 and 2019 ($ in Millions)				
	2018	**2019**					**2018**	**2019**
Assets				**Liabilities and Owners' Equity**				
Current assets				Current liabilities				
Cash	$ 104	$ 160		Accounts payable			$ 232	$ 266
Accounts receivable	455	688		Notes payable			196	123
Inventory	553	555		Total			$ 428	$ 389
Total	$1,112	$1,403						
Fixed assets								
Net fixed assets	$1,644	$1,709		Long-term debt			$ 408	$ 454
				Owners' equity				
				Common stock and paid-in surplus			600	640
				Retained earnings			1,320	1,629
				Total			$1,920	$2,269
Total assets	$2,756	$3,112		Total liabilities and owners' equity			$2,756	$3,112

balance sheet "balances" because the value of the left-hand side always equals the value of the right-hand side. That is, the value of the firm's assets is equal to the sum of its liabilities and shareholders' equity:[1]

$$\text{Assets} = \text{Liabilities} + \text{Shareholders' equity} \qquad \text{[2.1]}$$

This is the balance sheet identity, or equation, and it always holds because shareholders' equity is defined as the difference between assets and liabilities.

Net Working Capital

net working capital
Current assets less current liabilities.

As shown in Figure 2.1, the difference between a firm's current assets and its current liabilities is called **net working capital**. Net working capital is positive when current assets exceed current liabilities. Based on the definitions of current assets and current liabilities, this means that the cash that will become available over the next 12 months exceeds the cash that must be paid over that same period. For this reason, net working capital is usually positive in a healthy firm.

Table 2.1 shows simplified balance sheets for the fictitious U.S. Corporation. There are three particularly important things to keep in mind when examining a balance sheet: liquidity, debt versus equity, and market value versus book value.

EXAMPLE 2.1   **Building the Balance Sheet**

A firm has current assets of $100, net fixed assets of $500, short-term debt of $70, and long-term debt of $200. What does the balance sheet look like? What is shareholders' equity? What is net working capital?

    In this case, total assets are $100 + 500 = $600 and total liabilities are $70 + 200 = $270, so shareholders' equity is the difference: $600 − 270 = $330. The balance sheet would thus look like:

(continued)

---

[1]The terms *owners' equity, shareholders' equity,* and *stockholders' equity* are used interchangeably to refer to the equity in a corporation. The term *net worth* also is used. Variations exist in addition to these.

Assets		Liabilities and Shareholders' Equity	
Current assets	$100	Current liabilities	$ 70
Net fixed assets	500	Long-term debt	200
		Shareholders' equity	330
Total assets	$600	Total liabilities and shareholders' equity	$600

Net working capital is the difference between current assets and current liabilities, or $100 − 70 = $30.

Liquidity

Liquidity refers to the speed and ease with which an asset can be converted to cash. Gold is a relatively liquid asset; a custom manufacturing facility is not. Liquidity really has two dimensions: ease of conversion versus loss of value. Any asset can be converted to cash quickly if we cut the price enough. A highly liquid asset, therefore, is one that can be quickly sold without significant loss of value. An illiquid asset is one that cannot be quickly converted to cash without a substantial price reduction.

Assets are normally listed on the balance sheet in order of decreasing liquidity, meaning that the most liquid assets are listed first. Current assets are relatively liquid and include cash and those assets that we expect to convert to cash over the next 12 months. Accounts receivable, for example, represent amounts not yet collected from customers on sales already made. Naturally, we hope these will convert to cash in the near future. Inventory is probably the least liquid of the current assets, at least for many businesses.

Fixed assets are, for the most part, relatively illiquid. These consist of tangible things such as buildings and equipment that don't convert to cash at all in normal business activity (they are, of course, used in the business to generate cash). Intangible assets, such as trademarks, have no physical existence but can be very valuable. Like tangible fixed assets, they won't ordinarily convert to cash and are generally considered illiquid.

Liquidity is valuable. The more liquid a business is, the less likely it is to experience financial distress (i.e., difficulty in paying debts or buying needed assets). Unfortunately, liquid assets are generally less profitable to hold. For example, cash holdings are the most liquid of all investments, but they sometimes earn no return at all—they just sit there. There is, therefore, a trade-off between the advantages of liquidity and forgone potential profits.

Annual and quarterly financial statements (and lots more) for most public U.S. corporations can be found in the EDGAR database at www.sec.gov.

Debt versus Equity

To the extent that a firm borrows money, it usually gives first claim to the firm's cash flow to creditors. Equity holders are entitled only to the residual value, the portion left after creditors are paid. The value of this residual portion is the shareholders' equity in the firm, which is the value of the firm's assets less the value of the firm's liabilities:

Shareholders' equity = Assets − Liabilities

This is true in an accounting sense because shareholders' equity is defined as this residual portion. More importantly, it is true in an economic sense: If the firm sells its assets and pays its debts, whatever cash is left belongs to the shareholders.

The home page for the Financial Accounting Standards Board (FASB) is www.fasb.org.

The use of debt in a firm's capital structure is called *financial leverage*. The more debt a firm has (as a percentage of assets), the greater is its degree of financial leverage. As we discuss in later chapters, debt acts like a lever in the sense that using it can greatly magnify both gains and losses. So, financial leverage increases the potential reward to shareholders, but it also increases the potential for financial distress and business failure.

Market Value versus Book Value

Generally Accepted Accounting Principles (GAAP)
The common set of standards and procedures by which audited financial statements are prepared.

The true value of any asset is its *market* value, which is the amount of cash we would get if we actually sold it. In contrast, the values shown on the balance sheet for the firm's assets are *book values* and generally are not what the assets are actually worth. Under **Generally Accepted Accounting Principles (GAAP)**, audited financial statements in the United States generally show assets at *historical cost*. In other words, assets are "carried on the books" at what the firm paid for them (minus accumulated depreciation), no matter how long ago they were purchased or how much they are worth today.

For current assets, market value and book value might be somewhat similar because current assets are bought and converted into cash over a relatively short span of time. In other circumstances, they might differ quite a bit. Moreover, for fixed assets, it would be purely a coincidence if the actual market value of an asset (what the asset could be sold for) were equal to its book value. For example, a railroad might own enormous tracts of land purchased a century or more ago. What the railroad paid for that land could be hundreds or thousands of times less than what it is worth today. The balance sheet would nonetheless show the historical cost. There are exceptions to this practice.

Managers and investors frequently will be interested in knowing the market value of the firm. This information is not on the balance sheet. The fact that balance sheet assets are listed at cost means that there is no necessary connection between the total assets shown and the market value of the firm. Indeed, many of the most valuable assets that a firm might have—good management, a good reputation, talented employees—don't appear on the balance sheet at all. To give one example, one of the most valuable assets for many well-known companies is their brand name. According to one source, the names "Coca-Cola," "Microsoft," and "IBM" are all worth in excess of $50 billion.

Similarly, the owners' equity figure on the balance sheet and the true market value of the equity need not be related. For financial managers, then, the accounting value of the equity is not an especially important concern; it is the market value that matters. Henceforth, whenever we speak of the value of an asset or the value of the firm, we will normally mean its *market value*. So, for example, when we say the goal of the financial manager is to increase the value of the stock, we mean the market value of the stock.

EXAMPLE 2.2   **Market versus Book Values**

The Klingon Corporation has fixed assets with a book value of $700 and an appraised market value of about $1,000. Current assets are $400 on the books, but approximately $600 would be realized if they were liquidated. Klingon has $500 in long-term debt, both book value and market value, and no current liabilities of any kind. What is the book value of the equity? What is the market value?

We can construct two simplified balance sheets, one in accounting (book value) terms and one in economic (market value) terms:

KLINGON CORPORATION Balance Sheets Market Value versus Book Value					
	Book	**Market**		**Book**	**Market**
Assets			**Liabilities and Shareholders' Equity**		
Current assets	$ 400	$ 600	Long-term debt	$ 500	$ 500
Net fixed assets	700	1,000	Shareholders' equity	600	1,100
	$1,100	$1,600		$1,100	$1,600

In this example, shareholders' equity is actually worth almost twice as much as what is shown on the books. The distinction between book and market values is important precisely because book values can be so different from true economic values.

CONCEPT QUESTIONS

2.1a What is the balance sheet identity?

2.1b What is liquidity? Why is it important?

2.1c What do we mean by financial leverage?

2.1d Explain the difference between accounting value and market value. Which is more important to the financial manager? Why?

2.2 THE INCOME STATEMENT

The **income statement** measures performance over some period of time, usually a quarter or a year. The income statement equation is:

Excel Master
coverage online

Revenues − Expenses = Income   [2.2]

If you think of the balance sheet as a snapshot, then you can think of the income statement as a video recording covering the period between a before and an after picture. Table 2.2 gives a simplified income statement for U.S. Corporation.

income statement
Financial statement summarizing a firm's performance over a period of time.

TABLE 2.2

Income statement for U.S. Corporation

U.S. CORPORATION 2019 Income Statement ($ in Millions)		
Net sales		$1,509
Cost of goods sold		750
Depreciation		89
Earnings before interest and taxes		$ 670
Interest paid		70
Taxable income		$ 600
Taxes (21%)		126
Net income		$ 474
Dividends	$165	
Addition to retained earnings	309	

The first thing reported on an income statement is usually revenue and expenses from the firm's principal operations. Subsequent parts include, among other things, financing expenses such as interest paid. Taxes paid are reported separately. The last item is *net income* (the so-called bottom line). Net income often is expressed on a per-share basis and called *earnings per share (EPS)*.

As indicated, U.S. paid cash dividends of $165. The difference between net income and cash dividends, $309, is the addition to retained earnings for the year. This amount is added to the cumulative retained earnings account on the balance sheet. If you look back at the two balance sheets for U.S. Corporation, you'll see that retained earnings did go up by this amount, $1,320 + 309 = $1,629.

EXAMPLE 2.3   **Earnings and Dividends per Share**

Suppose U.S. Corporation had 200 million shares outstanding at the end of 2019. Based on the income statement in Table 2.2, what was EPS? What were dividends per share?

From the income statement, U.S. Corporation had a net income of $474 million for the year. Total dividends were $165 million. Because 200 million shares were outstanding, we can calculate earnings per share and dividends per share as follows:

$$\text{Earnings per share} = \text{Net income/Total shares outstanding}$$
$$= \$474/200 = \$2.37 \text{ per share}$$

$$\text{Dividends per share} = \text{Total dividends/Total shares outstanding}$$
$$= \$165/200 = \$.825 \text{ per share}$$

When looking at an income statement, the financial manager needs to keep three things in mind: GAAP, cash versus noncash items, and time and costs.

GAAP and the Income Statement

An income statement prepared using GAAP will show revenue when it accrues. This is not necessarily when the cash comes in. The general rule (the recognition principle) is to recognize revenue when the earnings process is virtually complete and the value of an exchange of goods or services is known or can be reliably determined. In practice, this principle usually means that revenue is recognized at the time of sale, which need not be the same as the time of collection.

Expenses shown on the income statement are based on the matching principle. The basic idea here is to first determine revenues as described earlier and then match those revenues with the costs associated with producing them. So, if we manufacture a product and then sell it on credit, the revenue is recognized at the time of sale. The production and other costs associated with the sale of that product likewise would be recognized at that time. Once again, the actual cash outflows may have occurred at some very different times. Thus, as a result of the way revenues and expenses are reported, the figures shown on the income statement may not be at all representative of the actual cash inflows and outflows that occurred during a particular period.

Noncash Items

noncash items
Expenses charged against revenues that do not directly affect cash flow, such as depreciation.

A primary reason that accounting income differs from cash flow is that an income statement contains **noncash items**. The most important of these is *depreciation*. Suppose a firm purchases a fixed asset for $5,000 and pays in cash. Obviously, the firm has a $5,000 cash outflow at the time of purchase. However, instead of deducting the $5,000 as an expense, an accountant might depreciate the asset over a five-year period.

If the depreciation is straight-line and the asset is written down to zero over that period, then $5,000/5 = $1,000 would be deducted each year as an expense.[2] The important thing to recognize is that this $1,000 deduction isn't cash—it's an accounting number. The actual cash outflow occurred when the asset was purchased.

The depreciation deduction is another application of the matching principle in accounting. The revenues associated with an asset would generally occur over some length of time. So, the accountant seeks to match the expense of purchasing the asset with the benefits produced from owning it.

As we will see, for the financial manager, the actual timing of cash inflows and outflows is critical in coming up with a reasonable estimate of market value, so we need to learn how to separate the cash flows from the noncash accounting entries. In reality, the difference between cash flow and accounting income can be pretty dramatic. For example, in the third quarter of 2017, wireless infrastructure company Westell Technologies announced a net loss of $14.5 million. Sounds bad, but the company also reported a positive cash flow of $26.6 million, a difference of $41.1 million.

Time and Costs

It is often useful to think of the future as having two distinct parts: the short run and the long run. These are not precise time periods. The distinction has to do with whether costs are fixed or variable. In the long run, all business costs are variable. Given sufficient time, assets can be sold, debts can be paid, and so on.

If our time horizon is relatively short, however, some costs are effectively fixed—they must be paid no matter what (e.g., property taxes). Other costs, such as wages to laborers and payments to suppliers, are still variable. As a result, even in the short run, the firm can vary its output level by varying expenditures in these areas.

The distinction between fixed and variable costs is important, at times, to the financial manager, but the way costs are reported on the income statement is not a good guide as to which costs are which. The reason is that, in practice, accountants tend to classify costs as either product costs or period costs.

Product costs include such things as raw materials, direct labor expense, and manufacturing overhead. These are reported on the income statement as costs of goods sold, but they include both fixed and variable costs. Similarly, period costs are incurred during a particular time period and might be reported as selling, general, and administrative expenses. Once again, some of these period costs may be fixed and others may be variable. The company president's salary is a period cost and is probably fixed, at least in the short run.

The balance sheets and income statement we have been using thus far are hypothetical. Our nearby *Work the Web* box shows how to find actual balance sheets and income statements online for almost any public company.

---

[2]By "straight-line," we mean that the depreciation deduction is the same every year. By "written down to zero," we mean that the asset is assumed to have no value at the end of five years.

W🌐RK THE WEB

The U.S. Securities and Exchange Commission (SEC) requires that most public companies file regular reports, including annual and quarterly financial statements. The SEC has a public site named EDGAR that makes these reports available for free at www.sec.gov. We went to "Company Filings Search" and searched for "Microsoft." When we got our results, we limited our search to Form 10-K. Here is what we found:

Filings	Format		Description	Filing Date	File/Film Number
10-K	Documents	Interactive Data	Annual report [Section 13 and 15(d), not S-K Item 405] Acc-no: 0001564590-17-014900 (34 Act) Size: 28 MB	2017-08-02	001-37845 171000067
10-K	Documents	Interactive Data	Annual report [Section 13 and 15(d), not S-K Item 405] Acc-no: 0001193125-16-662229 (34 Act) Size: 13 MB	2016-07-28	001-37845 161790278
10-K	Documents	Interactive Data	Annual report [Section 13 and 15(d), not S-K Item 405] Acc-no: 0001193125-15-272806 (34 Act) Size: 14 MB	2015-07-31	000-14278 151019135
10-K	Documents	Interactive Data	Annual report [Section 13 and 15(d), not S-K Item 405] Acc-no: 0001193125-14-289961 (34 Act) Size: 18 MB	2014-07-31	000-14278 141007161
10-K	Documents	Interactive Data	Annual report [Section 13 and 15(d), not S-K Item 405] Acc-no: 0001193125-13-310205 (34 Act) Size: 24 MB	2013-07-30	000-14278 13996075
10-K	Documents	Interactive Data	Annual report [Section 13 and 15(d), not S-K Item 405] Acc-no: 0001193125-12-316848 (34 Act) Size: 17 MB	2012-07-26	000-14278 12967580
10-K	Documents	Interactive Data	Annual report [Section 13 and 15(d), not S-K Item 405] Acc-no: 0001193125-11-200680 (34 Act) Size: 16 MB	2011-07-28	000-14278 11953262
10-K	Documents	Interactive Data	Annual report [Section 13 and 15(d), not S-K Item 405] Acc-no: 0001193125-10-171791 (34 Act) Size: 20 MB	2010-07-30	000-14278 10960074
10-K	Documents		Annual report [Section 13 and 15(d), not S-K Item 405] Acc-no: 0001193125-09-158735 (34 Act) Size: 1 MB	2009-07-30	000-14278 09971824
10-K	Documents		Annual report [Section 13 and 15(d), not S-K Item 405] Acc-no: 0001193125-08-152768 (34 Act) Size: 1 MB	2008-07-31	000-14278 08962705
10-K	Documents		Annual report [Section 13 and 15(d), not S-K Item 405] Acc-no: 0001193125-07-170817 (34 Act) Size: 1 MB	2007-08-03	000-14278 071024829
10-K	Documents		Annual report [Section 13 and 15(d), not S-K Item 405] Acc-no: 0001193125-06-180008 (34 Act) Size: 1 MB	2006-08-25	000-14278 061056648
10-K	Documents		Annual report [Section 13 and 15(d), not S-K Item 405] Acc-no: 0001193125-05-174625 (34 Act) Size: 1 MB	2005-08-26	000-14278 051050009
10-K	Documents		Annual report [Section 13 and 15(d), not S-K Item 405] Acc-no: 0001193125-04-150689 Size: 1 MB	2004-09-01	000-14278 041011640
10-K	Documents		Annual report [Section 13 and 15(d), not S-K Item 405] Acc-no: 0001193125-03-045632 Size: 1 MB	2003-09-05	000-14278 03982442
10-K	Documents		Annual report [Section 13 and 15(d), not S-K Item 405] Acc-no: 0001032210-02-001351 Size: 1 MB	2002-09-06	000-14278 02757909
10-K	Documents		Annual report [Section 13 and 15(d), not S-K Item 405] Acc-no: 0001032210-01-501099 Size: 261 KB	2001-09-18	000-14278 1736790
10-K	Documents		Annual report [Section 13 and 15(d), not S-K Item 405] Acc-no: 0001032210-00-001961 Size: 457 KB	2000-09-28	000-14278 731256
10-K	Documents		Annual report [Section 13 and 15(d), not S-K Item 405] Acc-no: 0001022210-99-001375 Size: 289 KB	1999-09-28	000-14278 99719734
10-K	Documents		Annual report [Section 13 and 15(d), not S-K Item 405] Acc-no: 0001032210-98-001067 Size: 176 KB	1998-09-25	000-14278 98713364
10-K	Documents		Annual report [Section 13 and 15(d), not S-K Item 405] Acc-no: 0001017062-97-001764 Size: 198 KB	1997-09-29	000-14278 97687694
10-K	Documents		Annual report [Section 13 and 15(d), not S-K Item 405] Acc-no: 0000891020-96-001130 Size: 147 KB	1996-09-27	000-14278 96635668
10-K	Documents		Annual report [Section 13 and 15(d), not S-K Item 405] Acc-no: 0000891020-95-000423 Size: 189 KB	1995-09-25	000-14278 95575996
10-K	Documents		Annual report [Section 13 and 15(d), not S-K Item 405] Acc-no: 0000891020-94-000175 Size: 442 KB	1994-09-27	000-14278 94560472

Source: **www.sec.gov**

As of the date of this search, EDGAR had 24 of these reports for Microsoft available for downloading. The 10-K is the annual report filed with the SEC. It includes, among other things, the list of officers and their salaries, financial statements for the previous fiscal year, and an explanation by the company for the financial results. Here is an exercise for you: Go to the "Descriptions of SEC Forms" page and find the different forms companies must file with the SEC. What is a 10-Q report?

> **QUESTIONS**
> 1. *Before the popularization of computers, electronic filing of documents with the SEC was not available. Go to www.sec.gov and find the filings for General Electric. What is the date of the oldest 10-K available on the website for General Electric? Look up the 10-K forms for IBM and Apple to see if the year of the first electronic filing is the same for these companies.*
> 2. *Go to www.sec.gov and find out when the following forms are used: Form DEF 14A, Form 8-K, and Form 6-K.*

Earnings Management

The way that firms are required by GAAP to report financial results is intended to be objective and precise. In reality, there is plenty of wiggle room, and, as a result, companies have significant discretion over their reported earnings. For example, corporations frequently like to show investors that they have steadily growing earnings. To do this, they might take steps to overstate or understate earnings at various times to smooth out dips and surges. Doing so is called *earnings management*, and it is a controversial practice.

With the increasing globalization of business, accounting standards need to be more alike across countries. In recent years, U.S. accounting standards have increasingly become more closely tied to International Financial Reporting Standards (IFRS). In particular, the Financial Accounting Standards Board (in charge of U.S. GAAP) and the International Accounting Standards Board (in charge of IFRS) have been working toward a convergence of policies. Although GAAP and IFRS have become similar in several areas, as of 2018, it appears that a full convergence of accounting policies is off the table, at least for now.

For more information about IFRS, check out the website www.ifrs.org.

CONCEPT QUESTIONS

2.2a What is the income statement equation?

2.2b What are the three things to keep in mind when looking at an income statement?

2.2c Why is accounting income not the same as cash flow?

2.3 TAXES

Taxes can be one of the largest cash outflows a firm experiences. For example, for fiscal year 2018, Walmart's earnings before taxes were about $15.1 billion. Its tax bill, including all taxes paid worldwide, was a whopping $4.6 billion, or about 30 percent of its pretax earnings.

Excel Master coverage online

The size of a company's tax bill is determined through the tax code, an often-amended set of rules. In this section, we examine corporate tax rates and how taxes are calculated. If the various rules of taxation seem a little bizarre or convoluted to you, keep in mind that the tax code is the result of political, not economic, forces. As a result, there is no reason why it has to make economic sense.

Corporate Tax Rates

As we discussed in our chapter introduction, after the passage of the Tax Cuts and Jobs Act of 2017, the federal corporate tax rate in the United States became a flat 21 percent. However, tax rates on other forms of business such as proprietorships, partnerships, and LLCs did not become flat. To illustrate some important points about taxes for such entities, we take a look at personal tax rates in Table 2.3. As shown, in 2018, there are seven tax brackets, ranging from 10 percent to a high of 37 percent, down from 39.6 percent in 2017.

The IRS has a great website! (www.irs.gov)

Taxable Income		Tax Rate
$ 0–	9,525	10%
9,525–	38,700	12
38,700–	82,500	22
82,500–	157,500	24
157,500–	200,000	32
200,000–	500,000	35
500,000+		37

TABLE 2.3

Personal tax rates for 2018 (unmarried individuals)

Average versus Marginal Tax Rates

average tax rate
Total taxes paid divided by total taxable income.

marginal tax rate
Amount of tax payable on the next dollar earned.

In making financial decisions, it is frequently important to distinguish between average and marginal tax rates. Your **average tax rate** is your tax bill divided by your taxable income; in other words, the percentage of your income that goes to pay taxes. Your **marginal tax rate** is the extra tax you would pay if you earned one more dollar. The percentage tax rates shown in Table 2.3 are all marginal rates. Put another way, the tax rates in Table 2.3 apply to the part of income in the indicated range only, not all income.

The difference between average and marginal tax rates can be best illustrated with a simple example. Suppose you are single and your personal taxable income is $100,000. What is your tax bill? From Table 2.3, we can figure your tax bill like this:

$$
\begin{aligned}
.10(\$9,525) &= \$952.50 \\
.12(\$38,700 - 9,525) &= 3,501.00 \\
.22(\$82,500 - 38,700) &= 9,636.00 \\
.24(\$100,000 - 82,500) &= \underline{4,200.00} \\
&= \underline{\$18,289.50}
\end{aligned}
$$

Your total tax is $18,289.50.

In our example, what is the average tax rate? You had a taxable income of $100,000 and a tax bill of $18,289.50, so the average tax rate is $18,289.50/$100,000 = .1829, or 18.29%. What is the marginal tax rate? If you made one more dollar, the tax on that dollar would be 24 cents, so your marginal rate is 24 percent.

EXAMPLE 2.4　Deep in the Heart of Taxes

Algernon, a small proprietorship owned by an unmarried individual, has a taxable income of $80,000. What is its tax bill? What is its average tax rate? Its marginal tax rate?

From Table 2.3, we see that the tax rate applied to the first $9,525 is 10 percent; the rate applied over that up to $38,700 is 12 percent; the rate applied after that up to our total of $80,000 is 22 percent. So Algernon must pay .10 × $9,525 + .12 × ($38,700 − 9,525) + .22 × ($80,000 − 38,700) = $13,540. The average tax rate is thus $13,540/$80,000 = .1692, or 16.92%. The marginal rate is 22 percent because Algernon's taxes would rise by 22 cents if it earned another dollar in taxable income.

It will normally be the marginal tax rate that is relevant for financial decision making. The reason is that any new cash flows will be taxed at that marginal rate. Because financial decisions usually involve new cash flows or changes in existing ones, this rate will tell us the marginal effect on our tax bill.

With a flat-rate tax, such as the U.S. federal corporate tax (as of 2018), there is only one tax rate, so the rate is the same for all income levels. With such a tax system, the marginal tax rate is always the same as the average tax rate.

Before moving on, we should note that the tax rates we have discussed in this section relate to federal taxes only. Overall tax rates can be higher if state, local, and any other taxes are considered.

What Is Warren Buffett's Tax Rate?

In 2011, famed investor Warren Buffett, one of the wealthiest individuals in the world, created a stir when he publicly stated that his tax rate was lower than the tax rate paid by his secretary. The previous year, Buffett's gross income was about $63 million, on which he paid only a 15 percent tax rate. (Remember, this was before the Tax Cuts and Jobs Act of 2017.) His secretary (with a substantially lower income) had a 31 percent marginal tax rate. Also in 2011, when Republican presidential contender Mitt Romney released his income taxes, it was revealed that he, too, paid an income tax rate of only 15 percent on his $21 million annual income.

Why do Buffett's and Romney's tax rates appear so low? Currently, under the U.S. tax system, wage income is taxed at a much higher rate than dividends and long-term capital gains. In fact, in 2011, in the highest tax bracket, wage income was taxed at 37 percent, while dividends and long-term capital gains were taxed at 15 percent. For Buffett and Romney, most of their annual income comes from their investments, not wages, hence the 15 percent rate.

So do rich guys get all the (tax) breaks? Former U.S. President Barack Obama seems to think so. In his 2012 State of the Union Address, with Buffett's secretary Debbie Bosanek joining First Lady Michelle Obama in her box as a special guest, he called for the creation of a "Buffett tax." As he described it, such a tax would be an extra tax paid by very high-income individuals. Maybe President Obama was mad about the fact that he and the first lady paid (in 2013) $98,169 in federal taxes on their joint income of $481,098, implying an average tax rate of 20.4 percent.

Of course, you know that income received from dividends is already taxed. Dividends are paid from corporate income, which was taxed at 35 percent for larger dividend-paying companies. Effectively, any tax on dividends is double taxation on that money. The tax code realizes this. The lower tax rate on dividends lowers the double tax rate. The same thing is true for capital gains; taxes are paid on the money before the investment is made.

In Buffett's case, most of his wealth stems from his approximately 30 percent ownership of Berkshire Hathaway Corporation. Based on its 23,000 (no typo!)-page tax return, Berkshire's 2014 corporate tax bill was $7.9 billion on pretax income of $28.1 billion—a 28 percent average rate. Buffett's share of Berkshire's tax bill therefore amounts to something on the order of $2.37 billion! If we include Berkshire's corporate taxes, Buffett's average tax rate is more like 28 + 15 = 43 percent.

To give another example, consider the situation described by N. Gregory Mankiw, the well-known economist and textbook author. Mankiw considers taking a writing job for $1,000. He figures that if he earns an 8 percent return and there are no taxes, he would be able to leave his children about $10,000 in 30 years when he passes on. However, because of federal, state, and Medicare taxes, he would receive only about $523 after taxes today. And because of corporate taxes and personal income taxes, his return on the same investment would be only about 4 percent, which will result in a balance of $1,700 in 30 years. When he dies, his account will be taxed using the marginal estate tax rate, which is as high as 55 percent. As a result, his children will receive only about $1,000, implying a tax rate of 90 percent!

CONCEPT QUESTION

2.3a   What is the difference between a marginal and an average tax rate?

2.4 CASH FLOW

At this point, we are ready to discuss perhaps one of the most important pieces of financial information that can be gleaned from financial statements: *cash flow*. By cash flow, we mean the difference between the number of dollars that came in and the number that went out. For example, if you were the owner of a business, you might be very interested in how much cash you actually took out of your business in a given year. How to determine this amount is one of the things we discuss next.

There is no standard financial statement that presents this information in the way that we wish. We will, therefore, discuss how to calculate cash flow for U.S. Corporation and point out how the result differs from that of standard financial statement calculations.

Excel Master coverage online

Important note: There is a standard financial accounting statement called the *statement of cash flows*, but it is concerned with a somewhat different issue that should not be confused with what is discussed in this section.

From the balance sheet identity, we know that the value of a firm's assets is equal to the value of its liabilities plus the value of its equity. Similarly, the cash flow from the firm's assets must equal the sum of the cash flow to creditors and the cash flow to stockholders (or owners, if the business is not a corporation):

Cash flow from assets = Cash flow to creditors + Cash flow to stockholders   [2.3]

This is the cash flow identity. What it reflects is the fact that a firm generates cash through its various activities, and that cash either is used to pay creditors or else is paid out to the owners of the firm. We discuss the various things that make up these cash flows next.

Cash Flow from Assets

cash flow from assets
The total of cash flow to creditors and cash flow to stockholders, consisting of the following: operating cash flow, capital spending, and change in net working capital.

operating cash flow
Cash generated from a firm's normal business activities.

Cash flow from assets involves three components: operating cash flow, capital spending, and change in net working capital. **Operating cash flow** refers to the cash flow that results from the firm's day-to-day activities of producing and selling. Expenses associated with the firm's financing of its assets are not included because they are not operating expenses.

In the normal course of events, some portion of the firm's cash flow is reinvested in the firm. *Capital spending* refers to the net spending on fixed assets (purchases of fixed assets less sales of fixed assets). Finally, *the change in net working capital* is the amount spent on net working capital. It is measured as the change in net working capital over the period being examined and represents the net increase or decrease in current assets over current liabilities. The three components of cash flow are examined in more detail next. In all our examples, all amounts are in millions of dollars.

Operating Cash Flow   To calculate operating cash flow (OCF), we want to calculate revenues minus costs, but we don't want to include depreciation because it's not a cash outflow, and we don't want to include interest because it's a financing expense. We do want to include taxes because taxes are, unfortunately, paid in cash.

If we look at U.S. Corporation's income statement (Table 2.2), we see that earnings before interest and taxes (EBIT) are $670. This is almost what we want because it doesn't include interest paid. We need to make two adjustments. First, recall that depreciation is a noncash expense. To get cash flow, we first add back the $89 in depreciation because it wasn't a cash deduction. The other adjustment is to subtract the $126 in taxes because these were paid in cash. The result is operating cash flow:

U.S. CORPORATION 2019 Operating Cash Flow	
Earnings before interest and taxes	$670
+ Depreciation	89
− Taxes	126
Operating cash flow	**$633**

U.S. Corporation thus had a 2019 operating cash flow of $633.

Operating cash flow is an important number because it tells us, on a very basic level, whether or not a firm's cash inflows from its business operations are sufficient to cover its everyday cash outflows. For this reason, a negative operating cash flow is often a sign of trouble.

There is an unpleasant possibility for confusion when we speak of operating cash flow. In accounting practice, operating cash flow often is defined as net income plus depreciation. For U.S. Corporation, this would amount to $474 + 89 = $563. The accounting definition of operating cash flow differs from ours in one important way: Interest is deducted when net income is computed. Notice that the difference between the $633 operating cash flow we calculated and this $563 is $70, the amount of interest paid for the year. This definition of cash flow thus considers interest paid to be an operating expense. Our definition treats it properly as a financing expense. If there were no interest expense, the two definitions would be the same.

To finish our calculation of cash flow from assets for U.S. Corporation, we need to consider how much of the $633 operating cash flow was reinvested in the firm. We consider spending on fixed assets first.

Capital Spending   Net capital spending is money spent on fixed assets less money received from the sale of fixed assets. At the end of 2018, net fixed assets for U.S. Corporation (Table 2.1) were $1,644. During the year, we wrote off (depreciated) $89 worth of fixed assets on the income statement. So, if we didn't purchase any new fixed assets, net fixed assets would have been $1,644 − 89 = $1,555 at year's end. The 2019 balance sheet shows $1,709 in net fixed assets, so we must have spent a total of $1,709 − 1,555 = $154 on fixed assets during the year:

Ending net fixed assets	$1,709
− Beginning net fixed assets	1,644
+ Depreciation	89
Net investment in fixed assets	$ 154

This $154 is our net capital spending for 2019.

Could net capital spending be negative? The answer is yes. This would happen if the firm sold off more assets than it purchased. The *net* here refers to purchases of fixed assets net of any sales of fixed assets.

Change in Net Working Capital   In addition to investing in fixed assets, a firm also will invest in current assets. For example, going back to the balance sheet in Table 2.1, we see that at the end of 2019, U.S. had current assets of $1,403. At the end of 2018, current assets were $1,112, so, during the year, U.S. invested $1,403 − 1,112 = $291 in current assets.

As the firm changes its investment in current assets, its current liabilities usually will change as well. To determine the change in net working capital, the easiest approach is to take the difference between the beginning and ending net working capital (NWC) figures. Net working capital at the end of 2019 was $1,403 − 389 = $1,014. Similarly, at the end of 2018, net working capital was $1,112 − 428 = $684. So, given these figures, we have:

Ending NWC	$1,014
− Beginning NWC	684
Change in NWC	$ 330

Net working capital thus increased by $330. Put another way, U.S. Corporation had a net investment of $330 in NWC for the year.

Conclusion   Given the figures we've come up with, we're ready to calculate cash flow from assets. The total cash flow from assets is given by operating cash flow less the amounts invested in fixed assets and net working capital. So, for U.S., we have:

U.S. CORPORATION 2019 Cash Flow from Assets	
Operating cash flow	$633
− Net capital spending	154
− Change in NWC	330
Cash flow from assets	$ 149

From the cash flow identity above, this $149 cash flow from assets equals the sum of the firm's cash flow to creditors and its cash flow to stockholders. We consider these next.

It wouldn't be at all unusual for a growing corporation to have a negative cash flow. As we shall see below, a negative cash flow means that the firm raised more money by borrowing and selling stock than it paid out to creditors and stockholders that year.

A Note on "Free" Cash Flow   Cash flow from assets sometimes goes by a different name, **free cash flow**. Of course, there is no such thing as "free" cash (we wish!). Instead, the name refers to cash that the firm is free to distribute to creditors and stockholders because it is not needed for working capital or fixed asset investments. We will stick with "cash flow from assets" as our label for this important concept because, in practice, there is some variation in exactly how free cash flow is computed; different users calculate it in different ways. Nonetheless, whenever you hear the phrase "free cash flow," you should understand that what is being discussed is cash flow from assets or something quite similar.

free cash flow
Another name for cash flow from assets.

Cash Flow to Creditors and Stockholders

The cash flows to creditors and stockholders represent the net payments to creditors and owners during the year. They are calculated in a similar way. **Cash flow to creditors** is interest paid less net new borrowing; **cash flow to stockholders** is dividends paid less net new equity raised.

cash flow to creditors
A firm's interest payments to creditors less net new borrowing.

cash flow to stockholders
Dividends paid out by a firm less net new equity raised.

Cash Flow to Creditors   Looking at the income statement in Table 2.2, we see that U.S. Corporation paid $70 in interest to creditors. From the balance sheets in Table 2.1, long-term debt rose by $454 − 408 = $46. So, U.S. Corporation paid out $70 in interest, but it borrowed an additional $46. Net cash flow to creditors is thus:

U.S. CORPORATION 2019 Cash Flow to Creditors	
Interest paid	$70
− Net new borrowing	46
Cash flow to creditors	$24

Cash flow to creditors is sometimes called *cash flow to bondholders*; we will use these terms interchangeably.

Cash Flow to Stockholders   From the income statement, dividends paid to stockholders amount to $165. To get net new equity raised, we need to look at the common stock and paid-in surplus account. This account tells us how much stock the company has sold. During the year, this account rose by $40, so $40 in net new equity was raised. Given this, we have:

U.S. CORPORATION 2019 Cash Flow to Stockholders	
Dividends paid	$165
− Net new equity raised	40
Cash flow to stockholders	$125

The cash flow to stockholders for 2019 was thus $125.

TABLE **2.4**

Cash flow summary

I. **The cash flow identity**

Cash flow from assets = Cash flow to creditors (bondholders)
+ Cash flow to stockholders (owners)

II. **Cash flow from assets**

Cash flow from assets = Operating cash flow
− Net capital spending
− Change in net working capital (NWC)

where

Operating cash flow = Earnings before interest and taxes (EBIT)
+ Depreciation − Taxes

Net capital spending = Ending net fixed assets − Beginning net fixed assets
+ Depreciation

Change in NWC = Ending NWC − Beginning NWC

III. **Cash flow to creditors (bondholders)**

Cash flow to creditors = Interest paid − Net new borrowing

IV. **Cash flow to stockholders (owners)**

Cash flow to stockholders = Dividends paid − Net new equity raised

Conclusion

The last thing that we need to do is to verify that the cash flow identity holds to be sure that we didn't make any mistakes. From above, cash flow from assets is $149. Cash flow to creditors and stockholders is $24 + 125 = $149, so everything checks out. Table 2.4 contains a summary of the various cash flow calculations for future reference.

An Example: Cash Flows for Dole Cola

This extended example covers the various cash flow calculations discussed in the chapter. It also illustrates a few variations that may arise.

Operating Cash Flow   During the year, Dole Cola, Inc., had sales and cost of goods sold of $600 and $300, respectively. Depreciation was $150, and interest paid was $30. Taxes were calculated at a straight 21 percent. Dividends were $30. (All figures are in millions of dollars.) What was operating cash flow for Dole? Why is this different from net income?

The easiest thing to do here is to go ahead and create an income statement. We can then pick up the numbers we need. Dole Cola's income statement is given here:

DOLE COLA 2019 Income Statement	
Net sales	$600
Cost of goods sold	300
Depreciation	150
Earnings before interest and taxes	$150
Interest paid	30
Taxable income	$120
Taxes	25
Net income	$ 95
Dividends	$30
Addition to retained earnings	65

Net income for Dole was thus $95. We now have all the numbers we need. Referring back to the U.S. Corporation example and Table 2.4, we have:

DOLE COLA	
2019 Operating Cash Flow	
Earnings before interest and taxes	$150
+ Depreciation	150
− Taxes	25
Operating cash flow	$275

As this example illustrates, operating cash flow is not the same as net income because depreciation and interest are subtracted out when net income is calculated. If you recall our earlier discussion, we don't subtract these out in computing operating cash flow because depreciation is not a cash expense and interest paid is a financing expense, not an operating expense.

Net Capital Spending   Suppose beginning net fixed assets were $500 and ending net fixed assets were $750. What was the net capital spending for the year?

From the income statement for Dole, depreciation for the year was $150. Net fixed assets rose by $250. Dole thus spent $250 along with an additional $150, for a total of $400.

Change in NWC and Cash Flow from Assets   Suppose Dole Cola started the year with $2,130 in current assets and $1,620 in current liabilities. The corresponding ending figures were $2,260 and $1,710. What was the change in NWC during the year? What was cash flow from assets? How does this compare to net income?

Net working capital started out as $2,130 − 1,620 = $510 and ended up at $2,260 − 1,710 = $550. The change in NWC was thus $550 − 510 = $40. Putting together all the information for Dole Cola, we have:

DOLE COLA	
2019 Cash Flow from Assets	
Operating cash flow	$275
− Net capital spending	400
− Change in NWC	40
Cash flow from assets	−$165

Dole had cash flow from assets of −$165. Net income was positive at $95. Is the fact that cash flow from assets was negative a cause for alarm? Not necessarily. The cash flow here is negative primarily because of a large investment in fixed assets. If these are good investments, then the resulting negative cash flow is not a worry.

Cash Flow to Creditors and Stockholders   We saw that Dole Cola had cash flow from assets of −$165. The fact that this is negative means that Dole raised more money in the form of new debt and equity than it paid out for the year. For example, suppose we know that Dole didn't sell any new equity for the year. What was cash flow to stockholders? To creditors?

■ Answer to Chapter Review and Self-Test Problem

2.1   In preparing the balance sheets, remember that shareholders' equity is the residual. With this in mind, Rasputin's balance sheets are as follows:

| RASPUTIN CORPORATION | | | | | | |
Balance Sheets as of December 31, 2018 and 2019						
	2018	**2019**			**2018**	**2019**
Current assets	$2,140	$2,346	Current liabilities		$ 994	$1,126
Net fixed assets	6,770	7,087	Long-term debt		2,869	2,962
			Equity		5,047	5,345
			Total liabilities and			
Total assets	$8,910	$9,433	shareholders' equity		$8,910	$9,433

The income statement is straightforward:

| RASPUTIN CORPORATION | |
2019 Income Statement	
Sales	$3,990
Cost of goods sold	2,137
Depreciation	1,018
Earnings before interest and taxes	$ 835
Interest paid	267
Taxable income	$ 568
Taxes (21%)	119
Net income	$ 449
Dividends	$305
Addition to retained earnings	144

Notice that we've used a flat 21 percent tax rate. Also, notice that the addition to retained earnings is net income less cash dividends.

We can now pick up the figures we need to get operating cash flow:

| RASPUTIN CORPORATION | |
2019 Operating Cash Flow	
Earnings before interest and taxes	$ 835
+ Depreciation	1,018
− Current taxes	119
Operating cash flow	$1,734

Next, we get the capital spending for the year by looking at the change in fixed assets, remembering to account for the depreciation:

Ending fixed assets	$7,087
− Beginning fixed assets	6,770
+ Depreciation	1,018
Net investment in fixed assets	$1,335

After calculating beginning and ending NWC, we take the difference to get the change in NWC:

Ending NWC	$1,220
— Beginning NWC	1,146
Change in NWC	$ 74

We now combine operating cash flow, net capital spending, and the change in net working capital to get the total cash flow from assets:

RASPUTIN CORPORATION	
2019 Cash Flow from Assets	
Operating cash flow	$1,734
— Net capital spending	1,335
— Change in NWC	74
Cash flow from assets	$ 325

To get cash flow to creditors, notice that long-term borrowing increased by $93 during the year and that interest paid was $267, so:

RASPUTIN CORPORATION	
2019 Cash Flow to Creditors	
Interest paid	$267
— Net new borrowing	93
Cash flow to creditors	$174

Finally, dividends paid were $305. To get net new equity, we have to do some extra calculating. Total equity was up by $5,345 − 5,047 = $298. Of this increase, $144 was from additions to retained earnings, so $154 in new equity was raised during the year. Cash flow to stockholders was thus:

RASPUTIN CORPORATION	
2019 Cash Flow to Stockholders	
Dividends paid	$305
— Net new equity	154
Cash flow to stockholders	$ 151

As a check, notice that cash flow from assets ($325) does equal cash flow to creditors plus cash flow to stockholders ($174 + 151 = $325).

CRITICAL THINKING AND CONCEPTS REVIEW

LO 1   **2.1   Liquidity**   What does liquidity measure? Explain the trade-off a firm faces between high-liquidity and low-liquidity levels.

LO 2   **2.2   Accounting and Cash Flows**   Why is it that the revenue and cost figures shown on a standard income statement may not be representative of the actual cash inflows and outflows that occurred during a period?

LO 1   **2.3 Book Values versus Market Values**   In preparing a balance sheet, why do you think standard accounting practice focuses on historical cost rather than market value?

LO 2   **2.4 Operating Cash Flow**   In comparing accounting net income and operating cash flow, what two items do you find in net income that are not in operating cash flow? Explain what each is and why it is excluded in operating cash flow.

LO 1   **2.5 Book Values versus Market Values**   Under standard accounting rules, it is possible for a company's liabilities to exceed its assets. When this occurs, the owners' equity is negative. Can this happen with market values? Why or why not?

LO 4   **2.6 Cash Flow from Assets**   Suppose a company's cash flow from assets was negative for a particular period. Is this necessarily a good sign or a bad sign?

LO 4   **2.7 Operating Cash Flow**   Suppose a company's operating cash flow was negative for several years running. Is this necessarily a good sign or a bad sign?

LO 4   **2.8 Net Working Capital and Capital Spending**   Could a company's change in NWC be negative in a given year? (*Hint*: Yes.) Explain how this might come about. What about net capital spending?

LO 4   **2.9 Cash Flow to Stockholders and Creditors**   Could a company's cash flow to stockholders be negative in a given year? (*Hint*: Yes.) Explain how this might come about. What about cash flow to creditors?

LO 4   **2.10 Firm Values**   In February 2017, Toshiba announced that it was writing off $6.3 billion due to its acquisition of nuclear power plant construction firm CB&I Stone & Webster only a year before. We would argue that Toshiba's stockholders probably didn't suffer as a result of the reported loss.

QUESTIONS AND PROBLEMS

connect   Select problems are available in McGraw-Hill *Connect*. Please see the packaging options section of the preface for more information.

BASIC (Questions 1–12)

LO 1   **1. Building a Balance Sheet**   Grey Wolf, Inc., has current assets of $2,090, net fixed assets of $9,830, current liabilities of $1,710, and long-term debt of $4,520. What is the value of the shareholders' equity account for this firm? How much is net working capital?

LO 2   **2. Building an Income Statement**   Sidewinder, Inc., has sales of $634,000, costs of $328,000, depreciation expense of $73,000, interest expense of $38,000, and a tax rate of 21 percent. What is the net income for this firm?

LO 2   **3. Dividends and Retained Earnings**   Suppose the firm in Problem 2 paid out $68,000 in cash dividends. What is the addition to retained earnings?

LO 2   **4. Per-Share Earnings and Dividends**   Suppose the firm in Problem 3 had 35,000 shares of common stock outstanding. What is the earnings per share, or EPS, figure? What is the dividends per share figure?

LO 3   **5. Calculating Taxes**   Duela Dent is single and had $189,000 in taxable income. Using the rates from Table 2.3 in the chapter, calculate her income taxes.

LO 3   **6. Tax Rates**   In Problem 5, what is the average tax rate? What is the marginal tax rate?

LO 2   7. **Calculating OCF**   Benson, Inc., has sales of $38,530, costs of $12,750, depreciation expense of $2,550, and interest expense of $1,850. If the tax rate is 21 percent, what is the operating cash flow, or OCF?

LO 4   8. **Calculating Net Capital Spending**   Rottweiler Obedience School's December 31, 2018, balance sheet showed net fixed assets of $1,945,000, and the December 31, 2019, balance sheet showed net fixed assets of $2,137,000. The company's 2019 income statement showed a depreciation expense of $335,000. What was the company's net capital spending for 2019?

LO 4   9. **Calculating Additions to NWC**   The December 31, 2018, balance sheet of Justin's Golf Shop, Inc., showed current assets of $1,490 and current liabilities of $1,210. The December 31, 2019, balance sheet showed current assets of $1,675 and current liabilities of $1,290. What was the company's 2019 change in net working capital, or NWC?

LO 4   10. **Cash Flow to Creditors**   The December 31, 2018, balance sheet of Whelan, Inc., showed long-term debt of $1,350,000, and the December 31, 2019, balance sheet showed long-term debt of $1,470,000. The 2019 income statement showed an interest expense of $97,500. What was the firm's cash flow to creditors during 2019?

LO 4   11. **Cash Flow to Stockholders**   The December 31, 2018, balance sheet of Whelan, Inc., showed $120,000 in the common stock account and $2,289,000 in the additional paid-in surplus account. The December 31, 2019, balance sheet showed $137,000 and $2,568,000 in the same two accounts, respectively. If the company paid out $149,500 in cash dividends during 2019, what was the cash flow to stockholders for the year?

LO 4   12. **Calculating Cash Flows**   Given the information for Whelan, Inc., in Problems 10 and 11, suppose you also know that the firm's net capital spending for 2019 was $745,000 and that the firm reduced its net working capital investment by $94,300. What was the firm's 2019 operating cash flow, or OCF?

INTERMEDIATE (Questions 13–22)

LO 1   13. **Market Values and Book Values**   Klingon Widgets, Inc., purchased new cloaking machinery three years ago for $6 million. The machinery can be sold to the Romulans today for $4.6 million. Klingon's current balance sheet shows net fixed assets of $3.15 million, current liabilities of $830,000, and net working capital of $210,000. If all the current accounts were liquidated today, the company would receive $950,000 in cash. What is the book value of Klingon's total assets today? What is the sum of the market value of NWC and the market value of fixed assets?

LO 4   14. **Calculating Cash Flows**   Weiland Co. shows the following information on its 2019 income statement: sales = $178,000; costs = $103,600; other expenses = $5,100; depreciation expense = $12,100; interest expense = $8,900; taxes = $12,705; dividends = $10,143. In addition, you're told that the firm issued $2,900 in new equity during 2019 and redeemed $4,000 in outstanding long-term debt.

  a.   What is the 2019 operating cash flow?
  b.   What is the 2019 cash flow to creditors?

c. What is the 2019 cash flow to stockholders?

d. If net fixed assets increased by $23,140 during the year, what was the addition to NWC?

LO 2 **15. Using Income Statements**   Given the following information for Ted's Dread Co., calculate the depreciation expense: sales = $68,500; costs = $51,700; addition to retained earnings = $4,500; dividends paid = $2,420; interest expense = $2,130; tax rate = 21 percent.

LO 1 **16. Preparing a Balance Sheet**   Prepare a balance sheet for Alaskan Peach Corp. as of December 31, 2019, based on the following information: cash = $207,000; patents and copyrights = $871,000; accounts payable = $293,000; accounts receivable = $265,000; tangible net fixed assets = $5,270,000; inventory = $579,000; notes payable = $201,000; accumulated retained earnings = $4,676,000; long-term debt = $1,680,000.

LO 1 **17. Residual Claims**   Tremonti, Inc., is obligated to pay its creditors $7,900 during the year.

a. What is the value of the shareholders' equity if assets equal $9,100?

b. What if assets equal $6,900?

LO 2 **18. Net Income and OCF**   During the year, Belyk Paving Co. had sales of $2,275,000. Cost of goods sold, administrative and selling expenses, and depreciation expense were $1,285,000, $535,000, and $420,000, respectively. In addition, the company had an interest expense of $245,000 and a tax rate of 21 percent. (Ignore any tax loss carryforward provision and assume interest expense is fully deductible.)

a. What is the company's net income?

b. What is its operating cash flow?

c. Explain your results in parts (a) and (b).

LO 2 **19. Accounting Values versus Cash Flows**   In Problem 18, suppose Belyk Paving Co. paid out $370,000 in cash dividends. Is this possible? If net capital spending was zero, no new investments were made in net working capital, and no new stock was issued during the year, what do you know about the firm's long-term debt account?

LO 4 **20. Calculating Cash Flows**   Prescott Football Manufacturing had the following operating results for 2019: sales = $29,874; cost of goods sold = $21,632; depreciation expense = $3,470; interest expense = $514; dividends paid = $825. At the beginning of the year, net fixed assets were $19,872, current assets were $3,557, and current liabilities were $3,110. At the end of the year, net fixed assets were $22,987, current assets were $4,381, and current liabilities were $2,981. The tax rate for 2019 was 24 percent.

a. What is net income for 2019?

b. What is the operating cash flow for 2019?

c. What is the cash flow from assets for 2019? Is this possible? Explain.

d. If no new debt was issued during the year, what is the cash flow to creditors? What is the cash flow to stockholders? Explain and interpret the positive and negative signs of your answers in parts (a) through (d).

LO 4   **21. Calculating Cash Flows**   Consider the following abbreviated financial statements for Cabo Wabo, Inc.:

CABO WABO, INC. Partial Balance Sheets as of December 31, 2018 and 2019					
	2018	2019		2018	2019
Assets			**Liabilities and Owners' Equity**		
Current assets	$ 2,989	$ 3,169	Current liabilities	$1,291	$1,898
Net fixed assets	13,862	14,493	Long-term debt	7,161	8,221

CABO WABO, INC. 2019 Income Statement	
Sales	$44,730
Costs	22,432
Depreciation	3,777
Interest paid	1,032

a.   What is owners' equity for 2018 and 2019?

b.   What is the change in net working capital for 2019?

c.   In 2019, the company purchased $7,876 in new fixed assets. How much in fixed assets did the company sell? What is the cash flow from assets for the year? (The tax rate is 22 percent.)

d.   During 2019, the company raised $2,371 in new long-term debt. How much long-term debt must the company have paid off during the year? What is the cash flow to creditors?

LO 4   **22. Cash Flow Identity**   Graffiti Advertising, Inc., reported the following financial statements for the last two years. Construct the cash flow identity for the company. Explain what each number means.

2019 Income Statement	
Sales	$750,727
Cost of goods sold	430,821
Selling and administrative	165,676
Depreciation	72,489
EBIT	$ 81,741
Interest	25,630
EBT	$ 56,111
Taxes	14,028
Net income	$ 42,083
Dividends	$ 14,200
Addition to retained earnings	27,883

GRAFFITI ADVERTISING, INC. Balance Sheet as of December 31, 2018			
Cash	$ 17,691	Accounts payable	$ 12,721
Accounts receivable	25,228	Notes payable	19,149
Inventory	18,321	Current liabilities	$ 31,870
Current assets	$ 61,240	Long-term debt	$181,000
Net fixed assets	$457,454	Owners' equity	$305,824
		Total liabilities and	
Total assets	$518,964	owners' equity	$518,694

GRAFFITI ADVERTISING, INC.			
Balance Sheet as of December 31, 2019			
Cash	$ 19,003	Accounts payable	$ 13,962
Accounts receivable	28,025	Notes payable	21,872
Inventory	30,222	Current liabilities	$ 35,834
Current assets	$ 77,250	Long-term debt	$201,900
Net fixed assets	$539,679	Owners' equity	$379,195
		Total liabilities and	
Total assets	$616,929	owners' equity	$616,929

CHALLENGE (Question 23)

LO 4 **23. Net Fixed Assets and Depreciation**   On the balance sheet, the net fixed assets (NFA) account is equal to the gross fixed assets (FA) account (which records the acquisition cost of fixed assets) minus the accumulated depreciation (AD) account (which records the total depreciation taken by the firm against its fixed assets). Using the fact that $NFA = FA - AD$, show that the expression given in the chapter for net capital spending, $NFA_{end} - NFA_{beg} + D$ (where D is the depreciation expense during the year), is equivalent to $FA_{end} - FA_{beg}$.

WHAT'S ON THE WEB?

2.1 Change in Net Working Capital   Visit Alcoa at www.alcoa.com. Find the most recent annual report and locate the balance sheets for the past two years. Use these balance sheets to calculate the change in net working capital. How do you interpret this number?

2.2 Book Values versus Market Values   The home page for The Coca-Cola Company can be found at www.coca-cola.com. Locate the most recent annual report, which contains a balance sheet for the company. What is the book value of equity for Coca-Cola? The market value of a company is the number of shares of stock outstanding times the price per share. This information can be found at finance.yahoo.com using the ticker symbol for Coca-Cola (KO). What is the market value of equity? Which number is more relevant for shareholders?

2.3 Net Working Capital   Duke Energy is one of the world's largest energy companies. Go to the company's home page at www.duke-energy.com, follow the link to the investors' page, and locate the annual reports. What was Duke Energy's net working capital for the most recent year? Does this number seem low to you given Duke's current liabilities? Does this indicate that Duke Energy may be experiencing financial problems? Why or why not?

2.4 Cash Flows to Stockholders and Creditors   Cooper Tire & Rubber Company provides financial information for investors on its website at www.coopertire.com. Follow the "Investors" link and find the most recent annual report. Using the consolidated statement of cash flows, calculate the cash flow to stockholders and the cash flow to creditors.

EXCEL *MASTER IT!* PROBLEM

Excel
Master
coverage online

Using Excel to find the marginal tax rate can be accomplished using the VLOOKUP function. However, calculating the total tax bill is a little more difficult. Here we show a copy of the IRS tax table for an individual for 2018 (the income thresholds are indexed to inflation and change through time). Often, tax tables are presented in this format.

If taxable income is over...	But not over...	The tax is:
$ 0	$ 9,525	10% of the amount over $0
9,525	38,700	$952.50 plus 12% of the amount over $9,525
38,700	82,500	$4,453.50 plus 22% of the amount over $38,700
82,500	157,500	$14,089.50 plus 24% of the amount over $82,500
157,500	200,000	$32,089.50 plus 32% of the amount over $157,500
200,000	500,000	$45,689.50 plus 35% of the amount over $200,000
500,000		$150,689.50 plus 37% of the amount over $500,00

In reading this table, the marginal tax rate for taxable income less than $9,525 is 10%. If the taxable income is between $9,525 and $38,700, the tax bill is $952.50 plus the marginal taxes. The marginal taxes are calculated as the taxable income minus $9,525 times the marginal tax rate of 12%.

Below, we have the tax table for a married couple filing jointly.

Taxable income is greater than or equal to...	But less than...	Tax rate
$ 0	$ 19,050	10%
19,050	77,400	12
77,400	165,000	22
165,000	315,000	24
315,000	400,000	32
400,000	600,000	35
600,000		37

a. Create a tax table in Excel for a married couple similar to the individual tax table shown earlier. Your spreadsheet should then calculate the marginal tax rate, the average tax rate, and the tax bill for any level of taxable income input by a user.

b. For a taxable income of $335,000, what is the marginal tax rate?

c. For a taxable income of $335,000, what is the total tax bill?

d. For a taxable income of $335,000, what is the average tax rate?

CHAPTER CASE
Cash Flows and Financial Statements at Sunset Boards, Inc.

Sunset Boards is a small company that manufactures and sells surfboards in Malibu. Tad Marks, the founder of the company, is in charge of the design and sale of the surfboards, but his background is in surfing, not business. As a result, the company's financial records are not well maintained.

The initial investment in Sunset Boards was provided by Tad and his friends and family. Because the initial investment was relatively small, and the company has made surfboards only for its own store, the investors haven't required detailed financial statements from Tad. But thanks to word of mouth among professional surfers, sales have picked up recently, and Tad is considering a major expansion. His plans include opening another surfboard store in Hawaii, as well as supplying his "sticks" (surfer lingo for boards) to other sellers.

Tad's expansion plans require a significant investment, which he plans to finance with a combination of additional funds from outsiders plus some money borrowed from banks. Naturally, the new investors and creditors require more organized and detailed financial statements than Tad has previously prepared. At the urging of his investors, Tad has hired financial analyst Jameson Reid to evaluate the performance of the company over the past year.

After rooting through old bank statements, sales receipts, tax returns, and other records, Jameson has assembled the following information:

	2018	2019
Cost of goods sold	$224,359	$283,281
Cash	32,372	34,394
Depreciation	63,334	71,584
Interest expense	13,783	15,780
Selling and administrative expenses	44,121	57,586
Accounts payable	57,220	63,479
Net fixed assets	279,419	348,508
Sales	440,122	536,483
Accounts receivable	22,939	29,755
Notes payable	26,079	28,474
Long-term debt	141,040	158,368
Inventory	48,272	66,244
New equity	0	27,157

Sunset Boards currently pays out 50 percent of net income as dividends to Tad and the other original investors and has a 21 percent tax rate. You are Jameson's assistant, and he has asked you to prepare the following:

1. An income statement for 2018 and 2019.
2. A balance sheet for 2018 and 2019.
3. Operating cash flow for each year.
4. Cash flow from assets for 2019.
5. Cash flow to creditors for 2019.
6. Cash flow to stockholders for 2019.

QUESTIONS

1. How would you describe Sunset Boards's cash flows for 2019? Write a brief discussion.

2. In light of your discussion in the previous question, what do you think about Tad's expansion plans?

Working with Financial Statements | 3

In June 2018, shares of jet manufacturer Boeing were trading for about $370. At that price, Boeing had a price-earnings, or PE, ratio of 24, meaning that investors were willing to pay $24 for every dollar in income earned by Boeing. At the same time, investors were willing to pay $274 for each dollar earned by Amazon.com, but only a meager $6 and $7 for each dollar earned by Ford and Comcast, respectively. And then there were stocks like Tesla, which, despite having no earnings (a loss actually), had a stock price of about $318 per share. Meanwhile, the average stock in the Standard & Poor's (S&P) 500 index, which contains 500 of the largest publicly traded companies in the United States, had a PE ratio of about 24, so Boeing was average in this regard.

As we look at these numbers, an obvious question arises: Why were investors willing to pay so much for a dollar of Amazon's earnings but so much less for a dollar earned by Comcast? To understand the answer, we need to delve into subjects such as relative profitability and growth potential, and we also need to know how to compare financial and operating information across companies. By a remarkable coincidence, that is precisely what this chapter is about.

The PE ratio is just one example of a financial ratio. As we will see in this chapter, there are a wide variety of such ratios, all designed to summarize specific aspects of a firm's financial position. In addition to discussing financial ratios and what they mean, we will have quite a bit to say about who uses this information and why.

Everybody needs to understand ratios. Managers will find that almost every business characteristic, from profitability to employee productivity, is summarized in some kind of ratio. Marketers examine ratios dealing with costs, markups, and margins. Production

Please visit us at essentialsofcorporatefinance.blogspot.com for the latest developments in the world of corporate finance.

personnel focus on ratios dealing with issues such as operating efficiency. Accountants need to understand ratios because, among other things, ratios are one of the most common and important forms of financial statement information.

In fact, regardless of your field, you very well may find that your compensation is tied to some ratio or group of ratios. Perhaps that is the best reason to study up!

In Chapter 2, we discussed some of the essential concepts of financial statements and cash flows. This chapter continues where our earlier discussion left off. Our goal here is to expand your understanding of the uses (and abuses) of financial statement information.

A good working knowledge of financial statements is desirable because such statements, and numbers derived from those statements, are the primary means of communicating financial information both within the firm and outside the firm. In short, much of the language of business finance is rooted in the ideas we discuss in this chapter.

In the best of all worlds, the financial manager has full market value information about all of the firm's assets. This will rarely (if ever) happen. So, the reason we rely on accounting figures for much of our financial information is that we are almost always unable to obtain all (or even part) of the market information that we want. The only meaningful yardstick for evaluating business decisions is whether or not they create economic value (see Chapter 1). However, in many important situations, it will not be possible to make this judgment directly because we can't see the market value effects.

We recognize that accounting numbers are often a pale reflection of economic reality, but they frequently are the best available information. For privately held corporations, not-for-profit businesses, and smaller firms, for example, very little direct market value information exists at all. The accountants' reporting function is crucial in these circumstances.

Clearly, one important goal of an accountant is to report financial information to the user in a form useful for decision making. Ironically, the information frequently does not come to the user in such a form. In other words, financial statements don't come with a user's guide. This chapter is a first step in filling this gap.

Company financial information can be found in many places on the web, including www.sec.gov and finance.google.com.

3.1 STANDARDIZED FINANCIAL STATEMENTS

Excel Master coverage online

One obvious thing we might want to do with a company's financial statements is to compare them to those of other, similar companies. We would immediately have a problem, however. It's almost impossible to directly compare the financial statements for two companies because of differences in size.

For example, Ford and GM are obviously serious rivals in the auto market, but GM was historically much larger (in terms of assets), so it was difficult to compare them directly. For that matter, it's difficult to even compare financial statements from different points in time for the same company if the company's size has changed. The size problem is compounded if we try to compare GM and, say, Toyota. If Toyota's financial statements are denominated in yen, then we have a size *and* a currency difference.

TABLE 3.1

PRUFROCK CORPORATION Balance Sheets as of December 31, 2018 and 2019 ($ in millions)		
	2018	**2019**
Assets		
Current assets		
Cash	$ 84	$ 98
Accounts receivable	165	188
Inventory	393	422
Total	$ 642	$ 708
Fixed assets		
Net plant and equipment	$2,731	$2,922
Total assets	$3,373	$3,620
Liabilities and Owners' Equity		
Current liabilities		
Accounts payable	$ 312	$ 344
Notes payable	231	204
Total	$ 543	$ 548
Long-term debt	$ 531	$ 457
Owners' equity		
Common stock and paid-in surplus	$ 500	$ 510
Retained earnings	1,799	2,115
Total	$2,299	$2,625
Total liabilities and owners' equity	$3,373	$3,630

To start making comparisons, one obvious thing we might try to do is to somehow standardize the financial statements. One very common and useful way of doing this is to work with percentages instead of total dollars. The resulting financial statements are called **common-size statements**. We consider these next.

common-size statement
A standardized financial statement presenting all items in percentage terms. Balance sheet items are shown as a percentage of assets and income statement items as a percentage of sales.

Common-Size Balance Sheets

For easy reference, Prufrock Corporation's 2018 and 2019 balance sheets are provided in Table 3.1. Using these, we construct common-size balance sheets by expressing each item as a percentage of total assets. Prufrock's 2018 and 2019 common-size balance sheets are shown in Table 3.2.

Notice that some of the totals don't check exactly because of rounding errors. Also notice that the total change has to be zero because the beginning and ending numbers must add up to 100 percent.

In this form, financial statements are relatively easy to read and compare. For example, looking at the two balance sheets for Prufrock, we see that current assets were 19.5 percent of total assets in 2019, up from 19.0 percent in 2018. Current liabilities declined from 16.1 percent to 15.1 percent of total liabilities and equity over that same time. Similarly, total equity rose from 68.2 percent of total liabilities and equity to 72.3 percent.

IBM's website has a good guide to reading financial statements. Visit www.ibm.com/investor.

Overall, Prufrock's liquidity, as measured by current assets compared to current liabilities, increased over the year. Simultaneously, Prufrock's indebtedness diminished as a percentage of total assets. We might be tempted to conclude that the balance sheet has grown "stronger."

TABLE 3.2

PRUFROCK CORPORATION
Common-Size Balance Sheets
December 31, 2018 and 2019

	2018	2019	Change
Assets			
Current assets			
Cash	2.5%	2.7%	+ .2%
Accounts receivable	4.9	5.2	+ .3
Inventory	11.7	11.6	+ .0
Total	19.0%	19.5%	+ .5%
Fixed assets			
Net plant and equipment	81.0%	80.5%	− .5%
Total assets	100.0%	100.0%	0%
Liabilities and Owners' Equity			
Current liabilities			
Accounts payable	9.2%	9.5%	+ .2%
Notes payable	6.8	5.6	− 1.2
Total	16.1%	15.1%	− 1.0%
Long-term debt	15.7%	12.6%	− 3.2%
Owners' equity			
Common stock and paid-in surplus	14.8%	14.0%	− .8%
Retained earnings	53.3	58.3	+ 4.9
Total	68.2%	72.3%	+ 4.2%
Total liabilities and owners' equity	100.0%	100.0%	0%

Common-Size Income Statements

A useful way of standardizing the income statement shown in Table 3.3 is to express each item as a percentage of total sales, as illustrated for Prufrock in Table 3.4.

This income statement tells us what happens to each dollar in sales. For Prufrock, interest expense eats up $.060 out of every sales dollar, and taxes take another $.053. When all is said and done, $.201 of each dollar flows through to the bottom line (net income), and that amount is split into $.134 retained in the business and $.067 paid out in dividends.

TABLE 3.3

PRUFROCK CORPORATION
2019 Income Statement
($ in millions)

Sales		$2,361
Cost of goods sold		1,344
Depreciation		276
Earnings before interest and taxes		$ 741
Interest paid		141
Taxable income		$ 600
Taxes (21%)		126
Net income		$ 474
Dividends	$158	
Addition to retained earnings	316	

TABLE 3.4

PRUFROCK CORPORATION Common-Size Income Statement 2019		
Sales		100.0%
Cost of goods sold		56.9
Depreciation		11.7
Earnings before interest and taxes		31.4%
Interest paid		6.0
Taxable income		25.4%
Taxes (21%)		5.3
Net income		20.1%
Dividends	6.7%	
Addition to retained earnings	13.4	

These percentages are very useful in comparisons. For example, a relevant figure is the cost percentage. For Prufrock, $.569 of each $1.00 in sales goes to pay for goods sold. It would be interesting to compute the same percentage for Prufrock's main competitors to see how Prufrock stacks up in terms of cost control.

CONCEPT QUESTIONS

3.1a   Why is it often necessary to standardize financial statements?

3.1b   Describe how common-size balance sheets and income statements are formed.

3.2 RATIO ANALYSIS

Excel Master
coverage online

financial ratios
Relationships determined from a firm's financial information and used for comparison purposes.

Another way of avoiding the problems involved in comparing companies of different sizes is to calculate and compare **financial ratios**. Such ratios are ways of comparing and investigating the relationships between different pieces of financial information. We cover some of the more common ratios next, but there are many others that we don't touch on.

One problem with ratios is that different people and different sources frequently don't compute them in exactly the same way, and this leads to much confusion. The specific definitions we use here may or may not be the same as ones you have seen or will see elsewhere. If you are ever using ratios as a tool for analysis, you should be careful to document how you calculate each one, and, if you are comparing your numbers to those of another source, be sure you know how their numbers are computed.

We will defer much of our discussion of how ratios are used and some problems that come up with using them until a bit later in the chapter. For now, for each of the ratios we discuss, several questions come to mind:

1. How is it computed?
2. What is it intended to measure, and why might we be interested?
3. What is the unit of measurement?
4. What might a high or low value be telling us? How might such values be misleading?
5. How could this measure be improved?

Financial ratios are traditionally grouped into the following categories:

1. Short-term solvency, or liquidity, ratios.
2. Long-term solvency, or financial leverage, ratios.
3. Asset management, or turnover, ratios.
4. Profitability ratios.
5. Market value ratios.

We will consider each of these in turn. In calculating these numbers for Prufrock, we will use the ending balance sheet (2019) figures unless we explicitly say otherwise. Also notice that the various ratios are color-keyed to indicate which numbers come from the income statement and which come from the balance sheet.

Short-Term Solvency, or Liquidity, Measures

As the name suggests, short-term solvency ratios as a group are intended to provide information about a firm's liquidity, and these ratios are sometimes called *liquidity measures*. The primary concern is the firm's ability to pay its bills over the short run without undue stress. Consequently, these ratios focus on current assets and current liabilities.

For obvious reasons, liquidity ratios are particularly interesting to short-term creditors. Because financial managers are constantly working with banks and other short-term lenders, an understanding of these ratios is essential.

One advantage of looking at current assets and liabilities is that their book values and market values are likely to be similar. Often (though not always), these assets and liabilities don't live long enough for the two to get seriously out of step. On the other hand, like any type of near cash, current assets and liabilities can and do change fairly rapidly, so today's amounts may not be a reliable guide to the future.

Current Ratio   One of the best-known and most widely used ratios is the *current ratio*. As you might guess, the current ratio is defined as:

$$\text{Current ratio} = \frac{\text{Current assets}}{\text{Current liabilities}} \qquad [3.1]$$

For Prufrock, the 2019 current ratio is:

$$\text{Current ratio} = \frac{\$708}{\$548} = 1.29 \text{ times}$$

Because current assets and liabilities are, in principle, converted to cash over the following 12 months, the current ratio is a measure of short-term liquidity. The unit of measurement is either dollars or times. So, we could say Prufrock has $1.29 in current assets for every $1 in current liabilities, or we could say Prufrock has its current liabilities covered 1.29 times over.

To a creditor, particularly a short-term creditor such as a supplier, the higher the current ratio, the better. To the firm, a high current ratio indicates liquidity, but it also may indicate an inefficient use of cash and other short-term assets. Absent some extraordinary circumstances, we would expect to see a current ratio of at least 1 because a current ratio of less than 1 would mean that net working capital (current assets less current liabilities) is negative. This would be unusual in a healthy firm, at least for most types of businesses.

The current ratio, like any ratio, is affected by various types of transactions. For example, suppose the firm borrows over the long term to raise money. The short-run effect would be an increase in cash from the issue proceeds and an increase in long-term debt. Current liabilities would not be affected, so the current ratio would rise.

Finally, note that an apparently low current ratio may not be a bad sign for a company with a large reserve of untapped borrowing power.

EXAMPLE 3.1 | **Current Events**

Suppose a firm were to pay off some of its suppliers and short-term creditors. What would happen to the current ratio? Suppose a firm buys some inventory. What happens in this case? What happens if a firm sells some merchandise?

The first case is a trick question. What happens is that the current ratio moves away from 1. If it is greater than 1 (the usual case), it will get bigger, but if it is less than 1, it will get smaller. To see this, suppose the firm has $4 in current assets and $2 in current liabilities for a current ratio of 2. If we use $1 in cash to reduce current liabilities, then the new current ratio is ($4 − 1)/($2 − 1) = 3. If we reverse the original situation to $2 in current assets and $4 in current liabilities, then the change will cause the current ratio to fall to 1/3 from 1/2.

The second case is not quite as tricky. Nothing happens to the current ratio because cash goes down while inventory goes up—total current assets are unaffected.

In the third case, the current ratio would usually rise because inventory is normally shown at cost, and the sale would normally be at something greater than cost (the difference is the markup). The increase in either cash or receivables is therefore greater than the decrease in inventory. This increases current assets, and the current ratio rises.

Quick (or Acid-Test) Ratio   Inventory is often the least liquid current asset. It's also the one for which the book values are least reliable as measures of market value because the quality of the inventory isn't considered. Some of the inventory may later turn out to be damaged, obsolete, or lost.

More to the point, relatively large inventories are often a sign of short-term trouble. The firm may have overestimated sales and overbought or overproduced as a result. In this case, the firm may have a substantial portion of its liquidity tied up in slow-moving inventory.

To further evaluate liquidity, the *quick*, or *acid-test*, *ratio* is computed like the current ratio, except inventory is omitted:

$$\text{Quick ratio} = \frac{\text{Current assets} - \text{Inventory}}{\text{Current liabilities}} \qquad [3.2]$$

Notice that using cash to buy inventory does not affect the current ratio, but it reduces the quick ratio. Again, the idea is that inventory is relatively illiquid compared to cash. For Prufrock, this ratio in 2019 was:

$$\text{Quick ratio} = \frac{\$708 - 422}{\$548} = .52 \text{ times}$$

The quick ratio here tells a somewhat different story than the current ratio because inventory accounts for more than half of Prufrock's current assets. To exaggerate the point, if this inventory consisted of, say, unsold nuclear power plants, then this would be a cause for concern.

To give an example of current versus quick ratios, based on recent financial statements, Walmart and ManpowerGroup had current ratios of .85 and 1.39, respectively. However, ManpowerGroup carries no inventory to speak of, whereas Walmart's current assets are virtually all inventory. As a result, Walmart's quick ratio was only .22, and ManpowerGroup's was 1.39, the same as its current ratio.

Cash Ratio   A very short-term creditor might be interested in the *cash ratio*.

$$\text{Cash ratio} = \frac{\text{Cash}}{\text{Current liabilities}} \qquad [3.3]$$

You can verify that this works out to be .18 times for Prufrock.

Long-Term Solvency Measures

Long-term solvency ratios are intended to address the firm's long-run ability to meet its obligations, or, more generally, its financial leverage. These ratios are sometimes called *financial leverage ratios* or *leverage ratios*. We consider three commonly used measures and some variations.

Total Debt Ratio   The *total debt ratio* takes into account all debts of all maturities to all creditors. It can be defined in several ways, the easiest of which is:

$$\text{Total debt ratio} = \frac{\text{Total assets} - \text{Total equity}}{\text{Total assets}} \qquad \text{[3.4]}$$

$$= \frac{\$3,630 - 2,625}{\$3,630} = .28 \text{ times}$$

In this case, an analyst might say that Prufrock uses 28 percent debt.[1] Whether this is high or low or whether it even makes any difference depends on whether or not capital structure matters, a subject we discuss in a later chapter.

Prufrock has $.28 in debt for every $1 in total assets. Therefore, there is $.72 in equity (= $1 − .28) for every $.28 in debt. With this in mind, we can define two useful variations on the total debt ratio, the *debt-equity ratio* and the *equity multiplier*:

$$\text{Debt-equity ratio} = \text{Total debt}/\text{Total equity} \qquad \text{[3.5]}$$

$$= \$.28/\$.72 = .38 \text{ times}$$

$$\text{Equity multiplier} = \text{Total assets}/\text{Total equity} \qquad \text{[3.6]}$$

$$= \$1/\$.72 = 1.38 \text{ times}$$

The fact that the equity multiplier is 1 plus the debt-equity ratio is not a coincidence:

$$\text{Equity multiplier} = \text{Total assets}/\text{Total equity} = \$1/\$.72 = 1.38 \text{ times}$$

$$= (\text{Total equity} + \text{Total debt})/\text{Total equity}$$

$$= 1 + \text{Debt-equity ratio} = 1.38 \text{ times}$$

The thing to notice here is that given any one of these three ratios, you can immediately calculate the other two, so they all say exactly the same thing.

Times Interest Earned   Another common measure of long-term solvency is the *times interest earned* (TIE) *ratio*. Once again, there are several possible (and common) definitions, but we'll stick with the most traditional:

$$\text{Times interest earned ratio} = \frac{\text{EBIT}}{\text{Interest}} \qquad \text{[3.7]}$$

$$= \frac{\$741}{\$141} = 5.26 \text{ times}$$

As the name suggests, this ratio measures how well a company has its interest obligations covered, and it is often called the interest coverage ratio. For Prufrock, the interest bill is covered 5.26 times over.

---

[1]Total equity here includes preferred stock (discussed in Chapter 7), if there is any. An equivalent numerator in this ratio would be (Current liabilities + Long-term debt).

Cash Coverage   A problem with the TIE ratio is that it is based on EBIT, which is not really a measure of cash available to pay interest. The reason is that depreciation, a noncash expense, has been deducted out. Because interest is most definitely a cash outflow (to creditors), one way to define the *cash coverage ratio* is:

$$\text{Cash coverage ratio} = \frac{\text{EBIT} + \text{Depreciation}}{\text{Interest}} \qquad [3.8]$$

$$= \frac{\$741 + 276}{\$141} = \frac{\$1,017}{\$141} = 7.21 \text{ times}$$

The numerator here, EBIT plus depreciation, is often abbreviated EBITD (earnings before interest, taxes, and depreciation—say "ebbit-dee"). It is a basic measure of the firm's ability to generate cash from operations, and it is frequently used as a measure of cash flow available to meet financial obligations.

A common variation on EBITD is earnings before interest, taxes, depreciation, and amortization (EBITDA—say "ebbit-dah"). Here *amortization* refers to a noncash deduction similar conceptually to depreciation, except it applies to an intangible asset (such as a patent) rather than a tangible asset (such as a machine). Note that the word *amortization* here does not refer to the repayment of debt, a subject we discuss in a later chapter.

Asset Management, or Turnover, Measures

We next turn our attention to the efficiency with which Prufrock uses its assets. The measures in this section are sometimes called *asset utilization ratios*. The specific ratios we discuss all can be interpreted as measures of turnover. What they are intended to describe is how efficiently, or intensively, a firm uses its assets to generate sales. We first look at two important current assets: inventory and receivables.

Inventory Turnover and Days' Sales in Inventory   During the year, Prufrock had a cost of goods sold of $1,344. Inventory at the end of the year was $422. With these numbers, *inventory turnover* can be calculated as:

$$\text{Inventory turnover} = \frac{\text{Cost of goods sold}}{\text{Inventory}} \qquad [3.9]$$

$$= \frac{\$1,344}{\$422} = 3.18 \text{ times}$$

In a sense, we sold off, or turned over, the entire inventory 3.18 times. As long as we are not running out of stock and thereby forgoing sales, the higher this ratio is, the more efficiently we are managing inventory.

If we know that we turned our inventory over 3.18 times during the year, then we can immediately figure out how long it took us to turn it over, on average. The result is the average *days' sales in inventory:*

$$\text{Days' sales in inventory} = \frac{365 \text{ days}}{\text{Inventory turnover}} \qquad [3.10]$$

$$= \frac{365}{3.18} = 114.61 \text{ days}$$

This tells us that, roughly speaking, inventory sits about 115 days, on average, before it is sold. Alternatively, assuming we used the most recent inventory and cost figures, it will take about 115 days to work off our current inventory.

For example, in early 2018, the auto industry had a 35-day supply of cars and trucks. Of course, not all manufacturers had the same inventory level. At that same time, General

Motors had a 68-day supply. This inventory level means that at the then-current rate of sales, it would have taken General Motors 68 days to deplete the available supply, or, equivalently, that General Motors had 68 days of vehicle sales in inventory. At the same time, Ford had a 115-day supply. This type of information is useful to auto manufacturers in planning future marketing and production decisions. Historically, a 60-day supply of inventory has been considered normal in the automobile industry, so these figures pointed to manufacturing continuing at the same level for GM, and likely decreasing for Ford, in 2018.

It might make more sense to use the average inventory in calculating turnover. Inventory turnover would then be $1,344/[($393 + 422)/2] = 3.30 times.[2] Whether we use the ending inventory or average inventory depends on the purpose of the calculation. If we are interested in how long it will take us to sell our current inventory, then using the ending figure (as we did initially) is probably better.

In many of the ratios we discuss in the following pages, average figures could just as well be used. Again, it depends on whether we are worried about the past, in which case averages are appropriate, or the future, in which case ending figures might be better. Also, using ending figures is common in reporting industry averages; so, for comparison purposes, ending figures should be used in such cases. In any event, using ending figures is definitely less work, so we'll continue to use them.

Receivables Turnover and Days' Sales in Receivables   Our inventory measures give some indication of how fast we can sell products. We now look at how fast we collect on those sales. The *receivables turnover* is defined in the same way as inventory turnover:

$$\text{Receivables turnover} = \frac{\text{Sales}}{\text{Accounts receivable}} \qquad [3.11]$$

$$= \frac{\$2,361}{\$188} = 12.56 \text{ times}$$

Loosely speaking, we collected our outstanding credit accounts and reloaned the money 12.56 times during the year.[3]

This ratio makes more sense if we convert it to days, so the *days' sales in receivables* is:

$$\text{Days' sales in receivables} = \frac{365 \text{ days}}{\text{Receivables turnover}} \qquad [3.12]$$

$$= \frac{365}{12.56} = 29.06 \text{ days}$$

Therefore, on average, we collect on our credit sales in about 30 days. For obvious reasons, this ratio is very frequently called the *average collection period* (ACP).

Also note that if we are using the most recent figures, we can say that we have 30 days' worth of sales currently uncollected. We will learn more about this subject when we study credit policy in a later chapter.

---

[2]Notice that we calculated the average as (Beginning value + Ending value)/2.

[3]Here we have implicitly assumed that all sales are credit sales. If they were not, then we would use total credit sales in these calculations, not total sales.

> **EXAMPLE 3.2** **Payables Turnover**
>
> Here is a variation on the receivables collection period. How long, on average, does it take for Prufrock Corporation to pay its bills? To answer, we need to calculate the accounts payable turnover rate using cost of goods sold. We will assume that Prufrock purchases everything on credit.
>
> The cost of goods sold is $1,344, and accounts payable are $344. The turnover is therefore $1,344/$344 = 3.91 times. So, days' costs in payables was about 365/3.91 = 93.42 days. On average, then, Prufrock takes about 93 days to pay. As a potential creditor, we might take note of this fact.

Total Asset Turnover Moving away from specific accounts like inventory or receivables, we can consider an important "big picture" ratio, the *total asset turnover* ratio. As the name suggests, total asset turnover is:

$$\text{Total asset turnover} = \frac{\text{Sales}}{\text{Total assets}} \qquad \text{[3.13]}$$

$$= \frac{\$2,361}{\$3,630} = .65 \text{ times}$$

In other words, for every dollar in assets, we generated $.65 in sales.

A closely related ratio, the *capital intensity ratio*, is the reciprocal of (that is, 1 divided by) total asset turnover. It can be interpreted as the dollar investment in assets needed to generate $1 in sales. High values correspond to capital-intensive industries (such as public utilities). For Prufrock, total asset turnover is .65, so, if we flip this over, we get that capital intensity is $1/.65 = $1.54. That is, it takes Prufrock $1.54 in assets to create $1 in sales.

It might seem that a high total asset turnover ratio is always a good sign for a company, but it isn't necessarily. Consider a company with old assets. The assets would be almost fully depreciated and might be very outdated. In this case, the book value of assets is low, contributing to a higher asset turnover. Plus, the high turnover might mean that the company will need to make major capital outlays in the near future. A low asset turnover might seem bad, but it could indicate the opposite: The company could have just purchased a lot of new equipment, which implies that the book value of assets is relatively high. These new assets could be more productive and efficient than those used by the company's competitors.

The eXtensible Business Reporting Language (XBRL) is designed to make extracting EDGAR data easier. You can learn more about it at www.xbrl.org.

> **EXAMPLE 3.3** **More Turnover**
>
> Suppose you find that a particular company generates $.40 in sales for every dollar in total assets. How often does this company turn over its total assets?
>
> The total asset turnover here is .40 times per year. It takes 1/.40 = 2.5 years to turn assets over completely.

Profitability Measures

The three measures we discuss in this section are probably the best known and most widely used of all financial ratios. In one form or another, they are intended to measure how efficiently the firm uses its assets and how efficiently the firm manages its operations. The focus in this group is on the bottom line—net income.

Profit Margin Companies pay a great deal of attention to their *profit margin*:

$$\text{Profit margin} = \frac{\text{Net income}}{\text{Sales}} \tag{3.14}$$

$$= \frac{\$474}{\$2,361} = .2008, \text{ or } 20.08\%$$

This tells us that Prufrock, in an accounting sense, generates about 20 cents in profit for every dollar in sales.

All other things being equal, a relatively high profit margin is obviously desirable. This situation corresponds to low expense ratios relative to sales. However, we hasten to add that other things are often not equal.

For example, lowering our sales price usually will increase unit volume, but normally will cause profit margins to shrink. Total profit (or, more importantly, operating cash flow) may go up or down, so the fact that margins are smaller isn't necessarily bad. After all, isn't it possible that, as the saying goes, "Our prices are so low that we lose money on everything we sell, but we make it up in volume!"?[4]

Return on Assets *Return on assets* (ROA) is a measure of profit per dollar of assets. It can be defined several ways, but the most common is:

$$\text{Return on assets} = \frac{\text{Net income}}{\text{Total assets}} \tag{3.15}$$

$$= \frac{\$474}{\$3,630} = .1306, \text{ or } 13.06\%$$

Return on Equity *Return on equity* (ROE) is a measure of how the stockholders fared during the year. Because benefiting shareholders is our goal, ROE is, in an accounting sense, the true bottom-line measure of performance. ROE is usually measured as:

$$\text{Return on equity} = \frac{\text{Net income}}{\text{Total equity}} \tag{3.16}$$

$$= \frac{\$474}{\$2,625} = .1806, \text{ or } 18.06\%$$

Therefore, for every dollar in equity, Prufrock generated 18.06 cents in profit, but, again, this is only correct in accounting terms.

Because ROA and ROE are such commonly cited numbers, we stress that it is important to remember they are accounting rates of return. For this reason, these measures should properly be called *return on book assets* and *return on book equity*. In addition, ROE is sometimes called *return on net worth*. Whatever it's called, it would be inappropriate to compare the result to, for example, an interest rate observed in the financial markets.

The fact that ROE exceeds ROA reflects Prufrock's use of financial leverage. We will examine the relationship between these two measures in more detail later.

Market Value Measures

Our final group of measures is based, in part, on information not necessarily contained in financial statements—the market price per share of the stock. Obviously, these measures can be calculated directly only for publicly traded companies.

---

[4]No, it's not; margins can be small, but they do need to be positive!

We assume that Prufrock has 33 million shares outstanding and the stock sold for $115 per share at the end of the year. If we recall that Prufrock's net income was $474 million, then we can calculate that its earnings per share were:

$$\text{EPS} = \frac{\text{Net income}}{\text{Shares outstanding}} = \frac{\$474}{33} = \$14.36 \qquad [3.17]$$

Price-Earnings Ratio

The first of our market value measures, the *price-earnings*, or PE, *ratio* (or multiple), is defined as:

$$\text{PE ratio} = \frac{\text{Price per share}}{\text{Earnings per share}} \qquad [3.18]$$

$$= \frac{\$115}{\$14.36} = 8.01 \text{ times}$$

In the vernacular, we would say that Prufrock shares sell for about eight times earnings, or we might say that Prufrock shares have, or "carry," a PE multiple of 8.

Because the PE ratio measures how much investors are willing to pay per dollar of current earnings, higher PEs are often taken to mean that the firm has significant prospects for future growth. Of course, if a firm had no or almost no earnings, its PE would probably be quite large; so, as always, care is needed in interpreting this ratio.

Price-Sales Ratio

In some cases, companies will have negative earnings for extended periods, so their PE ratios are not very meaningful. A good example is a recent start-up. Such companies usually do have some revenues, so analysts will often look at the *price-sales ratio*:

$$\text{Price-sales ratio} = \text{Price per share}/\text{Sales per share} \qquad [3.19]$$

In Prufrock's case, sales were $2,361, so here is the price-sales ratio:

$$\text{Price-sales ratio} = \$115/(\$2,361/33) = \$115/\$71.55 = 1.61 \text{ times}$$

As with PE ratios, whether a particular price-sales ratio is high or low depends on the industry involved.

Market-to-Book Ratio

A second commonly quoted measure is the *market-to-book ratio*:

$$\text{Market-to-book ratio} = \frac{\text{Market value per share}}{\text{Book value per share}} \qquad [3.20]$$

$$= \frac{\$115}{\$2,625/33} = \frac{\$115}{\$79.55} = 1.45 \text{ times}$$

Notice that book value per share is total equity (not just common stock) divided by the number of shares outstanding.

Because book value per share is an accounting number, it reflects historical costs. Therefore, in a loose sense, the market-to-book ratio compares the market value of the firm's investments to their costs. A value less than 1 could mean that the firm has not been successful overall in creating value for its stockholders.

Enterprise Value-EBITDA Ratio

A company's enterprise value is an estimate of the market value of the company's operating assets. By operating assets, we mean all the assets of the firm except cash. Of course, it's not practical to work with the individual assets of a firm because market values would usually not be available. Instead, we can use the right-hand side of the balance sheet and calculate the enterprise value as:

Enterprise value = Total market value of the stock + Book value of all liabilities − Cash   [3.21]

We use the book value for liabilities because we typically can't get the market values, at least not for all of them. However, book value is usually a reasonable approximation for market value when it comes to liabilities, particularly short-term debts. Notice that the sum of the market values of the stock and all liabilities equals the value of the firm's assets from the balance sheet identity. Once we have this number, we subtract the cash to get the enterprise value.

Enterprise value is frequently used to calculate the EBITDA ratio (or multiple):

EBITDA ratio = Enterprise value/EBITDA   [3.22]

This ratio is similar in spirit to the PE ratio, but it relates the value of all the operating assets (the enterprise value) to a measure of the operating cash flow generated by those assets (EBITDA).

This completes our definition of some common ratios. We could tell you about more of them, but these are enough for now. We'll leave it here and go on to discuss some ways of using these ratios instead of just how to calculate them. Table 3.5 summarizes the ratios we've discussed. Table 3.6 provides some information for the well-known home supply stores Lowe's and The Home Depot for their fiscal years ending in 2018. As you can see,

TABLE 3.5   Common financial ratios

I. Short-term solvency, or liquidity, ratios

$$\text{Current ratio} = \frac{\text{Current assets}}{\text{Current liabilities}}$$

$$\text{Quick ratio} = \frac{\text{Current assets} - \text{Inventory}}{\text{Current liabilities}}$$

$$\text{Cash ratio} = \frac{\text{Cash}}{\text{Current liabilities}}$$

II. Long-term solvency, or financial leverage, ratios

$$\text{Total debt ratio} = \frac{\text{Total assets} - \text{Total equity}}{\text{Total assets}}$$

Debt-equity ratio = Total debt/Total equity

Equity multiplier = Total assests/Total equity

$$\text{Times interest earned ratio} = \frac{\text{EBIT}}{\text{Interest}}$$

$$\text{Cash coverage ratio} = \frac{\text{EBIT} + \text{Depreciation}}{\text{Interest}}$$

III. Asset utilization, or turnover, ratios

$$\text{Inventory turnover} = \frac{\text{Cost of goods sold}}{\text{Inventory}}$$

$$\text{Days' sales in inventory} = \frac{365 \text{ days}}{\text{Inventory turnover}}$$

$$\text{Receivables turnover} = \frac{\text{Sales}}{\text{Accounts receivable}}$$

$$\text{Payables turnover} = \frac{\text{Cost of goods sold}}{\text{Accounts payable}}$$

$$\text{Days' sales in receivables} = \frac{365 \text{ days}}{\text{Receivables turnover}}$$

$$\text{Days' costs in payables} = \frac{365 \text{ days}}{\text{Payables turnover}}$$

$$\text{Total asset turnover} = \frac{\text{Sales}}{\text{Total assets}}$$

$$\text{Capital intensity} = \frac{\text{Total assets}}{\text{Sales}}$$

IV. Profitability ratios

$$\text{Profit margin} = \frac{\text{Net income}}{\text{Sales}}$$

$$\text{Return on assets (ROA)} = \frac{\text{Net income}}{\text{Total assets}}$$

$$\text{Return on equity (ROE)} = \frac{\text{Net income}}{\text{Total equity}}$$

$$\text{ROE} = \frac{\text{Net income}}{\text{Sales}} \times \frac{\text{Sales}}{\text{Assets}} \times \frac{\text{Assets}}{\text{Equity}}$$

V. Market value ratios

$$\text{Price-earnings ratio} = \frac{\text{Price per share}}{\text{Earnings per share}}$$

$$\text{Price-sales ratio} = \frac{\text{Price per share}}{\text{Sales per share}}$$

$$\text{Market-to-book ratio} = \frac{\text{Market value per share}}{\text{Book value per share}}$$

$$\text{EBITDA ratio} = \frac{\text{Enterprise value}}{\text{EBITDA}}$$

Financial information from 2018 for Lowe's and The Home Depot (numbers in millions except for per-share data)

	Lowe's	The Home Depot
Sales	$68,819	$100,904
Net income	3,447	8,630
Current assets	12,772	18,933
Current liabilities	12,096	16,194
Total assets	35,291	44,529
Total debt	29,418	43,075
Total equity	5,873	1,454
Price per share	100.50	199.64
Book value per share	7.12	1.25
Earnings per share	4.18	7.44
Current ratio	1.06	1.17
Debt-equity ratio	5.01	29.63
Total asset turnover	1.95	2.27
Profit margin	5.01%	8.55%
ROE	58.69%	593.54%
ROA	9.77%	19.38%
Market-to-book ratio	14.11	159.27
Price-earnings ratio	24.04	26.83

Source: **Lowe's; Home Depot.**

The Home Depot has a higher current ratio, debt-equity ratio, and total asset turnover. The Home Depot also has higher profitability ratios. Because of its increased use of leverage and better profitability, The Home Depot has a higher ROE, something we will discuss in the next section.

The price-earnings ratio is similar for Lowe's and The Home Depot, although The Home Depot's market-to-book ratio is more than 10 times as large as Lowe's. Overall, The Home Depot appears to be performing better than Lowe's based on this abbreviated financial analysis. Of course, if we really want to examine these two companies, we would want to look at more ratios than the ones presented here.

CONCEPT QUESTIONS

3.2a   What are the five groups of ratios? Give two or three examples of each kind.

3.2b   Turnover ratios all have one of two figures as the numerator. What are these two figures? What do these ratios measure? How do you interpret the results?

3.2c   Profitability ratios all have the same figure in the numerator. What is it? What do these ratios measure? How do you interpret the results?

3.2d   Given the total debt ratio, what other two ratios can be computed? Explain how.

3.3 THE DUPONT IDENTITY

Excel Master
coverage online

As we mentioned in discussing ROA and ROE, the difference between these two profitability measures is a reflection of the use of debt financing, or financial leverage. We illustrate the relationship between these measures in this section by investigating a famous way of decomposing ROE into its component parts.

To begin, let's recall the definition of ROE:

$$\text{Return on equity} = \frac{\text{Net income}}{\text{Total equity}}$$

If we were so inclined, we could multiply this ratio by Assets/Assets without changing anything:

$$\text{Return on equity} = \frac{\text{Net income}}{\text{Total equity}} = \frac{\text{Net income}}{\text{Total equity}} \times \frac{\text{Assets}}{\text{Assets}}$$

$$= \frac{\text{Net income}}{\text{Assets}} \times \frac{\text{Assets}}{\text{Total equity}}$$

Notice that we have expressed the ROE as the product of two other ratios—ROA and the equity multiplier:

$$\text{ROE} = \text{ROA} \times \text{Equity multiplier} = \text{ROA} \times (1 + \text{Debt-equity ratio})$$

Looking back at Prufrock, we see that the debt-equity ratio was .38 and ROA was 13.06 percent. Our work here implies that Prufrock's ROE, as we previously calculated, is:

$$\text{ROE} = .1306 \times 1.38 = .1806, \text{ or } 18.06\%$$

We can further decompose ROE by multiplying the top and bottom by total sales:

$$\text{ROE} = \frac{\text{Sales}}{\text{Sales}} \times \frac{\text{Net income}}{\text{Assets}} \times \frac{\text{Assets}}{\text{Total equity}}$$

If we rearrange things a bit, ROE is

$$\text{ROE} = \underbrace{\frac{\text{Net income}}{\text{Sales}} \times \frac{\text{Sales}}{\text{Assets}}}_{\text{Return on assets}} \times \frac{\text{Assets}}{\text{Total equity}} \qquad [3.23]$$

$$= \text{Profit margin} \times \text{Total asset turnover} \times \text{Equity multiplier}$$

What we have now done is to partition ROA into its two component parts, profit margin and total asset turnover. This last expression is called the **DuPont identity**, after the DuPont Corporation, which popularized its use.

We can check this relationship for Prufrock by noting that the profit margin was 20.08 percent and the total asset turnover was .65. ROE should thus be:

$$\text{ROE} = \text{Profit margin} \times \text{Total asset turnover} \times \text{Equity multiplier}$$
$$= \quad .2008 \quad \times \quad .65 \quad \times \quad 1.38$$
$$= .1806, \text{ or } 18.06\%$$

This 18.06 percent ROE is exactly what we had before.

The DuPont identity tells us that ROE is affected by three things:

1. Operating efficiency (as measured by profit margin).
2. Asset use efficiency (as measured by total asset turnover).
3. Financial leverage (as measured by the equity multiplier).

Weakness in either operating or asset use efficiency (or both) will show up in a diminished return on assets, which will translate into a lower ROE.

Considering the DuPont identity, it appears that a firm could leverage up its ROE by increasing its amount of debt. It turns out this will happen only if the ratio of EBIT to total assets is greater than the interest rate. More importantly, the use of debt financing has a

DuPont identity
Popular expression breaking ROE into three parts: operating efficiency, asset use efficiency, and financial leverage.

TABLE 3.7	Amazon.com						
DuPont analysis for Amazon and Alibaba	Year	ROE	=	Profit margin	×	Total asset turnover	×	Equity multiplier

Year	ROE	=	Profit margin	×	Total asset turnover	×	Equity multiplier
2017	15.0%	=	2.3%	×	1.355	×	4.74
2016	21.7%	=	3.1%	×	1.631	×	4.32
2015	16.7%	=	2.1%	×	1.653	×	4.84

Alibaba							
Year	ROE	=	Profit margin	×	Total asset turnover	×	Equity multiplier
2017	15.7%	=	27.6%	×	.312	×	1.82
2016	32.9%	=	70.7%	×	.278	×	1.68
2015	16.7%	=	31.8%	×	.298	×	1.76

number of other effects, and, as we discuss at some length in later chapters, the amount of leverage a firm uses is governed by its capital structure policy.

The decomposition of ROE we've discussed in this section is a convenient way of systematically approaching financial statement analysis. If ROE is unsatisfactory by some measure, then the DuPont identity tells you where to start looking for the reasons. To give an example, take a look at the information about Internet marketplace companies Amazon and Alibaba in Table 3.7. As you can see, in 2017, Amazon had an ROE of 15.0 percent, down from its ROE in 2015 of 16.7 percent. In contrast, also in 2017, Alibaba had an ROE of 15.7 percent, down from its ROE in 2015 of 16.7 percent. Given this information, it would appear that the two companies operate in a similar fashion, but as we see, that is not true.

Looking at the DuPont breakdown, we see that Amazon's profit margin is in the 2 to 3 percent range, while Alibaba's profit has ranged from 27.6 percent to an astounding 70.7 percent. However, Amazon's ROE is similar to Alibaba's because Amazon has a higher asset utilization, as measured by total asset turnover, and a higher leverage, as measured by the equity multiplier.

An Expanded DuPont Analysis

The regulatory filings of publicly traded corporations may be found at www.sec.gov.

So far, we've seen how the DuPont equation lets us break down ROE into its basic three components: profit margin, total asset turnover, and financial leverage. We now extend this analysis to take a closer look at how key parts of a firm's operations feed into ROE. To get going, we went to the SEC website (www.sec.gov) and found the 10-K for chemical products giant DowDuPont. In the 10-K, we located the financial statements for 2017. What we found is summarized in Table 3.8.

Using the information in Table 3.8, Figure 3.1 shows how we can construct an expanded DuPont analysis for DowDuPont and present that analysis in chart form. The advantage of the extended DuPont chart is that it lets us examine several ratios at once, thereby getting a better overall picture of a company's performance and also allowing us to determine possible items to improve.

Looking at the left-hand side of our DuPont chart in Figure 3.1, we see items related to profitability. As always, profit margin is calculated as net income divided by sales. But, as our chart emphasizes, net income depends on sales and a variety of costs, such as cost of goods sold (CoGS) and selling, general, and administrative (SG&A) expenses. DuPont can increase its ROE by increasing sales and also by reducing one or more of these costs. In

TABLE **3.8**

FINANCIAL STATEMENTS FOR DOWDUPONT 12 months ending December 31, 2017 (All numbers are in millions)				
Income Statement		**Balance Sheet**		
Sales	$62,484	Current assets		Current liabilities	
CoGS	48,008	Cash	$ 16,088	Accounts payable	$ 11,601
Gross profit	$14,476	Accounts receivable	16,813	Notes payable	50,203
SG&A expense	7,232	Inventory	16,992	Total	$ 61,804
R&D expense	4,017	Total	$ 49,893	Total long-term debt	$ 30,030
EBIT	$ 3,227	Fixed assets	$142,271	Total equity	$100,330
Interest	1,082	Total assets	$192,164	Total liabilities and equity	$192,164
EBT	$ 2,145				
Taxes	476				
Net income	$ 1,669				

FIGURE **3.1**   **Extended DuPont chart for DowDuPont**

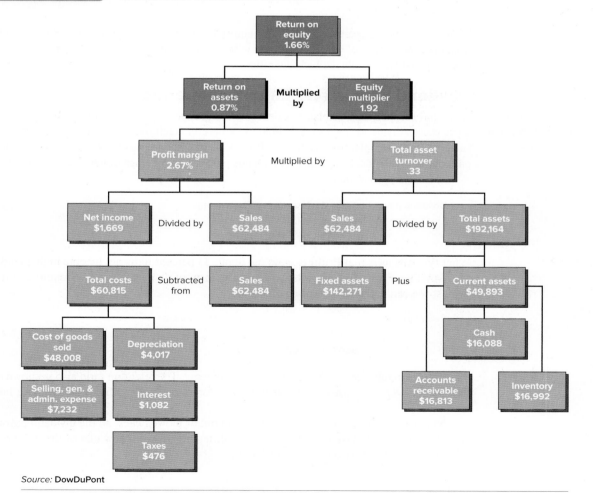

Source: **DowDuPont**

other words, if we want to improve profitability, our chart clearly shows us the areas on which we should focus.

Turning to the right-hand side of Figure 3.1, we have an analysis of the key factors underlying total asset turnover. Thus, we see that reducing inventory holdings through more efficient management reduces current assets, which reduces total assets, which then improves total asset turnover.

CONCEPT QUESTIONS

3.3a   Return on assets, or ROA, can be expressed as the product of two ratios. Which two?

3.3b   Return on equity, or ROE, can be expressed as the product of three ratios. Which three?

3.4 INTERNAL AND SUSTAINABLE GROWTH

A firm's return on assets and return on equity are frequently used to calculate two additional numbers, both of which have to do with the firm's ability to grow. We examine these next, but first we introduce two basic ratios.

Dividend Payout and Earnings Retention

You can find growth rates under the "Analysis" link at finance.yahoo.com.

As we have seen in various places, a firm's net income gets divided into two pieces. The first piece is cash dividends paid to stockholders. Whatever is left over is the addition to retained earnings. For example, from Table 3.3, Prufrock's net income was $474, of which $158 was paid out in dividends. If we express dividends paid as a percentage of net income, the result is the *dividend payout ratio*:

$$\text{Dividend payout ratio} = \text{Cash dividends}/\text{Net income} \qquad [3.24]$$
$$= \$158/\$474$$
$$= .3333, \text{ or } 33.33\%$$

What this tells us is that Prufrock pays out about 33 percent of its net income in dividends.

Anything Prufrock does not pay out in the form of dividends must be retained in the firm, so we can define the *retention ratio* as:

$$\text{Retention ratio} = \text{Addition to retained earnings}/\text{Net income}$$
$$= \$316/\$474 \qquad [3.25]$$
$$= .6667, \text{ or } 66.67\%$$

So, Prufrock retains about 67 percent of its net income. The retention ratio also is known as the *plowback ratio* because it is, in effect, the portion of net income that is plowed back into the business.

Notice that net income must be either paid out or plowed back, so the dividend payout and plowback ratios have to add up to 1. Put differently, if you know one of these figures, you can figure the other one out immediately.

EXAMPLE 3.4   **Payout and Retention**

The Manson-Marilyn Corporation routinely pays out 40 percent of net income in the form of dividends. What is its plowback ratio? If net income was $800, how much did stockholders actually receive?

   If the payout ratio is 40 percent, then the retention, or plowback, ratio must be 60 percent because the two have to add up to 100 percent. Dividends were 40 percent of $800, or $320.

ROA, ROE, and Growth

Investors and others are frequently interested in knowing how rapidly a firm's sales can grow. The important thing to recognize is that if sales are to grow, assets have to grow as well, at least over the long run. Further, if assets are to grow, then the firm must somehow obtain the money to pay for the needed acquisitions. In other words, growth has to be financed, and as a direct corollary, a firm's ability to grow depends on its financing policies.

   A firm has two broad sources of financing: *internal* and *external*. Internal financing refers to what the firm earns and subsequently plows back into the business. External financing refers to funds raised by either borrowing money or selling stock.

The Internal Growth Rate   Suppose a firm has a policy of financing growth using only internal financing. This means that the firm won't borrow any funds and won't sell any new stock. How rapidly can the firm grow? The answer is given by the **internal growth rate**:

$$\text{Internal growth rate} = \frac{\text{ROA} \times b}{1 - \text{ROA} \times b} \qquad [3.26]$$

internal growth rate
The maximum possible growth rate a firm can achieve without external financing of any kind.

where ROA is, as usual, return on assets and b is the retention, or plowback, ratio we just discussed.

   For Prufrock Corporation, we earlier calculated ROA as 13.06 percent. We also saw that the retention ratio is 66.67 percent, so the internal growth rate is:

$$\begin{aligned}\text{Internal growth rate} &= \frac{\text{ROA} \times b}{1 - \text{ROA} \times b} \\ &= \frac{.1306 \times .6667}{1 - .1306 \times .6667} \\ &= .0954, \text{ or } 9.54\%\end{aligned}$$

Thus, if Prufrock relies solely on internally generated financing, it can grow at a maximum rate of 9.54 percent per year.

The Sustainable Growth Rate   If a firm only relies on internal financing, then, through time, its total debt ratio will decline. The reason is that assets will grow, but total debt will remain the same (or even fall if some is paid off). Frequently, firms have a particular total debt ratio or equity multiplier that they view as optimal (why this is so is the subject of Chapter 13).

   With this in mind, we now consider how rapidly a firm can grow if (1) it wishes to maintain a particular total debt ratio and (2) it is unwilling to sell new stock. There are various reasons a firm might wish to avoid selling stock, and equity sales by established firms are actually a relatively rare occurrence. Given these two assumptions, the maximum growth rate that can be achieved, called the **sustainable growth rate**, is:

$$\text{Sustainable growth rate} = \frac{\text{ROE} \times b}{1 - \text{ROE} \times b} \qquad [3.27]$$

sustainable growth rate
The maximum possible growth rate a firm can achieve without external equity financing while maintaining a constant debt-equity ratio.

Notice that this is the same as the internal growth rate, except that ROE is used instead of ROA.

Looking at Prufrock, we earlier calculated ROE as 18.06 percent, and we know that the retention ratio is 66.67 percent, so we can easily calculate sustainable growth as:

$$\text{Sustainable growth rate} = \frac{\text{ROE} \times b}{1 - \text{ROE} \times b}$$

$$= \frac{.1806 \times .6667}{1 - .1806 \times .6667}$$

$$= .1369, \text{ or } 13.69\%$$

If you compare this sustainable growth rate of 13.69 percent to the internal growth rate of 9.54 percent, you might wonder why it is larger. The reason is that, as the firm grows, it will have to borrow additional funds if it is to maintain a constant debt ratio. This new borrowing is an extra source of financing in addition to internally generated funds, so Prufrock can expand more rapidly.

Determinants of Growth   In our previous section, we saw that the return on equity, or ROE, could be decomposed into its various components using the DuPont identity. Because ROE appears so prominently in the determination of the sustainable growth rate, the factors important in determining ROE are also important determinants of growth.

As we saw, ROE can be written as the product of three factors:

ROE = Profit margin × Total asset turnover × Equity multiplier

If we examine our expression for the sustainable growth rate, we see that anything that increases ROE will increase the sustainable growth rate by making the numerator larger and the denominator smaller. Increasing the plowback ratio will have the same effect.

Putting it all together, what we have is that a firm's ability to sustain growth depends explicitly on the following four factors:

1. *Profit margin.* An increase in profit margin will increase the firm's ability to generate funds internally and thereby increase its sustainable growth.
2. *Total asset turnover.* An increase in the firm's total asset turnover increases the sales generated for each dollar in assets. This decreases the firm's need for new assets as sales grow and thereby increases the sustainable growth rate. Notice that increasing total asset turnover is the same thing as decreasing capital intensity.
3. *Financial policy.* An increase in the debt-equity ratio increases the firm's financial leverage. Because this makes additional debt financing available, it increases the sustainable growth rate.
4. *Dividend policy.* A decrease in the percentage of net income paid out as dividends will increase the retention ratio. This increases internally generated equity and thus increases internal and sustainable growth.

The sustainable growth rate is a very useful number. What it illustrates is the explicit relationship between the firm's four major areas of concern: its operating efficiency as measured by profit margin, its asset use efficiency as measured by total asset turnover, its financial policy as measured by the debt-equity ratio, and its dividend policy as measured by the retention ratio. If sales are to grow at a rate higher than the sustainable growth rate, the firm must increase profit margins, increase total asset turnover, increase financial leverage, increase earnings retention, or sell new shares.

The two growth rates, internal and sustainable, are summarized in Table 3.9. The nearby *Finance Matters* box discusses some issues related to growth rates.

How Fast Is Too Fast?

Growth rates are an important tool for evaluating a company, and, as we will see later, an important tool for valuing a company's stock. When thinking about (and calculating) growth rates, a little common sense goes a long way. For example, in 2018, retailing giant Walmart had about 785 million square feet of stores, distribution centers, and so forth. Suppose the company wants to expand its square footage by 6 percent over the next year. This increase doesn't sound too outrageous, but can Walmart grow its square footage at 6 percent indefinitely?

We'll get into the calculation in our next chapter, but if you assume that Walmart grows at 6 percent per year over the next 202 years, the company will have about 100 trillion square feet of property, which is about the total land mass of the entire United States! In other words, if Walmart keeps growing at 6 percent, the entire country will eventually be one big Walmart. Scary.

Facebook is another example. The company had total revenues of about $1.97 billion in 2010 and $40.65 billion in 2017. This represents an annual rate of increase of 54 percent! How likely do you think it is that the company can continue this growth rate? If this growth continued, the company would have revenues of about $26.67 trillion in just 15 years, which exceeds the gross domestic product (GDP) of the United States. Obviously, Facebook's growth rate will slow substantially in the next several years.

What about growth in cash flow? As of the beginning of 2018, cash flow for Internet travel booking website Priceline.com grew at an annual rate of about 37 percent for the past 10 years. The company was expected to generate about $4.48 billion in cash flow for 2018. If Priceline.com's cash flow grew at the same rate for the next 19 years, the company would generate about $1.77 trillion per year, or slightly more than the $1.63 trillion of U.S. currency circulating in the world.

As these examples show, growth rates can be deceiving. It is fairly easy for a small company to grow very fast. If a company has $100 in sales, it only has to increase sales by another $100 to have a 100 percent increase in sales. If the company's sales are $10 billion, it has to increase sales by another $10 billion to achieve the same 100 percent increase. So, long-term growth rate estimates must be chosen very carefully. As a rule of thumb, for really long-term growth estimates, you should probably assume that a company will not grow much faster than the economy as a whole, which is about 1 to 3 percent (inflation-adjusted).

TABLE 3.9

Summary of internal and sustainable growth rates

I. Internal growth rate

$$\text{Internal growth rate} = \frac{\text{ROA} \times b}{1 - \text{ROA} \times b}$$

where:

ROA = Return on assets = Net income/Total assets

b = Plowback (retention) ratio

= Addition to retained earnings/Net income

= 1 − Dividend payout ratio

The internal growth rate is the maximum growth rate that can be achieved with no external financing of any kind.

II. Sustainable growth rate

$$\text{Sustainable growth rate} = \frac{\text{ROE} \times b}{1 - \text{ROE} \times b}$$

where:

ROE = Return on equity = Net income/Total equity

b = Plowback (retention) ratio

= Addition to retained earnings/Net income

= 1 − Dividend payout ratio

The sustainable growth rate is the maximum growth rate that can be achieved with no external equity financing while maintaining a constant debt-equity ratio.

A Note on Sustainable Growth Rate Calculations   Very commonly, the sustainable growth rate is calculated using just the numerator in our expression, ROE × b. This causes some confusion, which we can clear up here. The issue has to do with how ROE is computed. Recall that ROE is calculated as net income divided by total equity. If total equity is taken from an ending balance sheet (as we have done consistently, and is commonly done in practice), then our formula is the right one. However, if total equity is from the beginning of the period, then the simpler formula is the correct one.

In principle, you'll get exactly the same sustainable growth rate regardless of which way you calculate it (as long as you match up the ROE calculation with the right formula). In reality, you may see some differences because of accounting-related complications. By the way, if you use the average of beginning and ending equity (as some advocate), yet another formula is needed. Also, all of our comments here apply to the internal growth rate as well.

A simple example is useful to illustrate these points. Suppose a firm has a net income of $20 and a retention ratio of .60. Beginning assets are $100. The debt-equity ratio is .25, so beginning equity is $80.

If we use beginning numbers, we get the following:

ROE = $20/$80 = .25, or 25%
Sustainable growth = .25 × .60 = .15, or 15%

For the same firm, ending equity is $80 + .60 × $20 = $92. So, we can calculate this:

ROE = $20/$92 = .2174, or 21.74%
Sustainable growth = .2174 × .60/(1 − .2174 × .60) = .15, or 15%

These growth rates are exactly the same. See if you don't agree that the internal growth rate is 12 percent.

CONCEPT QUESTIONS

3.4a   What does a firm's internal growth rate tell us?

3.4b   What does a firm's sustainable growth rate tell us?

3.4c   Why is the sustainable growth rate likely to be larger than the internal growth rate?

3.5 USING FINANCIAL STATEMENT INFORMATION

Excel Master
coverage online

Our last task in this chapter is to discuss in more detail some practical aspects of financial statement analysis. In particular, we will look at reasons for doing financial statement analysis, how to go about getting benchmark information, and some of the problems that come up in the process.

Why Evaluate Financial Statements?

As we have discussed, the primary reason for looking at accounting information is that we don't have, and can't reasonably expect to get, market value information. It is important to emphasize that, whenever we have market information, we will use it instead of accounting data. Also, if there is a conflict between accounting and market data, market data should be given precedence.

Financial statement analysis is essentially an application of "management by exception." In many cases, such analysis will boil down to comparing ratios for one business with some kind of average or representative ratios. Those ratios that seem to differ the most from the averages are tagged for further study.

Internal Uses Financial statement information has a variety of uses within a firm. Among the most important of these is performance evaluation. For example, managers are frequently evaluated and compensated on the basis of accounting measures of performance such as profit margin and return on equity. Also, firms with multiple divisions frequently compare the performance of those divisions using financial statement information.

Another important internal use of financial statement information involves planning for the future. Historical financial statement information is very useful for generating projections about the future and for checking the realism of assumptions made in those projections.

External Uses Financial statements are useful to parties outside the firm, including short-term and long-term creditors and potential investors. For example, we would find such information quite useful in deciding whether or not to grant credit to a new customer.

We also would use this information to evaluate suppliers, and suppliers would use our statements before deciding to extend credit to us. Large customers use this information to decide if we are likely to be around in the future. Credit-rating agencies rely on financial statements in assessing a firm's overall creditworthiness. The common theme here is that financial statements are a prime source of information about a firm's financial health.

We also would find such information useful in evaluating our main competitors. We might be thinking of launching a new product. A prime concern would be whether the competition would jump in shortly thereafter. In this case, we would be interested in our competitors' financial strength to see if they could afford the necessary development.

Finally, we might be thinking of acquiring another firm. Financial statement information would be essential in identifying potential targets and deciding what to offer.

Choosing a Benchmark

Given that we want to evaluate a division or a firm based on its financial statements, a basic problem immediately comes up. How do we choose a benchmark, or a standard of comparison? We describe in this section some ways of getting started.

Time-Trend Analysis One standard we could use is history. Suppose we found that the current ratio for a particular firm is 2.4 based on the most recent financial statement information. Looking back over the last 10 years, we might find that this ratio has declined fairly steadily over that period.

Based on this, we might wonder if the liquidity position of the firm has deteriorated. It could be, of course, that the firm has made changes that allow it to use its current assets more efficiently, that the nature of the firm's business has changed, or that business practices have changed. If we investigate, we might find any of these possible explanations. This is an example of what we mean by management by exception—a deteriorating time trend may not be bad, but it does merit investigation.

Peer Group Analysis The second means of establishing a benchmark is to identify firms similar in the sense that they compete in the same markets, have similar assets, and operate in similar ways. In other words, we need to identify a *peer group*. There are obvious problems with doing this since no two companies are identical. Ultimately, the choice of which companies to use as a basis for comparison is subjective.

One common way of identifying potential peers is based on **Standard Industrial Classification (SIC) codes**. These are four-digit codes established by the U.S. government for statistical reporting purposes. Firms with the same SIC code are frequently assumed to be similar.

Standard Industrial Classification (SIC) code
U.S. government code used to classify a firm by its type of business operations.

TABLE 3.10		

Selected two-digit SIC codes	Agriculture, Forestry, and Fishing
	  01 Agriculture production: crops
	  02 Forestry
	Mining
	  10 Metal mining
	  13 Oil and gas extraction
	Construction
	  15 Building construction
	  16 Construction other than building
	Manufacturing
	  28 Chemicals and allied products
	  29 Petroleum refining
	  35 Machinery, except electrical
	  37 Transportation equipment
	Transportation, Communication, Electric, Gas, and Sanitary Service
	  45 Transportation by air
	  49 Electric, gas, and sanitary services
		Retail Trade
		  54 Food stores
		  55 Auto dealers and gas stations
		  58 Eating and drinking places
		Finance, Insurance, and Real Estate
		  60 Banking
		  63 Insurance
		  65 Real Estate
		Services
		  78 Motion pictures
		  80 Health services
		  82 Educational services

The first digit in an SIC code establishes the general type of business. For example, firms engaged in finance, insurance, and real estate have SIC codes beginning with 6. Each additional digit narrows down the industry. So, companies with SIC codes beginning with 60 are mostly banks and banklike businesses; those with codes beginning with 602 are mostly commercial banks; and SIC code 6025 is assigned to national banks that are members of the Federal Reserve system. Table 3.10 is a list of selected two-digit codes (the first two digits of the four-digit SIC codes) and the industries they represent.

Beginning in 1997, a new industry classification system was instituted. Specifically, the North American Industry Classification System (NAICS, pronounced "nakes") is intended to replace the older SIC codes, and it probably will eventually. Currently, however, SIC codes are widely used.

Learn more about NAICS at www.naics.com.

SIC codes are far from perfect. Suppose you were examining financial statements for Walmart, the largest retailer in the United States. In a quick scan of the nearest financial database, you might find about 20 large, publicly owned corporations with this same SIC code, but you might not be too comfortable with some of them. Target would seem to be a reasonable peer, but Neiman Marcus also carries the same industry code. Are Walmart and Neiman Marcus really comparable?

As this example illustrates, it is probably not appropriate to blindly use SIC code-based averages. Instead, analysts often identify a set of primary competitors and then compute a set of averages based on this group. Also, we may be more concerned with a group of the top firms in an industry, not the average firm. Such a group is called an *aspirant group* because we aspire to be like them. In this case, a financial statement analysis reveals how far we have to go.

We can now take a look at a specific industry. Suppose we are in the retail hardware business. Table 3.11 contains some condensed common-size financial statements for this industry from RMA, one of many sources of such information. Table 3.12 contains selected ratios from the same source.

There is a large amount of information here, most of which is self-explanatory. On the right in Table 3.11, we have current information reported for different groups based on sales. Within each sales group, common-size information is reported. For example,

TABLE **3.11**	Selected financial statement information

Manufacturing—Wineries NAICS 312130								
Comparative Historical Data				Current Data Sorted by Sales					

			Type of Statement						
38	33	29	Unqualified	1			2	4	22
40	53	41	Reviewed		2		15	15	9
17	15	12	Compiled	1	2	3	3	2	1
24	25	26	Tax Returns	11	6	4	4	1	
100	150	150	Other	24	35	20	18	26	27
				31 (4/1–9/30/15)			227 (10/1/15–3/31/16)		
4/1/13– 3/31/14 ALL 219	4/1/14– 3/31/15 ALL 276	4/1/15 – 3/31/16 ALL 258	NUMBER OF STATEMENTS	0-1 MM 37	1-3 MM 45	3-5 MM 27	5-10 MM 42	10-25 MM 48	25MM & OVER 59
			Assets						
5.2%	5.3%	5.0%	Cash & Equivalents	6.8%	5.0%	8.7%	5.2%	2.0%	4.4%
8.4	8.1	9.2	Trade Receivables (net)	5.6	7.3	7.5	9.0	11.0	12.3
44.4	47.4	47.3	Inventory	52.0	50.1	49.4	42.6	47.0	44.9
2.4	1.9	1.7	All Other Current	.6	1.6	.7	1.8	1.6	2.8
60.5	62.7	63.1	Total Current	65.0	64.0	66.3	58.6	61.6	64.3
32.0	29.2	29.8	Fixed Assets (net)	28.4	32.6	22.9	36.3	29.4	27.6
3.5	4.0	3.7	Intangibles (net)	4.5	1.5	3.7	3.1	5.0	4.1
4.0	4.1	3.4	All Other Non-Current	2.0	2.0	7.1	2.0	3.9	4.0
100.0	100.0	100.0	Total	100.0	100.0	100.0	100.0	100.0	100.0
			Liabilities						
14.1	16.8	15.7	Notes Payable—Short Term	17.7	14.3	10.0	12.3	18.8	18.1
2.1	1.8	1.3	Cur. Mat.-L.T.D.	.9	1.0	.9	2.0	1.4	1.6
8.8	8.9	8.8	Trade Payables	5.9	9.0	7.2	7.8	12.2	9.3
.2	.2	.2	Income Taxes Payable	.4	.3	.0	.3	.0	.1
6.0	6.0	6.5	All Other Current	7.6	4.8	6.0	4.1	8.7	7.4
31.2	33.8	32.6	Total Current	32.5	29.3	24.1	26.5	41.2	36.5
19.8	17.4	18.5	Long-Term Debt	20.5	17.5	17.8	22.5	17.4	16.6
.4	.3	.4	Deferred Taxes	.0	.0	.2	.7	.7	.4
6.3	6.7	6.6	All Other Non-Current	13.5	5.6	17.8	7.5	4.4	3.6
42.2	41.8	41.9	Net Worth	33.5	17.5	50.1	42.8	36.3	42.9
100.0	100.0	100.0	Total Liabilities & Net Worth	100.0	100.0	100.0	100.0	100.0	100.0
			Income Data						
100.0	100.0	100.0	Net Sales	100.0	100.0	100.0	100.0	100.0	100.0
48.9	50.0	49.3	Gross Profit	57.1	54.1	55.8	49.5	45.0	41.0
37.2	37.9	37.9	Operating Expenses	51.4	44.5	39.4	38.2	32.5	27.8
11.7	12.0	11.4	Operating Profit	5.7	9.7	16.4	11.3	12.5	13.3
2.7	2.6	2.6	All Other Expenses (net)	3.4	1.9	1.1	4.3	2.9	2.1
9.0	9.5	8.8	Profit Before Taxes	2.3	7.8	15.3	7.1	9.6	11.2

M = $ thousand; MM = $ million.

Interpretation of Statement Studies Figures: RMA cautions that the studies be regarded only as a general guideline and not as an absolute industry norm. This is due to limited samples within categories, the categorization of companies by their primary NAICS code only, and different methods of operations by companies within the same industry. For these reasons, RMA recommends that the figures be used only as general guidelines in addition to other methods of financial analysis.

TABLE 3.12	Selected ratios

Manufacturing—Wineries NAICS 312130

Comparative Historical Data				Current Data Sorted by Sales					
			Type of Statement	1					
38	33	29	Unqualified				2	4	22
40	53	41	Reviewed		2		15	15	9
17	15	12	Compiled	1	2	3	3	2	1
24	25	26	Tax Returns	11	6	4	4	1	
100	150	150	Other	29	35	20	18	26	27
				31 (4/1–9/30/15)			227 (10/1/15–3/31/16)		
4/1/13–3/31/14 ALL 219	4/1/14–3/31/15 ALL 276	4/1/15–3/31/16 ALL 258	NUMBER OF STATEMENTS	0–1 MM 37	1–3 MM 45	3–5 MM 27	5–10 MM 42	10–25 MM 48	25 MM & OVER 59
			Ratios						
4.0	4.5	4.0		4.1	5.8	5.9	3.8	2.4	3.4
2.1	2.0	2.1	Current	2.7	2.3	3.3	2.3	1.5	1.9
1.4	1.4	1.4		1.4	1.5	1.8	1.8	1.2	1.3
.9	.9	.9		1.2	1.1	1.9	1.2	.6	.7
.3	.3	.3	Quick	.3	.3	.5	.4	.3	.4
.2	.2	.2		.1	.2	.2	.2	.1	.2
16 23.0	15 24.8	15 23.7		0 UND	2 49.3	11 32.8	16 22.4	21 17.2	28 13.1
30 12.2	34 10.6	31 11.8	Sales/Receivables	10 35.6	28 12.9	20 18.3	29 12.6	37 9.8	41 8.9
51 7.1	52 7.0	52 7.0		46 7.9	50 7.3	39 9.4	57 6.4	56 6.5	59 6.2
261 1.4	332 1.1	304 1.2		192 1.9	304 1.2	261 1.4	304 1.2	365 1.0	261 1.4
456 .8	521 .7	521 .7	Cost of Sales/Inventory	608 .6	608 .6	608 .6	608 .6	521 .7	365 1.0
730 .5	912 .4	730 .5		912 .4	912 .4	730 .5	730 .5	730 .5	608 .6
14 14.4	26 14.0	21 17.3		0 UND	10 36.2	21 17.2	23 16.0	36 10.1	23 16.1
24 6.6	59 6.2	51 7.2	Cost of Sales/Payables	48 7.6	53 6.9	35 10.3	47 7.8	69 5.3	51 7.2
38 3.6	122 3.0	107 3.4		166 2.2	146 2.5	70 5.2	122 3.0	122 3.0	76 4.8
1.4	1.3	1.3		1.2	1.2	1.1	1.3	2.0	1.9
2.7	2.4	2.6	Sales/Working Capital	2.0	2.8	2.3	2.1	3.7	2.9
6.6	5.1	5.2		7.8	5.8	4.0	2.8	6.7	6.0
9.7	11.4	14.3		4.5	7.9	31.5	12.3	13.0	19.9
(200) 3.9	(252) 4.7	(235) 3.7	EBIT/Interest	(31) 1.0	(36) 3.60	(25) 9.0	(40) 2.3	(46) 4.1	(57) 5.7
1.9	1.7	1.3		−2.1	1.2	2.1	1.1	1.2	2.8
8.0	9.1	9.5	Net Profit + Depr.,					6.9	17.3
(42) 4.8	(55) 5.0	(45) 5.9	Dep., Amort./				(10)	3.5 (24)	7.7
1.9	2.6	2.6	Cur. Mat. L/T/D					1.8	4.3
.3	.2	.2		.2	.2	.1	.4	.2	.3
.8	.7	.7	Fixed/Worth	.6	.7	.4	1.0	.8	.8
1.6	1.4	1.5		4.5	1.5	1.1	1.5	1.9	1.3
.6	.6	.6		.5	.5	.4	.6	1.2	.8
1.5	1.4	1.4	Debt/Worth	2.6	1.0	1.2	1.4	2.1	1.1
4.1	3.0	3.9		24.2	2.7	4.3	2.8	4.3	3.2
32.8	33.9	32.7	% Profit Before	34.2	25.0	47.0	20.0	42.2	27.9
(194) 14.8	(253) 15.6	(230) 13.6	Taxes/Tangible	(29) 5.5	(41) 11.8	(25) 20.5	(38) 7.4	(43) 19.6	(54) 18.3
2.7	3.3	2.7	Net Worth	−8.9	4.6	3.3	.4	3.7	10.2

TABLE 3.12   Selected ratios *(continued)*

| | | | | 43 (4/1–9/30/10) | | | 326 (10/1/10–3/31/11) | | |
4/1/13– 3/31/14 ALL 219	4/1/14– 3/31/15 ALL 276	4/1/15– 3/31/16 ALL 258	NUMBER OF STATEMENTS	0–1 MM 37	1–3 MM 45	3–5 MM 27	5–10 MM 42	10–25 MM 48	25 MM & OVER 59
12.0	12.8	12.1	% Profit	13.6	9.1	23.9	8.7	13.4	13.1
5.1	5.6	4.8	Before Taxes/	1.4	5.2	7.2	2.7	4.4	7.0
.7	.9	.6	Total Assets	−5.0	.8	1.5	.2	.8	3.0
7.4	9.5	8.6	Sales/Net	7.3	6.8	13.9	3.9	33.5	9.0
2.5	3.0	2.9	Fixed Assets	5.0	2.3	5.1	1.4	2.1	3.3
1.1	1.1	1.2		2.4	1.5	1.7	.9	1.0	1.4
1.1	1.0	1.1	Sales/Total	1.1	1.1	1.2	1.0	1.1	1.1
.7	.7	.7	Assets	.7	.7	.8	.6	.7	.7
.5	.5	.5		.5	.5	.5	.4	.4	.5
2.4	2.4	2.1	% Depr.,	3.4	1.6	1.1	2.7	2.3	1.4
(171) 5.2	(270) 5.1	(199) 5.3	Dep., Amort./	(22) 5.9	(31) 5.8	(40) 3.9	(35) 7.1	(29) 6.1	(56) 4.0
8.3	8.1	8.4	Sales	14.3	8.7	9.6	9.1	9.3	7.1
3.1	2.7	2.6	% Officers',						
(27) 4.3	(201) 4.1	(33) 4.1	Directors', Owners'						
7.7	9.5	7.3	Comp/Sales						
4892971M	8360552M	5519014M	Net Sales ($)	19825M	82307M	103312M	287163M	774866M	4251541M
6963108M	8811913M	8435750M	Total Assets ($)	49293M	161278M	147637M	602723M	1722233M	5752586M

M = $ thousand; MM = $ million.

firms with sales in the $10 million to $25 million range have cash and equivalents equal to 2.0 percent of total assets. There are 48 companies in this group, out of 258 in all.

On the left, we have three years' worth of summary historical information for the entire group. For example, operating profit decreased slightly from 11.7 percent of sales to 11.4 percent over that time.

Table 3.12 contains some selected ratios, again reported by sales groups on the right and time period on the left. To see how we might use this information, suppose our firm has a current ratio of 2. Based on the ratios, is this value unusual?

Looking at the current ratio for the overall group for the most recent year (third column from the left in Table 3.12), we see that three numbers are reported. The one in the middle, 2.1, is the median, meaning that half of the 258 firms had current ratios that were lower and half had higher current ratios. The other two numbers are the upper and lower quartiles. So, 25 percent of the firms had a current ratio larger than 4.0 and 25 percent had a current ratio smaller than 1.4. Our value of 2 falls comfortably within these bounds, so it doesn't appear too unusual. This comparison illustrates how knowledge of the range of ratios is important in addition to knowledge of the average. Notice how stable the current ratio has been for the last three years.

EXAMPLE 3.5	**More Ratios**

Take a look at the most recent numbers reported for Cost of Sales/Inventory and EBIT/Interest in Table 3.12. What are the overall median values? What are these ratios?

    If you look back at our discussion, you will see that these are the inventory turnover and the times interest earned, or TIE, ratios. The median value for inventory turnover for the entire group is .7 times. So, the days' sales in inventory would be 365/.7 = 521 days, which is the boldfaced number reported. While this is long compared to other industries, this doesn't seem like very long for fine wines. The median for the TIE is 3.7 times. The number in parentheses indicates that the calculation is meaningful for, and therefore based on, only 235 of the 258 companies. In this case, the reason is that only 235 companies paid any significant amount of interest.

There are many sources of ratio information in addition to the one we examine here. The nearby *Work the Web* box shows how to get this information for most publicly traded companies, along with some very useful benchmarking information. Be sure to look it over and then benchmark your favorite company.

W🌐RK THE WEB

As we discussed in this chapter, ratios are an important tool for examining a company's performance, but gathering the necessary information can be tedious and time-consuming. Fortunately, many sites on the web provide this information for free. We went to www.reuters.com, entered the ticker symbol "BBY" (for Best Buy), and then went to the financials page. Here is an abbreviated look at the results:

MANAGEMENT EFFECTIVENESS

	Company	industry	sector
Return on Assets (TTM)	10.40	4.84	6.44
Return on Assets - 5 Yr. Avg.	7.32	4.12	7.05
Return on Investment (TTM)	22.62	10.03	10.59
Return on Investment - 5 Yr. Avg.	16.04	7.53	11.45
Return on Equity (TTM)	32.88	12.66	12.74
Return on Equity - 5 Yr. Avg.	24.47	11.20	14.92

Source: www.reuters.com

    In looking at the Management Effectiveness ratios (or what we call profitability ratios), Best Buy has outperformed the company and sector for both the 1-year and 5-year periods reported.

QUESTIONS

1. Go to www.reuters.com and find the major ratio categories listed on this website. How do the categories differ from the categories listed in the textbook?
2. Go to www.reuters.com and find all the ratios for Best Buy. How is the company performing in each ratio category presented on this website?

What's in a Ratio?

Abraham Briloff, a well-known financial commentator, famously remarked that "financial statements are like fine perfume; to be sniffed but not swallowed." As you probably have figured out by now, his point is that information gleaned from financial statements—and ratios and growth rates computed from that information—should be taken with a grain of salt.

For example, looking back at our chapter opener regarding PE ratios, investors must really think that Amazon.com will have extraordinary growth. After all, they are willing to pay about $274 for every dollar the company currently earns, which definitely makes it look like a growth company. Looking back, from 2012 to 2017, Amazon's revenue increased by 22 percent per year. More important, looking ahead, the well-known independent investment research company Value Line projected revenue growth of 21 percent per year and earnings growth of 48 percent per year over the next five years for Amazon.

A problem that can occur with ratio analysis is negative equity. Let's look at retailer Sears Holdings, for example. The company reported a loss of about $383 million during 2017, and its book value of equity was negative $3.7 billion. If you calculate the ROE for the company, you will find that it is about 10 percent, which is pretty good. Unfortunately, if you examine the ROE a little closer, you will find something unusual: The more the company loses, the higher the ROE becomes. Also, in this case, both the market-to-book and PE ratios are negative. How do you interpret a negative PE? We're not really sure either. Whenever a company has a negative book value of equity, it means the losses for the company have been so large that it has erased all the book equity. In this case, ROE, PE ratios, and market-to-book ratios are usually not reported because they lack meaning.

Even if a company's book equity is positive, you still have to be careful. For example, consider Boeing, which had a market-to-book ratio of about 500 in early 2018. Because this ratio measures the value created by the company for shareholders, things look pretty good for the company. But a closer look shows that Boeing's book value of equity per share was $19.90 in 2013, but it dropped to $.60 in 2017 even though the company posted a positive net income for the year. As it happens, the drop was due to accounting charges related to the company's 747, 747-8, and KC-46A programs.

Financial ratios are important tools used in evaluating companies of all types, but you cannot take a number as given. Instead, before doing any analysis, the first step is to ask whether the number actually makes sense.

Problems with Financial Statement Analysis

We close out our chapter on working with financial statements by discussing some additional problems that can arise in using financial statements. In one way or another, the basic problem with financial statement analysis is that there is no underlying theory to help us identify which items or ratios to look at and to guide us in establishing benchmarks.

As we discuss in other chapters, there are many cases in which financial theory and economic logic provide guidance in making judgments about value and risk. Very little such help exists with financial statements. This is why we can't say which ratios matter the most and what a high or low value might be.

One particularly severe problem is that many firms, such as General Electric (GE), are conglomerates owning more or less unrelated lines of business. The consolidated financial statements for such firms don't really fit any neat industry category. More generally, the kind of peer group analysis we have been describing is going to work best when the firms are strictly in the same line of business, the industry is competitive, and there is only one way of operating.

Another problem that is becoming increasingly common is that major competitors and natural peer group members in an industry may be scattered around the globe. The automobile industry is an obvious example. The problem here is that financial statements from outside the United States do not necessarily conform at all to GAAP (more precisely, different countries can have different GAAPs). The existence of different standards and procedures makes it very difficult to compare financial statements across national borders.

Even companies that are clearly in the same line of business may not be comparable. For example, electric utilities engaged primarily in power generation are all classified in the same group (SIC 4911). This group is often thought to be relatively homogeneous. However, utilities generally operate as regulated monopolies, so they don't compete with each other. Many have stockholders, and many are organized as cooperatives with no stockholders. There are several different ways of generating power, ranging from hydroelectric to nuclear, so the operating activities can differ quite a bit. Finally, profitability is strongly affected by the regulatory environment, so utilities in different locations can be very similar but show very different profits.

Several other general problems frequently crop up. First, different firms use different accounting procedures—for inventory, for example. This makes it difficult to compare statements. Second, different firms end their fiscal years at different times. For firms in seasonal businesses (such as a retailer with a large Christmas season), this can lead to difficulties in comparing balance sheets because of fluctuations in accounts during the year. Finally, for any particular firm, unusual or transient events, such as a one-time profit from an asset sale, may affect financial performance. In comparing firms, such events can give misleading signals. Our nearby *Finance Matters* box discusses some additional issues.

CONCEPT QUESTIONS

3.5a   What are some uses for financial statement analysis?
3.5b   What are SIC codes and how might they be useful?
3.5c   Why do we say that financial statement analysis is management by exception?
3.5d   What are some of the problems that can arise with financial statement analysis?

SUMMARY AND CONCLUSIONS

This chapter has discussed aspects of financial statement analysis, including:

1. Standardized financial statements. We explained that differences in firm size make it difficult to compare financial statements, and we discussed how to form common-size statements to make comparisons easier.

2. Ratio analysis. Evaluating ratios of accounting numbers is another way of comparing financial statement information. We therefore defined and discussed a number of the most commonly reported and used financial ratios. We also discussed the famous DuPont identity as a way of analyzing financial performance, and we examined the connection between profitability, financial policy, and growth.

3. Using financial statements. We described how to establish benchmarks for comparison purposes and discussed some of the types of information that are available. We then examined some of the potential problems that can arise.

After you have studied this chapter, we hope that you will have some perspective on the uses and abuses of financial statements. You also should find that your vocabulary of business and financial terms has grown substantially.

▣connect® POP QUIZ!

Can you answer the following questions? If your class is using *Connect*, log on to SmartBook to see if you know the answers to these and other questions, check out the study tools, and find out what topics require additional practice!

Section 3.1 A common-size balance sheet expresses all accounts as a percentage of what?

Section 3.2 What are the categories of traditional financial ratios?

Section 3.3 According to the DuPont identity, what factors affect ROE?

Section 3.4 Bubbles, Inc., has a return on equity of 12 percent and its retention ratio is 60 percent. What is its sustainable growth rate?

Section 3.5 When should market information be used when analyzing financial transactions?

CHAPTER REVIEW AND SELF-TEST PROBLEMS

3.1   Common-Size Statements   Here are the most recent financial statements for Wildhack. Prepare a common-size income statement based on this information. How do you interpret the standardized net income? What percentage of sales goes to cost of goods sold? (See Problem 15.)

WILDHACK CORPORATION 2019 Income Statement ($ in millions)	
Sales	$3,756
Cost of goods sold	2,453
Depreciation	490
Earnings before interest and taxes	$ 813
Interest paid	613
Taxable income	$ 200
Taxes (21%)	42
Net income	$ 158
Dividends	$72
Addition to retained earnings	86

	2018	2019		2018	2019
Assets			**Liabilities and Owners' Equity**		
Current assets			Current liabilities		
Cash	$ 120	$ 88	Accounts payable	$ 124	$ 144
Accounts receivable	224	192	Notes payable	1,412	1,039
Inventory	424	368	Total	$1,536	$1,183
Total	$ 768	$ 648	Long-term debt	$1,804	$2,077
Fixed assets			Owners' equity		
Net plant and equipment	$5,228	$5,354	Common stock and paid-in surplus	$ 300	$ 300
			Retained earnings	2,356	2,442
Total assets	$5,996	$6,002	Total	$2,656	$2,742
			Total liabilities and owners' equity	$5,996	$6,002

WILDHACK CORPORATION
Balance Sheets as of December 31, 2018 and 2019
($ in millions)

3.2 Financial Ratios   Based on the balance sheets and income statement in the previous problem, calculate the following ratios for 2019: (See Problem 35.)

Current ratio
Quick ratio
Cash ratio
Inventory turnover
Receivables turnover
Days' sales in inventory
Days' sales in receivables
Total debt ratio
Times interest earned ratio
Cash coverage ratio

3.3 ROE and the DuPont Identity   Calculate the 2019 ROE for the Wildhack Corporation and then break down your answer into its component parts using the DuPont identity. (See Problem 36.)

3.4 Sustainable Growth   Based on the following information, what growth rate can Corwin maintain if no external financing is used? What is the sustainable growth rate? (See Problems 20, 21.)

CORWIN COMPANY
Financial Statements

Income Statement		Balance Sheet			
Sales	$2,750	Current assets	$ 600	Long-term debt	$ 200
Cost of sales	2,450	Net fixed assets	800	Equity	1,200
Tax (21%)	63	Total	$1,400	Total	$1,400
Net income	$ 237				
Dividends	$ 79				

■ Answers to Chapter Review and Self-Test Problems

3.1   We've calculated the common-size income statement below. Remember that we divide each item by total sales.

WILDHACK CORPORATION 2019 Common-Size Income Statement		
Sales		100.0%
Cost of goods sold		65.3
Depreciation		13.0
Earnings before interest and taxes		21.6
Interest paid		16.3
Taxable income		5.3
Taxes (21%)		1.1
Net income		4.2%
Dividends	1.9%	
Addition to retained earnings	2.3	

Net income is 4.2 percent of sales. Because this is the percentage of each sales dollar that makes its way to the bottom line, the standardized net income is the firm's profit margin. Cost of goods sold is 65.3 percent of sales.

3.2   We've calculated the ratios below based on the ending figures. If you don't remember a definition, refer back to Table 3.5.

Current ratio	$648/$1,183	= .55 times
Quick ratio	$280/$1,183	= .24 times
Cash ratio	$88/$1,183	= .07 times
Inventory turnover	$2,453/$368	= 6.67 times
Receivables turnover	$3,756/$192	= 19.56 times
Days' sales in inventory	365/6.67	= 54.76 days
Days' sales in receivables	365/19.56	= 18.66 days
Total debt ratio	$3,260/$6,002	= .54 times
Times interest earned ratio	$813/$613	= 1.33 times
Cash coverage ratio	$1,303/$613	= 2.13 times

3.3   The return on equity is the ratio of net income to total equity. For Wildhack, this is $158/$2,742 = .0576, or 5.76%, which is not outstanding. Given the DuPont identity, ROE can be written as:

ROE = Profit margin × Total asset turnover × Equity multiplier
     = $158/$3,756 × $3,756/$6,002   × $6,002/$2,742
     = .0421   ×   .6258   ×   2.1889
     = .0576, or 5.76%

Notice that return on assets, ROA, is .0421 × .6258 = .0263, or 2.63%.

3.4   Corwin retains $158/$237 = $\frac{2}{3}$ ≈ .6667 of net income. Return on assets is $237/$1,400 = .1693, or 16.93%. The internal growth rate is

$$\frac{ROA \times b}{1 - ROA \times b} = \frac{.1693 \times .6667}{1 - .1693 \times .6667} = .1272, \text{ or } 12.72\%$$

Return on equity for Corwin is $237/$1,200 = .1975, or 19.75%, so we can calculate the sustainable growth rate as:

$$\frac{\text{ROE} \times b}{1 - \text{ROE} \times b} = \frac{.1975 \times .6667}{1 - .1975 \times .6667} = .1516, \text{ or } 15.16\%$$

CRITICAL THINKING AND CONCEPTS REVIEW

LO 2   **3.1**   **Current Ratio**   What effect would the following actions have on a firm's current ratio? Assume that net working capital is positive.

    a.   Inventory is purchased.

    b.   A supplier is paid.

    c.   A short-term bank loan is repaid.

    d.   A long-term debt is paid off early.

    e.   A customer pays off a credit account.

    f.   Inventory is sold at cost.

    g.   Inventory is sold for a profit.

LO 2   **3.2**   **Current Ratio and Quick Ratio**   In recent years, Dixie Co. has greatly increased its current ratio. At the same time, the quick ratio has fallen. What has happened? Has the liquidity of the company improved?

LO 2   **3.3**   **Current Ratio**   Explain what it means for a firm to have a current ratio equal to .50. Would the firm be better off if the current ratio were 1.50? What if it were 15.0? Explain your answers.

LO 2   **3.4**   **Financial Ratios**   Fully explain the kind of information the following financial ratios provide about a firm:

    a.   Quick ratio

    b.   Cash ratio

    c.   Capital intensity ratio

    d.   Total asset turnover

    e.   Equity multiplier

    f.   Times interest earned ratio

    g.   Profit margin

    h.   Return on assets

    i.   Return on equity

    j.   Price-earnings ratio

LO 1   **3.5**   **Standardized Financial Statements**   What types of information do common-size financial statements reveal about the firm? What is the best use for these common-size statements?

LO 2   **3.6**   **Peer Group Analysis**   Explain what peer group analysis means. As a financial manager, how could you use the results of peer group analysis to evaluate the performance of your firm? How is a peer group different from an aspirant group?

LO 3   **3.7**   **DuPont Identity**   Why is the DuPont identity a valuable tool for analyzing the performance of a firm? Discuss the types of information it reveals as compared to ROE considered by itself.

LO 2 3.8 **Industry-Specific Ratios** Specialized ratios are sometimes used in specific industries. For example, the so-called book-to-bill ratio is closely watched for semiconductor manufacturers. A ratio of .93 indicates that for every $100 worth of chips shipped over some period, only $93 worth of new orders were received. In the first quarter of 2018, the North American semiconductor equipment industry's book-to-bill ratio was 1.14, down from 1.27 in the first quarter of 2017. The most recent low occurred in October 2016 when it reached .91. What is this ratio intended to measure? Why do you think it is so closely followed?

LO 2 3.9 **Industry-Specific Ratios** So-called same-store sales are a very important measure for companies as diverse as McDonald's and Target. As the name suggests, examining same-store sales means comparing revenues from the same stores or restaurants at two different points in time. Why might companies focus on same-store sales rather than total sales?

LO 2 3.10 **Industry-Specific Ratios** There are many ways of using standardized financial information beyond those discussed in this chapter. The usual goal is to put firms on an equal footing for comparison purposes. For example, for auto manufacturers, it is common to express sales, costs, and profits on a per-car basis. For each of the following industries, give an example of an actual company and discuss one or more potentially useful means of standardizing financial information:

a. Public utilities

b. Large retailers

c. Airlines

d. Online services

e. Hospitals

f. College textbook publishers

LO 2 3.11 **Financial Statement Analysis** You are examining the common-size income statements for a company for the past five years and have noticed that the cost of goods as a percentage of sales has been increasing steadily. At the same time, EBIT as a percentage of sales has been decreasing. What might account for the trends in these ratios?

LO 2 3.12 **Financial Statement Analysis** In the previous question, what actions might managers take to improve these ratios?

QUESTIONS AND PROBLEMS

Select problems are available in McGraw-Hill *Connect*. Please see the packaging options section of the Preface for more information.

BASIC (Questions 1–26)

LO 2 1. **Calculating Liquidity Ratios** SDJ, Inc., has net working capital of $2,135, current liabilities of $5,320, and inventory of $2,470. What is the current ratio? What is the quick ratio?

LO 2 2. **Calculating Profitability Ratios** Wims, Inc., has sales of $15.2 million, total assets of $9.8 million, and total debt of $3.7 million. If the profit margin is 6 percent, what is net income? What is ROA? What is ROE?

LO 2
3. **Calculating the Average Collection Period**   Trout Lumber Yard has a current accounts receivable balance of $527,164. Credit sales for the year just ended were $6,787,626. What is the receivables turnover? The days' sales in receivables? How long did it take, on average, for credit customers to pay off their accounts during the past year?

LO 2
4. **Calculating Inventory Turnover**   A7X Corporation has ending inventory of $625,817, and cost of goods sold for the year just ended was $9,758,345. What is the inventory turnover? The days' sales in inventory? How long, on average, did a unit of inventory sit on the shelf before it was sold?

LO 2
5. **Calculating Leverage Ratios**   Bello, Inc., has a total debt ratio of .43. What is its debt-equity ratio? What is its equity multiplier?

LO 2
6. **Calculating Market Value Ratios**   Dove, Inc., had additions to retained earnings for the year just ended of $486,000. The firm paid out $175,000 in cash dividends, and it has ending total equity of $6.825 million. If the company currently has 335,000 shares of common stock outstanding, what are earnings per share? Dividends per share? What is book value per share? If the stock currently sells for $46 per share, what is the market-to-book ratio? The price-earnings ratio? If total sales were $15.4 million, what is the price-sales ratio?

LO 3
7. **DuPont Identity**   If jPhone, Inc., has an equity multiplier of 1.67, total asset turnover of 1.45, and a profit margin of 5.9 percent, what is its ROE?

LO 3
8. **DuPont Identity**   Croc Gator Removal has a profit margin of 6.4 percent, total asset turnover of 1.73, and ROE of 14.3 percent. What is this firm's debt-equity ratio?

LO 2
9. **Calculating Average Payables Period**   For the past year, Hawkeye, Inc., had a cost of goods sold of $95,318. At the end of the year, the accounts payable balance was $22,816. How long, on average, did it take the company to pay off its suppliers during the year? What might a large value for this ratio imply?

LO 2
10. **Equity Multiplier and Return on Equity**   Pickler Company has a debt-equity ratio of .65. Return on assets is 7.2 percent, and total equity is $815,000. What is the equity multiplier? Return on equity? Net income?

LO 3
11. **Internal Growth**   If Levine, Inc., has an ROA of 7.8 percent and a payout ratio of 25 percent, what is its internal growth rate?

LO 3
12. **Sustainable Growth**   If the Crash Davis Driving School has an ROE of 14.6 percent and a payout ratio of 20 percent, what is its sustainable growth rate?

LO 3
13. **Sustainable Growth**   Based on the following information, calculate the sustainable growth rate for Northern Lights Co.:

$$\text{Profit margin} = 6.7\%$$
$$\text{Capital intensity ratio} = .45$$
$$\text{Debt–equity ratio} = .35$$
$$\text{Net income} = \$135,000$$
$$\text{Dividends} = \$65,000$$

LO 3   **14. Sustainable Growth**   Assuming the following ratios are constant, what is the sustainable growth rate?

Total asset turnover $=2.95$

Profit margin $=5.9\%$

Equity multiplier $=1.31$

Payout ratio $=40\%$

Bethesda Mining Company reports the following balance sheet information for 2018 and 2019. Use this information to work Problems 15 through 17.

| | | | | BETHESDA MINING COMPANY | | |
| | | | | Balance Sheets as of December 31, 2018 and 2019 | | |

	2018	2019		2018	2019
Assets			**Liabilities and Owners' Equity**		
Current assets			Current liabilities		
Cash	$ 21,182	$ 24,141	Accounts payable	$180,108	$190,767
Accounts receivable	51,036	59,935	Notes payable	83,179	98,175
Inventory	120,589	142,718	Total	$263,287	$288,942
Total	$192,807	$226,794	Long-term debt	$305,000	$340,000
			Owners' equity		
			Common stock and paid-in surplus	$165,000	$178,000
Fixed assets			Accumulated retained earnings	235,445	283,578
Net plant and equipment	$775,925	$863,726	Total	$400,445	$461,578
Total assets	$968,732	$1,090,520	Total liabilities and owners' equity	$968,732	$1,090,520

LO 1   **15. Preparing Standardized Financial Statements**   Prepare the 2018 and 2019 common-size balance sheets for Bethesda Mining.

LO 2   **16. Calculating Financial Ratios**   Based on the balance sheets given for Bethesda Mining, calculate the following financial ratios for each year:

    a.   Current ratio

    b.   Quick ratio

    c.   Cash ratio

    d.   Debt-equity ratio and equity multiplier

    e.   Total debt ratio

LO 3   **17. DuPont Identity**   Suppose that the Bethesda Mining Company had sales of $2,751,332 and net income of $86,432 for the year ending December 31, 2019. Calculate the DuPont identity.

LO 3   **18. DuPont Identity**   The Taylor Company has an ROA of 7.6 percent, a profit margin of 5.2 percent, and an ROE of 14 percent. What is the company's total asset turnover? What is the equity multiplier?

LO 2   **19. Return on Assets**   Borland, Inc., has a profit margin of 5.6 percent on sales of $13.6 million. If the firm has debt of $6.4 million and total assets of $9.8 million, what is the firm's ROA?

LO 3   **20. Calculating Internal Growth**   The most recent financial statements for Minnie's Manufacturing Co. are shown here:

Income Statement		Balance Sheet			
Sales	$87,600	Current assets	$ 29,000	Debt	$ 38,400
Costs	64,350	Fixed assets	91,400	Equity	82,000
Taxable income	$23,250	Total	$120,400	Total	$120,400
Tax (21%)	4,883				
Net Income	$18,368				

Assets and costs are proportional to sales. Debt and equity are not. The company maintains a constant 40 percent dividend payout ratio. No external financing is possible. What is the internal growth rate?

LO 3   21. **Calculating Sustainable Growth**   For Minnie's Manufacturing in Problem 20, what is the sustainable growth rate?

LO 2   22. **Total Asset Turnover**   Kaleb's Karate Supply had a profit margin of 6.7 percent, sales of $14.2 million, and total assets of $6.75 million. What was total asset turnover? If management set a goal of increasing total asset turnover to 2.75 times, what would the new sales figure need to be, assuming no increase in total assets?

LO 2   23. **Return on Equity**   Barrett, Inc., has a total debt ratio of .65, total debt of $353,000, and net income of $20,750. What is the company's return on equity?

LO 2   24. **Market Value Ratios**   Wilson, Inc., has a current stock price of $64. For the past year, the company had net income of $9.1 million, total equity of $24.7 million, sales of $49.6 million, and 4.9 million shares of stock outstanding. What are earnings per share (EPS)? Price-earnings ratio? Price-sales ratio? Book value per share? Market-to-book ratio?

LO 3   25. **Profit Margin**   PXG Co. has total assets of $8.42 million and a total asset turnover of 1.5 times. If the return on assets is 8.3 percent, what is its profit margin?

LO 2   26. **Enterprise Value-EBITDA Multiple**   The market value of the equity of Skipper, Inc., is $745,000. The balance sheet shows $46,000 in cash and $235,000 in debt, while the income statement has EBIT of $96,700 and a total of $144,000 in depreciation and amortization. What is the enterprise value-EBITDA multiple for this company?

INTERMEDIATE (Questions 27–46)

LO 3   27. **Using the DuPont Identity**   Y3K, Inc., has sales of $12,840, total assets of $4,730, and a debt-equity ratio of .25. If its return on equity is 14 percent, what is its net income?

LO 2   28. **Ratios and Fixed Assets**   The Plainfield Company has a long-term debt ratio (i.e., the ratio of long-term debt to long-term debt plus equity) of .35 and a current ratio of 1.25. Current liabilities are $2,510, sales are $12,840, profit margin is 8 percent, and ROE is 12.8 percent. What is the amount of the firm's net fixed assets?

LO 2   **29. Profit Margin**   In response to complaints about high prices, a grocery chain runs the following advertising campaign: "If you pay your child $2 to go buy $50 worth of groceries, then your child makes twice as much on the trip as we do." You've collected the following information from the grocery chain's financial statements:

(in millions)	
Sales	$685.00
Net income	13.70
Total assets	365.00
Total debt	229.80

Evaluate the grocery chain's claim. What is the basis for the statement? Is this claim misleading? Why or why not?

LO 3   **30. Using the DuPont Identity**   The Moraine Company has net income of $158,230. There are currently 28.45 days' sales in receivables. Total assets are $804,320, total receivables are $155,218, and the debt-equity ratio is .25. What is the company's profit margin? Its total asset turnover? Its ROE?

LO 2   **31. Calculating the Cash Coverage Ratio**   Delectable Parsnip, Inc.'s, net income for the most recent year was $8,417. The tax rate was 21 percent. The firm paid $4,632 in total interest expense and deducted $5,105 in depreciation expense. What was the company's cash coverage ratio for the year?

LO 2   **32. Calculating the Times Interest Earned Ratio**   For the most recent year, Camargo, Inc., had sales of $534,000, cost of goods sold of $241,680, depreciation expense of $60,400, and additions to retained earnings of $72,800. The firm currently has 20,000 shares of common stock outstanding, and the previous year's dividends per share were $1.35. Assuming a 22 percent income tax rate, what was the times interest earned ratio?

LO 2   **33. Return on Assets**   A fire has destroyed a large percentage of the financial records of the Inferno Company. You have the task of piecing together information in order to release a financial report. You have found the return on equity to be 11.6 percent. Sales were $1.79 million, the total debt ratio was .43, and total debt was $693,000. What is the return on assets (ROA)?

LO 2   **34. Ratios and Foreign Companies**   Prince Albert Canning PLC had a net loss of £32,415 on sales of £515,380. What was the company's profit margin? Does the fact that these figures are quoted in a foreign currency make any difference? Why? In dollars, sales were $689,785. What was the net loss in dollars?

Some recent financial statements for Smolira Golf, Inc., follow. Use this information to work Problems 35 through 38.

SMOLIRA GOLF, INC. Balance Sheets as of December 31, 2018 and 2019					
	2018	**2019**		**2018**	**2019**
Assets			**Liabilities and Owners' Equity**		
Current assets			Current liabilities		
Cash	$ 5,298	5,827	Accounts payable	$ 3,754	$ 3,986
Accounts receivable	7,707	8,477	Notes payable	3,045	3,318
Inventory	12,150	21,956	Other	152	179
Total	$ 25,155	$ 36,260	Total	$ 6,951	$ 7,483
			Long-term debt	$ 24,700	$ 16,000
			Owners' equity		
			Common stock and paid-in surplus	$ 40,000	$ 37,000
Fixed assets			Accumulated retained earnings	28,805	55,189
Net plant and equipment	$ 75,301	$ 79,412	Total	$ 68,805	$ 92,189
Total assets	$100,456	$115,672	Total liabilities and owners' equity	$100,456	$115,672

SMOLIRA GOLF, INC. 2019 Income Statement	
Sales	$229,854
Cost of goods sold	184,317
Depreciation	8,730
EBIT	$ 36,807
Interest paid	1,811
Taxable income	$ 34,996
Taxes	7,349
Net income	$ 27,647
Dividends	$16,000
Addition to retained earnings	11,647

LO 2

35. Calculating Financial Ratios   Find the following financial ratios for Smolira Golf (use year-end figures rather than average values where appropriate):

Short-term solvency ratios

    a.   Current ratio   _____

    b.   Quick ratio   _____

    c.   Cash ratio   _____

Asset utilization ratios

    d.   Total asset turnover   _____

    e.   Inventory turnover   _____

    f.   Receivables turnover   _____

Long-term solvency ratios

    g.   Total debt ratio   _____

    h.   Debt–equity ratio   _____

    i.   Equity multiplier   _____

    j.   Times interest earned ratio _____

    k.   Cash coverage ratio   _____

Profitability ratios

  l. Profit margin   _____

  m. Return on assets   _____

  n. Return on equity   _____

LO 3   **36. DuPont Identity** Construct the DuPont identity for Smolira Golf.

LO 2   **37. Market Value Ratios** Smolira Golf has 10,000 shares of common stock outstanding, and the market price for a share of stock at the end of 2019 was $73. What is the price-earnings ratio? What is the price-sales ratio? What are the dividends per share? What is the market-to-book ratio at the end of 2019?

LO 2   **38. Interpreting Financial Ratios** After calculating the ratios for Smolira Golf, you have uncovered the following industry ratios for 2019:

	Lower Quartile	Median	Upper Quartile
Current ratio	1.3	2.6	5.3
Total asset turnover	2.1	2.7	4.1
Debt-equity ratio	.23	.50	.60
Profit margin	8.4%	11.2%	16.3%

How is Smolira Golf performing based on these ratios?

LO 3   **39. Growth and Profit Margin** Jasmine Manufacturing wishes to maintain a sustainable growth rate of 7 percent a year, a debt-equity ratio of .65, and a dividend payout ratio of 25 percent. The ratio of total assets to sales is constant at 1.25. What profit margin must the firm achieve?

LO 2   **40. Market Value Ratios** Abercrombie & Fitch and American Eagle Outfitters (AEO) reported the following numbers (in millions except for the share price) for fiscal year 2018. Calculate the earnings per share, market-to-book ratio, and price-earnings ratio for each company.

	Abercrombie	AEO
Net income	$ 7.09	$ 302.79
Shares outstanding	67.79	176.61
Stock price	$ 26.43	$ 24.56
Total equity	$1,242.38	$1,246.79

LO 3   **41. Growth and Assets** A firm wishes to maintain an internal growth rate of 5.3 percent and a dividend payout ratio of 40 percent. The current profit margin is 6.8 percent and the firm uses no external financing sources. What must total asset turnover be?

LO 3   **42. Sustainable Growth** Based on the following information, calculate the sustainable growth rate for Groot, Inc.:

    Profit margin $= 7.1\%$

  Total asset turnover $= 1.90$

   Total debt ratio $= .45$

    Payout ratio $= 20\%$

What is the ROA here?

LO 3 **43. Sustainable Growth and Outside Financing** You've collected the following information about Gandalf, Inc.:

$$Sales = \$295{,}000$$
$$Net\ income = \$18{,}400$$
$$Dividends = \$9{,}100$$
$$Total\ debt = \$68{,}000$$
$$Total\ equity = \$94{,}000$$

What is the sustainable growth rate for the company? If it does grow at this rate, how much new borrowing will take place in the coming year, assuming a constant debt-equity ratio? What growth rate could be supported with no outside financing at all?

LO 4 **44. Constraints on Growth** High Flyer, Inc., wishes to maintain a growth rate of 12 percent per year and a debt-equity ratio of .25. The profit margin is 5 percent, and total asset turnover is constant at 1.20. Is this growth rate possible? To answer, determine what the dividend payout ratio must be. How do you interpret the result?

LO 3 **45. Internal and Sustainable Growth Rates** Best Buy reported the following numbers (in millions) for the years ending January 28, 2017, and February 3, 2018. What are the internal and sustainable growth rates? What are the internal and sustainable growth rates using ROE × b and ROA × b and the end-of-period equity (assets)? What are the growth rates if you use the beginning of period equity in this equation? Why aren't the growth rates the same? What is your best estimate of the internal and sustainable growth rates?

	2017	2018
Net income		$ 1,000
Dividends		409
Total assets	$13,856	13,049
Total equity	4,709	3,612

LO 3 **46. Expanded DuPont Identity** Hershey Co. reported the following income statement and balance sheet (in millions) for 2017. Construct the expanded DuPont identity similar to Figure 3.1. What is the company's return on equity?

Income Statement	
Sales	$7,515.426
CoGS	4,065.760
SG&A	1,896.643
Other costs	344.043
EBIT	$1,208.980
Interest	98.282
EBT	$1,110.698
Taxes	354.131
Net income	$ 756.567

Balance Sheet			
Assets		**Liabilities & Equity**	
Current assets		Current liabilities	$2,076.543
Cash	$ 380.179		
Accounts receivable	588.262	Long-term debt	$2,545.618
Inventory	1,033.469		
Total	$2,001.910	Shareholders' equity	$ 931.565
Fixed assets	$3,551.816		
Total assets	$5,553.726	Total liabilities and shareholders' equity	$5,553.726

Source: **Hershey Co.**

WHAT'S ON THE WEB?

3.1 DuPont Identity   You can find financial statements for The Walt Disney Company at Disney's home page, thewaltdisneycompany.com. For the three most recent years, calculate the DuPont identity for Disney. How has ROE changed over this period? How have changes in each component of the DuPont identity affected ROE over this period?

3.2 Ratio Analysis   You want to examine the financial ratios for Johnson & Johnson. Go to www.reuters.com and type in the ticker symbol for the company (JNJ). Next, go to the financials link.

a.   What do TTM and MRQ mean?

b.   How do JNJ's recent profitability ratios compare to their values over the past five years? To the industry averages? To the sector averages? To the S&P 500 averages? Which is the better comparison group for JNJ: the industry, sector, or S&P 500 averages? Why?

c.   In what areas does JNJ seem to outperform its competitors based on the financial ratios? Where does JNJ seem to lag behind its competitors?

3.3 Standardized Financial Statements   Go to www.att.com and find the income statements and balance sheets for the two most recent years at this link. Using this information, prepare the common-size income statements and balance sheets for the two years.

3.4 Asset Utilization Ratios   Find the most recent financial statements for Walmart at www.walmart.com and Boeing at www.boeing.com. Calculate the asset utilization ratio for these two companies. What does this ratio measure? Is the ratio similar for both companies? Why or why not?

EXCEL *MASTER IT!* PROBLEM

Excel Master
coverage online

The eXtensible Business Reporting Language (XBRL) is likely the future of financial reporting. XBRL is a computer language that "tags" each item and specifies what that item is. XBRL reporting already has been adopted for use in Australia, Japan, and the United Kingdom. XBRL reporting will allow investors to quickly download financial statements for analysis.

Currently, several companies voluntarily submit financial statements in XBRL format. For this assignment, go to the SEC website at www.sec.gov. When you click the link for a particular filing, the XBRL results are shown at the bottom of the page. Download the income statement and balance sheet from the annual report for a company of your choice. Using these reports, calculate the financial ratios for the company from the data available for the past two years. Do you notice any changes in these ratios that might indicate the need for further investigation?

CHAPTER CASE
Ratios and Financial Planning at S&S Air, Inc.

Chris Guthrie was recently hired by S&S Air, Inc., to assist the company with its financial planning and to evaluate the company's performance. Chris graduated from college five years ago with a finance degree. He has been employed in the finance department of a Fortune 500 company since then.

S&S Air was founded 10 years ago by friends Mark Sexton and Todd Story. The company has manufactured and sold light airplanes over this period, and the company's products have received high reviews for safety and reliability. The company has a niche market in that it sells primarily to individuals who own and fly their own airplanes. The company has two models: the Birdie, which sells for $53,000, and the Eagle, which sells for $78,000.

While the company manufactures aircraft, its operations are different from commercial aircraft companies. S&S Air builds aircraft to order. By using prefabricated parts, the company is able to complete the manufacture of an airplane in only five weeks. The company also receives a deposit on each order, as well as another partial payment before the order is complete. In contrast, a commercial airplane may take one and one-half to two years to manufacture once the order is placed.

Mark and Todd have provided the following financial statements. Chris has gathered the industry ratios for the light airplane manufacturing industry.

S&S AIR, INC. 2019 Income Statement	
Sales	$26,501,600
Cost of goods sold	19,780,200
Other expenses	3,166,700
Depreciation	864,500
EBIT	$ 2,690,200
Interest	479,200
Taxable income	$ 2,211,000
Taxes (21%)	464,310
Net income	$ 1,746,690

Dividends	$270,600	
Additions to retained earnings	1,476,090	

S&S AIR, INC. 2019 Balance Sheet			
Assets		**Liabilities and Equity**	
Current assets		Current liabilities	
Cash	$ 481,852	Accounts payable	$ 944,698
Accounts receivable	2,025,778	Notes payable	1,909,248
Inventory	1,634,820	Total current liabilities	$ 2,853,946
Total current assets	$ 4,142,450		
Fixed assets		Long-term debt	$ 5,060,000
Net plant and equipment	$16,256,698	Shareholder equity	
		Common stock	$ 190,000
		Retained earnings	12,295,202
		Total equity	$12,485,202
Total assets	$20,399,148	Total liabilities and equity	$20,399,148

Light Airplane Industry Ratios			
	Lower Quartile	Median	Upper Quartile
Current ratio	.50	1.43	1.89
Quick ratio	.64	.84	1.05
Cash ratio	.08	.21	.39
Total asset turnover	.68	.85	1.13
Inventory turnover	4.89	6.15	10.89
Receivables turnover	6.27	9.82	11.51
Total debt ratio	.31	.52	.61
Debt-equity ratio	.58	1.08	1.56
Equity multiplier	1.58	2.08	2.56
Times interest earned	5.18	8.06	9.83
Cash coverage ratio	5.84	8.43	10.27
Profit margin	4.05%	6.75%	8.47%
Return on assets	6.05%	10.53%	13.21%
Return on equity	9.93%	16.54%	26.15%

QUESTIONS

1. Calculate the ratios for S&S Air that are shown for the industry.

2. Mark and Todd agree that a ratio analysis can provide a measure of the company's performance. They have chosen Boeing as an aspirant company. Would you choose Boeing as an aspirant company? Why or why not?

3. Compare the performance of S&S Air to the industry. For each ratio, comment on why it might be viewed as positive or negative relative to the industry. Suppose you create an inventory ratio calculated by inventory divided by current liabilities. How do you think S&S Air's ratio would compare to the industry average?

4. Calculate the internal growth rate and sustainable growth rate for S&S Air. What do these numbers mean?

4 | Introduction to Valuation: The Time Value of Money

As you are probably aware, the U.S. government has a significant amount of debt. That debt, which is widely owned by investors, comes in different varieties, including Series EE U.S. Treasury savings bonds. With a Series EE bond, you pay a particular amount today of, say, $25, and the bond accrues interest over the time you hold it. In the middle of 2018, the U.S. Treasury promised to pay .10 percent per year on EE savings bonds. In an interesting (and important) wrinkle, if you hold the bond for 20 years, the Treasury promises to "step up" the value to double your cost. That is, if the $25 bond you purchased and all the accumulated interest earned is worth less than $50, the Treasury will automatically increase the value of the bond to $50.

Is giving up $25 in exchange for $50 in 20 years a good deal? On the plus side, you get back $2 for every $1 you put up. That probably sounds good, but, on the downside, you have to wait 20 years to get it. What you need to know is how to analyze this trade-off. This chapter gives you the tools you need.

Specifically, our goal here is to introduce you to one of the most important principles in finance, the time value of money. What you will learn is how to determine the value today of some cash flow to be received later. This is a very basic business skill, and it underlies the analysis of many different types of investments and financing arrangements. In fact, almost all business activities, whether they originate in marketing, management, operations, or strategy, involve comparing outlays made today to benefits projected for the future. How to do this comparison is something everyone needs to understand; this chapter gets you started.

LEARNING OBJECTIVES

After studying this chapter, you should be able to:

LO 1 Determine the future value of an investment made today.

LO 2 Determine the present value of cash to be received at a future date.

LO 3 Calculate the return on an investment.

LO 4 Predict how long it takes for an investment to reach a desired value.

Please visit us at essentialsofcorporatefinance.blogspot.com for the latest developments in the world of corporate finance.

One of the basic problems faced by the financial manager is how to determine the value today of cash flows expected in the future. For example, the jackpot in a PowerBall™ lottery drawing was $110 million. Does this mean the winning ticket was worth $110 million? The answer is no because the jackpot was actually going to pay out over a 20-year period at a rate of $5.5 million per year. How much was the ticket worth then? The answer depends on the time value of money, the subject of this chapter.

In the most general sense, the phrase *time value of money* refers to the fact that a dollar in hand today is worth more than a dollar promised at some time in the future. On a practical level, one reason for this is that you could earn interest while you waited; so, a dollar today would grow to more than a dollar later. The trade-off between money now and money later thus depends on, among other things, the rate you can earn by investing. Our goal in this chapter is to explicitly evaluate this trade-off between dollars today and dollars at some future time.

A thorough understanding of the material in this chapter is critical to understanding material in subsequent chapters, so you should study it with particular care. We present a number of examples in this chapter. In many problems, your answer may differ from ours slightly. This can happen because of rounding and is not a cause for concern.

To find out more about U.S. savings bonds and other government securities, go to www .treasurydirect.gov.

4.1 FUTURE VALUE AND COMPOUNDING

Excel Master coverage online

The first thing we will study is future value. **Future value (FV)** refers to the amount of money an investment will grow to over some period of time at some given interest rate. Put another way, future value is the cash value of an investment at some time in the future. We start out by considering the simplest case, a single-period investment.

future value (FV)
The amount an investment is worth after one or more periods. Also *compound value.*

Investing for a Single Period

Suppose you were to invest $100 in a savings account that pays 10 percent interest per year. How much would you have in one year? You would have $110. This $110 is equal to your original *principal* of $100 plus $10 in interest that you earn. We say that $110 is the future value of $100 invested for one year at 10 percent, and we mean that $100 today is worth $110 in one year, given that 10 percent is the interest rate.

In general, if you invest for one period at an interest rate of r, your investment will grow to $(1 + r)$ per dollar invested. In our example, r is 10 percent, so your investment grows to $1 + .10 = 1.10$ dollars per dollar invested. You invested $100 in this case, so you ended up with $100 \times 1.10 = $110.

Investing for More Than One Period

Going back to our $100 investment, what will you have after two years, assuming the interest rate doesn't change? If you leave the entire $110 in the bank, you will earn $110 \times .10 = $11 in interest during the second year, so you will have a total of $110 + 11 = $121. This $121 is the future value of $100 in two years at 10 percent. Another way of looking at it is that one year from now you are effectively investing $110 at 10 percent for a year. This is a single-period problem, so you'll end up with $1.10 for every dollar invested, or $110 \times 1.1 = $121 total.

This $121 has four parts. The first part is the $100 original principal. The second part is the $10 in interest you earn in the first year, and the third part is another $10 you earn in the second year, for a total of $120. The last $1 you end up with (the fourth part) is interest you earn in the second year on the interest paid in the first year: $10 \times .10 = $1.

This process of leaving your money and any accumulated interest in an investment for more than one period, thereby reinvesting the interest, is called **compounding**. Compounding the interest means earning **interest on interest**, so we call the result **compound interest**. With **simple interest**, the interest is not reinvested, so interest is earned each period only on the original principal.

compounding
The process of accumulating interest in an investment over time to earn more interest.

interest on interest
Interest earned on the reinvestment of previous interest payments.

compound interest
Interest earned on both the initial principal and the interest reinvested from prior periods.

simple interest
Interest earned only on the original principal amount invested.

EXAMPLE 4.1 **Interest on Interest**

Suppose you locate a two-year investment that pays 14 percent per year. If you invest $325, how much will you have at the end of the two years? How much of this is simple interest? How much is compound interest?

At the end of the first year, you will have $325 × 1.14 = $370.50. If you reinvest this entire amount, and thereby compound the interest, you will have $370.50 × 1.14 = $422.37 at the end of the second year. The total interest you earn is thus $422.37 − 325 = $97.37. Your $325 original principal earns $325 × .14 = $45.50 in interest each year, for a two-year total of $91 in simple interest. The remaining $97.37 − 91 = $6.37 results from compounding. You can check this by noting that the interest earned in the first year is $45.50. The interest on interest earned in the second year thus amounts to $45.50 × .14 = $6.37, as we calculated.

We now take a closer look at how we calculated the $121 future value. We multiplied $110 by 1.1 to get $121. The $110, however, was $100 also multiplied by 1.1. In other words:

$$\$121 = \$110 \times 1.1$$
$$= (\$100 \times 1.1) \times 1.1$$
$$= \$100 \times (1.1 \times 1.1)$$
$$= \$100 \times 1.1^2$$
$$= \$100 \times 1.21$$

At the risk of belaboring the obvious, let's ask: How much would our $100 grow to after three years? Once again, in two years, we'll be investing $121 for one period at 10 percent. We'll end up with $1.1 for every dollar we invest, or $121 × 1.1 = $133.1 total. This $133.1 is thus:

$$\$133.1 = \$121 \times 1.1$$
$$= (\$110 \times 1.1) \times 1.1$$
$$= (\$100 \times 1.1) \times 1.1 \times 1.1$$
$$= \$100 \times (1.1 \times 1.1 \times 1.1)$$
$$= \$100 \times 1.1^3$$
$$= \$100 \times 1.331$$

You're probably noticing a pattern to these calculations, so we can now go ahead and state the general result. As our examples suggest, the future value of $1 invested for t periods at a rate of r per period is:

$$\text{Future value} = \$1 \times (1 + r)^t \qquad [4.1]$$

The expression $(1 + r)^t$ is sometimes called the *future value interest factor* (or *future value factor*) for $1 invested at r percent for t periods. It can be abbreviated as FVIF(r, t).

In our example, what would your $100 be worth after five years? We can first compute the relevant future value factor as:

$$(1 + r)^t = (1 + .10)^5 = 1.1^5 = 1.6105$$

Year	Beginning Amount	Interest Earned	Ending Amount
1	$100.00	$10.00	$110.00
2	110.00	11.00	121.00
3	121.00	12.10	133.10
4	133.10	13.31	146.41
5	146.41	14.64	161.05
		Total interest $61.05	

Your $100 will thus grow to:

$100 × 1.6105 = $161.05

The growth of your $100 each year is illustrated in Table 4.1. As shown, the interest earned in each year is equal to the beginning amount multiplied by the interest rate of 10 percent.

In Table 4.1, notice that the total interest you earn is $61.05. Over the five-year span of this investment, the simple interest is $100 × .10 = $10 per year, so you accumulate $50 this way. The other $11.05 is from compounding.

A brief introduction to key financial concepts is available at www .teachmefinance.com.

Figure 4.1 illustrates the growth of the compound interest in Table 4.1. Notice how the simple interest is constant each year, but the compound interest you earn gets bigger every year. The size of the compound interest keeps increasing because more and more interest builds up and there is thus more to compound.

Future values depend critically on the assumed interest rate, particularly for long-lived investments. Figure 4.2 illustrates this relationship by plotting the growth of $1 for different rates and lengths of time. Notice that the future value of $1 after 10 years is about $6.20 at a 20 percent rate, but it is only about $2.60 at 10 percent. In this case, doubling the interest rate more than doubles the future value.

FIGURE 4.1

Future value, simple interest, and compound interest

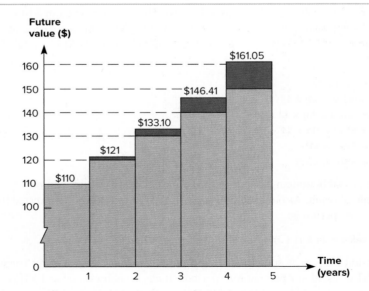

Growth of $100 original amount at 10% per year. Blue shaded area represents the portion of the total that results from compounding of interest.

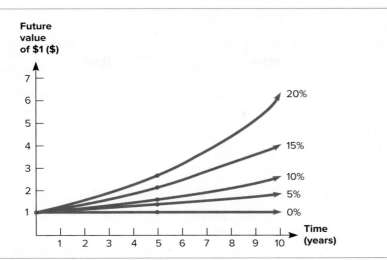

FIGURE 4.2

Future value of $1 for different periods and rates

To solve future value problems, we need to come up with the relevant future value factors. There are several different ways of doing this. In our example, we could have multiplied 1.1 by itself five times. This would work fine, but it would get to be very tedious for, say, a 30-year investment.

Fortunately, there are several easier ways to get future value factors. Most calculators have a key labeled "y^x". You can usually enter 1.1, press this key, enter 5, and press the "=" key to get the answer. This is an easy way to calculate future value factors because it's quick and accurate.

Alternatively, you can use a table that contains future value factors for some common interest rates and time periods. Table 4.2 contains some of these factors. Table A.1 in Appendix A at the end of the book contains a much larger set. To use the table, find the column that corresponds to 10 percent. Then look down the rows until you come to five periods. You should find the factor that we calculated, 1.6105.

Tables such as Table 4.2 are not as common as they once were because they predate inexpensive calculators and are only available for a relatively small number of rates. Interest rates often are quoted to three or four decimal places, so the tables needed to deal with these accurately would be quite large. As a result, the "real world" has moved away from using them. We will emphasize the use of a calculator in this chapter.

These tables still serve a useful purpose. To make sure you are doing the calculations correctly, pick a factor from the table and then calculate it yourself to see that you get the same answer. There are plenty of numbers to choose from.

Number of Periods	Interest Rates				
	5%	10%	15%	20%	
1	1.0500	1.1000	1.1500	1.2000	
2	1.1025	1.2100	1.3225	1.4400	
3	1.1576	1.3310	1.5209	1.7280	
4	1.2155	1.4641	1.7490	2.0736	
5	1.2763	1.6105	2.0114	2.4883	

TABLE 4.2

Future value interest factors

EXAMPLE 4.2 **Compound Interest**

You've located an investment that pays 12 percent. That rate sounds good to you, so you invest $400. How much will you have in three years? How much will you have in seven years? At the end of seven years, how much interest have you earned? How much of that interest results from compounding?

Based on our discussion, we can calculate the future value factor for 12 percent and three years as:

$(1 + r)^t = 1.12^3 = 1.4049$

Your $400 thus grows to:

$400 \times 1.4049 = 561.97

After seven years, you will have:

$400 \times 1.12^7 = $400 \times 2.2107 = 884.27

Thus, you will more than double your money over seven years.

Because you invested $400, the interest in the $884.27 future value is $884.27 − 400 = $484.27. At 12 percent, your $400 investment earns $400 × .12 = $48 in simple interest every year. Over seven years, the simple interest thus totals 7 × $48 = $336. The other $484.27 − 336 = $148.27 is from compounding.

How much do you need at retirement? Locate the "Retirement Calculator" link at www.bankrate.com.

The effect of compounding is not great over short time periods, but it really starts to add up as the time horizon grows. To take an extreme case, suppose one of your more frugal ancestors had invested $5 for you at a 6 percent interest rate 200 years ago. How much would you have today? The future value factor is a substantial $1.06^{200} = 115,125.90$ (you won't find this one in a table), so you would have $5 × 115,125.90 = $575,629.52 today. Notice that the simple interest is $5 × .06 = $.30 per year. After 200 years, this amounts to $60. The rest is from reinvesting. Such is the power of compound interest!

EXAMPLE 4.3 **How Much for That Island?**

To further illustrate the effect of compounding for long horizons, consider the case of Peter Minuit and the Indians. In 1626, Minuit bought all of Manhattan Island for about $24 in goods and trinkets. This sounds cheap, but the Indians may have gotten the better end of the deal. To see why, suppose the Indians had sold the goods and invested the $24 at 10 percent. How much would it be worth today?

Roughly 392 years have passed since the transaction. At 10 percent, $24 will grow by quite a bit over that time. How much? The future value factor is approximately:

$(1 + r)^t = 1.1^{392} \simeq 16,824,000,000,000,000$

That is, 17 followed by 15 zeroes. The future value is thus on the order of $24 × 16.824 quadrillion, or about $404 quadrillion (give or take a few hundreds of trillions).

Well, $404 quadrillion is a lot of money. How much? If you had it, you could buy the United States. All of it. Cash. With money left over to buy Canada, Mexico, and the rest of the world, for that matter.

This example is something of an exaggeration, of course. In 1626, it would not have been easy to locate an investment that would pay 10 percent every year without fail for the next 392 years.

USING A FINANCIAL CALCULATOR

Although there are the various ways of calculating future values we have described so far, many of you will decide that a financial calculator is the way to go. If you are planning on using one, you should read this extended hint; otherwise, skip it.

A financial calculator is an ordinary calculator with a few extra features. In particular, it knows some of the most commonly used financial formulas, so it can directly compute things like future values.

Financial calculators have the advantage that they handle a lot of the computation, but that is really all. In other words, you still have to understand the problem; the calculator does some of the arithmetic. In fact, there is an old joke (somewhat modified) that goes like this: Anyone can make a mistake on a time value of money problem, but to really screw one up takes a financial calculator! We therefore have two goals for this section. First, we'll discuss how to compute future values. After that, we'll show you how to avoid the most common mistakes people make when they start using financial calculators.

How to Calculate Future Values with a Financial Calculator   Examining a typical financial calculator, you will find five keys of particular interest. They usually look like this:

| N | I/Y | PMT | PV | FV |

For now, we need to focus on four of these. The keys labeled **PV** and **FV** are what you would guess: present value and future value. The key labeled **N** refers to the number of periods, which is what we have been calling t. Finally, **I/Y** stands for the interest rate, which we have called r.[1]

If we have the financial calculator set up correctly (see our next section), then calculating a future value is very simple. Take a look back at our question involving the future value of $100 at 10 percent for five years. We have seen that the answer is $161.05. The exact keystrokes will differ depending on what type of calculator you use, but here is basically all you do:

1. Enter −100. Press the **PV** key. (The negative sign is explained below.)
2. Enter 10. Press the **I/Y** key. (Notice that we entered 10, not .10; see below.)
3. Enter 5. Press the **N** key.

Now we have entered all of the relevant information. To solve for the future value, we need to ask the calculator what the **FV** is. Depending on your calculator, you either press the button labeled "CPT" (for compute) and then press **FV**, or else you press **FV**. Either way, you should get 161.05. If you don't (and you probably won't if this is the first time you have used a financial calculator!), we offer some help in our next section.

Before we explain the kinds of problems that you are likely to run into, we want to establish a standard format for showing you how to use a financial calculator. Using the example we just looked at, in the future, we will illustrate such problems like this:

Enter	5	10		−100	
	N	I/Y	PMT	PV	FV
Solve for					161.05

Here is an important tip: Appendix D in the back of the book contains more detailed instructions for the most common types of financial calculators. See if yours is included, and, if it is, follow the instructions there if you need help. Of course, if all else fails, you can read the manual that came with the calculator.

How to Get the Wrong Answer Using a Financial Calculator   There are a couple of common (and frustrating) problems that cause a lot of trouble with financial calculators. In this section, we provide some important *dos* and *don'ts*. If you can't seem to get a problem to work out, you should refer back to this section.

---

[1]The reason financial calculators use N and I/Y is that the most common use for these calculators is determining loan payments. In this context, N is the number of payments and I/Y is the interest rate on the loan. But, as we will see, there are many other uses of financial calculators that don't involve loan payments and interest rates.

(continued)

There are two categories we examine: three things you need to do only once and three things you need to do every time you work a problem. The things you need to do only once deal with the following calculator settings:

1. *Make sure your calculator is set to display a large number of decimal places.* Most financial calculators only display two decimal places; this causes problems because we frequently work with numbers—like interest rates—that are very small.

2. *Make sure your calculator is set to assume only one payment per period or per year.* Some financial calculators assume monthly payments (12 per year) unless you say otherwise.

3. *Make sure your calculator is in "end" mode.* This is usually the default, but you can accidentally change to "begin" mode.

If you don't know how to set these three things, see Appendix D or your calculator's operating manual. There are also three things you need to do *every time you work a problem:*

1. *Before you start, completely clear out the calculator.* This is very important. Failure to do this is the number one reason for wrong answers; you must get in the habit of clearing the calculator every time you start a problem. How you do this depends on the calculator (see Appendix D), but you must do more than just clear the display. For example, on a Texas Instruments BA II Plus, you must press **2nd** then **CLR TVM** for *clear time value of money.* There is a similar command on your calculator. Learn it!

   Note that turning the calculator off and back on won't do it. Most financial calculators remember everything you enter, even after you turn them off. In other words, they remember all your mistakes unless you explicitly clear them out. Also, if you are in the middle of a problem and make a mistake, *clear it out and start over.* Better to be safe than sorry.

2. *Put a negative sign on cash outflows.* Most financial calculators require you to put a negative sign on cash outflows and a positive sign on cash inflows. As a practical matter, this usually means that you should enter the present value amount with a negative sign (because normally the present value represents the amount you give up today in exchange for cash inflows later). You enter a negative value on the BA II Plus by first entering a number and then pressing the **+/−** key. By the same token, when you solve for a present value, you shouldn't be surprised to see a negative sign.

3. *Enter the rate correctly.* Financial calculators assume that rates are quoted in percent, so if the rate is .08 (or 8 percent), you should enter 8, not .08.

If you follow these guidelines (especially the one about clearing out the calculator), you should have no problem using a financial calculator to work almost all of the problems in this and the next few chapters. We'll provide some additional examples and guidance where appropriate.

CONCEPT QUESTIONS

4.1a What do we mean by the future value of an investment?

4.1b What does it mean to compound interest? How does compound interest differ from simple interest?

4.1c In general, what is the future value of $1 invested at r per period for t periods?

4.2 PRESENT VALUE AND DISCOUNTING

When we discuss future value, we are thinking of questions such as the following: What will my $2,000 investment grow to if it earns a 6.5 percent return every year for the next six years? The answer to this question is what we call the future value of $2,000 invested at 6.5 percent for six years (verify that the answer is about $2,918).

There is another type of question that comes up even more often in financial management that is obviously related to future value. Suppose you need to have $10,000 in 10 years, and you can earn 6.5 percent on your money. How much do you have to invest today to reach your goal? You can verify that the answer is $5,327.26. How do we know this? Read on.

The Single-Period Case

We've seen that the future value of $1 invested for one year at 10 percent is $1.10. We now ask a slightly different question: How much do we have to invest today at 10 percent to get $1 in one year? In other words, we know the future value here is $1, but what is the **present value (PV)**? The answer isn't too hard to figure out. Whatever we invest today will be 1.1 times bigger at the end of the year. Because we need $1 at the end of the year:

present value (PV)
The current value of future cash flows discounted at the appropriate discount rate.

Present value × 1.1 = $1

Or solving for the present value:

Present value = $1/1.1 = $.909

In this case, the present value is the answer to the following question: What amount, invested today, will grow to $1 in one year if the interest rate is 10 percent? Present value is thus the reverse of future value. Instead of compounding the money forward into the future, we **discount** it back to the present.

discount
Calculation of the present value of some future amount.

EXAMPLE 4.4 **Single-Period PV**

Suppose you need $800 to buy textbooks next year. You can earn 7 percent on your money. How much do you have to put up today?

We need to know the PV of $800 in one year at 7 percent. Proceeding as earlier:

Present value × 1.07 = $800

We can now solve for the present value:

Present value = $800 × (1/1.07) = $747.66

Thus, $747.66 is the present value. Again, this means that investing this amount for one year at 7 percent will result in a future value of $800.

From our examples, the present value of $1 to be received in one period is generally given as:

PV = $1 × [1/(1 + *r*)] = $1/(1 + *r*)

We next examine how to get the present value of an amount to be paid in two or more periods into the future.

Present Values for Multiple Periods

Suppose you need to have $1,000 in two years. If you can earn 7 percent, how much do you have to invest to make sure that you have the $1,000 when you need it? In other words, what is the present value of $1,000 in two years if the relevant rate is 7 percent?

Based on your knowledge of future values, you know that the amount invested must grow to $1,000 over the two years. In other words, it must be the case that:

$1,000 = PV × 1.07 × 1.07
= PV × 1.07²
= PV × 1.1449

Given this, we can solve for the present value:

Present value = $1,000/1.1449 = $873.44

Therefore, $873.44 is the amount you must invest in order to achieve your goal.

EXAMPLE 4.5   Saving Up

You would like to buy a new automobile. You have $50,000, but the car costs $68,500. If you can earn 9 percent, how much do you have to invest today to buy the car in two years? Do you have enough? Assume the price will stay the same.

What we need to know is the present value of $68,500 to be paid in two years, assuming a 9 percent rate. Based on our discussion, this is:

PV = $68,500/1.09² = $68,500/1.1881 = $57,655.08

You're still about $7,655 short, even if you're willing to wait two years.

As you have probably recognized by now, calculating present values is quite similar to calculating future values, and the general result looks much the same. The present value of $1 to be received t periods into the future at a discount rate of r is:

$$PV = \$1 \times [1/(1 + r)^t] = \$1/(1 + r)^t \qquad [4.2]$$

The quantity in brackets, $1/(1 + r)^t$, goes by several different names. Because it's used to discount a future cash flow, it is often called a *discount factor*. With this name, it is not surprising that the rate used in the calculation is often called the **discount rate**. We tend to call it this in talking about present values. The quantity in brackets also is called the *present value interest factor* (or just *present value factor*) for $1 at r percent for t periods and is sometimes abbreviated as PVIF(r, t). Finally, calculating the present value of a future cash flow to determine its worth today is commonly called **discounted cash flow (DCF) valuation**.

To illustrate, suppose you need $1,000 in three years. You can earn 15 percent on your money. How much do you have to invest today? To find out, we have to determine the present value of $1,000 in three years at 15 percent. We do this by discounting $1,000 back three periods at 15 percent. With these numbers, the discount factor is:

$1/1.15³ = 1/1.5209 = .6575$

The amount you must invest is thus:

$1,000 × .6575 = $657.52

We say that $657.52 is the present, or discounted, value of $1,000 to be received in three years at 15 percent.

There are tables for present value factors as there are tables for future value factors, and you use them in the same way (if you use them at all). Table 4.3 contains a small set of these factors. A much larger set can be found in Table A.2 in Appendix A.

discount rate
The rate used to calculate the present value of future cash flows.

discounted cash flow (DCF) valuation
(a) Calculating the present value of a future cash flow to determine its value today. (b) The process of valuing an investment by discounting its future cash flows.

TABLE **4.3**

Present value interest factors

Number of Periods	Interest Rates			
	5%	10%	15%	20%
1	.9524	.9091	.8696	.8333
2	.9070	.8264	.7561	.6944
3	.8638	.7513	.6575	.5787
4	.8227	.6830	.5718	.4823
5	.7835	.6209	.4972	.4019

In Table 4.3, the discount factor we calculated, .6575, can be found by looking down the column labeled "15%" until you come to the third row. Of course, you could use a financial calculator, as we illustrate nearby.

As the length of time until payment grows, present values decline. As Example 4.6 illustrates, present values tend to become small as the time horizon grows. If you look out far enough, they will always get close to zero. Also, for a given length of time, the higher the discount rate is, the lower is the present value. Put another way, present values and discount rates are inversely related. Increasing the discount rate decreases the PV and vice versa.

CALCULATOR HINTS

You solve present value problems on a financial calculator like you do future value problems. For the example we just examined (the present value of $1,000 to be received in three years at 15 percent), you would do the following:

Enter	3	15			1,000
	N	I/Y	PMT	PV	FV

Solve for   −657.52

Notice that the answer has a negative sign; as we discussed earlier, that's because it represents an outflow today in exchange for the $1,000 inflow later.

EXAMPLE 4.6   **Deceptive Advertising**

Recently, some businesses have been saying things like "Come try our product. If you do, we'll give you $100 just for coming by!" If you read the fine print, what you find out is that they will give you a savings certificate that will pay you $100 in 25 years or so. If the going interest rate on such certificates is 10 percent per year, how much are they really giving you today?

What you're actually getting is the present value of $100 to be paid in 25 years. If the discount rate is 10 percent per year, then the discount factor is:

$$1/1.1^{25} = 1/10.8347 = .0923$$

This tells you that a dollar in 25 years is worth a little more than nine cents today, assuming a 10 percent discount rate. Given this, the promotion is actually paying you about .0923 × $100 = $9.23. Maybe this is enough to draw customers, but it's not $100.

The relationship between time, discount rates, and present values is illustrated in Figure 4.3. Notice that by the time we get to 10 years, the present values are all substantially smaller than the future amounts.

FIGURE 4.3

Present value of $1 for different periods and rates

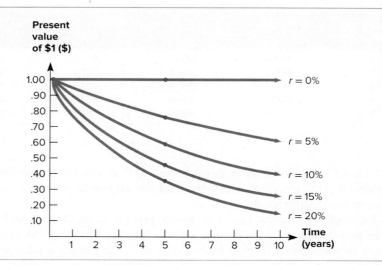

CONCEPT QUESTIONS

4.2a What do we mean by the present value of an investment?

4.2b The process of discounting a future amount back to the present is the opposite of doing what?

4.2c What do we mean by discounted cash flow, or DCF, valuation?

4.2d In general, what is the present value of $1 to be received in t periods, assuming a discount rate of r per period?

4.3 MORE ON PRESENT AND FUTURE VALUES

Excel Master
coverage online

If you look back at the expressions we came up with for present and future values, you will see there is a very simple relationship between the two. We explore this relationship and some related issues in this section.

Present versus Future Value

For a downloadable, Windows-based financial calculator, go to www.calculator.org.

What we called the present value factor is just the reciprocal of (that is, 1 divided by) the future value factor:

> **Future value factor = $(1 + r)^t$**
> **Present value factor = $1/(1 + r)^t$**

In fact, the easy way to calculate a present value factor on many calculators is to first calculate the future value factor and then press the **1/X** key to flip it over.

If we let FV_t stand for the future value after t periods, then the relationship between future value and present value can be written as one of the following:

> **$PV \times (1 + r)^t = FV_t$**
> **$PV = FV_t/(1 + r)^t = FV_t \times [1/(1 + r)^t]$**   [4.3]

We will call this last result the *basic present value equation*, and we use it throughout the text. There are a number of variations that come up, but this simple equation underlies many of the most important ideas in finance.

EXAMPLE 4.7   **Evaluating Investments**

To give you an idea of how we will be using present and future values, consider the following simple investment. Your company proposes to buy an asset for $335. This investment is very safe. You will sell the asset in three years for $400. You know you could invest the $335 elsewhere at 10 percent with very little risk. What do you think of the proposed investment?

This is not a good investment. Why not? Because you can invest the $335 elsewhere at 10 percent. If you do, after three years it will grow to:

$$\$335 \times (1 + r)^t = \$335 \times 1.1^3$$
$$= \$335 \times 1.331$$
$$= \$445.89$$

Because the proposed investment only pays out $400, it is not as good as other alternatives we have. Another way of saying the same thing is to notice that the present value of $400 in three years at 10 percent is:

$$\$400 \times [1/(1 + r)^t] = \$400/1.1^3 = \$400/1.331 = \$300.53$$

This tells us that we only have to invest about $300 to get $400 in three years, not $335. We will return to this type of analysis later on.

Determining the Discount Rate

It will turn out that we frequently need to determine what discount rate is implicit in an investment. We can do this by looking at the basic present value equation:

$$PV = FV_t/(1 + r)^t$$

There are only four parts to this equation: the present value (PV), the future value (FV_t), the discount rate (r), and the life of the investment (t). Given any three of these, we can always find the fourth.

EXAMPLE 4.8   **Finding *r* for a Single-Period Investment**

You are considering a one-year investment. If you put up $1,250, you will get back $1,350. What rate is this investment paying?

First, in this single-period case, the answer is fairly obvious. You are getting a total of $100 in addition to your $1,250. The implicit rate on this investment is thus $100/$1,250 = .08, or 8 percent.

More formally, from the basic present value equation, the present value (the amount you must put up today) is $1,250. The future value (what the present value grows to) is $1,350. The time involved is one period, so we have:

$$\$1,250 = \$1,350/(1 + r)^t$$
$$1 + r = \$1,350/\$1,250 = 1.08$$
$$r = .08, \text{ or } 8\%$$

In this simple case, of course, there was no need to go through this calculation, but, as we describe later, it gets a little harder when there is more than one period.

To illustrate what happens with multiple periods, let's say that we are offered an investment that costs us $100 and will double our money in eight years. To compare this to other investments, we would like to know what discount rate is implicit in these numbers. This discount rate is called the *rate of return*, or sometimes just *return*, on the investment. In this case, we have a present value of $100, a future value of $200 (double our money), and an eight-year life. To calculate the return, we can write the basic present value equation as:

$$PV = FV/(1 + r)^t$$
$$\$100 = \$200/(1 + r)^8$$

It also could be written as:

$$(1 + r)^8 = \$200/\$100 = 2$$

We now need to solve for *r*. There are three ways we could do it:

1. Use a financial calculator. (See below.)
2. Solve the equation for $1 + r$ by taking the eighth root of both sides. Because this is the same thing as raising both sides to the power of ⅛, or .125, this is actually easy to do with the $\boxed{y^x}$ key on a calculator. Just enter 2, then press $\boxed{y^x}$, enter .125, and press the $\boxed{=}$ key. The eighth root should be about 1.09, which implies that *r* is 9 percent.
3. Use a future value table. The future value factor for eight years is equal to 2. If you look across the row corresponding to eight periods in Table A.1, you will see that a future value factor of 2 corresponds to the 9 percent column, again implying that the return here is 9 percent.

Why does the Rule of 72 work? See www.money chimp.com.

Actually, in this particular example, there is a useful "back of the envelope" means of solving for *r*—the Rule of 72. For reasonable rates of return, the time it takes to double your money is given approximately by 72/*r*%. In our example, this means that 72/*r*% = 8 years, implying that *r* is 9 percent as we calculated. This rule is fairly accurate for discount rates in the 5 percent to 20 percent range.

The nearby *Finance Matters* box provides some examples of rates of return on collectibles. See if you can verify the numbers reported there.

EXAMPLE 4.9   **Double Your Fun**

You have been offered an investment that promises to double your money every 10 years. What is the approximate rate of return on the investment?

From the Rule of 72, the rate of return is given approximately by 72/*r*% = 10, so the rate is approximately 72/10 = .072, or 7.2%. Verify that the exact answer is 7.177 percent.

A slightly more extreme example involves money bequeathed by Benjamin Franklin, who died on April 17, 1790. In his will, he gave 1,000 pounds sterling to Massachusetts and the city of Boston. He gave a like amount to Pennsylvania and the city of Philadelphia. The money was paid to Franklin when he held political office, but he believed that politicians should not be paid for their service (it appears that this view is not widely shared by modern-day politicians).

Franklin originally specified that the money should be paid out 100 years after his death and used to train young people. Later, however, after some legal wrangling, it was agreed that the money would be paid out in 1990, 200 years after Franklin's death. By that

Collectibles as Investments?

It used to be that trading in collectibles such as baseball cards, art, and old toys occurred mostly at auctions, swap meets, and collectible shops, all of which were limited to regional traffic. However, with the growing popularity of online auctions such as eBay, trading in collectibles has expanded to an international arena. The most visible form of collectible is probably the baseball card, but Furbies, Beanie Babies, and Pokémon cards have been extremely hot collectibles in the recent past. However, it's not just fad items that spark interest from collectors; virtually anything of sentimental value from days gone by is considered collectible, and, more and more, collectibles are being viewed as investments.

Collectibles typically provide no cash flows until they are sold, and condition and buyer sentiment are the major determinants of value. The rates of return have been amazing at times, but care is needed in interpreting them. For example, in 2018, a 1915-S Panama-Pacific Round $50 Gold Piece sold for $336,000. While that looks like a whopping price increase to the untrained eye, check for yourself that the actual return on the investment was only about 8.93 percent per year. Not too bad, but nowhere near the return most people expect from looking at the sales price.

Comic books have recently grown in popularity among collectors. The first issue of *Batman* was the Spring 1940 issue, sold at a cover price of 10 cents. In 2018, one of the original comics was auctioned off for $227,050. This gain seems like a very high return to the untrained eye, and indeed it is! See if you don't agree that the return was about 20.64 percent per year.

Stamp collecting (or philately) is another popular activity. Possibly the most famous stamp in the world is the British Guiana One-Cent Black on Magenta stamp, issued in 1856. There is only one known example of this stamp left in existence and it has been out of public view since 1986. In June 2014, the stamp sold at auction for $9,480,000. Although this is almost 1 billion times the original price of the stamp, verify for yourself that the annual return is about 13.98 percent.

time, the Pennsylvania bequest had grown to about $2 million; the Massachusetts bequest had grown to $4.5 million. The money was used to fund the Franklin Institutes in Boston and Philadelphia. Assuming that 1,000 pounds sterling was equivalent to 1,000 dollars (the dollar did not become the official U.S. currency until 1792), what rate of return did the two states earn?

For Pennsylvania, the future value is $2 million and the present value is $1,000. There are 200 years involved, so we need to solve for r in the following:

$$\$1,000 = \$2,000,000/(1 + r)^{200}$$
$$(1 + r)^{200} = 2,000$$

Solving for r, we see that the Pennsylvania money grew at about 3.87 percent per year. The Massachusetts money did better; verify that the rate of return in this case was 4.3 percent. Small differences can add up!

We can illustrate how to calculate unknown rates using a financial calculator with these numbers. For Pennsylvania, you would do the following:

CALCULATOR HINTS

Enter	200			−1,000	2,000,000
	N	**I/Y**	**PMT**	**PV**	**FV**
Solve for		3.87			

As in our previous examples, notice the minus sign on the present value, representing Franklin's outlay made many years ago. What do you change to work the problem for Massachusetts?

EXAMPLE 4.10 **Saving for College**

You estimate that you will need about $80,000 to send your child to college in eight years. You have about $35,000 now. If you can earn 20 percent per year, will you make it? At what rate will you just reach your goal?

If you can earn 20 percent, the future value of your $35,000 in eight years will be:

$$FV = \$35,000 \times 1.20^8 = \$35,000 \times 4.2998 = \$150,493.59$$

So, you will make it easily. The minimum rate is the unknown r in the following:

$$FV = \$35,000 \times (1 + r)^8 = \$80,000$$
$$(1 + r)^8 = \$80,000/35,000 = 2.2857$$

Therefore, the future value factor is 2.2857. Looking at the row in Table A.1 that corresponds to eight periods, we see that our future value factor is roughly halfway between the ones shown for 10 percent (2.1436) and 12 percent (2.4760), so you will reach your goal if you earn approximately 11 percent. To get the exact answer, we could use a financial calculator or we could solve for r:

$$(1 + r)^8 = \$80,000/35,000 = 2.2857$$
$$1 + r = 2.2857^{(1/8)} = 2.2857^{.125} = 1.1089$$
$$r = 10.89\%$$

EXAMPLE 4.11 **Only 18,262.5 Days to Retirement**

You would like to retire in 50 years as a millionaire. If you have $10,000 today, what rate of return do you need to earn to achieve your goal?

The future value is $1,000,000. The present value is $10,000, and there are 50 years until retirement. We need to calculate the unknown discount rate in the following:

$$\$10,000 = \$1,000,000/(1 + r)^{50}$$
$$(1 + r)^{50} = 100$$

The future value factor is thus 100. You can verify that the implicit rate is about 9.65 percent.

Finding the Number of Periods

Suppose we were interested in purchasing an asset that costs $50,000. We currently have $25,000. If we can earn 12 percent on this $25,000, how long until we have the $50,000? Finding the answer involves solving for the last variable in the basic present value equation, the number of periods. You already know how to get an approximate answer to this particular problem. Notice that we need to double our money. From the Rule of 72, this will take about $72/12 = 6$ years at 12 percent.

To come up with the exact answer, we again can manipulate the basic present value equation. The present value is $25,000, and the future value is $50,000. With a 12 percent discount rate, the basic equation takes one of the following forms:

$$\$25,000 = \$50,000/1.12^t$$
$$\$50,000/\$25,000 = 1.12^t = 2$$

We thus have a future value factor of 2 for a 12 percent rate. We now need to solve for t. If you look down the column in Table A.1 that corresponds to 12 percent, you will see that a future value factor of 1.9738 occurs at six periods. It will thus take about six years, as we calculated. To get the exact answer, we have to explicitly solve for t (or use a financial calculator). If you do this, you will find that the answer is 6.1163 years, so our approximation was quite close in this case.

If you do use a financial calculator, here are the relevant entries:

CALCULATOR HINTS

Enter		12		−25,000	50,000
	N	I/Y	PMT	PV	FV
Solve for	6.1163				

EXAMPLE 4.12	**Waiting for Godot**

You've been saving up to buy the Godot Company. The total cost will be $10 million. You currently have about $2.3 million. If you can earn 5 percent on your money, how long will you have to wait? At 16 percent, how long must you wait?

At 5 percent, you'll have to wait a long time. From the basic present value equation:

$2.3 = $10/1.05^t$

$1.05^t = 4.35$

$t = 30.12$ years

At 16 percent, things are a little better. Verify for yourself that it will take about 10 years.

This example finishes our introduction to basic time value of money concepts. Table 4.4 summarizes present value and future value calculations for future reference. As the *Work the Web* box in this section shows, online calculators are widely available to handle these calculations, but it is still important to know what is going on.

TABLE 4.4

Summary of time value of money calculations

 I. **Symbols**

   PV = Present value, what future cash flows are worth today

   FV_t = Future value, what cash flows are worth in the future

   r = Interest rate, rate of return, or discount rate per period—typically, but not always, one year

   t = Number of periods—typically, but not always, the number of years

   C = Cash amount

 II. **Future value of C invested at r percent per period for t periods**

   $FV_t = C \times (1 + r)^t$

   The term $(1 + r)^t$ is called the *future value factor.*

 III. **Present value of C to be received in t periods at r percent per period**

   $PV = C/(1 + r)^t$

   The term $1/(1 + r)^t$ is called the *present value factor.*

 IV. **The basic present value equation giving the relationship between present and future value is:**

   $PV = FV_t /(1 + r)^t$

W🌐RK THE WEB

How important is the time value of money? A recent web search returned more than 996 million hits! It is important to understand the calculations behind the time value of money, but the advent of financial calculators and spreadsheets has eliminated the need for tedious calculations. In fact, many websites offer time value of money calculators. The following is an example from Moneychimp's website, www.moneychimp.com. You need $150,000 in 25 years and will invest your money at 9.2 percent. How much do you need to deposit today? To use the calculator, you enter the values and hit "Calculate." The results look like this:

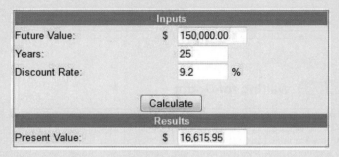

Who said time value of money calculations are hard?

QUESTIONS

1. Use the present value calculator on this website to answer the following: Suppose you want to have $140,000 in 25 years. If you can earn a 10 percent return, how much do you have to invest today?

2. Use the future value calculator on this website to answer the following question: Suppose you have $8,000 today that you plan to save for your retirement in 40 years. If you earn a return of 10.8 percent per year, how much will this account be worth when you are ready to retire?

SPREADSHEET STRATEGIES	

USING A SPREADSHEET FOR TIME VALUE OF MONEY CALCULATIONS

Learn more about using Excel for time value of money and other calculations at www .studyfinance.com.

More and more, businesspeople from many different areas (and not just finance and accounting) rely on spreadsheets to do all the different types of calculations that come up in the real world. As a result, in this section, we show you how to use a spreadsheet to handle the various time value of money problems we presented in this chapter. We will use Microsoft Excel™, but the commands are similar for other types of software. We assume you are already familiar with basic spreadsheet operations.

As we have seen, you can solve for any one of the following four potential unknowns: future value, present value, the discount rate, or the number of periods. With a spreadsheet, there is a separate formula for each. In Excel, these are as follows:

To Find	Enter This Formula
Future value	= FV(rate, nper, pmt, pv)
Present value	= PV(rate, nper, pmt, fv)
Discount rate	= RATE(nper, pmt, pv, fv)
Number of periods	= NPER(rate, pmt, pv, fv)

In these formulas, pv and fv are present and future value; nper is the number of periods; and rate is the discount, or interest, rate.

There are two things that are a little tricky here. First, unlike a financial calculator, the spreadsheet requires that the rate be entered as a decimal. Second, as with most financial calculators, you have to put a negative sign on either the present value or the future value to solve for the rate or the number of periods. For the same reason, if you solve for a present value, the answer will have a negative sign unless you input a negative future value. The same is true when you compute a future value.

To illustrate how you might use these formulas, we will go back to an example in the chapter. If you invest $25,000 at 12 percent per year, how long until you have $50,000? You might set up a spreadsheet like this:

	A	B	C	D	E	F	G	H
1								
2		Using a spreadsheet for time value of money calculations						
3								
4	If we invest $25,000 at 12 percent, how long until we have $50,000? We need to solve for the							
5	unknown number of periods, so we use the formula NPER (rate, pmt, pv, fv).							
6								
7	Present value (pv):	$25,000						
8	Future value (fv):	$50,000						
9	Rate:	.12						
10								
11	Periods:	6.116255						
12								
13	The formula entered in cell B11 is =NPER(B9,0,-B7,B8); notice that pmt is zero and that pv has a							
14	negative sign on it. Also notice that the rate is entered as a decimal, not a percentage.							

CONCEPT QUESTIONS

4.3a   What is the basic present value equation?

4.3b   What is the Rule of 72?

SUMMARY AND CONCLUSIONS

This chapter has introduced you to the basic principles of present value and discounted cash flow valuation. In it, we explained a number of things about the time value of money, including:

1. For a given rate of return, the value at some point in the future of an investment made today can be determined by calculating the future value of that investment.

2. The current worth of a future cash flow can be determined for a given rate of return by calculating the present value of the cash flow involved.

3. The relationship between present value and future value for a given rate, r, and time, t, is given by the basic present value equation:

$$PV = FV_t/(1 + r)^t$$

As we have shown, it is possible to find any one of the four components (PV, FV_t, r, or t) given the other three.

The principles developed in this chapter will figure prominently in the chapters to come. The reason for this is that most investments, whether they involve real assets or financial assets, can be analyzed using the discounted cash flow, or DCF, approach. As a result, the DCF approach is broadly applicable and widely used in practice. Before going on, therefore, you might want to do some of the problems below.

connect POP QUIZ!

Can you answer the following questions? If your class is using *Connect*, log on to SmartBook to see if you know the answers to these and other questions, check out the study tools, and find out what topics require additional practice!

Section 4.1 If you invest $500 for one year at a rate of 8 percent per year, how much interest will you earn?

Section 4.2 What is the formula used to calculate the present value of a future amount?

Section 4.3 Suppose you invest $100 now and receive $259.37 in 10 years. What rate of interest did you earn?

CHAPTER REVIEW AND SELF-TEST PROBLEMS

4.1   **Calculating Future Values**   Assume you deposit $1,000 today in an account that pays 8 percent interest. How much will you have in four years? (See Problem 2.)

4.2   **Calculating Present Values**   Suppose you have just celebrated your 19th birthday. A rich uncle set up a trust fund for you that will pay you $100,000 when you turn 25. If the relevant discount rate is 11 percent, how much is this fund worth today? (See Problem 3.)

4.3   **Calculating Rates of Return**   You've been offered an investment that will double your money in 12 years. What rate of return are you being offered? Check your answer using the Rule of 72. (See Problem 4.)

4.4   **Calculating the Number of Periods**   You've been offered an investment that will pay you 7 percent per year. If you invest $10,000, how long until you have $20,000? How long until you have $30,000? (See Problem 5.)

■ Answers to Chapter Review and Self-Test Problems

4.1   We need to calculate the future value of $1,000 at 8 percent for four years. The future value factor is:

$$1.08^4 = 1.3605$$

The future value is thus $1,000 \times 1.3605 = \$1,360.49$.

4.2   We need the present value of $100,000 to be paid in six years at 11 percent. The discount factor is:

$$1/1.11^6 = 1/1.8704 = .5346$$

The present value is thus about $53,464.

4.3   Suppose you invest, say, $100. You will have $200 in 12 years with this investment. So, $100 is the amount you have today, the present value, and $200 is the amount you will have in 12 years, or the future value. From the basic present value equation, we have:

$$\$200 = \$100 \times (1 \times r)^{12}$$
$$2 = (1 \times r)^{12}$$

From here, we need to solve for r, the unknown rate. As shown in the chapter, there are several different ways to do this. We will take the 12th root of 2 (by raising 2 to the power of 1/12):

$$2^{1/12} = 1 + r$$
$$1.0595 = 1 + r$$
$$r = .0595, \text{ or } 5.95\%$$

Using the Rule of 72, we have $72/t = r\%$, or $72/12 = 6\%$, so our answer looks good (remember that the Rule of 72 is only an approximation).

4.4 The basic equation is:

$$\$20,000 = \$10,000 \times (1 + .07)^{t}$$
$$2 = (1 + 07)^{t}$$

If we solve for t, we get that $t = 10.24$ years. Using the Rule of 72, we get $72/7 = 10.29$ years, so, once again, our answer looks good. To get \$30,000, verify for yourself that you will have to wait 16.24 years.

CRITICAL THINKING AND CONCEPTS REVIEW

LO 1 4.1 **Compounding** What is compounding? What is discounting?

LO 1 4.2 **Compounding and Periods** As you increase the length of time involved, what happens to future values? What happens to present values?

LO 1 4.3 **Compounding and Interest Rates** What happens to a future value if you increase the rate, r? What happens to a present value?

LO 1 4.4 **Future Values** Suppose you deposit a large sum in an account that earns a low interest rate and simultaneously deposit a small sum in an account with a high interest rate. Which account will have the larger future value?

LO 3 4.5 **Ethical Considerations** Take a look back at Example 4.6. Is it deceptive advertising? Is it unethical to advertise a future value like this without a disclaimer?

Use the following information for the next five questions: On March 28, 2008, Toyota Motor Credit Corporation (TMCC), a subsidiary of Toyota Motor, offered some securities for sale to the public. Under the terms of the deal, TMCC promised to repay the owner of one of these securities \$100,000 on March 28, 2038, but investors would receive nothing until then. Investors paid TMCC \$24,099 for each of these securities; so they gave up \$24,099 on March 28, 2008, for the promise of a \$100,000 payment 30 years later.

LO 2 4.6 **Time Value of Money** Why would TMCC be willing to accept such a small amount today (\$24,099) in exchange for a promise to repay about four times that amount (\$100,000) in the future?

LO 3 4.7 **Call Provisions** TMCC has the right to buy back the securities on the anniversary date at a price established when the securities were issued (this feature is a term of this particular deal). What impact does this feature have on the desirability of this security as an investment?

LO 3   **4.8** **Time Value of Money**   Would you be willing to pay $24,099 today in exchange for $100,000 in 30 years? What would be the key considerations in answering yes or no? Would your answer depend on who is making the promise to repay?

LO 3   **4.9** **Investment Comparison**   Suppose that when TMCC offered the security for $24,099, the U.S. Treasury had offered an essentially identical security. Do you think it would have had a higher or lower price? Why?

LO 3   **4.10** **Length of Investment**   The TMCC security is bought and sold on the New York Stock Exchange. If you looked at the price today, do you think the price would exceed the $24,099 original price? Why? If you looked in 2022, do you think the price would be higher or lower than today's price? Why?

QUESTIONS AND PROBLEMS

connect   Select problems are available in McGraw-Hill *Connect*. Please see the packaging options section of the Preface for more information.

BASIC (Questions 1–15)

LO 1   **1. Simple Interest versus Compound Interest**   First City Bank pays 7 percent simple interest on its savings account balances, whereas Second City Bank pays 7 percent interest compounded annually. If you made a deposit of $7,900 in each bank, how much more money would you earn from your Second City Bank account at the end of 10 years?

LO 1   **2. Calculating Future Values**   For each of the following, compute the future value:

Present Value	Years	Interest Rate	Future Value
$ 2,960	7	13%	
7,846	16	7	
85,381	19	9	
221,614	26	5	

LO 2   **3. Calculating Present Values**   For each of the following, compute the present value:

Present Value	Years	Interest Rate	Future Value
	15	7%	$ 19,415
	8	11	47,382
	13	10	312,176
	25	13	629,381

LO 3   **4. Calculating Interest Rates**   Solve for the unknown interest rate in each of the following:

Present Value	Years	Interest Rate	Future Value
$ 715	9		$ 1,381
905	12		1,718
15,000	26		141,832
70,300	15		312,815

LO 4 **5. Calculating the Number of Periods**   Solve for the unknown number of years in each of the following:

Present Value	Years	Interest Rate	Future Value
$ 195		8%	$ 873
2,105		11	3,500
47,800		10	326,500
38,650		15	213,380

LO 3 **6. Calculating Rates of Return**   Assume the total cost of a college education will be $235,000 when your child enters college in 18 years. You presently have $53,000 to invest. What annual rate of interest must you earn on your investment to cover the cost of your child's college education?

LO 4 **7. Calculating the Number of Periods**   At 5.3 percent interest, how long does it take to double your money? To quadruple it?

LO 3 **8. Calculating Rates of Return**   In 2018, one of the first copper pennies struck at the Philadelphia mint in 1793 was sold for $300,000. What was the rate of return on this investment?

LO 4 **9. Calculating the Number of Periods**   You're trying to save to buy a new $175,000 Ferrari. You have $35,000 today that can be invested at your bank. The bank pays 2.9 percent annual interest on its accounts. How long will it be before you have enough to buy the car?

LO 2 **10. Calculating Present Values**   Imprudential, Inc., has an unfunded pension liability of $645 million that must be paid in 25 years. To assess the value of the firm's stock, financial analysts want to discount this liability back to the present. If the relevant discount rate is 5.5 percent, what is the present value of this liability?

LO 2 **11. Calculating Present Values**   You have just received notification that you have won the $1 million first prize in the Centennial Lottery. However, the prize will be awarded on your 100th birthday (assuming you're around to collect), 80 years from now. What is the present value of your windfall if the appropriate discount rate is 8.45 percent?

LO 1 **12. Calculating Future Values**   Your coin collection contains fifty 1952 silver dollars. If your grandparents purchased them for their face value when they were new, how much will your collection be worth when you retire in 2063, assuming they appreciate at an annual rate of 4.8 percent?

LO 1
LO 3 **13. Calculating Growth Rates and Future Values**   In 1895, the first U.S. Open Golf Championship was held. The winner's prize money was $150. In 2018, the winner's check was $2,160,000. What was the annual percentage increase in the winner's check over this period? If the winner's prize increases at the same rate, what will it be in 2048?

LO 3 **14. Calculating Rates of Return**   In 2018, an *Action Comics* No. 1, featuring the first appearance of Superman, was sold at auction for $573,600. The comic book was originally sold in 1938 for $.10. What was the annual increase in the value of this comic book?

LO 3 **15. Calculating Rates of Return**   Although appealing to more refined tastes, art as a collectible has not always performed so profitably. During 2010, Deutscher-Menzies sold *Arkie under the Shower*, a painting by renowned Australian painter Brett Whiteley, at auction for a price of $1,100,000.

Unfortunately for the previous owner, he had purchased it 3 years earlier at a price of $1,680,000. What was his annual rate of return on this painting?

INTERMEDIATE (Questions 16–25)

LO 3   **16. Calculating Rates of Return**   Refer back to the Series EE savings bonds we discussed at the very beginning of the chapter.

    a. Assuming you purchased a $50 face value bond, what rate of return would you earn if you held the bond for 20 years until it doubled in value?

    b. If you purchased a $50 face value bond in early 2018 at the then-current interest rate of .10 percent per year, how much would the bond be worth in 2028?

    c. In 2028, instead of cashing the bond in for its then-current value, you decide to hold the bond until it doubles in face value in 2038. What rate of return will you earn over the last 10 years?

LO 2   **17. Calculating Present Values**   Suppose you are still committed to owning a $175,000 Ferrari (see Question 9). If you believe your mutual fund can achieve an annual return of 11.2 percent, and you want to buy the car in 10 years on the day you turn 30, how much must you invest today?

LO 1   **18. Calculating Future Values**   You have just made your first $5,000 contribution to your individual retirement account. Assuming you earn an annual rate of return of 10.2 percent and make no additional contributions, what will your account be worth when you retire in 45 years? What if you wait 10 years before contributing? (Does this suggest an investment strategy?)

LO 1   **19. Calculating Future Values**   You are scheduled to receive $10,000 in two years. When you receive it, you will invest it for six more years at 7.5 percent per year. How much will you have in eight years?

LO 4   **20. Calculating the Number of Periods**   You expect to receive $30,000 at graduation in two years. You plan on investing it at 7 percent until you have $125,000. How long will you wait from now? (Better than the situation in Question 9, but still no Ferrari.)

LO 1   **21. Calculating Future Values**   You have $5,800 to deposit. Regency Bank offers 12 percent per year compounded monthly (1 percent per month), while King Bank offers 12 percent but will only compound annually. How much will your investment be worth in 20 years at each bank?

LO 3   **22. Calculating Rates of Return**   An investment offers to triple your money in 24 months (don't believe it). What rate per three months are you being offered?

LO 4   **23. Calculating the Number of Periods**   You can earn .31 percent per month at your bank. If you deposit $1,800, how long must you wait until your account has grown to $3,100?

LO 2   **24. Calculating Present Values**   You need $85,000 in 10 years. If you can earn .78 percent per month, how much will you have to deposit today?

LO 2   **25. Calculating Present Values**   You have decided that you want to be a millionaire when you retire in 45 years. If you can earn an annual return of 11.4 percent, how much do you have to invest today? What if you can earn 5.7 percent?

CHALLENGE (Question 26)

LO 1   **26. Calculating Future Values**   You have $20,000 you want to invest for the next 40 years. You are offered an investment plan that will pay you 6 percent per year for the next 20 years and 10 percent per year for the last 20 years. How much will you have at the end of the 40 years? Does it matter if the investment plan pays you 10 percent per year for the first 20 years and 6 percent per year for the next 20 years? Why or why not?

WHAT'S ON THE WEB?

4.1 Calculating Future Values   Go to www.dinkytown.net and find the "Savings Calculators" link. If you currently have $10,000 and invest this money at 9 percent, how much will you have in 30 years? Assume you will not make any additional contributions. How much will you have if you can earn 11 percent?

4.2 Calculating the Number of Periods   Go to www.dinkytown.net and find the "Cool Million" calculator. You want to be a millionaire. You can earn 11.5 percent per year. Using your current age, at what age will you become a millionaire if you have $25,000 to invest, assuming you make no other deposits (ignore inflation)?

4.3 Calculating the Number of Periods   Go to www.moneychimp.com and find the "Compound Interest" calculator. You want to buy a Lamborghini Murciélago. Assume the price of the car is $330,000 and you have $35,000. If you can earn an 11 percent return, how long must you wait to buy this car (assuming the price stays the same)?

4.4 Calculating Rates of Return   Use the "Return Rate" calculator at www.moneychimp.com to solve the following problem. You still want to buy the Lamborghini Murciélago, but you have $60,000 to invest and want to buy the car in 15 years. What interest rate do you have to earn to accomplish this (assuming the price stays the same)?

4.5 Future Values and Taxes   Taxes can greatly affect the future value of your investment. The website at www.financialcalculators.com has a financial calculator that adjusts your return for taxes. Go to this web page and find this calculator. Suppose you have $50,000 to invest today. If you can earn a 12 percent return, and you have no additional savings, how much will you have in 20 years? (Enter 0 percent as the tax rate.) Now, assume that your marginal tax rate is 27.5 percent. How much will you have at this tax rate?

EXCEL *MASTER IT!* PROBLEM

Excel Master coverage online

Before the advent of financial calculators (and Excel), tables often were used in the calculation of present values and future values. Using a two-way data table, create a future value table and a present value table. To make the table a little more interesting, make sure that it will calculate the future values and present values for different dollar amounts. One thing we should note here is that you will not be able to copy and paste the tables presented earlier in this workbook. When a data table is created, you cannot insert or delete rows or columns at a later point in time.

Discounted Cash Flow Valuation | 5

LEARNING OBJECTIVES

After studying this chapter, you should be able to:

LO 1 Determine the future value and present value of investments with multiple cash flows.

LO 2 Calculate loan payments, and find the interest rate on a loan.

LO 3 Describe how loans are amortized or paid off.

LO 4 Explain how interest rates are quoted (and misquoted).

What do professional athletes Alex Avila, Yu Darvish, and Jimmy Garoppolo have in common? All three signed big contracts in 2018. The contract values were reported as $8.25 million, $126 million, and $137.5 million, respectively. That's definitely major league money, but, even so, reported numbers like these can be misleading. For example, in January 2018, Avila signed with the Arizona Diamondbacks. His contract called for a salary of $4 million in 2018 and $4.25 million for 2019. Not bad, especially for someone who makes a living using the "tools of ignorance" (jock jargon for a catcher's equipment).

A closer look at the numbers shows that Alex, Yu, and Jimmy did pretty well, but nothing like the quoted figures. Using Yu's contract as an example, although the value was reported to be $126 million, it was actually payable over several years. The contract consisted of $25 million to be paid in 2018, but only $18 million in 2023. Because the payments were spread out over time, we must consider the time value of money, which means his contract was worth less than reported. How much did he really get? This chapter gives you the "tools of knowledge" to answer this question.

In our previous chapter, we learned how to examine single, lump-sum future payments to determine their current, or present, value. This is a useful skill, but we need to go further and figure out how to handle multiple future payments because that is the much more common situation. For example, most loans (including student loans) involve receiving a lump sum today and making future payments.

More generally, most types of business decisions, including decisions concerning marketing, operations, and strategy, involve the comparison of costs incurred today with cash

Please visit us at essentialsofcorporatefinance.blogspot.com for the latest developments in the world of corporate finance.

inflows hoped for later. Evaluating the cost-benefit trade-off requires the tools that we develop in this chapter.

Because discounted cash flow valuation is so important, students who learn this material well will find that life is much easier down the road. Getting it straight now will save you a lot of headaches later.

In our previous chapter, we covered the basics of discounted cash flow valuation. However, so far, we have only dealt with single cash flows. In reality, most investments have multiple cash flows. If Target is thinking of opening a new department store, there will be a large cash outlay in the beginning and then cash inflows for many years. In this chapter, we begin to explore how to value such investments.

When you finish this chapter, you should have some very practical skills. For example, you will know how to calculate your own car payments or student loan payments. You also will be able to determine how long it will take to pay off a credit card if you make the minimum payment each month (a practice we do not recommend). We will show you how to compare interest rates to determine which are the highest and which are the lowest, and we also will show you how interest rates can be quoted in different, and at times deceptive, ways.

5.1 FUTURE AND PRESENT VALUES OF MULTIPLE CASH FLOWS

Excel
Master
coverage online

Thus far, we have restricted our attention to either the future value of a lump-sum present amount or the present value of some single future cash flow. In this section, we begin to study ways to value multiple cash flows. We start with future value.

Future Value with Multiple Cash Flows

Suppose you deposit $100 today in an account paying 8 percent. In one year, you will deposit another $100. How much will you have in two years? This particular problem is relatively easy. At the end of the first year, you will have $108 plus the second $100 you deposit, for a total of $208. You leave this $208 on deposit at 8 percent for another year. At the end of this second year, the account is worth:

$208 × 1.08 = $224.64

Figure 5.1 is a *time line* that illustrates the process of calculating the future value of these two $100 deposits. Figures such as this one are very useful for solving complicated problems. Any time you are having trouble with a present or future value problem, drawing a time line will usually help you to see what is happening.

In the first part of Figure 5.1, we show the cash flows on the time line. The most important thing is that we write them down where they actually occur. Here, the first cash flow occurs today, which we label as Time 0. We therefore put $100 at Time 0 on the time line. The second $100 cash flow occurs one year from today, so we write it down at the point labeled as Time 1. In the second part of Figure 5.1, we calculate the future values one period at a time to come up with the final $224.64.

FIGURE **5.1** **Drawing and using a time line**

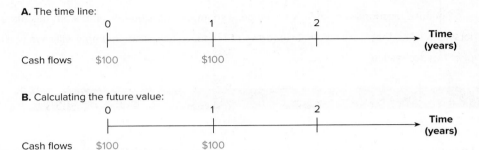

A. The time line:

B. Calculating the future value:

EXAMPLE 5.1 **Saving Up Revisited**

You think you will be able to deposit $4,000 at the end of each of the next three years in a bank account paying 8 percent interest. You currently have $7,000 in the account. How much will you have in three years? In four years?

At the end of the first year, you will have:

$7,000 × 1.08 + 4,000 = $11,560

At the end of the second year, you will have:

$11,560 × 1.08 + 4,000 = $16,484.80

Repeating this for the third year gives:

$16,484.80 × 1.08 + 4,000 = $21,803.58

Therefore, you will have $21,803.58 in three years. If you leave this on deposit for one more year (and don't add to it), at the end of the fourth year, you'll have:

$21,803.58 × 1.08 = $23,547.87

When we calculated the future value of the two $100 deposits, we calculated the balance as of the beginning of each year and then rolled that amount forward to the next year. We could have done it another, quicker way. The first $100 is on deposit for two years at 8 percent, so its future value is:

$100 × 1.08² = $100 × 1.1664 = $116.64

The second $100 is on deposit for one year at 8 percent, and its future value is thus:

$100 × 1.08 = $108.00

The total future value, as we previously calculated, is equal to the sum of these two future values:

$116.64 + 108 = $224.64

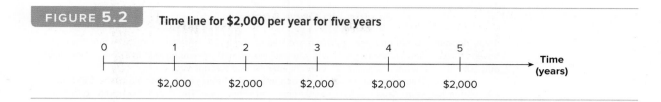

FIGURE 5.2   Time line for $2,000 per year for five years

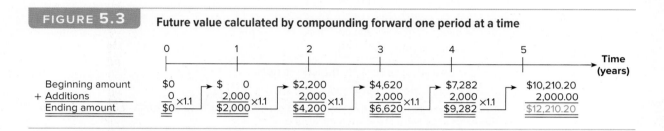

FIGURE 5.3   Future value calculated by compounding forward one period at a time

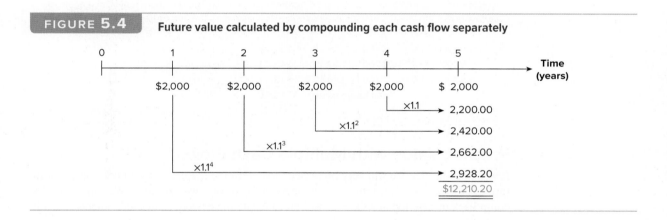

FIGURE 5.4   Future value calculated by compounding each cash flow separately

Based on this example, there are two ways to calculate future values for multiple cash flows: (1) compound the accumulated balance forward one year at a time or (2) calculate the future value of each cash flow first and then add these up. Both give the same answer, so you can do it either way.

To illustrate the two different ways of calculating future values, consider the future value of $2,000 invested at the end of each of the next five years. The current balance is zero, and the rate is 10 percent. We first draw a time line as shown in Figure 5.2.

On the time line, notice that nothing happens until the end of the first year when we make the first $2,000 investment. This first $2,000 earns interest for the next four (not five) years. Also, notice that the last $2,000 is invested at the end of the fifth year, so it earns no interest at all.

Figure 5.3 illustrates the calculations involved if we compound the investment one period at a time. As illustrated, the future value is $12,210.20.

Figure 5.4 goes through the same calculations, but it uses the second technique. Naturally, the answer is the same.

EXAMPLE 5.2   **Saving Up Once Again**

If you deposit $100 in one year, $200 in two years, and $300 in three years, how much will you
have in three years? How much of this is interest? How much will you have in five years if you don't
add additional amounts? Assume a 7 percent interest rate throughout.

We will calculate the future value of each amount in three years. Notice that the $100 earns
interest for two years, and the $200 earns interest for one year. The final $300 earns no interest.
The future values are thus:

$$
\begin{aligned}
\$100 \times 1.07^2 &= \$114.49 \\
\$200 \times 1.07 &= 214.00 \\
+ \$300 &= \underline{300.00} \\
\text{Total future value} &= \underline{\underline{\$628.49}}
\end{aligned}
$$

The future value is thus $628.49. The total interest is:

$$\$628.49 - (100 + 200 + 300) = \$28.49$$

How much will you have in five years? We know that you will have $628.49 in three years. If you
leave that in for two more years, it will grow to:

$$\$628.49 \times 1.07^2 = \$628.49 \times 1.1449 = \$719.56$$

Notice that we could have calculated the future value of each amount separately. Once again, be
careful about the lengths of time. As we previously calculated, the first $100 earns interest for only
four years, the second deposit earns three years' interest, and the last earns two years' interest:

$$
\begin{aligned}
\$100 \times 1.07^4 &= \$100 \times 1.3108 = \$131.08 \\
\$200 \times 1.07^3 &= \$200 \times 1.2250 = 245.01 \\
+\$300 \times 1.07^2 &= \$300 \times 1.1449 = \underline{343.47} \\
\text{Total future value} &= \underline{\underline{\$719.56}}
\end{aligned}
$$

Present Value with Multiple Cash Flows

It will turn out that we will very often need to determine the present value of a series of future cash flows. As with future values, there are two ways we can do it. We can either discount back one period at a time, or we can calculate the present values individually and add them up.

Suppose you need $1,000 in one year and $2,000 more in two years. If you can earn 9 percent on your money, how much do you have to put up today to exactly cover these amounts in the future? In other words, what is the present value of the two cash flows at 9 percent?

The present value of $2,000 in two years at 9 percent is:

$2,000/1.09² = $1,683.36

The present value of $1,000 in one year is:

$1,000/1.09 = $917.43

Therefore, the total present value is:

$1,683.36 + 917.43 = $2,600.79

To see why $2,600.79 is the right answer, we can check to see that after the $2,000 is paid out in two years, there is no money left. If we invest $2,600.79 for one year at 9 percent, we will have:

$2,600.79 × 1.09 = $2,834.86

We take out $1,000, leaving $1,834.86. This amount earns 9 percent for another year, leaving us with:

$1,834.86 × 1.09 = $2,000

This is as we planned. As this example illustrates, the present value of a series of future cash flows is the amount that you would need today in order to exactly duplicate those future cash flows (for a given discount rate).

An alternative way of calculating present values for multiple future cash flows is to discount back to the present one period at a time. To illustrate, suppose we had an investment that was going to pay $1,000 at the end of every year for the next five years. To find the present value, we could discount each $1,000 back to the present separately and then add the results up. Figure 5.5 illustrates this approach for a 6 percent discount rate. As shown, the answer is $4,212.36.

Alternatively, we could discount the last cash flow back one period and add it to the next-to-the-last cash flow:

$1,000/1.06 + 1,000 = $943.40 + 1,000 = $1,943.40

We could then discount this amount back one period and add it to the Year 3 cash flow:

$1,943.40/1.06 + 1,000 = $1,833.39 + 1,000 = $2,833.39

This process could be repeated as necessary. Figure 5.6 illustrates this approach and the remaining calculations.

As the accompanying *Finance Matters* box shows, calculating present values is a vital step in comparing alternative cash flows. We will have much more to say on this subject in subsequent chapters.

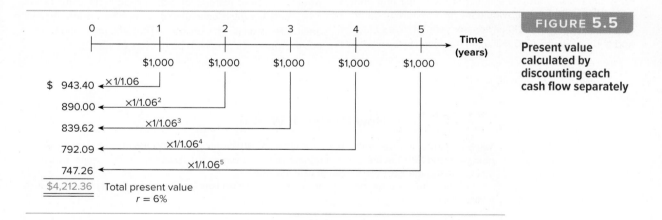

FIGURE 5.5

Present value calculated by discounting each cash flow separately

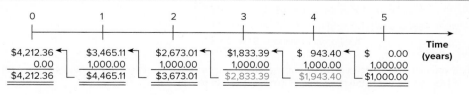

FIGURE 5.6

Present value calculated by discounting back one period at a time

FINANCE MATTERS

Jackpot!

If you, or someone you know, is a regular lottery player, you probably already understand that you are 20 times more likely to be killed by a lightning bolt than to win a big lottery jackpot. How bad are the odds? Below you will find a table comparing your chances of winning the Mega Millions Lottery to other events.

Big Game: Is It Worth the Gamble?	
Odds of winning Mega Millions jackpot	1:135,145,920*
Odds of being killed by a venomous spider	1:57,018,763
Odds of being killed by a dog bite	1:11,403,753
Odds of being killed by lightning	1:6,479,405
Odds of being killed by drowning	1:690,300
Odds of being killed by falling from a bed or other furniture	1:388,411
Odds of being killed in a car crash	1:6,029

Source: Virginia Lottery website. All other odds from the National Safety Council.

Sweepstakes may have different odds than lotteries, but the odds may not be much better. Probably the largest advertised grand prize ever was Pepsi's "Play for a Billion," which, you guessed it, had a $1 billion (*billion!*) prize. Not bad for a day's work, but you still have to read the fine print. It turns out that the winner would be paid $5 million per year for the next 20 years, $10 million per year for Years 21 to 39, and a lump sum of $710 million in 40 years. From what you have learned, you know the value of the sweepstakes wasn't even close to $1 billion. In fact, at an interest rate of 10 percent, the present value was about $70.7 million.

Lottery jackpots are often paid out over 20 or more years, but the winner can usually choose to take a lump-sum cash payment instead. For example, in June 2018, a Hackensack, New Jersey, man won the $315 million Powerball lottery. The man had the option of a single cash payment of $183 million or payments of $10.5 million over the next 30 years. In this case, the man chose the cash option.

Some lotteries make your decision a little tougher. The Ontario Lottery will pay you either $1,000 a day for the rest of your life or $7 million now. (That's in Canadian dollars, by the way.) The fine print tells you that the lottery determines the payout frequency. Assuming a payment of $365,000 is made at the beginning of each year, if you only receive payments for 20 years, the break-even interest rate is about .45 percent. Of course, if you manage to invest the $7 million lump sum at a rate of return of about 5.5 percent per year, you can have your cake and eat it, too, because the investment will return $365,000 at the beginning of each year forever! A Quebec 18-year-old was faced with such a decision when she went to buy a bottle of champagne to celebrate her birthday and won $1,000 a week for life. She took the weekly payment instead of a $1 million lump sum. Taxes complicate the decision in this case because the lottery payments are all on an aftertax basis. Thus, the rates of return in this example would have to be aftertax as well.

EXAMPLE 5.3   How Much Is It Worth?

You are offered an investment that will pay you $200 in one year, $400 the next year, $600 the next year, and $800 at the end of the next year. You can earn 12 percent on very similar investments. What is the most you should pay for this one?

We need to calculate the present value of these cash flows at 12 percent. Taking them one at a time gives:

$$
\begin{aligned}
\$200 \times 1/1.12^1 &= \$200/1.1200 = \$ \ \ 178.57 \\
\$400 \times 1/1.12^2 &= \$400/1.2544 = \ \ \ \ 318.88 \\
\$600 \times 1/1.12^3 &= \$600/1.4049 = \ \ \ \ 427.07 \\
+\$800 \times 1/1.12^4 &= \$800/1.5735 = \ \ \underline{\ \ \ 508.41} \\
\text{Total present value} &= \underline{\underline{\$1,432.93}}
\end{aligned}
$$

If you can earn 12 percent on your money, then you can duplicate this investment's cash flows for $1,432.93, so this is the most you should be willing to pay.

EXAMPLE 5.4   **How Much Is It Worth? Part 2**

You are offered an investment that will make three $5,000 payments. The first payment will occur four years from today. The second will occur in five years, and the third will follow in six years. If you can earn 11 percent, what is the most this investment is worth today? What is the future value of the cash flows?

We answer the questions in reverse order to illustrate a point. The future value of the cash flows in six years is:

$$\$5,000 \times 1.11^2 + 5,000 \times 1.11 + 5,000 = \$6,160.50 + 5,550 + 5,000$$
$$= \$16,710.50$$

The present value must be:

$$\$16,710.50/1.11^6 = \$8,934.12$$

Let's check this. Taking them one at a time, the PVs of the cash flows are:

$$\$5,000 \times 1/1.11^6 = \$5,000/1.8704 = \$2,673.20$$
$$\$5,000 \times 1/1.11^5 = \$5,000/1.6851 = \ \ 2,967.26$$
$$+\$5,000 \times 1/1.11^4 = \$5,000/1.5181 = \ \ \underline{3,293.65}$$
$$\text{Total present value} = \underline{\underline{\$8,934.12}}$$

This is as we previously calculated. The point we want to make is that we can calculate present and future values in any order and convert between them using whatever way seems most convenient. The answers will always be the same as long as we stick with the same discount rate and are careful to keep track of the right number of periods.

HOW TO CALCULATE PRESENT VALUES WITH MULTIPLE FUTURE CASH FLOWS USING A FINANCIAL CALCULATOR

CALCULATOR HINTS

To calculate the present value of multiple cash flows with a financial calculator, we will discount the individual cash flows one at a time using the same technique we used in our previous chapter, so this is not really new. There is a shortcut, however, that we can show you. We will use the numbers in Example 5.3 to illustrate.

To begin, of course, we first remember to clear out the calculator! Next, from Example 5.3, the first cash flow is $200 to be received in one year and the discount rate is 12 percent, so we do the following:

Enter	1	12			200
	N	**I/Y**	**PMT**	**PV**	**FV**
Solve for				−178.57	

Now, you can write down this answer to save it, but that's inefficient. All calculators have a memory where you can store numbers. Why not save it there? Doing so cuts way down on mistakes because you don't have to write down and/or rekey numbers, and it's much faster.

Next, we value the second cash flow. We need to change N to 2 and FV to 400. As long as we haven't changed anything else, we don't have to reenter I/Y or clear out the calculator, so we have:

Enter	2				400
	N	**I/Y**	**PMT**	**PV**	**FV**
Solve for				−318.88	

(*continued*)

You save this number by adding it to the one you saved in our first calculation, and so on, for the remaining two calculations.

As we will see in a later chapter, some financial calculators will let you enter all of the future cash flows at once, but we'll discuss that subject when we get to it.

A Note on Cash Flow Timing

In working present and future value problems, cash flow timing is critically important. In almost all such calculations, it is implicitly assumed that the cash flows occur at the end of each period. In fact, all the formulas we have discussed, all the numbers in a standard present value or future value table, and, very importantly, all the preset (or default) settings on a financial calculator or spreadsheet assume that cash flows occur at the end of each period. Unless you are very explicitly told otherwise, you always should assume that this is what is meant.

As a quick illustration of this point, suppose you are told that a three-year investment has a first-year cash flow of $100, a second-year cash flow of $200, and a third-year cash flow of $300. You are asked to draw a time line. Without further information, you should always assume that the time line looks like this:

On our time line, notice how the first cash flow occurs at the end of the first period, the second at the end of the second period, and the third at the end of the third period.

We will close this section by answering the question we posed at the beginning of the chapter concerning baseball player Yu Darvish's contract. The contract called for payments of $25 million in 2018, $20 million in 2019, $22 million in 2020, $22 million in 2021, $19 million in 2022, and $18 million in 2023. If 12 percent is the appropriate discount rate, what kind of deal did the Cubs' pitcher hurl?

To answer, we can calculate the present value by discounting each year's salary back to the present as follows (notice we assume that all the payments are made at year-end):

Year 1 (2018): $25,000,000 \times 1/1.12 = \$22,321,428.57$
Year 2 (2019): $20,000,000 \times 1/1.12^2 = \$15,943,877.55$
Year 3 (2020): $22,000,000 \times 1/1.12^3 = \$15,659,165.45$

.   .   .
.   .   .
.   .
.   .   .

Year 6 (2023): $18,000,000 \times 1/1.12^6 = \$9,119,360.18$

If you fill in the missing rows and then add (do it for practice), you will see that Yu's contract had a present value of about $87.8 million, or only about 70 percent of the stated $126 million value (but still pretty good).

HOW TO CALCULATE PRESENT VALUES WITH MULTIPLE FUTURE CASH FLOWS USING A SPREADSHEET

SPREADSHEET STRATEGIES

As we did in our previous chapter, we can set up a basic spreadsheet to calculate the present values of the individual cash flows as follows. Notice that we have calculated the present values one at a time and added them up.

	A	B	C	D	E	F
1						
2			**Using a spreadsheet to value multiple cash flows**			
3						
4	What is the present value of $200 in one year, $400 the next year, $600 the next year, and					
5	$800 the last year if the discount rate is 12 percent?					
6						
7	Rate:	.12				
8						
9	Year	Cash flows	Present values	Formula used		
10	1	$200	$178.57	= PV($B$7, A10,0,-B10)		
11	2	$400	$318.88	= PV($B$7, A11,0,-B11)		
12	3	$600	$427.07	= PV($B$7, A12,0,-B12)		
13	4	$800	$508.41	= PV($B$7, A13,0,-B13)		
14						
15		Total PV:	$1,432.93	= SUM(C10:C13)		
16						
17	Notice the negative signs inserted in the PV formulas. These make the present values have					
18	positive signs. Also, the reference to the discount rate in cell B7 is entered as $B$7					
19	(an "absolute" reference) because it is used over and over. We could have entered ".12" instead,					
20	but our approach is more flexible.					
21						
22						

CONCEPT QUESTIONS

5.1a   Describe how to calculate the future value of a series of cash flows.

5.1b   Describe how to calculate the present value of a series of cash flows.

5.1c   Unless we are explicitly told otherwise, what do we always assume about the timing of cash flows in present and future value problems?

5.2 VALUING LEVEL CASH FLOWS: ANNUITIES AND PERPETUITIES

We frequently encounter situations in which we have multiple cash flows that are all the same amount. For example, a very common type of loan repayment plan calls for the borrower to repay the loan by making a series of equal payments for some length of time. Almost all consumer loans (such as car loans) and home mortgages feature equal payments, usually made each month.

Excel Master
coverage online

annuity
A level stream of cash flows for a fixed period of time.

More generally, a series of constant, or level, cash flows that occur at the end of each period for some fixed number of periods is called an ordinary **annuity**; or, more correctly, the cash flows are said to be in ordinary annuity form. Annuities appear very frequently in financial arrangements, and there are some useful shortcuts for determining their values. We consider these next.

Present Value for Annuity Cash Flows

Suppose we were examining an asset that promised to pay $500 at the end of each of the next three years. The cash flows from this asset are in the form of a three-year, $500 ordinary annuity. If we wanted to earn 10 percent on our money, how much would we offer for this annuity?

From the previous section, we know that we can discount each of these $500 payments back to the present at 10 percent to determine the total present value:

$$\text{Present value} = \$500/1.1^1 + 500/1.1^2 + 500/1.1^3$$
$$= \$500/1.10 + 500/1.21 + 500/1.331$$
$$= \$454.55 + 413.22 + 375.66$$
$$= \$1,243.43$$

This approach works fine. However, we will often encounter situations where the number of cash flows is quite large. For example, a typical home mortgage calls for monthly payments over 30 years, for a total of 360 payments. If we were trying to determine the present value of those payments, it would be useful to have a shortcut.

Because the cash flows on an annuity are all the same, we can come up with a very useful variation on the basic present value equation. It turns out that the present value of an annuity of C dollars per period for t periods when the rate of return, or interest rate, is r is given by:

$$\text{Annuity present value} = C \times \left(\frac{1 - \text{Present value factor}}{r} \right)$$
$$= C \times \left\{ \frac{1 - [1/(1 + r)^t]}{r} \right\} \qquad [5.1]$$

The term in parentheses on the first line is sometimes called the present value interest factor for annuities and abbreviated PVIFA(r, t).

The expression for the annuity present value may look a little complicated, but it isn't difficult to use. Notice that the term in square brackets on the second line, $1/(1 + r)^t$, is the same present value factor we've been calculating. In the preceding example, the interest rate is 10 percent and there are three years involved. The usual present value factor is thus:

$$\text{Present value factor} = 1/1.1^3 = 1/1.331 = .751315$$

To calculate the annuity present value factor, we plug this in:

$$\text{Annuity present value factor} = (1 - \text{Present value factor})/r$$
$$= (1 - .751315)/.10$$
$$= .248685/.10 = 2.48685$$

As we calculated before, the present value of our $500 annuity is then:

$$\text{Annuity present value} = \$500 \times 2.48685 = \$1,243.43$$

| Number of | Interest Rates | | | |
Periods	5%	10%	15%	20%
1	.9524	.9091	.8696	.8333
2	1.8594	1.7355	1.6257	1.5278
3	2.7232	2.4869	2.2832	2.1065
4	3.5460	3.1699	2.8550	2.5887
5	4.3295	3.7908	3.3522	2.9906

TABLE 5.1

Annuity present value interest factors

EXAMPLE 5.5   **How Much Can You Afford?**

After carefully going over your budget, you have determined you can afford to pay $632 per month toward a new sports car. You call up your local bank and find out that the going rate is 1 percent per month for 48 months. How much can you borrow?

To determine how much you can borrow, we need to calculate the present value of $632 per month for 48 months at 1 percent per month. The loan payments are in ordinary annuity form, so the annuity present value factor is:

$$\text{Annuity PV factor} = (1 - \text{Present value factor})/r$$
$$= [1 - (1/1.01^{48})]/.01$$
$$= (1 - .62026)/.01$$
$$= 37.9740$$

With this factor, we can calculate the present value of the 48 payments of $632 each as:

$$\text{Present value} = \$632 \times 37.9740 = \$24,000$$

Therefore, $24,000 is about what you can afford to borrow and repay.

Annuity Tables   Just as there are tables for ordinary present value factors, there are tables for annuity factors as well. Table 5.1 contains a few such factors; Appendix A.3 contains a larger set. To find the annuity present value factor we just calculated, look for the row corresponding to three periods and then find the column for 10 percent. The number you see at that intersection should be 2.4869 (rounded to four decimal places), as we calculated. Once again, try calculating a few of these factors yourself and compare your answers to the ones in the table to make sure you know how to do it. If you are using a financial calculator, enter $1 as the payment and calculate the present value; the result should be the annuity present value factor.

ANNUITY PRESENT VALUES

CALCULATOR HINTS

To find annuity present values with a financial calculator, we need to use the **PMT** key (you were probably wondering what it was for). Compared to finding the present value of a single amount, there are two important differences. First, we enter the annuity cash flow using the **PMT** key, and, second, we don't enter anything for the future value, **FV**. So, for example, the problem we have been examining is a three-year, $500 annuity. If the discount rate is 10 percent, we need to do the following (after clearing out the calculator!):

Enter	3	10	500		
	N	**I/Y**	**PMT**	**PV**	**FV**
Solve for				−1,243.43	

As usual, we get a negative sign on the PV.

ANNUITY PRESENT VALUES

Using a spreadsheet to work the same problem goes like this:

	A	B	C	D	E	F	G
1							
2	Using a spreadsheet to find annuity present values						
3							
4	What is the present value of $500 per year for 3 years if the discount rate is 10 percent?						
5	We need to solve for the unknown present value, so we use the formula PV(rate, nper, pmt, fv).						
6							
7	Payment amount per period:	$500					
8	Number of payments:	3					
9	Discount rate:	.1					
10							
11	Annuity present value:	$1,243.43					
12							
13	The formula entered in cell B11 is =PV(B9, B8, −B7, 0); notice that fv is zero and that pmt has a						
14	negative sign on it. Also notice that the discount rate is entered as a decimal, not a percentage.						
15							

Finding the Payment   Suppose you wish to start a new business that specializes in the latest health food trend, frozen yak milk. To produce and market your product, the Yakee Doodle Dandy, you need to borrow $100,000. Because it strikes you as unlikely that this particular fad will be long-lived, you propose to pay off the loan quickly by making five equal annual payments. If the interest rate is 18 percent, what will the payments be?

In this case, we know that the present value is $100,000. The interest rate is 18 percent, and there are five years to make payments. The payments are all equal, so we need to find the relevant annuity factor and solve for the unknown cash flow:

$$\text{Annuity present value} = \$100,000 = C \times (1 - \text{Present value factor})/r$$
$$\$100,000 = C \times (1 - 1/1.18^5)/.18$$
$$= C \times (1 - .4371)/.18$$
$$= C \times 3.1272$$
$$C = \$100,000/3.1272 = \$31,977.78$$

Therefore, you'll make five payments of just under $32,000 each.

ANNUITY PAYMENTS

Finding annuity payments is easy with a financial calculator. In our example above, the PV is $100,000, the interest rate is 18 percent, and there are five years. We find the payment as follows:

Enter	5	18		100,000	
	N	I/Y	PMT	PV	FV
Solve for			−31,977.78		

Here we get a negative sign on the payment because the payment is an outflow for us.

ANNUITY PAYMENTS

Using a spreadsheet to work the same problem goes like this:

	A	B	C	D	E	F	
1							
2		Using a spreadsheet to find annuity payments					
3							
4	What is the annuity payment if the present value is $100,000, the interest rate is 18 percent, and						
5	there are 5 periods? We need to solve for the unknown payment in an annuity, so we use the						
6	formula PMT(rate, nper, pv, fv)						
7							
8	Annuity present value:	$100,000					
9	Number of payments:	5					
10	Discount rate:	.18					
11							
12	Annuity payment:	($31,977.78)					
13							
14	The formula entered in cell B12 is =PMT(B10, B9, B8); notice that the						
15	payment is negative because it is an outflow to us.						

EXAMPLE 5.6   Finding the Number of Payments

You ran a little short on your spring break vacation, so you put $1,000 on your credit card. You can afford to make only the minimum payment of $20 per month. The interest rate on the credit card is 1.5 percent per month. How long will you need to pay off the $1,000?

What we have here is an annuity of $20 per month at 1.5 percent per month for some unknown length of time. The present value is $1,000 (the amount you owe today). We need to do a little algebra (or else use a financial calculator):

$$\$1,000 = \$20 \times (1 - \text{Present value factor})/.015$$
$$(\$1,000/20) \times .015 = 1 - \text{Present value factor}$$
$$\text{Present value factor} = .25 = 1/(1 + r)^t$$
$$1.015^t = 1/.25 = 4$$

At this point, the problem boils down to asking the following question: How long does it take for your money to quadruple at 1.5 percent per month? Based on our previous chapter, the answer is about 93 months:

$$1.015^{93} \approx 4$$

It will take you about 93/12 = 7.75 years at this rate.

FINDING THE NUMBER OF PAYMENTS

To solve this one on a financial calculator, do the following:

Enter		1.5	−20	1,000	
	N	I/Y	PMT	PV	FV

Solve for   93.11

Notice that we put a negative sign on the payment you must make, and we have solved for the number of months. You still have to divide by 12 to get our answer. Also, some financial calculators won't report a fractional value for N; they automatically (without telling you) round up to the next whole period (not to the nearest value). With a spreadsheet, use the function =NPER(rate, pmt, pv, fv); be sure to put in a zero for fv and to enter −20 as the payment.

Finding the Rate   The last question we might want to ask concerns the interest rate implicit in an annuity. For example, an insurance company offers to pay you $1,000 per year for 10 years if you pay $6,710 up front. What rate is implicit in this 10-year annuity?

In this case, we know the present value ($6,710), we know the cash flows ($1,000 per year), and we know the life of the investment (10 years). What we don't know is the discount rate:

$$\$6{,}710 = \$1{,}000 \times (1 - \text{Present value factor})/r$$
$$\$6{,}710/1{,}000 = 6.71 = \{1 - [1/(1 + r)^{10}]\}/r$$

So, the annuity factor for 10 periods is equal to 6.71, and we need to solve this equation for the unknown value of r. Unfortunately, this is mathematically impossible to do directly. The only way to do it is to use a table or trial and error to find a value for r.

If you look across the row corresponding to 10 periods in Appendix A.3, you will see a factor of 6.7101 for 8 percent, so we see right away that the insurance company is offering about 8 percent. Alternatively, we could start trying different values until we got very close to the answer. Using this trial-and-error approach can be a little tedious, but, fortunately, machines are good at that sort of thing.[1]

To illustrate how to find the answer by trial and error, suppose a relative of yours wants to borrow $3,000. She offers to repay you $1,000 every year for four years. What interest rate are you being offered?

The cash flows here have the form of a four-year, $1,000 annuity. The present value is $3,000. We need to find the discount rate, r. Our goal in doing so is primarily to give you a feel for the relationship between annuity values and discount rates.

We need to start somewhere, and 10 percent is probably as good a place as any to begin. At 10 percent, the annuity factor is:

$$\text{Annuity present value factor} = (1 - 1/1.10^4)/.10 = 3.1699$$

The present value of the cash flows at 10 percent is thus:

$$\text{Present value} = \$1{,}000 \times 3.1699 = \$3{,}169.87$$

You can see that we're already in the right ballpark.

Is 10 percent too high or too low? Recall that present values and discount rates move in opposite directions: Increasing the discount rate lowers the PV and vice versa. Our present value here is too high, so the discount rate is too low. If we try 12 percent:

$$\text{Present value} = \$1{,}000 \times (1 - 1/1.12^4)/.12 = \$3{,}037.35$$

Now we're almost there. We are still a little low on the discount rate (because the PV is a little high), so we'll try 13 percent:

$$\text{Present value} = \$1{,}000 \times (1 - 1/1.13^4)/.13 = \$2{,}974.47$$

This is less than $3,000, so we now know that the answer is between 12 percent and 13 percent, and it looks to be about 12.5 percent. For practice, work at it for a while longer and see if you find that the answer is about 12.59 percent.

---

[1]Financial calculators rely on trial and error to find the answer. That's why they sometimes appear to be "thinking" before coming up with the answer. Actually, it is possible to directly solve for r if there are fewer than five periods, but it's usually not worth the trouble.

FINDING THE RATE

CALCULATOR HINTS

Alternatively, you could use a financial calculator to do the following:

Enter	4		1,000	−3,000	
	N	**I/Y**	**PMT**	**PV**	**FV**
Solve for		12.59			

Notice that we put a negative sign on the present value (why?). With a spreadsheet, use the function =RATE(nper, pmt, pv, fv); be sure to put in a zero for fv and to enter 1,000 as the payment and −3,000 as the present value.

Future Value for Annuities

On occasion, it's also handy to know a shortcut for calculating the future value of an annuity. As you might guess, there are future value factors for annuities as well as present value factors. In general, the future value factor for an annuity is given by:

$$\text{Annuity FV factor} = \text{(Future value factor} - 1)/r$$
$$= [(1 + r)^t - 1]/r \qquad [5.2]$$

To see how we use annuity future value factors, suppose you plan to contribute $2,000 every year into a retirement account paying 8 percent. If you retire in 30 years, how much will you have?

The number of years here, t, is 30, and the interest rate, r, is 8 percent, so we can calculate the annuity future value factor as:

$$\begin{aligned}
\text{Annuity FV factor} &= \text{(Future value factor} - 1)/r \\
&= (1.08^{30} - 1)/.08 \\
&= (10.0627 - 1)/.08 \\
&= 113.2832
\end{aligned}$$

The future value of this 30-year, $2,000 annuity is thus:

$$\begin{aligned}
\text{Annuity future value} &= \$2,000 \times 113.2832 \\
&= \$226,566.42
\end{aligned}$$

ANNUITY FUTURE VALUES

CALCULATOR HINTS

Of course, you could solve this problem using a financial calculator by doing the following:

Enter	30	8	−2,000		
	N	**I/Y**	**PMT**	**PV**	**FV**
Solve for					226,566.42

Notice that we put a negative sign on the payment (why?). With a spreadsheet, use the function =FV(rate, nper, pmt, pv); be sure to put in a zero for pv and to enter −2,000 as the payment.

A Note on Annuities Due

So far, we only have discussed ordinary annuities. These are the most important, but there is a variation that is fairly common. Remember that with an ordinary annuity, the cash flows occur at the end of each period. When you take out a loan with monthly payments, for example, the first loan payment normally occurs one month after you get the loan. However, when you lease an apartment, the first lease payment is usually due immediately. The second payment is due at the beginning of the second month, and so on. A lease is an example of an **annuity due**. An annuity due is an annuity for which the cash flows occur at the beginning of each period. Almost any type of arrangement in which we have to prepay the same amount each period is an annuity due.

annuity due
An annuity for which the cash flows occur at the beginning of the period.

There are several different ways to calculate the value of an annuity due. With a financial calculator, you switch it into "due" or "beginning" mode. It is very important to remember to switch it back when you are finished! Another way to calculate the present value of an annuity due can be illustrated with a time line. Suppose an annuity due has five payments of $400 each, and the relevant discount rate is 10 percent. The time line looks like this:

Notice how the cash flows here are the same as those for a *four*-year ordinary annuity, except that there is an extra $400 at Time 0. For practice, verify that the present value of a four-year $400 ordinary annuity at 10 percent is $1,267.95. If we add on the extra $400, we get $1,667.95, which is the present value of this annuity due.

Time value applications abound on the web. See, for example, www.college board.org and www .fidelity.com/calculators -tools/overview.

There is an even easier way to calculate the present or future value of an annuity due. If we assume that cash flows occur at the end of each period when they really occur at the beginning, then we discount each one by one period too many. We could fix this by multiplying our answer by $(1 + r)$, where r is the discount rate. In fact, the relationship between the value of an annuity due and an ordinary annuity with the same number of payments is:

$$\text{Annuity due value} = \text{Ordinary annuity value} \times (1 + r) \qquad \text{[5.3]}$$

This works for both present and future values, so calculating the value of an annuity due involves two steps: (1) calculate the present or future value as though it were an ordinary annuity and (2) multiply your answer by $(1 + r)$.

Perpetuities

We've seen that a series of level cash flows can be valued by treating those cash flows as an annuity. An important special case of an annuity arises when the level stream of cash flows continues forever. Such an asset is called a **perpetuity** because the cash flows are perpetual. Perpetuities also are called **consols**, particularly in Canada and the United Kingdom. See Example 5.7 for an important example of a perpetuity.

perpetuity
An annuity in which the cash flows continue forever.

consol
A type of perpetuity.

Because a perpetuity has an infinite number of cash flows, we obviously can't compute its value by discounting each one. Fortunately, valuing a perpetuity turns out to be the easiest possible case. The present value of a perpetuity is:

$$\text{Perpetuity PV} = C/r \qquad \text{[5.4]}$$

For example, an investment offers a perpetual cash flow of $500 every year. The return you require on such an investment is 8 percent. What is the value of this investment? The value of this perpetuity is:

$$\text{Perpetuity PV} = C/r = \$500/.08 = \$6,250$$

This concludes our discussion of valuing investments with multiple cash flows. For future reference, Table 5.2 contains a summary of the annuity and perpetuity basic calculations we described. By now, you probably think that you'll use online calculators to handle annuity problems. Before you do, see our nearby *Work the Web* box.

I. **Symbols**
   PV = Present value, what future cash flows are worth today
   FV_t = Future value, what cash flows are worth in the future at Time t
   r = Interest rate, rate of return, or discount rate per period—typically, but not always, one year
   t = Number of periods—typically, but not always, the number of years
   C = Cash amount

II. **Future value of C invested per period for t periods at r percent per period**
   $FV_t = C \times [(1 + r)^t - 1]/r$
   A series of identical cash flows paid for a set number of periods is called an annuity, and the term $[(1 + r)^t - 1]/r$ is called the *annuity future value factor*.

III. **Present value of C per period for t periods at r percent per period**
   $PV = C \times \{1 - [1/(1 + r)^t]\}/r$
   The term $\{1 - [1/(1 + r)^t]\}/r$ is called the *annuity present value factor*.

IV. **Present value of a perpetuity of C per period**
   $PV = C/r$
   A perpetuity has the same cash flow every period forever.

W🌐RK THE WEB

As we discussed in our previous chapter, many websites have financial calculators. One of these sites is Calculatoredge, which is located at www.calculatoredge.com. Suppose you retire with $1,500,000 and want to withdraw an equal amount each year for the next 30 years. If you can earn a 9.5 percent return, how much can you withdraw each year? Here is what Calculatoredge says:

Enter your values:

Currency:	US Dollars
Starting Principal:	1500000 **US Dollars**
Annual Interest Rate:	9.5 %
Repayment Period:	30 **Years**

Calculate   Clear

Results:
   Annuity Payment: 139288.47   **US Dollars / Year**

According to the Calculatoredge calculator, the answer is $139,288.47. How important is it to understand what you are doing? Calculate this one for yourself, and you should get $152,520.88. Which one is right? You are, of course! What's going on is that Calculatoredge assumes (but tells you on a different page) that the annuity is in the form of an annuity due, not an ordinary annuity. Recall that with an annuity due the payments occur at the beginning of the period rather than at the end of the period. The moral of the story is clear: *Caveat calculator.*

QUESTIONS

1. Go to the calculator at www.calculatoredge.com and find out how much the website says you could withdraw each year if you have $2,500,000, earn an 8 percent interest rate, and make annual withdrawals for 35 years. How much more are the withdrawals if they are in the form of an ordinary annuity?

2. Suppose you have $500,000 and want to make withdrawals each month for the next 10 years. The first withdrawal is today and the appropriate interest rate is 9 percent compounded monthly. Using this website, how much are your withdrawals?

EXAMPLE 5.7   **Preferred Stock**

Preferred stock (or preference stock) is an important example of a perpetuity. When a corporation sells preferred stock, the buyer is promised a fixed cash dividend every period (usually every quarter) forever. This dividend must be paid before any dividend can be paid to regular stockholders, hence the term *preferred*.

Suppose the Fellini Co. wants to sell preferred stock at $100 per share. A very similar issue of preferred stock already outstanding has a price of $40 per share and offers a dividend of $1 every quarter. What dividend will Fellini have to offer if the preferred stock is going to sell?

The issue that is already out has a present value of $40 and a cash flow of $1 every quarter forever. Because this is a perpetuity:

> Present value = $40 = $1 × (1/$r$)
> r = .025, or 2.5%

To be competitive, the new Fellini issue also will have to offer 2.5 percent *per quarter*; so, if the present value is to be $100, the dividend must be such that:

> Present value = $100 = C × (1/.025)
> C = $2.5 (per quarter)

CONCEPT QUESTIONS

5.2a   In general, what is the present value of an annuity of *C* dollars per period at a discount rate of *r* per period? The future value?

5.2b   In general, what is the present value of a perpetuity?

5.3 COMPARING RATES: THE EFFECT OF COMPOUNDING PERIODS

Excel
Master
coverage online

An important issue we need to discuss has to do with the way interest rates are quoted. This subject causes a fair amount of confusion because rates are quoted in many different ways. Sometimes the way a rate is quoted is the result of tradition, and sometimes it's the result of legislation. Unfortunately, at times, rates are quoted in deliberately deceptive ways to mislead borrowers and investors. We discuss these topics in this section.

Effective Annual Rates and Compounding

If a rate is quoted as 10 percent compounded semiannually, then what this means is that the investment actually pays 5 percent every six months. A natural question then arises: Is 5 percent every six months the same thing as 10 percent per year? It's easy to see that it is not. If you invest $1 at 10 percent per year, you will have $1.10 at the end of the year. If you invest at 5 percent every six months, then you'll have the future value of $1 at 5 percent for two periods, or:

> **$1 × 1.05² = $1.1025**

This is $.0025 more. The reason is very simple. What has occurred is that your account was credited with $1 × .05 = 5 cents in interest after six months. In the following six months, you earned 5 percent on that nickel, for an extra .05 × .05 = .0025 = .25 cents.

As our example illustrates, 10 percent compounded semiannually is actually equivalent to 10.25 percent per year. Put another way, we would be indifferent between 10 percent compounded semiannually and 10.25 percent compounded annually. Any time we have compounding during the year, we need to be concerned about what the rate really is.

In our example, the 10 percent is called a **stated**, or **quoted, interest rate**. Other names are used as well. The 10.25 percent, which is actually the rate that you will earn, is called the **effective annual rate (EAR)**. To compare different investments or interest rates, we will always need to convert to effective rates. Some general procedures for doing this are discussed next.

Calculating and Comparing Effective Annual Rates

To see why it is important to work only with effective rates, suppose you've shopped around and come up with the following three rates:

Bank A: 15 percent, compounded daily

Bank B: 15.5 percent, compounded quarterly

Bank C: 16 percent, compounded annually

Which of these is the best if you are thinking of opening a savings account? Which of these is best if they represent loan rates?

To begin, Bank C is offering 16 percent per year. Because there is no compounding during the year, this is the effective rate. Bank B is actually paying .155/4 = .03875, or 3.875 percent, per quarter. At this rate, an investment of $1 for four quarters would grow to:

$$\$1 \times 1.03875^4 = \$1.1642$$

The EAR, therefore, is 16.42 percent. For a saver, this is much better than the 16 percent rate Bank C is offering; for a borrower, it's worse.

Bank A is compounding every day. This may seem a little extreme, but it is very common to calculate interest daily. In this case, the daily interest rate is actually:

$$.15/365 = .000411$$

This is .0411 percent per day. At this rate, an investment of $1 for 365 periods would grow to:

$$\$1 \times 1.000411^{365} = \$1.1618$$

The EAR is 16.18 percent. This is not as good as Bank B's 16.42 percent for a saver and not as good as Bank C's 16 percent for a borrower.

This example illustrates two things. First, the highest quoted rate is not necessarily the best. Second, compounding during the year can lead to a significant difference between the quoted rate and the effective rate. Remember that the effective rate is what you get or what you pay.

If you look at our examples, you see that we computed the EARs in three steps. We first divided the quoted rate by the number of times that the interest is compounded. We then added 1 to the result and raised it to the power of the number of times the interest is compounded. Finally, we subtracted the 1. If we let m be the number of times the interest is compounded during the year, these steps can be summarized as:

$$\text{EAR} = (1 + \text{Quoted rate}/m)^m - 1 \qquad [5.5]$$

Suppose you were offered 12 percent compounded monthly. In this case, the interest is compounded 12 times a year, so m is 12. You can calculate the effective rate as:

$$
\begin{aligned}
\text{EAR} &= (1 + \text{Quoted rate}/m)^m - 1 \\
&= (1 + .12/12)^{12} - 1 \\
&= 1.01^{12} - 1 \\
&= 1.126825 - 1 \\
&= .126825, \text{ or } 12.6825\%
\end{aligned}
$$

stated interest rate
The interest rate expressed in terms of the interest payment made each period. Also *quoted interest rate.*

quoted interest rate
The interest rate expressed in terms of the interest payment made each period. Also *stated interest rate.*

effective annual rate (EAR)
The interest rate expressed as if it were compounded once per year.

EXAMPLE 5.8	**What's the EAR?**

A bank is offering 12 percent compounded quarterly. If you put $100 in an account, how much will you have at the end of one year? What's the EAR? How much will you have at the end of two years?

The bank is effectively offering 12%/4 = 3% every quarter. If you invest $100 for four periods at 3 percent per period, the future value is:

$$\text{Future value} = \$100 \times 1.03^4$$
$$= \$100 \times 1.1255$$
$$= \$112.55$$

The EAR is 12.55 percent, so at the end of one year you will have $100 × 1.1255 = $112.55.

We can determine what you would have at the end of two years in two different ways. One way is to recognize that two years is the same as eight quarters. At 3 percent per quarter, after eight quarters, you would have:

$$\$100 \times 1.03^8 = \$100 \times 1.2668 = \$126.68$$

Alternatively, we could determine the value after two years by using an EAR of 12.55 percent; so after two years you would have:

$$\$100 \times 1.1255^2 = \$100 \times 1.2668 = \$126.68$$

Thus, the two calculations produce the same answer. This illustrates an important point. Any time we do a present or future value calculation, the rate we use must be an actual or effective rate. In this case, the actual rate is 3 percent per quarter. The effective annual rate is 12.55 percent. It doesn't matter which one we use once we know the EAR.

EXAMPLE 5.9	**Quoting a Rate**

Now that you know how to convert a quoted rate to an EAR, consider going the other way. As a lender, you know you want to actually earn 18 percent on a particular loan. You want to quote a rate that features monthly compounding. What rate do you quote?

In this case, we know that the EAR is 18 percent, and we know that this is the result of monthly compounding. Let q stand for the quoted rate. We thus have:

$$\text{EAR} = (1 + \text{Quoted rate}/m)^m - 1$$
$$.18 = (1 + q/12)^{12} - 1$$
$$1.18 = (1 + q/12)^{12}$$

We need to solve this equation for the quoted rate. This calculation is the same as the ones we did to find an unknown interest rate in Chapter 4:

$$1.18^{(1/12)} = 1 + q/12$$
$$1.18^{.08333} = 1 + q/12$$
$$1.0139 = 1 + q/12$$
$$q = .0139 \times 12$$
$$= .1667, \text{ or } 16.67\%$$

Therefore, the rate you would quote is 16.67 percent, compounded monthly.

annual percentage rate (APR)
The interest rate charged per period multiplied by the number of periods per year.

EARs and APRs

Sometimes it's not altogether clear whether a rate is an effective annual rate or not. A case in point concerns what is called the **annual percentage rate (APR)** on a loan. Truth-in-lending laws in the United States require that lenders disclose an APR on virtually all consumer loans. This rate must be displayed on a loan document in a prominent and unambiguous way.[2]

Given that an APR must be calculated and displayed, an obvious question arises: Is an APR an effective annual rate? Put another way: If a bank quotes a car loan at 12 percent APR, is the consumer actually paying 12 percent interest? Surprisingly, the answer is no. There is some confusion over this point, which we discuss next.

The confusion over APRs arises because lenders are required by law to compute the APR in a particular way. By law, the APR is equal to the interest rate per period multiplied by the number of periods in a year. For example, if a bank is charging 1.2 percent per month on car loans, then the APR that must be reported is $1.2\% \times 12 = 14.4\%$. So, an APR is in fact a quoted, or stated, rate in the sense we've been discussing. For example, an APR of 12 percent on a loan calling for monthly payments is really 1 percent per month. The EAR on such a loan is thus:

$$\begin{aligned} \text{EAR} &= (1 + \text{APR}/12)^{12} - 1 \\ &= 1.01^{12} - 1 \\ &= .126825, \text{ or } 12.6825\% \end{aligned}$$

EXAMPLE 5.10 **What Rate Are You Paying?**

A typical credit card agreement quotes an interest rate of 18 percent APR. Monthly payments are required. What is the actual interest rate you pay on such a credit card?

Based on our discussion, an APR of 18 percent with monthly payments is really $.18/12 = .015$, or 1.5 percent, per month. The EAR is thus:

$$\begin{aligned} \text{EAR} &= (1 + .18/12)^{12} - 1 \\ &= 1.015^{12} - 1 \\ &= 1.1956 - 1 \\ &= .1956, \text{ or } 19.56\% \end{aligned}$$

This is the rate you actually pay.

The difference between an APR and an EAR probably won't be all that great (as long as the rates are relatively low), but it is somewhat ironic that truth-in-lending laws sometimes require lenders to be *un*truthful about the actual rate on a loan.

There can be a huge difference between the APR and EAR when interest rates are large. Consider "payday loans." Payday loans are short-term loans made to consumers, often for less than two weeks, and are offered by companies such as Check Into Cash and National Payday. The loans work like this: You write a check today that is postdated (i.e., the date on the check is in the future) and give it to the company. They give you some cash. When the check date arrives, you either go to the store and pay the cash amount of the check, or the company cashes it (or else automatically renews the loan).

---

[2]By law, lenders are required to report the APR on all consumer loans. We normally compute the APR as the interest rate per period multiplied by the number of periods in a year. According to federal law, the APR is a measure of the cost of consumer credit expressed as a yearly rate, and it includes interest and certain noninterest charges and fees. In practice, the APR can be much higher than the interest rate on the loan if the lender charges substantial fees that must be included in the federally mandated APR calculation.

For example, as of 2018 in one particular state, Check Into Cash allows you to write a check for $352.94 dated 14 days in the future, for which they give you $300 today. So what are the APR and EAR of this arrangement? First, we need to find the interest rate, which we can find by the FV equation as follows:

$$\text{FV} = \text{PV} \times (1 + r)^1$$
$$\$352.94 = \$300 \times (1 + r)^1$$
$$1.1765 = (1 + r)$$
$$r = .1765, \text{ or } 17.65\%$$

That doesn't seem too bad until you remember this is the interest rate for *14 days*! The APR of the loan is:

$$\text{APR} = .1765 \times 365/14$$
$$\text{APR} = 4.6007, \text{ or } 460.07\%$$

And the EAR for this loan is:

$$\text{EAR} = (1 + \text{Quoted rate}/m)^m - 1$$
$$\text{EAR} = (1 + .1765)^{365/14} - 1$$
$$\text{EAR} = 68.20089, \text{ or } 6{,}820.09\%$$

Now that's an interest rate! Just to see what an impact a small difference in fees can make, in another state, Check Into Cash will make you write a check for $335 for the same amount. Check for yourself that the APR of this arrangement is 304.17 percent and the EAR is 1,675.97 percent.

EARs, APRs, Financial Calculators, and Spreadsheets

A financial calculator will convert a quoted rate (or an APR) to an EAR and back. Unfortunately, the specific procedures are too different from calculator to calculator for us to illustrate in general terms; you'll have to consult Appendix D or your calculator's operating manual. Typically, however, what we have called EAR is labeled "EFF "(for *effective*) on a calculator. More troublesome is the fact that what we have called a quoted rate (or an APR) is labeled "NOM" (for *nominal*). Unfortunately, the term *nominal rate* has come to have a different meaning that we will see in our next chapter. So, remember that *nominal* in this context means quoted or APR.

With a spreadsheet, we can easily do these conversions. To convert a quoted rate (or an APR) to an effective rate in Excel, for example, use the formula EFFECT(nominal_ rate, npery), where nominal_rate is the quoted rate or APR and npery is the number of compounding periods per year. Similarly, to convert an EAR to a quoted rate, use NOMINAL(effect_rate, npery), where effect_rate is the EAR.

CONCEPT QUESTIONS

5.3a   If an interest rate is given as 12 percent, compounded daily, what do we call this rate?

5.3b   What is an APR? What is an EAR? Are they the same thing?

5.3c   In general, what is the relationship between a stated interest rate and an effective interest rate? Which is more relevant for financial decisions?

5.4 LOAN TYPES AND LOAN AMORTIZATION

Excel
Master
coverage online

Whenever a lender extends a loan, some provision will be made for repayment of the principal (the original loan amount). A loan might be repaid in equal installments, for example, or it might be repaid in a single lump sum. Because the way that the principal and interest are paid is up to the parties involved, there are actually an unlimited number of possibilities.

In this section, we describe a few forms of repayment that come up quite often; more complicated forms usually can be built up from these. The three basic types of loans are pure discount loans, interest-only loans, and amortized loans. Working with these loans is a very straightforward application of the present value principles that we already have developed.

Pure Discount Loans

The pure discount loan is the simplest form of loan. With such a loan, the borrower receives money today and repays a single lump sum at some time in the future. A one-year, 10 percent pure discount loan, for example, would require the borrower to repay $1.1 in one year for every dollar borrowed today.

Because a pure discount loan is so simple, we already know how to value one. Suppose a borrower was able to repay $25,000 in five years. If we, acting as the lender, wanted a 12 percent interest rate on the loan, how much would we be willing to lend? Put another way, what value would we assign today to that $25,000 to be repaid in five years? Based on our work in Chapter 4, we know that the answer is the present value of $25,000 at 12 percent for five years:

$$\text{Present value} = \$25{,}000/1.12^5$$
$$= \$25{,}000/1.7623$$
$$= \$14{,}186$$

Pure discount loans are very common when the loan term is short, say, a year or less. In recent years, they have become increasingly common for much longer periods.

EXAMPLE 5.11   Treasury Bills

When the U.S. government borrows money on a short-term basis (a year or less), it does so by selling what are called *Treasury bills*, or *T-bills* for short. A T-bill is a promise by the government to repay a fixed amount at some time in the future, for example, 3 months or 12 months.

Treasury bills are pure discount loans. If a T-bill promises to repay $10,000 in 12 months, and the market interest rate is 7 percent, how much will the bill sell for in the market?

The going rate is 7 percent, so the T-bill will sell for the present value of $10,000 to be paid in one year at 7 percent, or:

$$\text{Present value} = \$10{,}000/1.07 = \$9{,}345.79$$

Interest-Only Loans

A second type of loan has a repayment plan that calls for the borrower to pay interest each period and to repay the entire principal (the original loan amount) at some point in the future. Such loans are called *interest-only loans*. Notice that if there is just one period, a pure discount loan and an interest-only loan are the same thing.

For example, with a three-year, 10 percent, interest-only loan of $1,000, the borrower would pay $1,000 × .10 = $100 in interest at the end of the first and second years. At the end of the third year, the borrower would return the $1,000 along with another $100 in interest for that year. Similarly, a 50-year interest-only loan would call for the borrower to pay interest every year for the next 50 years and then repay the principal. In the extreme, the borrower pays the interest every period forever and never repays any principal. As we discussed earlier in the chapter, the result is a perpetuity.

Most corporate bonds have the general form of an interest-only loan. Because we will be considering bonds in some detail in the next chapter, we defer a further discussion of them for now.

Amortized Loans

With a pure discount or interest-only loan, the principal is repaid all at once. An alternative is an *amortized loan*, with which the lender may require the borrower to repay parts of the loan amount over time. The process of paying off a loan by making regular principal reductions is called *amortizing* the loan.

A simple way of amortizing a loan is to have the borrower pay the interest each period plus some fixed amount. This approach is common with medium-term business loans. Suppose a business takes out a $5,000, five-year loan at 9 percent. The loan agreement calls for the borrower to pay the interest on the loan balance each year and to reduce the loan balance each year by $1,000. Because the loan amount declines by $1,000 each year, it is fully paid in five years.

In the case we are considering, notice that the total payment will decline each year. The reason is that the loan balance goes down, resulting in a lower interest charge each year, while the $1,000 principal reduction is constant. For example, the interest in the first year will be $5,000 × .09 = $450. The total payment will be $1,000 + 450 = $1,450. In the second year, the loan balance is $4,000, so the interest is $4,000 × .09 = $360, and the total payment is $1,360. We can calculate the total payment in each of the remaining years by preparing an *amortization schedule* as follows:

Year	Beginning Balance	Total Payment	Interest Paid	Principal Paid	Ending Balance
1	$5,000	$1,450	$ 450	$1,000	$4,000
2	4,000	1,360	360	1,000	3,000
3	3,000	1,270	270	1,000	2,000
4	2,000	1,180	180	1,000	1,000
5	1,000	1,090	90	1,000	0
Totals		$6,350	$1,350	$5,000	

Notice that, in each year, the interest paid is given by the beginning balance multiplied by the interest rate. Also, notice that the beginning balance is given by the ending balance from the previous year.

Probably the most common way of amortizing a loan is to have the borrower make a single, fixed payment every period. Almost all consumer loans (such as car loans) and mortgages work this way. Suppose our five-year, 9 percent, $5,000 loan was amortized this way. How would the amortization schedule look?

We first need to determine the payment. From our discussion earlier in the chapter, we know that this loan's cash flows are in the form of an ordinary annuity. In this case, we can solve for the payment as follows:

$$\$5,000 = C \times (1 - 1/1.09^5)/.09$$
$$= C \times (1 - .6499)/.09$$

This gives us:

$$C = \$5,000/3.8897$$
$$= \$1,285.46$$

The borrower will, therefore, make five equal payments of $1,285.46. Will this pay off the loan? We check by filling in an amortization schedule.

In our previous example, we knew the principal reduction each year. We then calculated the interest owed to get the total payment. In this example, we know the total payment. We thus calculate the interest and then subtract it from the total payment to get the principal portion in each payment.

In the first year, the interest is $450, as we calculated before. Because the total payment is $1,285.46, the principal paid in the first year must be:

Principal paid = $1,285.46 − 450 = $835.46

The ending loan balance is thus:

Ending balance = $5,000 − 835.46 = $4,164.54

The interest in the second year is $4,164.54 × .09 = $374.81, and the loan balance declines by $1,285.46 − 374.81 = $910.65. We can summarize all of the relevant calculations in the following schedule:

Year	Beginning Balance	Total Payment	Interest Paid	Principal Paid	Ending Balance
1	$5,000.00	$1,285.46	$ 450.00	$ 835.46	$4,164.54
2	4,164.54	1,285.46	374.81	910.65	3,253.88
3	3,253.88	1,285.46	292.85	992.61	2,261.27
4	2,261.27	1,285.46	203.51	1,081.95	1,179.32
5	1,179.32	1,285.46	106.14	1,179.32	.00
Totals		$6,427.31	$1,427.31	$5,000.00	

Because the loan balance declines to zero, the five equal payments do pay off the loan. Notice that the interest paid declines each period. This isn't surprising because the loan balance is going down. Given that the total payment is fixed, the principal paid must be rising each period.

If you compare the two loan amortizations in this section, you see that the total interest is greater for the equal total payment case, $1,427.31 versus $1,350. The reason for this is that the loan is repaid more slowly early on, so the interest is somewhat higher. This doesn't mean that one loan is better than the other; it means that one is effectively paid off faster than the other. For example, the principal reduction in the first year is $835.46 in the equal total payment case compared to $1,000 in the first case. Many websites offer loan amortization schedules. See our nearby *Work the Web* box for an example.

You can find a good loan amortization schedule online at www.myamor tizationchart.com.

W🌐RK THE WEB

Preparing an amortization table is one of the more tedious time value of money applications. Using a spreadsheet makes it relatively easy, but there are also websites available that will prepare an amortization table very quickly. One such site is www.bankrate.com. The website has a mortgage calculator for home loans, but the same calculations apply to most other types of loans such as car loans and student loans. According to one source, college graduates in 2017 left school with an average of $39,400 in student loans. Suppose you graduate with the average student loan and decide to pay the loan off over the next 15 years at 6.8 percent, the maximum interest rate for unsubsidized Stafford loans. What are your monthly payments? Using the calculator, for the first year, we get:

Start Date				Estimated Payoff Date	
06/14/2018				**June 14, 2033**	

Amortization Schedule

Payment Date	Payment	Principal	Interest	Total Interest	Balance
Jul 2018	$349.75	$126.48	$223.27	$223.27	$39,273.52
Aug 2018	$349.75	$127.20	$222.55	$445.82	$39,146.32
Sep 2018	$349.75	$127.92	$221.83	$667.65	$39,018.40
Oct 2018	$349.75	$128.64	$221.10	$888.75	$38,889.76
Nov 2018	$349.75	$129.37	$220.38	$1,109.13	$38,760.39
Dec 2018	$349.75	$130.11	$219.64	$1,328.77	$38,630.28
Jan 2019	$349.75	$130.84	$218.90	$1,547.67	$38,499.44
Feb 2019	$349.75	$131.58	$218.16	$1,765.84	$38,367.86
Mar 2019	$349.75	$132.33	$217.42	$1,983.25	$38,235.53
Apr 2019	$349.75	$133.08	$216.67	$2,199.92	$38,102.45
May 2019	$349.75	$133.83	$215.91	$2,415.84	$37,968.61
Jun 2019	$349.75	$134.59	$215.16	$2,630.99	$37,834.02

As you can see, the monthly payment will be $349.75. The first payment will consist of $126.48 in principal and $223.27 in interest. Over the life of the loan you will pay a total of $23,554.54 in interest.

QUESTIONS

1. Suppose you take out a 30-year mortgage for $250,000 at an interest rate of 4.8 percent. Use this website to construct an amortization table for the loan. What are the interest payment and principal amounts in the 110th payment? How much in total interest will you pay over the life of the loan?

2. You take out a 30-year mortgage for $275,000 at an interest rate of 5.1 percent. How much will you pay in interest over the life of this loan? Now assume you pay an extra $100 per month on this loan. How much is your total interest now? How much sooner will the mortgage be paid off?

LOAN AMORTIZATION USING A SPREADSHEET

Loan amortization is a very common spreadsheet application. To illustrate, we will set up the problem that we have just examined, a five-year, $5,000, 9 percent loan with constant payments. Our spreadsheet looks like this:

	A	B	C	D	E	F	G	H
1								
2				Using a spreadsheet to amortize a loan				
3								
4			Loan amount:	$5,000				
5			Interest rate:	.09				
6			Loan term:	5				
7			Loan payment:	$1,285.46				
8				Note: payment is calculated using PMT(rate, nper, -pv, fv).				
9		Amortization table:						
10								
11		Year	Beginning	Total	Interest	Principal	Ending	
12			Balance	Payment	Paid	Paid	Balance	
13		1	$5,000.00	$1,285.46	$450.00	$835.46	$4,164.54	
14		2	4,164.54	1,285.46	374.81	910.65	3,253.88	
15		3	3,253.88	1,285.46	292.85	992.61	2,261.27	
16		4	2,261.27	1,285.46	203.51	1,081.95	1,179.32	
17		5	1,179.32	1,285.46	106.14	1,179.32	.00	
18		Totals		$6,427.31	$1,427.31	$5,000.00		
19								
20		Formulas in the amortization table:						
21								
22		Year	Beginning	Total	Interest	Principal	Ending	
23			Balance	Payment	Paid	Paid	Balance	
24		1	=+D4	=$D$7	=+$D$5*C13	=+D13-E13	=+C13-F13	
25		2	=+G13	=$D$7	=+$D$5*C14	=+D14-E14	=+C14-F14	
26		3	=+G14	=$D$7	=+$D$5*C15	=+D15-E15	=+C15-F15	
27		4	=+G15	=$D$7	=+$D$5*C16	=+D16-E16	=+C16-F16	
28		5	=+G16	=$D$7	=+$D$5*C17	=+D17-E17	=+C17-F17	
29								
30		Note: totals in the amortization table are calculated using the SUM formula.						
31								

We close out this discussion by noting that one type of loan may be particularly important to you. Student loans are an important source of financing for many college students, helping to cover the cost of tuition, books, new cars, condominiums, and many other things. Sometimes students do not seem to fully realize that such loans have a serious drawback: They must be repaid. See our nearby *Finance Matters* box for a discussion.

CONCEPT QUESTIONS

5.4a   What is a pure discount loan?

5.4b   What does it mean to amortize a loan?

An Unwelcome Christmas Present

If you are reading this, we can assume that you are a college student. While you will receive an education in college, and studies show that college graduates earn higher salaries on average than nongraduates, you might receive an unwelcome Christmas present when you graduate: student loan payments. About one-half of all college students graduate with student loans, and more than 90 percent of the loans are Stafford loans. Stafford loans are available through lenders such as Sallie Mae, online lenders, or, in some cases, your college. Stafford loans must be paid off in 10 years, but there is a six-month grace period from the time you graduate until the first payment must be made. The maximum interest rate on unsubsidized Stafford loans made after July 1, 2006, is 6.8 percent.

If you have student loans, you went through an introductory program. In case you forgot, here are several of the repayment options. First, you can make equal monthly payments like most other loans. A second option is to pay only the interest on the loan for up to four years, and then begin making principal and interest payments. This means your payments at the end of the loan are higher than the equal payment option. A third option is to make payments based on a percentage of your salary. A fourth option is a graduated payment option that increases your monthly payments on a predetermined schedule. Finally, you can consolidate your loans one time. If the loan balance is high enough, you may be able to extend your payment for up to 30 years.

While we do not recommend it, some students rack up an extraordinary amount of debt. For example, the son of former Federal Reserve Chairman Ben Bernanke was reported to be on track to graduate medical school with more than $400,000 in student loans. That's a lot, but it is estimated that there are 101 individuals in the U.S. with student loans greater than $1 million!

So how do student loans work in practice? A recent graduate from the University of Maryland with a master's degree in creative writing graduated with $40,000 in student loans. Her loan payments were $442 a month, a payment that was difficult to make on her salary as a fund-raiser. She considered the percentage of salary option, which would have lowered her monthly payments to about $200 per month. However, she realized that this was only putting off the inevitable, so she took a second job to make up the difference.

A dentist from Utah, who has more than $1 million in student loans, is using a government program to help out. He has agreed to pay 10 percent of his discretionary income each month for the next 25 years. Without the government program, his monthly payments would be about $10,500 per month. In 25 years, he will have repaid about $1.6 million toward his loan, but because his current payments don't cover the interest payments, the loan balance will be about $2 million. This will be forgiven by the U.S. government, but unfortunately will result in a tax bill of about $700,000.

A Chicago couple is using a third solution. Both the husband and wife are doctors. The wife is out of her residency and employed full time, while the husband is finishing his last year of residency. What is most unusual about this couple is the amount of student loan debt. The wife's student loan balance is $234,000, the husband's student loan balance is $310,000, and the couple has a $156,000 mortgage! The wife's student loan repayments already have started and amount to $1,750 per month. So how is the couple handling this? They are paying a total of $2,250 per month toward the wife's student loans. This will reduce the repayment period from 22 years to 13 years. The couple also is paying an additional $100 per month on their $1,500 mortgage payment. Fortunately, when the husband's residency ends, he expects his salary to triple. The couple will need it. His loan payments will be $2,349 per month. And you thought your student loan was high! Maybe MD stands for "mucho debt"!

SUMMARY AND CONCLUSIONS

This chapter rounds out your understanding of fundamental concepts related to the time value of money and discounted cash flow valuation. Several important topics were covered, including:

1. There are two ways of calculating present and future values when there are multiple cash flows. Both approaches are straightforward extensions of our earlier analysis of single cash flows.

2. A series of constant cash flows that arrive or are paid at the end of each period is called an ordinary annuity, and we described some useful shortcuts for determining the present and future values of annuities.

3. Interest rates can be quoted in a variety of ways. For financial decisions, it is important that any rates being compared first be converted to effective rates. The relationship between a quoted rate, such as an annual percentage rate, or APR, and an effective annual rate, or EAR, is given by:

$$EAR = (1 + \text{Quoted rate}/m)^m - 1$$

where m is the number of times during the year the money is compounded, or, equivalently, the number of payments during the year.

4. Many loans are annuities. The process of paying off a loan gradually is called amortizing the loan, and we discussed how amortization schedules are prepared and interpreted.

▮connect POP QUIZ!

Can you answer the following questions? If your class is using *Connect*, log on to SmartBook to see if you know the answers to these and other questions, check out the study tools, and find out what topics require additional practice!

Section 5.1 In multiple cash flow calculations, when is it assumed that cash flows occur?

Section 5.2 What is the present value of an ordinary annuity that pays $100 per year for three years if the discount rate is 6 percent per year?

Section 5.3 You agree to repay $1,200 in two weeks for a $1,000 payday loan. What is your EAR assuming that there are 52 weeks in a year?

Section 5.4 What is the simplest form of loan?

CHAPTER REVIEW AND SELF-TEST PROBLEMS

5.1 **Present Values with Multiple Cash Flows**   A first-round draft choice quarterback has been signed to a three-year, $10 million contract. The details provide for an immediate cash bonus of $1 million. The player is to receive $2 million in salary at the end of the first year, $3 million the next, and $4 million at the end of the last year. Assuming a 10 percent discount rate, is this package worth $10 million? How much is it worth? (See Problem 1.)

5.2 **Future Value with Multiple Cash Flows**   You plan to make a series of deposits in an interest-bearing account. You will deposit $1,000 today, $2,000 in two years, and $8,000 in five years. If you withdraw $3,000 in three years and $5,000 in seven years, how much will you have after eight years if the interest rate is 9 percent? What is the present value of these cash flows? (See Problem 3.)

5.3 **Annuity Present Value**   You are looking into an investment that will pay you $12,000 per year for the next 10 years. If you require a 15 percent return, what is the most you would pay for this investment? (See Problem 2.)

5.4 **APR versus EAR**   The going rate on student loans is quoted as 9 percent APR. The terms of the loan call for monthly payments. What is the effective annual rate, or EAR, on such a student loan? (See Problem 19.)

5.5   It's the Principal That Matters   Suppose you borrow $10,000. You are going to repay the loan by making equal annual payments for five years. The interest rate is 14 percent per year. Prepare an amortization schedule for the loan. How much interest will you pay over the life of the loan? (See Problem 55.)

5.6   Just a Little Bit Each Month   You've recently finished your MBA at the Darnit School. Naturally, you must purchase a new BMW immediately. The car costs about $42,000. The bank quotes an interest rate of 15 percent APR for a 72-month loan with a 10 percent down payment. What will your monthly payment be? What is the effective interest rate on the loan? (See Problem 20.)

■ Answers to Chapter Review and Self-Test Problems

5.1   Obviously, the package is not worth $10 million because the payments are spread out over three years. The bonus is paid today, so it's worth $1 million. The present values for the three subsequent salary payments are:

$$\$2/1.1 + \$3/1.1^2 + \$4/1.1^3 = \$2/1.1 + \$3/1.21 + \$4/1.331$$
$$= \$7.3028$$

The package is worth a total of $8.3028 million.

5.2   We will calculate the future value for each of the cash flows separately and then add the results. Notice that we treat the withdrawals as negative cash flows:

$$\$1,000 \times 1.09^8 = \quad \$1,000 \times 1.9926 = \$\ 1,992.56$$
$$\$2,000 \times 1.09^6 = \quad \$2,000 \times 1.6771 = \quad 3,354.20$$
$$-\$3,000 \times 1.09^5 = -\$3,000 \times 1.5386 = \ -4,615.87$$
$$\$8,000 \times 1.09^3 = \quad \$8,000 \times 1.2950 = \ 10,360.23$$
$$-\$5,000 \times 1.09^1 = -\$5,000 \times 1.0900 = \ \underline{-5,450.00}$$
$$\text{Total future value} = \$\ \underline{5,641.12}$$

To calculate the present value, we could discount each cash flow back to the present or we could discount back a single year at a time. However, because we already know that the future value in eight years is $5,641.12, the easy way to get the PV is to discount this amount back eight years:

$$\text{Present value} = \$5,641.12/1.09^8$$
$$= \$5,641.12/1.9926$$
$$= \$2,831.09$$

For practice, you can verify that this is what you get if you discount each cash flow back separately.

5.3   The most you would be willing to pay is the present value of $12,000 per year for 10 years at a 15 percent discount rate. The cash flows here are in ordinary annuity form, so the relevant present value factor is:

$$\text{Annuity present value factor} = [1 - (1/1.15^{10})]/.15$$
$$= (1 - .2472)/.15$$
$$= 5.0188$$

The present value of the 10 cash flows is thus:

Present value = $12,000 × 5.0188

            = $60,225

This is the most you would pay.

5.4   A rate of 9 percent with monthly payments is actually $9\%/12 = .75\%$ per month. The EAR is thus:

$$\text{EAR} = (1 + .09/12)^{12} - 1 = .0938, \text{ or } 9.38\%$$

5.5   We first need to calculate the annual payment. With a present value of $10,000, an interest rate of 14 percent, and a term of five years, the payment can be determined from:

$$\$10,000 = \text{Payment} \times (1 - 1/1.14^5)/.14$$

$$= \text{Payment} \times 3.4331$$

Therefore, the payment is $10,000/3.4331 = $2,912.84 (actually, it's $2,912.8355; this will create some small rounding errors in the accompanying schedule). We can now prepare the amortization schedule as follows:

Year	Beginning Balance	Total Payment	Interest Paid	Principal Paid	Ending Balance
1	$10,000.00	$ 2,912.84	$1,400.00	$ 1,512.84	$8,487.16
2	8,487.16	2,912.84	1,188.20	1,724.63	6,762.53
3	6,762.53	2,912.84	946.75	1,966.08	4,796.45
4	4,796.45	2,912.84	671.50	2,241.33	2,555.12
5	2,555.12	2,912.84	357.72	2,555.12	.00
Totals		$14,564.18	$4,564.18	$10,000.00	

5.6   The cash flows on the car loan are in annuity form, so we only need to find the payment. The interest rate is $15\%/12 = 1.25\%$ per month, and there are 72 months. The first thing we need is the annuity factor for 72 periods at 1.25 percent per period:

$$\text{Annuity present value factor} = (1 - \text{Present value factor})/r$$

$$= [1 - (1/1.0125^{72})]/.0125$$

$$= [1 - (1/2.4459)]/.0125$$

$$= (1 - .4088)/.0125$$

$$= 47.2925$$

The present value is the amount we finance. With a 10 percent down payment, we will be borrowing 90 percent of $42,000, or $37,800.

So, to find the payment, we need to solve for C in the following:

$$\$37,800 = C \times \text{Annuity present value factor}$$

$$= C \times 47.2925$$

Rearranging things a bit, we have:

$$C = \$37,800 \times (1/47.2925)$$

$$= \$37,800 \times .02115$$

$$= \$799.28$$

Your payment is just under $800 per month.

The actual interest rate on this loan is 1.25 percent per month. Based on our work in the chapter, we can calculate the effective annual rate as:

$$EAR = 1.0125^{12} - 1 = .1608, \text{ or } 16.08\%$$

The effective rate is about one point higher than the quoted rate.

CRITICAL THINKING AND CONCEPTS REVIEW

LO 1   **5.1**   **Annuity Period**   As you increase the length of time involved, what happens to the present value of an annuity? What happens to the future value?

LO 1   **5.2**   **Interest Rates**   What happens to the future value of an annuity if you increase the rate, r? What happens to the present value?

LO 1 **LO 2**   **5.3**   **Annuity Present Values**   Tri-State Megabucks Lottery advertises a $10 million grand prize. The winner receives $500,000 today and 19 annual payments of $500,000. A lump-sum option of $5 million payable immediately is also available. Is this deceptive advertising?

LO 1   **5.4**   **Annuity Present Values**   Suppose you won the Tri-State Megabucks Lottery in the previous question. What factors should you take into account in deciding whether you should take the annuity option or the lump-sum option?

LO 1   **5.5**   **Present Value**   If you were an athlete negotiating a contract, would you want a big signing bonus payable immediately and smaller payments in the future, or vice versa? How about looking at it from the team's perspective?

LO 1   **5.6**   **Present Value**   Suppose two athletes sign 10-year contracts for $80 million. In one case, we're told that the $80 million will be paid in 10 equal installments. In the other case, we're told that the $80 million will be paid in 10 installments, but the installments will increase by 5 percent per year. Who got the better deal?

LO 4   **5.7**   **APR and EAR**   Should lending laws be changed to require lenders to report EARs instead of APRs? Why or why not?

LO 3   **5.8**   **Time Value**   On subsidized Stafford loans, a common source of financial aid for college students, interest does not begin to accrue until repayment begins. Who receives a bigger subsidy, a freshman or a senior? Explain.

LO 3   **5.9**   **Time Value**   In words, how would you go about valuing the subsidy on a subsidized Stafford loan?

LO 3   **5.10**   **Time Value**   Eligibility for a subsidized Stafford loan is based on current financial need. However, both subsidized and unsubsidized Stafford loans are repaid out of future income. Given this, do you see a possible objection to having two types?

QUESTIONS AND PROBLEMS

connect   Select problems are available in McGraw-Hill *Connect*. Please see the packaging options section of the Preface for more information.

BASIC (Questions 1–28)

LO 1   **1.**   **Present Value and Multiple Cash Flows**   Fox Co. has identified an investment project with the following cash flows. If the discount rate is 10 percent, what is the present value of these cash flows? What is the present value at 18 percent? At 24 percent?

Year	Cash Flow
1	$ 570
2	430
3	840
4	1,230

LO 1   **2. Present Value and Multiple Cash Flows**   Investment X offers to pay you $3,100 per year for 9 years, whereas Investment Y offers to pay you $4,800 per year for 5 years. Which of these cash flow streams has the higher present value if the discount rate is 6 percent? If the discount rate is 22 percent?

LO 1   **3. Future Value and Multiple Cash Flows**   Wells, Inc., has identified an investment project with the following cash flows. If the discount rate is 8 percent, what is the future value of these cash flows in Year 4? What is the future value at an interest rate of 11 percent? At 24 percent?

Year	Cash Flow
1	$ 865
2	1,040
3	1,290
4	1,385

LO 1   **4. Calculating Annuity Present Values**   An investment offers $6,125 per year for 15 years, with the first payment occurring one year from now. If the required return is 8 percent, what is the value of the investment? What would the value be if the payments occurred for 40 years? For 75 years? Forever?

LO 1   **5. Calculating Annuity Cash Flows**   For each of the following annuities, calculate the annual cash flow.

Present Value	Years	Interest Rate
$ 15,000	6	11%
21,400	8	7
145,300	15	8
325,000	20	6

LO 1   **6. Calculating Annuity Values**   For each of the following annuities, calculate the present value.

Annuity Payment	Years	Interest Rate
$ 1,560	7	5%
1,280	9	10
20,000	18	8
53,200	28	14

LO 1   7. **Calculating Annuity Cash Flows**   For each of the following annuities, calculate the annuity payment.

Future Value	Years	Interest Rate
$ 21,800	8	5%
1,500,000	40	7
520,000	25	8
98,700	13	4

LO 1   8. **Calculating Annuity Values**   For each of the following annuities, calculate the future value.

Annual Payment	Years	Interest Rate
$2,100	10	8%
6,500	40	9
1,100	9	6
5,000	30	10

LO 1   9. **Calculating Annuity Values**   If you deposit $5,000 at the end of each year for the next 20 years into an account paying 10.1 percent interest, how much money will you have in the account in 20 years? How much will you have if you make deposits for 40 years?

LO 1   10. **Calculating Perpetuity Values**   Larry's Life Insurance Co. is trying to sell you an investment policy that will pay you and your heirs $25,000 per year forever. If the required return on this investment is 4 percent, how much will you pay for the policy?

LO 1   11. **Calculating Perpetuity Values**   In the previous problem, suppose Larry's told you the policy costs $645,000. At what interest rate would this be a fair deal?

LO 4   12. **Calculating EAR**   Find the EAR in each of the following cases.

Stated Rate (APR)	Number of Times Compounded	Effective Rate (EAR)
10.2%	Quarterly	
18.0	Monthly	
13.5	Daily	
9.5	Semiannually	

LO 4   13. **Calculating APR**   Find the APR, or stated rate, in each of the following cases.

Stated Rate (APR)	Number of Times Compounded	Effective Rate (EAR)
	Semiannually	15.3%
	Monthly	8.7
	Weekly	9.4
	Daily	14.9

LO 4 14. **Calculating EAR** First National Bank charges 14.3 percent compounded monthly on its business loans. First United Bank charges 14.7 percent compounded semiannually. As a potential borrower, which bank would you go to for a new loan?

LO 4 15. **Calculating APR** Vandermark Credit Corp. wants to earn an effective annual return on its consumer loans of 13.9 percent per year. The bank uses daily compounding on its loans. What interest rate is the bank required by law to report to potential borrowers? Explain why this rate is misleading to an uninformed borrower.

LO 4 16. **Calculating Future Values** What is the future value of $1,150 in 16 years assuming an interest rate of 7.9 percent compounded semiannually?

LO 4 17. **Calculating Future Values** Streamsong Credit Bank is offering 4.7 percent compounded daily on its savings accounts. If you deposit $4,750 today, how much will you have in the account in 5 years? In 10 years? In 20 years?

LO 4 18. **Calculating Present Values** An investment will pay you $100,000 in 9 years. If the appropriate discount rate is 5.5 percent compounded daily, what is the present value?

LO 4 19. **EAR versus APR** Ricky Ripov's Pawn Shop charges an interest rate of 12.1 percent per month on loans to its customers. Like all lenders, Ricky must report an APR to consumers. What rate should the shop report? What is the effective annual rate?

LO 2 20. **Calculating Loan Payments** You want to buy a new sports coupe for $78,500, and the finance office at the dealership has quoted you a loan with an APR of 4.9 percent for 60 months to buy the car. What will your monthly payments be? What is the effective annual rate on this loan?

LO 2 21. **Calculating Number of Periods** One of your customers is delinquent on his accounts payable balance. You've mutually agreed to a repayment schedule of $400 per month. You will charge 1.4 percent per month interest on the overdue balance. If the current balance is $17,320, how long will it take for the account to be paid off?

LO 4 22. **Calculating EAR** Friendly's Quick Loans, Inc., offers you "Five for four, or I knock on your door." This means you get $4 today and repay $5 when you get your paycheck in one week (or else). What's the effective annual return Friendly's earns on this lending business? If you were brave enough to ask, what APR would Friendly's say you were paying?

LO 1 23. **Valuing Perpetuities** Maybepay Life Insurance Co. is selling a perpetual annuity contract that pays $2,750 monthly. The contract currently sells for $400,000. What is the monthly return on this investment vehicle? What is the APR? The effective annual return?

LO 1 24. **Calculating Annuity Future Values** You are to make monthly deposits of $500 into a retirement account that earns an APR of 9.5 percent compounded monthly. If your first deposit will be made one month from now, how large will your retirement account be in 35 years?

LO 1 25. **Calculating Annuity Future Values** In the previous problem, suppose you make $6,000 annual deposits into the same retirement account. How large will your account balance be in 35 years?

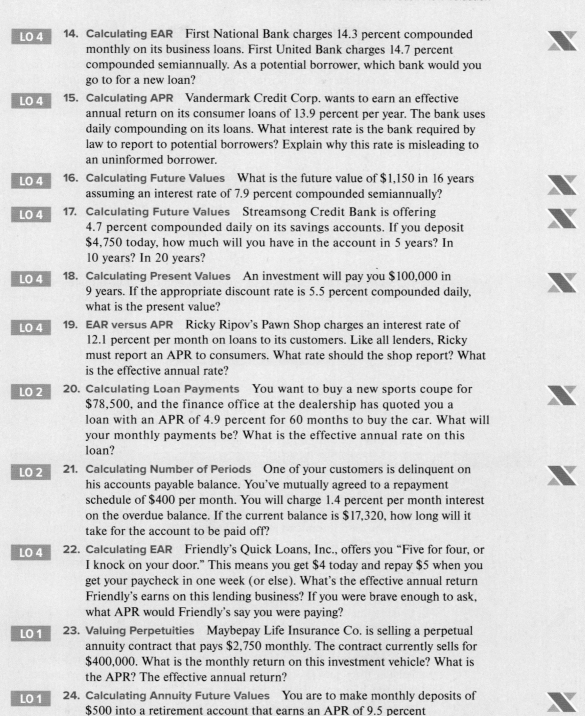

LO 1   26. **Calculating Annuity Present Values**   Beginning three months from now, you want to be able to withdraw $2,500 each quarter from your bank account to cover college expenses over the next 4 years. If the account pays .47 percent interest per quarter, how much do you need to have in your bank account today to meet your expense needs over the next 4 years?

LO 1   27. **Discounted Cash Flow Analysis**   If the appropriate discount rate for the following cash flows is 8.15 percent, what is the present value of the cash flows?

Year	Cash Flow
1	$1,200
2	1,100
3	800
4	600

LO 1   28. **Discounted Cash Flow Analysis**   If the appropriate discount rate for the following cash flows is 4.78 percent per year, what is the present value of the cash flows?

Year	Cash Flow
1	$1,400
2	1,900
3	3,400
4	4,300

INTERMEDIATE (Questions 29–56)

LO 4   29. **Simple Interest versus Compound Interest**   First Simple Bank pays 6.3 percent simple interest on its investment accounts. If First Complex Bank pays interest on its accounts compounded annually, what rate should the bank set if it wants to match First Simple Bank over an investment horizon of 10 years?

LO 2   30. **Calculating Annuities Due**   You want to buy a new sports car from Muscle Motors for $68,500. The contract is in the form of a 60-month annuity due at an APR of 4.5 percent. What will your monthly payment be?

LO 4   31. **Calculating Interest Expense**   You receive a credit card application from Shady Banks Savings and Loan offering an introductory rate of .9 percent per year, compounded monthly for the first six months, increasing thereafter to 18.5 percent compounded monthly. Assuming you transfer the $10,000 balance from your existing credit card and make no subsequent payments, how much interest will you owe at the end of the first year?

LO 4   32. **Calculating the Number of Periods**   You are saving to buy a $255,000 house. There are two competing banks in your area, both offering certificates of deposit yielding 4.8 percent. How long will it take your initial $95,000 investment to reach the desired level at First Bank, which pays simple interest? How long at Second Bank, which compounds interest monthly?

LO 4 33. **Calculating Future Values** You have an investment that will pay you 1.38 percent per month. How much will you have per dollar invested in one year? In two years?

LO 4 34. **Calculating Annuity Interest Rates** Although you may know William Shakespeare from his classic literature, what is not well-known is that he was an astute investor. In 1604, when he was 40 and writing *King Lear*, Shakespeare grew worried about his eventual retirement. Afraid that he would become like King Lear in his retirement and beg hospitality from his children, he purchased grain "tithes," or shares in farm output, for 440 pounds. The tithes paid him 60 pounds per year for 31 years. Even though he died at the age of 52, his children received the remaining payments. What interest rate did the Bard of Avon receive on this investment?

LO 1 35. **Comparing Cash Flow Streams** You've just joined the investment banking firm of Dewey, Cheatum, and Howe. They've offered you two different salary arrangements. You can have $6,100 per month for the next two years, or you can have $5,100 per month for the next two years, along with a $25,000 signing bonus today. If the interest rate is 7 percent compounded monthly, which do you prefer?

LO 1 36. **Calculating Present Value of Annuities** Peter Lynchpin wants to sell you an investment contract that pays equal $22,500 amounts at the end of each year for the next 20 years. If you require an effective annual return of 8 percent on this investment, how much will you pay for the contract today?

LO 4 37. **Calculating Rates of Return** You're trying to choose between two different investments, both of which have up-front costs of $30,000. Investment G returns $65,000 in six years. Investment H returns $98,000 in nine years. Which of these investments has the higher return?

LO 1 38. **Present Value and Interest Rates** What is the relationship between the value of an annuity and the level of interest rates? Suppose you just bought a 10-year annuity of $5,200 per year at the current interest rate of 10 percent per year. What happens to the value of your investment if interest rates suddenly drop to 5 percent? What if interest rates suddenly rise to 15 percent?

LO 1 39. **Calculating the Number of Payments** You're prepared to make monthly payments of $250, beginning at the end of this month, into an account that pays 8 percent interest compounded monthly. How many payments will you have made when your account balance reaches $50,000?

LO 2 40. **Calculating Annuity Present Values** You want to borrow $75,000 from your local bank to buy a new sailboat. You can afford to make monthly payments of $1,475, but no more. Assuming monthly compounding, what is the highest rate you can afford on a 60-month APR loan?

LO 1 41. **Calculating Present Values** In March 2018, the Buffalo Bills signed Star Lotulelei to a contract reportedly worth $50 million. Lotulelei's salary (including bonuses) was to be paid as $17.1 million in 2018, $8.9 million in 2019, $7.5 million in 2020, and $8.25 million in 2021 and 2022. If the appropriate interest rate is 11 percent, what kind of deal did the defensive tackle sack? Assume all payments are paid at the end of each year.

LO 1 42. **Calculating Present Values** The contract signed in February 2018 by Jimmy Garoppolo that we discussed at the beginning of the chapter was actually paid as a $35 million signing bonus to be paid immediately and a $7.6 million salary for 2018. The remaining salary was $18.6 million in 2019, $25.2 million in 2020, $25.5 million in 2021, and $25.6 million in 2022. If the appropriate interest rate is 11 percent, what kind of deal did the quarterback toss? Assume all payments other than the first $35 million are paid at the end of each year.

LO 4 43. **EAR versus APR**   You have just purchased a new warehouse. To finance the purchase, you've arranged for a 30-year mortgage loan for 80 percent of the $3,500,000 purchase price. The monthly payment on this loan will be $15,100. What is the APR on this loan? The EAR?

LO 1 44. **Annuity Values**   You are planning your retirement in 10 years. You currently have $50,000 in a bond account and $250,000 in a stock account. You plan to add $9,000 per year at the end of each of the next 10 years to your bond account. The stock account will earn a return of 10.5 percent and the bond account will earn a return of 7 percent. When you retire, you plan to withdraw an equal amount for each of the next 25 years at the end of each year and have nothing left. Additionally, when you retire you will transfer your money to an account that earns 6.25 percent. How much can you withdraw each year?

LO 4 45. **Calculating Annuities Due Interest Rates**   You have arranged for a loan on your new car that will require the first payment today. The loan is for $28,500, and the monthly payments are $525. If the loan will be paid off over the next 60 months, what is the APR of the loan?

LO 1 46. **Calculating Annuities Due**   Suppose you are going to receive $7,800 per year for five years. The appropriate discount rate is 7.5 percent.

    a. What is the present value of the payments if they are in the form of an ordinary annuity? What is the present value if the payments are an annuity due?

    b. Suppose you plan to invest the payments for five years. What is the future value if the payments are an ordinary annuity? What if the payments are an annuity due?

    c. Which has the higher present value, the ordinary annuity or annuity due? Which has the higher future value? Will this always be true?

LO 1 47. **Annuity and Perpetuity Values**   Mary is going to receive a 30-year annuity of $9,500. Nancy is going to receive a perpetuity of $9,500. If the appropriate discount rate is 5.4 percent, how much more is Nancy's cash flow worth?

LO 1 48. **Calculating Present Values**   A 6-year annuity of twelve $7,375 semiannual payments will begin 9 years from now, with the first payment coming 9.5 years from now. If the discount rate is 9 percent compounded semiannually, what is the value of this annuity five years from now? What is the value three years from now? What is the current value of the annuity?

LO 1 49. **Present Value and Multiple Cash Flows**   What is the present value of $2,625 per year, at a discount rate of 6.9 percent, if the first payment is received six years from now and the last payment is received 20 years from now?

LO 1 50. **Variable Interest Rates**   A 10-year annuity pays $1,725 per month, and payments are made at the end of each month. If the interest rate is 9 percent compounded monthly for the first four years, and 7 percent compounded monthly thereafter, what is the value of the annuity today?

CHAPTER 5 Discounted Cash Flow Valuation

LO 1 **51. Comparing Cash Flow Streams** You have your choice of two investment accounts. Investment A is a 10-year annuity that features end-of-month $1,525 payments and has an interest rate of 7 percent compounded monthly. Investment B is an annually compounded lump-sum investment with an interest rate of 9 percent, also good for 10 years. How much money would you need to invest in B today for it to be worth as much as Investment A 10 years from now?

LO 1 **52. Calculating Present Value of a Perpetuity** Given an interest rate of 6.35 percent per year, what is the value at Year 7 of a perpetual stream of $7,000 payments that begin at Year 20?

LO 4 **53. Calculating EAR** A local finance company quotes an interest rate of 16.7 percent on one-year loans. So, if you borrow $25,000, the interest for the year will be $4,175. Because you must repay a total of $29,175 in one year, the finance company requires you to pay $29,175/12, or $2,431.25 per month over the next 12 months. Is the interest rate on this loan 16.7 percent? What rate would legally have to be quoted? What is the effective annual rate?

LO 1 **54. Calculating Future Values** If today is Year 0, what is the future value of the following cash flows five years from now? What is the future value 10 years from now? Assume an interest rate of 6.1 percent per year.

Year	Cash Flow
2	$15,000
3	24,000
5	33,000

LO 3 **55. Amortization with Equal Payments** Prepare an amortization schedule for a three-year loan of $57,000. The interest rate is 8 percent per year, and the loan calls for equal annual payments. How much interest is paid in the third year? How much total interest is paid over the life of the loan?

LO 3 **56. Amortization with Equal Principal Payments** Rework Problem 55 assuming that the loan agreement calls for a principal reduction of $19,000 every year instead of equal annual payments.

CHALLENGE (Questions 57–60)

LO 4 **57. Discount Interest Loans** This question illustrates what is known as *discount interest.* Imagine you are discussing a loan with a somewhat unscrupulous lender. You want to borrow $18,000 for one year. The interest rate is 14.6 percent. You and the lender agree that the interest on the loan will be .146 × $18,000 = $2,628. So, the lender deducts this interest amount from the loan up front and gives you $15,372. In this case, we say that the discount is $2,628. What's wrong here?

LO 1 **58. Calculating Annuity Values** You are serving on a jury. A plaintiff is suing the city for injuries sustained after a freak street-sweeper accident. In the trial, doctors testified that it will be five years before the plaintiff is able to return to work. The jury already has decided in favor of the plaintiff. You are the foreperson of the jury and propose that the jury give the plaintiff an award to cover the following: (a) The present value of two years' back pay. The plaintiff's annual salary for the last two years would have been $44,000 and $47,000, respectively. (b) The present value of five years' future salary. You assume the salary will be $51,000 per year. (c) $200,000 for pain and suffering. (d) $25,000 for court costs. Assume that the salary payments are equal amounts paid at the end of each month. If the interest rate you choose is an EAR of 7 percent, what is the size of the settlement? If you were the plaintiff, would you like to see a higher or lower interest rate?

LO 4   **59. Calculating EAR with Points**   You are looking at a one-year loan of $15,000. The interest rate is quoted as 12 percent plus two points. A *point* on a loan is 1 percent (one percentage point) of the loan amount. Quotes similar to this one are common with home mortgages. The interest rate quotation in this example requires the borrower to pay two points to the lender up front and repay the loan later with 12 percent interest. What rate would you actually be paying here?

LO 1   **60. Future Value and Multiple Cash Flows**   An insurance company is offering a new policy to its customers. Typically, the policy is bought by a parent or grandparent for a child at the child's birth. The details of the policy are as follows: The purchaser (say, the parent) makes the following six payments to the insurance company:

First birthday:	$ 800
Second birthday:	$ 800
Third birthday:	$ 900
Fourth birthday:	$ 900
Fifth birthday:	$1,000
Sixth birthday:	$1,000

After the child's sixth birthday, no more payments are made. When the child reaches age 65, he or she receives $150,000. If the relevant interest rate is 10 percent for the first six years and 5.75 percent for all subsequent years, is the policy worth buying?

WHAT'S ON THE WEB?

5.1 Annuity Future Value   The Federal Reserve Bank of St. Louis has files listing historical interest rates on its website www.stlouisfed.org. Find the link for "FRED®" (Federal Reserve Economic Data). You will find listings for Moody's Seasoned Aaa Corporate Bond Yield and Moody's Seasoned Baa Corporate Bond Yield. (These rates are discussed in the next chapter.) If you invest $2,000 per year for the next 40 years at the most recent Aaa yield, how much will you have? What if you invest the same amount at the Baa yield?

5.2 Loan Payments   Finding the time necessary until you pay off a loan is simple if you make equal payments each month. However, when paying off credit cards, many individuals only make the minimum monthly payment, which is generally $10 or 2 percent to 3 percent of the balance, whichever is greater. You can find a credit card calculator at www.financialcalculators.com. You currently owe $10,000 on a credit card with a 17 percent interest rate and a minimum payment of $10 or 2 percent of your balance, whichever is greater. How soon will you pay off this debt if you make the minimum payment each month? How much total interest will you pay?

(continued)

5.3 Annuity Payments Find the retirement calculator at www.moneychimp.com to answer the following question: Suppose you have $1,500,000 when you retire and want to withdraw an equal amount each year for the next 30 years. How much can you withdraw each year if you earn 7 percent? What if you can earn 9 percent?

5.4 Annuity Payments The Federal Reserve Bank of St. Louis has files listing historical interest rates on its website www.stlouisfed.org. Find the link for "FRED®" (Federal Reserve Economic Data). You will find a listing for the Bank Prime Loan Rate. The file lists the monthly prime rates since January 1949 (1949.01). What is the most recent prime rate? What is the highest prime rate over this period? If you buy a house for $150,000 at the current prime rate on a 30-year mortgage with monthly payments, how much are your payments? If you had purchased the house at the same price when the prime rate was at its highest, what would your monthly payments have been?

5.5 Loan Amortization Bankrate, located at www.bankrate.com, has a financial calculator that will prepare an amortization table based on your inputs. First, find the APR quoted on the website for a 30-year fixed rate mortgage. You want to buy a home for $200,000 on a 30-year mortgage with monthly payments at the rate quoted on the site. What percentage of your first month's payment is principal? What percentage of your last month's payment is principal? What is the total interest paid on the loan?

EXCEL *MASTER IT!* PROBLEM

Excel
Master
coverage online

This is a classic retirement problem. A friend is celebrating her birthday and wants to start saving for her anticipated retirement. She has the following years to retirement and retirement spending goals:

Years until retirement:	30
Amount to withdraw each year:	$90,000
Years to withdraw in retirement:	20
Interest rate:	8%

Because your friend is planning ahead, the first withdrawal will not take place until one year after she retires. She wants to make equal annual deposits into her account for her retirement fund.

a. If she starts making these deposits in one year and makes her last deposit on the day she retires, what amount must she deposit annually to be able to make the desired withdrawals at retirement?

b. Suppose your friend just inherited a large sum of money. Rather than making equal annual payments, she decided to make one lump-sum deposit today to cover her retirement needs. What amount does she have to deposit today?

c. Suppose your friend's employer will contribute to the account each year as part of the company's profit-sharing plan. In addition, your friend expects a distribution from a family trust several years from now. What amount must she deposit annually now to be able to make the desired withdrawals at retirement?

Employer's annual contribution:	$ 1,500
Years until trust fund distribution:	20
Amount of trust fund distribution:	$25,000

CHAPTER CASE
S&S Air's Mortgage

Mark Sexton and Todd Story, the owners of S&S Air, Inc., were impressed by the work Chris had done on financial planning. Using Chris's analysis, and looking at the demand for light aircraft, they have decided that their existing fabrication equipment is sufficient, but it is time to acquire a bigger manufacturing facility. Mark and Todd have identified a suitable structure that is currently for sale, and they believe they can buy and refurbish it for about $35 million. Mark, Todd, and Chris are now ready to meet with Christie Vaughan, the loan officer for First United National Bank. The meeting is to discuss the mortgage options available to the company to finance the new facility.

Christie begins the meeting by discussing a 30-year mortgage. The loan would be repaid in equal monthly installments. Because of the previous relationship between S&S Air and the bank, there would be no closing costs for the loan. Christie states that the APR of the loan would be 6.1 percent. Todd asks if a shorter mortgage loan is available. Christie says that the bank does have a 20-year mortgage available at the same APR.

Mark decides to ask Christie about a "smart loan" he discussed with a mortgage broker when he was refinancing his home loan. A smart loan works as follows: Every two weeks a mortgage payment is made that is exactly one-half of the traditional monthly mortgage payment. Christie informs him that the bank does have smart loans. The APR of the smart loan would be the same as the APR of the traditional loan. Mark nods his head. He then states this is the best mortgage option available to the company because it saves interest payments.

Christie agrees with Mark, but then suggests that a bullet loan, or balloon payment, would result in the greatest interest savings. At Todd's prompting, she goes on to explain a bullet loan. The monthly payments of a bullet loan would be calculated using a 30-year traditional mortgage. In this case, there would be a 5-year bullet. This means that the company would make the mortgage payments for the traditional 30-year mortgage for the first five years, but immediately after the company makes the 60th payment, the bullet payment would be due. The bullet payment is the remaining principal of the loan. Chris then asks how the bullet payment is calculated. Christie tells him that the remaining principal can be calculated using an amortization table, but it is also the present value of the remaining 25 years of mortgage payments for the 30-year mortgage.

Todd also has heard of an interest-only loan and asks if this loan is available and what the terms would be. Christie says that the bank offers an interest-only loan with a term of 10 years and an APR of 3.5 percent. She goes on to further explain the terms. The company would be responsible for making interest payments each month on the amount borrowed. No principal payments are required. At the end of the 10-year term, the company would repay the $35 million. However, the company can make principal payments at any time. The principal payments would work just like those on a traditional mortgage. Principal payments would reduce the principal of the loan and reduce the interest due on the next payment.

Mark and Todd are satisfied with Christie's answers, but they are still unsure of which loan they should choose. They have asked Chris to answer the following questions to help them choose the correct mortgage.

QUESTIONS

1. What are the monthly payments for a 30-year traditional mortgage? What are the payments for a 20-year traditional mortgage?
2. Prepare an amortization table for the first six months of the traditional 30-year mortgage. How much of the first payment goes toward principal?
3. How long would it take for S&S Air to pay off the smart loan assuming 30-year traditional mortgage payments? Why is this shorter than the time needed to pay off the traditional mortgage? How much interest would the company save?
4. Assume S&S Air takes out a bullet loan under the terms described. What are the payments on the loan?
5. What are the payments for the interest-only loan?
6. Which mortgage is the best for the company? Are there any potential risks in this action?

6 | Interest Rates and Bond Valuation

Generally, when you make an investment, you expect that you will get back more money in the future than you invested today. But in December 2017, this wasn't the case for many bond investors. The yield on a five-year German government bond was about negative .20 percent, and the yields on two-year and five-year Japanese government bonds were negative .14 percent and negative .09 percent, respectively. In fact, in 2016, the amount of debt worldwide that had a negative yield reached a record $13.4 trillion! And negative yields were not restricted to government bonds, as at one point the yield on a bond issued by chocolate maker Nestlé was negative as well.

So what happened? Central banks were in a race to the bottom, lowering interest rates in an attempt to improve their domestic economies.

This chapter takes what we have learned about the time value of money and shows how it can be used to value one of the most common of all financial assets, a bond. It then discusses bond features, bond types, and the operation of the bond market.

What we will see is that bond prices depend critically on interest rates, so we will go on to discuss some very fundamental issues regarding interest rates. Clearly, interest rates are important to everybody because they underlie what businesses of all types—small and large—must pay to borrow money.

LEARNING OBJECTIVES

After studying this chapter, you should be able to:

LO 1 Identify important bond features and types of bonds.

LO 2 Describe bond values and why they fluctuate.

LO 3 Discuss bond ratings and what they mean.

LO 4 Evaluate the impact of inflation on interest rates.

LO 5 Explain the term structure of interest rates and the determinants of bond yields.

Please visit us at essentialsofcorporatefinance.blogspot.com for the latest developments in the world of corporate finance.

Our goal in this chapter is to introduce you to bonds. We begin by showing how the techniques we developed in Chapters 4 and 5 can be applied to bond valuation. From there, we go on to discuss bond features and how bonds are bought and sold. One important thing we learn is that bond values depend, in large part, on interest rates. Thus, we close out the chapter with an examination of interest rates and their behavior.

6.1 BONDS AND BOND VALUATION

Excel
Master
coverage online

When a corporation (or government) wishes to borrow money from the public on a long-term basis, it usually does so by issuing, or selling, debt securities that are generically called bonds. In this section, we describe the various features of corporate bonds and some of the terminology associated with bonds. We then discuss the cash flows associated with a bond and how bonds can be valued using our discounted cash flow procedure.

Bond Features and Prices

As we mentioned in our previous chapter, a bond is normally an interest-only loan, meaning that the borrower will pay the interest every period, but none of the principal will be repaid until the end of the loan. Suppose the Beck Corporation wants to borrow $1,000 for 30 years. The interest rate on similar debt issued by similar corporations is 12 percent. Beck will thus pay $.12 \times \$1,000 = \$120$ in interest every year for 30 years. At the end of 30 years, Beck will repay the $1,000. As this example suggests, a bond is a fairly simple financing arrangement. There is, however, a rich jargon associated with bonds, so we will use this example to define some of the more important terms.

In our example, the $120 regular interest payments that Beck promises to make are called the bond's **coupons**. Because the coupon is constant and paid every year, the type of bond we are describing is sometimes called a *level coupon bond*. The amount that will be repaid at the end of the loan is called the bond's **face value** or **par value**. As in our example, this par value is usually $1,000 for corporate bonds, and a bond that sells for its par value is called a *par value bond*. Government bonds frequently have much larger face, or par, values. Finally, the annual coupon divided by the face value is called the **coupon rate** on the bond; in this case, because $120/$1,000 = .12, or 12 percent, the bond has a 12 percent coupon rate.

The number of years until the face value is paid is called the bond's time to **maturity**. A corporate bond will frequently have a maturity of 30 years when it is originally issued, but this varies. Once the bond has been issued, the number of years to maturity declines as time goes by.

Bond Values and Yields

As time passes, interest rates change in the marketplace. The cash flows from a bond, however, stay the same. As a result, the value of the bond will fluctuate. When interest rates rise, the present value of the bond's remaining cash flows declines, and the bond is worth less. When interest rates fall, the bond is worth more.

To determine the value of a bond at a particular point in time, we need to know the number of periods remaining until maturity, the face value, the coupon, and the market interest rate for bonds with similar features. This interest rate required in the market on a bond is called the bond's **yield to maturity (YTM)**. This rate is sometimes called the bond's *yield* for short. Given all this information, we can calculate the present value of the cash flows as an estimate of the bond's current market value.

For example, suppose the Xanth (pronounced "zanth") Co. were to issue a bond with 10 years to maturity. The Xanth bond has an annual coupon of $80. Similar bonds have a yield to maturity of 8 percent. Based on our preceding discussion, the Xanth bond will pay $80 per year for the next 10 years in coupon interest. In 10 years, Xanth will pay $1,000 to the owner of the bond. The cash flows from the bond are shown in Figure 6.1. What would this bond sell for?

As illustrated in Figure 6.1, the Xanth bond's cash flows have an annuity component (the coupons) and a lump sum (the face value paid at maturity). We thus estimate the market value of the bond by calculating the present value of these two components separately

coupon
The stated interest payment made on a bond.

face value
The principal amount of a bond that is repaid at the end of the term. Also *par value.*

par value
The principal amount of a bond that is repaid at the end of the term. Also *face value.*

coupon rate
The annual coupon divided by the face value of a bond.

maturity
Specified date on which the principal amount of a bond is paid.

yield to maturity (YTM)
The rate required in the market on a bond.

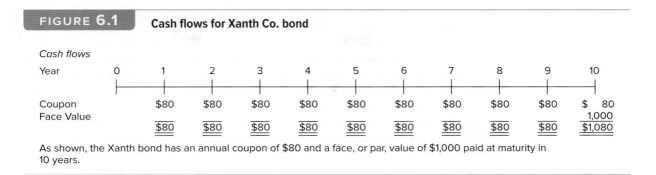

FIGURE **6.1**   **Cash flows for Xanth Co. bond**

As shown, the Xanth bond has an annual coupon of $80 and a face, or par, value of $1,000 paid at maturity in 10 years.

and adding the results together. First, at the going rate of 8 percent, the present value of the $1,000 paid in 10 years is:

Present value = $1,000/1.08¹⁰ = $1,000/2.1589 = $463.19

Second, the bond offers $80 per year for 10 years; the present value of this annuity stream is:

Annuity present value = $80 × (1 − 1/1.08¹⁰)/.08
= $80 × (1 − 1/2.1589)/.08
= $80 × 6.7101
= $536.81

We can now add the values for the two parts together to get the bond's value:

Total bond value = $463.19 + 536.81 = $1,000

This bond sells for exactly its face value. This is not a coincidence. The going interest rate in the market is 8 percent. Considered as an interest-only loan, what interest rate does this bond have? With an $80 coupon, this bond pays exactly 8 percent interest only when it sells for $1,000.

To illustrate what happens as interest rates change, suppose that a year has gone by. The Xanth bond now has 9 years to maturity. If the interest rate in the market has risen to 10 percent, what will the bond be worth? To find out, we repeat the present value calculations with 9 years instead of 10, and a 10 percent yield instead of an 8 percent yield. First, the present value of the $1,000 paid in 9 years at 10 percent is:

Present value = $1,000/1.10⁹ = $1,000/2.3579 = $424.10

Second, the bond now offers $80 per year for nine years; the present value of this annuity stream at 10 percent is:

Annuity present value = $80 × (1 − 1/1.10⁹)/.10
= $80 × (1 − 1/2.3579)/.10
= $80 × 5.7590
= $460.72

We can now add the values for the two parts together to get the bond's value:

Total bond value = $424.10 + 460.72 = $884.82

Therefore, the bond should sell for about $885. In the vernacular, we say that this bond, with its 8 percent coupon, is priced to yield 10 percent at $885.

The Xanth Co. bond now sells for less than its $1,000 face value. Why? The market interest rate is 10 percent. Considered as an interest-only loan of $1,000, this bond only pays 8 percent, its coupon rate. Because this bond pays less than the going rate, investors are only

A good bond site to visit is
www.bloomberg.com
/markets/rates-bonds,
which has loads of useful
information.

willing to lend something less than the $1,000 promised repayment. Because the bond sells for less than face value, it is said to be a *discount bond*.

The only way to get the interest rate up to 10 percent is to lower the price to less than $1,000 so that the purchaser, in effect, has a built-in gain. For the Xanth bond, the price of $885 is $115 less than the face value, so an investor who purchased and kept the bond would get $80 per year and would have a $115 gain at maturity as well. This gain compensates the lender for the below-market coupon rate.

Another way to see why the bond is discounted by $115 is to note that the $80 coupon is $20 below the coupon on a newly issued par value bond, based on current market conditions. The bond would be worth $1,000 only if it had a coupon of $100 per year. In a sense, an investor who buys and keeps the bond gives up $20 per year for nine years. At 10 percent, this annuity stream is worth:

$$\text{Annuity present value} = \$20 \times (1 - 1/1.10^9)/.10$$
$$= \$20 \times 5.7590$$
$$= \$115.18$$

This is the amount of the discount.

What would the Xanth bond sell for if interest rates had dropped by 2 percent instead of rising by 2 percent? As you might guess, the bond would sell for more than $1,000. Such a bond is said to sell at a *premium* and is called a *premium bond*.

This case is the opposite of that of a discount bond. The Xanth bond has a coupon rate of 8 percent when the market rate is now only 6 percent. Investors are willing to pay a premium to get this extra coupon amount. In this case, the relevant discount rate is 6 percent, and there are nine years remaining. The present value of the $1,000 face amount is:

$$\text{Present value} = \$1,000/1.06^9 = \$1,000/1.6895 = \$591.90$$

The present value of the coupon stream is:

$$\text{Annuity present value} = \$80 \times (1 - 1/1.06^9)/.06$$
$$= \$80 \times (1 - 1/1.6895)/.06$$
$$= \$80 \times 6.8017$$
$$= \$544.14$$

We can now add the values for the two parts together to get the bond's value:

$$\text{Total bond value} = \$591.90 + 544.14 = \$1,136.03$$

The total bond value is therefore about $136 in excess of par value. Once again, we can verify this amount by noting that the coupon is now $20 too high, based on current market conditions. The present value of $20 per year for nine years at 6 percent is:

$$\text{Annuity present value} = \$20 \times (1 - 1/1.06^9)/.06$$
$$= \$20 \times 6.8017$$
$$= \$136.03$$

This is as we calculated.

Based on our examples, we can now write the general expression for the value of a bond. If a bond has (1) a face value of F paid at maturity, (2) a coupon of C paid per period, (3) t periods to maturity, and (4) a yield of r per period, its value is:

$$\text{Bond value} = C \times [1 - 1/(1 + r)^t]/r + F/(1 + r)^t$$

$$\text{Bond value} = \underset{\text{of the coupons}}{\text{Present value}} + \underset{\text{of the face amount}}{\text{Present value}} \qquad [6.1]$$

EXAMPLE 6.1 **Semiannual Coupons**

In practice, bonds issued in the United States usually make coupon payments twice a year. So, if an ordinary bond has a coupon rate of 14 percent, then the owner will get a total of $140 per year, but this $140 will come in two payments of $70 each. Suppose we are examining such a bond. The yield to maturity is quoted at 16 percent.

Bond yields are quoted like APRs; the quoted rate is equal to the actual rate per period multiplied by the number of periods. In this case, with a 16 percent quoted yield and semiannual payments, the true yield is 8 percent per six months. The bond matures in seven years. What is the bond's price? What is the effective annual yield on this bond?

Based on our discussion, we know that the bond will sell at a discount because it has a coupon rate of 7 percent every six months when the market requires 8 percent every six months. So, if our answer is equal to or exceeds $1,000, we know that we have made a mistake.

To get the exact price, we first calculate the present value of the bond's face value of $1,000 paid in seven years. This seven-year period has 14 periods of six months each. At 8 percent per period, the value is:

$$\text{Present value} = \$1,000/1.08^{14} = \$1,000/2.9372 = \$340.46$$

The coupons can be viewed as a 14-period annuity of $70 per period. At an 8 percent discount rate, the present value of such an annuity is:

$$
\begin{aligned}
\text{Annuity present value} &= \$70 \times (1 - 1/1.08^{14})/.08 \\
&= \$70 \times (1 - .3405)/.08 \\
&= \$70 \times 8.2442 \\
&= \$577.10
\end{aligned}
$$

The total present value gives us what the bond should sell for:

$$\text{Total present value} = \$340.46 + 577.10 = \$917.56$$

To calculate the effective yield on this bond, note that 8 percent every six months is equivalent to:

$$\text{Effective annual rate} = (1 + .08)^2 - 1 = .1664, \text{ or } 16.64\%$$

The effective yield, therefore, is 16.64 percent.

As we have illustrated in this section, bond prices and interest rates always move in opposite directions. When interest rates rise, a bond's value, like any other present value, will decline. Similarly, when interest rates fall, bond values rise. Even if we are considering a bond that is riskless in the sense that the borrower is certain to make all the payments, there is still risk in owning a bond. We discuss this next.

Online bond calculators and interest rate information are available at money.cnn.com/data /bonds and www .bankrate.com.

Interest Rate Risk

The risk that arises for bond owners from fluctuating interest rates is called *interest rate risk*. How much interest rate risk a bond has depends on how sensitive its price is to interest rate changes. This sensitivity directly depends on two things: the time to maturity and the coupon rate. As we will see momentarily, you should keep the following in mind when looking at a bond:

1. All other things being equal, the longer the time to maturity, the greater the interest rate risk.
2. All other things being equal, the lower the coupon rate, the greater the interest rate risk.

FIGURE 6.2   Interest rate risk and time to maturity

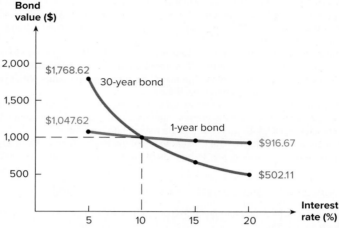

Value of a Bond with a 10 Percent Coupon Rate for Different Interest Rates and Maturities

	Time to Maturity	
Interest Rate	1 Year	30 Years
5%	$1,047.62	$1,768.62
10	1,000.00	1,000.00
15	956.52	67170
20	916.67	502.11

We illustrate the first of these two points in Figure 6.2. As shown, we compute and plot prices under different interest rate scenarios for 10 percent coupon bonds with maturities of 1 year and 30 years. Notice how the slope of the line connecting the prices is much steeper for the 30-year maturity bond than it is for the 1-year maturity bond. This steepness tells us that a relatively small change in interest rates will lead to a substantial change in the bond's value. In comparison, the one-year bond's price is relatively insensitive to interest rate changes.

Intuitively, we can see that the reason that longer-term bonds have greater interest rate sensitivity is that a large portion of a bond's value comes from the $1,000 face amount. The present value of this amount isn't greatly affected by a small change in interest rates if the amount is to be received in one year. Even a small change in the interest rate, however, once it is compounded for 30 years, can have a significant effect on the present value. As a result, the present value of the face amount will be much more volatile with a longer-term bond.

The other thing to know about interest rate risk is that, like most things in finance and economics, it increases at a decreasing rate. In other words, if we compared a 10-year bond to a 1-year bond, we would see that the 10-year bond has much greater interest rate risk. However, if you were to compare a 20-year bond to a 30-year bond, you would find that the 30-year bond has somewhat greater interest rate risk because it has a longer maturity, but the difference in the risk would be fairly small.

The reason that bonds with lower coupons have greater interest rate risk is easy to understand. As we discussed earlier, the value of a bond depends on the present value of its coupons and the present value of the face amount. If two bonds with different coupon rates have the same maturity, then the value of the one with the lower coupon is proportionately

Visit www.investorguide .com to learn more about bonds.

more dependent on the face amount to be received at maturity. As a result, all other things being equal, its value will fluctuate more as interest rates change. Put another way, the bond with the higher coupon has a larger cash flow early in its life, so its value is less sensitive to changes in the discount rate.

Bonds are usually not issued with maturities longer than 30 years. However, low interest rates have led to the issuance of bonds with much longer maturities. In the 1990s, Walt Disney issued "Sleeping Beauty" bonds with a 100-year maturity. Similarly, BellSouth (now known as AT&T), Coca-Cola, and Dutch banking giant ABN AMRO all issued bonds with 100-year maturities. These companies wanted to lock in the historically low interest rates for a *long* time. The current record holder for corporations appears to be Republic National Bank, which sold bonds with 1,000 years to maturity. Before these fairly recent issues, it appears the last time 100-year bonds were issued was in May 1954 by the Chicago and Eastern Railroad. And low interest rates in recent years have led to more 100-year bonds. For example, in 2017, Argentina joined Mexico, Ireland, and Belgium when it issued $2.75 billion in 100-year bonds. What made Argentina's bond sale unique was that the country had defaulted three times in the past 23 years.

We can illustrate the effect of interest rate risk using a 100-year BellSouth issue. The following table provides some basic information on this issue, along with its prices on December 31, 1995; May 6, 2008; and February 1, 2018.

Maturity	Coupon Rate	Price on 12/31/95	Price on 5/6/08	Percentage Change in Price 1995–2008	Price on 2/1/18	Percentage Change in Price 2008–2018
2095	7.00%	$1,000.00	$1,008.40	+.84%	$1,164.21	+15.5%

Several things emerge from this table. First, interest rates apparently fell slightly between December 31, 1995, and May 6, 2008 (why?). After that, however, they fell even more (why?). The bond's price first gained .84 percent and then gained an additional 15.5 percent. These swings illustrate that longer-term bonds have significant interest rate risk.

Finding the Yield to Maturity: More Trial and Error

Frequently, we will know a bond's price, coupon rate, and maturity date, but not its yield to maturity. Suppose we are interested in a six-year, 8 percent coupon bond. The coupons are paid annually. A broker quotes a price of $955.14. What is the yield on this bond?

We've seen that the price of a bond can be written as the sum of its annuity and lump-sum components. Knowing that there is an $80 coupon for six years and a $1,000 face value, we can say that the price is:

$$\$955.14 = \$80 \times [1 - 1/(1 + r)^6]/r + \$1,000/(1 + r)^6$$

where r is the unknown discount rate, or yield to maturity. We have one equation here and one unknown, but we cannot solve for r explicitly. The only way to find the answer is to use trial and error (or, better yet, a spreadsheet or financial calculator).

This problem is essentially identical to the one we examined in the last chapter when we tried to find the unknown interest rate on an annuity. However, finding the rate (or yield) on a bond is even more complicated because of the $1,000 face amount.

We can speed up the trial-and-error process by using what we know about bond prices and yields. In this case, the bond has an $80 coupon and is selling at a discount. We thus know that the yield is greater than 8 percent. If we compute the price at 10 percent:

$$\text{Bond value} = \$80 \times (1 - 1/1.10^6)/.10 + \$1{,}000/1.10^6$$
$$= \$80 \times 4.3553 + \$1{,}000/1.7716$$
$$= \$912.89$$

Current market rates are available at www .bankrate.com.

At 10 percent, the value we calculate is lower than the actual price, so 10 percent is too high. The true yield must be somewhere between 8 and 10 percent. At this point, it's "plug and chug" to find the answer. You would probably want to try 9 percent next. If you did, you would see that this is, in fact, the bond's yield to maturity.

current yield

A bond's coupon payment divided by its closing price.

A bond's yield to maturity should not be confused with its **current yield**, which is a bond's annual coupon divided by its price. In the example we just worked, the bond's annual coupon was $80 and its price was $955.14. Given these numbers, we see that the current yield is $80/$955.14 = .0838, or 8.38 percent, which is less than the yield to maturity of 9 percent. The reason the current yield is too low is that it only considers the coupon portion of your return; it doesn't consider the built-in gain from the price discount. For a premium bond, the reverse is true, meaning that current yield would be higher because it ignores the built-in loss.

Our discussion of bond valuation is summarized in Table 6.1.

EXAMPLE 6.2   Current Events

A bond has a quoted price of $1,080.42. It has a face value of $1,000, a semiannual coupon of $30, and a maturity of five years. What is its current yield? What is its yield to maturity? Which is bigger? Why?

Notice that this bond makes semiannual payments of $30, so the annual payment is $60. The current yield is thus $60/$1,080.42 = .0555, or 5.55 percent. To calculate the yield to maturity, refer back to Example 6.1. Now, in this case, the bond pays $30 every six months and it has 10 six-month periods until maturity. So, we need to find r as follows:

$$\$1{,}080.42 = \$30 \times [1 - 1/(1 + r)^{10}]/r + \$1{,}000/(1 + r)^{10}$$

After some trial and error, we find that r is equal to 2.1 percent. But the tricky part is that this 2.1 percent is the yield per *six months*. We have to double it to get the yield to maturity, so the yield to maturity is 4.2 percent, which is less than the current yield. The reason is that the current yield ignores the built-in loss of the premium between now and maturity.

TABLE 6.1

Summary of bond valuation

I. Finding the value of a bond
Bond value = $C \times [1 - 1/(1 + r)^t]/r + F/(1 + r)^t$
where:
    C = Coupon paid each period
    r = Rate per period
    t = Number of periods
    F = Bond's face value

II. Finding the yield on a bond
Given a bond value, coupon, time to maturity, and face value, it is possible to find the implicit discount rate, or yield to maturity, by trial and error only. To do this, try different discount rates in the preceding formula until the calculated bond value equals the given bond value. Remember that increasing the rate *decreases* the bond value.

EXAMPLE 6.3   **Bond Yields**

You're looking at two bonds identical in every way except for their coupons and, of course, their prices. Both have 12 years to maturity. The first bond has a 10 percent coupon rate and sells for $935.08. The second has a 12 percent coupon rate. What do you think it would sell for?

Because the two bonds are very similar, they will be priced to yield about the same rate. We first need to calculate the yield on the 10 percent coupon bond. Proceeding as before, we know that the yield must be greater than 10 percent because the bond is selling at a discount. The bond has a fairly long maturity of 12 years. We've seen that long-term bond prices are relatively sensitive to interest rate changes, so the yield is probably close to 10 percent. A little trial and error reveals that the yield is actually 11 percent:

$$\text{Bond value} = \$100 \times (1 - 1/1.11^{12})/.11 + \$1{,}000/1.11^{12}$$
$$= \$100 \times 6.4924 + \$1{,}000/3.4985$$
$$= \$649.24 + 285.84$$
$$= \$935.08$$

With an 11 percent yield, the second bond will sell at a premium because of its $120 coupon. Its value is:

$$\text{Bond value} = \$120 \times (1 - 1/1.11^{12})/.11 + \$1{,}000/1.11^{12}$$
$$= \$120 \times 6.4924 + \$1{,}000/3.4985$$
$$= \$779.08 + 285.84$$
$$= \$1{,}064.92$$

HOW TO CALCULATE BOND PRICES AND YIELDS USING A FINANCIAL CALCULATOR

CALCULATOR HINTS

Many financial calculators have fairly sophisticated built-in bond valuation routines. However, these vary quite a lot in implementation, and not all financial calculators have them. As a result, we will illustrate a simple way to handle bond problems that will work on just about any financial calculator.

To begin, of course, we first remember to clear out the calculator! Next, for Example 6.3, we have two bonds to consider, both with 12 years to maturity. The first one sells for $935.08 and has a 10 percent coupon rate. To find its yield, we can do the following:

Enter	12		100	−935.08	1,000
	N	**I/Y**	**PMT**	**PV**	**FV**
Solve for		11			

Notice that here we have entered both a future value of $1,000, representing the bond's face value, and a payment of 10 percent of $1,000, or $100, per year, representing the bond's annual coupon. Also notice that we have a negative sign on the bond's price, which we have entered as the present value.

For the second bond, we now know that the relevant yield is 11 percent. It has a 12 percent coupon and 12 years to maturity, so what's the price? To answer, we enter the relevant values and solve for the present value of the bond's cash flows:

Enter	12	11	120		1,000
	N	**I/Y**	**PMT**	**PV**	**FV**
Solve for				−1,064.92	

(continued)

There is an important detail that comes up here. Suppose we have a bond with a price of $902.29, 10 years to maturity, and a coupon rate of 6 percent. As we mentioned earlier, most bonds actually make semiannual payments. Assuming that this is the case for the bond here, what's the bond's yield to maturity? To answer, we need to enter the relevant numbers like this:

Enter	20		30	−902.29	1,000
	N	**I/Y**	**PMT**	**PV**	**FV**
Solve for		3.7			

Notice that we entered $30 as the payment because the bond actually makes payments of $30 every six months. Similarly, we entered 20 for N because there are actually 20 six-month periods. When we solve for the yield, we get 3.7 percent, but the tricky thing to remember is that this is the yield *per six months*, so we have to double it to get the right answer: $2 \times 3.7\% = 7.4$ percent, which would be the bond's reported yield.

SPREADSHEET STRATEGIES

HOW TO CALCULATE BOND PRICES AND YIELDS USING A SPREADSHEET

Like financial calculators, most spreadsheets have fairly elaborate routines available for calculating bond values and yields; many of these routines involve details that we have not discussed. However, setting up a simple spreadsheet to calculate prices or yields is straightforward, as our next two spreadsheets show:

	A	B	C	D	E	F	G	H
1								
2	Using a spreadsheet to calculate bond yields							
3								
4	Suppose we have a bond with 22 years to maturity, a coupon rate of 8 percent, and a price of							
5	$960.17. If the bond makes semiannual payments, what is its yield to maturity?							
6								
7	Settlement date:	1/1/00						
8	Maturity date:	1/1/22						
9	Annual coupon rate:	.08						
10	Bond price (% of par):	96.017						
11	Face value (% of par):	100						
12	Coupons per year:	2						
13	Yield to maturity:	**.084**						
14								
15	The formula entered in cell B13 is = YIELD(B7, B8, B9, B10, B11, B12); notice that face value and bond							
16	price are entered as a percentage of face value.							
17								

(continued)

	A	B	C	D	E	F	G	H
1								
2	Using a spreadsheet to calculate bond values							
3								
4	Suppose we have a bond with 22 years to maturity, a coupon rate of 8 percent, and a yield to							
5	maturity of 9 percent. If the bond makes semiannual payments, what is its price today?							
6								
7	Settlement date:	1/1/00						
8	Maturity date:	1/1/22						
9	Annual coupon rate:	.08						
10	Yield to maturity:	.09						
11	Face value (% of par):	100						
12	Coupons per year:	2						
13	Bond price (% of par):	**90.49**						
14								
15	The formula entered in cell B13 is = PRICE(B7, B8, B9, B10, B11, B12); notice that face value and bond							
16	price are entered as a percentage of face value.							
17								

In our spreadsheets, notice that we had to enter two dates, a settlement date and a maturity date. The settlement date is just the date you actually pay for the bond, and the maturity date is the day the bond actually matures. In most of our problems, we don't explicitly have these dates, so we have to make them up. For example, because our bond has 22 years to maturity, we just picked 1/1/2000 (January 1, 2000) as the settlement date and 1/1/2022 (January 1, 2022) as the maturity date. Any two dates would do as long as they were exactly 22 years apart, but these are particularly easy to work with. Finally, notice that we had to enter the coupon rate and yield to maturity in annual terms and then explicitly provide the number of coupon payments per year.

CONCEPT QUESTIONS

6.1a What are the cash flows associated with a bond?

6.1b What is the general expression for the value of a bond?

6.1c Is it true that the only risk associated with owning a bond is that the issuer will not make all the payments? Explain.

6.2 MORE ON BOND FEATURES

Excel Master coverage online

In this section, we continue our discussion of corporate debt by describing in some detail the basic terms and features that make up a typical long-term corporate bond. We discuss additional issues associated with long-term debt in subsequent sections.

Securities issued by corporations may be classified roughly as *equity securities* and *debt securities*. At the crudest level, a debt represents something that must be repaid; it is the result of borrowing money. When corporations borrow, they generally promise to make regularly scheduled interest payments and to repay the original amount borrowed (i.e., the principal). The person or firm making the loan is called the *creditor*, or *lender*. The corporation borrowing the money is called the *debtor*, or *borrower*.

From a financial point of view, the main differences between debt and equity are the following:

Information for bond investors can be found at www.investinginbonds .com.

1. Debt is not an ownership interest in the firm. Creditors generally do not have voting power.
2. The corporation's payment of interest on debt is considered a cost of doing business and is fully tax deductible. Dividends paid to stockholders are *not* tax deductible.
3. Unpaid debt is a liability of the firm. If it is not paid, the creditors can legally claim the assets of the firm. This action can result in liquidation or reorganization, two of the possible consequences of bankruptcy. Thus, one of the costs of issuing debt is the possibility of financial failure. This possibility does not arise when equity is issued.

Is It Debt or Equity?

Sometimes it is not clear if a particular security is debt or equity. Suppose a corporation issues a perpetual bond with interest payable solely from corporate income if, and only if, earned. Whether or not this is really a debt is hard to say and is primarily a legal and semantic issue. Courts and taxing authorities would have the final say.

Corporations are very adept at creating exotic, hybrid securities that have many features of equity but are treated as debt. Obviously, the distinction between debt and equity is very important for tax purposes. So, one reason that corporations try to create a debt security that is really equity is to obtain the tax benefits of debt and the bankruptcy benefits of equity.

As a general rule, equity represents an ownership interest, and it is a residual claim. This means that equity holders are paid after debt holders. As a result, the risks and benefits associated with owning debt and equity are different. To give one example, note that the maximum reward for owning a debt security is ultimately fixed by the amount of the loan, whereas there is no upper limit to the potential reward from owning an equity interest.

Long-Term Debt: The Basics

Ultimately, all long-term debt securities are promises made by the issuing firm to pay principal when due and to make timely interest payments on the unpaid balance. Beyond this, there are a number of features that distinguish these securities from one another. We discuss some of these features next.

The maturity of a long-term debt instrument is the length of time the debt remains outstanding with some unpaid balance. Debt securities can be short term (with maturities of one year or less) or long term (with maturities of more than one year).[1] Short-term debt is sometimes referred to as *unfunded debt*.[2]

Debt securities are typically called *notes*, *debentures*, or *bonds*. Strictly speaking, a bond is a secured debt. However, in common usage, the word *bond* refers to all kinds of secured and unsecured debt. We will, therefore, continue to use the term generically to refer to long-term debt.

The two major forms of long-term debt are public issue and private issue. We concentrate on public-issue bonds. Most of what we say about them holds true for private-issue, long-term debt as well. The main difference between public-issue and private-issue debt is

---

[1]There is no universally agreed-upon distinction between short-term and long-term debt. In addition, people often refer to intermediate-term debt, which has a maturity of more than 1 year and less than 3 to 5, or even 10, years.
[2]The word *funding* is part of the jargon of finance. It generally refers to the long term. Thus, a firm planning to "fund" its debt requirements may be replacing short-term debt with long-term debt.

that the latter is directly placed with a lender and not offered to the public. Because this is a private transaction, the specific terms are up to the parties involved.

There are many other dimensions to long-term debt, including such things as security, call features, sinking funds, ratings, and protective covenants. The following table illustrates these features for a bond issued by the cell phone company Sprint on February 22, 2018. If some of these terms are unfamiliar, have no fear. We discuss them all presently. Many of these features will be detailed in the bond indenture, so we discuss this first.

Features of a Sprint Bond		
Term		**Explanation**
Amount of issue	$1.5 billion	The company issued $1.5 billion worth of bonds.
Date of issue	02/22/2018	The bonds were sold on 02/22/2018.
Maturity	03/01/2026	The bonds mature on 03/01/2026.
Face value	$2,000	The denomination of the bonds is $2,000.
Annual coupon	7.625	Each bondholder will receive $152.50 per bond per year (7.625% of face value).
Offer price	100	The offer price will be 100% of the $2,000 face value, or $2,000, per bond.
Coupon payment dates	03/01, 09/01	Coupons of $152.50/2 = $76.25 will be paid on these dates.
Security	None	The bonds are not secured by specific assets.
Sinking fund	None	The bonds have no sinking fund.
Call provision	At any time	The bonds do not have a deferred call.
Call price	Treasury rate plus .50%.	The bonds have a "make-whole" call price.
Rating	Moody's B3; S&P B	The bonds have a "junk bond" credit rating.

The Indenture

The **indenture** is the written agreement between the corporation (the borrower) and its creditors. It is sometimes referred to as the *deed of trust*.[3] Usually, a trustee (a bank, perhaps) is appointed by the corporation to represent the bondholders. The trust company must (1) make sure the terms of the indenture are obeyed; (2) manage the sinking fund (described in the following pages); and (3) represent the bondholders in default, that is, if the company defaults on its payments to them.

indenture
The written agreement between the corporation and the lender detailing the terms of the debt issue.

The bond indenture is a legal document. It can run several hundred pages and generally makes for very tedious reading. It is an important document, however, because it generally includes the following provisions:

1. The basic terms of the bonds.
2. The total amount of bonds issued.
3. A description of property used as security.
4. The repayment arrangements.
5. The call provisions.
6. Details of the protective covenants.

We discuss these features next.

---

[3]The term *loan agreement* or *loan contract* is usually used for privately placed debt and term loans.

Terms of a Bond   Corporate bonds have historically had a face value (i.e., a denomination) of $1,000, although par values of $2,000 like the Sprint bond have become fairly common. This is called the *principal value*, and it is stated on the bond certificate. So, if a corporation wanted to borrow $1 million, 1,000 bonds with a face value of $1,000 would have to be sold. The par value (i.e., initial accounting value) of a bond is almost always the same as the face value, and the terms are used interchangeably in practice.

Corporate bonds are usually in **registered form**. For example, the indenture might read as follows:

> **Interest is payable semiannually on July 1 and January 1 of each year to the person in whose name the bond is registered at the close of business on June 15 or December 15, respectively.**

registered form
The registrar of a company records who owns each bond, and bond payments are made directly to the owner of record.

This means that the company has a registrar who will record the ownership of each bond and record any changes in ownership. The company will pay the interest and principal directly to the owner of record. Long ago, corporate bonds (and other types) had attached "coupons." To obtain an interest payment, the owner had to separate a coupon from the bond certificate and send it to the company registrar (the paying agent).

Alternatively, the bond could be in **bearer form**. This means that the certificate is the basic evidence of ownership, and the corporation will "pay the bearer." Ownership is not otherwise recorded, and, as with a registered bond with attached coupons, the holder of the bond certificate detaches the coupons and sends them to the company to receive payment.

bearer form
A bond issued without record of the owner's name; payment is made to whomever holds the bond.

There are two drawbacks to bearer bonds. First, they are difficult to recover if they are lost or stolen. Second, because the company does not know who owns its bonds, it cannot notify bondholders of important events. Bearer bonds were once the dominant type, but they are now much less common (in the United States) than registered bonds.

Security   Debt securities are classified according to the collateral and mortgages used to protect the bondholder.

Collateral is a general term that frequently means securities (e.g., bonds and stocks) that are pledged as security for payment of debt. For example, collateral trust bonds often involve a pledge of common stock held by the corporation. However, the term *collateral* is commonly used to refer to any asset pledged on a debt.

Mortgage securities are secured by a mortgage on the real property of the borrower. The property involved is usually real estate, for example, land or buildings. The legal document that describes the mortgage is called a *mortgage trust indenture* or *trust deed*. A "blanket" mortgage pledges all the real property owned by the company.[4]

debenture
Unsecured debt, usually with a maturity of 10 years or more.

Bonds frequently represent unsecured obligations of the company. A **debenture** is an unsecured bond, for which no specific pledge of property is made. The term **note** is generally used for such instruments if the maturity of the unsecured bond is less than 10 or so years from when the bond is originally issued. Debenture holders only have a claim on property not otherwise pledged; in other words, the property that remains after mortgages and collateral trusts are taken into account.

note
Unsecured debt, usually with a maturity of under 10 years.

The terminology that we use here and elsewhere in this chapter is standard in the United States. Outside the United States, these same terms can have different meanings.

---

[4]Real property includes land and things "affixed thereto." It does not include cash or inventories.

For example, bonds issued by the British government ("gilts") are called treasury "stock." Also, in the United Kingdom, a debenture is a *secured* obligation.

At the current time, almost all public bonds issued in the United States by industrial and financial companies are debentures. However, most utility and railroad bonds are secured by a pledge of assets.

Seniority   In general terms, *seniority* indicates preference in position over other lenders, and debts are sometimes labeled as *senior* or *junior* to indicate seniority. Some debt is *subordinated*, as in, for example, a subordinated debenture.

In the event of default, holders of subordinated debt must give preference to other specified creditors. Usually, this means that the subordinated lenders will be paid off only after the specified creditors have been compensated. However, debt cannot be subordinated to equity.

Repayment   Bonds can be repaid at maturity, at which time the bondholder will receive the stated, or face, value of the bond, or they may be repaid in part or in entirety before maturity. Early repayment in some form is more typical and often is handled through a sinking fund.

A **sinking fund** is an account managed by the bond trustee for the purpose of repaying the bonds. The company makes annual payments to the trustee, who then uses the funds to retire a portion of the debt. The trustee does this by either buying up some of the bonds in the market or calling in a fraction of the outstanding bonds. This second option is discussed in the next section.

There are many different kinds of sinking fund arrangements, and the details would be spelled out in the indenture. For example:

1. Some sinking funds start about 10 years after the initial issuance.
2. Some sinking funds establish equal payments over the life of the bond.
3. Some high-quality bond issues establish payments to the sinking fund that are insufficient to redeem the entire issue. As a consequence, there is the possibility of a large "balloon payment" at maturity.

The Call Provision   A **call provision** allows the company to repurchase, or "call," part or all of the bond issue at stated prices over a specific period. Corporate bonds are usually callable.

Generally, the call price is above the bond's stated value (that is, the par value). The difference between the call price and the stated value is the **call premium**. The amount of the call premium usually becomes smaller over time. One arrangement is to initially set the call premium equal to the annual coupon payment and then make it decline to zero as the call date moves closer to the time of maturity.

Call provisions are not usually operative during the first part of a bond's life. This makes the call provision less of a worry for bondholders in the bond's early years. For example, a company might be prohibited from calling its bonds for the first 10 years. This is a **deferred call provision**. During this period of prohibition, the bond is said to be **call protected**.

In the last few years, use of a new type of call provision, a "make-whole" call, has become very widespread in the corporate bond market. With such a feature, bondholders receive exactly what the bonds are worth if they are called. When bondholders don't suffer a loss in the event of a call, they are made whole.

To determine the make-whole call price, we calculate the present value of the remaining interest and principal payments at a rate specified in the indenture. For example, looking at

---

The Securities Industry and Financial Markets Association (SIFMA) website is www.sifma.org.

sinking fund
An account managed by the bond trustee for early bond redemption.

call provision
Agreement giving the issuer the option to repurchase a bond at a specific price prior to maturity.

call premium
The amount by which the call price exceeds the par value of the bond.

deferred call provision
Bond call provision prohibiting the company from redeeming the bond prior to a certain date.

call protected bond
Bond during period in which it cannot be redeemed by the issuer.

our Sprint issue, we see that the discount rate is "Treasury rate plus .50%." What this means is that we determine the discount rate by first finding a U.S. Treasury issue with the same maturity. We calculate the yield to maturity on the Treasury issue and then add on an additional .50 percent to get the discount rate we use.

Notice that, with a make-whole call provision, the call price is higher when interest rates are lower and vice versa (why?). Also notice that, as is common with a make-whole call, the Sprint issue does not have a deferred call feature. Why might investors not be too concerned about the absence of this feature?

protective covenant
A part of the indenture limiting certain actions that might be taken during the term of the loan, usually to protect the lender's interest.

Protective Covenants   A **protective covenant** is that part of the indenture or loan agreement that limits certain actions a company might otherwise wish to take during the term of the loan. Protective covenants can be classified into two types: negative covenants and positive (or affirmative) covenants.

A *negative covenant* is a "thou shalt not" type of covenant. It limits or prohibits actions that the company might take. Here are some typical examples:

1. The firm must limit the amount of dividends it pays according to some formula.
2. The firm cannot pledge any assets to other lenders.
3. The firm cannot merge with another firm.
4. The firm cannot sell or lease any major assets without approval by the lender.
5. The firm cannot issue additional long-term debt.

A *positive covenant* is a "thou shalt" type of covenant. It specifies an action that the company agrees to take or a condition the company must abide by. Here are some examples:

1. The company must maintain its working capital at or above some specified minimum level.
2. The company must periodically furnish audited financial statements to the lender.
3. The firm must maintain any collateral or security in good condition.

This is only a partial list of covenants; a particular indenture may feature many different ones.

Want detailed information on the amount and terms of the debt issued by a particular firm? Check out the firm's latest financial statements by searching SEC filings at www.sec.gov.

CONCEPT QUESTIONS

6.2a   What are the distinguishing features of debt as compared to equity?

6.2b   What is the indenture? What are protective covenants? Give some examples.

6.2c   What is a sinking fund?

6.3 BOND RATINGS

Firms frequently pay to have their debt rated. The two leading bond-rating firms are Moody's and Standard and Poor's (S&P). The debt ratings are an assessment of the creditworthiness of the corporate issuer. The definitions of creditworthiness used by Moody's and S&P are based on how likely the firm is to default and the protection creditors have in the event of a default.

It is important to recognize that bond ratings are concerned *only* with the possibility of default. Earlier, we discussed interest rate risk, which we defined as the risk of a change in the value of a bond resulting from a change in interest rates. Bond ratings do not address this issue. As a result, the price of a highly rated bond can still be quite volatile.

Bond ratings are constructed from information supplied by the corporation. The rating classes and some information concerning them are shown in the following table.

	Investment-Quality Bond Ratings				Low-Quality, Speculative, and/or "Junk" Bond Ratings					
	High Grade		Medium Grade		Low Grade		Very Low Grade			
Standard & Poor's	AAA	AA	A	BBB	BB	B	CCC	CC	C	D
Moody's	Aaa	Aa	A	Baa	Ba	B	Caa	Ca	C	

Moody's	S&P	
Aaa	AAA	Debt rated Aaa and AAA has the highest rating. Capacity to pay interest and principal is extremely strong.
Aa	AA	Debt rated Aa and AA has a very strong capacity to pay interest and repay principal. Together with the highest rating, this group constitutes the high-grade bond class.
A	A	Debt rated A has a strong capacity to pay interest and repay principal, although it is somewhat more susceptible to the adverse effects of changes in circumstances and economic conditions than debt in higher-rated categories.
Baa	BBB	Debt rated Baa and BBB is regarded as having an adequate capacity to pay interest and repay principal. Whereas it normally exhibits adequate protection parameters, adverse economic conditions or changing circumstances are more likely to lead to a weakened capacity to pay interest and repay principal for debt in this category than in higher-rated categories. These bonds are medium-grade obligations.
Ba; B Caa Ca C	BB; B CCC CC C	Debt rated in these categories is regarded, on balance, as predominantly speculative with respect to capacity to pay interest and repay principal in accordance with the terms of the obligation. BB and Ba indicate the lowest degree of speculation, and Ca, CC, and C the highest degree of speculation. Although such debt is likely to have some quality and protective characteristics, these are outweighed by large uncertainties or major risk exposures to adverse conditions. Issues rated C by Moody's are typically in default.
	D	Debt rated D is in default, and payment of interest and/or repayment of principal is in arrears.

Note: At times, both Moody's and S&P use adjustments (called notches) to these ratings. S&P uses plus and minus signs: A+ is the strongest A rating and A− the weakest. Moody's uses a 1, 2, or 3 designation, with 1 being the highest.

The highest rating a firm's debt can have is AAA or Aaa, and such debt is judged to be the best quality and to have the lowest degree of default risk. For example, the Sprint issue we discussed earlier was rated B. The AAA rating is not awarded very often: As of 2018, only two nonfinancial U.S. companies have AAA ratings, Johnson & Johnson and Microsoft. AA or Aa ratings indicate very good quality debt and are much more common. The lowest rating is D, for debt that is in default.

Beginning in the 1980s, a growing part of corporate borrowing has taken the form of low-grade, or "junk," bonds. If these low-grade corporate bonds are rated at all, they are rated below investment grade by the major rating agencies. Investment-grade bonds are bonds rated at least BBB by S&P or Baa by Moody's.

Some bonds are called "crossover" or "5B" bonds. The reason is that they are rated triple-B (or Baa) by one rating agency and double-B (or Ba) by another, a "split rating." For example, in February 2016, India-based textile and chemical company Standard Industries sold an issue of 10-year notes rated BBB− by S&P and Ba2 by Moody's.

Want to know what criteria are commonly used to rate corporate and municipal bonds? Go to www.standardandpoors .com, www.moodys.com, or www.fitchinv.com.

A bond's credit rating can change as the issuer's financial strength improves or deteriorates. For example, in January 2018, Moody's downgraded Teva Pharmaceuticals from investment grade to junk bond status. Bonds that drop into junk territory from above are called "fallen angels." Why was Teva downgraded? The reason given by Moody's was a much higher debt load because of an ill-timed acquisition and weakening sales of a major drug. Executives of the company also had been accused of collaborating with contractors to pay bribes to politicians.

Credit ratings are important because defaults really do occur, and, when they do, investors can lose heavily. For example, in 2000, AmeriServe Food Distribution, Inc., which supplied restaurants such as Burger King with everything from burgers to giveaway toys, defaulted on $200 million in junk bonds. After the default, the bonds traded at just 18 cents on the dollar, leaving investors with a loss of more than $160 million.

Even worse in AmeriServe's case, the bonds had been issued only four months earlier, thereby making AmeriServe an NCAA champion. While that might be a good thing for a college basketball team such as the University of Kentucky Wildcats, in the bond market it means "No Coupon At All," and it's not a good thing for investors.

CONCEPT QUESTIONS

6.3a   What is a junk bond?

6.3b   What does a bond rating say about the risk of fluctuations in a bond's value resulting from interest rate changes?

6.4   SOME DIFFERENT TYPES OF BONDS

Thus far, we have considered only "plain vanilla" corporate bonds. In this section, we briefly look at bonds issued by governments and also at bonds with unusual features.

Government Bonds

If you're nervous about the level of debt piled up by the U.S. government, don't go to www.public debt.treas.gov or to www.usdebtclock.org! Learn all about government bonds at www.newyorkfed.org.

The biggest borrower in the world—by a wide margin—is everybody's favorite family member, Uncle Sam. In mid-2018, the total debt of the U.S. government was more than $21.5 *trillion*, or about $64,500 per U.S. citizen (and growing rapidly). When the government wishes to borrow money for more than one year, it sells what are known as Treasury notes and bonds to the public (in fact, it does so every month). Treasury notes have original maturities ranging from 2 to 10 years, while Treasury bonds have longer maturities, extending out as far as 30 years.

Most U.S. Treasury issues are ordinary coupon bonds. There are two important things to keep in mind, however. First, U.S. Treasury issues, unlike essentially all other bonds, have no default risk because (we hope) the Treasury always can come up with the money to make the payments. Second, Treasury issues are exempt from state income taxes (though not federal income taxes). In other words, the coupons you receive on a Treasury note or bond are taxed only at the federal level.

State and local governments also borrow money by selling notes and bonds. Such issues are called *municipal* notes and bonds, or "munis." Unlike Treasury issues, munis have varying degrees of default risk, and, in fact, they are rated much like corporate issues. Also, they are almost always callable. The most intriguing thing about munis is that their coupons are exempt from federal income taxes (and state income taxes in some cases), which makes them very attractive to high-income, high-tax-bracket investors.

Because of the enormous tax break they receive, the yields on municipal bonds are much lower than the yields on taxable bonds. For example, in the middle of 2018, long-term, high-quality corporate bonds were yielding about 4.2 percent. At the same time, long-term, high-quality munis were yielding about 2.8 percent. Suppose an investor was in a 30 percent tax bracket. All else being the same, would this investor prefer an Aa corporate bond or an Aa municipal bond?

To answer, we need to compare the *aftertax* yields on the two bonds. Ignoring state and local taxes, the muni pays 2.8 percent on both a pretax and an aftertax basis. The corporate issue pays 4.2 percent before taxes, but it only pays $.042 \times (1 - .30) = .029$, or 2.9 percent, once we account for the 30 percent tax bite. Given this, the yields are quite close.

EXAMPLE 6.4 **Taxable versus Municipal Bonds**

Suppose taxable bonds are currently yielding 8 percent, while at the same time, munis of comparable risk and maturity are yielding 6 percent. Which is more attractive to an investor in a 40 percent tax bracket? What is the break-even tax rate? How do you interpret this rate?

For an investor in a 40 percent tax bracket, a taxable bond yields $8 \times (1 - .40) = 4.8$ percent after taxes, so the muni is much more attractive. The break-even tax rate is the tax rate at which an investor would be indifferent between a taxable and a nontaxable issue. If we let t^* stand for the break-even tax rate, then we can solve for it as follows:

$$.08 \times (1 - t^*) = .06$$
$$1 - t^* = .06/.08 = .75$$
$$t^* = .25 \text{ or } 25\%$$

Thus, an investor in a 25 percent tax bracket would make 6 percent after taxes from either bond.

Zero Coupon Bonds

A bond that pays no coupons at all must be offered at a price that is much lower than its stated value. Such bonds are called **zero coupon bonds**, or *zeroes*.[5]

Suppose the Eight-Inch Nails (EIN) Company issues a $1,000 face value, five-year zero coupon bond. The initial price is set at $508.35. Even though no interest payments are made on the bond, zero coupon bond calculations use semiannual periods to be consistent with coupon bond calculations. Using semiannual periods, it is straightforward to verify that, at this price, the bond yields 14 percent to maturity. The total interest paid over the life of the bond is $1,000 - 508.35 = $491.65.

For tax purposes, the issuer of a zero coupon bond deducts interest every year even though no interest is actually paid. Similarly, the owner must pay taxes on interest accrued every year, even though no interest is actually received.

zero coupon bond
A bond that makes no coupon payments, and thus is initially priced at a deep discount.

---

[5]A bond issued with a very low coupon rate (as opposed to a zero coupon rate) is an original-issue discount (OID) bond.

TABLE 6.2	Year	Beginning Value	Ending Value	Implicit Interest Expense	Straight-Line Interest Expense
Interest expense for EIN's zeroes	1	$508.35	$ 582.01	$ 73.66	$ 98.33
	2	582.01	666.34	84.33	98.33
	3	666.34	762.90	96.55	98.33
	4	762.90	873.44	110.54	98.33
	5	873.44	1,000.00	126.56	98.33
	Total			$491.65	$491.65

Another good bond market site is money.cnn.com.

The way in which the yearly interest on a zero coupon bond is calculated is governed by tax law. Before 1982, corporations could calculate the interest deduction on a straight-line basis. For EIN, the annual interest deduction would have been $491.65/5 = $98.33 per year.

Under current tax law, the implicit interest is determined by amortizing the loan. We do this by first calculating the bond's value at the beginning of each year. For example, after one year, the bond will have four years until maturity, so it will be worth $1,000/1.07^8 = $582.01; the value in two years will be $1,000/1.07^6 = $666.34; and so on. The implicit interest each year is the change in the bond's value for the year. The values and interest expenses for the EIN bond are listed in Table 6.2.

Notice that under the old rules, zero coupon bonds were more attractive for corporations because the deductions for interest expense were larger in the early years (compare the implicit interest expense with the straight-line expense).

Under current tax law, EIN could deduct $73.66 in interest paid the first year, and the owner of the bond would pay taxes on $73.66 of taxable income (even though no interest was actually received). This second tax feature makes taxable zero coupon bonds less attractive to individuals. However, they are still a very attractive investment for tax-exempt investors with long-term dollar-denominated liabilities, such as pension funds, because the future dollar value is known with relative certainty.

Some bonds are zero coupon bonds for only part of their lives. For example, at one time, General Motors had a debenture outstanding that matured on March 15, 2036. For the first 20 years, no coupon payments were scheduled, but 20 years into the bond's life, it was to begin paying coupons at a rate of 7.75 percent per year, payable semiannually.

Floating-Rate Bonds

The conventional bonds we have talked about in this chapter have fixed-dollar obligations because the coupon rate is set as a fixed percentage of the par value. Similarly, the principal is set equal to the par value. Under these circumstances, the coupon payment and principal are completely fixed.

With *floating-rate bonds (floaters)*, the coupon payments are adjustable. The adjustments are tied to an interest rate index such as the Treasury bill interest rate or the 30-year Treasury bond rate. The value of a floating-rate bond depends on exactly how the coupon payment adjustments are defined. In most cases, the coupon adjusts with a lag to some base rate. Suppose a coupon rate adjustment is made on June 1. The adjustment might be based on the simple average of Treasury bond yields during the previous three months.

In addition, the majority of floaters have the following features:

1. The holder has the right to redeem the note at par on the coupon payment date after some specified amount of time. This is called a *put* provision, and it is discussed in the following section.

2. The coupon rate has a floor and a ceiling, meaning that the coupon is subject to a minimum and a maximum. In this case, the coupon rate is said to be "capped," and the upper and lower rates are sometimes called the *collar*.

Official information on U.S. inflation-indexed bonds is at www .treasurydirect.gov.

A particularly interesting type of floating-rate bond is an *inflation-linked* bond. Such bonds have coupons that are adjusted according to the rate of inflation (the principal amount may be adjusted as well). The U.S. Treasury began issuing such bonds in January of 1997. The issues are sometimes called "TIPS," or Treasury Inflation-Protected Securities. Other countries, including Canada, Israel, and Britain, have issued similar securities.

Other Types of Bonds

Many bonds have unusual, or exotic, features. Unfortunately, there are far too many variations for us to cover in detail here. We therefore focus on only a few of the more common types.

Structured notes are bonds that are based on stocks, bonds, commodities, or currencies. One particular type of structured note has a return based on a stock market index. At expiration, if the stock index has declined, the bond returns the principal. However, if the stock index has increased, the bond will return a portion of the stock index return, say 80 percent. Another type of structured note will return twice the stock index return, but with the potential for loss of principal.

A *convertible bond* can be swapped for a fixed number of shares of stock anytime before maturity at the holder's option. Convertibles are relatively common, but the number has been decreasing in recent years.

A *put bond* allows the *holder* to force the issuer to buy the bond back at a stated price. The put feature is therefore the reverse of the call provision and is a relatively new development.

A given bond may have many unusual features. For example, two exotic bonds include CoCo bonds, which have a coupon payment, and NoNo bonds, which are zero coupon bonds. CoCo and NoNo bonds are contingent convertible, putable, callable, subordinated bonds. The contingent convertible clause is similar to the normal conversion feature, except the contingency feature must be met. For example, a contingency feature may require that the company stock trade at 110 percent of the conversion price for 20 out of 30 days. Valuing a bond of this sort can be quite complex, and the yield to maturity calculation is often meaningless. The nearby *Finance Matters* box provides some more examples of exotic bonds.

CONCEPT QUESTIONS

6.4a What do you think would be the effect of a call provision on a bond's coupon? Why might an investor want to buy a callable bond?

6.4b What do you think would be the effect of a put feature on a bond's coupon? How about a convertibility feature? Why?

Exotic Bonds

Bonds come in many flavors. The unusual types are called "exotics" and can range from the fairly simple to the truly esoteric. Take the case of mortgage-backed securities (MBSs). MBSs are a type of securitized financial instrument. In securitization, cash flows from financial assets are pooled together into securities, and the securities are sold to investors. With an MBS, banks or mortgage brokers who originate mortgages sell the mortgages to a trust. The trust pools the mortgages and sells bonds to investors. Bondholders receive payments based on the mortgage payments made by homeowners. During 2008, problems with MBSs skyrocketed due to the precipitous drop in real estate values and the sharply increased default rates on the underlying mortgages.

The reverse convertible is a relatively new type of structured note. One type generally offers a high coupon rate, but the redemption at maturity can be paid in cash at par value or paid in shares of stock. For example, one recent General Motors (GM) reverse convertible had a coupon rate of 16 percent, which is a very high coupon rate in today's interest rate environment. However, at maturity, if GM's stock declined sufficiently, bondholders would receive a fixed number of GM shares that were worth less than par value. So, while the income portion of the bond return would be high, the potential loss in par value easily could erode the extra return.

CAT bonds are issued to cover insurance companies against natural catastrophes. The type of natural catastrophe is outlined in the bond. For example, about 30 percent of all CAT bonds protect against a North Atlantic hurricane. The way these issues are structured is that the borrowers can suspend payment temporarily (or even permanently) if they have significant hurricane-related losses. These CAT bonds may seem like pretty risky investments, but, to date, only five have not been paid in full. Because of Hurricane Katrina, CAT bondholders lost $190 million. CAT bondholders also lost $300 million due to the 2011 tsunami in Japan. During 2011, two other CAT bond issues, each worth $100 million, were triggered due to an unusually active tornado season, and a CAT bond was triggered due to the 2017 earthquake in Mexico. This bond was issued on August 4th and the earthquake occurred on September 7th.

Perhaps the most unusual bond (and certainly the most ghoulish) is the "death bond." Companies such as Stone Street Financial purchase life insurance policies from individuals who are expected to die within the next 10 years. They then sell bonds that are paid off from the life insurance proceeds received when the policyholders die. The return on the bonds to investors depends on how long the policyholders live. A major risk is that if medical treatment advances quickly, it will raise the life expectancy of the policyholders, thereby decreasing the return to the bondholder.

6.5 BOND MARKETS

Excel
Master
coverage online

Bonds are bought and sold in enormous quantities every day. You may be surprised to learn that the trading volume in bonds on a typical day is many, many times larger than the trading volume in stocks (by trading volume, we mean the amount of money that changes hands). Here is a finance trivia question: What is the largest securities market in the world? Most people would guess the New York Stock Exchange. In fact, the largest securities market in the world in terms of trading volume is the U.S. Treasury market.

How Bonds Are Bought and Sold

As we mentioned all the way back in Chapter 1, most trading in bonds takes place over the counter, or OTC. Recall that this means that there is no particular place where buying and selling occur. Instead, dealers around the country (and around the world) stand ready to buy and sell. The various dealers are connected electronically.

One reason the bond markets are so big is that the number of bond issues far exceeds the number of stock issues. There are two reasons for this. First, a corporation would typically have only one common stock issue outstanding (there are exceptions to this that we discuss in our next chapter). However, a single large corporation could easily have a dozen or more note and bond issues outstanding. Beyond this, federal, state, and local borrowing is enormous. For example, even a small city would usually have a wide variety of notes and bonds outstanding, representing money borrowed to pay for things like roads, sewers, and schools. When you think about how many small cities there are in the United States, you begin to get the picture!

Because the bond market is almost entirely OTC, it has historically had little or no *transparency*. A financial market is transparent if it is possible to easily observe its prices and trading volume. On the New York Stock Exchange, for example, it is possible to see the price and quantity for every single transaction. In contrast, in the bond market, historically it was not possible to observe either. Transactions are privately negotiated between parties, and there is little or no centralized reporting of transactions.

Although the total volume of trading in bonds far exceeds that in stocks, only a very small fraction of the total bond issues that exist actually trade on a given day. This means that getting up-to-date prices on individual bonds is often difficult or impossible, particularly for smaller corporate or municipal issues. Instead, a variety of sources of estimated prices exist and are very commonly used.

W🌐RK THE WEB

Bond quotes have become more available with the rise of the web. One site where you can find current bond prices (from TRACE) is finra-markets.morningstar.com/BondCenter. We went to the site and entered "AZO" for AutoZone, the well-known auto parts company. We found a total of 10 bond issues outstanding. Here you see the information we pulled up.

Issuer Name	Symbol	Callable	Sub-Product Type	Coupon	Maturity	Ratings Moody's®	S&P	Last Sale Price	Yield
AUTOZONE INC	AZO3996669	Yes	Corporate Bond	3.125	07/15/2023	Baa1	BBB	97.564	3.655
AUTOZONE INC	AZO.GI	Yes	Corporate Bond	7.125	08/01/2018	Baa1	BBB	100.529	2.612
AUTOZONE INC	AZO3925874	Yes	Corporate Bond	2.875	01/15/2023	Baa1	BBB	96.504	3.711
AUTOZONE INC	AZO3844612	Yes	Corporate Bond	3.700	04/15/2022	Baa1	BBB	100.733	3.480
AUTOZONE INC	AZO4235546	Yes	Corporate Bond	2.500	04/15/2021	Baa1	BBB	97.586	3.403
AUTOZONE INC	AZO4354812	Yes	Corporate Bond	3.125	04/21/2026	Baa1	BBB	92.845	4.205
AUTOZONE INC	AZO4235610	Yes	Corporate Bond	3.250	04/15/2025	Baa1	BBB	95.108	4.078
AUTOZONE INC	AZO.GK	Yes	Corporate Bond	4.000	11/15/2020	Baa1	BBB	101.758	3.152
AUTOZONE INC	AZO4354853	Yes	Corporate Bond	1.625	04/21/2019	Baa1	BBB	99.448	2.290
AUTOZONE INC	AZO4482985	Yes	Corporate Bond	3.750	06/01/2027	Baa1	BBB	96.408	4.236

Most of the information is self-explanatory. The Price and Yield columns show the price and yield to maturity of the issues based on their most recent sales. If you need more information about a particular issue, clicking on it will give you more details such as coupon dates and call dates.

QUESTIONS

1. Go to this website and find the last bond shown in the accompanying table. When was this bond issued? What was the size of the bond issue? What were the yield to maturity and price when the bond was issued?

2. When you search for Chevron bonds (CVX), you will find bonds for several companies listed. Why do you think Chevron has bonds issued with different corporate names?

Bond Price Reporting

To learn more about TRACE, visit www.finra .org.

In 2002, transparency in the corporate bond market began to improve dramatically. Under new regulations, corporate bond dealers are now required to report trade information through what is known as the Trade Reporting and Compliance Engine (TRACE). A nearby *Work the Web* box shows how to get TRACE prices.

As we mentioned before, the U.S. Treasury market is the largest securities market in the world. As with bond markets in general, it is an OTC market, so there is limited transparency. However, unlike the situation with bond markets in general, trading in Treasury issues, particularly recently issued ones, is very heavy. Each day, representative prices for outstanding Treasury issues are reported.

To purchase newly issued corporate bonds, go to www.incapital.com.

Figure 6.3 shows a portion of the daily Treasury note and bond listings from *The Wall Street Journal* online. The only difference between a Treasury note and a Treasury bond is that notes have 10 years or less to maturity at the time of issuance. The entry that begins "5/15/2030" is highlighted. Reading from left to right, the "5/15/2030" tells us that the bond's maturity is May 15, 2030. The 6.250 is the bond's coupon rate. Treasury bonds all make semiannual payments and have a face value of $1,000, so this bond will pay $31.25 per six months until it matures.

To buy Treasury bonds directly from the government, go to www .treasurydirect.gov.

The next two pieces of information are the **bid** and **asked prices**. In general, in any OTC or dealer market, the bid price represents what a dealer is willing to pay for a security, and the asked price (or "ask" price) is what a dealer is willing to take for it. The difference between the two prices is called the **bid-ask spread** (or "spread"), and it represents the dealer's profit.

Treasury prices are quoted as a percentage of face value. The bid price, or what a dealer is willing to pay for the bond, on the 5/15/2030 bond is 132.8984. With a $1,000 face value, this quote represents $1,328.984. The asked price, or the price at which the dealer is willing to sell the bond, is 132.9609, or $1,329.609.

The next number quoted is the change in the asked price from the previous day, measured as a percentage of face value, so this issue's asked price rose by .4688 percent, or $4.688, in value from the previous day. Finally, the last number reported is the yield to maturity, based on the asked price. Notice that this is a premium bond because it sells for more than its face value. Not surprisingly, its yield to maturity (2.949 percent) is less than its coupon rate (6.25 percent).

The Federal Reserve Bank of St. Louis maintains dozens of online files containing macroeconomic data as well as rates on U.S. Treasury issues. Go to fred.stlouisfed.org.

The very last ordinary bond listed, in this case the 5/15/2048, is often called the "bellwether" bond. This bond's yield is the one that is usually reported in the evening news. So, for example, when you hear that long-term interest rates rose, what is really being said is that the yield on this bond went up (and its price went down).

If you examine the yields on the various issues in Figure 6.3, you clearly see that they vary by maturity. Why this occurs and what it might mean is one of the things we discuss in our next section.

bid price
The price a dealer is willing to pay for a security.

asked price
The price a dealer is willing to take for a security.

bid-ask spread
The difference between the bid price and the asked price.

EXAMPLE 6.5   Treasury Quotes

Locate the Treasury issue in Figure 6.3 maturing in February 2024. What is its coupon rate? What is its bid price? What was the *previous day's* asked price?

The bond listed as 2/29/2024 is the one we seek. Its coupon rate is 2.125 percent of face value. The bid price is 96.1172, or 96.1172 percent of face value. The ask price is 96.1328, which is up by .1484 from the previous day. This means that the ask price on the previous day was equal to 96.1328 − .1484 = 95.9844.

A Note on Bond Price Quotes   If you buy a bond between coupon payment dates, the price you pay is usually more than the price you are quoted. The reason is that standard convention in the bond market is to quote prices net of "accrued interest," meaning that

U.S. Treasury Quotes

Treasury note and bond data are representative over-the-counter quotations as of 3 p.m. Eastern time.

FIGURE 6.3

Sample *Wall Street Journal* U.S. Treasury note and bond prices

Maturity	Coupon	Bid	Asked	Chg	Asked Yield
1/31/2019	1.500	99.5469	99.5625	−0.0078	2.205
12/31/2021	2.125	97.8906	97.9063	0.0703	2.749
1/31/2022	1.500	95.6563	95.6719	0.0547	2.762
2/28/2023	2.625	99.2109	99.2266	0.1172	2.801
9/30/2023	1.375	92.7969	92.8125	0.1172	2.847
2/29/2024	2.125	96.1172	96.1328	0.1484	2.864
7/31/2024	2.125	95.7344	95.7500	0.1172	2.887
1/31/2025	2.500	97.6328	97.6484	0.1953	2.892
4/30/2025	2.875	99.8359	99.8516	0.2109	2.899
11/15/2026	6.500	126.6406	126.6563	0.3125	2.906
2/15/2029	5.250	120.9453	121.0078	0.4063	2.941
5/15/2030	6.250	132.8984	132.9609	0.4688	2.949
2/15/2036	4.500	120.9375	121.0000	0.5625	2.964
5/15/2037	5.000	129.0938	129.1563	0.6641	2.973
11/15/2039	4.375	121.3047	121.3672	0.6953	3.014
5/15/2040	4.375	121.5313	121.5938	0.7500	3.021
8/15/2041	3.750	111.6875	111.7500	0.7500	3.040
5/15/2042	3.000	99.1875	99.2188	0.7266	3.046
2/15/2043	3.125	101.1641	101.1953	0.7344	3.056
2/15/2044	3.625	110.0313	110.0625	0.6875	3.056
8/15/2046	2.250	84.6797	84.7109	0.6016	3.064
5/15/2047	3.000	98.7578	98.7891	0.6953	3.063
5/15/2048	3.125	101.1875	101.2188	0.7422	3.062

Source: www.wsj.com, 6/14/2018.

accrued interest is deducted to arrive at the quoted price. This quoted price is called the **clean price**. The price you actually pay, however, includes the accrued interest. This price is the **dirty price**, also known as the "full" or "invoice" price.

An example is the easiest way to understand these issues. Suppose you buy a bond with a 12 percent annual coupon, payable semiannually. You actually pay $1,080 for this bond, so $1,080 is the dirty, or invoice, price. Further, on the day you buy it, the next coupon is due in four months, so you are between coupon dates. Notice that the next coupon will be $60.

The accrued interest on a bond is calculated by taking the fraction of the coupon period that has passed, in this case two months out of six, and multiplying this fraction by the next coupon, $60. So, the accrued interest in this example is 2/6 × $60 = $20. The bond's quoted price (i.e., its clean price) would be $1,080 − 20 = $1,060.

clean price
The price of a bond net of accrued interest; this is the price that is typically quoted.

dirty price
The price of a bond including accrued interest, also known as the *full* or *invoice price*. This is the price the buyer actually pays.

CONCEPT QUESTIONS

6.5a Why do we say bond markets may have little or no transparency?

6.5b In general, what are bid and ask prices?

6.5c What is the difference between a bond's clean price and dirty price?

6.6 INFLATION AND INTEREST RATES

So far, we haven't considered the role of inflation in our various discussions of interest rates, yields, and returns. Because this is an important consideration, we consider the impact of inflation next.

Real versus Nominal Rates

real rates
Interest rates or rates of return that have been adjusted for inflation.

nominal rates
Interest rates or rates of return that have not been adjusted for inflation.

In examining interest rates, or any other financial market rates such as discount rates, bond yields, rates of return, and required returns, it is often necessary to distinguish between **real rates** and **nominal rates**. Nominal rates are called "nominal" because they have not been adjusted for inflation. Real rates are rates that have been adjusted for inflation.

To see the effect of inflation, suppose prices currently are rising by 5 percent per year. In other words, the rate of inflation is 5 percent. An investment is available that will be worth $115.50 in one year. It costs $100 today. Notice that with a present value of $100 and a future value in one year of $115.50, this investment has a 15.5 percent rate of return. In calculating this 15.5 percent return, we did not consider the effect of inflation, however, so this is the nominal return.

What is the impact of inflation here? To answer, suppose pizzas cost $5 apiece at the beginning of the year. With $100, we can buy 20 pizzas. Because the inflation rate is 5 percent, pizzas will cost 5 percent more, or $5.25, at the end of the year. If we take the investment, how many pizzas can we buy at the end of the year? Measured in pizzas, what is the rate of return on this investment?

Our $115.50 from the investment will buy us $115.50/5.25 = 22 pizzas. This is up from 20 pizzas, so our pizza rate of return is 10 percent. What this illustrates is that even though the nominal return on our investment is 15.5 percent, our buying power goes up by only 10 percent because of inflation. Put another way, we are really only 10 percent richer. In this case, we say that the real return is 10 percent.

Alternatively, we can say that with 5 percent inflation, each of the 115.50 nominal dollars we get is worth 5 percent less in real terms, so the real dollar value of our investment in a year is:

$115.50/1.05 = $110

What we have done is to *deflate* the $115.50 by 5 percent. Because we give up $100 in current buying power to get the equivalent of $110, our real return is again 10 percent. Now that we have removed the effect of future inflation, this $110 is said to be measured in current dollars.

The difference between nominal and real rates is important and bears repeating:

> **The nominal rate on an investment is the percentage change in the number of dollars you have.**
> **The real rate on an investment is the percentage change in how much you can buy with your dollars, in other words, the percentage change in your buying power.**

The Fisher Effect

Fisher effect
The relationship among nominal returns, real returns, and inflation.

Our discussion of real and nominal returns illustrates a relationship often called the **Fisher effect** (after the great economist Irving Fisher). Because investors are ultimately concerned with what they can buy with their money, they require compensation for inflation.

Let R stand for the nominal rate and r stand for the real rate. The Fisher effect tells us that the relationship between nominal rates, real rates, and inflation can be written as:

$$1 + R = (1 + r) \times (1 + h) \qquad\qquad\qquad [6.2]$$

where h is the inflation rate.

In the preceding example, the nominal rate was 15.50 percent, and the inflation rate was 5 percent. What was the real rate? We can determine it by plugging in these numbers:

$$
\begin{aligned}
1 + .1550 &= (1 + r) \times (1 + .05) \\
1 + r &= 1.1550/1.05 = 1.10 \\
r &= .10, \text{ or } 10\%
\end{aligned}
$$

This real rate is the same as we had before. If we take another look at the Fisher effect, we can rearrange things a little as follows:

$$
\begin{aligned}
1 + R &= (1 + r) \times (1 + h) \\
R &= r + h + r \times h \qquad\qquad\qquad [6.3]
\end{aligned}
$$

What this tells us is that the nominal rate has three components. First, there is the real rate on the investment, r. Next, there is the compensation for the decrease in the value of the money originally invested because of inflation, h. The third component represents compensation for the fact that the dollars earned on the investment also are worth less because of the inflation.

This third component is usually small, so it is often dropped. The nominal rate is then approximately equal to the real rate plus the inflation rate:

$$R \approx r + h \qquad\qquad\qquad [6.4]$$

EXAMPLE 6.6 The Fisher Effect

If investors require a 10 percent real rate of return, and the inflation rate is 8 percent, what must the approximate nominal rate be? The exact nominal rate?

First of all, the nominal rate is approximately equal to the sum of the real rate and the inflation rate: 10% + 8% = 18%. From the Fisher effect, we have:

$$
\begin{aligned}
1 + R &= (1 + r) \times (1 + h) \\
&= 1.10 \times 1.08 \\
&= 1.1880
\end{aligned}
$$

Therefore, the nominal rate will actually be closer to 19 percent.

It is important to note that financial rates, such as interest rates, discount rates, and rates of return, are almost always quoted in nominal terms. To remind you of this, we will henceforth use the symbol R instead of r in most of our discussions about such rates.

CONCEPT QUESTIONS

6.6a What is the difference between a nominal and a real return? Which is more important to a typical investor?

6.6b What is the Fisher effect?

6.7 DETERMINANTS OF BOND YIELDS

We are now in a position to discuss the determinants of a bond's yield. As we will see, the yield on any particular bond is a reflection of a variety of factors, some common to all bonds and some specific to the issue under consideration.

The Term Structure of Interest Rates

At any point in time, short-term and long-term interest rates will generally be different. Sometimes short-term rates are higher, sometimes lower. Figure 6.4 gives us a long-range perspective on this by showing over two centuries of short- and long-term interest rates. As shown, through time, the difference between short- and long-term rates has ranged from essentially zero to up to several percentage points, both positive and negative.

The relationship between short- and long-term interest rates is known as the **term structure of interest rates.** To be a little more precise, the term structure of interest rates tells us what *nominal* interest rates are on *default-free, pure discount* bonds of all maturities. These rates are, in essence, "pure" interest rates because they involve no risk of default and a single, lump-sum future payment. In other words, the term structure tells us the pure time value of money for different lengths of time.

When long-term rates are higher than short-term rates, we say that the term structure is upward sloping, and when short-term rates are higher, we say it is downward sloping. The term structure also can be "humped." When this occurs, it is usually because rates increase at first, but then begin to decline as we look at longer- and longer-term rates. The most common shape of the term structure, particularly in modern times, is upward sloping, but the degree of steepness has varied quite a bit.

term structure of interest rates

The relationship between nominal interest rates on default-free, pure discount securities and time to maturity; that is, the pure time value of money.

FIGURE 6.4   **U.S. interest rates: 1800 to mid-2018**

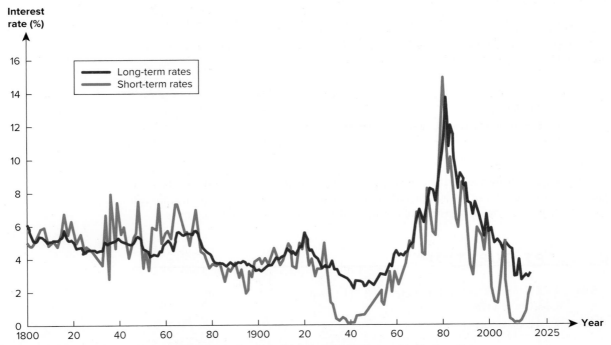

Source: Siegel, Jeremy J., *Stocks for the Long Run,* 3rd ed., New York, NY: McGraw-Hill, 2004, as updated by the authors.

What determines the shape of the term structure? There are three basic components. The first two are the ones we discussed in our previous section: the real rate of interest and the rate of inflation. The real rate of interest is the compensation investors demand for forgoing the use of their money. You can think of it as the pure time value of money after adjusting for the effects of inflation.

The real rate of interest is the basic component underlying every interest rate, regardless of the time to maturity. When the real rate is high, all interest rates will tend to be higher, and vice versa. Thus, the real rate doesn't really determine the shape of the term structure; instead, it mostly influences the overall level of interest rates.

In contrast, the prospect of future inflation very strongly influences the shape of the term structure. Investors thinking about loaning money for various lengths of time recognize that future inflation erodes the value of the dollars that will be returned. As a result, investors demand compensation for this loss in the form of higher nominal rates. This extra compensation is called the **inflation premium**.

If investors believe that the rate of inflation will be higher in the future, then long-term nominal interest rates will tend to be higher than short-term rates. Thus, an upward-sloping term structure may be a reflection of anticipated increases in inflation. Similarly, a downward-sloping term structure probably reflects the belief that inflation will be falling in the future.

The third, and last, component of the term structure has to do with interest rate risk. As we discussed earlier in the chapter, longer-term bonds have much greater risk of loss resulting from changes in interest rates than do shorter-term bonds. Investors recognize this risk, and they demand extra compensation in the form of higher rates for bearing it. This extra compensation is called the **interest rate risk premium**. The longer the term to maturity, the greater is the interest rate risk, so the interest rate risk premium increases with maturity. However, as we discussed earlier, interest rate risk increases at a decreasing rate, so the interest rate risk premium does as well.[6]

Putting the pieces together, we see that the term structure reflects the combined effect of the real rate of interest, the inflation premium, and the interest rate risk premium. Figure 6.5 shows how these can interact to produce an upward-sloping term structure (in the top part of Figure 6.5) or a downward-sloping term structure (in the bottom part).

In the top part of Figure 6.5, notice how the rate of inflation is expected to rise gradually. At the same time, the interest rate risk premium increases at a decreasing rate, so the combined effect is to produce a pronounced upward-sloping term structure. In the bottom part of Figure 6.5, the rate of inflation is expected to fall in the future, and the expected decline is enough to offset the interest rate risk premium and produce a downward-sloping term structure. Notice that if the rate of inflation was expected to decline by only a small amount, we could still get an upward-sloping term structure because of the interest rate risk premium.

We assumed in drawing Figure 6.5 that the real rate would remain the same. Actually, expected future real rates could be larger or smaller than the current real rate. Also, for simplicity, we used straight lines to show expected future inflation rates as rising or declining, but they do not necessarily have to look like this. They could, for example, rise and then fall, leading to a humped yield curve.

Bond Yields and the Yield Curve: Putting It All Together

Going back to Figure 6.3, recall that we saw that the yields on Treasury notes and bonds of different maturities are not the same. Each day, in addition to the Treasury prices and yields shown in Figure 6.3, *The Wall Street Journal* provides a plot of Treasury yields relative to

inflation premium
The portion of a nominal interest rate that represents compensation for expected future inflation.

interest rate risk premium
The compensation investors demand for bearing interest rate risk.

Online yield curve information is available at www.bloomberg.com /markets.

---

[6]In days of old, the interest rate risk premium was called a "liquidity" premium. Today, the term *liquidity premium* has an altogether different meaning, which we explore in our next section. Also, the interest rate risk premium is sometimes called a maturity risk premium. Our terminology is consistent with the modern view of the term structure.

FIGURE **6.5** **The term structure of interest rates**

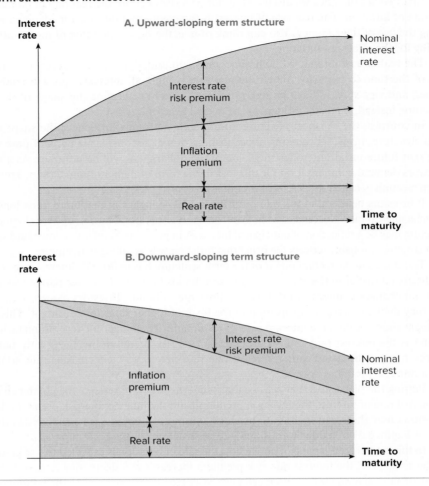

A. Upward-sloping term structure

B. Downward-sloping term structure

Treasury yield curve
A plot of the yields on
Treasury notes and bonds
relative to maturity.

Treasury yield curve
A plot of the yields on
Treasury notes and bonds
relative to maturity.

default risk premium
The portion of a nominal
interest rate or bond yield
that represents
compensation for the
possibility of default.

maturity. This plot is called the **Treasury yield curve** (or the yield curve). Figure 6.6 shows the yield curve as of June 2018. Note, the yield curve available on the Treasury website will display both the nominal and real yield curves.

As you probably now suspect, the shape of the yield curve is a reflection of the term structure of interest rates. In fact, the Treasury yield curve and the term structure of interest rates are almost the same thing. The only difference is that the term structure is based on pure discount bonds, whereas the yield curve is based on coupon bond yields. As a result, Treasury yields depend on the three components that underlie the term structure: the real rate, expected future inflation, and the interest rate risk premium.

Treasury notes and bonds have three important features that we need to remind you of: They are default-free, they are taxable, and they are highly liquid. This is not true of bonds in general, so we need to examine what additional factors come into play when we look at bonds issued by corporations or municipalities.

The first thing to consider is credit risk—that is, the possibility of default. Investors recognize that issuers other than the Treasury may or may not make all the promised payments on a bond, so they demand a higher yield as compensation for this risk. This extra compensation is called the **default risk premium**. Earlier in the chapter, we saw how bonds

Treasury Yield Curve

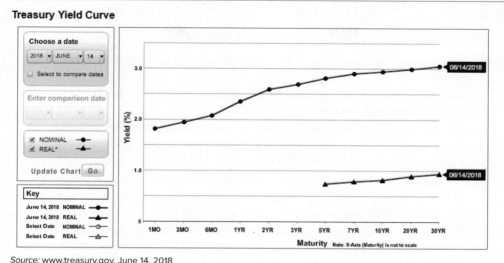

Source: www.treasury.gov, June 14, 2018

FIGURE 6.6

The Treasury yield curve

June 14, 2018

were rated based on their credit risk. What you will find if you start looking at bonds of different ratings is that lower-rated bonds have higher yields.

An important thing to recognize about a bond's yield is that it is calculated assuming that all the promised payments will be made. As a result, it is really a promised yield, and it may or may not be what you will earn. In particular, if the issuer defaults, your actual yield will be lower, probably much lower. This fact is particularly important when it comes to junk bonds. Thanks to a clever bit of marketing, such bonds are now commonly called high-yield bonds, which has a much nicer ring to it; but now you recognize that these are really high-*promised*-yield bonds.

Next, recall that we discussed earlier how municipal bonds are free from most taxes and, as a result, have much lower yields than taxable bonds. Investors demand the extra yield on a taxable bond as compensation for the unfavorable tax treatment. This extra compensation is the **taxability premium**.

Finally, bonds have varying degrees of liquidity. As we discussed earlier, there are an enormous number of bond issues, most of which do not trade on a regular basis. As a result, if you wanted to sell quickly, you would probably not get as good a price as you could otherwise. Investors prefer liquid assets to illiquid ones, so they demand a **liquidity premium** on top of all the other premiums we have discussed. As a result, all else being the same, less-liquid bonds will have higher yields than more-liquid bonds.

Conclusion

If we combine all of the things we have discussed regarding bond yields, we find that bond yields represent the combined effect of no fewer than six things. The first is the real rate of interest. On top of the real rate are five premiums representing compensation for (1) expected future inflation, (2) interest rate risk, (3) default risk, (4) taxability, and (5) lack of liquidity. As a result, determining the appropriate yield on a bond requires careful analysis of each of these effects.

taxability premium
The portion of a nominal interest rate or bond yield that represents compensation for unfavorable tax status.

liquidity premium
The portion of a nominal interest rate or bond yield that represents compensation for lack of liquidity.

CONCEPT QUESTIONS

6.7a What is the term structure of interest rates? What determines its shape?

6.7b What is the Treasury yield curve?

6.7c What are the six components that make up a bond's yield?

SUMMARY AND CONCLUSIONS

This chapter has explored bonds and bond yields. We saw that:

1. Determining bond prices and yields is an application of basic discounted cash flow principles.

2. Bond values move in the direction opposite that of interest rates, leading to potential gains or losses for bond investors.

3. Bonds have a variety of features spelled out in a document called the indenture.

4. Bonds are rated based on their default risk. Some bonds, such as Treasury bonds, have no risk of default, whereas so-called junk bonds have substantial default risk.

5. A wide variety of bonds exist, many of which contain exotic, or unusual, features.

6. Almost all bond trading is OTC, with little or no market transparency. As a result, bond price and volume information can be difficult to find.

7. Bond yields reflect the effect of six different things: the real rate and five premiums that investors demand as compensation for inflation, interest rate risk, default risk, taxability, and lack of liquidity.

In closing, we note that bonds are a vital source of financing to governments and corporations of all types. Bond prices and yields are a rich subject, and our one chapter, necessarily, touches on only the most important concepts and ideas. There is a great deal more we could say, but, instead, we move on to stocks in our next chapter.

▣ connect POP QUIZ!

Can you answer the following questions? If your class is using *Connect*, log on to SmartBook to see if you know the answers to these and other questions, check out the study tools, and find out what topics require additional practice!

Section 6.1 What is the coupon rate on a bond that has a par value of $1,000, a market value of $1,100, and a coupon interest rate of $100 per year?

Section 6.2 What is the provision in the bond indenture giving the issuing company the option to repurchase bonds prior to maturity?

Section 6.3 Do bond ratings consider default risk?

Section 6.4 What are the features of municipal bonds?

Section 6.5 What does the dirty price of a bond represent?

Section 6.6 What is the difference between a real and a nominal rate of return?

Section 6.7 What do historical data suggest about the nature of short-term and long-term interest rates?

CHAPTER REVIEW AND SELF-TEST PROBLEMS

6.1   **Bond Values**   A Microgates Industries bond has a 10 percent coupon rate and a $1,000 face value. Interest is paid semiannually, and the bond has 20 years to maturity. If investors require a 12 percent yield, what is the bond's value? What is the effective annual yield on the bond? (See Problem 6.)

6.2 Yields A Macrohard Corp. bond carries an 8 percent coupon, paid semiannually. The par value is $1,000, and the bond matures in six years. If the bond currently sells for $911.37, what is its yield to maturity? What is the effective annual yield? (See Problem 21.)

■ Answers to Chapter Review and Self-Test Problems

6.1 Because the bond has a 10 percent coupon yield and investors require a 12 percent return, we know that the bond must sell at a discount. Notice that, because the bond pays interest semiannually, the coupons amount to $100/2 = $50 every six months. The required yield is 12%/2 = 6% every six months. Finally, the bond matures in 20 years, so there are a total of 40 six-month periods.

The bond's value thus is equal to the present value of $50 every six months for the next 40 six-month periods, plus the present value of the $1,000 face amount:

$$\text{Bond value} = \$50 \times (1 - 1/1.06^{40})/.06 + 1,000/1.06^{40}$$
$$= \$50 \times 15.0463 + 1,000/10.2857$$
$$= \$849.54$$

Notice that we discounted the $1,000 back 40 periods at 6 percent per period, rather than 20 years at 12 percent. The reason is that the effective annual yield on the bond is $1.06^2 - 1 = .1236$, or 12.36%, not 12 percent. We thus could have used 12.36 percent per year for 20 years when we calculated the present value of the $1,000 face amount, and the answer would have been the same.

6.2 The present value of the bond's cash flows is its current price, $911.37. The coupon is $40 every six months for 12 periods. The face value is $1,000. So, the bond's yield is the unknown discount rate in the following:

$$\$911.37 = \$40 \times [1 - 1/(1 + r)^{12}]/r + \$1,000/(1 + r)^{12}$$

The bond sells at a discount. Because the coupon rate is 8 percent, the yield must be something in excess of that.

If we were to solve this by trial and error, we might try 12 percent (or 6 percent per six months):

$$\text{Bond value} = \$40 \times (1 - 1/1.06^{12})/.06 + \$1,000/1.06^{12}$$
$$= \$832.32$$

This is less than the actual value, so our discount rate is too high. We now know that the yield is somewhere between 8 and 12 percent. With further trial and error (or a little machine assistance), the yield works out to be 10 percent, or 5 percent every six months.

By convention, the bond's yield to maturity would be quoted as $2 \times 5\% = 10\%$. The effective yield is thus $1.05^2 - 1 = .1025$, or 10.25%.

CRITICAL THINKING AND CONCEPTS REVIEW

LO 1   **6.1 Treasury Bonds** Is it true that a U.S. Treasury security is risk free?

LO 2   **6.2 Interest Rate Risk** Which has greater interest rate risk, a 30-year Treasury bond or a 30-year BB corporate bond?

LO 1 **6.3 Treasury Pricing**   With regard to bid and ask prices on a Treasury bond, is it possible for the bid price to be higher? Why or why not?

LO 2 **6.4 Yield to Maturity**   Treasury bid and ask quotes are sometimes given in terms of yields, so there would be a bid yield and an ask yield. Which do you think would be larger? Explain.

LO 1 **6.5 Call Provisions**   A company is contemplating a long-term bond issue. It is debating whether or not to include a call provision. What are the benefits to the company from including a call provision? What are the costs? How do these answers change for a put provision?

LO 1 **6.6 Coupon Rate**   How does a bond issuer decide on the appropriate coupon rate to set on its bonds? Explain the difference between the coupon rate and the required return on a bond.

LO 4 **6.7 Real and Nominal Returns**   Are there any circumstances under which an investor might be more concerned about the nominal return on an investment than the real return?

LO 3 **6.8 Bond Ratings**   Companies pay rating agencies such as Moody's and S&P to rate their bonds, and the costs can be substantial. However, companies are not required to have their bonds rated in the first place; doing so is strictly voluntary. Why do you think they do it?

LO 3 **6.9 Bond Ratings**   Often, junk bonds are not rated. Why?

LO 3 **6.10 Crossover Bonds**   Looking back at the crossover bonds we discussed in the chapter, why do you think split ratings such as these occur?

LO 1 **6.11 Municipal Bonds**   Why is it that municipal bonds are not taxed at the federal level but are taxable across state lines? Why is it that U.S. Treasury bonds are not taxable at the state level? (You may need to dust off the history books for this one.)

LO 1 **6.12 Treasury Market**   All Treasury bonds are relatively liquid, but some are more liquid than others. Take a look back at Figure 6.3. Which issues appear to be the most liquid? The least liquid?

LO 3 **6.13 Rating Agencies**   Several years ago, a controversy erupted regarding bond-rating agencies when some agencies began to provide unsolicited bond ratings. Why do you think this is controversial?

LO 1 **6.14 Bonds as Equity**   The 100-year bonds we discussed in the chapter have something in common with junk bonds. Critics charge that, in both cases, the issuers are really selling equity in disguise. What are the issues here? Why would a company want to sell "equity in disguise"?

LO 2 **6.15 Bond Prices versus Yields**
   a. What is the relationship between the price of a bond and its YTM?
   b. Explain why some bonds sell at a premium over par value while other bonds sell at a discount. What do you know about the relationship between the coupon rate and the YTM for premium bonds? What about for discount bonds? For bonds selling at par value?
   c. What is the relationship between the current yield and YTM for premium bonds? For discount bonds? For bonds selling at par value?

QUESTIONS AND PROBLEMS

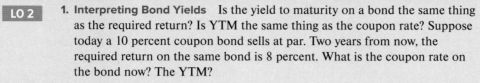

Select problems are available in McGraw-Hill *Connect*. Please see the packaging options section of the Preface for more information.

BASIC (Questions 1–17)

LO 2   **1. Interpreting Bond Yields**   Is the yield to maturity on a bond the same thing as the required return? Is YTM the same thing as the coupon rate? Suppose today a 10 percent coupon bond sells at par. Two years from now, the required return on the same bond is 8 percent. What is the coupon rate on the bond now? The YTM?

LO 2   **2. Interpreting Bond Yields**   Suppose you buy a 7 percent coupon, 20-year bond today when it's first issued. If interest rates suddenly rise to 15 percent, what happens to the value of your bond? Why?

LO 2   **3. Bond Prices**   Vulcan, Inc., has 7 percent coupon bonds on the market that have 13 years left to maturity. The bonds make annual payments and have a par value of $1,000. If the YTM on these bonds is 8.4 percent, what is the current bond price?

LO 2   **4. Bond Yields**   The Petit Chef Co. has 7 percent coupon bonds on the market with nine years left to maturity. The bonds make annual payments and have a par value of $1,000. If the bonds currently sell for $1,038.50, what is the YTM?

LO 2   **5. Coupon Rates**   Big Canyon Enterprises has bonds on the market making annual payments, with 12 years to maturity, a par value of $1,000, and a price of $1,030. At this price, the bonds yield 6.14 percent. What must the coupon rate be on the bonds?

LO 2   **6. Bond Prices**   Dufner Co. issued 15-year bonds one year ago at a coupon rate of 4.8 percent. The bonds make semiannual payments. If the YTM on these bonds is 5.3 percent, what is the current dollar price assuming a $1,000 par value?

LO 2   **7. Bond Yields**   Parkway Void Co. issued 15-year bonds two years ago at a coupon rate of 5.4 percent. The bonds make semiannual payments. If these bonds currently sell for 106 percent of par value, what is the YTM?

LO 2   **8. Coupon Rates**   Henley Corporation has bonds on the market with 10.5 years to maturity, a YTM of 5.7 percent, a par value of $1,000, and a current price of $945. The bonds make semiannual payments. What must the coupon rate be on the bonds?

LO 4   **9. Calculating Real Rates of Return**   If Treasury bills are currently paying 4.7 percent and the inflation rate is 1.9 percent, what is the approximate real rate of interest? The exact real rate?

LO 4   **10. Inflation and Nominal Returns**   Suppose the real rate is 1.8 percent and the inflation rate is 3.7 percent. What rate would you expect to see on a Treasury bill?

LO 4   **11. Nominal and Real Returns**   An investment offers a total return of 12 percent over the coming year. Alex Hamilton thinks the total real return on this investment will be only 9 percent. What does Alex believe the inflation rate will be over the next year?

LO 4   **12. Nominal versus Real Returns**   Say you own an asset that had a total return last year of 12.1 percent. If the inflation rate last year was 3.4 percent, what was your real return?

LO 2 13. **Using Treasury Quotes**   Locate the Treasury issue in Figure 6.3 maturing in February 2029. What is its coupon rate? What is the dollar bid price for a $1,000 par value bond? What was the *previous day's* asked price for a $1,000 par value bond?

LO 2 14. **Using Treasury Quotes**   Locate the Treasury bond in Figure 6.3 maturing in May 2037. Is this a premium or a discount bond? What is its current yield? What is its yield to maturity? What is the bid-ask spread for a $1,000 par value bond?

LO 2 15. **Zero Coupon Bonds**   You find a zero coupon bond with a par value of $10,000 and 13 years to maturity. If the yield to maturity on this bond is 4.7 percent, what is the price of the bond? Assume semiannual compounding periods.

LO 2 16. **Valuing Bonds**   Lion Corp. has a $2,000 par value bond outstanding with a coupon rate of 3.8 percent paid semiannually and 13 years to maturity. The yield to maturity of the bond is 4.9 percent. What is the dollar price of the bond?

LO 2 17. **Valuing Bonds**   Union Local School District has bonds outstanding with a coupon rate of 3.2 percent paid semiannually and 16 years to maturity. The yield to maturity on these bonds is 3.7 percent and the bonds have a par value of $5,000. What is the dollar price of the bonds?

INTERMEDIATE (Questions 18–33)

LO 2 18. **Bond Price Movements**   Bond X is a premium bond making semiannual payments. The bond has a coupon rate of 7.5 percent, a YTM of 6 percent, and 13 years to maturity. Bond Y is a discount bond making semiannual payments. This bond has a coupon rate of 6 percent, a YTM of 7.5 percent, and also 13 years to maturity. What are the prices of these bonds today assuming both bonds have a $1,000 par value? If interest rates remain unchanged, what do you expect the prices of these bonds to be in 1 year? In 3 years? In 8 years? In 12 years? In 13 years? What's going on here? Illustrate your answers by graphing bond prices versus time to maturity.

LO 2 19. **Interest Rate Risk**   Both Bond Bill and Bond Ted have 5.8 percent coupons, make semiannual payments, and are priced at par value. Bond Bill has 5 years to maturity, whereas Bond Ted has 25 years to maturity. If interest rates suddenly rise by 2 percent, what is the percentage change in the price of Bond Bill? Of Bond Ted? Both bonds have a par value of $1,000. If rates were to suddenly fall by 2 percent instead, what would the percentage change in the price of Bond Bill be then? Of Bond Ted? Illustrate your answers by graphing bond prices versus YTM. What does this problem tell you about the interest rate risk of longer-term bonds?

LO 2 20. **Interest Rate Risk**   Bond J has a coupon rate of 4 percent. Bond K has a coupon rate of 14 percent. Both bonds have 17 years to maturity, a par value of $1,000, and a YTM of 8 percent, and both make semiannual payments. If interest rates suddenly rise by 2 percent, what is the percentage price change of these bonds? What if rates suddenly fall by 2 percent instead? What does this problem tell you about the interest rate risk of lower-coupon bonds?

LO 2 21. **Bond Yields**   Bart Software has 5.7 percent coupon bonds on the market with 22 years to maturity. The bonds make semiannual payments and currently sell for 97 percent of par. What is the current yield? The YTM? The effective annual yield?

LO 2 22. **Bond Yields**   BDJ Co. wants to issue new 25-year bonds for some much-needed expansion projects. The company currently has 4.8 percent coupon bonds on the market that sell for $1,028, make semiannual payments, have a $1,000 par value, and mature in 25 years. What coupon rate should the company set on its new bonds if it wants them to sell at par?

LO 2 23. **Accrued Interest**   You purchase a bond with an invoice price of $1,043. The bond has a coupon rate of 4.7 percent, semiannual coupons, and a $1,000 par value, and there are five months to the next coupon date. What is the clean price of the bond?

LO 2 24. **Accrued Interest**   You purchase a bond with a coupon rate of 5.2 percent, semiannual coupons, and a clean price of $993. If the next coupon payment is due in two months, what is the invoice price?

LO 2 25. **Using Bond Quotes**   Suppose the following bond quote for IOU Corporation appears in the financial page of today's newspaper. Assume the bond has a face value of $1,000, and the current date is April 15, 2019. What is the yield to maturity of the bond? What is the current yield?

Company (Ticker)	Coupon	Maturity	Last Price	Last Yield	EST Vol (000s)
IOU (IOU)	7.60	Apr 15, 2031	91.645	??	1,827

LO 2 26. **Zero Coupon Bonds**   Suppose your company needs to raise $40 million and you want to issue 20-year bonds for this purpose. Assume the required return on your bond issue will be 5.7 percent, and you're evaluating two issue alternatives: a 5.7 percent semiannual coupon bond and a zero coupon bond. Your company's tax rate is 21 percent.

a.   How many of the coupon bonds would you need to issue to raise the $40 million? How many of the zeroes would you need to issue?

b.   In 20 years, what will your company's repayment be if you issue the coupon bonds? What if you issue the zeroes?

c.   Based on your answers in parts (a) and (b), why would you ever want to issue the zeroes? To answer, calculate the firm's aftertax cash outflows for the first year under the two different scenarios. Assume that the IRS amortization rules apply for the zero coupon bonds.

LO 2 27. **Finding the Maturity**   You've just found a 10 percent coupon bond on the market that sells for par value. What is the maturity on this bond? (Warning: possible trick question.)

Use the following Treasury bond quotes to answer Questions 28–30: To calculate the number of years until maturity, assume that it is currently May 2019. All of the bonds have a $1,000 par value and pay semiannual coupons.

Rate	Maturity Mo/Yr	Bid	Asked	Chg	Ask Yld
??	May 25	103.5362	103.8235	+.3204	2.18
5.850	May 27	103.1840	103.3215	+.4513	??
6.125	May 36	??	??	+.6821	3.87

LO 2   **28. Bond Yields**   In the table, find the Treasury bond that matures in May 2027. What is your yield to maturity if you buy this bond?

LO 2   **29. Bond Prices**   In the table, find the Treasury bond that matures in May 2036. What is the asked price of this bond in dollars? If the bid-ask spread for this bond is .0628, what is the bid price in dollars?

LO 2   **30. Coupon Rates**   Find the Treasury bond that matures in May 2025. What is the coupon rate for this bond?

Use the following corporate bond quotes to answer Questions 31–33: To calculate the number of years until maturity, assume that it is currently January 15, 2019. All of the bonds have a $2,000 par value and pay semiannual coupons.

Company (Ticker)	Coupon	Maturity	Last Price	Last Yield	EST $ Vol (000's)
Xenon, Inc. (XIC)	5.400	Jan 15, 2024	96.153	??	57,362
Kenny Corp. (KCC)	7.125	Jan 15, 2026	??	6.02	48,941
Williams Co. (WICO)	??	Jan 15, 2028	95.165	6.85	43,802

LO 2   **31. Bond Yields**   What is the yield to maturity for the bond issued by Xenon, Inc.?

LO 2   **32. Bond Prices**   What price would you expect to pay for the Kenny Corp. bond? What is the bond's current yield?

LO 2   **33. Coupon Rates**   What is the coupon rate for the Williams Co. bond?

CHALLENGE (Question 34–35)

LO 2   **34. Components of Bond Returns**   Bond P is a premium bond with a coupon rate of 8.2 percent. Bond D is a discount bond with a coupon rate of 5.9 percent. Both bonds make annual payments and have a YTM of 7 percent, a par value of $1,000, and five years to maturity. What is the current yield for Bond P? For Bond D? If interest rates remain unchanged, what is the expected capital gains yield over the next year for Bond P? For Bond D? Explain your answers and the interrelationships among the various types of yields.

LO 2   **35. Holding Period Yield**   The YTM on a bond is the interest rate you earn on your investment if interest rates don't change. If you actually sell the bond before it matures, your realized return is known as the *holding period yield* (HPY).

a.   Suppose that today you buy an annual coupon bond with a coupon rate of 6 percent for $915. The bond has 10 years to maturity and a par value of $1,000. What rate of return do you expect to earn on your investment?

b.   Two years from now, the YTM on your bond has declined by one percentage point, and you decide to sell. What price will your bond sell for? What is the HPY on your investment? Compare this yield to the YTM when you first bought the bond. Why are they different?

6.1 Bond Quotes You can find current bond prices at finra-markets.morningstar.com/ BondCenter. You want to find the bond prices and yields for bonds issued by Pfizer. Enter the ticker symbol "PFE" to do a search. What is the shortest-maturity bond issued by Pfizer that is outstanding? What is the longest-maturity bond? What is the credit rating for Pfizer's bonds? Do all of the bonds have the same credit rating? Why do you think this is?

6.2 Yield Curves You can find information regarding the most current bond yields at money.cnn.com. Go there and graph the yield curve for U.S. Treasury bonds. What is the general shape of the yield curve? What does this imply about expected future inflation? Now graph the yield curve for AAA-, AA-, and A-rated corporate bonds. Is the corporate yield curve the same shape as the Treasury yield curve? Why or why not?

6.3 Default Premiums The Federal Reserve Bank of St. Louis has files listing historical interest rates on its website www.stlouisfed.org. Find your way to the "FRED®" data, then "Interest Rates." You will find listings for Moody's Seasoned Aaa Corporate Bond Yield and Moody's Seasoned Baa Corporate Bond Yield. A default premium can be calculated as the difference between the Aaa bond yield and the Baa bond yield. Calculate the default premium using these two bond indexes for the most recent 36 months. Is the default premium the same for every month? Why do you think this is?

WHAT'S ON THE WEB?

EXCEL *MASTER IT!* PROBLEM

Excel Master coverage online

In an earlier worksheet, we discussed the difference between yield to maturity and yield to call. There is another yield that is commonly quoted, the yield to worst. The yield to worst is the lowest potential yield that can be received on a bond without the issuer actually defaulting. Yield to worst is calculated on all possible call dates. It is assumed that prepayment occurs if the bond has a call provision. The yield to worst will be the lower of yield to maturity or yield to call. The yield to worst may be the same as yield to maturity but never higher. Of course, with a traditional callable bond that has a call premium, the call premium can decline over time.

A company has the following bond outstanding. The bond is callable every year on May 1, the anniversary date of the bond. The bond has a deferred call with 3 years left. The call premium on the first call date is 1 year's interest. The call premium will decline by 10 percent of the original call premium for 10 years. Thirteen years from today, the call premium will be zero. Given the following information, what is the yield to worst for this bond?

Current date:	5/1/2019
Maturity date:	5/1/2039
Price (percent of par):	98.5%
Coupon rate:	10.00%
Par value (percent of par):	100%
Coupons per year:	2

Call date	Call premium
5/1/2022	$100
5/1/2023	90
5/1/2024	80
5/1/2025	70
5/1/2026	60
5/1/2027	50
5/1/2028	40
5/1/2029	30
5/1/2030	20
5/1/2031	10

CHAPTER CASE

Financing S&S Air's Expansion Plans with a Bond Issue

Mark Sexton and Todd Story, the owners of S&S Air, have decided to expand their operations. They instructed their newly hired financial analyst, Chris Guthrie, to enlist an underwriter to help sell $20 million in new 10-year bonds to finance construction. Chris has entered into discussions with Renata Harper, an underwriter from the firm of Crowe & Mallard, about which bond features S&S Air should consider and what coupon rate the issue will likely have.

Although Chris is aware of the bond features, he is uncertain as to the costs and benefits of some features, so he isn't clear on how each feature would affect the coupon rate of the bond issue. You are Renata's assistant, and she has asked you to prepare a memo to Chris describing the effect of each of the following bond features on the coupon rate of the bond. She also would like you to list any advantages or disadvantages of each feature.

QUESTIONS

1. The security of the bond—that is, whether the bond has collateral.

2. The seniority of the bond.

3. The presence of a sinking fund.

4. A call provision with specified call dates and call prices.

5. A deferred call accompanying the preceding call provision.

6. A make-whole call provision.

7. Any positive covenants. Also, discuss several possible positive covenants S&S Air might consider.

8. Any negative covenants. Also, discuss several possible negative covenants S&S Air might consider.

9. A conversion feature (note that S&S Air is not a publicly traded company).

10. A floating-rate coupon.

7 | Equity Markets and Stock Valuation

When the stock market closed on June 15, 2018, the common stock of biopharmaceutical company Gilead Sciences was selling for $70.23 per share. On that same day, well-known credit rating provider TransUnion closed at $71.16 per share, while oil and natural gas company PrimeEnergy closed at $70.00. Because the stock prices of these three companies were so similar, you might expect they would be offering similar dividends to their stockholders, but you would be wrong. In fact, Gilead Science's annual dividend was $2.28 per share, TransUnion's was $.30 per share, and PrimeEnergy was paying no dividend at all!

As we will see in this chapter, the dividends currently being paid are one of the primary factors we look at when we attempt to value common stocks. However, it is obvious from looking at PrimeEnergy that current dividends are not the end of the story, so this chapter explores dividends, stock values, and the connection between the two.

Going back to Chapter 1, we see that the goal of financial management is to maximize stock prices, so an understanding of what determines share values is obviously a key concern. When a corporation has publicly held stock, its shares often will be bought and sold on one or more of the major stock exchanges, so we will examine how stocks are traded. We also will see that the shareholders in a corporation have certain rights, and that how these rights are allocated can have a significant impact on corporate control and governance.

LEARNING OBJECTIVES

After studying this chapter, you should be able to:

LO 1 Assess how stock prices depend on future dividends and dividend growth.

LO 2 Identify the different ways corporate directors are elected to office.

LO 3 Explain how the stock markets work.

Please visit us at essentialsofcorporatefinance.blogspot.com for the latest developments in the world of corporate finance.

In our previous chapter, we introduced you to bonds and bond valuation. In this chapter, we turn to the other major source of financing for corporations, common and preferred stock. We first describe the cash flows associated with a share of stock and then go on to develop a very famous result, the dividend growth model. From there, we move on to examine various important features of common and preferred stock, focusing on shareholder rights. We close out the chapter with a discussion of how shares of stock are traded and how stock prices and other important information are reported in the financial press.

7.1 COMMON STOCK VALUATION

Excel
Master
coverage online

A share of common stock is more difficult to value in practice than a bond, for at least three reasons. First, with common stock, not even the promised cash flows are known in advance. Second, the life of the investment is essentially forever because common stock has no maturity. Third, there is no way to easily observe the rate of return that the market requires. Nonetheless, as we will see, there are cases in which we can come up with the present value of the future cash flows for a share of stock and thus determine its value.

Cash Flows

Imagine that you are considering buying a share of stock today. You plan to sell the stock in one year. You somehow know that the stock will be worth $70 at that time. You predict that the stock also will pay a $10 per share dividend at the end of the year. If you require a 25 percent return on your investment, what is the most you would pay for the stock? In other words, what is the present value of the $10 dividend along with the $70 ending value at 25 percent?

If you buy the stock today and sell it at the end of the year, you will have a total of $80 in cash. At 25 percent:

Present value = ($10 + 70)/1.25 = $64

Therefore, $64 is the value you would assign to the stock today.

More generally, let P_0 be the current price of the stock, and assign P_1 to be the price in one period. If D_1 is the cash dividend paid at the end of the period, then:

$$P_0 = (D_1 + P_1)/(1 + R) \qquad [7.1]$$

where R is the required return in the market on this investment.

Notice that we really haven't said much so far. If we wanted to determine the value of a share of stock today (P_0), we would first have to come up with the value in one year (P_1). This is even harder to do, so we've only made the problem more complicated.

What is the price in one period, P_1? We don't know in general. Instead, suppose we somehow knew the price in two periods, P_2. Given a predicted dividend in two periods, D_2, the stock price in one period would be:

$$P_1 = (D_2 + P_2)/(1 + R)$$

If we were to substitute this expression for P_1 into our expression for P_0, we would have:

$$P_0 = \frac{D_1 + P_1}{1 + R} = \frac{D_1 + \frac{D_2 + P_2}{1 + R}}{1 + R}$$

$$= \frac{D_1}{(1 + R)^1} + \frac{D_2}{(1 + R)^2} + \frac{P_2}{(1 + R)^2}$$

Now we need to get a price in two periods. We don't know this either, so we can procrastinate again and write:

$$P_2 = (D_3 + P_3)/(1 + R)$$

If we substitute this back in for P_2, we have:

$$P_0 = \frac{D_1}{(1+R)^1} + \frac{D_2}{(1+R)^2} + \frac{P_2}{(1+R)^2}$$

$$= \frac{D_1}{(1+R)^1} + \frac{D_2}{(1+R)^2} + \frac{\frac{D_3 + P_3}{1+R}}{(1+R)^2}$$

$$= \frac{D_1}{(1+R)^1} + \frac{D_2}{(1+R)^2} + \frac{D_3}{(1+R)^3} + \frac{P_3}{(1+R)^3}$$

You should start to notice that we can push the problem of coming up with the stock price off into the future forever. It is important to note that no matter what the stock price is, the present value is essentially zero if we push the sale of the stock far enough away. What we are eventually left with is the result that the current price of the stock can be written as the present value of the dividends beginning in one period and extending out forever:

$$P_0 = \frac{D_1}{(1+R)^1} + \frac{D_2}{(1+R)^2} + \frac{D_3}{(1+R)^3} + \frac{D_4}{(1+R)^4} + \frac{D_5}{(1+R)^5} + \cdots$$

We have illustrated here that the price of the stock today is equal to the present value of all of the future dividends. How many future dividends are there? In principle, there can be an infinite number. This means that we still can't compute a value for the stock because we would have to forecast an infinite number of dividends and then discount them all. In the next section, we consider some special cases in which we can get around this problem.

EXAMPLE 7.1   **Growth Stocks**

You might be wondering about shares of stock in companies such as eBay that currently pay no dividends. Small, growing companies frequently plow back everything and thus pay no dividends. Are such shares worth nothing? It depends. When we say that the value of the stock is equal to the present value of the future dividends, we don't rule out the possibility that some number of those dividends are zero. They just can't all be zero.

Imagine a company that has a provision in its corporate charter that prohibits the paying of dividends now or ever. The corporation never borrows any money, never pays out any money to stockholders in any form whatsoever, and never sells any assets. Such a corporation couldn't really exist because the IRS wouldn't like it, and the stockholders could always vote to amend the charter if they wanted to. If it did exist, however, what would the stock be worth?

The stock would be worth absolutely nothing. Such a company is a financial "black hole." Money goes in, but nothing valuable ever comes out. Because nobody would ever get any return on this investment, the investment has no value. This example is a little absurd, but it illustrates that when we speak of companies that don't pay dividends, what we really mean is that they are not *currently* paying dividends.

Some Special Cases

There are a few very useful special circumstances under which we can come up with a value for the stock. What we have to do is make some simplifying assumptions about the pattern of future dividends. The cases we consider are the following: (1) the dividend has a zero growth rate, (2) the dividend grows at a constant rate, and (3) the dividend grows at a non-constant rate. Finally, we examine stock pricing using comparables.

Zero Growth   The case of zero growth is one we've already seen. A share of common stock in a company with a constant dividend is much like a share of preferred stock. From Chapter 5 (Example 5.7), we know that the dividend on a share of preferred stock has zero growth and thus is constant through time. For a zero-growth share of common stock, this implies that:

$$D_1 = D_2 = D_3 = D = \text{constant}$$

So, the value of the stock is:

$$P_0 = \frac{D}{(1+R)^1} + \frac{D}{(1+R)^2} + \frac{D}{(1+R)^3} + \frac{D}{(1+R)^4} + \frac{D}{(1+R)^5} + \cdots$$

Because the dividend is always the same, the stock can be viewed as an ordinary perpetuity with a cash flow equal to D every period. The per-share value is thus given by:

$$P_0 = D/R \qquad\qquad\qquad [7.2]$$

where R is the required return.

For example, suppose the Paradise Prototyping Company has a policy of paying a $10 per-share dividend every year. If this policy is to be continued indefinitely, what is the value of a share of stock if the required return is 20 percent? The stock in this case amounts to an ordinary perpetuity, so the stock is worth $10/.20 = $50 per share.

> Students who are interested in equity valuation techniques should check out the Motley Fool at www.fool.com.

Constant Growth   Suppose we know that the dividend for some company always grows at a steady rate. Call this growth rate g. If we let D_0 be the dividend just paid, then the next dividend, D_1, is:

$$D_1 = D_0 \times (1 + g)$$

The dividend in two periods is:

$$D_2 = D_1 \times (1 + g)$$
$$= [D_0 \times (1 + g)] \times (1 + g)$$
$$= D_0 \times (1 + g)^2$$

We could repeat this process to come up with the dividend at any point in the future. In general, from our discussion of compound growth in Chapter 4, we know that the dividend t periods into the future, D_t, is given by:

$$D_t = D_0 \times (1 + g)^t$$

An asset with cash flows that grow at a constant rate forever is called a *growing perpetuity*. As we will see momentarily, there is a simple expression for determining the value of such an asset.

The assumption of steady dividend growth might strike you as peculiar. Why would the dividend grow at a constant rate? The reason is that, for many companies, steady growth in dividends is an explicit goal. This subject falls under the general heading of dividend policy, so we defer further discussion of it to a later chapter.

EXAMPLE 7.2   **Dividend Growth**

The Hedless Corporation has just paid a dividend of $3 per share. The dividend of this company grows at a steady rate of 8 percent per year. Based on this information, what will the dividend be in five years?

Here we have a $3 current amount that grows at 8 percent per year for five years. The future amount is thus:

$3 × 1.08^5 = $3 × 1.4693 = $4.41

The dividend, therefore, will increase by $4.41 − 3 = $1.41 over the coming five years.

If the dividend grows at a steady rate, then we have replaced the problem of forecasting an infinite number of future dividends with the problem of coming up with a single growth rate, a considerable simplification. In this case, if we take D_0 to be the dividend just paid and g to be the constant growth rate, the value of a share of stock can be written as:

$$P_0 = \frac{D_1}{(1+R)^1} + \frac{D_2}{(1+R)^2} + \frac{D_3}{(1+R)^3} + \cdots$$

$$= \frac{D_0(1+g)^1}{(1+R)^1} + \frac{D_0(1+g)^2}{(1+R)^2} + \frac{D_0(1+g)^3}{(1+R)^3} + \cdots$$

As long as the growth rate, g, is less than the discount rate, R, the present value of this series of cash flows can be written as:

$$P_0 = \frac{D_0 \times (1+g)}{R-g} = \frac{D_1}{R-g} \qquad [7.3]$$

This elegant result goes by a lot of different names. We will call it the **dividend growth model**. By any name, it is very easy to use. To illustrate, suppose D_0 is $2.30, R is 13 percent, and g is 5 percent. The price per share in this case is:

$$P_0 = D_0 \times (1+g)/(R-g)$$
$$= \$2.30 \times 1.05/(.13 - .05)$$
$$= \$2.415/.08$$
$$= \$30.19$$

dividend growth model
A model that determines the current price of a stock as its dividend next period divided by the discount rate less the dividend growth rate.

We can actually use the dividend growth model to get the stock price at any point in time, not just today. In general, the price of the stock as of Time t is:

$$P_t = \frac{D_t \times (1+g)}{R-g} = \frac{D_{t+1}}{R-g} \qquad [7.4]$$

In our example, suppose we are interested in the price of the stock in five years, P_5. We first need the dividend at Time 5, D_5. Because the dividend just paid is $2.30 and the growth rate is 5 percent per year, D_5 is:

$$D_5 = \$2.30 \times 1.05^5 = \$2.30 \times 1.2763 = \$2.935$$

From the dividend growth model, we get that the price of the stock in five years is:

$$P_5 = \frac{D_5 \times (1+g)}{R-g} = \frac{\$2.935 \times 1.05}{.13 - .05} = \frac{\$3.0822}{.08} = \$38.53$$

EXAMPLE 7.3   **Gordon Growth Company**

The next dividend for the Gordon Growth Company will be $4 per share. Investors require a 16 percent return on companies such as Gordon. Gordon's dividend increases by 6 percent every year. Based on the dividend growth model, what is the value of Gordon's stock today? What is the value in four years?

The only tricky thing here is that the next dividend, D_1, is given as $4, so we won't multiply this by $(1 + g)$. With this in mind, the price per share is given by:

$$P_0 = D_1/(R - g)$$
$$= \$4/(.16 - .06)$$
$$= \$4/.10$$
$$= \$40$$

Because we already have the dividend in one year, we know that the dividend in four years is equal to $D_1 \times (1 + g)^3 = \$4 \times 1.06^3 = \$4.764$. The price in four years is therefore:

$$P_4 = D_4 \times (1 + g)/(R - g)$$
$$= \$4.764 \times 1.06/(.16 - .06)$$
$$= \$5.05/.10$$
$$= \$50.50$$

Notice in this example that P_4 is equal to $P_0 \times (1 + g)^4$:

$$P_4 = \$50.50 = \$40 \times 1.06^4 = P_0 \times (1 + g)^4$$

To see why this is so, notice first that:

$$P_4 = D_5/(R - g)$$

However, D_5 is equal to $D_1 \times (1 + g)^4$, so we can write P_4 as:

$$P_4 = D_1 \times (1 + g)^4/(R - g)$$
$$= [D_1/(R - g)] \times (1 + g)^4$$
$$= P_0 \times (1 + g)^4$$

This last example illustrates that the dividend growth model makes the implicit assumption that the stock price will grow at the same constant rate as the dividend. This really isn't too surprising. What it tells us is that if the cash flows on an investment grow at a constant rate through time, so does the value of that investment.

You might wonder what would happen with the dividend growth model if the growth rate, g, were greater than the discount rate, R. It looks like we would get a negative stock price because $R - g$ would be less than zero. This is not what would happen.

Instead, if the constant growth rate exceeds the discount rate, then the stock price is infinitely large. Why? If the growth rate is bigger than the discount rate, then the present value of the dividends keeps on getting bigger and bigger. Essentially, the same is true if the growth rate and the discount rate are equal. In both cases, the simplification that allows us to replace the infinite stream of dividends with the dividend growth model is "illegal," so the answers we get from the dividend growth model are nonsense unless the growth rate is less than the discount rate.

Finally, the expression we came up with for the constant growth case will work for any growing perpetuity, not just dividends on common stock. If C_1 is the next cash flow on a growing perpetuity, then the present value of the cash flows is given by:

$$\text{Present value} = C_1/(R - g) = C_0(1 + g)/(R - g)$$

Notice that this expression looks like the result for an ordinary perpetuity except that we have $R - g$ on the bottom instead of only R.

Nonconstant Growth   The last case we consider is nonconstant growth. The main reason to consider this case is to allow for "supernormal" growth rates over some finite length of time. As we discussed earlier, the growth rate cannot exceed the required return indefinitely, but it certainly could do so for some number of years. To avoid the problem of having to forecast and discount an infinite number of dividends, we will require that the dividends start growing at a constant rate sometime in the future.

For a simple example of nonconstant growth, consider the case of a company that is currently not paying dividends. You predict that, in five years, the company will pay a dividend for the first time. The dividend will be $.50 per share. You expect that this dividend will then grow at a rate of 10 percent per year indefinitely. The required return on companies such as this one is 20 percent. What is the price of the stock today?

To see what the stock is worth today, we first find out what it will be worth once dividends are paid. We can then calculate the present value of that future price to get today's price. The first dividend will be paid in five years, and the dividend will grow steadily from then on. Using the dividend growth model, we can say that the price in four years will be:

$$P_4 = D_4 \times (1 + g)/(R - g)$$
$$= D_5/(R - g)$$
$$= \$.50/(.20 - .10)$$
$$= \$5$$

If the stock will be worth $5 in four years, then we can get the current value by discounting this price back four years at 20 percent:

$$P_0 = \$5/1.20^4 = \$5/2.0736 = \$2.41$$

The stock is therefore worth $2.41 today.

The problem of nonconstant growth is only slightly more complicated if the dividends are not zero for the first several years. Suppose that you have come up with the following dividend forecasts for the next three years:

Year	Expected Dividend
1	$1.00
2	$2.00
3	$2.50

After the third year, the dividend will grow at a constant rate of 5 percent per year. The required return is 10 percent. What is the value of the stock today?

In dealing with nonconstant growth, a time line can be very helpful. Figure 7.1 illustrates one for this problem. The important thing to notice is when constant growth starts. As we've shown, for this problem, constant growth starts at Time 3. This means that we can use our constant growth model to determine the stock price at Time 3, P_3. By far the most common mistake in this situation is to incorrectly identify the start of the constant growth phase and, as a result, calculate the future stock price at the wrong time.

FIGURE **7.1**

Nonconstant growth

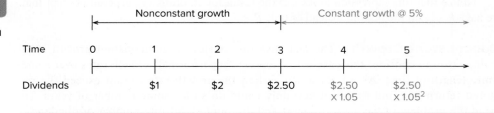

As always, the value of the stock is the present value of all the future dividends. To calculate this present value, we first have to compute the present value of the stock price three years down the road, as we did before. We then have to add in the present value of the dividends that will be paid between now and then. So, the price in three years is:

$$P_3 = D_3 \times (1 + g)/(R - g)$$
$$= \$2.50 \times 1.05/(.10 - .05)$$
$$= \$52.50$$

We can now calculate the total value of the stock as the present value of the first three dividends plus the present value of the price at Time 3, P_3:

$$P_0 = \frac{D_1}{(1 + R)^1} + \frac{D_2}{(1 + R)^2} + \frac{D_3}{(1 + R)^3} + \frac{P_3}{(1 + R)^3}$$
$$= \frac{\$1}{1.10} + \frac{2}{1.10^2} + \frac{2.50}{1.10^3} + \frac{52.50}{1.10^3}$$
$$= \$.91 + 1.65 + 1.88 + 39.44$$
$$= \$43.88$$

The value of the stock today is thus $43.88.

EXAMPLE 7.4   **Supernormal Growth**

Chain Reaction, Inc., has been growing at a phenomenal rate of 30 percent per year because of its rapid expansion and explosive sales. You believe that this growth rate will last for three more years and that the rate will then drop to 10 percent per year. If the growth rate then remains at 10 percent indefinitely, what is the total value of the stock? Total dividends just paid were $5 million, and the required return is 20 percent.

Chain Reaction's situation is an example of supernormal growth. It is unlikely that a 30 percent growth rate can be sustained for any extended length of time. To value the equity in this company, we first need to calculate the total dividends over the supernormal growth period:

Year	Total Dividends (in millions)
1	$5.00 × 1.3 = $ 6.500
2	6.50 × 1.3 = 8.450
3	8.45 × 1.3 = 10.985

The price at Time 3 can be calculated as:

$$P_3 = D_3 \times (1 + g)/(R - g)$$

(continued)

where g is the long-run growth rate. So we have:

$P_3 = \$10.985 \times 1.10/(.20 - .10) = \$120.835$

To determine the value today, we need the present value of this amount plus the present value of the total dividends:

$$P_0 = \frac{D_1}{(1 + R)^1} + \frac{D_2}{(1 + R)^2} + \frac{D_3}{(1 + R)^3} + \frac{P_3}{(1 + R)^3}$$

$$= \frac{\$6.50}{1.20} + \frac{8.45}{1.20^2} + \frac{10.985}{1.20^3} + \frac{120.835}{1.20^3}$$

$$= \$5.42 + 5.87 + 6.36 + 69.93$$

$$= \$87.57$$

The total value of the stock today is thus \$87.57 million. If there were 20 million shares, then the stock would be worth \$87.57/20 = \$4.38 per share.

Components of the Required Return

Thus far, we have taken the required return, or discount rate, R, as given. We will have quite a bit to say on this subject in Chapters 10 and 11. For now, we want to examine the implications of the dividend growth model for this required return. Earlier, we calculated P_0 as:

$$P_0 = D_1 / (R - g)$$

If we rearrange this to solve for R, we get:

$$R - g = D_1 / P_0$$
$$R = D_1 / P_0 + g \qquad\qquad \text{[7.5]}$$

This tells us that the total return, R, has two components. The first of these, D_1/P_0, is called the **dividend yield**. Because this is calculated as the expected cash dividend divided by the current price, it is conceptually similar to the current yield on a bond.

dividend yield
A stock's expected cash dividend divided by its current price.

The second part of the total return is the growth rate, g. We know that the dividend growth rate is also the rate at which the stock price grows (see Example 7.3). Thus, this growth rate can be interpreted as the **capital gains yield**, that is, the rate at which the value of the investment grows.[1]

capital gains yield
The dividend growth rate, or the rate at which the value of an investment grows.

To illustrate the components of the required return, suppose we observe a stock selling for \$20 per share. The next dividend will be \$1 per share. You think that the dividend will grow by 10 percent per year more or less indefinitely. What return does this stock offer you if this is correct?

The dividend growth model calculates the total return as:

$$R = \text{Dividend yield} + \text{Capital gains yield}$$
$$R = D_1 / P_0 + g$$

In this case, the total return works out to be:

$$R = \$1/\$20 + .10$$
$$= .05 + .10$$
$$= .15, \text{ or } 15\%$$

This stock, therefore, has a required return of 15 percent.

---

[1]Here and elsewhere, we use the term *capital gains* a little loosely. For the record, a capital gain (or loss) is, strictly speaking, something defined by the IRS. For our purposes, it would be more accurate (but less common) to use the term *price appreciation* instead of *capital gain*.

We can verify this answer by calculating the price in one year, P_1, using 15 percent as the required return. Based on the dividend growth model, this price is:

$$P_1 = D_1 \times (1 + g)/(R - g)$$
$$= \$1 \times 1.10/(.15 - .10)$$
$$= \$1.10/.05$$
$$= \$22$$

Notice that this $22 is $20 × 1.1, so the stock price has grown by 10 percent, as it should. If you pay $20 for the stock today, you will get a $1 dividend at the end of the year, and you will have a $22 − 20 = $2 gain. Your dividend yield is thus $1/$20 = .05, or 5 percent. Your capital gains yield is $2/$20 = .10, or 10 percent, so your total return would be 5% + 10% = 15%.

To get a feel for actual numbers in this context, consider that, according to the 2018 Value Line *Investment Survey*, The Hershey Company's dividends were expected to grow by 5.5 percent over the next 5 or so years, compared to a historical growth rate of 9 percent over the preceding 10 years. In 2018, the projected dividend for the coming year was given as $2.85. The stock price at that time was about $94 per share. What is the return investors require on Hershey? Here, the dividend yield is about 3 percent and the capital gains yield is 5.5 percent, giving a total required return of 8.5 percent on Hershey stock.

Stock Valuation Using Comparables, or Comps

An obvious problem with our dividend-based approach to stock valuation is that many companies don't pay dividends. What do we do in such cases? A common approach is to make use of the PE ratio, which we defined in Chapter 3 as the ratio of a stock's price per share to its earnings per share (EPS) over the previous year. The idea here is to have some sort of benchmark or reference PE ratio, which we then multiply by earnings to come up with a price:

$$\text{Price at Time } t = P_t = \text{Benchmark PE ratio} \times \text{EPS}_t \qquad [7.6]$$

The benchmark PE ratio could come from one of several possible sources. It could be based on similar companies (perhaps an industry average or median), or it could be based on a company's own historical values. Suppose we are trying to value Inactivision, Inc., a video game developer known for its hit *Slack Ops* series. Inactivision does not pay dividends, but after studying the industry, you feel that a PE ratio of 20 is appropriate for a company like this one. Total earnings over the four most recent quarters combined are $2 per share, so you think the stock should sell for 20 × $2 = $40. You might view it as an attractive purchase if it is going for less than $40, but not attractive if it sells for more than $40.

Security analysts spend a lot of time forecasting future earnings, particularly for the coming year. A PE ratio that is based on estimated future earnings is called a *forward* PE ratio. Suppose you felt that Inactivision's earnings for the coming year were going to be $2.50, reflecting the growing popularity of the company's *World of Slackcraft* massively multiplayer online role-playing game (MMORPG). In this case, if the current stock price is $40, the forward PE ratio is $40/$2.50 = 16.

Finally, notice that your benchmark PE of 20 applies to earnings over the previous year. If earnings over the coming year turn out to be $2.50, then the stock price one year from today should be 20 × $2.50 = $50. Forecast prices such as this one often are called *target* prices.

Often we will be interested in valuing newer companies that both don't pay dividends and are not yet profitable, meaning that earnings are negative. What do we do then? One answer is to use the price-sales ratio, which we also introduced in Chapter 3. As the name suggests, this

TABLE **7.1**

Summary of stock valuation

I.   **The general case**
In general, the price today of a share of stock, P_0, is the present value of all of its future dividends, $D_1, D_2, D_3, \dots$:

$$P_0 = \frac{D_1}{(1+R)^1} + \frac{D_2}{(1+R)^2} + \frac{D_3}{(1+R)^3} + \dots$$

where R is the required return.

II.   **Constant growth case**
If the dividend is constant and equal to D, then the price can be written as:

$$P_0 = \frac{D}{R}$$

If the dividend grows at a steady rate g, then the price can be written as:

$$P_0 = \frac{D_1}{R-g}$$

This result is called the *dividend growth model*.

III.   **Nonconstant Growth**
If the dividend grows steadily after t periods, then the price can be written as:

$$P_0 = \frac{D_1}{(1+R)^1} + \frac{D_2}{(1+R)^2} + \dots + \frac{D_t}{(1+R)^t} + \frac{P_t}{(1+R)^t}$$

where:

$$P_t = \frac{D_t \times (1+g)}{(R-g)}$$

IV.   **The required return, R, can be written as the sum of two things:**

$$R = D_1/P_0 + g$$

where D_1/P_0 is the *dividend yield* and g is the *capital gains yield* (which is the same thing as the growth rate in dividends for the steady growth case).

V.   **Valuation Using Comparables**
For stocks that don't pay dividends (or have erratic dividend growth rates), we can value them using the PE ratio and/or the price-sales ratio:

P_t = Benchmark PE ratio × EPS_t
P_t = Benchmark price–sales ratio × Sales per share$_t$

ratio is the price per share on the stock divided by sales per share. You use this ratio like you use the PE ratio, except you use sales per share instead of earnings per share. As with PE ratios, price-sales ratios vary depending on company age and industry. Typical values are in the .8–2.0 range, but they can be much higher for younger, faster-growing companies.

For future reference, our discussion of stock valuation techniques is summarized in Table 7.1.

CONCEPT QUESTIONS

7.1a   What are the relevant cash flows for valuing a share of common stock?

7.1b   Does the value of a share of stock depend on how long you expect to keep it?

7.1c   What is the value of a share of stock when the dividend grows at a constant rate?

7.1d   What is a "target price" on a stock? How is it determined?

7.2 SOME FEATURES OF COMMON AND PREFERRED STOCK

In discussing common stock features, we focus on shareholder rights and dividend payments. For preferred stock, we explain what "preferred" means, and we also debate whether preferred stock is really debt or equity.

Common Stock Features

common stock
Equity without priority for dividends or in bankruptcy.

The term **common stock** means different things to different people, but it is usually applied to stock that has no special preference either in paying dividends or in bankruptcy.

Shareholder Rights   The conceptual structure of the corporation assumes that shareholders elect directors who, in turn, hire management to carry out their directives. Shareholders, therefore, control the corporation through the right to elect the directors. Generally, only shareholders have this right.

Directors are elected each year at an annual meeting. Although there are exceptions (discussed in a moment), the general idea is "one share, one vote" (*not* one share*holder*, one vote). Corporate democracy is thus very different from our political democracy. With corporate democracy, the "golden rule" prevails absolutely.[2]

Directors are elected at an annual shareholders' meeting by a vote of the holders of a majority of shares who are present and entitled to vote. However, the exact mechanism for electing directors differs across companies. The most important difference is whether shares must be voted cumulatively or voted straight.

To illustrate the two different voting procedures, imagine that a corporation has two shareholders: Smith with 20 shares and Jones with 80 shares. Both want to be a director. Jones does not want Smith, however. We assume that there are a total of four directors to be elected.

cumulative voting
A procedure in which a shareholder may cast all votes for one member of the board of directors.

The effect of **cumulative voting** is to permit minority participation.[3] If cumulative voting is permitted, the total number of votes that each shareholder may cast is determined first. This is usually calculated as the number of shares (owned or controlled) multiplied by the number of directors to be elected.

With cumulative voting, the directors are elected all at once. In our example, this means that the top four vote-getters will be the new directors. Individual shareholders can distribute votes however they wish.

Will Smith get a seat on the board? If we ignore the possibility of a five-way tie, then the answer is yes. Smith will cast $20 \times 4 = 80$ votes, and Jones will cast $80 \times 4 = 320$ votes. If Smith gives all his votes to himself, he is assured of a directorship. The reason is that Jones can't divide 320 votes among four candidates in such a way as to give all of them more than 80 votes, so Smith will finish fourth at worst.

In general, if there are N directors up for election, then $1/(N + 1)$ percent of the stock plus one share will guarantee you a seat. In our current example, this is $1/(4 + 1) = .20$, or 20 percent (plus one share). So, the more seats that are up for election at one time, the easier (and cheaper) it is to win one.

straight voting
A procedure in which a shareholder may cast all votes for each member of the board of directors.

With **straight voting** the directors are elected one at a time. Each time, Smith can cast 20 votes and Jones can cast 80. As a consequence, Jones will elect all of the candidates. The only way to guarantee a seat is to own 50 percent plus one share. This also guarantees that you will win every seat, so it's really all or nothing.

---

[2]The golden rule: Whoever has the gold makes the rules.

[3]By minority participation, we mean participation by shareholders with relatively small amounts of stock.

| EXAMPLE 7.5 | **Buying the Election** |

Stock in JRJ Corporation sells for $20 per share and features cumulative voting. There are 10,000 shares outstanding. If three directors are up for election, how much does it cost to ensure yourself a seat on the board?

The question here is how many shares of stock it will take to get a seat. The answer is 2,501, so the cost is 2,501 × $20 = $50,020. Why 2,501? Because there is no way the remaining 7,499 votes can be divided among three people to give all of them more than 2,501 votes. For example, suppose two people receive 2,502 votes and the first two seats. A third person can receive at most 10,000 − 2,502 − 2,502 − 2,501 = 2,495, so the third seat is yours. Verify that we arrived at 2,501 using the formula described earlier.

As we've illustrated, straight voting can "freeze out" minority shareholders; that is the reason many states have mandatory cumulative voting. In states where cumulative voting is mandatory, devices have been worked out to minimize its impact.

Many companies have staggered elections for directors. With staggered elections, only a fraction of the directorships are up for election at a particular time. Thus, if only two directors are up for election at any one time, it will take $1/(2 + 1) = .3333$, or 33.33 percent of the stock plus one share to guarantee a seat. Staggered boards are often called "classified" boards because directors are placed into different classes with terms that expire at different times. In recent years, corporations have come under pressure to "declassify" their boards, meaning that all directors would stand for election every year, and many have done so.

Overall, staggering has two basic effects:

1. Staggering makes it more difficult for a minority shareholder to elect a director when there is cumulative voting because there are fewer directors to be elected at one time.

2. Staggering makes takeover attempts less likely to be successful because it makes it more difficult to vote in a majority of new directors.

We should note that staggering may serve a beneficial purpose. It provides "institutional memory," that is, continuity on the board of directors. This may be important for corporations with significant long-range plans and projects.

Proxy Voting   A **proxy** is the grant of authority by a shareholder to someone else to vote that shareholder's shares. For convenience, much of the voting in large public corporations is actually done by proxy.

As we have seen, with straight voting, each share of stock has one vote. The owner of 10,000 shares has 10,000 votes. Large companies have hundreds of thousands or even millions of shareholders. Shareholders can come to the annual meeting and vote in person, or they can transfer their right to vote to another party.

Obviously, management always tries to get as many proxies as possible transferred to it. However, if shareholders are not satisfied with management, an "outside" group of shareholders can try to obtain votes via proxy. They can vote by proxy in an attempt to replace management by electing enough directors. The resulting battle is called a *proxy fight*.

Classes of Stock   Some firms have more than one class of common stock. Often, the classes are created with unequal voting rights. The Ford Motor Company, for example, has Class B common stock, which is not publicly traded (it is held by Ford family interests and

proxy
A grant of authority by a shareholder allowing another individual to vote his or her shares.

trusts). This class has about 40 percent of the voting power, even though it represents less than 10 percent of the total number of shares outstanding.

There are many other cases of corporations with different classes of stock. For example, Google, the web search company, has three publicly traded classes of common stock, A, B, and C. The Class A shares are held by the public, and each share has one vote. The Class B shares are held by company insiders, and each Class B share has 10 votes. Then, in 2014, the company had a stock split of its Class B shares, creating Class C shares, which have no vote at all. As a result, Google's founders and managers control the company. The CEO of cable TV giant Comcast, Brian Roberts, owns about .04 percent of the company's equity, but he has a third of all the votes thanks to the creation of a special class of stock.

In principle, the New York Stock Exchange does not allow companies to create classes of publicly traded common stock with unequal voting rights. Exceptions (e.g., Ford) appear to have been made. In addition, many non-NYSE companies have dual classes of common stock.

A primary reason for creating dual or multiple classes of stock has to do with control of the firm. If such stock exists, management of a firm can raise equity capital by issuing nonvoting or limited-voting stock while maintaining control.

The subject of unequal voting rights is controversial in the United States, and the idea of one share, one vote has a strong following and a long history. Interestingly, however, shares with unequal voting rights are quite common in the United Kingdom and elsewhere around the world.

Other Rights   The value of a share of common stock in a corporation is directly related to the general rights of shareholders. In addition to the right to vote for directors, shareholders usually have the following rights:

1. The right to share proportionally in dividends paid.
2. The right to share proportionally in assets remaining after liabilities have been paid in a liquidation.
3. The right to vote on stockholder matters of great importance, such as a merger. Voting is usually done at the annual meeting or a special meeting.

In addition, shareholders sometimes have the right to share proportionally in any new stock sold. This is called the *preemptive right.*

Essentially, a preemptive right means that a company that wishes to sell stock must first offer it to the existing stockholders before offering it to the general public. The purpose is to give stockholders the opportunity to protect their proportionate ownership in the corporation.

Dividends   A distinctive feature of corporations is that they have shares of stock on which they are authorized by law to pay dividends to their shareholders. **Dividends** paid to shareholders represent a return on the capital directly or indirectly contributed to the corporation by the shareholders. The payment of dividends is at the discretion of the board of directors.

dividend
Payments by a corporation to shareholders, made in either cash or stock.

Some important characteristics of dividends include the following:

1. Unless a dividend is declared by the board of directors of a corporation, it is not a liability of the corporation. A corporation cannot default on an undeclared dividend. As a consequence, corporations cannot become bankrupt because of nonpayment of dividends. The amount of the dividend and even whether it is paid are decisions based on the business judgment of the board of directors.

2. The payment of dividends by the corporation is not a business expense. Dividends are not deductible for corporate tax purposes. In short, dividends are paid out of the corporation's aftertax profits.

3. Dividends received by individual shareholders are taxable. In 2018, the tax rate was 15 to 20 percent. However, corporations that own stock in other corporations are permitted to exclude 50 percent of the dividend amounts they receive and are taxed on only the remaining 50 percent (the 50 percent exclusion was reduced from 70 percent by the Tax Cuts and Jobs Act of 2017).[4]

Preferred Stock Features

Preferred stock differs from common stock because it has preference over common stock in the payment of dividends and in the distribution of corporation assets in the event of liquidation. *Preference* means only that the holders of the preferred shares must receive a dividend (in the case of an ongoing firm) before holders of common shares are entitled to anything.

Preferred stock is a form of equity from a legal and tax standpoint. It is important to note, however, that holders of preferred stock sometimes have no voting privileges.

preferred stock
Stock with dividend priority over common stock, normally with a fixed dividend rate, sometimes without voting rights.

Stated Value   Preferred shares have a stated liquidating value, usually $100 per share. The cash dividend is described in terms of dollars per share. For example, General Motors "$5 preferred" easily translates into a dividend yield of 5 percent of stated value.

Cumulative and Noncumulative Dividends   A preferred dividend is not like interest on a bond. The board of directors may decide not to pay the dividends on preferred shares, and their decision may have nothing to do with the current net income of the corporation.

Dividends payable on preferred stock are either *cumulative* or *noncumulative*; most are cumulative. If preferred dividends are cumulative and are not paid in a particular year, they will be carried forward as an *arrearage*. Usually, both the accumulated (past) preferred dividends and the current preferred dividends must be paid before the common shareholders can receive anything.

Unpaid preferred dividends are not debts of the firm. Directors elected by the common shareholders can defer preferred dividends indefinitely. However, in such cases, common shareholders also must forgo dividends. In addition, holders of preferred shares are often granted voting and other rights if preferred dividends have not been paid for some time. For example, at one point, US Airways had failed to pay dividends on one of its preferred stock issues for six quarters. As a consequence, the holders of the shares were allowed to nominate two people to represent their interests on the airline's board. Because preferred stockholders receive no interest on the accumulated dividends, some have argued that firms have an incentive to delay paying preferred dividends, but, as we have seen, this may mean sharing control with preferred stockholders.

Is Preferred Stock Really Debt?   A good case can be made that preferred stock is really debt in disguise, a kind of equity bond. Preferred shareholders are only entitled to receive a stated dividend, and, if the corporation is liquidated, preferred shareholders are only

---

[4]For the record, the 50 percent exclusion applies when the recipient owns less than 20 percent of the outstanding stock in a corporation. If a corporation owns more than 20 percent but less than 65 percent, the exclusion is 65 percent. If more than 65 percent is owned, the corporation can file a single "consolidated" return, and the exclusion is effectively 100 percent.

entitled to the stated value of their preferred shares. Often, preferred stocks carry credit ratings much like those of bonds. Furthermore, preferred stock is sometimes convertible into common stock, and preferred stocks are often callable.

In addition, in recent years, many new issues of preferred stock have had obligatory sinking funds. The existence of such a sinking fund effectively creates a final maturity because it means that the entire issue ultimately will be retired. For these reasons, preferred stock seems to be a lot like debt. However, for tax purposes, preferred dividends are treated like common stock dividends.

CONCEPT QUESTIONS

7.2a   What is a proxy?

7.2b   What rights do stockholders have?

7.2c   Why is preferred stock called preferred?

7.3 THE STOCK MARKETS

Excel Master coverage online

primary market
The market in which new securities are originally sold to investors.

secondary market
The market in which previously issued securities are traded among investors.

dealer
An agent who buys and sells securities from inventory.

broker
An agent who arranges security transactions among investors.

Back in Chapter 1, we very briefly mentioned that shares of stock are bought and sold on various stock exchanges, the two most important of which are the New York Stock Exchange and the NASDAQ. From our earlier discussion, recall that the stock market consists of a **primary market** and a **secondary market**. In the primary, or new-issue, market, shares of stock are first brought to the market and sold to investors. In the secondary market, existing shares are traded among investors.

In the primary market, companies sell securities to raise money. We will discuss this process in detail in a later chapter. We therefore focus mainly on secondary market activity in this section. We conclude with a discussion of how stock prices are quoted in the financial press.

Dealers and Brokers

Because most securities transactions involve dealers and brokers, it is important to understand exactly what is meant by the terms *dealer* and *broker*. A **dealer** maintains an inventory and stands ready to buy and sell at any time. In contrast, a **broker** brings buyers and sellers together but does not maintain an inventory. Thus, when we speak of used car dealers and real estate brokers, we recognize that the used car dealer maintains an inventory, whereas the real estate broker does not.

In the securities markets, a dealer stands ready to buy securities from investors wishing to sell them and sell securities to investors wishing to buy them. Recall from our previous chapter that the price the dealer is willing to pay is called the bid price. The price at which the dealer will sell is called the ask price (sometimes called the asked, offered, or offering price). The difference between the bid and ask prices is called the spread, and it is the basic source of dealer profits.

Dealers exist in all areas of the economy, not just the stock markets. For example, your local college bookstore is probably both a primary and a secondary market textbook dealer. If you buy a new book, this is a primary market transaction. If you buy a used book, this is a secondary market transaction, and you pay the store's ask price. If you sell the book back, you receive the store's bid price, often half of the ask price. The bookstore's spread is the difference between the two prices.

In contrast, a securities broker arranges transactions between investors, matching investors wishing to buy securities with investors wishing to sell securities. The distinctive characteristic of security brokers is that they do not buy or sell securities for their own accounts. Facilitating trades by others is their business.

Organization of the NYSE

The New York Stock Exchange, or NYSE, popularly known as the Big Board, was founded in 1792. It has occupied its current location on Wall Street since the turn of the twentieth century. Measured in terms of dollar volume of activity and the total value of shares listed, it is the largest stock market in the world.

Members   Historically, the NYSE had 1,366 exchange **members**. Prior to 2006, the exchange members were said to own "seats" on the exchange, and, collectively, the members of the exchange were also the owners. For this and other reasons, seats were valuable and were bought and sold fairly regularly. Seat prices reached a record $4 million in 2005.

> **member**
> As of 2006, a member is the owner of a trading license on the NYSE.

In 2006, all of this changed when the NYSE became a publicly owned corporation called NYSE Group, Inc. Naturally, its stock is listed on the NYSE. Now, instead of purchasing seats, exchange members must purchase trading licenses, the number of which is limited to 1,366. In 2018, a license would set you back a cool $50,000—per year. Having a license entitles you to buy and sell securities on the floor of the exchange. Different members play different roles in this regard.

On April 4, 2007, the NYSE grew even larger when it merged with Euronext to form NYSE Euronext. Euronext was a stock exchange in Amsterdam, with subsidiaries in Belgium, France, Portugal, and the United Kingdom. With the merger, NYSE Euronext became the world's "first global exchange." Further expansion occurred in 2008 when NYSE Euronext merged with the American Stock Exchange. Then, in November 2013, the acquisition of the NYSE by the Intercontinental Exchange (ICE) was completed. ICE, which was founded in May 2000, was originally a commodities exchange, but its rapid growth gave it the necessary $8.2 billion to acquire the NYSE.

As we briefly describe how the NYSE operates, keep in mind that other markets owned by NYSE Euronext and ICE may function differently. What makes the NYSE somewhat unique is that it is a *hybrid market*. In a hybrid market, trading takes place both electronically and face-to-face.

With electronic trading, orders to buy and orders to sell are submitted to the exchange. Orders are compared by a computer and whenever there is a match, the orders are executed with no human intervention. Most trades on the NYSE occur this way. For orders that are not handled electronically, the NYSE relies on its license holders. There are three different types of license holders, **designated market makers (DMMs)**, **floor brokers**, and **supplemental liquidity providers (SLPs)**, and we now discuss the role played by each.

> **designated market makers (DMMs)**
> NYSE members who act as dealers in particular stocks. Formerly known as "specialists."

> **floor brokers**
> NYSE members who execute customer buy and sell orders.

The DMMs, formerly known as "specialists," act as dealers in particular stocks. Typically, each stock on the NYSE is assigned to a single DMM. As a dealer, a DMM maintains a two-sided market, meaning that the DMM continually posts and updates bid and ask prices. By doing so, the DMM ensures that there is always a buyer or seller available, thereby promoting market liquidity.

> **supplemental liquidity providers (SLPs)**
> Investment firms that are active participants in stocks assigned to them. Their job is to make a one-sided market (i.e., offering to either buy or sell). They trade purely for their own accounts.

The job of a floor broker is to execute trades for customers, with an emphasis on getting the best price possible. Floor brokers are generally employees of large brokerage firms such as Merrill Lynch, the wealth management division of Bank of America. The interaction between floor brokers and DMMs is the key to nonelectronic trading on the NYSE. We discuss this interaction in detail in just a moment.

The SLPs are essentially investment firms that agree to be active participants in stocks assigned to them. Their job is to regularly make a one-sided market (i.e., offering to either buy or sell). They trade purely for their own accounts (using their own money), so they do not represent customers. They are given a small rebate on their buys and sells, thereby encouraging them to be more aggressive. The NYSE's goal is to generate as much liquidity as possible, which makes it easier for ordinary investors to quickly buy and sell at prevailing prices. Unlike DMMs and floor brokers, SLPs do not operate on the floor of the stock exchange.

In recent years, floor brokers have become less important on the exchange floor because of the efficient Pillar system, which allows orders to be transmitted electronically directly to the DMM. Additionally, the NYSE has an electronic platform called Arca, which accounts for a substantial percentage of all trading on the NYSE, particularly for smaller orders. The average time for a trade on the NYSE Arca is less than 1 second.

Finally, a small number of NYSE members are floor traders who independently trade for their own accounts. Floor traders try to anticipate temporary price fluctuations and profit from them by buying low and selling high. In recent decades, the number of floor traders has declined substantially, suggesting that it has become increasingly difficult to profit from short-term trading on the exchange floor.

Operations   Now that we have a basic idea of how the NYSE is organized and who the major players are, we turn to the question of how trading actually takes place. Fundamentally, the business of the NYSE is to attract and process **order flow**. The term *order flow* means the flow of customer orders to buy and sell stocks. The customers of the NYSE are the millions of individual investors and tens of thousands of institutional investors who place their orders to buy and sell shares in NYSE-listed companies. The NYSE has been quite successful in attracting order flow. Currently, it is common for more than one billion shares to change hands in a single day.

Floor Activity   It is quite likely that you have seen footage of the NYSE trading floor on television, or you may have visited the NYSE and viewed exchange floor activity from the visitors' gallery (it's worth the trip). Either way, you would have seen a big room, about the size of a basketball gym. This big room is called, technically, "the Big Room." There are a couple of other, smaller rooms that you normally don't see, one of which is called "the Garage" because that is literally what it was before it was taken over for trading.

On the floor of the exchange are a number of stations. These stations have multiple counters with numerous terminal screens above and on the sides. People operate behind and in front of the counters in relatively stationary positions.

Other people move around on the exchange floor. In all, you may be reminded of worker ants moving around an ant colony. It is natural to wonder: What are all those people doing down there (and why are so many wearing funny-looking coats)?

As an overview of exchange floor activity, here is a quick look at what goes on. Each of the counters is a **DMM's post**. DMMs normally operate in front of their posts to monitor and manage trading in the stocks assigned to them. Clerical employees working for the DMMs operate behind the counter. Moving from the many workstations lining the walls of the exchange out to the exchange floor and back again are swarms of floor

order flow
The flow of customer orders to buy and sell securities.

DMM's post
A fixed place on the exchange floor where the DMM operates.

brokers, receiving customer orders, walking out to DMMs' posts where the orders can be executed, and returning to confirm order executions and receive new customer orders.

To better understand activity on the NYSE trading floor, imagine yourself as a floor broker. Your clerk has just handed you an order to sell 2,000 shares of Walmart for a customer of the brokerage company that employs you. The customer wants to sell the stock at the best possible price as soon as possible. You immediately walk (running violates exchange rules) to the DMM's post where Walmart stock is traded.

As you approach the DMM's post where Walmart is traded, you check the terminal screen for information on the current market price. The screen reveals that the last executed trade was at $25.63 and that the DMM is bidding $25.50 per share. You could immediately sell to the DMM at $25.50, but that would be too easy.

Take a virtual field trip to the New York Stock Exchange at www.nyse.com.

Instead, as the customer's representative, you are obligated to get the best possible price. It is your job to "work" the order, and your job depends on providing satisfactory order execution service. So, you look around for another broker who represents a customer who wants to buy Walmart stock. Luckily, you quickly find another broker at the DMM's post with an order to buy 2,000 shares. Noticing that the dealer is asking $25.76 per share, you both agree to execute your orders with each other at a price of $25.63. This price is halfway between the DMM's bid and ask prices, and it saves each of your customers $.13 × 2,000 = $260 as compared to dealing at the posted prices.

For a very actively traded stock, there may be many buyers and sellers around the DMM's post, and most of the trading will be done directly between brokers. This is called trading in the "crowd." In such cases, the DMM's responsibility is to maintain order and to make sure that all buyers and sellers receive a fair price. In other words, the DMM essentially functions as a referee.

More often, however, there will be no crowd at the DMM's post. Going back to our Walmart example, suppose you are unable to quickly find another broker with an order to buy 2,000 shares. Because you have an order to sell immediately, you may have no choice but to sell to the DMM at the bid price of $25.50. In this case, the need to execute an order quickly takes priority, and the DMM provides the liquidity necessary to allow immediate order execution.

Finally, note that colored coats are worn by many of the people on the floor of the exchange. The color of the coat indicates the person's job or position. Clerks, runners, visitors, exchange officials, and so on wear particular colors to identify themselves. Also, things can get a little hectic on a busy day, with the result that good clothing doesn't last long; the cheap coats offer some protection.

NASDAQ Operations

In terms of the number of companies listed and, on many days, the number of shares traded, the NASDAQ (say "Naz-dak") is even bigger than the NYSE. As we mentioned in Chapter 1, the somewhat odd name is derived from the acronym *NASDAQ*, which stood for National Association of Securities Dealers Automated Quotations system; but NASDAQ is now a name in its own right.

How big is the bid-ask spread on your favorite NASDAQ stock? Check out the latest quotes at money.cnn.com!

Introduced in 1971, the NASDAQ market is a computer network of securities dealers who disseminate timely security price quotes to NASDAQ subscribers. These dealers act as market makers for securities listed on the NASDAQ. As market makers, NASDAQ dealers post bid and asked prices at which they accept sell and buy orders, respectively. With each price quote, they also post the number of stock shares that they obligate themselves to trade at their quoted prices.

Not to be outdone by the NYSE, the NASDAQ completed a merger in May 2007 when it finalized its deal to buy the OMX, which controlled seven Nordic and Baltic stock exchanges. Since the merger, the NASDAQ is officially the NASDAQ OMX Group, although it is still often referred to as NASDAQ.

Unlike the NYSE DMM system, NASDAQ relies on multiple market makers for actively traded stocks. Thus, there are two key differences between the NYSE and NAS-DAQ: (1) NASDAQ is a computer network and has no physical location where trading takes place and (2) NASDAQ has a multiple market maker system rather than a DMM system. Notice that there is no direct trading in the crowd as there may be on the NYSE.

About 3,400 companies are listed on the NASDAQ system, with an average of about a dozen market makers for each security. Traditionally, shares of stock in smaller companies were listed on the NASDAQ, and there was a tendency for companies to move from the NASDAQ to the NYSE once they became large enough. Today, however, giant companies such as Amazon, Microsoft, and Intel have chosen to remain on the NASDAQ.

The NASDAQ network operates with three levels of information access. Level 1 is designed to provide a timely, accurate source of price quotations. These prices are freely available over the Internet.

Level 2 allows users to view price quotes from all NASDAQ market makers. In particular, this level allows access to **inside quotes**. Inside quotes are the highest bid quotes and the lowest asked quotes for a NASDAQ-listed security. Level 2 is now available on the web, sometimes for a small fee. Level 3 is for the use of market makers only. This access level allows NASDAQ dealers to enter or change their price quote information.

The NASDAQ is actually made up of three separate markets: the NASDAQ Global Select Market, the NASDAQ Global Market, and the NASDAQ Capital Market. As the market for NASDAQ's larger and more actively traded securities, the Global Select Market lists about 1,600 companies (as of 2018), including some of the best-known companies in the world, such as Microsoft and Intel. The Global Market companies are somewhat smaller in size, and NASDAQ lists about 860 of these companies. Finally, the smallest companies listed on NASDAQ are in the NASDAQ Capital Market; about 940 are currently listed. Of course, as Capital Market companies become more established, they may move up to the Global Market or Global Select Market.

ECNs   In a very important development in the late 1990s, the NASDAQ system was opened to so-called **electronic communications networks (ECNs)**. ECNs are basically websites that allow investors to trade directly with one another. Investor buy and sell orders placed on ECNs are transmitted to the NASDAQ and displayed along with market maker bid and ask prices. Thus, the ECNs open up the NASDAQ by essentially allowing individual investors, not just market makers, to enter orders. As a result, the ECNs act to increase liquidity and competition. Our nearby *Work the Web* box describes one ECN, the CBOE Global Markets (markets.cboe.com/us/equities), and contains important information about ECN "order books." Be sure to read it.

NASDAQ
(www.nasdaq.com) has a great website; check it out!

inside quotes
The highest bid quotes and the lowest ask quotes for a security.

electronic communications networks (ECNs)
Websites that allow investors to trade directly with one another.

W🌐RK THE WEB

Y ou can actually watch trading taking place on the web by visiting markets.cboe.com/us/equities. This stock market was originally the BATS Exchange until it was purchased by the CBOE in 2016. This market is somewhat unique in that the "order book," meaning the list of all buy and sell orders, is public in real time. As shown, we have captured a sample of the order book for Intel (INTC). On the top in blue are sell orders (asks); buy orders (bids) are in green on the bottom. All orders are "limit" orders, which means the customer has specified the most he or she will pay (for buy orders) or the least he or she will accept (for sell orders). The inside quotes (the highest bid, or buy, and the lowest ask, or sell) in the market are shown in bold face.

Book Viewer ≫ BZX Equities BYX Equities EDGX Equities EDGA Equities				Market Quality Statistics
Shows the top bids and asks for any symbol				
INTC			Orders Accepted	Total Volume
INTEL CORP COM			401,142	2,778,405

	TOP OF BOOK			LAST 10 TRADES	
	Shares	Price	Time	Price	Shares
ASKS	800	**52.37**	14:35:40	52.34	100
	600	52.36	14:35:39	52.34	100
	700	52.35	14:35:32	52.32	100
	1,000	52.34	14:35:32	52.32	100
	800	52.33	14:35:30	52.32	100
BIDS	1,500	**52.32**	14:35:21	52.30	100
	1,500	52.31	14:35:19	52.29	100
	600	52.30	14:35:18	52.29	100
	1,000	52.29	14:35:17	52.29	100
	1,000	52.28	14:35:15	52.29	100

Source: **markets.cboe.com**

If you visit the site, you can see trading take place as orders are entered and executed. Notice that on this particular day, about 2.8 million shares of Intel had traded on the CBOE Market. At that time, the inside quotes for Intel were 1,500 shares bid at $52.32 and 800 shares offered at $52.33. This is not the entire order book for Intel as there are more buy orders below $52.28 and more sell orders above $52.37.

QUESTIONS

1. *Go to markets.cboe.com/us/equities and look up the order book for Microsoft (MSFT). What are the inside quotes for Microsoft?*
2. *Go to markets.cboe.com/us/equities. This website shows the 25 most active stocks. Looking down through this list, what are the bid-ask spreads for these stocks?*

Of course, the NYSE and NASDAQ are not the only places stocks are traded. See our nearby *Finance Matters* box for a discussion of somewhat wilder markets.

The Wild, Wild West of Stock Trading

Where do companies go when they can't (or don't want to) meet the listing requirements of the larger stock markets? Two options are the Over-the-Counter Bulletin Board (OTCBB) and the OTC Markets, formerly Pink Sheets. These two electronic markets are part of the Wild, Wild West of stock trading. The somewhat odd names have simple explanations. The OTCBB began as an electronic bulletin board that was created to facilitate OTC trading in nonlisted stocks. The name "Pink Sheets" reflects the fact that, at one time, prices for such stocks were quoted on pink sheets of paper.

The well-known markets such as the NASDAQ and the NYSE have relatively strict listing requirements. If a company fails to meet these requirements, it can be delisted. The OTCBB and the Pink Sheets, on the other hand, have no listing requirements. The OTCBB does require that companies file financial statements with the SEC (or other relevant agency), but the Pink Sheets does not.

Stocks traded on these markets often have very low prices and are frequently referred to as "penny stocks," "microcaps," or even "nanocaps." Relatively few brokers do any research on these companies, so information is often spread through word of mouth or the internet, not the most reliable of sources. In fact, for many stocks, these markets often look like big electronic rumor mills and gossip factories. To get a feel for what trading looks like, we captured a typical screen from the OTCBB website (finra-markets.morningstar.com/MarketData/EquityOptions/default.jsp).

First, let's look at the returns. Intelligent Highway Solutions, Inc. (IHSI), had a return on this day of 100 percent! Of course, the gain occurred because the stock price jumped by $.0001. The stock price of Sky440, Inc. (SKYF), fell about 43 percent, as its price dropped by $.0003. Stocks on the OTCBB tend to have large trading volumes when they do trade, but the dollar amount is quite a bit

Most Actives	% Gainers	% Losers		Exchange by	OOTC ▼
Symbol			Last	Chg	Chg %	Vol (mil) ▼
SKYF	▼	0.0004	-0.0003	-42.8571	617.1280
WSTI	▲	0.0015	0.0005	50.0000	206.7324
IHSI	▲	0.0002	0.0001	100.0000	196.4200
ALKM	▼	0.0019	-0.0004	-17.3913	182.6769
RBIZ	▼	0.0009	-0.0004	-30.7692	163.6658
ADTM	▼	0.0007	-0.0003	-30.0000	163.2937
ABWN	▼	0.0087	-0.0013	-13.0000	106.4823
LCLP	▲	0.0005	0.0000	0.0000	93.7315
SRMX	▼	0.0020	-0.0005	-20.0000	85.5750
BTGI	▲	0.0005	0.0000	0.0000	72.5206

Source: finra-markets.morningstar.com

lower than seen on the larger exchanges. For example, by the end of this same trading day, Advance Micro Devices (AMD) was the most active stock on the NYSE, with about 94 million shares changing hands. Sky440 (SKYF) traded about 632 million shares. However, the total dollar volume for the day was a whopping $340,000 or so. In contrast, about $1.48 billion worth of AMD stock was traded.

The OTC Markets (www.otcmarkets.com) is a publicly traded company. To be listed on the OTC Markets, a company just has to find a market maker willing to trade in the company's stock. Companies list on the OTC Markets for various reasons. Small companies that do not wish to meet listing requirements are one type. Foreign companies often list on the OTC Markets because they do not prepare their

financial statements according to GAAP, a requirement for listing on U.S. stock exchanges. There are many companies that were formerly listed on bigger stock markets that were either delisted involuntarily or chose to "go dark" for various reasons, including, as we discussed in Chapter 1, the costs associated with Sarbox compliance.

All in all, the OTCBB and OTC Markets can be pretty wild places to trade. Low stock prices allow huge percentage returns on small stock price movements. Be advised, however, that attempts at manipulation and fraud are commonplace. Also, stocks on these markets are often very thinly traded, meaning there is little volume. It is not unusual for a stock listed on either market to have no trades on a given day. Even two or three days in a row without a trade in a particular stock is not uncommon.

Stock Market Reporting

Like so many other things, stock price reporting has largely migrated to the web. You can get up-to-the-minute prices on stocks from many online servers, along with plenty of information about a stock. The following is a stock quote from finance.yahoo.com for famed motorcycle manufacturer Harley-Davidson (HOG) from June 21, 2018.

Harley-Davidson, Inc. (HOG)   ☆ Add to watchlist
NYSE - Nasdaq Real Time Price. Currency in USD

45.61 -0.07 (-0.15%)
As of 2:47PM EDT. Market open.

Summary | Chart | Conversations | Statistics | Profile | Financials | Options | Holders | Historical Data | Analysis | Sustainability NEW

Previous Close	45.68	Market Cap	7.518B
Open	45.46	Beta	0.62
Bid	45.57 x 1200	PE Ratio (TTM)	15.27
Ask	45.58 x 900	EPS (TTM)	2.99
Day's Range	45.10 - 45.84	Earnings Date	Jul 16, 2018 - Jul 20, 2018
52 Week Range	39.34 - 56.95	Forward Dividend & Yield	1.48 (3.22%)
Volume	1,326,553	Ex-Dividend Date	2018-05-30
Avg. Volume	2,160,600	1y Target Est	48.31

Source: finance.yahoo.com, 2018

In the upper left, we have a recent trade price of $45.61. Based on that price, the stock had fallen by $.07 during the day, or .15 percent. In the box below, more information is provided. For example, the "Previous Close" is the closing price from the previous trading day, and "Open" is the first price of the current day. The high price for this day so far, shown in "Day's Range," was $45.84, and the low price was $45.10. About 1.33 million shares of Harley-Davidson had traded, relative to an average volume over the last three months of 2.16 million shares. As always, the bid and ask are the highest price someone was willing to pay and the lowest price someone was willing to take. For example, 45.57 × 1,200 tells you that someone was willing to pay $45.57 for 1,200 shares. The "×" is read as "by." You also can see the number of shares at the ask price. The "52 Week Range" gives the highest and lowest stock prices over the past 52 weeks.

And there is even more information in the quote. "Beta" is an important number. We will have lots more to say about it in a later chapter. Harley-Davidson, like most dividend-paying companies, actually pays dividends quarterly. However, the dividend shown of $1.48 is the expected dividend for the coming year. The dividend yield is the annual dividend divided by the stock price. Harley-Davidson's EPS for the past year was $2.99. The PE ratio shown is calculated using the current stock price divided by the last 12 months' earnings. The "1y Target Est" is the projected price next year based on analysts' estimates. Finally, we are shown the "Market Cap" (market capitalization, or total value of Harley-Davidson's stock).

> You can get real-time stock quotes on the web. See finance.yahoo.com for details.

CONCEPT QUESTIONS

7.3a   What is the difference between a securities broker and a securities dealer?

7.3b   Which is bigger, the bid price or the ask price? Why?

7.3c   What are the three types of license holders of the New York Stock Exchange, or NYSE?

7.3d   How does NASDAQ differ from the NYSE?

SUMMARY AND CONCLUSIONS

This chapter has covered the basics of stocks and stock valuation. The key points include:

1. The cash flows from owning a share of stock come in the form of future dividends. We saw that in certain special cases it is possible to calculate the present value of all the future dividends and thus come up with a value for the stock.

2. As the owner of shares of common stock in a corporation, you have various rights, including the right to vote to elect corporate directors. Voting in corporate elections can be either cumulative or straight. Most voting actually is done by proxy, and a proxy battle breaks out when competing sides try to gain enough votes to have their candidates for the board elected.

3. In addition to common stock, some corporations have issued preferred stock. The name stems from the fact that preferred stockholders must be paid first, before common stockholders can receive anything. Preferred stock has a fixed dividend.

4. The two biggest stock markets in the United States are the NYSE and the NASDAQ. We discussed the organization and operation of these two markets, and we saw how stock price information is reported.

This chapter completes Part Four of our book. By now, you should have a good grasp of what we mean by present value. You also should be familiar with how to calculate present values, loan payments, and so on. In Part Five, we cover capital budgeting decisions. As you will see, the techniques you have learned in Chapters 4–7 form the basis for our approach to evaluating business investment decisions.

---

 connect POP QUIZ!

Can you answer the following questions? If your class is using *Connect*, log on to SmartBook to see if you know the answers to these and other questions, check out the study tools, and find out what topics require additional practice!

Section 7.1 What is the total return for a stock that currently sells for $50, just paid a $1.75 dividend, and has a constant growth rate of 8 percent?

Section 7.2 True or false: For tax purposes, preferred stock is considered a form of equity.

CHAPTER REVIEW AND SELF-TEST PROBLEMS

7.1. **Dividend Growth and Stock Valuation**   The Brigapenski Co. has just paid a cash dividend of $2 per share. Investors require a 16 percent return from investments such as this. If the dividend is expected to grow at a steady 8 percent per year, what is the current value of the stock? What will the stock be worth in five years? (See Problem 1.)

7.2. **Required Returns**   Suppose we observe a stock selling for $40 per share. The next dividend will be $1 per share, and you think the dividend will grow at 12 percent per year forever. What is the dividend yield in this case? The capital gains yield? The total required return? (See Problem 3.)

■ Answers to Chapter Review and Self-Test Problems

7.1   The last dividend, D_0, was \$2. The dividend is expected to grow steadily at 8 percent. The required return is 16 percent. Based on the dividend growth model, we can say that the current price is:

$$P_0 = D_1/(R - g)$$
$$= D_0 \times (1 + g)/(R - g)$$
$$= \$2 \times 1.08/(.16 - .08)$$
$$= \$2.16/.08$$
$$= \$27$$

We could calculate the price in five years by calculating the dividend in five years and then using the growth model again. Alternatively, we could recognize that the stock price will increase by 8 percent per year and calculate the future price directly. We'll do both. First, the dividend in five years will be:

$$D_5 = D_0 \times (1 + g)^5$$
$$= \$2 \times 1.08^5$$
$$= \$2.9387$$

The price in five years therefore would be:

$$P_5 = D_5 \times (1 + g)/(R - g)$$
$$= \$2.9387 \times 1.08/.08$$
$$= \$3.1738/.08$$
$$= \$39.67$$

Once we understand the dividend model, however, it's easier to notice that:

$$P_5 = P_0 \times (1 + g)^5$$
$$= \$27 \times 1.08^5$$
$$= \$27 \times 1.4693$$
$$= \$39.67$$

Notice that both approaches yield the same price in five years.

7.2   The dividend yield is the next dividend, D_1, divided by the current price, P_0, or \$1/\$40 = .025, or 2.5%. The capital gains yield is the same as the dividend growth rate, 12 percent. The total required return is the sum of the two, 2.5% + 12% = 14.5%.

CRITICAL THINKING AND CONCEPTS REVIEW

LO 1   **7.1**   **Stock Valuation**   Why does the value of a share of stock depend on dividends?

LO 1   **7.2**   **Stock Valuation**   A substantial percentage of the companies listed on the NYSE and the NASDAQ don't pay dividends, but investors are nonetheless willing to buy shares in them. How is this possible given your answer to the previous question?

LO 1   **7.3**   **Dividend Policy**   Referring to the previous questions, under what circumstances might a company choose not to pay dividends?

LO 1   **7.4**   **Dividend Growth Model**   Under what two assumptions can we use the dividend growth model presented in the chapter to determine the value of a share of stock? Comment on the reasonableness of these assumptions.

LO 1   **7.5**   **Common versus Preferred Stock**   Suppose a company has a preferred stock issue and a common stock issue. Both have just paid a $2 dividend. Which do you think will have a higher price, a share of the preferred or a share of the common?

LO 1   **7.6**   **Dividend Growth Model**   Based on the dividend growth model, what are the two components of the total return on a share of stock? Which do you think is typically larger?

LO 1   **7.7**   **Growth Rate**   In the context of the dividend growth model, is it true that the growth rate in dividends and the growth rate in the price of the stock are identical?

LO 1   **7.8**   **Dividends and Earnings**   Is it possible for a company to pay dividends when it has a negative net income for the year? Could this happen for longer periods?

LO 2   **7.9**   **Corporate Ethics**   Is it unfair or unethical for corporations to create classes of stock with unequal voting rights?

LO 2   **7.10**   **Voting Rights**   Some companies, such as Google, have created classes of stock with little or no voting rights at all. Why would investors buy such stock?

LO 2   **7.11**   **Stock Valuation**   Evaluate the following statement: Managers should not focus on the current stock value because doing so will lead to an overemphasis on short-term profits at the expense of long-term profits.

LO 1   **7.12**   **Constant Dividend Growth Model**   In the constant dividend growth model, what is the highest reasonable growth rate for a stock's dividend?

LO 2   **7.13**   **Voting Rights**   In the chapter, we mentioned that many companies have been under pressure to declassify their boards of directors. Why would investors want a board to be declassified? What are the advantages of a classified board?

LO 1   **7.14**   **Price Ratio Valuation**   What are the difficulties in using the PE ratio to value stock?

QUESTIONS AND PROBLEMS

 Select problems are available in McGraw-Hill *Connect*. Please see the packaging options section of the Preface for more information.

BASIC (Questions 1–14)

LO 1   **1. Stock Values**   Fowler, Inc., just paid a dividend of $2.55 per share on its stock. The dividends are expected to grow at a constant rate of 3.9 percent per year, indefinitely. If investors require a return of 10.4 percent on this stock, what is the current price? What will the price be in 3 years? In 15 years?

LO 1   **2. Stock Values**   The next dividend payment by Hoffman, Inc., will be $2.65 per share. The dividends are anticipated to maintain a growth rate of

4.5 percent forever. If the stock currently sells for $43.15 per share, what is the required return?

LO 1   3. **Stock Values**   For the company in the previous problem, what is the dividend yield? What is the expected capital gains yield?

LO 1   4. **Stock Values**   Poulter Corporation will pay a dividend of $3.25 per share next year. The company pledges to increase its dividend by 5.1 percent per year, indefinitely. If you require a return of 11 percent on your investment, how much will you pay for the company's stock today?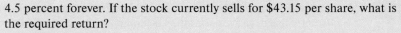

LO 1   5. **Stock Valuation**   Redan, Inc., is expected to maintain a constant 4.3 percent growth rate in its dividends, indefinitely. If the company has a dividend yield of 5.6 percent, what is the required return on the company's stock?

LO 1   6. **Stock Valuation**   Suppose you know that a company's stock currently sells for $67 per share and the required return on the stock is 10.8 percent. You also know that the total return on the stock is evenly divided between capital gains yield and dividend yield. If it's the company's policy to always maintain a constant growth rate in its dividends, what is the current dividend per share?

LO 1   7. **Stock Valuation**   Burkhardt Corp. pays a constant $15.25 dividend on its stock. The company will maintain this dividend for the next nine years and will then cease paying dividends forever. If the required return on this stock is 9.2 percent, what is the current share price?

LO 1   8. **Valuing Preferred Stock**   Smiling Elephant, Inc., has an issue of preferred stock outstanding that pays a $2.85 dividend every year, in perpetuity. If this issue currently sells for $77.32 per share, what is the required return?

LO 2   9. **Voting Rights**   After successfully completing your corporate finance class, you feel the next challenge ahead is to serve on the board of directors of Schenkel Enterprises. Unfortunately, you will be the only individual voting for you. If the company has 525,000 shares outstanding and the stock currently sells for $38, how much will it cost you to buy a seat if the company uses straight voting? Assume that the company uses cumulative voting and there are four seats in the current election; how much will it cost you to buy a seat now?

LO 1   10. **Growth Rates**   The stock price of Alps Co. is $67. Investors require a return of 10.5 percent on similar stocks. If the company plans to pay a dividend of $4.25 next year, what growth rate is expected for the company's stock price?

LO 1   11. **Valuing Preferred Stock**   E-Eyes.com has a new issue of preferred stock it calls 20/20 preferred. The stock will pay a $20 dividend per year, but the first dividend will not be paid until 20 years from today. If you require a return of 7.3 percent on this stock, how much should you pay today?

LO 1   12. **Stock Valuation**   Cape Corp. will pay a dividend of $2.64 next year. The company has stated that it will maintain a constant growth rate of 4.5 percent a year forever. If you want a return of 12 percent, how much will you pay for the stock? What if you want a return of 8 percent? What does this tell you about the relationship between the required return and the stock price?

LO 2   13. **Stock Valuation and PE Ratio**   The Blooming Flower Co. has earnings of $3.68 per share. The benchmark PE for the company is 18. What stock price would you consider appropriate? What if the benchmark PE were 21?

LO 2   **14. Stock Valuation and PS Ratio**   TwitterMe, Inc., is a new company and currently has negative earnings. The company's sales are $1.45 million and there are 130,000 shares outstanding. If the benchmark price-sales ratio is 3.9, what is your estimate of an appropriate stock price? What if the price-sales ratio were 3.2?

INTERMEDIATE (Questions 15–30)

LO 1   **15. Nonconstant Growth**   Metallica Bearings, Inc., is a young start-up company. No dividends will be paid on the stock over the next 9 years because the firm needs to plow back its earnings to fuel growth. The company will then pay a dividend of $23 per share 10 years from today and will increase the dividend by 5 percent per year thereafter. If the required return on this stock is 12 percent, what is the current share price?

LO 1   **16. Nonconstant Dividends**   Bon Chance, Inc., has an odd dividend policy. The company has just paid a dividend of $3 per share and has announced that it will increase the dividend by $5 per share for each of the next four years, and then never pay another dividend. If you require a return of 9.7 percent on the company's stock, how much will you pay for a share today?

LO 1   **17. Nonconstant Dividends**   Synovec Corporation is expected to pay the following dividends over the next four years: $7, $13, $18, and $3.25. Afterward, the company pledges to maintain a constant 5 percent growth rate in dividends forever. If the required return on the stock is 10.4 percent, what is the current share price?

LO 1   **18. Supernormal Growth**   Biarritz Corp. is growing quickly. Dividends are expected to grow at a rate of 25 percent for the next three years, with the growth rate falling off to a constant 4.5 percent thereafter. If the required return is 10.5 percent and the company just paid a dividend of $2.85, what is the current share price?

LO 1   **19. Negative Growth**   Antiques 'R' Us is a mature manufacturing firm. The company just paid a dividend of $16.30, but management expects to reduce the payout by 3.5 percent per year, indefinitely. If you require a return of 8 percent on this stock, what will you pay for a share today?

LO 2   **20. Finding the Dividend**   Dropshot Corporation stock currently sells for $68.98 per share. The market requires a return of 10.3 percent on the firm's stock. If the company maintains a constant 4.9 percent growth rate in dividends, what was the most recent dividend per share paid on the stock?

You've collected the following information from your favorite financial website. Use it to answer Questions 21–25 (the 52-week Hi and Lo are the highest and lowest stock prices over the previous 52 weeks).

52-Week Price		Stock (Div)	Div Yld %	PE Ratio	Close Price	Net Chg
Hi	Lo					
64.60	47.80	Abbott 1.12	1.9	235.6	62.91	−.05
145.94	70.28	Ralph Lauren 2.50	1.8	70.9	139.71	−.62
171.13	139.13	IBM 6.30	4.3	23.8	145.39	.19
91.80	71.96	Duke Energy 3.56	4.9	17.6	74.30	.84
113.19	96.20	Disney 1.68	1.7	15.5	??	.10

LO 3   21. **Dividend Yield**   Find the quote for Duke Energy. Assume that the dividend is constant. What was the highest dividend yield over the past year? What was the lowest dividend yield over the past year?

LO 1   22. **Stock Valuation**   According to the 2018 Value Line *Investment Survey*, the growth rate in dividends for IBM for the next five years is expected to be 5 percent. Suppose IBM meets this growth rate in dividends for the next five years and then the dividend growth rate falls to 3.5 percent indefinitely. Assume investors require a return of 10 percent on IBM stock. Is the stock priced correctly? What factors could affect your answer?

LO 1   23. **Stock Valuation**   According to the 2018 Value Line *Investment Survey*, the growth rate in dividends for Ralph Lauren for the next five years will be .5 percent. If investors feel this growth rate will continue, what is the required return for the company's stock?

LO 1   24. **Negative Growth**   According to the 2018 Value Line *Investment Survey*, the growth rate in dividends for Abbott Laboratories for the previous five years has been negative 11.5 percent. If investors feel this growth rate will continue, what is the required return for the company's stock? Does this number make sense? What are some of the potential reasons for the negative growth in dividends?

LO 1   25. **Stock Quotes**   Using the dividend yield, calculate the closing price for Walt Disney on this day. The actual closing price for Walt Disney was $108.85. Why is your closing price different? The Value Line *Investment Survey* projects a 4 percent dividend growth rate for Walt Disney. What is the required return for the stock using the dividend discount model and the actual stock price?

LO 1   26. **Stock Valuation and PE**   Sunset Corp. currently has an EPS of $3.85, and the benchmark PE for the company is 19. Earnings are expected to grow at 6 percent per year.

    a.   What is your estimate of the current stock price?

    b.   What is the target stock price in one year?

    c.   Assuming the company pays no dividends, what is the implied return on the company's stock over the next year? What does this tell you about the implied stock return using PE valuation?

LO 1   27. **Stock Valuation and PE**   You have found the following historical information for the Daniela Company:

	Year 1	Year 2	Year 3	Year 4
Stock price	$63.25	$71.94	$83.43	$88.27
EPS	3.15	3.35	3.60	3.85

Earnings are expected to grow at 7 percent for the next year. Using the company's historical average PE as a benchmark, what is the target stock price in one year?

LO 1   28. **Stock Valuation and PE**   In the previous problem, we assumed that the stock had a single stock price for the year. However, if you look at stock prices over any year, you will find a high and low stock price for the year. Instead of a single benchmark PE ratio, we now have a high and low PE ratio for each year. We can use these ratios to calculate a high and a low stock price for the next year. Suppose we have the following information on a particular company:

	Year 1	Year 2	Year 3	Year 4
High price	$48.60	$57.34	$69.46	$74.85
Low price	37.25	42.18	55.85	63.18
EPS	2.02	2.31	2.45	3.05

Earnings are projected to grow at 9 percent over the next year. What are your high and low target stock prices over the next year?

LO 1   **29. Stock Valuation and PE**   Berta, Inc., currently has an EPS of $3.85 and an earnings growth rate of 7 percent. If the benchmark PE ratio is 21, what is the target share price five years from now?

LO 1   **30. PE and Terminal Stock Price**   In practice, a common way to value a share of stock when a company pays dividends is to value the dividends over the next five years or so, then find the "terminal" stock price using a benchmark PE ratio. Suppose a company just paid a dividend of $1.15. The dividends are expected to grow at 10 percent over the next five years. The company has a payout ratio of 40 percent and a benchmark PE of 19. What is the target stock price in five years? What is the stock price today assuming a required return of 11 percent on this stock?

CHALLENGE (Questions 31–32)

LO 1   **31. Capital Gains versus Income**   Consider four different stocks, all of which have a required return of 19 percent and a most recent dividend of $2.40 per share. Stocks W, X, and Y are expected to maintain constant growth rates in dividends for the foreseeable future of 8 percent, 0 percent, and −5 percent per year, respectively. Stock Z is a growth stock that will increase its dividend by 20 percent for the next two years and then maintain a constant 12 percent growth rate, thereafter. What is the dividend yield for each of these four stocks? What is the expected capital gains yield? Discuss the relationship among the various returns that you find for each of these stocks.

LO 1   **32. Stock Valuation**   Most corporations pay quarterly dividends on their common stock rather than annual dividends. Barring any unusual circumstances during the year, the board raises, lowers, or maintains the current dividend once a year and then pays this dividend out in equal quarterly installments to its shareholders.

    a.   Suppose a company currently pays an annual dividend of $2.80 on its common stock in a single annual installment, and management plans on raising this dividend by 6 percent per year indefinitely. If the required return on this stock is 12 percent, what is the current share price?

    b.   Now suppose the company in part (a) actually pays its annual dividend in equal quarterly installments; thus, the company has just paid a dividend of $.70 per share, as it has for the previous three quarters. What is your value for the current share price now? (*Hint:* Find the equivalent annual end-of-year dividend for each year.) Comment on whether you think this model of stock valuation is appropriate.

WHAT'S ON THE WEB?

7.1 Dividend Discount Model   According to the 2018 Value Line *Investment Survey*, the dividend growth rate for ExxonMobil (XOM) is 3 percent. Find the current stock price quote and dividend information at finance.yahoo.com. If this dividend growth rate is correct, what is the required return for ExxonMobil? Does this number make sense to you?

7.2 Stock Quotes   What is the most expensive publicly traded stock in the United States? Go to finance.yahoo.com and enter BRKA (for Berkshire Hathaway Class A). What is the current price per share? What are the 52-week high and low? How many shares trade on an average day? How many shares have traded today?

7.3 Supernormal Growth   You are interested in buying stock in Coca-Cola (KO). You believe that the dividends will grow at 15 percent for the next four years and level off at 6 percent thereafter. Using the most recent dividend on finance.yahoo.com, if you want a 12 percent return, how much should you be willing to pay for a share of stock?

7.4 Market Operations   How does a stock trade take place? Go to www.nyse.com to find out. Describe the process of a trade on the NYSE.

EXCEL *MASTER IT!* PROBLEM

Excel Master coverage online

In practice, the use of the dividend discount model is refined from the method we presented in the textbook. Many analysts will estimate the dividend for the next 5 years and then estimate a perpetual growth rate at some point in the future, typically 10 years. Rather than have the dividend growth fall dramatically from the fast growth period to the perpetual growth period, linear interpolation is applied. That is, the dividend growth is projected to fall by an equal amount each year. For example, if the high growth period is 15 percent for the next 5 years and the dividends are expected to fall to a 5 percent perpetual growth rate 5 years later, the dividend growth rate would decline by 2 percent each year.

The Value Line *Investment Survey* provides information for investors. Below, you will find information for Microsoft (MSFT) found in the 2018 edition of Value Line:

2018 dividend:	**$1.56**
Five-year dividend growth rate:	**12.0%**

a.   Assume that a perpetual growth rate of 5 percent begins 10 years from now and use linear interpolation between the high growth rate and perpetual growth rate. Construct a table that shows the dividend growth rate and dividend each year. What is the stock price at Year 10? What is the stock price today?

b.   Instead of applying the constant dividend growth model to find the stock price in the future, analysts will often combine the dividend discount method with price ratio valuation, often with the PE ratio. Remember that the PE ratio is the price per share divided by the earnings per share. So, if we know what the PE ratio is, we can solve for the stock price. Suppose we also have the following information about MSFT:

Payout ratio:	**20%**
PE at constant growth rate:	**15**

Use the PE ratio to calculate the stock price when MSFT reaches a perpetual growth rate in dividends. Now supply the value of the stock today by finding the present value of the dividends during the supernormal growth rate and the price you calculated using the PE ratio.

c.   How sensitive is the current stock price to changes in PE ratio when the stock reaches the perpetual growth rate? Graph the current stock price against the PE ratio in 10 years to find out.

CHAPTER CASE
Stock Valuation at Ragan, Inc.

Ragan, Inc., was founded nine years ago by brother and sister Carrington and Genevieve Ragan. The company manufactures and installs commercial heating, ventilation, and cooling (HVAC) units. Ragan, Inc., has experienced rapid growth because of a proprietary technology that increases the energy efficiency of its units. The company is equally owned by Carrington and Genevieve. The original partnership agreement between the siblings gave each 50,000 shares of stock. In the event either wished to sell stock, the shares first had to be offered to the other at a discounted price.

Although neither sibling wants to sell, they have decided they should value their holdings in the company. To get started, they have gathered the following information about their main competitors:

Ragan, Inc. — Competitors					
	EPS	Div.	Stock Price	ROE	R
Arctic Cooling, Inc.	$1.30	$.16	$25.34	8.50%	10.00%
National Heating & Cooling	1.95	.23	29.85	10.50	13.00
Expert HVAC Corp.	−.37	.14	22.13	9.78	12.00
Industry average	$.96	$.18	$25.77	9.59%	11.67

Expert HVAC Corporation's negative earnings per share were the result of an accounting write-off last year. Without the write-off, earnings per share for the company would have been $1.10.

Last year, Ragan, Inc., had an EPS of $3.15 and paid a dividend to Carrington and Genevieve of $45,000 each. The company also had a return on equity of 17 percent. The siblings believe that 14 percent is an appropriate required return for the company.

QUESTIONS

1. Assuming the company continues its current growth rate, what is the value per share of the company's stock?

2. To verify their calculations, Carrington and Genevieve have hired Josh Schlessman as a consultant. Josh was previously an equity analyst and covered the HVAC industry. Josh has examined the company's financial statements, as well as those of its competitors. Although Ragan, Inc., currently has a technological advantage, his research indicates that other companies are investigating methods to improve efficiency. Given this, Josh believes that the company's technological advantage will last only for the next five years. After that period, the company's growth will likely slow to the industry growth average. Additionally, Josh believes that the required return used by the company is too high. He believes the industry average required return is more appropriate. Under this growth rate assumption, what is your estimate of the stock price?

8 | Net Present Value and Other Investment Criteria

Is there green in green? General Electric (GE) thinks so. Through its "Ecomagination" program, the company planned to double research and development spending on green products. In fact, by 2016, GE already had invested more than $20 billion in its Ecomagination program, with plans to invest another $5 billion by 2020.

With products such as a hybrid railroad locomotive (described as a 200-ton, 6,000-horsepower "Prius on rails"), GE's green initiative seems to be paying off. Revenue from the company's green products was more than $200 billion from 2005 to 2016. Further, revenues from Ecomagination products were growing twice as fast as the company's other revenues. GE's internal commitment to reduced energy consumption through green "Treasure Hunts" saved it more than $100 million, and, by 2016, the company had reduced water consumption by 53 percent relative to its 2006 baseline, another considerable cost savings.

While GE was in part motivated by the desire to go green, from a financial perspective the decision only makes sense if the company *makes* some green. Given that GE plans to spend about $2 billion per year on such undertakings, it is obviously a major financial decision, and the risks and rewards must be carefully weighed. In this chapter, we discuss the basic tools used in making such decisions.

This chapter introduces you to the practice of capital budgeting. Back in Chapter 1, we saw that increasing the value of the stock in a company is the goal of financial management. Thus, what we need to learn is how to tell whether a particular investment will achieve that or not. This chapter considers a variety of techniques that are actually used in practice. More importantly, it shows how many of these techniques can be misleading, and it explains why the net present value approach is the right one.

LEARNING OBJECTIVES

After studying this chapter, you should be able to:

LO 1 Summarize the payback rule and some of its shortcomings.

LO 2 Discuss accounting rates of return and some of the problems with them.

LO 3 Explain the internal rate of return criterion and its associated strengths and weaknesses.

LO 4 Evaluate proposed investments by using the net present value criterion.

LO 5 Apply the modified internal rate of return.

LO 6 Calculate the profitability index and understand its relation to net present value.

Please visit us at essentialsofcorporatefinance.blogspot.com for the latest developments in the world of corporate finance.

In Chapter 1, we identified the three key areas of concern to the financial manager. The first of these was the following: What long-term investments should we make? We called this the *capital budgeting decision.* In this chapter, we begin to deal with the issues that arise in answering this question.

The process of allocating, or budgeting, capital is usually more involved than just deciding whether or not to buy a particular fixed asset. We frequently will face broader issues like whether or not we should launch a new product or enter a new market. Decisions such as these will determine the nature of a firm's operations and products for years to come, primarily because fixed asset investments are generally long-lived and not easily reversed once they are made.

For these reasons, the capital budgeting question is probably the most important issue in corporate finance. How a firm chooses to finance its operations (the capital structure question) and how a firm manages its short-term operating activities (the working capital question) are certainly issues of concern, but it is the fixed assets that define the business of the firm. Airlines, for example, are airlines because they operate airplanes, regardless of how they finance them.

Any firm possesses a huge number of possible investments. Each possible investment is an option available to the firm. Some options are valuable and some are not. The essence of successful financial management, of course, is learning to identify which are which. With this in mind, our goal in this chapter is to introduce you to the techniques used to analyze potential business ventures to decide which are worth undertaking.

We present and compare several different procedures used in practice. Our primary goal is to acquaint you with the advantages and disadvantages of the various approaches. As we shall see, the most important concept in this area is the idea of net present value. We consider this next.

8.1 NET PRESENT VALUE

Excel Master coverage online

In Chapter 1, we argued that the goal of financial management is to create value for the stockholders. The financial manager must therefore examine a potential investment in light of its likely effect on the price of the firm's shares. In this section, we describe a widely used procedure for doing this, the net present value approach.

The Basic Idea

An investment is worth undertaking if it creates value for its owners. In the most general sense, we create value by identifying an investment worth more in the marketplace than it costs us to acquire. How can something be worth more than it costs? It's a case of the whole being worth more than the cost of the parts.

Suppose you buy a run-down house for $75,000 and spend another $75,000 on painters, plumbers, and so on to get it fixed up. Your total investment is $150,000. When the work is completed, you place the house back on the market and find that it's worth $170,000. The market value ($170,000) exceeds the cost ($150,000) by $20,000. What you have done here is to act as a manager and bring together some fixed assets (a house), some labor (plumbers, carpenters, and others), and some materials (carpeting, paint, and so on). The net result is that you have created $20,000 in value. Put another way, this $20,000 is the *value added* by management.

With our house example, it turned out *after the fact* that $20,000 in value was created. Things thus worked out very nicely. The real challenge, of course, would have been to somehow identify *ahead of time* whether or not investing the necessary $150,000 was a good idea in the first place. This is what capital budgeting is all about, namely, trying to determine whether a proposed investment or project will be worth more than it costs once it is in place.

For reasons that will be obvious in a moment, the difference between an investment's market value and its cost is called the **net present value**, or **NPV**, of the investment. In other words, net present value is a measure of how much value is created or added today by undertaking an investment. Given our goal of creating value for the stockholders, the capital budgeting process can be viewed as a search for investments with positive net present values.

With our run-down house, you probably can imagine how we would go about making the capital budgeting decision. We first would look at what comparable, fixed-up properties were selling for in the market. We then would get estimates of the cost of buying a particular property, fixing it up, and bringing it to market. At this point, we have an estimated total cost and an estimated market value. If the difference is positive, then this investment is worth undertaking because it has a positive estimated net present value. There is risk, of course, because there is no guarantee that our estimates will turn out to be correct.

As our example illustrates, investment decisions are greatly simplified when there is a market for assets similar to the investment we are considering. Capital budgeting becomes much more difficult when we cannot observe the market price for at least roughly comparable investments. The reason is that we are then faced with the problem of estimating the value of an investment using only indirect market information. Unfortunately, this is precisely the situation the financial manager usually encounters. We examine this issue next.

> **net present value (NPV)**
> The difference between an investment's market value and its cost.

Estimating Net Present Value

Imagine we are thinking of starting a business to produce and sell a new product, say, organic fertilizer. We can estimate the start-up costs with reasonable accuracy because we know what we will need to buy to begin production. Would this be a good investment? Based on our discussion, you know that the answer depends on whether or not the value of the new business exceeds the cost of starting it. In other words, does this investment have a positive NPV?

This problem is much more difficult than our "fixer-upper" house example because entire fertilizer companies are not routinely bought and sold in the marketplace; so it is essentially impossible to observe the market value of a similar investment. As a result, we must somehow estimate this value by other means.

Based on our work in Chapters 4 and 5, you may be able to guess how we will go about estimating the value of our fertilizer business. We first will try to estimate the future cash flows we expect the new business to produce. We then will apply our basic discounted cash flow procedure to estimate the present value of those cash flows. Once we have this estimate, we then estimate NPV as the difference between the present value of the future cash flows and the cost of the investment. As we mentioned in Chapter 5, this procedure is often called **discounted cash flow**, *or* **DCF**, valuation.

To see how we might go about estimating NPV, suppose we believe the cash revenues from our fertilizer business will be $20,000 per year, assuming everything goes as expected. Cash costs (including taxes) will be $14,000 per year. We will wind down the business in eight years. The plant, property, and equipment will be worth $2,000 as salvage at that time. The project costs $30,000 to launch. We use a 15 percent discount rate on new projects such as this one. Is this a good investment? If there are 1,000 shares of stock outstanding, what will be the effect on the price per share from taking the investment?

From a purely mechanical perspective, we need to calculate the present value of the future cash flows at 15 percent. The net cash inflow will be $20,000 cash income less $14,000 in costs per year for eight years. These cash flows are illustrated in Figure 8.1.

> **discounted cash flow (DCF) valuation**
> (a) Calculating the present value of a future cash flow to determine its value today. (b) The process of valuing an investment by discounting its future cash flows.

FIGURE **8.1**

Project cash flows
($000)

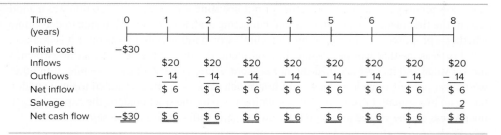

Time (years)	0	1	2	3	4	5	6	7	8
Initial cost	−$30								
Inflows		$20	$20	$20	$20	$20	$20	$20	$20
Outflows		− 14	− 14	− 14	− 14	− 14	− 14	− 14	− 14
Net inflow		$ 6	$ 6	$ 6	$ 6	$ 6	$ 6	$ 6	$ 6
Salvage									2
Net cash flow	−$30	$ 6	$ 6	$ 6	$ 6	$ 6	$ 6	$ 6	$ 8

As Figure 8.1 suggests, we effectively have an eight-year annuity of $20,000 − 14,000 = $6,000 per year along with a single lump-sum inflow of $2,000 in eight years. Calculating the present value of the future cash flows thus comes down to the same type of problem we considered in Chapter 5. The total present value is:

Present value = $6,000 × (1 − 1/1.15^8)/.15 + 2,000/1.15^8

$$= \$6{,}000 \times 4.4873 + 2{,}000/3.0590$$
$$= \$26{,}924 + 654$$
$$= \$27{,}578$$

When we compare this to the $30,000 estimated cost, the NPV is:

NPV = −$30,000 + 27,578 = −$2,422

Therefore, this is *not* a good investment. Based on our estimates, taking it would *decrease* the total value of the stock by $2,422. With 1,000 shares outstanding, our best estimate of the impact of taking this project is a loss of value of $2,422/1,000 = $2.422 per share.

Our fertilizer example illustrates how NPV estimates can be used to determine whether or not an investment is desirable. From our example, notice that if the NPV is negative, the effect on share value will be unfavorable. If the NPV were positive, the effect would be favorable. As a consequence, all we need to know about a particular proposal for the purpose of making an accept-reject decision is whether the NPV is positive or negative.

Given that the goal of financial management is to increase share value, our discussion in this section leads us to the *net present value rule*:

> **An investment should be accepted if the net present value is positive and rejected if it is negative.**

In the unlikely event that the net present value turned out to be exactly zero, we would be indifferent between taking the investment and not taking it.

Two comments about our example are in order. First and foremost, it is not the rather mechanical process of discounting the cash flows that is important. Once we have the cash flows and the appropriate discount rate, the required calculations are fairly straightforward. The task of coming up with the cash flows and the discount rate in the first place is much more challenging. We will have much more to say about this in our next chapter. For the remainder of this chapter, we take it as given that we have estimates of the cash revenues and costs and, where needed, an appropriate discount rate.

The second thing to keep in mind about our example is that the −$2,422 NPV is an estimate. Like any estimate, it can be high or low. The only way to find out the true NPV would be to place the investment up for sale and see what we could get for it. We generally won't be doing this, so it is important that our estimates be reliable. Once again, we will have more to say about this later. For the rest of this chapter, we will assume that the estimates are accurate.

EXAMPLE 8.1	**Using the NPV Rule**

Suppose we are asked to decide whether or not a new consumer product should be launched. Based on projected sales and costs, we expect that the cash flows over the five-year life of the project will be $2,000 in the first two years, $4,000 in the next two, and $5,000 in the last year. It will cost about $10,000 to begin production. We use a 10 percent discount rate to evaluate new products. What should we do here?

Given the cash flows and discount rate, we can calculate the total value of the product by discounting the cash flows back to the present:

$$\text{Present value} = \$2,000/1.1 + 2,000/1.1^2 + 4,000/1.1^3 + 4,000/1.1^4 + 5,000/1.1^5$$
$$= \$1,818 + 1,653 + 3,005 + 2,732 + 3,105$$
$$= \$12,313$$

The present value of the expected cash flows is $12,313, but the cost of getting those cash flows is only $10,000, so the NPV is $12,313 − 10,000 = $2,313. This is positive; so, based on the net present value rule, we should take on the project.

Calculating NPVs with a Spreadsheet

Spreadsheets and financial calculators are commonly used to calculate NPVs. The procedures used by various financial calculators are too different for us to illustrate here, so we will focus on using a spreadsheet (financial calculators are covered in Appendix D). Examining the use of spreadsheets in this context also allows us to issue an important warning. Let's rework Example 8.1:

SPREADSHEET STRATEGIES

	A	B	C	D	E	F	G	H
1								
2		Using a spreadsheet to calculate net present values						
3								
4		From Example 8.1, the project's cost is $10,000. The cash flows are $2,000 per year for the first two						
5		years, $4,000 per year for the next two, and $5,000 in the last year. The discount rate is						
6		10 percent; what's the NPV?						
7								
8			Year	Cash flow				
9			0	−$10,000	Discount rate =		10%	
10			1	2,000				
11			2	2,000		NPV =	$2,102.72	(*wrong* answer)
12			3	4,000		NPV =	$2,312.99	(*right* answer)
13			4	4,000				
14			5	5,000				
15								
16		The formula entered in cell F11 is = NPV(F9,C9:C14). This gives the wrong answer because the						
17		NPV function actually calculates present values, not net present values.						
18								
19		The formula entered in cell F12 is = NPV(F9,C10:C14) + C9. This gives the right answer because the						
20		NPV function is used to calculate the present value of the cash flows and then the initial cost is						
21		subtracted to calculate the answer. Notice that we added cell C9 because it is already negative.						

As we have seen in this section, estimating NPV is one way of assessing the profitability of a proposed investment. It is certainly not the only way profitability is assessed, and we now turn to some alternatives. As we will see, when compared to NPV, each of the ways of assessing profitability that we examine is flawed in some key way; so, NPV is the preferred approach in principle, if not always in practice.

In our nearby *Spreadsheet Strategies* box, we rework Example 8.1. Notice that we have provided two answers. By comparing the answers to that found in Example 8.1, we see that the first answer is wrong even though we used the spreadsheet's NPV formula. What happened is that the "NPV" function in our spreadsheet is actually a PV function; unfortunately, one of the original spreadsheet programs many years ago got the definition wrong, and subsequent spreadsheets have copied it! Our second answer shows how to use the formula properly.

The example here illustrates the danger of blindly using calculators or computers without understanding what is going on; we shudder to think of how many capital budgeting decisions in the real world are based on incorrect use of this particular function. We see another example of something that can go wrong with a spreadsheet later in the chapter.

CONCEPT QUESTIONS

8.1a   What is the net present value rule?

8.1b   If we say an investment has an NPV of $1,000, what exactly do we mean?

8.2 THE PAYBACK RULE

Excel Master
coverage online

It is very common in practice to talk of the payback on a proposed investment. Loosely, the *payback* is the length of time it takes to recover our initial investment, or "get our bait back." Because this idea is widely understood and used, we examine it in some detail.

Defining the Rule

We can illustrate how to calculate a payback with an example. Figure 8.2 shows the cash flows from a proposed investment. How many years do we have to wait until the accumulated cash flows from this investment equal or exceed the cost of the investment? As Figure 8.2 indicates, the initial investment is $50,000. After the first year, the firm has recovered $30,000, leaving $20,000 outstanding. The cash flow in the second year is exactly $20,000, so this investment "pays for itself" in exactly two years. Put another way, the **payback period** (or just payback) is two years. If we require a payback of, say, three years or less, then this investment is acceptable. This illustrates the *payback period rule*:

payback period
The amount of time required for an investment to generate cash flows sufficient to recover its initial cost.

> **Based on the payback rule, an investment is acceptable if its calculated payback period is less than some prespecified number of years.**

FIGURE 8.2

Net project cash flows

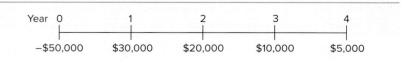

Year	0	1	2	3	4
	−$50,000	$30,000	$20,000	$10,000	$5,000

In our example, the payback works out to be exactly two years. This usually won't happen, of course. When the numbers don't work out exactly, it is customary to work with fractional years. Suppose the initial investment is $60,000, and the cash flows are $20,000 in the first year and $90,000 in the second. The cash flows over the first two years are $110,000, so the project obviously pays back sometime in the second year. After the first year, the project has paid back $20,000, leaving $40,000 to be recovered. To figure out the fractional year, note that this $40,000 is $40,000/$90,000 = 4/9 of the second year's cash flow. Assuming that the $90,000 cash flow is paid uniformly throughout the year, the payback would thus be 1⁴/₉ years.

EXAMPLE 8.2   Calculating Payback

The projected cash flows from a proposed investment are:

Year	Cash Flow
1	$100
2	200
3	500

This project costs $500. What is the payback period for this investment?

The initial cost is $500. After the first two years, the cash flows total $300. After the third year, the total cash flow is $800, so the project pays back sometime between the end of Year 2 and the end of Year 3. Because the accumulated cash flows for the first two years are $300, we need to recover $200 in the third year. The third-year cash flow is $500, so we will have to wait $200/$500 = .40 year to do this. The payback period is thus 2.4 years, or about two years and five months.

Now that we know how to calculate the payback period on an investment, using the payback period rule for making decisions is straightforward. A particular cutoff time is selected, say, two years, and all investment projects that have payback periods of two years or less are accepted, and all of those that pay back in more than two years are rejected.

Table 8.1 illustrates cash flows for five different projects. The figures shown as the Year 0 cash flows are the cost of the investment. We examine these to indicate some peculiarities that can, in principle, arise with payback periods.

The payback for the first project, A, is easily calculated. The sum of the cash flows for the first two years is $70, leaving us with $100 − 70 = $30 to go. The cash flow in the third year is $50, so the payback occurs sometime in that year. When we compare the $30 we need to the $50 that will be coming in, we get $30/$50 = .60; so, payback will occur 60 percent of the way into the year. The payback period is thus 2.6 years.

Project B's payback also is easy to calculate: It *never* pays back because the cash flows never total up to the original investment. Project C has a payback of exactly four years because it supplies the $130 that B is missing in Year 4. Project D is a little strange. Because of

Year	A	B	C	D	E
0	−$100	−$200	−$200	−$200	−$ 50
1	30	40	40	100	100
2	40	20	20	100	−50,000,000
3	50	10	10	− 200	
4	60		130	200	

TABLE 8.1

Expected cash flows for Projects A through E

the negative cash flow in Year 3, you can easily verify that it has two different payback periods, two years and four years. Which of these is correct? Both of them; the way the payback period is calculated doesn't guarantee a single answer. Finally, Project E is obviously unrealistic, but it does pay back in six months, thereby illustrating the point that a rapid payback does not guarantee a good investment.

Analyzing the Rule

When compared to the NPV rule, the payback period rule has some rather severe shortcomings. First, the payback period is calculated by adding up the future cash flows. There is no discounting involved, so the time value of money is completely ignored. The payback rule also fails to consider risk differences. The payback would be calculated the same way for both very risky and very safe projects.

Perhaps the biggest problem with the payback period rule is coming up with the right cutoff period because we don't really have an objective basis for choosing a particular number. Put another way, there is no economic rationale for looking at payback in the first place, so we have no guide as to how to pick the cutoff. As a result, we end up using a number that is arbitrarily chosen.

Suppose we have somehow decided on an appropriate payback period, say, two years or less. As we have seen, the payback period rule ignores the time value of money for the first two years. More seriously, cash flows after the second year are ignored entirely. To see this, consider the two investments, Long and Short, in Table 8.2. Both projects cost $250. Based on our discussion, the payback on Long is 2 + $50/$100 = 2.5 years, and the payback on Short is 1 + $150/$200 = 1.75 years. With a cutoff of two years, Short is acceptable and Long is not.

Is the payback period rule giving us the right decisions? Maybe not. Suppose again that we require a 15 percent return on this type of investment. We can calculate the NPVs for these two investments as:

NPV (Short) = −$250 + 100/1.15 + 200/1.15^2 = −$11.81
NPV (Long) = −$250 + 100 × (1 − 1/1.15^4)/.15 = $35.50

Now we have a problem. The NPV of the shorter-term investment is actually negative, meaning that taking it diminishes the value of the shareholders' equity. The opposite is true for the longer-term investment—it increases share value.

Our example illustrates two primary shortcomings of the payback period rule. First, by ignoring time value, we may be led to take investments (like Short) that actually are worth less than they cost. Second, by ignoring cash flows beyond the cutoff, we may be led to reject profitable long-term investments (like Long). More generally, using a payback period rule will tend to bias us toward shorter-term investments.

Redeeming Qualities of the Rule

Despite its shortcomings, the payback period rule is often used by large and sophisticated companies when they are making relatively minor decisions. There are several reasons for

TABLE 8.2

Investment projected cash flows

Year	Long	Short
0	−$250	−$250
1	100	100
2	100	200
3	100	0
4	100	0

this. The primary reason is that many decisions do not warrant detailed analysis because the cost of the analysis would exceed the possible loss from a mistake. As a practical matter, an investment that pays back rapidly and has benefits extending beyond the cutoff period probably has a positive NPV.

Small investment decisions are made by the hundreds every day in large organizations. Moreover, they are made at all levels. As a result, it would not be uncommon for a corporation to require, for example, a two-year payback on all investments of less than $10,000. Investments larger than this are subjected to greater scrutiny. The requirement of a two-year payback is not perfect for reasons we have seen, but it does exercise some control over expenditures and thus has the effect of limiting possible losses.

In addition to its simplicity, the payback rule has two other positive features. First, because it is biased toward short-term projects, it is biased toward liquidity. In other words, a payback rule tends to favor investments that free up cash for other uses more quickly. This could be very important for a small business; it would be less so for a large corporation. Second, the cash flows that are expected to occur later in a project's life are probably more uncertain. Arguably, a payback period rule adjusts for the extra riskiness of later cash flows, but it does so in a rather draconian fashion—by ignoring them altogether.

We should note here that some of the apparent simplicity of the payback rule is an illusion. The reason is that we still must come up with the cash flows first, and, as we discuss above, this is not at all easy to do. Thus, it would probably be more accurate to say that the *concept* of a payback period is both intuitive and easy to understand.

Summary of the Rule

To summarize, the payback period is a kind of "break-even" measure. Because time value is ignored, you can think of the payback period as the length of time it takes to break even in an accounting sense, but not in an economic sense. The biggest drawback to the payback period rule is that it doesn't ask the right question. The relevant issue is the impact an investment will have on the value of our stock, not how long it takes to recover the initial investment.

Nevertheless, because it is so simple, companies often use it as a screen for dealing with the myriad of minor investment decisions they have to make. There is certainly nothing wrong with this practice. Like any rule of thumb, there will be some errors in using it, but it wouldn't have survived all this time if it weren't useful. Now that you understand the rule, you can be on the alert for those circumstances under which it might lead to problems. To help you remember, the following table lists the pros and cons of the payback period rule:

Advantages and Disadvantages of the Payback Period Rule	
Advantages	**Disadvantages**
1. Easy to understand.	1. Ignores the time value of money.
2. Adjusts for uncertainty of later cash flows.	2. Requires an arbitrary cutoff point.
3. Biased toward liquidity.	3. Ignores cash flows beyond the cutoff date.
	4. Biased against long-term projects, such as research and development, and new projects.

CONCEPT QUESTIONS

8.2a   In words, what is the payback period? The payback period rule?

8.2b   Why do we say that the payback period is, in a sense, an accounting break-even measure?

8.3 THE AVERAGE ACCOUNTING RETURN

average accounting return (AAR)
An investment's average net income divided by its average book value.

Excel Master
coverage online

Another attractive, but flawed, approach to making capital budgeting decisions involves the **average accounting return (AAR)**. There are many different definitions of the AAR. However, in one form or another, the AAR is always defined as:

$$\frac{\text{Some measure of average accounting profit}}{\text{Some measure of average accounting value}}$$

The specific definition we will use is:

$$\frac{\text{Average net income}}{\text{Average book value}}$$

To see how we might calculate this number, suppose we are deciding whether or not to open a store in a new shopping mall. The required investment in improvements is $500,000. The store would have a five-year life because everything reverts to the mall owners after that time. The required investment would be 100 percent depreciated (straight-line) over five years, so the depreciation would be $500,000/5 = $100,000 per year. The tax rate is 25 percent. Table 8.3 contains the projected revenues and expenses. Based on these figures, net income in each year also is shown.

To calculate the average book value for this investment, we note that we started out with a book value of $500,000 (the initial cost) and ended up at $0. The average book value during the life of the investment is thus ($500,000 + 0)/2 = $250,000. As long as we use straight-line depreciation and a zero salvage value, the average investment will always be one-half of the initial investment.[1]

TABLE 8.3		Year 1	Year 2	Year 3	Year 4	Year 5
Projected yearly revenues and costs for average accounting return	Revenue	$433,333	$450,000	$266,667	$200,000	$133,333
	Expenses	200,000	150,000	100,000	100,000	100,000
	Earnings before depreciation	$233,333	$300,000	$166,667	$100,000	$ 33,333
	Depreciation	100,000	100,000	100,000	100,000	100,000
	Earnings before taxes	$133,333	$200,000	$ 66,667	$ 0	-$ 66,667
	Taxes (25%)	33,333	50,000	16,667	0	– 16,667
	Net income	$100,000	$150,000	$ 50,000	$ 0	-$ 50,000

$$\text{Average net income} = \frac{(\$100,000 + 150,000 + 50,000 + 0 - 50,000)}{5} = \$50,000$$

$$\text{Average book value} = \frac{\$500,000 + 0}{2} = \$250,000$$

---

[1]We could, of course, calculate the average of the six book values directly. In thousands, we would have ($500 + 400 + 300 + 200 + 100 + 0)/6 = $250.

Looking at Table 8.3, we see that net income is $100,000 in the first year, $150,000 in the second year, $50,000 in the third year, $0 in Year 4, and −$50,000 in Year 5. The average net income, then, is:

$$[\$100{,}000 + 150{,}000 + 50{,}000 + 0 + (-50{,}000)]/5 = \$50{,}000$$

The average accounting return is:

$$\text{AAR} = \frac{\text{Average net income}}{\text{Average book value}} = \frac{\$50{,}000}{\$250{,}000} = .20, \text{ or } 20\%$$

If the firm has a target AAR less than 20 percent, then this investment is acceptable; otherwise, it is not. The *average accounting return rule* is thus:

> **Based on the average accounting return rule, a project is acceptable if its average accounting return exceeds a target average accounting return.**

As we will see next, this rule has a number of problems.

You should recognize the chief drawback to the AAR immediately. Above all else, the AAR is not a rate of return in any meaningful economic sense. Instead, it is the ratio of two accounting numbers, and it is not comparable to the returns offered, for example, in financial markets.[2]

One of the reasons the AAR is not a true rate of return is that it ignores time value. When we average figures that occur at different times, we are treating the near future and the more distant future the same way. There was no discounting involved when we computed the average net income, for example.

The second problem with the AAR is similar to the problem we had with the payback period rule concerning the lack of an objective cutoff period. A calculated AAR is really not comparable to a market return, so the target AAR must somehow be specified. There is no generally agreed-upon way to do this. One way of doing it is to calculate the AAR for the firm as a whole and use this as a benchmark, but there are lots of other ways as well.

The third, and perhaps worst, flaw in the AAR is that it doesn't even look at the right things. Instead of cash flow and market value, it uses net income and book value. These are both poor substitutes. As a result, an AAR doesn't tell us what the effect on share price will be from taking an investment, so it doesn't tell us what we really want to know.

Does the AAR have any redeeming features? About the only one is that it almost always can be computed. The reason is that accounting information almost always will be available, both for the project under consideration and for the firm as a whole. We hasten to add that once the accounting information is available, we always can convert it to cash flows, so even this is not a particularly important fact. The AAR is summarized in the table that follows:

Advantages and Disadvantages of the Average Accounting Return	
Advantages	**Disadvantages**
1. Easy to calculate. 2. Needed information will usually be available.	1. Not a true rate of return; time value of money is ignored. 2. Uses an arbitrary benchmark cutoff rate. 3. Based on accounting net income and book values, not cash flows and market values.

---

[2]The AAR is closely related to the return on assets, or ROA, discussed in Chapter 3. In practice, the AAR is sometimes computed by first calculating the ROA for each year and then averaging the results. This produces a number that is similar, but not identical, to the one we computed.

CONCEPT QUESTIONS

8.3a   What is an average accounting rate of return, or AAR?

8.3b   What are the weaknesses of the AAR rule?

8.4   THE INTERNAL RATE OF RETURN

internal rate of return (IRR)
The discount rate that makes the net present value of an investment zero.

Excel
Master
coverage online

We now come to the most important alternative to NPV, the **internal rate of return**, or **IRR**. As we will see, the IRR is closely related to NPV. With the IRR, we try to find a single rate of return that summarizes the merits of a project. Furthermore, we want this rate to be an "internal" rate in the sense that it only depends on the cash flows of a particular investment, not on rates offered elsewhere.

To illustrate the idea behind the IRR, consider a project that costs $100 today and pays $110 in one year. Suppose you were asked, "What is the return on this investment?" What would you say? It seems both natural and obvious to say that the return is 10 percent because, for every dollar we put in, we get $1.10 back. In fact, as we will see in a moment, 10 percent is the internal rate of return, or IRR, on this investment.

Is this project with its 10 percent IRR a good investment? Once again, it would seem apparent that this is a good investment only if our required return is less than 10 percent. This intuition is also correct and illustrates the *IRR rule*:

> **Based on the IRR rule, an investment is acceptable if the IRR exceeds the required return. It should be rejected otherwise.**

Imagine that we wanted to calculate the NPV for our simple investment. At a discount rate of R, the NPV is:

$$NPV = -\$100 + 110/(1 + R)$$

Now, suppose we didn't know the discount rate. This presents a problem, but we could still ask how high the discount rate would have to be before this project was unacceptable. We know that we are indifferent between taking and not taking this investment when its NPV is just equal to zero. In other words, this investment is *economically* a break-even proposition when the NPV is zero because value is neither created nor destroyed. To find the break-even discount rate, we set NPV equal to zero and solve for R:

$$NPV = 0 = -\$100 + 110/(1 + R)$$
$$\$100 = \$110/(1 + R)$$
$$1 + R = \$110/100 = 1.10$$
$$R = .10, \text{ or } 10\%$$

This 10 percent is what we already have called the return on this investment. What we have now illustrated is that the internal rate of return on an investment (or "return" for short) is the discount rate that makes the NPV equal to zero. This is an important observation, so it bears repeating:

> **The IRR on an investment is the required return that results in a zero NPV when it is used as the discount rate.**

FIGURE 8.3

Project cash flows

The fact that the IRR is the discount rate that makes the NPV equal to zero is important because it tells us how to calculate the returns on more complicated investments. As we have seen, finding the IRR turns out to be relatively easy for a single-period investment. However, suppose you were now looking at an investment with the cash flows shown in Figure 8.3. As illustrated, this investment costs $100 and has a cash flow of $60 per year for two years, so it's only slightly more complicated than our single-period example. However, if you were asked for the return on this investment, what would you say? There doesn't seem to be any obvious answer (at least to us). However, based on what we now know, we can set the NPV equal to zero and solve for the discount rate:

$$\text{NPV} = 0 = -\$100 + 60/(1 + \text{IRR}) + 60/(1 + \text{IRR})^2$$

Unfortunately, the only way to find the IRR in general is by trial and error, either by hand or by calculator. This is precisely the same problem that came up in Chapter 5 when we found the unknown rate for an annuity and in Chapter 6 when we found the yield to maturity on a bond. In fact, we now see that, in both of those cases, we were finding an IRR.

In this particular case, the cash flows form a two-period, $60 annuity. To find the unknown rate, we can try some different rates until we get the answer. If we were to start with a 0 percent rate, the NPV would obviously be $120 − 100 = $20. At a 10 percent discount rate, we would have:

$$\text{NPV} = -\$100 + 60/1.1 + 60/1.1^2 = \$4.13$$

Now, we're getting close. We can summarize these and some other possibilities as shown in Table 8.4. From our calculations, the NPV appears to be zero between 10 percent and 15 percent, so the IRR is somewhere in that range. With a little more effort, we can find that the IRR is about 13.1 percent. So, if our required return is less than 13.1 percent, we would take this investment. If our required return exceeds 13.1 percent, we would reject it.

By now, you have probably noticed that the IRR rule and the NPV rule appear to be quite similar. In fact, the IRR is sometimes called the *discounted cash flow*, or *DCF*, *return*. The easiest way to illustrate the relationship between NPV and IRR is to plot the numbers we calculated in Table 8.4. We put the different NPVs on the vertical axis, or *y*-axis, and the discount rates on the horizontal axis, or *x*-axis. If we had a very large number of points, the resulting picture would be a smooth curve called a

Discount Rate	NPV
0%	$20.00
5	11.56
10	4.13
15	− 2.46
20	− 8.33

TABLE 8.4

NPV at different discount rates

FIGURE 8.4

An NPV profile

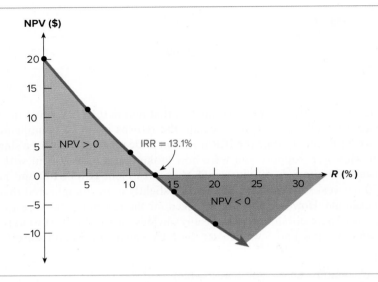

net present value profile

A graphical representation of the relationship between an investment's net present value and various discount rates.

net present value profile. Figure 8.4 illustrates the NPV profile for this project. Beginning with a 0 percent discount rate, we have $20 plotted directly on the *y*-axis. As the discount rate increases, the NPV declines smoothly. Where will the curve cut through the *x*-axis? This will occur where the NPV is equal to zero, so it will happen right at the IRR of 13.1 percent.

In our example, the NPV rule and the IRR rule lead to identical accept-reject decisions. We will accept an investment using the IRR rule if the required return is less than 13.1 percent. As Figure 8.4 illustrates, however, the NPV is positive at any discount rate less than 13.1 percent, so we would accept the investment using the NPV rule as well. The two rules are equivalent in this case.

EXAMPLE 8.3 **Calculating the IRR**

A project has a total up-front cost of $435.44. The cash flows are $100 in the first year, $200 in the second year, and $300 in the third year. What's the IRR? If we require an 18 percent return, should we take this investment?

We'll describe the NPV profile and find the IRR by calculating some NPVs at different discount rates. You should check our answers for practice. Beginning with 0 percent, we have:

Discount Rate	NPV
0%	$164.56
5	100.36
10	46.15
15	.00
20	− 39.61

The NPV is zero at 15 percent, so 15 percent is the IRR. If we require an 18 percent return, then we should not take the investment. The reason is that the NPV is negative at 18 percent (verify that it is −$24.47). The IRR rule tells us the same thing in this case. We shouldn't take this investment because its 15 percent return is below our required 18 percent return.

At this point, you may be wondering whether the IRR and NPV rules always lead to identical decisions. The answer is yes as long as two very important conditions are met. First, the project's cash flows must be *conventional*, meaning that the first cash flow (the initial investment) is negative and all the rest are positive. Second, the project must be *independent*, meaning that the decision to accept or reject this project does not affect the decision to accept or reject any other. The first of these conditions is typically met, but the second often is not. In any case, when one or both of these conditions are not met, problems can arise. We discuss some of these in a moment.

CALCULATING IRRs WITH A SPREADSHEET

Because IRRs are so tedious to calculate by hand, financial calculators and, especially, spreadsheets are generally used. The procedures used by various financial calculators are too different for us to illustrate here, so we will focus on using a spreadsheet (financial calculators are covered in Appendix D). As the following example illustrates, using a spreadsheet is very easy:

	A	B	C	D	E	F	G	H
1								
2	Using a spreadsheet to calculate internal rates of return							
3								
4	Suppose we have a four-year project that costs $500. The cash flows over the four-year life will be							
5	$100, $200, $300, and $400. What is the IRR?							
6								
7		Year	Cash flow					
8		0	−$500					
9		1	100		IRR =	27.3%		
10		2	200					
11		3	300					
12		4	400					
13								
14								
15	The formula entered in cell F9 is = IRR(C8:C12). Notice that the Year 0 cash flow has a negative sign,							
16	representing the initial cost of the project.							
17								

Problems with the IRR

The problems with the IRR come about when the cash flows are not conventional or when we are trying to compare two or more investments to see which is best. In the first case, surprisingly, the simple question "What's the return?" can become very difficult to answer. In the second case, the IRR can be a misleading guide.

Nonconventional Cash Flows   Suppose we have a strip-mining project that requires a $60 investment. Our cash flow in the first year will be $155. In the second year, the mine is depleted, but we have to spend $100 to restore the terrain. As Figure 8.5 illustrates, both the first and third cash flows are negative.

To find the IRR on this project, we can calculate the NPV at various rates:

Discount Rate	NPV
0%	−$5.00
10	− 1.74
20	− .28
30	.06
40	− .31

The NPV appears to be behaving in a very peculiar fashion here. First, as the discount rate increases from 0 percent to 30 percent, the NPV starts out negative and becomes positive. This seems backward because the NPV is rising as the discount rate rises. It then starts getting smaller and becomes negative again. What's the IRR? To find out, we draw the NPV profile in Figure 8.6.

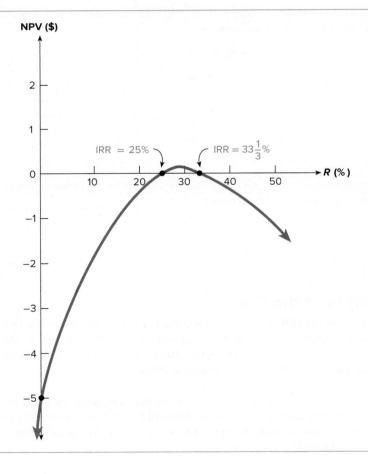

In Figure 8.6, notice that the NPV is zero when the discount rate is 25 percent, so this is the IRR. Or is it? The NPV is also zero at 33⅓ percent. Which of these is correct? The answer is both or neither; more precisely, there is no unambiguously correct answer. This is the **multiple rates of return** problem. Many computer spreadsheet packages aren't aware of this problem and just report the first IRR that is found. Others report only the smallest positive IRR, even though this answer is no better than any other. For example, if you enter this problem in our spreadsheet example, it will report that the IRR is 25 percent.

In our current example, the IRR rule breaks down completely. Suppose our required return was 10 percent. Should we take this investment? Both IRRs are greater than 10 percent, so, by the IRR rule, maybe we should. However, as Figure 8.6 shows, the NPV is negative at any discount rate less than 25 percent, so this is not a good investment. When should we take it? Looking at Figure 8.6 one last time, we see that the NPV is positive only if our required return is between 25 percent and 33⅓ percent.

The moral of the story is that when the cash flows aren't conventional, strange things can start to happen to the IRR. This is not anything to get upset about, however, because the NPV rule, as always, works fine. This illustrates that, oddly enough, the obvious question "What's the rate of return?" may not always have a good answer.

multiple rates of return

The possibility that more than one discount rate will make the net present value of an investment zero.

EXAMPLE 8.4   What's the IRR?

You are looking at an investment that requires you to invest $51 today. You'll get $100 in one year, but you must pay out $50 in two years. What is the IRR on this investment?

You're on the alert now to the nonconventional cash flow problem, so you probably wouldn't be surprised to see more than one IRR. However, if you start looking for an IRR by trial and error, it will take you a long time. The reason is that there is no IRR. The NPV is negative at every discount rate, so we shouldn't take this investment under any circumstances. What's the return on this investment? Your guess is as good as ours.

Mutually Exclusive Investments   Even if there is a single IRR, another problem can arise concerning mutually exclusive investment decisions. If two investments, X and Y, are mutually exclusive, then taking one of them means that we cannot take the other. Two projects that are not mutually exclusive are said to be independent. For example, if we own one corner lot, then we can build a gas station or an apartment building, but not both. These are mutually exclusive alternatives.

Thus far, we have asked whether or not a given investment is worth undertaking. There is a related question that comes up very often: Given two or more mutually exclusive investments, which one is the best? The answer is simple enough: The best one is the one with the largest NPV. Can we also say that the best one has the highest return? As we show, the answer is no.

To illustrate the problem with the IRR rule and mutually exclusive investments, consider the cash flows from the following two mutually exclusive investments:

Year	Investment A	Investment B
0	−$100	−$100
1	50	20
2	40	40
3	40	50
4	30	60

The IRR for A is 24 percent, and the IRR for B is 21 percent. Because these investments are mutually exclusive, we only can take one of them. Simple intuition suggests that Investment A is better because of its higher return. Unfortunately, simple intuition is not always correct.

To see why Investment A is not necessarily the better of the two investments, we've calculated the NPV of these investments for different required returns:

Discount Rate	NPV (A)	NPV (B)
0%	$60.00	$70.00
5	43.13	47.88
10	29.06	29.79
15	17.18	14.82
20	7.06	2.31
25	− 1.63	− 8.22

The IRR for A (24 percent) is larger than the IRR for B (21 percent). However, if you compare the NPVs, you'll see that which investment has the higher NPV depends on our required return. B has greater total cash flow, but it pays back more slowly than A. As a result, it has a higher NPV at lower discount rates.

In our example, the NPV and IRR rankings conflict for some discount rates. If our required return is 10 percent, for instance, then B has the higher NPV and is thus the better of the two, even though A has the higher IRR. If our required return is 15 percent, then there is no ranking conflict: A is better.

The conflict between the IRR and NPV for mutually exclusive investments can be illustrated by plotting their NPV profiles as we have done in Figure 8.7. In Figure 8.7, notice

FIGURE 8.7

NPV profiles for mutually exclusive investments

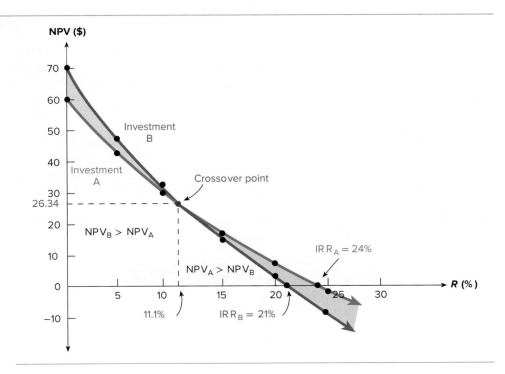

that the NPV profiles cross at about 11.1 percent. Notice also that at any discount rate less than 11.1 percent, the NPV for B is higher. In this range, taking B benefits us more than taking A, even though A's IRR is higher. At any rate greater than 11.1 percent, Investment A has the greater NPV.

This example illustrates that whenever we have mutually exclusive projects, we shouldn't rank them based on their returns. More generally, any time we are comparing investments to determine which is best, IRRs can be misleading. Instead, we need to look at the relative NPVs to avoid the possibility of choosing incorrectly. Remember, we're ultimately interested in creating value for the shareholders, so the option with the higher NPV is preferred, regardless of the relative returns.

If this seems counterintuitive, think of it this way. Suppose you have two investments. One has a 10 percent return and makes you $100 richer immediately. The other has a 20 percent return and makes you $50 richer immediately. Which one do you like better? We would rather have $100 than $50, regardless of the returns, so we like the first one better.

As we saw from Figure 8.7, the crossover rate for Investment A and Investment B is 11.1 percent. You might be wondering how we got this number. Actually, the calculation is fairly easy. We begin by subtracting the cash flows from one project from the cash flows of the second project. In this case, we will subtract Investment B from Investment A. Doing so, we get:

Year	Investment A	Investment B	Cash Flow Difference (A − B)
0	−$100	−$100	$ 0
1	50	20	30
2	40	40	0
3	40	50	− 10
4	30	60	− 30

Now all we have to do is calculate the IRR for these differential cash flows, which works out to be 11.1 percent. Verify for yourself that if you subtract Investment A's cash flows from Investment B's cash flows, the crossover rate is still 11.1 percent, so it doesn't matter which one you subtract from which.

Redeeming Qualities of the IRR

Despite its flaws, the IRR is very popular in practice, more so than even the NPV. It probably survives because it fills a need that the NPV does not. In analyzing investments, people in general, and financial analysts in particular, seem to prefer talking about rates of return rather than dollar values.

In a similar vein, the IRR also appears to provide a simple way of communicating information about a proposal. One manager might say to another, "Remodeling the clerical wing has a 20 percent return." This may somehow be simpler than saying, "At a 10 percent discount rate, the net present value is $4,000."

Finally, under certain circumstances, the IRR may have a practical advantage over the NPV. We can't estimate the NPV unless we know the appropriate discount rate, but we can still estimate the IRR. Suppose we didn't know the required return on an investment, but we found, for example, that it had a 40 percent return. We would probably be inclined to take it because it is very unlikely that the required return would be that high. The advantages and disadvantages of the IRR are summarized in the following table.

Advantages and Disadvantages of the Internal Rate of Return	
Advantages	**Disadvantages**
1. Closely related to NPV, often leading to identical decisions. 2. Easy to understand and communicate.	1. May result in multiple answers with nonconventional cash flows. 2. May lead to incorrect decisions in comparisons of mutually exclusive investments.

The Modified Internal Rate of Return (MIRR)

To address some of the problems that can crop up with the standard IRR, it is often proposed that a modified version be used. As we will see, there are several different ways of calculating a modified IRR, or MIRR, but the idea is to modify the cash flows first and then calculate IRR using the modified cash flows.

To illustrate, let's go back to the cash flows in Figure 8.5: −$60, +$155, and −$100. As we saw, there are two IRRs, 25 percent and 33⅓ percent. We next illustrate three different MIRRs, all of which have the property that only one answer will result, thereby eliminating the multiple IRR problem.

Method 1: The Discounting Approach   With the discounting approach, the idea is to discount all negative cash flows back to the present at the required return and add them to the initial cost. Then, calculate the IRR. Because only the first modified cash flow is negative, there will be only one IRR. The discount rate used might be the required return, or it might be some other externally supplied rate. We use the project's required return.

If the required return on the project is 20 percent, then the modified cash flows look like this:

Time 0: $-\$60 + \dfrac{-\$100}{1.20^2} = -\$129.44$

Time 1: $+\$155$
Time 2: $+\$0$

If you calculate the MIRR now, you should get 19.74 percent.

Method 2: The Reinvestment Approach   With the reinvestment approach, we compound *all* cash flows (positive and negative) except the first out to the end of the project's life and then calculate the IRR. In a sense, we are "reinvesting" the cash flows and not taking them out of the project until the very end. The rate we use could be the required return on the project, or it could be a separately specified "reinvestment rate." We use the project's required return. When we do, here are the modified cash flows:

Time 0:   −$60
Time 1:   +0
Time 2:   −$100 + ($155 × 1.2) = $86

The MIRR on this set of cash flows is 19.72 percent, or a little lower than we got using the discounting approach.

Method 3: The Combination Approach   As the name suggests, the combination approach blends our first two methods. Negative cash flows are discounted back to the present, and positive cash flows are compounded to the end of the project. In practice, different discount or compounding rates might be used, but we again stick with the project's required return.

With the combination approach, the modified cash flows are as follows:

Time 0: $-\$60 + \dfrac{-\$100}{1.20^2} = -\$129.44$

Time 1: $+0$

Time 2: $\$155 \times 1.2 = \$186$

See if you don't agree that the MIRR is 19.87, the highest of the three.

MIRR or IRR: Which Is Better? MIRRs are controversial. At one extreme are those who claim that MIRRs are superior to IRRs, period. For example, by design, they clearly don't suffer from the multiple rate of return problem.

At the other end, detractors say that MIRR should stand for "meaningless internal rate of return." As our example makes clear, one problem with MIRRs is that there are different ways of calculating them, and there is no clear reason to say one of our three methods is better than any other. The differences are small with our simple cash flows, but they could be much larger for a more complex project. Further, it's unclear how to interpret an MIRR. It may look like a rate of return; but it's a rate of return on a modified set of cash flows, not the project's actual cash flows.

We're not going to take sides. However, notice that calculating an MIRR requires discounting, compounding, or both, which leads to two obvious observations. First, if we have the relevant discount rate, why not calculate the NPV and be done with it? Second, because an MIRR depends on an externally supplied discount (or compounding) rate, the answer you get is not truly an "internal" rate of return, which, by definition, depends on only the project's cash flows.

We *will* take a stand on one issue that frequently comes up in this context. The value of a project does not depend on what the firm does with the cash flows generated by that project. A firm might use a project's cash flows to fund other projects, to pay dividends, or to buy an executive jet. It doesn't matter: How the cash flows are spent in the future does not affect their value today. As a result, there is generally no need to consider reinvestment of interim cash flows.

CONCEPT QUESTIONS

8.4a Under what circumstances will the IRR and NPV rules lead to the same accept-reject decisions? When might they conflict?

8.4b Is it generally true that an advantage of the IRR rule over the NPV rule is that we don't need to know the required return to use the IRR rule?

8.5 THE PROFITABILITY INDEX

Excel
Master
coverage online

profitability index (PI)

The present value of an investment's future cash flows divided by its initial cost. Also benefit-cost ratio.

Another method used to evaluate projects involves the **profitability index (PI)**, or benefit-cost ratio. This index is defined as the present value of the future cash flows divided by the initial investment. So, if a project costs $200 and the present value of its future cash flows is $220, the profitability index value would be $220/$200 = 1.10. Notice that the NPV for this investment is $20, so it is a desirable investment.

More generally, if a project has a positive NPV, then the present value of the future cash flows must be bigger than the initial investment. The profitability index thus would be bigger than 1.00 for a positive NPV investment and less than 1.00 for a negative NPV investment.

How do we interpret the profitability index? In our example, the PI was 1.10. This tells us that, per dollar invested, $1.10 in value, or $.10 in NPV, results. The profitability index thus measures "bang for the buck," that is, the value created per dollar invested. For this reason, it is often proposed as a measure of performance for government or other not-for-profit investments. Also, when capital is scarce, it may make sense to allocate it to those projects with the highest PIs.

The PI is obviously very similar to the NPV. However, consider an investment that costs $5 and has a $10 present value and an investment that costs $100 with a $150 present value. The first of these investments has an NPV of $5 and a PI of 2. The second has an NPV of $50 and a PI of 1.50. If these are mutually exclusive investments, then the second one is preferred, even though it has a lower PI. This ranking problem is very similar to the IRR ranking problem we saw in the previous section. In all, there seems to be little reason to rely on the PI instead of the NPV. Our discussion of the PI is summarized here:

Advantages and Disadvantages of the Profitability Index	
Advantages	**Disadvantages**
1. Closely related to NPV, generally leading to identical decisions.	1. May lead to incorrect decisions in comparisons of mutually exclusive investments.
2. Easy to understand and communicate.	
3. May be useful when available investment funds are limited.	

CONCEPT QUESTIONS

8.5a   What does the profitability index measure?

8.5b   How would you state the profitability index rule?

8.6 THE PRACTICE OF CAPITAL BUDGETING

Given that NPV seems to be telling us directly what we want to know, you might be wondering why there are so many other procedures and why alternative procedures are commonly used. Recall that we are trying to make an investment decision and that we are frequently operating under considerable uncertainty about the future. We can only *estimate* the NPV of an investment in this case. The resulting estimate can be very "soft," meaning that the true NPV might be quite different.

Because the true NPV is unknown, the astute financial manager seeks clues to assess whether the estimated NPV is reliable. For this reason, firms would typically use multiple criteria for evaluating a proposal. Suppose we have an investment with a positive estimated NPV. Based on our experience with other projects, this one appears to have a short payback and a very high AAR. In this case, the different indicators seem to agree that it's "all systems go." Put another way, the payback and the AAR are consistent with the conclusion that the NPV is positive.

On the other hand, suppose we had a positive estimated NPV, a long payback, and a low AAR. This still could be a good investment, but it looks like we need to be much more careful in making the decision because we are getting conflicting signals. If the estimated NPV is based on projections in which we have little confidence, then further analysis is probably in order. We consider how to go about this analysis in more detail in the next chapter.

Capital expenditures by individual corporations can add up to enormous sums for the economy as a whole. For example, for 2018, ExxonMobil announced that it expected to have about $25 billion in capital outlays during the year, down from its record $42.5 billion in 2013. About the same time, competitor Chevron announced that it would decrease its capital spending for 2018 to $18.3 billion, down from about $19.1 billion in 2017. Other companies with large capital spending budgets included Walmart, which projected capital spending of about $6.9 billion for 2018, and Apple, which projected capital spending of about $16 billion for 2018.

Large-scale capital spending is often an industrywide occurrence. For example, in 2018, capital spending in the semiconductor industry was expected to reach $77.4 billion. This tidy sum also was spent by the industry in 2017.

According to information released by the Census Bureau in 2018, capital investment for the economy as a whole was $1.576 trillion in 2016, $1.642 trillion in 2015, and $1.507 trillion in 2014. The totals for the three years therefore exceeded $4.7 trillion! Given the sums at stake, it is not too surprising that careful analysis of capital expenditures is something at which successful businesses seek to become adept.

There have been a number of surveys conducted asking firms what types of investment criteria they actually use. Table 8.5 summarizes the results of several of these. The first part of the table is a historical comparison looking at the primary capital budgeting techniques used by large firms through time. In 1959, only 19 percent of the firms surveyed used either IRR or NPV, and 68 percent used either payback periods or accounting returns. It is clear that, by the 1980s, IRR and NPV had become the dominant criteria.

| TABLE 8.5 | Capital budgeting techniques in practice |

A. Historical Comparison of the Primary Use of Various Capital Budgeting Techniques							
	1959	1964	1970	1975	1977	1979	1981
Payback period	34%	24%	12%	15%	9%	10%	5.0%
Average accounting return (AAR)	34	30	26	10	25	14	10.7
Internal rate of return (IRR)	19	38	57	37	54	60	65.3
Net present value (NPV)	—	—	—	26	10	14	16.5
IRR or NPV	19	38	57	63	64	74	81.8

B. Percentage of CFOs Who Always or Almost Always Use a Given Technique in 1999				
Capital Budgeting Technique	Percentage Always or Almost Always Use	Overall	Average Score Scale Is 4 (always) to 0 (never) Large Firms	Small Firms
Internal rate of return	76%	3.09	3.41	2.87
Net present value	75	3.08	3.42	2.83
Payback period	57	2.53	2.25	2.72
Accounting rate of return	20	1.34	1.25	1.41
Profitability index	12	.83	.75	.88

Sources: Graham, J.R. and Harvey, C.R., "The Theory and Practice of Corporate Finance: Evidence from the Field," *Journal of Financial Economics,* May–June 2001, pp. 187–244; Moore, J.S. and Reichert, A.K., "An Analysis of the Financial Management Techniques Currently Employed by Large U.S. Corporations," *Journal of Business Finance and Accounting,* Winter 1983, pp. 623–45; Stanley, M.T. and Block, S.B., "A Survey of Multinational Capital Budgeting," *The Financial Review,* March 1984, pp. 36–51.

TABLE **8.6**

Summary of
investment criteria

I.   **Discounted cash flow criteria**
   A. *Net present value (NPV)*. The NPV of an investment is the difference between its market value and its cost. The NPV rule is to take a project if its NPV is positive. NPV is frequently estimated by calculating the present value of the future cash flows (to estimate market value) and then subtracting the cost. NPV has no serious flaws; it is the preferred decision criterion.
   B. *Internal rate of return (IRR)*. The IRR is the discount rate that makes the estimated NPV of an investment equal to zero; it is sometimes called the *discounted cash flow (DCF) return*. The IRR rule is to take a project when its IRR exceeds the required return. IRR is closely related to NPV, and it leads to exactly the same decisions as NPV for conventional, independent projects. When project cash flows are unconventional there may be no IRR or there may be more than one. More seriously, the IRR cannot be used to rank mutually exclusive projects; the project with the highest IRR is not necessarily the preferred investment.
   C. *Modified internal rate of return (MIRR)*. The MIRR is a modification to the IRR. A project's cash flows are modified by (1) discounting the negative cash flows back to the present; (2) compounding all cash flows to the end of the project's life; or (3) combining (1) and (2). An IRR is then computed on the modified cash flows. MIRRs are guaranteed to avoid the multiple rate of return problem. But, it is unclear how to interpret them, and they are not truly "internal" because they depend on externally supplied discounting or compounding rates.
   D. *Profitability index (PI)*. The PI, also called the *benefit-cost ratio,* is the ratio of present value to cost. The PI rule is to take an investment if the index exceeds 1. The PI measures the present value of an investment per dollar invested. It is quite similar to NPV, but, like IRR, it cannot be used to rank mutually exclusive projects. However, it is sometimes used to rank projects when a firm has more positive NPV investments than it can currently finance.

II. **Payback criteria**
   Payback period. The payback period is the length of time until the sum of an investment's cash flows equals its cost. The payback period rule is to take a project if its payback is *less* than some cutoff. The payback period is a flawed criterion primarily because it ignores risk, the time value of money, and cash flows beyond the cutoff point.

III. **Accounting criteria**
   Average accounting return (AAR). The AAR is a measure of accounting profit relative to book value. It is *not* related to the IRR, but it is similar to the accounting return on assets (ROA) measure in Chapter 3. The AAR rule is to take an investment if its AAR exceeds a benchmark AAR. The AAR is seriously flawed for a variety of reasons, and it has little to recommend it.

Panel B of Table 8.5 summarizes the results of a 1999 survey of chief financial officers (CFOs) at both large and small firms in the United States. A total of 392 CFOs responded. What is shown is the percentage of CFOs who always or almost always use the various capital budgeting techniques we described in this chapter. Not surprisingly, IRR and NPV are the two most widely used techniques, particularly at larger firms. However, over half of the respondents always, or almost always, use the payback criterion as well. In fact, among smaller firms, payback is used about as much as NPV and IRR. Less commonly used are accounting rate of return and the profitability index. For quick reference, these criteria are briefly summarized in Table 8.6.

CONCEPT QUESTIONS

8.6a   What are the most commonly used capital budgeting procedures?

8.6b   If NPV is conceptually the best tool for capital budgeting, why do you think multiple measures are used in practice?

SUMMARY AND CONCLUSIONS

This chapter has covered the different criteria used to evaluate proposed investments. The criteria, in the order in which we discussed them, are:

1. Net present value (NPV)
2. Payback period
3. Average accounting return (AAR)
4. Internal rate of return (IRR)
5. Modified internal rate of return (MIRR)
6. Profitability index (PI)

We illustrated how to calculate each of these and discussed the interpretation of the results. We also described the advantages and disadvantages of each of them. Ultimately, a good capital budgeting criterion must tell us two things. First, is a particular project a good investment? Second, if we have more than one good project, but we can only take one of them, which one should we take? The main point of this chapter is that only the NPV criterion can always provide the correct answer to both questions.

For this reason, NPV is one of the two or three most important concepts in finance, and we refer to it many times in the chapters ahead. When we do, keep two things in mind: (1) NPV is always the difference between the market value of an asset or project and its cost and (2) the financial manager acts in the shareholders' best interests by identifying and taking positive NPV projects.

Finally, we noted that NPVs can't normally be observed in the market; instead, they must be estimated. Because there is always the possibility of a poor estimate, financial managers use multiple criteria for examining projects. These other criteria provide additional information about whether a project truly has a positive NPV.

connect POP QUIZ!

Can you answer the following questions? If your class is using *Connect*, log on to SmartBook to see if you know the answers to these and other questions, check out the study tools, and find out what topics require additional practice!

Section 8.1 Describe the basic NPV investment rule.

Section 8.2 What are the advantages of the payback period method for management?

Section 8.3 How would you define the average accounting return rule?

CHAPTER REVIEW AND SELF-TEST PROBLEMS

8.1 Investment Criteria This problem will give you some practice calculating NPVs and paybacks. A proposed overseas expansion has the following cash flows:

Year	Cash Flow
0	−$100
1	50
2	40
3	40
4	15

Calculate the payback and NPV at a required return of 15 percent. (See Problem 21.)

8.2 Mutually Exclusive Investments Consider the following two mutually exclusive investments. Calculate the IRR for each. Under what circumstances will the IRR and NPV criteria rank the two projects differently? (See Problem 10.)

Year	Investment A	Investment B
0	−$100	−$100
1	50	70
2	70	75
3	40	10

8.3 Average Accounting Return You are looking at a three-year project with a projected net income of $1,000 in Year 1, $2,000 in Year 2, and $4,000 in Year 3. The cost is $9,000, which will be depreciated straight-line to zero over the three-year life of the project. What is the average accounting return, or AAR? (See Problem 4.)

■ Answers to Chapter Review and Self-Test Problems

8.1 In the following table, we have listed the cash flows and their discounted values (at 15 percent).

	Cash Flow	
Year	Undiscounted	Discounted (at 15%)
1	$ 50	$ 43.48
2	40	30.25
3	40	26.30
4	15	8.58
Total	$145	$108.60

Recall that the initial investment is $100. Examining the undiscounted cash flows, we see that the payback occurs between Years 2 and 3. The cash flows for the first two years are $90 total, so, going into the third year, we are short by $10. The total cash flow in Year 3 is $40, so the payback is $2 + \$10/\$40 = 2.25$ years.

Looking at the discounted cash flows, we see that the sum is $108.60, so the NPV is $8.60.

8.2   To calculate the IRR, we might try some guesses as in the following table:

Discount Rate	NPV(A)	NPV(B)
0%	$60.00	$55.00
10	33.36	33.13
20	13.43	16.20
30	− 1.91	2.78
40	− 13.99	− 8.09

Several things are immediately apparent from our guesses. First, the IRR on A must be just a little less than 30 percent (why?). With some more effort, we find that it's 28.61 percent. For B, the IRR must be a little more than 30 percent (again, why?); it works out to be 32.37 percent. Also, notice that at 10 percent, the NPVs are very close, indicating that the NPV profiles cross in that vicinity. Verify that the NPVs are the same at 10.61 percent.

Now, the IRR for B is always higher. As we've seen, A has the larger NPV for any discount rate less than 10.61 percent, so the NPV and IRR rankings will conflict in that range. Remember, if there's a conflict, we will go with the higher NPV. Our decision rule is thus very simple: Take A if the required return is less than 10.61 percent, take B if the required return is between 10.61 percent and 32.37 percent (the IRR on B), and take neither if the required return is more than 32.37 percent.

8.3   Here we need to calculate the ratio of average net income to average book value to get the AAR. Average net income is:

Average net income = ($1,000 + 2,000 + 4,000)/3

= $2,333.33

Average book value is:

Average book value = $9,000/2 = $4,500

So, the average accounting return is:

AAR = $2,333.33/$4,500 = .5185, or 51.85%

This is an impressive return. Remember, however, that it isn't really a rate of return like an interest rate or an IRR, so the size doesn't tell us a lot. In particular, our money is probably not going to grow at 51.85 percent per year, sorry to say.

CRITICAL THINKING AND CONCEPTS REVIEW

LO 4
LO 1   8.1   **Payback Period and Net Present Value**   If a project with conventional cash flows has a payback period less than its life, can you definitively state the algebraic sign of the NPV? Why or why not?

LO 4   8.2   **Net Present Value**   Suppose a project has conventional cash flows and a positive NPV. What do you know about its payback? Its profitability index? Its IRR? Explain.

LO 1   **8.3**   **Payback Period**   Concerning payback:

    a.   Describe how the payback period is calculated and describe the information this measure provides about a sequence of cash flows. What is the payback criterion decision rule?

    b.   What are the problems associated with using the payback period as a means of evaluating cash flows?

    c.   What are the advantages of using the payback period to evaluate cash flows? Are there any circumstances under which using payback might be appropriate? Explain.

LO 2   **8.4**   **Average Accounting Return**   Concerning AAR:

    a.   Describe how the average accounting return is usually calculated and describe the information this measure provides about a sequence of cash flows. What is the AAR criterion decision rule?

    b.   What are the problems associated with using the AAR as a means of evaluating a project's cash flows? What underlying feature of AAR is most troubling to you from a financial perspective? Does the AAR have any redeeming qualities?

LO 4   **8.5**   **Net Present Value**   Concerning NPV:

    a.   Describe how NPV is calculated and describe the information this measure provides about a sequence of cash flows. What is the NPV criterion decision rule?

    b.   Why is NPV considered to be a superior method of evaluating the cash flows from a project? Suppose the NPV for a project's cash flows is computed to be $2,500. What does this number represent with respect to the firm's shareholders?

LO 3   **8.6**   **Internal Rate of Return**   Concerning IRR:

    a.   Describe how the IRR is calculated, and describe the information this measure provides about a sequence of cash flows. What is the IRR criterion decision rule?

    b.   What is the relationship between IRR and NPV? Are there any situations in which you might prefer one method over the other? Explain.

    c.   Despite its shortcomings in some situations, why do most financial managers use IRR along with NPV when evaluating projects? Can you think of a situation in which IRR might be a more appropriate measure to use than NPV? Explain.

LO 6   **8.7**   **Profitability Index**   Concerning the profitability index:

    a.   Describe how the profitability index is calculated and describe the information this measure provides about a sequence of cash flows. What is the profitability index decision rule?

    b.   What is the relationship between the profitability index and the NPV? Are there any situations in which you might prefer one method over the other? Explain.

LO 3
LO 1   **8.8**   **Payback and Internal Rate of Return**   A project has perpetual cash flows of C per period, a cost of I, and a required return of R. What is the relationship between the project's payback and its IRR? What implications does your answer have for long-lived projects with relatively constant cash flows?

LO 4   **8.9**   **International Investment Projects**   In June 2017, automobile manufacturer BMW announced plans to invest $600 million to expand production at its South Carolina plant. BMW apparently felt that it would better be able to compete and create value with a U.S.-based facility. In fact, BMW expected to export 70 percent of the vehicles produced in South Carolina. Also in 2017, noted Taiwanese iPhone supplier Foxconn announced plans to build a $10 billion plant in Wisconsin, and Chinese tire manufacturer Wanli Tire Corp. announced plans to build a $1 billion plant in South Carolina. What are some of the reasons that foreign manufacturers of products as diverse as automobiles, cell phones, and tires might arrive at this same conclusion?

LO 4   **8.10**   **Capital Budgeting Problems**   What are some of the difficulties that might come up in actual applications of the various criteria we discussed in this chapter? Which one would be the easiest to implement in actual applications? The most difficult?

LO 4   **8.11**   **Capital Budgeting in Not-for-Profit Entities**   Are the capital budgeting criteria we discussed applicable to not-for-profit corporations? How should such entities make capital budgeting decisions? What about the U.S. government? Should it evaluate spending proposals using these techniques?

LO 3   **8.12**   **Internal Rate of Return**   In a previous chapter, we discussed the yield to maturity (YTM) of a bond. In what ways are the IRR and the YTM similar? How are they different?

LO 5   **8.13**   **Modified Internal Rate of Return**   One of the less flattering interpretations of the acronym MIRR is "meaningless internal rate of return." Why do you think this term is applied to MIRR?

LO 4   **8.14**   **Net Present Value**   It is sometimes stated that "the net present value approach assumes reinvestment of the intermediate cash flows at the required return." Is this claim correct? To answer, suppose you calculate the NPV of a project in the usual way. Next, suppose you do the following:

   a.   Calculate the future value (as of the end of the project) of all the cash flows other than the initial outlay assuming they are reinvested at the required return, producing a single future value figure for the project.

   b.   Calculate the NPV of the project using the single future value calculated in the previous step and the initial outlay. It is easy to verify that you will get the same NPV as in your original calculation only if you use the required return as the reinvestment rate in the previous step.

LO 3   **8.15**   **Internal Rate of Return**   It is sometimes stated that "the internal rate of return approach assumes reinvestment of the intermediate cash flows at the internal rate of return." Is this claim correct? To answer, suppose you calculate the IRR of a project in the usual way. Next, suppose you do the following:

   a.   Calculate the future value (as of the end of the project) of all the cash flows other than the initial outlay assuming they are reinvested at the IRR, producing a single future value figure for the project.

   b.   Calculate the IRR of the project using the single future value calculated in the previous step and the initial outlay. It is easy to verify that you will get the same IRR as in your original calculation only if you use the IRR as the reinvestment rate in the previous step.

QUESTIONS AND PROBLEMS

McGraw Hill Education connect   Select problems are available in McGraw-Hill *Connect*. Please see the packaging options section of the Preface for more information.

LO 1   **1. Calculating Payback**   What is the payback period for the following set of cash flows?

Year	Cash Flow
0	−$7,800
1	3,100
2	3,200
3	2,200
4	1,400

LO 1   **2. Calculating Payback**   An investment project provides cash inflows of $865 per year for eight years. What is the project payback period if the initial cost is $3,100? What if the initial cost is $4,300? What if it is $7,900?

LO 1   **3. Calculating Payback**   Stenson, Inc., imposes a payback cutoff of three years for its international investment projects. If the company has the following two projects available, should it accept either of them?

Year	Cash Flow (A)	Cash Flow (B)
0	−$75,000	−$125,000
1	33,000	29,000
2	36,000	32,000
3	19,000	35,000
4	9,000	240,000

LO 2   **4. Calculating AAR**   You're trying to determine whether or not to expand your business by building a new manufacturing plant. The plant has an installation cost of $10.8 million, which will be depreciated straight-line to zero over its four-year life. If the plant has projected net income of $1,293,000, $1,725,000, $1,548,000, and $1,310,000 over these four years, what is the project's average accounting return (AAR)?

LO 3   **5. Calculating IRR**   A firm evaluates all of its projects by applying the IRR rule. If the required return is 11 percent, should the firm accept the following project?

Year	Cash Flow
0	−$157,300
1	74,000
2	87,000
3	46,000

LO 4   **6. Calculating NPV**   For the cash flows in the previous problem, suppose the firm uses the NPV decision rule. At a required return of 9 percent, should the firm accept this project? What if the required return was 21 percent?

LO 3
LO 4

7. Calculating NPV and IRR   A project that provides annual cash flows of $2,620 for eight years costs $9,430 today. Is this a good project if the required return is 8 percent? What if it's 24 percent? At what discount rate would you be indifferent between accepting the project and rejecting it?

LO 3

8. Calculating IRR   What is the IRR of the following set of cash flows?

Year	Cash Flow
0	−$19,400
1	10,400
2	9,320
3	6,900

LO 4

9. Calculating NPV   For the cash flows in the previous problem, what is the NPV at a discount rate of 0 percent? What if the discount rate is 10 percent? If it is 20 percent? If it is 30 percent?

LO 3
LO 4

10. NPV versus IRR   Piercy, LLC, has identified the following two mutually exclusive projects:

Year	Cash Flow (A)	Cash Flow (B)
0	−$77,500	−$77,500
1	43,000	21,000
2	29,000	28,000
3	23,000	34,000
4	21,000	41,000

a. What is the IRR for each of these projects? If you apply the IRR decision rule, which project should the company accept? Is this decision necessarily correct?

b. If the required return is 11 percent, what is the NPV for each of these projects? Which project will you choose if you apply the NPV decision rule?

c. Over what range of discount rates would you choose Project A? Project B? At what discount rate would you be indifferent between these two projects? Explain.

LO 3
LO 4

11. NPV versus IRR   Consider the following two mutually exclusive projects:

Year	Cash Flow (X)	Cash Flow (Y)
0	−$23,900	−$23,900
1	13,100	9,300
2	9,480	10,620
3	7,890	11,180

Sketch the NPV profiles for X and Y over a range of discount rates from 0 to 25 percent. What is the crossover rate for these two projects?

LO 3   **12. Problems with IRR**   Howell Petroleum, Inc., is trying to evaluate a generation project with the following cash flows:

Year	Cash Flow
0	−$38,000,000
1	56,000,000
2	− 9,000,000

a. If the company requires a return of 10 percent on its investments, should it accept this project? Why?

b. Compute the IRR for this project. How many IRRs are there? If you apply the IRR decision rule, should you accept the project or not? What's going on here?

LO 6   **13. Calculating Profitability Index**   What is the profitability index for the following set of cash flows if the relevant discount rate is 10 percent? What if the discount rate is 15 percent? If it is 22 percent?

Year	Cash Flow
0	−$29,500
1	16,900
2	13,600
3	8,300

LO 4
LO 6   **14. Problems with Profitability Index**   The Whenworth Corporation is trying to choose between the following two mutually exclusive design projects:

Year	Cash Flow (I)	Cash Flow (II)
0	−$84,000	−$29,800
1	30,600	10,500
2	36,900	17,400
3	43,700	15,600

a. If the required return is 11 percent and the company applies the profitability index decision rule, which project should the firm accept?

b. If the company applies the NPV decision rule, which project should it take?

c. Explain why your answers in parts (a) and (b) are different.

LO 1
LO 3
LO 4
LO 6   **15. Comparing Investment Criteria**   Consider the following two mutually exclusive projects:

Year	Cash Flow (A)	Cash Flow (B)
0	−$245,000	−$53,000
1	34,000	31,900
2	49,000	21,800
3	51,000	17,300
4	325,000	16,200

Whichever project you choose, if any, you require a return of 13 percent on your investment.

    a. If you apply the payback criterion, which investment will you choose? Why?

    b. If you apply the NPV criterion, which investment will you choose? Why?

    c. If you apply the IRR criterion, which investment will you choose? Why?

    d. If you apply the profitability index criterion, which investment will you choose? Why?

    e. Based on your answers in parts (a) through (d), which project will you finally choose? Why?

LO 3
LO 4
16. NPV and IRR   Bausch Company is presented with the following two mutually exclusive projects. The required return for both projects is 15 percent.

Year	Project M	Project N
0	−$140,000	−$359,000
1	61,500	159,300
2	73,400	168,400
3	68,100	154,800
4	40,500	110,400

    a. What is the IRR for each project?

    b. What is the NPV for each project?

    c. Which, if either, of the projects should the company accept?

LO 4
LO 6
17. NPV and Profitability Index   Coore Manufacturing has the following two possible projects. The required return is 12 percent.

Year	Project Y	Project Z
0	−$47,600	−$81,000
1	23,900	34,000
2	18,600	32,800
3	20,700	30,500
4	14,600	27,300

    a. What is the profitability index for each project?

    b. What is the NPV for each project?

    c. Which, if either, of the projects should the company accept?

LO 3
18. Crossover Point   Crenshaw Enterprises has gathered projected cash flows for two projects. At what interest rate would the company be indifferent between the two projects? Which project is better if the required return is above this interest rate? Why?

Year	Project I	Project J
0	−$189,000	−$189,000
1	93,500	73,600
2	84,600	72,800
3	63,200	76,800
4	57,800	84,000

LO 1
LO 3

19. Payback Period and IRR   Suppose you have a project with a payback period exactly equal to the life of the project. What do you know about the IRR of the project? Suppose that the payback period is never. What do you know about the IRR of the project now?

LO 4

20. NPV and Discount Rates   An investment has an installed cost of $787,350. The cash flows over the four-year life of the investment are projected to be $312,615, $304,172, $245,367, and $229,431. If the discount rate is zero, what is the NPV? If the discount rate is infinite, what is the NPV? At what discount rate is the NPV equal to zero? Sketch the NPV profile for this investment based on these three points.

LO 1
LO 4

21. NPV and Payback Period   Kaleb Konstruction, Inc., has the following mutually exclusive projects available. The company has historically used a three-year cutoff for projects. The required return is 10 percent.

Year	Project F	Project G
0	−$195,000	−$298,000
1	98,400	71,600
2	86,300	94,500
3	81,600	123,600
4	72,000	166,800
5	64,800	187,200

   a. Calculate the payback period for both projects.
   b. Calculate the NPV for both projects.
   c. Which project, if any, should the company accept?

LO 5

22. MIRR   Doak Corp. is evaluating a project with the following cash flows:

Year	Cash Flow
0	−$32,600
1	11,520
2	14,670
3	11,270
4	10,940
5	− 4,230

The company uses an interest rate of 10 percent on all of its projects. Calculate the MIRR of the project using all three methods.

INTERMEDIATE (Questions 23–27)

LO 5

23. MIRR   Suppose the company in the previous problem uses a discount rate of 11 percent and a reinvestment rate of 8 percent on all of its projects. Calculate the MIRR of the project using all three methods with these rates.

LO 4

24. Crossover and NPV   Hanse, Inc., has the following two mutually exclusive projects available.

Year	Project R	Project S
0	−$51,000	−$76,000
1	19,000	20,000
2	19,000	20,000
3	24,000	35,000
4	11,000	30,000
5	7,000	10,000

What is the crossover rate for these two projects? What is the NPV of each project at the crossover rate?

LO 3
LO 4

25. Calculating IRR   A project has the following cash flows:

Year	Cash Flow
0	$112,000
1	− 67,000
2	− 57,000

What is the IRR for this project? If the required return is 10 percent, should the firm accept the project? What is the NPV of this project? What is the NPV of the project if the required return is 0 percent? 24 percent? What is going on here? Sketch the NPV profile to help you with your answer.

LO 4
LO 6

26. NPV and the Profitability Index   If we define the NPV index as the ratio of NPV to cost, what is the relationship between this index and the profitability index?

LO 1
LO 4
LO 6

27. Cash Flow Intuition   A project has an initial cost of I, has a required return of R, and pays C annually for N years.

   a. Find C in terms of I and N such that the project has a payback period equal to its life.

   b. Find C in terms of I, N, and R such that this is a profitable project according to the NPV decision rule.

   c. Find C in terms of I, N, and R such that the project has a benefit-cost ratio of 2.

CHALLENGE (Questions 28–30)

LO 4

28. NPV Valuation   The Yurdone Corporation wants to set up a private cemetery business. According to the CFO, Barry M. Deep, business is "looking up." As a result, the cemetery project will provide a net cash inflow of $164,000 for the firm during the first year, and the cash flows are projected to grow at a rate of 4.7 percent per year forever. The project requires an initial investment of $1,825,000.

   a. If the company requires a return of 12 percent on such undertakings, should the cemetery business be started?

   b. The company is somewhat unsure about the assumption of a 4.7 percent growth rate in its cash flows. At what constant growth rate would the company just break even if it still required a return of 12 percent on its investment?

LO 3

29. Problems with IRR   Koepka Corp. has a project with the following cash flows:

Year	Cash Flow
0	$35,000
1	− 27,000
2	29,000

What is the IRR of the project? What is happening here?

30. NPV and IRR   Anderson International Limited is evaluating a project in Erewhon. The project will create the following cash flows:

Year	Cash Flow
0	−$875,000
1	306,900
2	287,600
3	285,300
4	259,300

All cash flows will occur in Erewhon and are expressed in dollars. In an attempt to improve its economy, the Erewhonian government has declared that all cash flows created by a foreign company are "blocked" and must be reinvested with the government for one year. The reinvestment rate for these funds is 4 percent. If Anderson uses a required return of 10 percent on this project, what are the NPV and IRR of the project? Is the IRR you calculated the MIRR of the project? Why or why not?

WHAT'S ON THE WEB?

8.1 Net Present Value   You have a project that has an initial cash outflow of −$20,000 and cash inflows of $6,000, $5,000, $4,000, and $3,000, respectively, for the next four years. Go to www.vindeep.com and find the IRR calculator. Enter the cash flows. If the required return is 12 percent, what is the IRR of the project? The NPV?

8.2 Internal Rate of Return   Using the online calculator from the previous problem, find the IRR for a project with cash flows of −$500, $1,200, and −$400. What is going on here?

EXCEL *MASTER IT!* PROBLEM

Excel Master coverage online

As you have already seen, Excel does not have a function to calculate the payback period. We have shown three ways to calculate the payback period, but there are numerous other methods as well. Below, the cash flows for a project are shown. You need to calculate the payback period using two different methods.

a.   Calculate the payback period in a table. The first three columns of the table will be the year, the cash flow for that year, and the cumulative cash flow. The fourth column will show the whole year for the payback. In other words, if the payback period is 3+ years, this column will have a 3, otherwise it will be a zero. The next column will calculate the fractional part of the payback period, or else it will display zero. The last column will add the previous two columns and display the final payback period calculation. You should also have a cell that displays the final payback period by itself, and a cell that returns the correct accept or reject decision based on the payback criteria.

b.   Write a nested IF statement that calculates the payback period using only the project cash flow column. The IF statement should return a value of "Never" if the project has no payback period. In contrast to the example we showed previously, the nested IF function should test for the payback period starting with shorter payback periods and working toward longer payback periods. Another cell should display the correct accept or reject decision based on the payback criteria.

Year	Cash Flow
0	−$250,000
1	41,000
2	48,000
3	63,000
4	79,000
5	88,000
6	64,000
7	41,000

CHAPTER CASE
Bullock Gold Mining

Seth Bullock, the owner of Bullock Gold Mining, is evaluating a new gold mine in South Dakota. Dan Dority, the company's geologist, has just finished his analysis of the mine site. He has estimated that the mine would be productive for eight years, after which the gold would be completely mined. Dan has taken an estimate of the gold deposits to Alma Garrett, the company's financial officer. Alma has been asked by Seth to perform an analysis of the new mine and present her recommendation on whether the company should open the new mine.

Alma has used the estimates provided by Dan to determine the revenues that could be expected from the mine. She also has projected the expense of opening the mine and the annual operating expenses. If the company opens the mine, it will cost $625 million today, and it will have a cash outflow of $90 million nine years from today in costs associated with closing the mine and reclaiming the area surrounding it. The expected cash flows each year from the mine are shown in the nearby table. Bullock Gold Mining has a 12 percent required return on all of its gold mines.

Year	Cash Flow
0	−$625,000,000
1	70,000,000
2	129,000,000
3	183,000,000
4	235,000,000
5	210,000,000
6	164,000,000
7	108,000,000
8	86,000,000
9	− 90,000,000

QUESTIONS

1. Construct a spreadsheet to calculate the payback period, internal rate of return, modified internal rate of return, and net present value of the proposed mine.

2. Based on your analysis, should the company open the mine?

3. Bonus question: Most spreadsheets do not have a built-in formula to calculate the payback period. Write a VBA script that calculates the payback period for a project.

9 | Making Capital Investment Decisions

Even having a major star is no guarantee of success for a movie release. In 2018, the film *Gotti*, which starred John Travolta, slept with the fishes as it debuted with a 0.0 rating on Rotten Tomatoes. The critics all said, "fugeddaboudit!" Fortunately for the production company, Oasis Films, the film didn't lose a lot of money (it only cost $10 million to make). Not all films are as lucky. Take *Monster Trucks*, the children's film about the monsters that live in trucks. According to critics, just watching the movie amounted to a crushing experience. One called it a "clueless family caper." Another was even more harsh, saying "*Monster Trucks* is a wreck, fueled by the crazy belief that noise and repetition can disguise the lack of credible writing, directing, acting and FX."

Looking at the numbers, Paramount Pictures spent close to $125 million making the movie, plus millions more for marketing and distribution. Paramount was so negative about movie ticket sales that it wrote off $115 million *before* the movie was released! And the movie subsequently crashed, pulling in only $64.5 million worldwide. Of course, there are movies that do quite well. Also in 2018, the superhero hit *Black Panther* raked in about $1.4 billion worldwide at a production cost of about $200 million.

Obviously, Paramount didn't *plan* to lose $60 or so million on *Monster Trucks*, but it happened. As that movie's box office crack-up shows, projects don't always go as companies think they will. This chapter explores how this can happen and what companies can do to analyze and possibly avoid these situations.

In broader terms, this chapter follows up on our previous one by delving more deeply into capital budgeting. We have two main tasks. First, recall that in the last chapter, we saw that cash flow estimates are the critical input into a net present value analysis, but we didn't say very much about where these cash flows come from; so, we will now examine this question in some detail. Our second goal is to learn how to critically examine NPV estimates and, in particular, how to evaluate the sensitivity of NPV estimates to assumptions made about the uncertain future.

LEARNING OBJECTIVES

After studying this chapter, you should be able to:

LO 1 Determine the relevant cash flows for a proposed investment.

LO 2 Analyze a project's expected cash flows.

LO 3 Evaluate an estimated NPV.

Please visit us at essentialsofcorporatefinance.blogspot.com for the latest developments in the world of corporate finance.

So far, we've covered various parts of the capital budgeting decision. Our task in this chapter is to start bringing these pieces together. In particular, we will show you how to "spread the numbers" for a proposed investment or project and, based on those numbers, make an initial assessment about whether or not the project should be undertaken.

In the discussion that follows, we focus on the process of setting up a discounted cash flow analysis. From the last chapter, we know that the projected future cash flows are the key element in such an evaluation. Accordingly, we emphasize working with financial and accounting information to come up with these figures.

In evaluating a proposed investment, we pay special attention to deciding what information is relevant to the decision at hand and what information is not. As we shall see, it is easy to overlook important pieces of the capital budgeting puzzle. We also describe how to go about evaluating the results of our discounted cash flow analysis.

9.1 PROJECT CASH FLOWS: A FIRST LOOK

The effect of taking a project is to change the firm's overall cash flows today and in the future. To evaluate a proposed investment, we must consider these changes in the firm's cash flows and then decide whether or not they add value to the firm. The first (and most important) step, therefore, is to decide which cash flows are relevant and which are not.

Relevant Cash Flows

What is a relevant cash flow for a project? The general principle is simple enough: A relevant cash flow for a project is a change in the firm's overall future cash flow that comes about as a direct consequence of the decision to take that project. Because the relevant cash flows are defined in terms of changes in, or increments to, the firm's existing cash flow, they are called the **incremental cash flows** associated with the project.

incremental cash flows
The difference between a firm's future cash flows with a project and those without the project.

The concept of incremental cash flow is central to our analysis, so we will state a general definition and refer back to it as needed:

> The incremental cash flows for project evaluation consist of *any and all* changes in the firm's future cash flows that are a direct consequence of taking the project.

This definition of incremental cash flows has an obvious and important corollary: Any cash flow that exists regardless of whether or not a project is undertaken is *not* relevant.

The Stand-Alone Principle

In practice, it would be very cumbersome to actually calculate the future total cash flows to the firm with and without a project, especially for a large firm. Fortunately, it is not really necessary to do so. Once we identify the effect of undertaking the proposed project on the firm's cash flows, we need only focus on the project's resulting incremental cash flows. This is called the **stand-alone principle**.

stand-alone principle
The assumption that evaluation of a project may be based on the project's incremental cash flows.

What the stand-alone principle says is that, once we have determined the incremental cash flows from undertaking a project, we can view that project as a kind of "minifirm" with its own future revenues and costs, its own assets, and, of course, its own cash flows. We will then be primarily interested in comparing the cash flows from this minifirm to the cost of acquiring it. An important consequence of this approach is that we will be evaluating the proposed project purely on its own merits, in isolation from any other activities or projects.

CONCEPT QUESTIONS

9.1a What are the relevant incremental cash flows for project evaluation?

9.1b What is the stand-alone principle?

9.2 INCREMENTAL CASH FLOWS

We are concerned here only with those cash flows that are incremental and that result from a project. Looking back at our general definition, it seems easy enough to decide whether or not a cash flow is incremental. Even so, there are a few situations where mistakes are easy to make. In this section, we describe some of these common pitfalls and how to avoid them.

Sunk Costs

A **sunk cost**, by definition, is a cost we have already paid or have already incurred the liability to pay. Such a cost cannot be changed by the decision today to accept or reject a project. Put another way, the firm will have to pay this cost no matter what. Based on our general definition of incremental cash flow, such a cost is clearly irrelevant to the decision at hand. So, we will always be careful to exclude sunk costs from our analysis.

That a sunk cost is irrelevant seems obvious given our discussion. Nonetheless, it's easy to fall prey to the sunk cost fallacy. Suppose General Milk Company hires a financial consultant to help evaluate whether or not a line of chocolate milk should be launched. When the consultant turns in the report, General Milk objects to the analysis because the consultant did not include the hefty consulting fee as a cost of the chocolate milk project.

Who is correct? By now, we know that the consulting fee is a sunk cost because the consulting fee must be paid whether or not the chocolate milk line is actually launched (this is an attractive feature of the consulting business).

sunk cost
A cost that has already been incurred and cannot be recouped and therefore should not be considered in an investment decision.

Opportunity Costs

When we think of costs, we normally think of out-of-pocket costs, namely, those that require us to actually spend some amount of cash. An **opportunity cost** is slightly different; it requires us to give up a benefit. A common situation arises where a firm already owns some of the assets a proposed project will be using. For example, we might be thinking of converting an old rustic cotton mill we bought years ago for $100,000 into "upmarket" condominiums.

If we undertake this project, there will be no direct cash outflow associated with buying the old mill since we already own it. For purposes of evaluating the condo project, should we then treat the mill as "free"? The answer is no. The mill is a valuable resource used by the project. If we didn't use it here, we could do something else with it. Like what? The obvious answer is that, at a minimum, we could sell it. Using the mill for the condo complex thus has an opportunity cost: We give up the valuable opportunity to do something else with it.[1]

opportunity cost
The most valuable alternative that is given up if a particular investment is undertaken.

---

[1]Economists sometimes use the acronym *TANSTAAFL*, which is short for "There ain't no such thing as a free lunch," to describe the fact that only very rarely is something truly free.

There is another issue here. Once we agree that the use of the mill has an opportunity cost, how much should the condo project be charged? Given that we paid $100,000, it might seem that we should charge this amount to the condo project. Is this correct? The answer is no, and the reason is based on our discussion concerning sunk costs.

The fact that we paid $100,000 some years ago is irrelevant. That cost is sunk. At a minimum, the opportunity cost that we charge the project is what the mill would sell for today (net of any selling costs) because this is the amount that we give up by using it instead of selling it.

Side Effects

Remember that the incremental cash flows for a project include all the changes in the *firm's* future cash flows. It would not be unusual for a project to have side, or spillover, effects, both good and bad. For example, if the Innovative Motors Company (IMC) introduces a new car, some of the sales might come at the expense of other IMC cars. This is called **erosion**, and the same general problem could occur for any multiline producer or seller.[2] In this case, the cash flows from the new line should be adjusted downward to reflect lost profits on other lines.

In accounting for erosion, it is important to recognize that any sales lost as a result of our launching a new product might be lost anyway because of future competition. Erosion is only relevant when the sales would not otherwise be lost.

erosion
The cash flows of a new project that come at the expense of a firm's existing projects.

Net Working Capital

Normally, a project will require that the firm invest in net working capital in addition to long-term assets. For example, a project will generally need some amount of cash on hand to pay any expenses that arise. In addition, a project will need an initial investment in inventories and accounts receivable (to cover credit sales). Some of this financing will be in the form of amounts owed to suppliers (accounts payable), but the firm will have to supply the balance. This balance represents the investment in net working capital.

It's easy to overlook an important feature of net working capital in capital budgeting. As a project winds down, inventories are sold, receivables are collected, bills are paid, and cash balances can be drawn down. These activities free up the net working capital originally invested. So, the firm's investment in project net working capital closely resembles a loan. The firm supplies working capital at the beginning and recovers it toward the end.

Financing Costs

In analyzing a proposed investment, we will not include interest paid or any other financing costs such as dividends or principal repaid because we are interested in the cash flow generated by the assets of the project. As we mentioned in Chapter 2, interest paid, for example, is a component of cash flow to creditors, not cash flow from assets.

More generally, our goal in project evaluation is to compare the cash flow from a project to the cost of acquiring that project in order to estimate NPV. The particular mixture of debt and equity a firm actually chooses to use in financing a project is a managerial variable and primarily determines how project cash flow is divided between owners and creditors. This is not to say that financing arrangements are unimportant. They are something to be analyzed separately. We will cover this in later chapters.

---

[2]More colorfully, erosion is sometimes called *piracy* or *cannibalism*.

Other Issues

There are some other things to watch out for. First, we are only interested in measuring cash flow. Moreover, we are interested in measuring it when it actually occurs, not when it accrues in an accounting sense. Second, we are always interested in *aftertax* cash flow because taxes are definitely a cash outflow. In fact, whenever we write "incremental cash flows," we mean aftertax incremental cash flows. Remember, however, that aftertax cash flow and accounting profit, or net income, are entirely different things.

CONCEPT QUESTIONS

9.2a   What is a sunk cost? An opportunity cost?

9.2b   Explain what erosion is, and why it is relevant.

9.2c   Explain why interest paid is not a relevant cash flow for project evaluation.

9.3 PRO FORMA FINANCIAL STATEMENTS AND PROJECT CASH FLOWS

The first thing we need when we begin evaluating a proposed investment is a set of pro forma, or projected, financial statements. Given these, we can develop the projected cash flows from the project. Once we have the cash flows, we can estimate the value of the project using the techniques we described in the previous chapter.

Excel Master
coverage online

Getting Started: Pro Forma Financial Statements

Pro forma financial statements are a convenient and easily understood means of summarizing much of the relevant information for a project. To prepare these statements, we will need estimates of quantities such as unit sales, the selling price per unit, the variable cost per unit, and total fixed costs. We also will need to know the total investment required, including any investment in net working capital.

pro forma financial statements
Financial statements projecting future years' operations.

To illustrate, suppose we think we can sell 50,000 cans of shark attractant per year at a price of $4.00 per can. It costs us about $2.50 per can to make the attractant, and a new product such as this one typically has only a three-year life (perhaps because the customer base dwindles rapidly). We require a 20 percent return on new products.

Fixed costs for the project, including such things as rent on the production facility, will run $17,430 per year. Further, we will need to invest a total of $90,000 in manufacturing equipment. For simplicity, we will assume that this $90,000 will be 100 percent depreciated over the three-year life of the project. Furthermore, the cost of removing the equipment will roughly equal its actual value in three years, so it will be essentially worthless on a market value basis as well. Finally, the project will require an initial $20,000 investment in net working capital, and the tax rate is 21 percent.

In Table 9.1, we organize these initial projections by first preparing the pro forma income statement for each of the three years. Once again, notice that we have not deducted any interest expense. This will always be so. As we described earlier, interest paid is a financing expense, not a component of operating cash flow.

We also can prepare a series of abbreviated balance sheets that show the capital requirements for the project. as we've done in Table 9.2. Here we have net working capital of

TABLE 9.1 Projected income statement, shark attractant project, Years 1–3	Sales (50,000 units at $4.00/unit) $200,000 Variable costs ($2.50/unit) 125,000 Fixed costs 17,430 Depreciation (= $90,000/3) 30,000 EBIT $ 27,570 Taxes (21%) 5,790 Net income $ 21,780

TABLE 9.2

Projected capital requirements, shark attractant project

		Year		
	0	**1**	**2**	**3**
Net working capital	$ 20,000	$20,000	$20,000	$20,000
Net fixed assets	90,000	60,000	30,000	0
Total investment	$110,000	$80,000	$50,000	$20,000

$20,000 in each year. Fixed assets are $90,000 at the start of the project's life (Year 0), and they decline by the $30,000 in depreciation each year, ending up at zero. Notice that the total investment given here for future years is the total book, or accounting, value, not market value.

At this point, we need to start converting this accounting information into cash flows. We consider how to do this next.

Project Cash Flows

To develop the cash flows from a project, we need to recall (from Chapter 2) that cash flow from assets has three components: operating cash flow, capital spending, and additions to net working capital. To evaluate a project, or minifirm, we need to arrive at estimates for each of these.

Once we have estimates of the components of cash flow, we will calculate cash flow for our minifirm as we did in Chapter 2 for an entire firm:

> **Project cash flow = Project operating cash flow**
> **— Project change in net working capital**
> **— Project capital spending**

We consider these components next.

Project Operating Cash Flow   To determine the operating cash flow associated with a project, we first need to recall the definition of operating cash flow:

> **Operating cash flow = Earnings before interest and taxes**
> **+ Depreciation**
> **— Taxes**

To illustrate the calculation of operating cash flow, we will use the projected information from the shark attractant project. For ease of reference, Table 9.3 repeats the income statement.

Sales	$200,000
Variable costs	125,000
Fixed costs	17,430
Depreciation	30,000
EBIT	$ 27,570
Taxes (21%)	5,790
Net income	$ 21,780

TABLE 9.3

Projected income statement, shark attractant project, Years 1–3

EBIT	$27,570
Depreciation	+30,000
Taxes	−5,790
Operating cash flow	$ 51,780

TABLE 9.4

Projected operating cash flow, shark attractant project

	Year			
	0	**1**	**2**	**3**
Operating cash flow		$51,780	$51,780	$51,780
Change in NWC	− $ 20,000			+20,000
Capital spending	− 90,000			
Total project cash flow	−$110,000	$51,780	$51,780	$71,780

TABLE 9.5

Projected total cash flows, shark attractant project

Given the income statement in Table 9.3, calculating the operating cash flow is straight-forward. As we see in Table 9.4, projected operating cash flow for the shark attractant project is $51,780.

Project Net Working Capital and Capital Spending   We next need to take care of the fixed asset and net working capital requirements. Based on our balance sheets above, the firm must spend $90,000 up front for fixed assets and invest an additional $20,000 in net working capital. The immediate outflow is thus $110,000. At the end of the project's life, the fixed assets will be worthless (the salvage value will be zero), but the firm will recover the $20,000 that was tied up in working capital. This will lead to a $20,000 cash *inflow* in the last year.

On a purely mechanical level, notice that whenever we have an investment in net working capital, that same investment has to be recovered; in other words, the same number needs to appear at some time in the future with the opposite sign.

Projected Total Cash Flow and Value

Given the information we've accumulated, we can finish the preliminary cash flow analysis as illustrated in Table 9.5.

Now that we have cash flow projections, we are ready to apply the various criteria we discussed in the last chapter. First, the NPV at the 20 percent required return is:

$$\text{NPV} = -\$110,000 + 51,780/1.2 + 51,780/1.2^2 + 71,780/1.2^3$$
$$= \$10,648$$

So, based on these projections, the project creates more than $10,000 in value and should be accepted. Also, the return on this investment obviously exceeds 20 percent (because the NPV is positive at 20 percent). After some trial and error, we find that the IRR works out to be about 25.76 percent.

In addition, if required, we could go ahead and calculate the payback and the average accounting return, or AAR. Inspection of the cash flows shows that the payback on this project is a little over two years (verify that it's about 2.1 years).

From the last chapter, we know that the AAR is average net income divided by average book value. The net income each year is $21,780. The average of the four book values (from Table 9.2) is ($110,000 + 80,000 + 50,000 + 20,000)/4 = $65,000, so the AAR is $21,780/$65,000 = .3351, or 33.51 percent. We've already seen that the return on this investment (the IRR) is about 26 percent. The fact that the AAR is larger illustrates again why the AAR cannot be meaningfully interpreted as the return on a project.

The Tax Shield Approach

A useful variation on our basic definition of operating cash flow (OCF) is the *tax shield* approach. The tax shield definition of OCF is:

$$\text{OCF} = (\text{Sales} - \text{Costs}) \times (1 - T_c) + \text{Depreciation} \times T_c$$

where T_c is the corporate tax rate. Assuming that $T_c = 21\%$, the OCF works out to be:

$$\text{OCF} = (\$200,000 - 142,430) \times .79 + 30,000 \times .21$$
$$= \$45,480 + 6,300$$
$$= \$51,780$$

This is as we had before.

This approach views OCF as having two components. The first part is what the project's cash flow would be if there were no depreciation expense. In this case, this would-have-been cash flow is $45,480.

depreciation tax shield

The tax saving that results from the depreciation deduction, calculated as depreciation multiplied by the corporate tax rate.

The second part of OCF in this approach is the depreciation deduction multiplied by the tax rate. This is called the **depreciation tax shield**. We know that depreciation is a non-cash expense. The only cash flow effect of deducting depreciation is to reduce our taxes, a benefit to us. At the current 21 percent corporate tax rate, every dollar in depreciation expense saves us 21 cents in taxes. In our example, the $30,000 depreciation deduction saves us $30,000 × .21 = $6,300 in taxes.

The tax shield approach will always give the same answer as our basic approach, so you might wonder why we bother. The answer is that it is sometimes a little simpler to use, particularly for projects that involve cost-cutting.

CONCEPT QUESTIONS

9.3a   What is the definition of project operating cash flow? How does this differ from net income?

9.3b   In the shark attractant project, why did we add back the firm's net working capital investment in the final year?

9.3c   What is the "depreciation tax shield"?

9.4 MORE ON PROJECT CASH FLOW

In this section, we take a closer look at some aspects of project cash flow. In particular, we discuss project net working capital in more detail. We then examine current tax laws regarding depreciation.

Excel
Master
coverage online

A Closer Look at Net Working Capital

In calculating operating cash flow, we did not explicitly consider the fact that some of our sales might be on credit. Also, we may not actually have paid some of the costs shown. In either case, the cash flow has not yet occurred. We show here that these possibilities are not a problem as long as we don't forget to include additions to net working capital in our analysis. This discussion thus emphasizes the importance and the effect of doing so.

Suppose during a particular year of a project we have the following simplified income statement:

Sales	$500
Costs	310
Net income	$190

Depreciation and taxes are zero. No fixed assets are purchased during the year. Also, to illustrate a point, we assume that the only components of net working capital are accounts receivable and payable. The beginning and ending amounts for these accounts are:

	Beginning of Year	End of Year	Change
Accounts receivable	$880	$910	+$30
Accounts payable	550	605	+ 55
Net working capital	$330	$305	−$25

Based on this information, what is total cash flow for the year? We first can mechanically apply what we have been discussing to come up with the answer. Operating cash flow in this particular case is the same as EBIT because there are no taxes or depreciation, and thus equals $190. Also, notice that net working capital actually declined by $25, so the change in net working capital is negative. This means that $25 was freed up during the year. There was no capital spending, so the total cash flow for the year is:

Total cash flow = Operating cash flow − Change in NWC − Capital spending

$$= \$190 - (-25) - 0$$

$$= \$215$$

Now, we know that this $215 total cash flow has to be "dollars in" less "dollars out" for the year. We, therefore, could ask a different question: What were cash revenues for the year? Also, what were cash costs?

To determine cash revenues, we need to look more closely at net working capital. During the year, we had sales of $500. However, accounts receivable rose by $30 over the same time period. What does this mean? The $30 increase tells us that sales exceeded collections by $30. In other words, we haven't yet received the cash from $30 of the $500 in sales. As a result, our cash inflow is $500 − 30 = $470. In general, cash inflow is sales minus the increase in accounts receivable.

Cash outflows can be determined similarly. We show costs of $310 on the income statement, but accounts payable increased by $55 during the year. This means that we have not yet paid $55 of the $310, so cash costs for the period are $310 − 55 = $255. In other words, in this case, cash costs equal costs less the increase in accounts payable.

Putting this information together, cash inflows less cash outflows is $470 − 255 = $215, as we had before. Notice that:

Cash flow = Cash inflow − Cash outflow
$$= (\$500 - 30) - (310 - 55)$$
$$= (\$500 - 310) - (30 - 55)$$
$$= \text{Operating cash flow} - \text{Change in NWC}$$
$$= \$190 - (-25)$$
$$= \$215$$

More generally, this example illustrates that including net working capital changes in our calculations has the effect of adjusting for the discrepancy between accounting sales and costs and actual cash receipts and payments.

EXAMPLE 9.1	**Cash Collections and Costs**

For the year just completed, the Combat Wombat Telestat Co. (CWT) reports sales of $998 and costs of $734. You have collected the following beginning and ending balance sheet information:

	Beginning	Ending
Accounts receivable	$100	$110
Inventory	100	80
Accounts payable	100	70
Net working capital	$100	$120

Based on these figures, what are cash inflows? Cash outflows? What happened to each account? What is net cash flow?

Sales were $998, but receivables rose by $10. So, cash collections were $10 less than sales, or $988. Costs were $734, but inventories fell by $20. This means that we didn't replace $20 worth of inventory, so costs are actually overstated by this amount. Also, payables fell by $30. This means that, on a net basis, we actually paid our suppliers $30 more than we received from them, resulting in a $30 understatement of costs. Adjusting for these events, cash costs are $734 − 20 + 30 = $744. Net cash flow is $988 − 744 = $244.

Finally, notice that net working capital increased by $20 overall. We can check our answer by noting that the original accounting sales less costs of $998 − 734 is $264. In addition, CWT spent $20 on net working capital, so the net result is a cash flow of $264 − 20 = $244, as we calculated.

Depreciation

Accelerated Cost Recovery System (ACRS)

Depreciation method under U.S. tax law allowing for the accelerated write-off of property under various classifications.

As we note elsewhere, accounting depreciation is a noncash deduction. As a result, depreciation has cash flow consequences only because it influences the tax bill. The way that depreciation is computed for tax purposes is thus the relevant method for capital investment decisions. Not surprisingly, the procedures are governed by tax law. We now discuss some specifics of the depreciation system enacted by the Tax Reform Act of 1986. This system is a modification of the **Accelerated Cost Recovery System (ACRS)** instituted in 1981.

Class	Examples
3-year	Equipment used in research
5-year	Autos, computers
7-year	Most industrial equipment

TABLE 9.6

Modified ACRS
property classes

Year	3-Year	5-Year	7-Year
		Property Class	
1	33.33%	20.00%	14.29%
2	44.45	32.00	24.49
3	14.81	19.20	17.49
4	7.41	11.52	12.49
5		11.52	8.93
6		5.76	8.92
7			8.93
8			4.46

TABLE 9.7

Modified ACRS
depreciation
allowances

Modified ACRS (MACRS) Depreciation   Calculating depreciation is normally very mechanical. While there are a number of ifs, ands, and buts involved, the basic idea is that every asset is assigned to a particular class. An asset's class establishes its life for tax purposes. Once an asset's tax life is determined, we compute the depreciation for each year by multiplying the cost of the asset by a fixed percentage. The expected salvage value (what we think the asset will be worth when we dispose of it) and the actual expected economic life (how long we expect the asset to be in service) are not explicitly considered in the calculation of depreciation.

Some typical depreciation classes are described in Table 9.6, and associated percentages (rounded to two decimal places) are shown in Table 9.7. Remember that land cannot be depreciated.

To illustrate how depreciation is calculated, we consider an automobile costing $35,000. Autos are normally classified as five-year property. Looking at Table 9.7, we see that the relevant figure for the first year of a five-year asset is 20 percent. The depreciation in the first year is thus $35,000 × .20 = $7,000. The relevant percentage in the second year is 32 percent, so the depreciation in the second year is $35,000 × .32 = $11,200, and so on. We can summarize these calculations as follows:

Year	MACRS Percentage	Depreciation
1	20.00%	.2000 × $35,000 = $ 7,000
2	32.00	.3200 × 35,000 = 11,200
3	19.20	.1920 × 35,000 = 6,720
4	11.52	.1152 × 35,000 = 4,032
5	11.52	.1152 × 35,000 = 4,032
6	5.76	.0576 × 35,000 = 2,016
	100.00%	$35,000

	Year	Beginning Book Value	Depreciation	Ending Book Value
TABLE 9.8	1	$35,000	$ 7,000	$28,000
	2	28,000	11,200	16,800
MACRS book values	3	16,800	6,720	10,080
	4	10,080	4,032	6,048
	5	6,048	4,032	2,016
	6	2,016	2,016	0

Notice that the MACRS percentages sum up to 100 percent. As a result, we write off 100 percent of the cost of the asset, or $35,000 in this case.

Bonus Depreciation   For a number of years prior to 2018, various tax rules and regulations were enacted that allowed "bonus" depreciation. Based on the Protecting Americans from Tax Hikes (PATH) Act of 2015, the size of the bonus in 2017 was 50 percent. What this meant is that a firm could take a depreciation deduction of 50 percent of the cost on an eligible asset in the first year and then depreciate the remaining 50 percent using the MACRS schedules as we have just described. Significantly, in late 2017, Congress passed the Tax Cuts and Jobs Act, which increased the bonus depreciation to 100 percent for 2018, lasting until the end of 2022. After that, it drops by 20 percent per year until it reaches zero after 2026. The implication is that most firms will not use the MACRS schedules until 2023 unless they wish to (taking the bonus depreciation is optional). Of course, future legislation may change things.

Book Value versus Market Value   In calculating depreciation under current tax law, the economic life and future market value of the asset are not an issue. As a result, the book value of an asset can differ substantially from its actual market value. For example, with our $35,000 car, book value after the first year is $35,000 less the first year's depreciation of $7,000, or $28,000. The remaining book values are summarized in Table 9.8. After six years, the book value of the car is zero.

Suppose we wanted to sell the car after five years. Based on historical averages, it will be worth, say, 25 percent of the purchase price, or .25 × $35,000 = $8,750. If we actually sold it for this, then we would have to pay taxes at the ordinary income tax rate on the difference between the sale price of $8,750 and the book value of $2,016. For a corporation in the 21 percent bracket, the tax liability is .21 × $6,734 = $1,414.14.

The reason that taxes must be paid in this case is that the difference in market value and book value is "excess" depreciation, and it must be "recaptured" when the asset is sold. What this means is that, as it turns out, we overdepreciated the asset by $8,750 − 2,016 = $6,734. Because we deducted $6,734 too much in depreciation, we paid $1,414.14 too little in taxes, and we have to make up the difference.

Notice that this is not a tax on a capital gain. As a general (albeit rough) rule, a capital gain only occurs if the market price exceeds the original cost. However, what is and what is not a capital gain is ultimately up to taxing authorities, and the specific rules can be very complex. We will ignore capital gains taxes for the most part.

Finally, if the book value exceeds the market value, then the difference is treated as a loss for tax purposes. For example, if we sell the car after two years for $15,000, then the book value exceeds the market value by $1,800. In this case, a tax savings of .21 × $1,800 = $378 occurs.

EXAMPLE 9.2	**MACRS Depreciation**

The Staple Supply Co. has just purchased a new computerized information system with an installed cost of $160,000. The computer is treated as five-year property. What are the yearly depreciation allowances? Based on historical experience, we think that the system will be worth only $10,000 when we get rid of it in four years. What are the tax consequences of the sale? What is the total aftertax cash flow from the sale?

The yearly depreciation allowances are calculated by multiplying $160,000 by the five-year percentages in Table 9.7:

Year	MACRS Percentage	Depreciation		Ending Book Value
1	20.00%	.2000 × $160,000 =	$ 32,000	$128,000
2	32.00	.3200 × 160,000 =	51,200	76,800
3	19.20	.1920 × 160,000 =	30,720	46,080
4	11.52	.1152 × 160,000 =	18,432	27,648
5	11.52	.1152 × 160,000 =	18,432	9,216
6	5.76	.0576 × 160,000 =	9,216	0
	100.00%		$160,000	

Notice that we also have computed the book value of the system as of the end of each year. The book value at the end of Year 4 is $27,648. If we sell the system for $10,000 at that time, we will have a loss of $17,648 (the difference) for tax purposes. This loss, of course, is like depreciation because it isn't a cash expense.

What really happens? Two things. First: We get $10,000 from the buyer. Second: We save .21 × $17,648 = $3,706 in taxes. So, the total aftertax cash flow from the sale is a $13,706 cash inflow.

An Example: The Majestic Mulch and Compost Company (MMCC)

At this point, we want to go through a somewhat more involved capital budgeting analysis. Keep in mind as you read that the basic approach here is exactly the same as that in our earlier shark attractant example. We have only added some more "real-world" detail (and a lot more numbers).

MMCC is investigating the feasibility of a new line of power mulching tools aimed at the growing number of home composters. Based on exploratory conversations with buyers for large garden shops, it projects unit sales as follows:

Year	Unit Sales
1	3,000
2	5,000
3	6,000
4	6,500
5	6,000
6	5,000
7	4,000
8	3,000

The new power mulcher will be priced to sell at $120 per unit to start. When the competition catches up after three years, however, MMCC anticipates that the price will drop to $110.

The power mulcher project will require $20,000 in net working capital at the start. Subsequently, total net working capital at the end of each year will be about 15 percent of sales for that year. The variable cost per unit is $60, and total fixed costs are $25,000 per year.

It will cost about $800,000 to buy the equipment necessary to begin production. This investment is primarily in industrial equipment and thus qualifies as seven-year MACRS property. The equipment actually will be worth about 20 percent of its cost in eight years, or .20 × $800,000 = $160,000. The relevant tax rate is 21 percent, and the required return is 15 percent. Based on this information, should MMCC proceed?

Operating Cash Flows   There is a lot of information here that we need to organize. The first thing we can do is calculate projected sales. Sales in the first year are projected at 3,000 units at $120 apiece, or $360,000 total. The remaining figures are shown in Table 9.9.

Next, we compute the depreciation on the $800,000 investment in Table 9.10. With this information, we can prepare the pro forma income statements, as shown in Table 9.11. From here, computing the operating cash flows is straightforward. The results are illustrated in the first part of Table 9.13.

Changes in NWC   Now that we have the operating cash flows, we need to determine the changes in NWC. By assumption, net working capital requirements change as sales change. In each year, we generally will either add to or recover some of our project net working capital. Recalling that NWC starts out at $20,000 and then rises to 15 percent of sales, we can calculate the amount of NWC for each year as illustrated in Table 9.12.

TABLE 9.9

Projected revenues, power mulcher project

Year	Unit Price	Unit Sales	Revenues
1	$120	3,000	$360,000
2	120	5,000	600,000
3	120	6,000	720,000
4	110	6,500	715,000
5	110	6,000	660,000
6	110	5,000	550,000
7	110	4,000	440,000
8	110	3,000	330,000

TABLE 9.10

Annual depreciation, power mulcher project

Year	MACRS Percentage	Depreciation	Ending Book Value
1	14.29%	.1429 × $800,000 = $114,320	$685,680
2	24.49	.2449 × 800,000 = 195,920	489,760
3	17.49	.1749 × 800,000 = 139,920	349,840
4	12.49	.1249 × 800,000 = 99,920	249,920
5	8.93	.0893 × 800,000 = 71,440	178,480
6	8.92	.0892 × 800,000 = 71,360	107,120
7	8.93	.0893 × 800,000 = 71,440	35,680
8	4.46	.0446 × 800,000 = 35,680	0
	100.00%	$800,000	

TABLE 9.11		Pro forma income statements, power mulcher project						
	Year							
	1	**2**	**3**	**4**	**5**	**6**	**7**	**8**
Unit price	$ 120	$ 120	$ 120	$ 110	$ 110	$ 110	$ 110	$ 110
Unit sales	3,000	5,000	6,000	6,500	6,000	5,000	4,000	3,000
Revenues	$360,000	$600,000	$720,000	$715,000	$660,000	$550,000	$440,000	$330,000
Variable costs	180,000	300,000	360,000	390,000	360,000	300,000	240,000	180,000
Fixed costs	25,000	25,000	25,000	25,000	25,000	25,000	25,000	25,000
Depreciation	114,320	195,920	139,920	99,920	71,440	71,360	71,440	35,680
EBIT	$ 40,680	$ 79,080	$195,080	$200,080	$203,560	$153,640	$103,560	$ 89,320
Taxes (21%)	8,543	16,607	40,967	42,017	42,748	32,264	21,748	18,757
Net income	$ 32,137	$ 62,473	$154,113	$ 158,063	$160,812	$121,376	$ 81,812	$ 70,563

Year	Revenues	Net Working Capital	Cash Flow
0		$ 20,000	−$20,000
1	$360,000	54,000	− 34,000
2	600,000	90,000	− 36,000
3	720,000	108,000	− 18,000
4	715,000	107,250	750
5	660,000	99,000	8,250
6	550,000	82,500	16,500
7	440,000	66,000	16,500
8	330,000	49,500	16,500

TABLE 9.12

Changes in net working capital, power mulcher project

As illustrated, during the first year, net working capital grows from $20,000 to .15 × $360,000 = $54,000. The increase in net working capital for the year is thus $54,000 − 20,000 = $34,000. The remaining figures are calculated the same way.

Remember that an increase in net working capital is a cash outflow, so we use a negative sign in this table to indicate an additional investment that the firm makes in net working capital. A positive sign represents net working capital returning to the firm. Thus, for example, $16,500 in NWC flows back to the firm in Year 6. Over the project's life, net working capital builds to a peak of $108,000 and declines from there as sales begin to drop off.

We show the result for changes in net working capital in the second part of Table 9.13. Notice that at the end of the project's life, there is $49,500 in net working capital still to be recovered. Therefore, in the last year, the project returns $16,500 of NWC during the year and then returns the remaining $49,500 at the end of the year for a total of $66,000.

Capital Spending   Finally, we have to account for the long-term capital invested in the project. In this case, we invest $800,000 at Year 0. By assumption, this equipment will be worth $160,000 at the end of the project. It will have a book value of zero at that time. As we discussed above, this $160,000 excess of market value over book value is taxable, so the aftertax proceeds will be $160,000 × (1 − .21) = $126,400. These figures are shown in the third part of Table 9.13.

Total Cash Flow and Value   We now have all the cash flow pieces, and we put them together in Table 9.14. In addition to the total project cash flows, we have calculated the

TABLE 9.13 — Projected cash flows, power mulcher project

I. Operating Cash Flow

	0	1	2	3	4	5	6	7	8
EBIT		$40,680	$79,080	$195,080	$200,080	$203,560	$153,640	$103,560	$89,320
Depreciation		114,320	195,920	139,920	99,920	71,440	71,360	71,440	35,680
Taxes		− 8,543	− 16,607	− 40,967	− 42,017	− 42,748	− 32,264	− 21,748	− 18,757
Operating cash flow		$146,457	$258,393	$294,033	$257,983	$232,252	$192,736	$153,252	$106,243

II. Net Working Capital

	0	1	2	3	4	5	6	7	8
Initial NWC	−$ 20,000								
Increases in NWC		−$ 34,000	−$ 36,000	−$ 18,000	$ 750	$ 8,250	$ 16,500	$ 16,500	$ 16,500
NWC recovery									49,500
Changes in NWC	−$ 20,000	−$ 34,000	−$ 36,000	−$ 18,000	$ 750	$ 8,250	$ 16,500	$ 16,500	$ 66,000

III. Capital Spending

	0	1	2	3	4	5	6	7	8
Initial outlay	−$800,000								
Aftertax salvage									$126,400
Capital spending	−$800,000								$126,400

TABLE 9.14 — Projected total cash flows, power mulcher project

	0	1	2	3	4	5	6	7	8
Operating cash flow		$146,457	$258,393	$294,033	$257,983	$232,252	$192,736	$153,252	$106,243
Changes in NWC	−$ 20,000	− 34,000	− 36,000	− 18,000	750	8,250	16,500	16,500	66,000
Capital spending	− 800,000								126,400
Total project cash flow	−$820,000	$112,457	$222,393	$276,033	$258,733	$240,502	$209,236	$169,752	$298,643
Cumulative cash flow	−$820,000	−$707,543	−$485,150	−$209,116	$ 49,617	$290,119	$499,355	$669,107	$967,750

Net present value (15%) = $146,852
Internal rate of return = 19.86%
Payback = 3.81 years

cumulative cash flows. At this point, it's essentially plug-and-chug to calculate the net present value, internal rate of return, and payback.

If we sum the discounted cash flows and the initial investment, the net present value (at 15 percent) works out to be $146,852. This is positive; so, based on these preliminary projections, the power mulcher project is acceptable. The internal, or DCF, rate of return is greater than 15 percent because the NPV is positive. It works out to be 19.86 percent, again indicating that the project is acceptable.

Looking at the cumulative cash flows, we see that the project has been paid back somewhere between three and four years because the cumulative cash flow is almost zero at that time. As indicated, the fractional year works out to be $209,116/$258,733 = .81, so the payback is 3.81 years. We can't say whether or not this is good because we don't have a benchmark for MMCC. This is the usual problem with payback periods.

Conclusion

This completes our preliminary DCF analysis. Where do we go from here? If we have a great deal of confidence in our projections, then there is no further analysis to be done. We should begin production and marketing immediately. It is unlikely that this will be the case. It is important to remember that the result of our analysis is an estimate of NPV, and we usually will have less than complete confidence in our projections. This means we have more work to do. In particular, we almost surely will want to spend some time evaluating the quality of our estimates. We take up this subject in the next several sections.

CONCEPT QUESTIONS

9.4a Why is it important to consider changes in net working capital in developing cash flows? What is the effect of doing so?

9.4b How is depreciation calculated for fixed assets under current tax law? What effect do expected salvage value and estimated economic life have on the calculated depreciation deduction?

9.5 EVALUATING NPV ESTIMATES

As we discussed in Chapter 8, an investment has a positive net present value if its market value exceeds its cost. Such an investment is desirable because it creates value for its owner. The primary problem in identifying such opportunities is that, most of the time, we can't actually observe the relevant market value. Instead, we estimate it. Having done so, it is only natural to wonder whether or not our estimates are at least close to the true values. We consider this question next.

The Basic Problem

Suppose we are working on a preliminary DCF analysis along the lines we described in previous sections. We carefully identify the relevant cash flows, avoiding such things as sunk costs, and we remember to consider working capital requirements. We add back any depreciation, we account for possible erosion, and we pay attention to opportunity costs. Finally, we double-check our calculations, and, when all is said and done, the bottom line is that the estimated NPV is positive.

When Things Go Wrong . . .

If you think about it, the decision by a company to acquire another company is a capital budgeting decision. One important difference, however, is that an acquisition may be more expensive than a typical project and, possibly, much more expensive. Of course, as with any other project, acquisitions can fail. When they do, the losses can be huge.

For example, in April 2014, Microsoft announced it was acquiring Nokia for $7.2 billion. The acquisition of Nokia was supposed to give Microsoft the hardware necessary to boost the company's mobile operating system. Of course, the acquisition did not go as planned. In July 2015, Microsoft announced that it was writing off $7.6 billion due to the acquisition, which was more than the acquisition price.

In another example, in early 2018, Teva Pharmeceutical announced it would write off $17 billion in assets. Much of the write-off was due to the company's 2016 acquisition of Allergan's generic drug business. Teva spent $40 billion on the acquisition but soon found it couldn't charge as much as expected for new generic drugs because of competition and price pressure.

One of the largest acquisitions in U.S. history was America Online's (AOL's) purchase of Time Warner in 2001. AOL purchased Time Warner under the assumption that AOL was part of the "new economy" and primed for fast growth. Time Warner was the "old" communications company, owning cable stations and a music label, among other things. But things didn't work as well as planned. Infighting among employees from the two companies hurt production and morale. In 2002, accounting irregularities were uncovered at AOL, and, as a result of the acquisition costs, the company was saddled with massive debt. To make matters worse, AOL began to lose customers and money. Although AOL was the acquirer, and the once-dominant partner, things got so bad at AOL that the company changed its name back to Time Warner. To cap things off, in 2002, Time Warner wrote off a stunning $54 billion in assets associated with the acquisition, which was, at the time, the largest such write-off in history. Finally, in 2016, Time Warner was acquired by Charter Communications for about $79 billion.

Now what? Do we stop here and move on to the next proposal? Probably not. The fact that the estimated NPV is positive is definitely a good sign, but, more than anything, this tells us that we need to take a closer look.

If you think about it, there are two circumstances under which a discounted cash flow analysis could lead us to conclude that a project has a positive NPV. The first possibility is that the project really does have a positive NPV. That's the good news. The bad news is the second possibility: A project may appear to have a positive NPV because our estimate is inaccurate.

Notice that we also could err in the opposite way. If we conclude that a project has a negative NPV when the true NPV is positive, then we lose a valuable opportunity.

Forecasting Risk

The key inputs into a DCF analysis are projected future cash flows. If these projections are seriously in error, then we have a classic GIGO, or garbage-in, garbage-out, system. In this case, no matter how carefully we arrange the numbers and manipulate them, the resulting answer still can be grossly misleading. This is the danger in using a relatively sophisticated technique like DCF. It is sometimes easy to get caught up in number crunching and forget the underlying nuts-and-bolts economic reality.

forecasting risk
The possibility that errors in projected cash flows will lead to incorrect decisions. Also *estimation risk*.

The possibility that we will make a bad decision because of errors in the projected cash flows is called **forecasting risk** (or *estimation risk*). Because of forecasting risk, there is the danger that we will think a project has a positive NPV when it really does not. How is this possible? It occurs if we are overly optimistic about the future, and, as a result, our projected cash flows don't realistically reflect the possible future cash flows. Our nearby *Finance Matters* box shows what can happen in such cases.

So far, we have not explicitly considered what to do about the possibility of errors in our forecasts, so our goal is to develop some tools that will be useful in identifying areas where potential errors exist and where they might be especially damaging. In one form or another, we will be trying to assess the economic "reasonableness" of our estimates. We also will be wondering how much damage will be done by errors in those estimates.

Sources of Value

The first line of defense against forecasting risk is to ask: What is it about this investment that leads to a positive NPV? We should be able to point to something specific as the source of value. For example, if the proposal under consideration involved a new product, then we might ask questions such as the following: Are we certain that our new product is significantly better than that of the competition? Can we truly manufacture at lower cost, or distribute more effectively, or identify undeveloped market niches, or gain control of a market?

These are just a few of the potential sources of value. There are many others. A key factor to keep in mind is the degree of competition in the market. It is a basic principle of economics that positive NPV investments will be rare in a highly competitive environment. Therefore, proposals that appear to show significant value in the face of stiff competition are particularly troublesome, and the likely reaction of the competition to any innovations must be closely examined.

The point to remember is that positive NPV investments are probably not all that common, and the number of positive NPV projects is almost certainly limited for any given firm. If we can't articulate some sound economic basis for thinking ahead of time that we have found something special, then the conclusion that our project has a positive NPV should be viewed with some suspicion.

CONCEPT QUESTIONS

9.5a   What is forecasting risk? Why is it a concern for the financial manager?

9.5b   What are some potential sources of value in a new project?

9.6 SCENARIO AND OTHER WHAT-IF ANALYSES

Excel
Master
coverage online

Our basic approach to evaluating cash flow and NPV estimates involves asking what-if questions. Accordingly, we discuss some organized ways of going about a what-if analysis. Our goal in doing so is to assess the degree of forecasting risk and to identify those components most critical to the success or failure of an investment.

Getting Started

We are investigating a new project. Naturally, the first thing we do is estimate NPV based on our projected cash flows. We will call this the *base case*. Now, however, we recognize the possibility of error in those cash flow projections. After completing the base case, we thus wish to investigate the impact of different assumptions about the future on our estimates.

One way to organize this investigation is to put an upper and lower bound on the various components of the project. Suppose we forecast sales at 100 units per year. We know this estimate may be high or low, but we are relatively certain it is not off by more than 10 units in either direction. We thus would pick a lower bound of 90 and an upper bound of 110. We go on to assign such bounds to any other cash flow components we are unsure about.

When we pick these upper and lower bounds, we are not ruling out the possibility that the actual values could be outside this range. What we are saying, loosely speaking, is that it is unlikely that the true average (as opposed to our estimated average) of the possible values is outside this range.

An example is useful to illustrate the idea here. The project under consideration costs $200,000, has a five-year life, and has no salvage value. Depreciation is straight-line to zero. The required return is 12 percent, and the tax rate is 21 percent. In addition, we have compiled the following information:

	Base Case	Lower Bound	Upper Bound
Unit sales	6,000	5,500	6,500
Price per unit	$80	$75	$85
Variable cost per unit	$60	$58	$62
Fixed costs per year	$50,000	$45,000	$55,000

With this information, we can calculate the base-case NPV by first calculating net income:

Sales	$480,000
Variable costs	360,000
Fixed costs	50,000
Depreciation	40,000
EBIT	$ 30,000
Taxes (21%)	6,300
Net income	$ 23,700

Operating cash flow is thus $30,000 + 40,000 − 6,300 = $63,700 per year. At 12 percent, the five-year annuity factor is 3.6048, so the base-case NPV is:

Base-case NPV = −$200,000 + 63,700 × 3.6048
            = $29,624

Thus, the project looks good so far.

Scenario Analysis

The basic form of what-if analysis is called **scenario analysis**. What we do is investigate the changes in our NPV estimates that result from asking questions like: "What if unit sales realistically should be projected at 5,500 units instead of 6,000?"

Once we start looking at alternative scenarios, we might find that most of the plausible ones result in positive NPVs. In this case, we have some confidence in proceeding with the project. If a substantial percentage of the scenarios look bad, then the degree of forecasting risk is high and further investigation is in order.

There are a number of possible scenarios we could consider. A good place to start is with the worst-case scenario. This will tell us the minimum NPV of the project. If this is positive, we will be in good shape. While we are at it, we will go ahead and determine the other extreme, the best case. This puts an upper bound on our NPV.

To get the worst case, we assign the least favorable value to each item. This means *low* values for items such as units sold and price per unit and *high* values for costs. We do the reverse for the best case. For our project, these values would be:

	Worst Case	Best Case
Unit sales	5,500	6,500
Price per unit	$75	$85
Variable cost per unit	$62	$58
Fixed costs	$55,000	$45,000

With this information, we can calculate the net income and cash flows under each scenario (check these for yourself):

Scenario	Net Income	Cash Flow	Net Present Value	IRR
Base case	$23,700	$63,700	$ 29,624	17.8%
Worst case*	− 18,565	21,435	− 122,732	−17.7
Best case	71,495	111,495	201,915	47.9

* We assume a tax credit is created in our worst-case scenario.

What we learn is that under the worst scenario, the cash flow is still positive at $21,435. That's good news. The bad news is that the return is −17.7 percent in this case, and the NPV is −$122,732. Because the project costs $200,000, we stand to lose more than half of the original investment under the worst possible scenario. The best case offers an attractive 47.9 percent return.

The terms *best case* and *worst case* are very commonly used, and we will stick with them, but we should note that they are somewhat misleading. The absolute best thing that could happen would be something absurdly unlikely, such as launching a new diet soda and subsequently learning that our (patented) formulation also happens to cure the common cold. Of course, on rare occasions, things do go very, very wrong. For example, in April 2010, BP's Gulf of Mexico oil rig *Deepwater Horizon* caught fire and sank following an explosion, leading to a massive oil spill. The leak was finally stopped in July after releasing more than 200 million gallons of crude oil into the Gulf. In 2018, BP took a charge of $1.7 billion related to closing claims from the accident, raising the total costs associated with the disaster to about $65 billion, not including opportunity costs such as lost government contracts. And the company noted that there were numerous claims yet to be settled. Nonetheless, our point is that in assessing the reasonableness of an NPV estimate, we need to stick to cases that are reasonably likely to occur.

Instead of *best* and *worst*, then, it is probably more accurate to say *optimistic* and *pessimistic*. In broad terms, if we were thinking about a reasonable range for, say, unit sales, then what we call the best case would correspond to something near the upper end of that range. The worst case would correspond to the lower end.

As we have mentioned, there are an unlimited number of different scenarios that we could examine. At a minimum, we might want to investigate two intermediate cases by going halfway between the base amounts and the extreme amounts. This would give us five scenarios in all, including the base case.

Beyond this point, it is hard to know when to stop. As we generate more and more possibilities, we run the risk of "paralysis of analysis." The difficulty is that no matter how many scenarios we run, all we can learn are possibilities, some good and some bad. Beyond that, we don't get any guidance as to what to do. Scenario analysis is thus useful in telling us what can happen and in helping us gauge the potential for disaster, but it does not tell us whether or not to take the project.

FIGURE 9.1

Sensitivity analysis
for unit sales

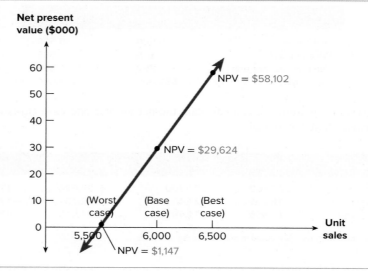

Sensitivity Analysis

sensitivity analysis
Investigation of what happens to net present value when only one variable is changed.

Sensitivity analysis is a variation on scenario analysis that is useful in pinpointing the areas where forecasting risk is especially severe. The basic idea with a sensitivity analysis is to freeze all of the variables except one and then see how sensitive our estimate of NPV is to changes in that one variable. If our NPV estimate turns out to be very sensitive to relatively small changes in the projected value of some component of project cash flow, then the fore-casting risk associated with that variable is high.

To illustrate how sensitivity analysis works, we go back to our base case for every item except unit sales. We then can calculate cash flow and NPV using the largest and smallest unit sales figures.

Scenario	Unit Sales	Cash Flow	Net Present Value	IRR
Base case	6,000	$63,700	$29,624	17.8%
Worst case	5,500	55,800	1,147	12.2
Best case	6,500	71,600	58,102	23.2

The results of our sensitivity analysis for unit sales can be illustrated graphically as in Figure 9.1. Here we place NPV on the vertical axis and unit sales on the horizontal axis. When we plot the combinations of unit sales versus NPV, we see that all possible combinations fall on a straight line. The steeper the resulting line is, the greater is the sensitivity of the estimated NPV to the projected value of the variable being investigated.

By way of comparison, we now freeze everything except fixed costs and repeat the analysis:

Scenario	Fixed Costs	Cash Flow	Net Present Value	IRR
Base case	$50,000	$63,700	$29,624	17.8%
Worst case	55,000	59,750	15,385	15.1
Best case	45,000	67,650	43,863	20.5

What we see here is that, given our ranges, the estimated NPV of this project is more sensitive to projected unit sales than it is to projected fixed costs. In fact, under the worst case for fixed costs, the NPV is still positive.

As we have illustrated, sensitivity analysis is useful in pinpointing those variables that deserve the most attention. If we find that our estimated NPV is especially sensitive to a variable that is difficult to forecast (such as unit sales), then the degree of forecasting risk is high. We might decide that further market research would be a good idea in this case.

Because sensitivity analysis is a form of scenario analysis, it suffers from the same drawbacks. Sensitivity analysis is useful for pointing out where forecasting errors will do the most damage, but it does not tell us what to do about possible errors.

CONCEPT QUESTIONS

9.6a   What are scenario and sensitivity analyses?

9.6b   What are the drawbacks to what-if analyses?

9.7   ADDITIONAL CONSIDERATIONS IN CAPITAL BUDGETING

Our final task for this chapter is a brief discussion of two additional considerations in capital budgeting: managerial options and capital rationing. Both of these can be very important in practice, but, as we will see, explicitly dealing with either of them is difficult.

Managerial Options and Capital Budgeting

In our capital budgeting analysis thus far, we have more or less ignored the possibility of future managerial actions. Implicitly, we have assumed that once a project is launched, its basic features cannot be changed. For this reason, we say that our analysis is *static* (as opposed to dynamic).

In reality, depending on what actually happens in the future, there always will be ways to modify a project. We will call these opportunities **managerial options**. Because they involve real (as opposed to financial) assets, such options are often called "real" options. There are a great number of these options. The way a product is priced, manufactured, advertised, and produced all can be changed, and these are just a few of the possibilities. We discuss some of the most important managerial options in the next few sections.

managerial options
Opportunities that managers can exploit if certain things happen in the future. Also known as "real" options.

Contingency Planning   The various what-if procedures in this chapter have another use. We also can view them as primitive ways of exploring the dynamics of a project and investigating managerial options. What we think about in this case are some of the possible futures that could come about and what actions we might take if they do.

For example, we might find that a project fails to break even when sales drop below 10,000 units. This is a fact that is interesting to know, but the more important thing is then to go on and ask, "What actions are we going to take if this actually occurs?" This is called **contingency planning**, and it amounts to an investigation of some of the managerial options implicit in a project.

contingency planning
Taking into account the managerial options implicit in a project.

There is no limit to the number of possible futures, or contingencies, that we could investigate. However, there are some broad classes, and we consider these next.

The Option to Expand   One particularly important option we have not explicitly addressed is the option to expand. If we truly find a positive NPV project, then there is an obvious consideration: Can we expand the project or repeat it to get an even larger NPV? Our static analysis implicitly assumes that the scale of the project is fixed.

For example, if the sales demand for a particular product were to greatly exceed expectations, we might investigate increasing production. If this were not feasible for some reason, then we could always increase cash flow by raising the price. Either way, the potential cash flow is higher than we have indicated because we have implicitly assumed that no expansion or price increase is possible. Overall, because we ignore the option to expand in our analysis, we *underestimate* NPV (all other things being equal).

The Option to Abandon   At the other extreme, the option to scale back or even abandon a project is also quite valuable. For example, if a project does not even cover its own expenses, we might be better off if we abandoned it. Our DCF analysis implicitly assumes that we would keep operating even in this case.

In reality, if sales demand were significantly below expectations, we might be able to sell off some capacity or put it to another use. Maybe the product or service could be redesigned or otherwise improved. Regardless of the specifics, we once again *underestimate* NPV if we assume that the project must last for some fixed number of years, no matter what happens in the future.

The Option to Wait   Implicitly, we have treated proposed investments as if they were "go or no-go" decisions. Actually, there is a third possibility. The project can be postponed, perhaps in hope of more favorable conditions. We call this the option to wait.

For example, suppose an investment costs $120 and has a perpetual cash flow of $10 per year. If the discount rate is 10 percent, then the NPV is $10/.10 − $120 = −$20, so the project should not be undertaken now. However, this does not mean that we should forget about the project forever because in the next period, the appropriate discount rate could be different. If it fell to, say, 5 percent, then the NPV would be $10/.05 − $120 = $80, and we would take the project.

More generally, as long as there is some possible future scenario under which a project has a positive NPV, then the option to wait is valuable.

To illustrate some of these ideas, consider the case of Euro Disney (known today as Disneyland Paris). The deal to open Euro Disney occurred in 1987, and the park opened its doors outside of Paris in 1992. Disney's management thought Europeans would go goofy over the new park, but trouble soon began. The number of visitors never met expectations, in part because the company priced tickets too high. Disney also decided not to serve alcohol in a country that was accustomed to wine with meals. French labor inspectors fought Disney's strict dress codes, and so on.

After several years of operations, the park began serving wine in its restaurants, lowered ticket prices, and made other adjustments. In other words, management exercised its option to reformulate the product. The park began to make a small profit. Then, the company exercised the option to expand by adding a "second gate," which was another theme park next to Euro Disney named Walt Disney Studios. The second gate was intended to encourage visitors to extend their stays. But the new park flopped. The reasons ranged from high ticket prices, attractions geared toward Hollywood rather than European filmmaking, labor strikes in Paris, and a summer heat wave.

By the summer of 2003, Euro Disney was close to bankruptcy again. Executives discussed a variety of options. These options ranged from letting the company go broke (the option to abandon) to pulling the Disney name from the park. In 2005, the company finally agreed to a restructuring with the help of the French government.

After all the changes made at Euro Disney, the park gained momentum for several years, almost breaking even in 2008. In 2017, the resort posted revenues of $6.5 billion and a net income of $1.8 billion. And then, in 2018, Walt Disney announced plans to invest €2 billion in Disneyland Paris.

Disney hopes to leverage the lessons learned in its other theme parks around the world. For example, in 2014, Hong Kong Disneyland had a total of 7.5 million visitors for the year, resulting in a record revenue of $5.5 billion and a record net income of $332 million. And in April 2011, the groundbreaking occurred on a new $4.4 billion theme park in Shanghai that opened in the spring of 2016.

The whole idea of managerial options was summed up aptly by Jay Rasulo, the overseer of Disney's theme parks, when he said: "One thing we know for sure is that you never get it 100 percent right the first time. We open every one of our parks with the notion that we're going to add content."

Strategic Options   Companies sometimes undertake new projects just to explore possibilities and evaluate potential future business strategies. This is a little like testing the water by sticking a toe in before diving. Such projects are difficult to analyze using conventional DCF methods because most of the benefits come in the form of **strategic options**, that is, options for future, related business moves. Projects that create such options may be very valuable, but that value is difficult to measure. Research and development, for example, is an important and valuable activity for many firms precisely because it creates options for new products and procedures.

To give another example, a large manufacturer might decide to open a retail outlet as a pilot study. The primary goal is to gain some market insight. Because of the high start-up costs, this one operation won't break even. However, based on the sales experience from the pilot, we can then evaluate whether or not to open more outlets, change the product mix, enter new markets, and so on. The information gained and the resulting options for actions are all valuable, but coming up with a reliable dollar figure is probably not feasible.

> **strategic options**
> Options for future, related business products or strategies.

Conclusion   We have seen that incorporating options into capital budgeting analysis is not easy. What can we do about them in practice? The answer is that we can only keep them in the back of our minds as we work with the projected cash flows. We will tend to underestimate NPV by ignoring options. The damage might be small for a highly structured, very specific proposal, but it might be great for an exploratory one.

Capital Rationing

Capital rationing is said to exist when we have profitable (positive NPV) investments available but we can't get the needed funds to undertake them. For example, as division managers for a large corporation, we might identify $5 million in excellent projects but find that, for whatever reason, we can spend only $2 million. Now what? Unfortunately, for reasons we will discuss, there may be no truly satisfactory answer.

> **capital rationing**
> The situation that exists if a firm has positive net present value projects but cannot obtain the necessary financing.

Soft Rationing   The situation we have just described is **soft rationing**. This occurs when, for example, different units in a business are allocated some fixed amount of money each year for capital spending. Such an allocation is primarily a means of controlling and keeping track of overall spending. The important thing about soft rationing is that the corporation as a whole isn't short of capital; more can be raised on ordinary terms if management so desires.

> **soft rationing**
> The situation that occurs when units in a business are allocated a certain amount of financing for capital budgeting.

If we face soft rationing, the first thing to do is try and get a larger allocation. Failing that, one common suggestion is to generate as large a net present value as possible within the existing budget. This amounts to choosing those projects with the largest benefit-cost ratio (profitability index).

Strictly speaking, this is the correct thing to do only if the soft rationing is a one-time event; that is, it won't exist next year. If the soft rationing is a chronic problem, then something is amiss. The reason goes all the way back to Chapter 1. Ongoing soft rationing means we are constantly bypassing positive NPV investments. This contradicts our goal of the firm. If we are not trying to maximize value, then the question of which projects to take becomes ambiguous because we no longer have an objective goal in the first place.

hard rationing
The situation that occurs when a business cannot raise financing for a project under any circumstances.

Hard Rationing   With **hard rationing**, a business cannot raise capital for a project under any circumstances. For large, healthy corporations, this situation probably does not occur very often. This is fortunate because with hard rationing, our DCF analysis breaks down, and the best course of action is ambiguous.

The reason DCF analysis breaks down has to do with the required return. Suppose we say that our required return is 20 percent. Implicitly, we are saying that we will take a project with a return that exceeds this. However, if we face hard rationing, then we are not going to take a new project no matter what the return on that project is, so the whole concept of a required return is ambiguous. About the only interpretation we can give this situation is that the required return is so large that no project has a positive NPV in the first place.

Hard rationing can occur when a company experiences financial distress, meaning that bankruptcy is a possibility. Also, a firm may not be able to raise capital without violating a pre-existing contractual agreement. We discuss these situations in greater detail in a later chapter.

CONCEPT QUESTIONS

9.7a   Why do we say that our standard discounted cash flow analysis is static?

9.7b   What are managerial options in capital budgeting? Give some examples.

9.7c   What is capital rationing? What types are there? What problems does capital rationing create for discounted cash flow analysis?

SUMMARY AND CONCLUSIONS

This chapter has described how to go about putting together a discounted cash flow analysis and evaluating the results. In it, we covered:

1. The identification of relevant project cash flows. We discussed project cash flows and described how to handle some issues that often come up, including sunk costs, opportunity costs, financing costs, net working capital, and erosion.

2. Preparing and using pro forma, or projected, financial statements. We showed how pro forma financial statement information is useful in coming up with projected cash flows.

3. The use of scenario and sensitivity analysis. These tools are widely used to evaluate the impact of assumptions made about future cash flows and NPV estimates.

4. Additional issues in capital budgeting. We examined the managerial options implicit in many capital budgeting situations. We also discussed the capital rationing problem.

The discounted cash flow analysis we've covered here is a standard tool in the business world. It is a very powerful tool, so care should be taken in its use. The most important thing is to get the cash flows identified in a way that makes economic sense. This chapter gives you a good start on learning to do this.

≡connect POP QUIZ!

Can you answer the following questions? If your class is using *Connect*, log on to SmartBook to see if you know the answers to these and other questions, check out the study tools, and find out what topics require additional practice!

Section 9.1 What is the first step in estimating cash flow?

Section 9.2 What are sunk costs?

Section 9.3 What investment criteria can be applied to estimated cash flows?

Section 9.4 If a firm's current assets are $150,000, its total assets are $320,000, and its current liabilities are $80,000, what is its net working capital?

Section 9.5 A project has a positive NPV. What could drive this result?

Section 9.6 If a firm's variable cost per unit estimate used in its base case analysis is $50 per unit and it anticipates the upper and lower bounds to be ±10 percent, what is the "worst case" for variable cost per unit?

Section 9.7 Capital rationing exists when a company has identified positive NPV projects but can't or won't find what?

CHAPTER REVIEW AND SELF-TEST PROBLEMS

9.1 Calculating Operating Cash Flow   Mater Pasta, Inc., has projected a sales volume of $1,432 for the second year of a proposed expansion project. Costs normally run 70 percent of sales, or about $1,002 in this case. The depreciation expense will be $80, and the tax rate is 22 percent. What is the operating cash flow? (See Problem 9.)

9.2 Scenario Analysis   A project under consideration costs $500,000, has a five-year life, and has no salvage value. Depreciation is straight-line to zero. The required return is 15 percent, and the tax rate is 21 percent. Sales are projected at 400 units per year. Price per unit is $3,000, variable cost per unit is $1,900, and fixed costs are $250,000 per year. No net working capital is required.

Suppose you think the unit sales, price, variable cost, and fixed cost projections are accurate to within 5 percent. What are the upper and lower bounds for these projections? What is the base-case NPV? What are the best- and worst-case scenario NPVs? (See Problem 21.)

■ Answers to Chapter Review and Self-Test Problems

9.1   First, we can calculate the project's EBIT, its tax bill, and its net income.

$$\text{EBIT} = \$1,432 - 1,002 - 80 = \$350$$
$$\text{Taxes} = \$350 \times .22 = \$77$$
$$\text{Net income} = \$350 - 77 = \$273$$

With these numbers, operating cash flow is:

$$\text{OCF} = \text{EBIT} + \text{Depreciation} - \text{Taxes}$$
$$= \$350 + 80 - 77$$
$$= \$353$$

9.2   We can summarize the relevant information as follows:

	Base Case	Lower Bound	Upper Bound
Unit sales	400	380	420
Price per unit	$3,000	$2,850	$3,150
Variable cost per unit	$1,900	$1,805	$1,995
Fixed costs	$250,000	$237,500	$262,500

The depreciation is $100,000 per year, and the tax rate is 21 percent, so we can calculate the cash flows under each scenario. Remember that we assign high costs and low prices and volume under the worst case and the opposite for the best case.

Scenario	Unit Sales	Price	Variable Costs	Fixed Costs	Cash Flow
Base case	400	$3,000	$1,900	$250,000	$171,100
Best case	420	3,150	1,805	237,500	279,646
Worst case	380	2,850	1,995	262,500	70,296

At 15 percent, the five-year annuity factor is 3.35216, so the NPVs are:

$$\text{Base-case NPV} = -\$500,000 + 171,100 \times 3.35216 = \$73,554$$
$$\text{Best-case NPV} = -\$500,000 + 279,646 \times 3.35216 = \$437,417$$
$$\text{Worst-case NPV} = -\$500,000 + 70,296 \times 3.35216 = -\$264,357$$

CRITICAL THINKING AND CONCEPTS REVIEW

LO 1   **9.1**   **Opportunity Cost**   In the context of capital budgeting, what is an opportunity cost?

LO 1   **9.2**   **Depreciation**   Given the choice, would a firm prefer to use MACRS depreciation or straight-line depreciation? Why?

LO 1   **9.3**   **Net Working Capital**   In our capital budgeting examples, we assumed that a firm would recover all of the working capital it invested in a project. Is this a reasonable assumption? When might it not be valid?

LO 1   **9.4**   **Stand-Alone Principle**   Suppose a financial manager is quoted as saying, "Our firm uses the stand-alone principle. Because we treat projects like minifirms in our evaluation process, we include financing costs because they are relevant at the firm level." Critically evaluate this statement.

LO 1   **9.5   Cash Flow and Depreciation**   "When evaluating projects, we're only concerned with the relevant incremental aftertax cash flows. Therefore, because depreciation is a noncash expense, we should ignore its effects when evaluating projects." Critically evaluate this statement.

LO 1   **9.6   Capital Budgeting Considerations**   A major college textbook publisher has an existing finance textbook. The publisher is debating whether or not to produce an "essentialized" version, meaning a shorter (and lower-priced) book. What are some of the considerations that should come into play?

To answer the next three questions, refer to the following example. In 2003, Porsche unveiled its new sports-utility vehicle (SUV), the Cayenne. With a price tag of more than $40,000, the Cayenne went from zero to 62 mph in 9.7 seconds. Porsche's decision to enter the SUV market was in response to the runaway success of other high-priced SUVs such as the Mercedes-Benz M-class. Vehicles in this class had generated years of very high profits. The Cayenne certainly spiced up the market, and Porsche subsequently introduced the Cayenne Turbo S, which goes from zero to 60 mph in 4.8 seconds and has a top speed of 168 mph. The price tag for the Cayenne Turbo S? The price started at $124,600 in 2018.

Some analysts questioned Porsche's entry into the luxury SUV market. The analysts were concerned not only that Porsche was a late entry into the market, but also that the introduction of the Cayenne would damage Porsche's reputation as a maker of high-performance automobiles.

LO 1   **9.7   Erosion**   In evaluating the Cayenne, would you consider the possible damage to Porsche's reputation?

LO 1   **9.8   Capital Budgeting**   Porsche was one of the last manufacturers to enter the sports-utility vehicle market. Why would one company decide to proceed with a product when other companies, at least initially, decide not to enter the market?

LO 1   **9.9   Capital Budgeting**   In evaluating the Cayenne, what do you think Porsche needs to assume regarding the substantial profit margins that exist in this market? Is it likely they will be maintained as the market becomes more competitive, or will Porsche be able to maintain the profit margin because of its image and the performance of the Cayenne?

LO 2   **9.10   Sensitivity Analysis and Scenario Analysis**   What is the essential difference between sensitivity analysis and scenario analysis?

LO 1   **9.11   Marginal Cash Flows**   A co-worker claims that looking at all this marginal this and incremental that is a bunch of nonsense and states: "Listen, if our average revenue doesn't exceed our average cost, then we will have a negative cash flow, and we will go broke!" How do you respond?

LO 1   **9.12   Capital Rationing**   Going all the way back to Chapter 1, recall that we saw that partnerships and proprietorships can face difficulties when it comes to raising capital. In the context of this chapter, the implication is that small businesses will generally face what problem?

LO 2   **9.13   Forecasting Risk**   What is forecasting risk? In general, would the degree of forecasting risk be greater for a new product or a cost-cutting proposal? Why?

LO 2   **9.14   Options and NPV**   What is the option to abandon? The option to expand? Explain why we tend to underestimate NPV when we ignore these options.

QUESTIONS AND PROBLEMS

connect Select problems are available in McGraw-Hill *Connect*. Please see the packaging options section of the Preface for more information.

BASIC (Questions 1–22)

LO 1
1. **Relevant Cash Flows** Kenny, Inc., is looking at setting up a new manufacturing plant in South Park. The company bought some land six years ago for $5.3 million in anticipation of using it as a warehouse and distribution site, but the company has since decided to rent facilities elsewhere. The land would net $7.7 million if it were sold today. The company now wants to build its new manufacturing plant on this land; the plant will cost $29.3 million to build, and the site requires $1.41 million worth of grading before it is suitable for construction. What is the proper cash flow amount to use as the initial investment in fixed assets when evaluating this project? Why?

LO 1
2. **Relevant Cash Flows** Winnebagel Corp. currently sells 28,000 motor homes per year at $84,000 each and 7,000 luxury motor coaches per year at $135,000 each. The company wants to introduce a new portable camper to fill out its product line; it hopes to sell 29,000 of these campers per year at $24,700 each. An independent consultant has determined that if the company introduces the new campers, it could boost the sales of its existing motor homes by 2,500 units per year and reduce the sales of its motor coaches by 750 units per year. What is the amount to use as the annual sales figure when evaluating this project? Why?

LO 2
3. **Calculating Projected Net Income** A proposed new investment has projected sales of $635,000. Variable costs are 40 percent of sales, and fixed costs are $168,000; depreciation is $83,000. Prepare a pro forma income statement assuming a tax rate of 23 percent. What is the projected net income?

LO 2
4. **Calculating OCF** Consider the following income statement:

Sales	$537,200
Costs	346,800
Depreciation	94,500
EBIT	?
Taxes (21%)	?
Net income	?

Fill in the missing numbers and then calculate the OCF. What is the depreciation tax shield?

LO 2
5. **Calculating Depreciation** A piece of newly purchased industrial equipment costs $745,000 and is classified as seven-year property under MACRS. Calculate the annual depreciation allowances and end-of-the-year book values for this equipment.

LO 2
6. **Calculating Salvage Value** Consider an asset that costs $635,000 and is depreciated straight-line to zero over its eight-year tax life. The asset is to be used in a five-year project; at the end of the project, the asset can be sold for $105,000. If the relevant tax rate is 22 percent, what is the aftertax cash flow from the sale of this asset?

LO 2 7. **Calculating Salvage Value**   An asset used in a four-year project falls in the five-year MACRS class for tax purposes. The asset has an acquisition cost of $6.8 million and will be sold for $1.46 million at the end of the project. If the tax rate is 23 percent, what is the aftertax salvage value of the asset?

LO 2 8. **Calculating Project OCF**   Cusic Music Company is considering the sale of a new sound board used in recording studios. The new board would sell for $26,400, and the company expects to sell 1,500 per year. The company currently sells 1,850 units of its existing model per year. If the new model is introduced, sales of the existing model will fall to 1,520 units per year. The old board retails for $24,900. Variable costs are 55 percent of sales, depreciation on the equipment to produce the new board will be $1.875 million per year, and fixed costs are $2.9 million per year. If the tax rate is 22 percent, what is the annual OCF for the project?

LO 2 9. **Calculating Project OCF**   H. Cochran, Inc., is considering a new three-year expansion project that requires an initial fixed asset investment of $2.15 million. The fixed asset will be depreciated straight-line to zero over its three-year tax life, after which time it will be worthless. The project is estimated to generate $2.23 million in annual sales, with costs of $1.25 million. If the tax rate is 23 percent, what is the OCF for this project?

LO 2 10. **Calculating Project NPV**   In the previous problem, suppose the required return on the project is 14 percent. What is the project's NPV?

LO 2 11. **Calculating Project Cash Flow from Assets**   In the previous problem, suppose the project requires an initial investment in net working capital of $150,000, and the fixed asset will have a market value of $185,000 at the end of the project. What is the project's Year 0 net cash flow? Year 1? Year 2? Year 3? What is the new NPV?

LO 2 12. **NPV and Modified ACRS**   In the previous problem, suppose the fixed asset actually falls into the three-year MACRS class. All the other facts are the same. What is the project's Year 1 net cash flow now? Year 2? Year 3? What is the new NPV?

LO 2 13. **NPV and Bonus Depreciation**   In the previous problem, suppose the fixed asset actually qualifies for 100 percent bonus depreciation. All the other facts are the same. What is the project's Year 1 net cash flow now? Year 2? Year 3? What is the new NPV?

LO 2 14. **Project Evaluation**   Kolby's Korndogs is looking at a new sausage system with an installed cost of $655,000. This cost will be depreciated straight-line to zero over the project's five-year life, at the end of which the sausage system can be scrapped for $85,000. The sausage system will save the firm $183,000 per year in pretax operating costs, and the system requires an initial investment in net working capital of $35,000. If the tax rate is 22 percent and the discount rate is 8 percent, what is the NPV of this project?

LO 2 15. **NPV and Bonus Depreciation**   In the previous problem, suppose the fixed asset actually qualifies for 100 percent bonus depreciation. All the other facts are the same. What is the new NPV?

LO 2 16. **Project Evaluation**   Your firm is contemplating the purchase of a new $395,000 computer-based order entry system. The system will be depreciated straight-line to zero over its five-year life. It will be worth $30,000 at the end of that time. You will save $125,000 before taxes per year in order processing costs, and you will be able to reduce working capital by $35,000 at the beginning of the project. Working capital will revert back to normal at the end of the project. If the tax rate is 21 percent, what is the IRR for this project?

LO 2   **17. Project Evaluation**   In the previous problem, suppose your required return on the project is 10 percent and your pretax cost savings are $135,000 per year. Will you accept the project? What if the pretax cost savings are only $95,000 per year?

LO 3   **18. Scenario Analysis**   Automatic Transmissions, Inc., has the following estimates for its new gear assembly project: price = $940 per unit; variable cost = $340 per unit; fixed costs = $3.4 million; quantity = 53,000 units. Suppose the company believes all of its estimates are accurate only to within ±15 percent. What values should the company use for the four variables given here when it performs its best-case scenario analysis? What about the worst-case scenario?

LO 3   **19. Sensitivity Analysis**   For the company in the previous problem, suppose management is most concerned about the impact of its price estimate on the project's profitability. How could you address this concern for Automatic Transmissions? Describe how you would calculate your answer. What values would you use for the other forecast variables?

LO 3   **20. Sensitivity Analysis**   We are evaluating a project that costs $1.68 million, has a six-year life, and has no salvage value. Assume that depreciation is straight-line to zero over the life of the project. Sales are projected at 90,000 units per year. Price per unit is $37.95, variable cost per unit is $23.20, and fixed costs are $815,000 per year. The tax rate is 21 percent, and we require a return of 11 percent on this project.

   a.   Calculate the base-case cash flow and NPV. What is the sensitivity of NPV to changes in the sales figure? Explain what your answer tells you about a 500-unit decrease in projected sales.

   b.   What is the sensitivity of OCF to changes in the variable cost figure? Explain what your answer tells you about a $1 decrease in estimated variable costs.

LO 3   **21. Scenario Analysis**   In the previous problem, suppose the projections given for price, quantity, variable costs, and fixed costs are all accurate to within ±10 percent. Calculate the best-case and worst-case NPV figures.

LO 2   **22. Calculating Project Cash Flows and NPV**   Pappy's Potato has come up with a new product, the Potato Pet (they are freeze-dried to last longer). Pappy's paid $120,000 for a marketing survey to determine the viability of the product. It is felt that Potato Pet will generate sales of $835,000 per year. The fixed costs associated with this will be $204,000 per year, and variable costs will amount to 20 percent of sales. The equipment necessary for production of the Potato Pet will cost $865,000 and will be depreciated in a straight-line manner for the four years of the product life (as with all fads, it is felt the sales will end quickly). This is the only initial cost for the production. Pappy's has a tax rate of 23 percent and a required return of 13 percent. Calculate the payback period, NPV, and IRR.

INTERMEDIATE (Questions 23–28)

LO 2   **23. Cost-Cutting Proposals**   CSM Machine Shop is considering a four-year project to improve its production efficiency. Buying a new machine press for $395,000 is estimated to result in $144,000 in annual pretax cost savings. The press falls in the MACRS five-year class, and it will have a salvage value at the end of the project of $45,000. The press also requires an initial investment in spare parts inventory of $15,000, along with an additional $2,000 in inventory for each succeeding year of the project. If the shop's tax rate is 22 percent and its discount rate is 11 percent, should the company buy and install the machine press?

LO 2 24. **NPV and Bonus Depreciation** In the previous problem, suppose the fixed asset actually qualifies for 100 percent bonus depreciation. All the other facts are the same. What is the new NPV?

LO 2 25. **NPV and Bonus Depreciation** Eggz, Inc., is considering the purchase of new equipment that will allow the company to collect loose hen feathers for sale. The equipment will cost $425,000 and will be eligible for 100 percent bonus depreciation. The equipment can be sold for $45,000 at the end of the project in five years. Sales would be $275,000 per year, with annual fixed costs of $47,000 and variable costs equal to 35 percent of sales. The project would require an investment of $25,000 in NWC that would be returned at the end of the project. The tax rate is 22 percent, and the required return is 9 percent. What is the project's NPV?

LO 2 26. **Sensitivity Analysis** Consider a three-year project with the following information: initial fixed asset investment = $665,000; straight-line depreciation to zero over the five-year life; zero salvage value; price = $39.20; variable costs = $29.85; fixed costs = $315,000; quantity sold = 85,000 units; tax rate = 23 percent. How sensitive is OCF to changes in quantity sold?

LO 2 27. **Project Analysis** You are considering a new product launch. The project will cost $780,000, have a four-year life, and have no salvage value; depreciation is straight-line to zero. Sales are projected at 170 units per year, price per unit will be $16,300, variable cost per unit will be $11,100, and fixed costs will be $535,000 per year. The required return on the project is 11 percent, and the relevant tax rate is 21 percent.

    a. Based on your experience, you think the unit sales, variable cost, and fixed cost projections given here are probably accurate to within ±10 percent. What are the best and worst cases for these projections? What is the base-case NPV? What are the best-case and worst-case scenarios?

    b. Evaluate the sensitivity of your base-case NPV to changes in fixed costs.

LO 2 28. **Project Analysis** McGilla Golf has decided to sell a new line of golf clubs. The clubs will sell for $925 per set and have a variable cost of $480 per set. The company has spent $150,000 for a marketing study that determined the company will sell 75,000 sets per year for seven years. The marketing study also determined that the company will lose sales of 8,800 sets per year of its high-priced clubs. The high-priced clubs sell at $1,325 and have variable costs of $640. The company also will increase sales of its cheap clubs by 11,000 sets per year. The cheap clubs sell for $385 and have variable costs of $160 per set. The fixed costs each year will be $14.65 million. The company also has spent $1 million on research and development for the new clubs. The plant and equipment required will cost $30.1 million and will be depreciated on a straight-line basis. The new clubs also will require an increase in net working capital of $3.5 million that will be returned at the end of the project. The tax rate is 23 percent, and the cost of capital is 14 percent. Calculate the payback period, the NPV, and the IRR.

CHALLENGE (Questions 29–30)

LO 2   **29. Project Evaluation**   Aria Acoustics, Inc. (AAI), projects unit sales for a new seven-octave voice emulation implant as follows:

Year	Unit Sales
1	71,500
2	87,800
3	104,300
4	89,200
5	75,300

Production of the implants will require $1.5 million in net working capital to start and additional net working capital investments each year equal to 15 percent of the projected sales increase for the following year. Total fixed costs are $2.15 million per year, variable production costs are $230 per unit, and the units are priced at $375 each. The equipment needed to begin production has an installed cost of $20.5 million. Because the implants are intended for professional singers, this equipment is considered industrial machinery and thus qualifies as seven-year MACRS property. In five years, this equipment can be sold for about 20 percent of its acquisition cost. AAI has a 21 percent tax rate and a required return on all its projects of 15 percent. Based on these preliminary project estimates, what is the NPV of the project? What is the IRR?

LO 2   **30. Calculating Required Savings**   A proposed cost-saving device has an installed cost of $565,000. The device will be used in a five-year project but is classified as three-year MACRS property for tax purposes. The required initial net working capital investment is $40,000, the tax rate is 23 percent, and the project discount rate is 12 percent. The device has an estimated Year 5 salvage value of $55,000. What level of pretax cost savings do we require for this project to be profitable?

EXCEL *MASTER IT!* PROBLEM

Excel
Master
coverage online

For this *Master It!* assignment, refer to the Conch Republic Electronics case at the end of Chapter 9. For your convenience, we have entered the relevant values in the case, such as the price and variable cost, already. For this project, answer the following questions.

a.   What is the profitability index of the project?

b.   What is the IRR of the project?

c.   What is the NPV of the project?

d.   How sensitive is the NPV to changes in the price of the new smartphone? Construct a one-way data table to help you.

e.   How sensitive is the NPV to changes in the quantity sold?

CHAPTER CASE
Conch Republic Electronics

Conch Republic Electronics is a midsized electronics manufacturer located in Key West, Florida. The company president is Shelly Couts, who inherited the company. The company originally repaired radios and other household appliances when it was founded more than 70 years ago. Over the years, the company has expanded, and it is now a reputable manufacturer of various specialty electronic items. Jay McCanless, a recent MBA graduate, has been hired by the company in its finance department.

One of the major revenue-producing items manufactured by Conch Republic is a smartphone. Conch Republic currently has one smartphone model on the market and sales have been excellent. The smartphone is a unique item in that it comes in a variety of tropical colors and is preprogrammed to play Jimmy Buffett music. However, as with any electronic item, technology changes rapidly, and the current smartphone has limited features in comparison with newer models. Conch Republic spent $1.2 million to develop a prototype for a new smartphone that has all the features of the existing one but adds new features such as Wifi tethering. The company has spent a further $250,000 for a marketing study to determine the expected sales figures for the new smartphone.

Conch Republic can manufacture the new smartphone for $210 each in variable costs. Fixed costs for the operation are estimated to run $5.3 million per year. The estimated sales volumes are 64,000, 106,000, 87,000, 78,000, and 54,000 per year for each of the next five years, respectively. The unit price of the new smartphone will be $515. The necessary equipment can be purchased for $38.5 million and will be depreciated on a seven-year MACRS schedule. It is believed the value of the equipment in five years will be $5.8 million.

Net working capital for the smartphones will be 20 percent of sales and will occur with the timing of the cash flows for the year (i.e., there is no initial outlay for NWC). Changes in NWC thus will occur first in Year 1 with the first year's sales. Conch Republic has a 22 percent corporate tax rate and a required return of 12 percent.

Shelly has asked Jay to prepare a report that answers the following questions:

QUESTIONS

1. What is the payback period of the project?
2. What is the profitability index of the project?
3. What is the IRR of the project?
4. What is the NPV of the project?
5. How sensitive is the NPV to changes in the price of the new smartphone?
6. How sensitive is the NPV to changes in the quantity sold?
7. Should Conch Republic produce the new smartphone?
8. Suppose Conch Republic loses sales on other models because of the introduction of the new model. How would this affect your analysis?

Some Lessons from Capital Market History | 10

LEARNING OBJECTIVES

After studying this chapter, you should be able to:

LO 1 Calculate the return on an investment.

LO 2 Discuss the historical returns on various important types of investments.

LO 3 Explain the historical risks on various important types of investments.

LO 4 Assess the implications of market efficiency.

With the S&P 500 Index returning about 19 percent and the NASDAQ Composite Index up about 28 percent in 2017, stock market performance overall was very good. In particular, investors in biopharmaceutical company Madrigal Pharmaceuticals, Inc., had to be happy about the 516 percent gain in that stock, and investors in genomic therapy company Sangamo Therapeutics had to feel pretty good following that company's 438 percent gain. Of course, not all stocks increased in value during the year. Stock in Sears Holdings fell 61 percent, and stock in Under Armour dropped 48 percent. These examples show that there were tremendous potential profits to be made during 2017, but there was also the risk of losing money—and lots of it. So what should you, as a stock market investor, expect when you invest your own money? In this chapter, we study more than eight decades of market history to find out.

This chapter and the next take us into new territory: the relation between risk and return. As you will see, this chapter has a lot of very practical information for anyone thinking of investing in financial assets such as stocks and bonds. For example, suppose you were to start investing in stocks today. Do you think your money would grow at an average rate of 5 percent per year? Or 10 percent? Or 20 percent? This chapter gives you an idea of what to expect (the answer may surprise you). The chapter also shows how risky certain investments can be, and it gives you the tools to think about risk in an objective way.

Please visit us at essentialsofcorporatefinance.blogspot.com for the latest developments in the world of corporate finance.

Thus far, we haven't had much to say about what determines the required return on an investment. In one sense, the answer is very simple: The required return depends on the risk of the investment. The greater the risk, the greater is the required return.

Having said this, we are left with a somewhat more difficult problem. How can we measure the amount of risk present in an investment? Put another way, what does it mean to say that one investment is riskier than another? Obviously, we need to define what we mean by risk if we are going to answer these questions. This is our task in the next two chapters.

From the last several chapters, we know that one of the responsibilities of the financial manager is to assess the value of proposed investments. In doing this, it is important that we first look at what financial investments have to offer. At a minimum, the return we require from a proposed nonfinancial investment must be at least as large as what we can get from buying financial assets of similar risk.

Our goal in this chapter is to provide a perspective on what capital market history can tell us about risk and return. The most important thing to get out of this chapter is a feel for the numbers. What is a high return? What is a low one? More generally, what returns should we expect from financial assets and what are the risks from such investments? This perspective is essential for understanding how to analyze and value risky investment projects.

We start our discussion of risk and return by describing the historical experience of investors in the U.S. financial markets. In 1931, for example, the stock market lost 43 percent of its value. Just two years later, the stock market gained 54 percent. In more recent memory, the market lost about 25 percent of its value on October 19, 1987, alone, and stocks lost almost 40 percent in 2008. What lessons, if any, can financial managers learn from such shifts in the stock market? We will explore the last half century (and then some) of market history to find out.

Not everyone agrees on the value of studying history. On the one hand, there is philosopher George Santayana's famous comment: "Those who cannot remember the past are condemned to repeat it." On the other hand, there is industrialist Henry Ford's equally famous comment: "History is more or less bunk." Nonetheless, perhaps everyone would agree with the following observation from Mark Twain: "October. This is one of the peculiarly dangerous months to speculate in stocks. The others are July, January, September, April, November, May, March, June, December, August, and February."

There are two central lessons that emerge from our study of market history. First: There is a reward for bearing risk. Second: The greater the potential reward, the greater is the risk. To understand these facts about market returns, we devote much of this chapter to reporting the statistics and numbers that make up the modern capital market history of the United States. In the next chapter, these facts provide the foundation for our study of how financial markets put a price on risk.

10.1 RETURNS

We wish to discuss historical returns on different types of financial assets. The first thing we need to do, then, is to briefly discuss how to calculate the return from investing.

Excel Master coverage online

Dollar Returns

If you buy an asset of any sort, your gain (or loss) from that investment is called your *return on investment*. This return will usually have two components. First: You may receive some cash directly while you own the investment. This is called the income component of

FIGURE 10.1

Dollar returns

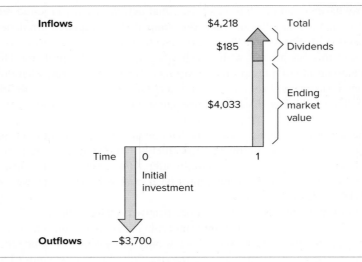

your return. Second: The value of the asset you purchase often will change. In this case, you have a capital gain or capital loss on your investment.[1]

To illustrate, suppose the Video Concept Company has several thousand shares of stock outstanding. You purchased some of these shares of stock in the company at the beginning of the year. It is now year-end, and you want to determine how well you have done on your investment.

First, over the year, a company may pay cash dividends to its shareholders. As a stockholder in Video Concept Company, you are a part owner of the company. If the company is profitable, it may choose to distribute some of its profits to shareholders (we discuss the details of dividend policy in a later chapter). So, as the owner of some stock, you will receive some cash. This cash is the income component from owning the stock.

In addition to the dividend, the other part of your return is the capital gain or capital loss on the stock. This part arises from changes in the value of your investment. For example, consider the cash flows illustrated in Figure 10.1. At the beginning of the year, the stock is selling for $37 per share. If you buy 100 shares, you have a total outlay of $3,700. Suppose, over the year, the stock pays a dividend of $1.85 per share. By the end of the year, then, you will have received income of:

Dividend = $1.85 × 100 = $185

Also, the value of the stock rises to $40.33 per share by the end of the year. Your 100 shares are worth $4,033, so you have a capital gain of:

Capital gain = ($40.33 − 37) × 100 = $333

On the other hand, if the price had dropped to, say, $34.78, you would have had a capital loss of:

Capital loss = ($34.78 − 37) × 100 = −$222

Notice that a capital loss is the same thing as a negative capital gain.

How did the market do today? Find out at finance.yahoo.com.

---

[1]As we mentioned in an earlier chapter, strictly speaking, what is and what is not a capital gain (or loss) is determined by the IRS. We thus use the terms loosely.

The total dollar return on your investment is the sum of the dividend and the capital gain:

Total dollar return = Dividend income + Capital gain (or loss)   [10.1]

In our first example, the total dollar return is thus given by:

Total dollar return = $185 + 333 = $518

Notice that, if you sold the stock at the end of the year, the total amount of cash you would have would be your initial investment plus the total return. In the preceding example, then:

Total cash if stock is sold = Initial investment + Total return   [10.2]
= $3,700 + 518
= $4,218

As a check, notice that this is the same as the proceeds from the sale of the stock plus the dividends:

Proceeds from stock sale + Dividends = $40.33 × 100 + 185
= $4,033 + 185
= $4,218

Suppose you hold on to your Video Concept stock and don't sell it at the end of the year. Should you still consider the capital gain as part of your return? Isn't this only a "paper" gain and not really a return if you don't sell the stock?

The answer to the first question is a strong yes, and the answer to the second is an equally strong no. The capital gain is every bit as much a part of your return as the dividend, and you should certainly count it as part of your return. That you actually decided to keep the stock and not sell (you don't "realize" the gain) is irrelevant because you could have converted it to cash if you had wanted to. Whether you choose to do so or not is up to you.

After all, if you insisted on converting your gain to cash, you could always sell the stock at year-end and immediately reinvest by buying the stock back. There is no net difference between doing this and not selling (assuming, of course, that there are no tax consequences from selling the stock). Again, the point is that whether you actually cash out and buy sodas (or whatever) or reinvest by not selling doesn't affect the return you earn.

Percentage Returns

It is usually more convenient to summarize information about returns in percentage terms, rather than dollar terms, because that way your return doesn't depend on how much you actually invest. The question we want to answer is this: How much do we get for each dollar we invest?

To answer this question, let P_t be the price of the stock at the beginning of the year and let D_{t+1} be the dividend paid on the stock during the year. Consider the cash flows in Figure 10.2. These are the same as those in Figure 10.1, except that we have now expressed everything on a per-share basis.

In our example, the price at the beginning of the year was $37 per share and the dividend paid during the year on each share was $1.85. As we discussed in Chapter 7, expressing the dividend as a percentage of the beginning stock price results in the dividend yield:

Dividend yield = D_{t+1}/P_t
= $1.85/$37 = .05, or 5%

This says that, for each dollar we invest, we get five cents in dividends.

FIGURE 10.2

Dollar returns per share

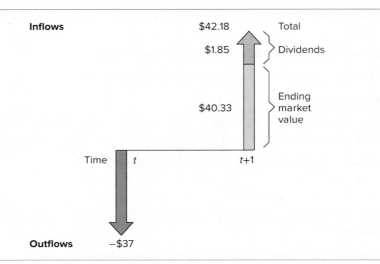

The second component of our percentage return is the capital gains yield. Recall (from Chapter 7) that this is calculated as the change in the price during the year (the capital gain) divided by the beginning price:

$$\text{Capital gains yield} = (P_{t+1} - P_t)/P_t$$
$$= (\$40.33 - 37)/\$37$$
$$= \$3.33/\$37$$
$$= .09, \text{ or } 9\%$$

So, per dollar invested, we get nine cents in capital gains.

Putting it together, per dollar invested, we get 5 cents in dividends and 9 cents in capital gains; so, we get a total of 14 cents. Our percentage return is 14 cents on the dollar, or 14 percent.

To check this, notice that we invested $3,700 and ended up with $4,218. By what percentage did our $3,700 increase? As we saw, we picked up $4,218 − 3,700 = $518. This is a $518/$3,700 = .14, or 14 percent increase.

To give a more concrete example, stock in Microsoft began 2017 at $62.14 per share. Microsoft paid dividends of $1.59 during 2017 and the stock price at the end of the year was $85.54. What was the return on Microsoft for the year? For practice, see if you agree that the answer is 40.22 percent. Of course, negative returns occur as well. For example, again in 2017, GameStop's stock price at the end of the year was $17.95 per share and dividends of $1.52 were paid. The stock began the year at $25.26 per share. Verify that the loss was 22.92 percent for the year.

EXAMPLE 10.1   Calculating Returns

Suppose you buy some stock for $25 per share. At the end of the year, the price is $35 per share. During the year, you get a $2 dividend per share. This is the situation illustrated in Figure 10.3. What is the dividend yield? The capital gains yield? The percentage return? If your total investment was $1,000, how much do you have at the end of the year?

Your $2 dividend per share works out to a dividend yield of:

$$\text{Dividend yield} = D_{t+1}/P_t$$
$$= \$2/\$25 = .08, \text{ or } 8\%$$

The per-share capital gain is $10, so the capital gains yield is:

$$\text{Capital gains yield} = (P_{t+1} - P_t)/P_t$$
$$= (\$35 - 25)/\$25$$
$$= \$10/\$25$$
$$= .40, \text{ or } 40\%$$

The total percentage return is thus 48 percent.

If you had invested $1,000, you would have had $1,480 at the end of the year, representing a 48 percent increase. To check this, note that your $1,000 would have bought you $1,000/$25 = 40 shares. Your 40 shares would then have paid you a total of 40 × $2 = $80 in cash dividends. Your $10 per share gain would have given you a total capital gain of $10 × 40 = $400. Add these together, and you get the $480 increase.

FIGURE 10.3

Cash flow: An investment example

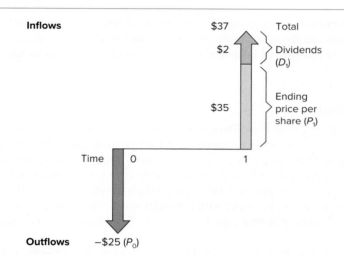

Inflows

$37 — Total

$2 — Dividends ($D_1$)

$35 — Ending price per share (P_1)

Time — 0 — 1

Outflows — −$25 ($P_0$)

CONCEPT QUESTIONS

10.1a What are the two parts of total return?

10.1b Why are unrealized capital gains or losses included in the calculation of returns?

10.1c What is the difference between a dollar return and a percentage return? Why are percentage returns more convenient?

10.2 THE HISTORICAL RECORD

Excel Master coverage online

Roger Ibbotson and Rex Sinquefield conducted a famous set of studies dealing with rates of return in U.S. financial markets.[2] They presented year-to-year historical rates of return on five important types of financial investments. The returns can be interpreted as what you would have earned if you had held portfolios of the following:

1. *Large-company stocks.* The large-company stock portfolio is based on the Standard & Poor's 500 index, which contains 500 of the largest companies (in terms of total market value of outstanding stock) in the United States.

---

[2]R. G. Ibbotson and R. A. Sinquefield, *Stocks, Bonds, Bills, and Inflation* [SBBI] (Charlottesville, VA: Financial Analysis Research Foundation, 1982).

2. *Small-company stocks.* This is a stock portfolio composed of smaller companies, where "small" corresponds to the smallest 20 percent of the companies listed on the New York Stock Exchange, again as measured by market value of outstanding stock.

3. *Long-term corporate bonds.* This is a portfolio of high-quality bonds with 20 years to maturity.

4. *Long-term U.S. government bonds.* This is a portfolio of U.S. government bonds with 20 years to maturity.

5. *U.S. Treasury bills.* This is based on Treasury bills (T-bills for short) with a one-month maturity.

For more on market history, visit www.globalfinancialdata .com, where you can download free sample data.

These returns are not adjusted for inflation or taxes; thus, they are nominal, pretax returns.

In addition to the year-to-year returns on these financial instruments, the year-to-year percentage change in the consumer price index (CPI) also is computed. This is a commonly used measure of inflation, so we can calculate real returns using this as the inflation rate.

A First Look

Go to www.bigcharts.com to see both intraday and long-term charts.

Before looking closely at the different portfolio returns, we take a look at the big picture. Figure 10.4 shows what happened to $1 invested in these different portfolios at the beginning of 1926. The growth in value for each of the different portfolios over the 92-year period ending in 2017 is given separately (the long-term corporate bonds are omitted). Notice that to get everything on a single graph, some modification in scaling is used. As is commonly done with financial series, the vertical axis is scaled such that equal distances measure equal percentage (as opposed to dollar) changes in values.

Looking at Figure 10.4, we see that the small-company, or "small-cap" (short for small-capitalization), investment did the best overall. Every dollar invested grew to a remarkable $36,931.00 over the 92 years. The larger common stock portfolio did less well; a dollar invested in it grew to $7,346.15.

At the other end, the T-bill portfolio grew to only $20.78. This is even less impressive when we consider the inflation over this period. As illustrated, the increase in the price level was such that $13.78 is needed just to replace the original $1.

Given the historical record, why would anybody buy anything other than small-cap stocks? If you look closely at Figure 10.4, you will probably see the answer. The T-bill portfolio and the long-term government bond portfolio grew more slowly than did the stock portfolios, but they also grew much more steadily. The small stocks ended up on top, but, as you can see, they grew quite erratically at times. For example, small stocks were the worst performers for about the first 10 years and had a smaller return than long-term government bonds for almost 15 years.

A Closer Look

To illustrate the variability of the different investments, Figures 10.5 through 10.8 plot the year-to-year percentage returns in the form of vertical bars drawn from the horizontal axis. The height of the bar tells us the return for the particular year. Looking at the long-term government bonds (Figure 10.7), we see that the largest historical return (40.35 percent) occurred in 1982. This was a good year for bonds. In comparing these charts, notice the differences in the vertical axis scales. With these differences in mind,

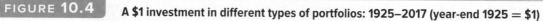

FIGURE 10.4   **A $1 investment in different types of portfolios: 1925–2017 (year-end 1925 = $1)**

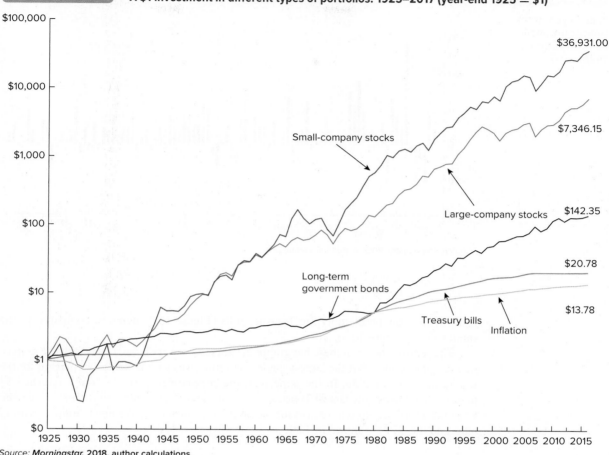

Source: *Morningstar,* **2018**, author calculations.

FIGURE 10.5

Year-to-year total returns on large-company stocks: 1926–2017

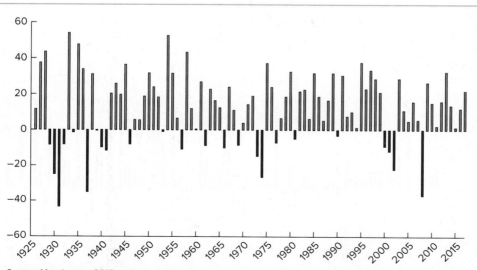

Source: *Morningstar,* **2018**, author calculations.

FIGURE 10.6

Year-to-year total returns on small-company stocks: 1926–2017

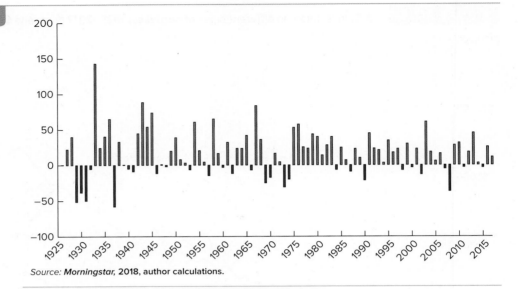

Source: *Morningstar,* 2018, author calculations.

you can see how predictably the Treasury bills (Figure 10.7) behaved compared to the small stocks (Figure 10.6).

The returns shown in these bar graphs are sometimes very large. Looking at the graphs, we see, for example, that the largest single-year return was a remarkable 143 percent for the small-cap stocks in 1933. In the same year, the large-company stocks "only" returned 53 percent. In contrast, the largest Treasury bill return was 15 percent in 1981. For future reference, the actual year-to-year returns for the S&P 500, long-term government bonds, Treasury bills, and the CPI are shown in Table 10.1.

FIGURE 10.7

Year-to-year total returns on bonds and bills: 1926–2017

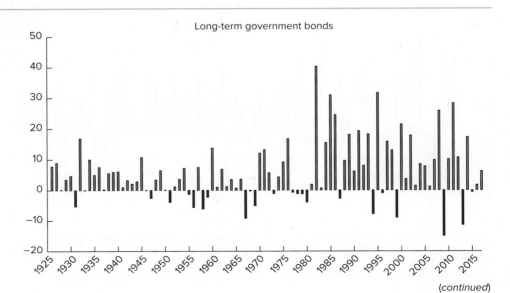

Long-term government bonds

(continued)

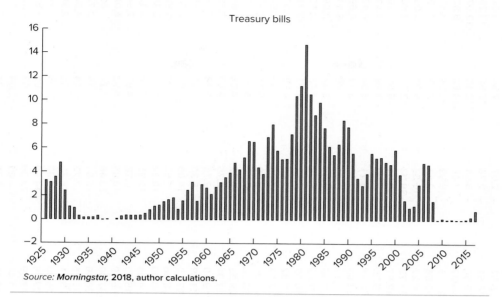

Treasury bills

Source: *Morningstar,* 2018, author calculations.

FIGURE 10.8

Year-to-year inflation: 1926–2017

Source: *Morningstar,* 2018, author calculations.

CONCEPT QUESTIONS

10.2a With 20-20 hindsight, what was the best investment for the period 1926–1935?

10.2b Why doesn't everyone buy only small stocks as investments?

10.2c What was the smallest return observed over the 92 years for each of these investments? Approximately when did it occur?

10.2d About how many times did large stocks (common stocks) return more than 30 percent? How many times did they return less than −20 percent?

10.2e What was the longest "winning streak" (years without a negative return) for large stocks? For long-term government bonds?

10.2f How often did the T-bill portfolio have a negative return?

TABLE 10.1 Year-to-year total returns: 1926–2017

Year	Large-Company Stocks	Long-Term Government Bonds	U.S. Treasury Bills	Consumer Price Index
1926	11.14%	7.90%	3.30%	−1.12%
1927	37.13	10.36	3.15	−2.26
1928	43.31	−1.37	4.05	−1.16
1929	−8.91	5.23	4.47	.58
1930	−25.26	5.80	2.27	−6.40
1931	−43.86	−8.04	1.15	−9.32
1932	−8.85	14.11	.88	−10.27
1933	52.88	.31	.52	.76
1934	−2.34	12.98	.27	1.52
1935	47.22	5.88	.17	2.99
1936	32.80	8.22	.17	1.45
1937	−35.26	.13	.27	2.86
1938	33.20	6.26	.06	−2.78
1939	.91	5.71	.04	.00
1940	−10.08	10.34	.04	.71
1941	−11.77	−8.66	.14	9.93
1942	21.07	2.67	.34	9.03
1943	25.76	2.50	.38	2.96
1944	19.69	2.88	.38	2.30
1945	36.46	5.17	.38	2.25
1946	−8.18	4.07	.38	18.13
1947	5.24	−1.15	.62	8.84
1948	5.10	2.10	1.06	2.99
1949	18.06	7.02	1.12	−2.07
1950	30.58	−1.44	1.22	5.93
1951	24.55	−3.53	1.56	6.00
1952	18.50	1.82	1.75	.75
1953	−1.10	.88	1.87	.75
1954	52.40	7.89	.93	−.74
1955	31.43	−1.03	1.80	.37
1956	6.63	−3.14	2.66	2.99
1957	−10.85	5.25	3.28	2.90
1958	43.34	−6.70	1.71	1.76
1959	11.90	−1.35	3.48	1.73
1960	.48	7.74	2.81	1.36
1961	26.81	3.02	2.40	.67
1962	−8.78	4.63	2.82	1.33
1963	22.69	1.37	3.23	1.64
1964	16.36	4.43	3.62	.97
1965	12.36	1.40	4.06	1.92
1966	−10.10	1.61	4.94	3.46
1967	23.94	−6.38	4.39	3.04
1968	11.00	5.33	5.49	4.72
1969	−8.47	−7.45	6.90	6.20
1970	3.94	12.24	6.50	5.57
1971	14.30	12.67	4.36	3.27

Year	Large-Company Stocks	Long-Term Government Bonds	U.S. Treasury Bills	Consumer Price Index
1972	18.99	9.15	4.23	3.41
1973	−14.69	−12.66	7.29	8.71
1974	−26.47	3.28	7.99	12.34
1975	37.23	4.67	5.87	6.94
1976	23.93	18.34	5.07	4.86
1977	−7.16	2.31	5.45	6.70
1978	6.57	−2.07	7.64	9.02
1979	18.61	−2.76	10.56	13.29
1980	32.50	−5.91	12.10	12.52
1981	−4.92	−.16	14.60	8.92
1982	21.55	49.99	10.94	3.83
1983	22.56	−2.11	8.99	3.79
1984	6.27	16.53	9.90	3.95
1985	31.73	39.03	7.71	3.80
1986	18.67	32.51	6.09	1.10
1987	5.25	−8.09	5.88	4.43
1988	16.61	8.71	6.94	4.42
1989	31.69	22.15	8.44	4.65
1990	−3.10	5.44	7.69	6.11
1991	30.46	20.04	5.43	3.06
1992	7.62	8.09	3.48	2.90
1993	10.08	22.32	3.03	2.75
1994	1.32	−11.46	4.39	2.67
1995	37.58	37.28	5.61	2.54
1996	22.96	−2.59	5.14	3.32
1997	33.36	17.70	5.19	1.70
1998	28.58	19.22	4.86	1.61
1999	21.04	−12.76	4.80	2.68
2000	−9.10	22.16	5.98	3.39
2001	−11.89	5.30	3.33	1.55
2002	−22.10	14.08	1.61	2.38
2003	28.68	1.62	1.03	1.88
2004	10.88	10.34	1.43	3.26
2005	4.91	10.35	3.30	3.42
2006	15.79	.28	4.97	2.54
2007	5.49	10.85	4.52	4.08
2008	−37.00	39.46	1.24	.09
2009	26.46	−25.61	.15	2.72
2010	15.06	7.73	.14	1.50
2011	2.11	35.75	.06	2.96
2012	16.00	1.80	.08	1.74
2013	32.39	−14.69	.05	1.50
2014	13.69	22.60	.03	.76
2015	1.41	−.64	.04	.74
2016	11.98	1.76	.21	2.11
2017	19.57	5.78	.75	1.58

Source: Author calculations based on data from *Global Financial Data* and other sources.

10.3 AVERAGE RETURNS: THE FIRST LESSON

As you've probably begun to notice, the history of capital market returns is too complicated to be of much use in its undigested form. We need to begin summarizing all these numbers. Accordingly, we discuss how to go about condensing the detailed data. We start out by calculating average returns.

Calculating Average Returns

The obvious way to calculate the average returns on the different investments in Table 10.1 is to add up the yearly returns and divide by 92. The result is the historical average of the individual values.

If you add up the returns for the large-company common stocks for the 92 years, you will get about 11.09. The average annual return is thus 11.09/92 = .121, or 12.1%. You interpret this 12.1 percent like any other average. If you picked a year at random from the 92-year history and you had to guess the return in that year, the best guess would be 12.1 percent.

Average Returns: The Historical Record

Table 10.2 shows the average returns for the investments we have discussed. As shown, in a typical year, the small stocks increased in value by 16.5 percent. Notice also how much larger the stock returns are than the bond returns.

These averages are, of course, nominal since we haven't worried about inflation. Notice that the average inflation rate was 3.0 percent per year over this 92-year span. The nominal return on U.S. Treasury bills was 3.4 percent per year. The average real return on Treasury bills was thus approximately .4 percent per year; so, the real return on T-bills has been quite low historically.

At the other extreme, small stocks had an average real return of about 16.5% − 3.0% = 13.5%, which is relatively large. If you remember the Rule of 72 (Chapter 4), then you recall that a quick back-of-the-envelope calculation tells us that 13.5 percent real growth doubles your buying power about every five years. Notice also that the real value of the large stock portfolio increased by 9.1 percent in a typical year.

Risk Premiums

Now that we have computed some average returns, it seems logical to see how they compare with each other. Based on our previous discussion, one such comparison involves government-issued securities. These are free of much of the variability we see in, for example, the stock market.

The government borrows money by issuing bonds. These bonds come in different forms. The ones we will focus on are Treasury bills. These have the shortest time to

Investment	Average Return
Large stocks	12.1%
Small stocks	16.5
Long-term corporate bonds	6.4
Long-term government bonds	6.0
U.S. Treasury bills	3.4
Inflation	3.0

TABLE 10.2

Average annual returns: 1926–2017

Source: Morningstar, 2018, author calculations.

TABLE 10.3	Investment	Average Return	Risk Premium
Average annual returns and risk premiums: 1926–2017	Large stocks	12.1%	8.7%
	Small stocks	16.5	13.1
	Long-term corporate bonds	6.4	3.0
	Long-term government bonds	6.0	2.6
	U.S. Treasury bills	3.4	—

Source: *Morningstar*, 2018, author calculations.

maturity of the different government bonds. Because the government always can raise taxes to pay its bills, this debt is virtually free of any default risk over its short life. Thus, we will call the rate of return on such debt the *risk-free return*, and we will use it as a kind of benchmark.

A particularly interesting comparison involves the virtually risk-free return on T-bills and the very risky return on common stocks. The difference between these two returns can be interpreted as a measure of the *excess return* on the average risky asset (assuming the stock of a large U.S. corporation has about average risk compared to all risky assets).

We call this the "excess" return because it is the additional return we earn by moving from a relatively risk-free investment to a risky one. Because it can be interpreted as a reward for bearing risk, we will call it a **risk premium**.

risk premium

The excess return required from an investment in a risky asset over that required from a risk-free investment.

From Table 10.2, we can calculate the risk premiums for the different investments. We report only the nominal risk premium in Table 10.3 because there is only a slight difference between the historical nominal and real risk premiums.

The risk premium on T-bills is shown as zero in the table because we have assumed that they are riskless.

The First Lesson

Looking at Table 10.3, we see that the average risk premium earned by a typical large common stock is $12.1\% - 3.4\% = 8.7\%$. This is a significant reward. The fact that it exists historically is an important observation, and it is the basis for our first lesson: Risky assets, on average, earn a risk premium. Put another way: There is a reward for bearing risk.

Why is this so? Why, for example, is the risk premium for small stocks so much larger than the risk premium for large stocks? More generally, what determines the relative sizes of the risk premiums for the different assets? The answers to these questions are at the heart of modern finance, and the next chapter is devoted to them. For now, part of the answer can be found by looking at the historical variability of the returns of these different investments. So, to get started, we now turn our attention to measuring variability in returns.

CONCEPT QUESTIONS

10.3a What do we mean by excess return and risk premium?

10.3b What was the real (as opposed to nominal) risk premium on the common stock portfolio?

10.3c What was the nominal risk premium on corporate bonds? The real risk premium?

10.3d What is the first lesson from capital market history?

10.4 THE VARIABILITY OF RETURNS: THE SECOND LESSON

We already have seen that the year-to-year returns on common stocks tend to be more volatile than the returns on, say, long-term government bonds. We now discuss measuring this variability so we can begin examining the subject of risk.

Excel Master
coverage online

Frequency Distributions and Variability

To get started, we can draw a *frequency distribution* for the common stock returns like the one in Figure 10.9. What we have done here is to count up the number of times the annual return on the large stock portfolio falls within each 10 percent range. For example, in Figure 10.9, the height of 15 in the range 20 percent to 30 percent means that 15 of the 92 annual returns were in that range. Notice also that the returns are very concentrated between −10 and 40 percent.

What we need to do now is to actually measure the spread in returns. We know, for example, that the return on small stocks in a typical year was 16.5 percent. We now want to know how far the actual return deviates from this average in a typical year. In other words, we need a measure of how volatile the return is. The **variance** and its square root, the **standard deviation**, are the most commonly used measures of volatility. We describe how to calculate them next.

variance
The average squared difference between the actual return and the average return.

standard deviation
The positive square root of the variance.

The Historical Variance and Standard Deviation

The variance essentially measures the average squared difference between the actual returns and the average return. The bigger this number is, the more the actual returns tend to differ from the average return. Also, the larger the variance or standard deviation is, the more spread out the returns will be.


```
                                        2016
                                        2014
                                        2012
                                        2010
                              2015 2006 2017
                              2011 2004 2009 2013
                    2000 2007 1988 2003 1997
                    1990 2005 1986 1999 1995
                    1981 1994 1979 1998 1991
                    1977 1993 1972 1996 1989
                    1969 1992 1971 1983 1985
                    1962 1987 1968 1982 1980
                    1953 1984 1965 1976 1975
                    1946 1978 1964 1967 1955
               2001 1940 1970 1959 1963 1950
               1973 1939 1960 1952 1961 1945
          2002 1966 1934 1956 1949 1951 1938 1958
     2008 1974 1957 1932 1948 1944 1943 1936 1935 1954
1931 1937 1930 1941 1929 1947 1926 1942 1927 1928 1933
−80 −70 −60 −50 −40 −30 −20 −10  0  10  20  30  40  50  60  70  80  90
                         Percent
```

FIGURE 10.9

Frequency distribution of returns on common stocks: 1926–2017

Source: Morningstar, 2018, author calculations.

For an easy-to-read review of basic stats, check out www .robertniles.com/stats.

The way we will calculate the variance and standard deviation depends on the specific situation. In this chapter, we are looking at historical returns; so, the procedure we describe here is the correct one for calculating the *historical* variance and standard deviation. If we were examining projected future returns, then the procedure would be different. We describe this procedure in the next chapter.

To illustrate how we calculate the historical variance, suppose a particular investment had returns of 10 percent, 12 percent, 3 percent, and −9 percent over the last four years. The average return is $(.10 + .12 + .03 − .09)/4 = .04$, or 4%. Notice that the return is never actually equal to 4 percent. Instead, the first return deviates from the average by $.10 − .04 = .06$, the second return deviates from the average by $.12 − .04 = .08$, and so on. To compute the variance, we square each of these deviations, add up the squares, and divide the result by the number of returns less 1, or 3 in this case. This information is summarized in the following table:

Year	(1) Actual Return	(2) Average Return	(3) Deviation (1) − (2)	(4) Squared Deviation
1	.10	.04	.06	.0036
2	.12	.04	.08	.0064
3	.03	.04	−.01	.0001
4	−.09	.04	−.13	.0169
Totals	.16		.00	.0270

In the first column, we write down the four actual returns. In the third column, we calculate the difference between the actual returns and the average by subtracting out 4 percent. Finally, in the fourth column, we square the numbers in Column 3 to get the squared deviations from the average.

The variance can now be calculated by dividing .0270, the sum of the squared deviations, by the number of returns less 1. Let Var(R), or σ^2 (read this as "sigma squared"), stand for the variance of the return:

$$\text{Var}(R) = \sigma^2 = .027/(4 − 1) = .009$$

The standard deviation is the square root of the variance. So, if SD(R), or σ, stands for the standard deviation of the return:

$$\text{SD}(R) = \sigma = \sqrt{.009} = .09487, \text{ or } 9.487\%$$

The square root of the variance is used because the variance is measured in "squared" percentages and thus is hard to interpret. The standard deviation is an ordinary percentage, so the answer here could be written as 9.487 percent.

In the preceding table, notice that the sum of the deviations is equal to zero. This will always be the case, and it provides a good way to check your work. In general, if we have T historical returns, where T is some number, we can write the historical variance as:

$$\text{Var}(R) = \frac{1}{T−1}[(R_1 − \bar{R})^2 + \cdots + (R_T − \bar{R})^2] \qquad [10.3]$$

This formula tells us to do what we did above: Take each of the T individual returns $(R_1, R_2, \ldots)$ and subtract the average return, $\bar{R}$; square the results, and add up all these squares; and, finally, divide this total by the number of returns less 1 ($= T − 1$). The standard deviation is always the square root of Var(R). Standard deviations are a widely used measure of volatility. Our nearby *Work the Web* box gives a real-world example.

W🌐RK THE WEB

Standard deviations are widely reported for mutual funds. For example, the Fidelity Magellan Fund is a large mutual fund. How volatile is it? To find out, we went to www.morningstar.com, entered the ticker symbol FMAGX, and hit the "Ratings & Risk" link. Here is what we found:

MPT Statistics FMAGX

3-Year	5-Year	10-Year	15-Year

3-Year Trailing	Index	R-Squared	Beta	Alpha	Treynor Ratio	Currency
vs. Best-Fit Index						
FMAGX	Morningstar US Large Cap TR USD	94.89	1.08	-0.48	—	USD
vs. Standard Index						
FMAGX	S&P 500 TR USD	93.96	1.08	-0.25	9.98	USD
Category: LG	S&P 500 TR USD	82.63	1.03	0.22	10.34	USD

05/31/2018

Volatility Measures FMAGX

3-Year	5-Year	10-Year	15-Year

3-Year Trailing	Standard Deviation	Return	Sharpe Ratio	Sortino Ratio	Bear Market Percentile Rank
FMAGX	11.54	11.52	0.95	1.62	—
S&P 500 TR USD	—	—	—	—	—
Category: LG	11.86	11.47	0.92	1.65	—

05/31/2018

Source: www.morningstar.com

The standard deviation for the Fidelity Magellan Fund is 11.54 percent. When you consider the average stock has a standard deviation of about 50 percent, this seems like a low number. The reason for the low standard deviation has to do with the power of diversification, a topic we discuss in the next chapter. The return is the average return, so over the last three years, investors in the Magellan Fund gained 11.52 percent per year. Also under the Volatility Measures section, you will see the Sharpe ratio. The Sharpe ratio is calculated as the risk premium of the asset divided by the standard deviation. As such, it is a measure of return to the level of risk taken (as measured by standard deviation). The "beta" for the Fidelity Magellan Fund is 1.08. We will have more to say about this number—lots more—in the next chapter.

QUESTIONS

1. Go to the Morningstar website at www.morningstar.com. What does the Bear Market Percentile Rank measure?
2. Get a quote for the Fidelity Magellan fund at Morningstar. What are the five sectors that have the highest percentage investment for this fund? What are the five stocks with the highest percentage investment?

EXAMPLE 10.2	Calculating the Variance and Standard Deviation

Suppose the Supertech Company and the Hyperdrive Company have experienced the following returns in the last four years:

Year	Supertech Returns	Hyperdrive Returns
2016	−.20	.05
2017	.50	.09
2018	.30	−.12
2019	.10	.20

What are the average returns? The variances? The standard deviations? Which investment was more volatile?

To calculate the average returns, we add up the returns and divide by 4. The results are:

Supertech average return $= \overline{R} = .70/4 = .175$, or 17.5%
Hyperdrive average return $= \overline{R} = .22/4 = .055$, or 5.5%

To calculate the variance for Supertech, we can summarize the relevant calculations as follows:

Year	(1) Actual Return	(2) Average Return	(3) Deviation (1) − (2)	(4) Squared Deviation
2016	−.20	.175	−.375	.140625
2017	.50	.175	.325	.105625
2018	.30	.175	.125	.015625
2019	.10	.175	−.075	.005625
Totals	.70		.000	.267500

Because there are four years of returns, we calculate the variance by dividing .2675 by $(4 − 1) = 3$:

	Supertech	Hyperdrive
Variance (σ^2)	$.2675/3 = .0892$	$.0529/3 = .0176$
Standard deviation (σ)	$\sqrt{.0892} = .2986$	$\sqrt{.0176} = .1328$

For practice, verify that you get the same answer as we do for Hyperdrive. Notice that the standard deviation for Supertech, 29.86 percent, is a little more than twice Hyperdrive's 13.28 percent; Supertech was thus the more volatile investment.

The Historical Record

Figure 10.10 summarizes much of our discussion of capital market history so far. It displays average returns, standard deviations, and frequency distributions of annual returns on a common scale. In Figure 10.10, notice, for example, that the standard deviation for the small-stock portfolio (31.7 percent per year) is about 10 times larger than the T-bill portfolio's standard deviation (3.1 percent per year). We will return to these figures momentarily.

FIGURE 10.10	Historical average returns, standard deviations, and frequency distributions: 1926–2017

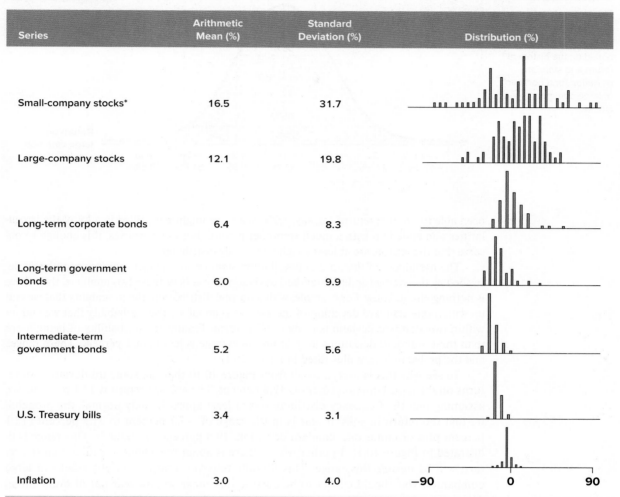

Series	Arithmetic Mean (%)	Standard Deviation (%)	Distribution (%)
Small-company stocks*	16.5	31.7	
Large-company stocks	12.1	19.8	
Long-term corporate bonds	6.4	8.3	
Long-term government bonds	6.0	9.9	
Intermediate-term government bonds	5.2	5.6	
U.S. Treasury bills	3.4	3.1	
Inflation	3.0	4.0	−90 0 90

*The 1933 small-company stocks total return was 142.9 percent.

Source: Morningstar, 2018, author calculations.

Normal Distribution

For many different random events in nature, a particular frequency distribution, the **normal distribution** (or *bell curve*), is useful for describing the probability of ending up in a given range. For example, the idea behind "grading on a curve" comes from the fact that exam scores often resemble a bell curve.

Figure 10.11 illustrates a normal distribution and its distinctive bell shape. As you can see, this distribution has a much cleaner appearance than the actual return distributions illustrated in Figure 10.10. Even so, like the normal distribution, the actual distributions do appear to be at least roughly mound-shaped and symmetric. When this is true, the normal distribution is often a very good approximation.

Also, keep in mind that the distributions in Figure 10.10 are based on only 92 yearly observations, while Figure 10.11 is, in principle, based on an infinite number. So, if we had

normal distribution
A symmetric, bell-shaped frequency distribution that is completely defined by its average and standard deviation.

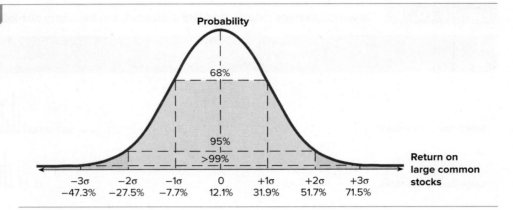

FIGURE **10.11**

The normal distribution

Illustrated returns are based on the historical return and standard deviation for a portfolio of large common stocks.

been able to observe returns for, say, 1,000 years, we might have filled in a lot of the irregularities and ended up with a much smoother picture. For our purposes, it is enough to observe that the returns are at least roughly normally distributed.

The usefulness of the normal distribution stems from the fact that it is completely described by the average and the standard deviation. If you have these two numbers, then there is nothing else to know. For example, with a normal distribution, the probability that we end up within one standard deviation of the average is about ⅔. The probability that we end up within two standard deviations is about 95 percent. Finally, the probability of being more than three standard deviations away from the average is less than 1 percent. These ranges and the probabilities are illustrated in Figure 10.11.

To see why this is useful, recall from Figure 10.10 that the standard deviation of returns on the large common stocks is 19.8 percent. The average return is 12.1 percent. So, assuming that the frequency distribution is at least approximately normal, the probability that the return in a given year is in the range of −7.7 percent to 31.9 percent (12.1 percent plus or minus one standard deviation, 19.8 percent) is about ⅔. This range is illustrated in Figure 10.11. In other words, there is about one chance in three that the return will be *outside* this range. This literally tells you that, if you buy stocks in large companies, you should expect to be outside this range in one year out of every three. This reinforces our earlier observations about stock market volatility. However, there is only a 5 percent chance (approximately) that we would end up outside the range of −27.5 percent to 51.7 percent (12.1 percent plus or minus 2 × 19.8%). These points also are illustrated in Figure 10.11.

The Second Lesson

Our observations concerning the year-to-year variability in returns are the basis for our second lesson from capital market history. On average, bearing risk is handsomely rewarded, but, in a given year, there is a significant chance of a dramatic change in value. Thus, our second lesson is this: The greater the potential reward, the greater is the risk.

Thus far in this chapter, we have emphasized the year-to-year variability in returns. We should note that even day-to-day movements can exhibit considerable volatility. For example, on September 17, 2001, the Dow Jones Industrial Average (DJIA) plummeted 684.81 points, or 7.13 percent. By historical standards, it was one of the worst days ever for the 30 stocks that comprise the DJIA (as well as for a majority of stocks in the market). Still, while the drop was the largest decrease in the DJIA ever in terms of points at the time, it actually wasn't quite in the top 12 largest one-day percentage decreases in history, as illustrated in the following table:

Top 12 One-Day Percentage Changes in the Dow Jones Industrial Average		
1	October 19, 1987	−22.61
2	October 28, 1929	−12.82
3	October 29, 1929	−11.73
4	November 6, 1929	− 9.92
5	December 18, 1899	− 8.72
6	August 12, 1932	− 8.40
7	March 14, 1907	− 8.29
8	October 26, 1987	− 8.04
9	October 15, 2008	− 7.87
10	July 21, 1933	− 7.84
11	October 18, 1937	− 7.75
12	December 1, 2008	− 7.70

Source: http://online.wsj.com/mdc/public/page/2_3047
-djia_alltime.html.

This discussion also highlights the importance of looking at returns in terms of percentages rather than dollar amounts or index points. For example, the biggest one-day loss in terms of points was on September 29, 2008, when the DJIA declined by 778 points. The second worst was the 733-point drop of October 15, 2008. In contrast, the 5.57-point drop in the DJIA on December 18, 1899, marked the fifth worst day in the history of the index, but a 5.6-point loss in the DJIA in today's market would hardly be noticed. This is precisely why we relied on percentage returns when we examined market history in this chapter.[3]

2008: The Bear Growled and Investors Howled

To reinforce our point concerning stock market volatility, consider that a few short years ago, 2008 entered the record books as one of the worst years for stock market investors in U.S. history. How bad was it? As shown in several exhibits in the chapter (e.g., Table 10.1), the widely followed S&P 500 index plunged 37 percent. Of the 500 stocks in the index, 485 were down for the year.

Over the period 1926–2017, only the year 1931 had a lower return than 2008 (−44 percent versus −37 percent). Making matters worse, the downdraft continued with a further decline of 8.43 percent in January 2009. In all, from November 2007 (when the decline began) through March 2009 (when it ended), the S&P 500 lost 50 percent of its value.

Figure 10.12 shows the month-by-month performance of the S&P 500 during 2008. As indicated, returns were negative in 8 of the 12 months. Most of the damage occurred in the fall, with investors losing almost 17 percent in October alone. Small stocks fared no better. They also fell 37 percent for the year (with a 21 percent drop in October), their worst performance since losing 58 percent in 1937.

As Figure 10.12 suggests, stock prices were highly volatile during the year. Oddly, the S&P had 126 up days and 126 down days (remember the markets are closed weekends and

---

[3]By the way, as you may have noticed, what's kind of weird is that 6 of the 12 worst days in the history of the DJIA occurred in October, including the top 3. We have no clue as to why. Furthermore, looking back at the Mark Twain quote near the beginning of the chapter, how do you suppose he knew? Sounds like a case for *CSI: Wall Street.*

FIGURE **10.12**

S&P 500 monthly returns: 2008

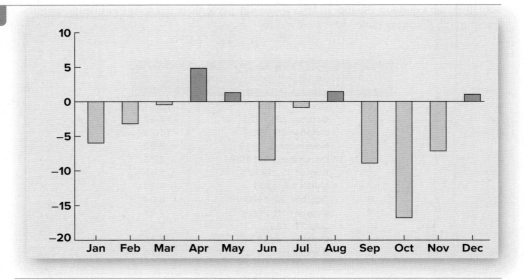

holidays). Of course, the down days were much worse on average. To see how extraordinary volatility was in 2008, consider that there were 18 days during which the value of the S&P changed by more than five percent. There were only 17 such moves between 1956 and 2007!

The drop in stock prices was a global phenomenon, and many of the world's major markets were off by much more than the S&P. China, India, and Russia, for example, all experienced declines of more than 50 percent. Tiny Iceland saw share prices drop by more than 90 percent for the year. Trading on the Icelandic exchange was temporarily suspended on October 9. In what has to be a modern record for a single day, stocks fell by 76 percent when trading resumed on October 14.

Were there any bright spots in 2008 for U.S. investors? The answer is yes because, as stocks tanked, bonds soared, particularly U.S. Treasury bonds. In fact, long-term Treasuries gained 40 percent, while shorter-term Treasury bonds were up 13 percent. Long-term corporate bonds did less well, but still managed to finish in positive territory, up 9 percent. These returns were especially impressive considering that the rate of inflation, as measured by the CPI, was essentially zero.

Of course, stock prices can be volatile in both directions. From March 2009 through February 2011, a period of about 700 days, the S&P 500 doubled in value. This climb was the fastest doubling since 1936 when the S&P did it in just 500 days. So, what lessons should investors take away from this very recent, and very turbulent, bit of capital market history? First, and most obviously, stocks have significant risk! But there is a second, equally important lesson. Depending on the mix, a diversified portfolio of stocks and bonds might have suffered in 2008, but the losses would have been much smaller than those experienced by an all-stock portfolio. In other words, diversification matters, a point we will examine in detail in our next chapter.

Using Capital Market History

Based on the discussion in this section, you should begin to have an idea of the risks and rewards from investing. For example, in the middle of 2018, Treasury bills were paying about 2.3 percent. Suppose we had an investment that we thought had about the same risk as a

The Super Guide to Investing

Every year, in late January or early February, about 90 million people in the United States watch television for a prediction of how well the stock market is going to do in the upcoming year. So you missed it this year? Maybe not. The stock market predictor we're talking about is the Super Bowl!

The Super Bowl indicator has become one of the more famous (or infamous) indicators of stock market performance. Here's how it works. In the 1960s, the original National Football League (NFL) and the upstart American Football League (AFL) were fighting for dominance. The Super Bowl indicator says that if a team from the original AFL wins the Super Bowl, the market posts a negative return for the year, and, if a team from the original NFL wins, the market will post a gain for the year.

So are you ready to bet the ranch on the Super Bowl indicator? Maybe that's not a super idea. Between 1997 and 2017, the Super Bowl indicator has only been right 10 out of 20 years. Of course, you could follow the second Super Bowl indicator. When there are 50 points or more scored in the game, the stock market had an average return of 18.6 percent. When 39 points or fewer are scored, the average market return is only 3.7 percent.

The Philadelphia Eagles won the Super Bowl in 2018. This was the Eagles' first Super Bowl victory and the team is an original NFL team. Was the Super Bowl predictor correct in 2018?

For those of you who like horse racing, there is the Triple Crown winner indicator. According to this indicator, if a horse wins the Kentucky Derby, Preakness, and Belmont Stakes, better known as the Triple Crown, the stock market will fall dramatically. However, when you consider that the youngest of these races, the Kentucky Derby, began in 1875 and to date there have only been 13 Triple Crown winners, what do you do in the 100+ years when there is no Triple Crown winner? Of course, Justify won the Triple Crown in 2018, a negative market indicator, but the Super Bowl indicator is positive. Which one should you follow?

So you want more predictors? How about the hemline indicator, also known as the "bull markets and bare knees" indicator? Through much of the nineteenth century, long skirts dominated women's fashion, and the stock market experienced many bear markets. In the 1920s, flappers revealed their knees and the stock market boomed. Even the stock market crash of October 1987 was predicted by hemlines. During the 1980s, miniskirts flourished, but by October 1987 a fashion shift had women wearing longer skirts.

These are only three examples of what are known as "technical" trading rules. There are lots of others. How seriously should you take them? That's up to you, but our advice is to keep in mind that life is full of odd coincidences. Just because a bizarre stock market predictor seems to have worked well in the past doesn't mean that it's going to work in the future.

portfolio of large-company common stocks. At a minimum, what return would this investment have to offer for us to be interested?

From Table 10.3, the risk premium on larger common stocks has been 8.7 percent historically, so a reasonable estimate of our required return would be this premium plus the T-bill rate, $8.7\% + 2.3\% = 11.0\%$. If we were thinking of starting a new business, then the risks of doing so might resemble those of investing in small-company stocks. In this case, the risk premium is 13.1 percent, so we might require more like 15.4 percent from such an investment, at a minimum.

We will discuss the relationship between risk and required return in more detail in the next chapter. For now, you should notice that a projected internal rate of return, or IRR, on a risky investment in the 10 percent to 20 percent range isn't particularly outstanding. It depends on how much risk there is. This, too, is an important lesson from capital market history.

The discussion in this section shows that there is much to be learned from capital market history. As the accompanying *Finance Matters* box describes, capital market history also provides some odd coincidences.

EXAMPLE 10.3   **Investing in Growth Stocks**

The term *growth stock* is frequently a euphemism for small-company stock. Are such investments suitable for "widows and orphans"? Before answering, you should consider the historical volatility. For example, from the historical record, what is the approximate probability that you will actually lose 15 percent or more of your money in a single year if you buy a portfolio of such companies?

Looking back at Figure 10.10, we see that the average return on small stocks is 16.5 percent, and the standard deviation is 31.7 percent. Assuming that the returns are approximately normal, there is about a ⅓ probability that you will experience a return outside the range of –15.2 percent to 48.2 percent (= 16.5% ± 31.7%).

Because the normal distribution is symmetric, the odds of being above or below this range are equal. There is thus a ⅙ chance (half of ⅓) that you will lose more than 15.2 percent. So, you should expect this to happen once in every six years, on average. Such investments thus can be very volatile, and they are not well suited for those who cannot afford the risk.

More on the Stock Market Risk Premium

As we have discussed, the historical stock market risk premium has been substantial. In fact, based on standard economic models, it has been argued that the historical risk premium is too big and is thus an overestimate of what is likely to happen in the future.

Of course, any time we use the past to predict the future, there is the danger that the past period we observe isn't representative of what the future will hold. For example, in this chapter, we studied the period 1926–2017. Perhaps investors got lucky over this period and earned particularly high returns. Data from earlier years are available, though they are not of the same quality. With that caveat in mind, researchers have traced returns back to 1802, and the risk premiums seen in the pre-1926 era are perhaps a little smaller, but not dramatically so.

Another possibility is that the U.S. stock market experience was unusually good. Investors in at least some other major countries did not do as well because their financial markets were nearly or completely wiped out because of revolution, war, and/or hyperinflation. A recent study addresses this issue by examining data from 1900–2010 for 17 countries.

Figure 10.13 shows the historical average stock market risk premium for all 17 countries over the 111-year period. Looking at the numbers, the U.S. risk premium is the 7th highest at 7.2 percent (which differs from our earlier estimate because of the differing time periods examined). The overall average risk premium is 6.9 percent. These numbers make it clear that U.S. investors did well, but not exceptionally so relative to investors in many other countries.

So, is the U.S. stock market risk premium estimated from 1926–2017 too high? The evidence seems to suggest that the answer is "maybe a little." One thing we haven't stressed so far is that even with 111 years of data, the average risk premium is still not measured with great precision. From a statistical standpoint, the standard error associated with the U.S. estimated risk premium of 7.2 percent is about 2 percent.[4] So, even one standard error range covers 5.2 to 9.2 percent.

---

[4]Recall from basic "sadistics" that the standard error of a sample mean is the sample standard deviation divided by the square root of the sample size. In our case, the standard deviation over the 1900–2010 period (not shown) was 19.8 percent, so the standard error is $.198/\sqrt{111} = .019$.

| FIGURE 10.13 | Stock market risk premiums for 17 countries: 1900–2010 |

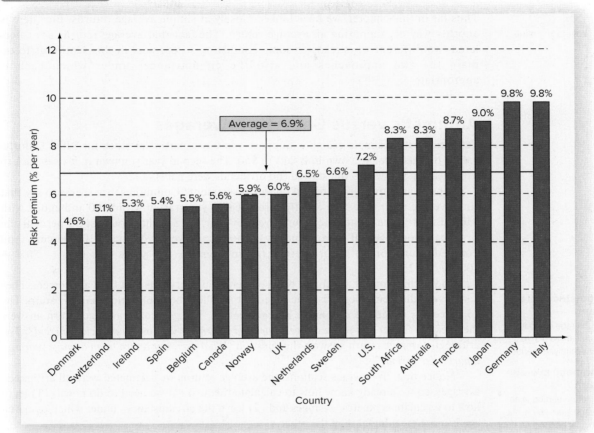

Source: Based on information in Dimson, Elroy, Marsh, Paul and Staunton, Michael, "The Worldwide Equity Premium: A Smaller Puzzle," in *Handbook of the Equity Risk Premium*, Mehra, Rajnish, ed., Elsevier: 2007. Updates by the authors.

CONCEPT QUESTIONS

10.4a In words, how do we calculate a variance? A standard deviation?

10.4b With a normal distribution, what is the probability of ending up more than one standard deviation below the average?

10.4c Assuming that long-term corporate bonds have an approximately normal distribution, what is the approximate probability of earning 14.6 percent or more in a given year? With T-bills, approximately what is this probability?

10.4d What is the second lesson from capital market history?

10.5 MORE ON AVERAGE RETURNS

Excel
Master
coverage online

Thus far in this chapter, we have looked closely at simple average returns. But there is another way of computing an average return. The fact that average returns are calculated two different ways leads to some confusion, so our goal in this section is to explain the two approaches and also the circumstances under which each is appropriate.

Arithmetic versus Geometric Averages

Let's start with a simple example. Suppose you buy a particular stock for $100. Unfortunately, the first year you own it, it falls to $50. The second year you own it, it rises back to $100, leaving you where you started (no dividends were paid).

What was your average return on this investment? Common sense seems to say that your average return must be exactly zero because you started with $100 and ended with $100. But if we calculate the returns year-by-year, we see that you lost 50 percent the first year (you lost half of your money). The second year, you made 100 percent (you doubled your money). Your average return over the two years was thus $(-50\% + 100\%)/2 = 25\%$!

geometric average return
The average compound return earned per year over a multiyear period.

So which is correct, 0 percent or 25 percent? The answer is that both are correct: They just answer different questions. The 0 percent is called the **geometric average return**. The 25 percent is called the **arithmetic average return**. The geometric average return answers the question *"What was your average compound return per year over a particular period?"* The arithmetic average return answers the question *"What was your return in an average year over a particular period?"*

arithmetic average return
The return earned in an average year over a particular period.

Notice that, in previous sections, the average returns we calculated were all arithmetic averages, so we already know how to calculate them. What we need to do now is (1) learn how to calculate geometric averages and (2) learn the circumstances under which one average is more meaningful than the other.

Calculating Geometric Average Returns

First, to illustrate how we calculate a geometric average return, suppose a particular investment had annual returns of 10 percent, 12 percent, 3 percent, and −9 percent over the last four years. The geometric average return over this four-year period is calculated as $(1.10 \times 1.12 \times 1.03 \times .91)^{1/4} - 1 = .0366$, or 3.66%. In contrast, the average arithmetic return we have been calculating is $(.10 + .12 + .03 - .09)/4 = .040$, or 4.0%.

In general, if we have T years of returns, the geometric average return over these T years is calculated using this formula:

$$\text{Geometric average return} = [(1 + R_1) \times (1 + R_2) \times \ldots \times (1 + R_T)]^{1/T} - 1 \qquad [10.4]$$

This formula tells us that four steps are required:

1. Take each of the T annual returns $R_1, R_2, \ldots, R_T$ and add a one to each (after converting them to decimals!).
2. Multiply all the numbers from Step 1 together.
3. Take the result from Step 2 and raise it to the power of $1/T$.
4. Finally, subtract one from the result of Step 3. The result is the geometric average return.

EXAMPLE 10.4   Calculating the Geometric Average Return

Calculate the geometric average return for the S&P 500 using the returns given below. To do so, convert percentages to decimal returns, add one, and then calculate their product:

S&P 500 Returns	Product
11.14%	1.1114
37.13	× 1.3713
43.31	× 1.4331
− 8.91	× .9109
−25.26	× .7474
	1.4870

Notice that the number 1.4870 is what our investment is worth after five years if we started with a $1 investment. The geometric average return is then calculated as:

Geometric average return = $1.4870^{1/5} - 1 = .0826$, or 8.26%

Thus the geometric average return is about 8.26 percent in this example. Here is a tip: If you are using a financial calculator, you can put $1 in as the present value, $1.4870 as the future value, and 5 as the number of periods. Then, solve for the unknown rate. You should get the same answer we did.

One thing you may have noticed in our examples thus far is that the geometric average returns seem to be smaller. It turns out that this will always be true (as long as the returns are not all identical, in which case the two "averages" would be the same). To illustrate, Table 10.4 shows the arithmetic averages and standard deviations from Figure 10.10, along with the geometric average returns.

As shown in Table 10.4, the geometric averages are all smaller, but the magnitude of the difference varies quite a bit. The reason is that the difference is greater for more volatile investments. In fact, there is a useful approximation. Assuming all the numbers are expressed in decimals (as opposed to percentages), the geometric average return is approximately equal to the arithmetic average return minus half the variance. For example, looking at the large-company stocks, the arithmetic average is .121 and the standard deviation is .198, implying that the variance is .0392. The approximate geometric average is thus $.121 - \frac{.0392}{2} = .101$, which, in this case, is close to the actual value.

TABLE 10.4

Geometric versus arithmetic average returns: 1926–2017

	Average Return		
Series	Geometric	Arithmetic	Standard Deviation
Large-company stocks	10.2%	12.1%	19.8%
Small-company stocks	12.1	16.5	31.7
Long-term corporate bonds	6.1	6.4	8.3
Long-term government bonds	5.5	6.0	9.9
Intermediate-term government bonds	5.1	5.2	5.6
U.S. Treasury bills	3.4	3.4	3.1
Inflation	2.9	3.0	4.0

> ### EXAMPLE 10.5   More Geometric Averages
>
> Take a look back at Figure 10.4. There, we showed the value of a $1 investment after 92 years. Use the value for the large-company stock investment to check the geometric average in Table 10.4.
>
> In Figure 10.4, the large-company investment grew to $7,346.15 over 92 years. The geometric average return is thus:
>
> Geometric average return $= 7{,}346.15^{1/92} - 1 = .102$, or 10.2%
>
> This 10.2% is the value shown in Table 10.4. For practice, check some of the other numbers in Table 10.4 the same way.

Arithmetic Average Return or Geometric Average Return?

When we look at historical returns, the difference between the geometric and arithmetic average returns isn't too hard to understand. To put it slightly differently, the geometric average tells you what you actually earned per year on average, compounded annually. The arithmetic average tells you what you earned in a typical year. You should use whichever one answers the question you want answered.

A somewhat trickier question concerns which average return to use when forecasting future wealth levels, and there's a lot of confusion on this point among analysts and financial planners. First, let's get one thing straight: If you *know* the true arithmetic average return, then this is what you should use in your forecast. So, for example, if you know the arithmetic return is 10 percent, then your best guess of the value of a $1,000 investment in 10 years is the future value of $1,000 at 10 percent for 10 years, or $2,593.74.

The problem we face, however, is that we usually only have *estimates* of the arithmetic and geometric returns, and estimates have errors. In this case, the arithmetic average return is probably too high for longer periods and the geometric average is probably too low for shorter periods. So, you should regard long-run projected wealth levels calculated using arithmetic averages as optimistic. Short-run projected wealth levels calculated using geometric averages are probably pessimistic.

As a practical matter, if you are using averages calculated over a long period of time (such as the 92 years we use) to forecast up to a decade or so into the future, then you should use the arithmetic average. If you are forecasting a few decades into the future (such as you might do for retirement planning), then you should split the difference between the arithmetic and geometric average returns. Finally, if for some reason you are doing very long forecasts covering many decades, use the geometric average.

This concludes our discussion of geometric versus arithmetic averages. One last note: In the future, when we say "average return," we mean arithmetic average unless we explicitly say otherwise.

CONCEPT QUESTIONS

10.5a   If you want to forecast what the stock market is going to do over the next year, should you use an arithmetic or geometric average?

10.5b   If you want to forecast what the stock market is going to do over the next century, should you use an arithmetic or geometric average?

10.6   CAPITAL MARKET EFFICIENCY

Capital market history suggests that the market values of stocks and bonds can fluctuate widely from year to year. Why does this occur? At least part of the answer is that prices change because new information arrives, and investors reassess asset values based on that information.

The behavior of market prices has been extensively studied. A question that has received particular attention is whether prices adjust quickly and correctly when new information arrives. A market is said to be *efficient* if this is the case. To be more precise, in an **efficient capital market**, current market prices fully reflect available information. By this we mean that, based on available information, there is no reason to believe that the current price is too low or too high.

The concept of market efficiency is a rich one, and much has been written about it. A full discussion of the subject goes beyond the scope of our study of business finance. However, because the concept figures so prominently in studies of market history, we briefly describe the key points here.

efficient capital market
Market in which security prices reflect available information.

Price Behavior in an Efficient Market

To illustrate how prices behave in an efficient market, suppose the F-Stop Camera Corporation (FCC), through years of secret research and development, has developed a camera whose autofocusing system will double the speed of those now available. FCC's capital budgeting analysis suggests that launching the new camera is a highly profitable move; in other words, the NPV appears to be positive and substantial. The key assumption thus far is that FCC has not released any information about the new system, so the fact of its existence is "inside" information only.

Now, consider a share of stock in FCC. In an efficient market, its price reflects what is known about FCC's current operations and profitability, and it reflects market opinion about FCC's potential for future growth and profits. The value of the new autofocusing system is not reflected, however, because the market is unaware of its existence.

If the market agrees with FCC's assessment of the value of the new project, FCC's stock price will rise when the decision to launch is made public. Assume the announcement is made in a press release on Wednesday morning. In an efficient market, the price of shares in FCC will adjust quickly to this new information. Investors should not be able to buy the stock on Wednesday afternoon and make a profit on Thursday. This would imply that it took the stock market a full day to realize the implication of the FCC press release. If the market is efficient, the price of shares of FCC stock on Wednesday afternoon already will reflect the information contained in the Wednesday morning press release.

Figure 10.14 presents three possible stock price adjustments for FCC. In the figure, Day 0 represents the announcement day. As illustrated, before the announcement, FCC's stock sells for $140 per share. The NPV per share of the new system is, say, $40, so the new price will be $180 once the value of the new project is fully reflected.

The solid line in Figure 10.14 represents the path taken by the stock price in an efficient market. In this case, the price adjusts immediately to the new information and no further changes in the price of the stock take place. The broken line in Figure 10.14 depicts a delayed reaction. Here, it takes the market eight days or so to fully absorb the information. Finally, the dotted line illustrates an overreaction and subsequent adjustment to the correct price.

The broken line and the dotted line in Figure 10.14 illustrate paths that the stock price might take in an inefficient market. If, for example, stock prices don't adjust immediately to new information (the broken line), then buying stock immediately following the release of new information and then selling it several days later would be a positive NPV activity because the price is too low for several days after the announcement.

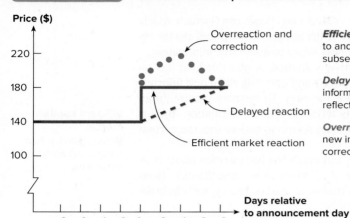

FIGURE 10.14   **Reaction of stock price to new information in efficient and inefficient markets**

Efficient market reaction: The price instantaneously adjusts to and fully reflects new information; there is no tendency for subsequent increases and decreases.

Delayed reaction: The price partially adjusts to the new information; eight days elapse before the price completely reflects the new information.

Overreaction and correction: The price overadjusts to the new information; it overshoots the new price and subsequently corrects.

The Efficient Markets Hypothesis

efficient markets hypothesis (EMH)
The hypothesis that actual capital markets, such as the New York Stock Exchange, are efficient.

The **efficient markets hypothesis (EMH)** asserts that well-organized capital markets, such as the NYSE, are efficient markets, at least as a practical matter. In other words, an advocate of the EMH might argue that while inefficiencies may exist, they are relatively small and uncommon.

If a market is efficient, then there is a very important implication for market participants: All investments in an efficient market are zero NPV investments. The reason is not complicated. If prices are neither too low nor too high, then the difference between the market value of an investment and its cost is zero; hence, the NPV is zero. As a result, in an efficient market, investors get exactly what they pay for when they buy securities, and firms receive exactly what their stocks and bonds are worth when they sell them.

What makes a market efficient is competition among investors. Many individuals spend their entire lives trying to find mispriced stocks. For any given stock, they study what has happened in the past to the stock's price and its dividends. They learn, to the extent possible, what a company's earnings have been, how much it owes to creditors, what taxes it pays, what businesses it is in, what new investments are planned, how sensitive it is to changes in the economy, and so on.

Not only is there a great deal to know about any particular company, there is a powerful incentive for knowing it, namely, the profit motive. If you know more about some company than other investors in the marketplace, you can profit from that knowledge by investing in the company's stock if you have good news and by selling it if you have bad news.

Look under the "contents" link at www.investorhome.com for more info on the EMH.

The logical consequence of all this information being gathered and analyzed is that mispriced stocks will become fewer and fewer. In other words, because of competition among investors, the market will become increasingly efficient. A kind of equilibrium comes into being where there is just enough mispricing around for those who are best at identifying it to make a living at it. For most other investors, the activity of information gathering and analysis will not pay.[5] Having said this, the accompanying *Finance Matters* box indicates how hard it is for *anybody* to "beat the market."

[5]The idea behind the EMH can be illustrated by the following short story: A student was walking down the hall with her finance professor when they both saw a $20 bill on the ground. As the student bent down to pick it up, the professor shook her head slowly and, with a look of disappointment on her face, said patiently to the student, "Don't bother. If it were really there, someone else would have picked it up already." The moral of the story reflects the logic of the efficient markets hypothesis: If you think you have found a pattern in stock prices or a simple device for picking winners, you probably have not.

Can the Pros Beat the Market?

2017 was a good year for investors in the Quantified STF mutual fund, which posted a gain of about 70 percent for the year, one of the highest returns for any mutual fund. In an industry where literally millions of dollars are at stake for mutual fund managers, it would seem that mutual funds should be able to consistently outperform the market. Unfortunately for investors, during 2017, only 43 percent of mutual funds outperformed their benchmarks for the year. The performance of mutual funds was even worse in 2016 as only 26 percent outperformed.

Other facts point to the difficulty that mutual funds have in beating the market. For example, over the past 50 years, the stock market had an average return of 13.5 percent, while the average mutual fund returned 11.8 percent. And during the past five years, only 11 percent of mutual fund managers had a performance each year that was in the top half of the funds in their respective category. This underperformance is not limited to mutual fund managers. The *Hulbert Financial Digest*, which tracks the performance of investment letters, reported that 80 percent of investment letters underperformed the stock market over the long term.

The year 2017 also saw the end of the "Buffett Challenge." In 2008, famed investor Warren Buffett made a $1 million bet with Ted Seides, founder of the Protégé hedge fund. A hedge fund is a limited partnership that pools investors' money, similar in this respect to a mutual fund. The wager, the proceeds of which went to the charity of the winner's choice, was that a portfolio of five hedge funds picked by Seides could not outperform the S&P 500. Seides conceded defeat in September 2017, about four months early. At that point, the S&P 500 had a cumulative return of about 85 percent over the previous nine plus years, while the five hedge funds had a cumulative return of about 22 percent.

One thing we know for sure is that past performance is no predictor of future returns. For example, in July 1994, the American Century Giftrust fund had been the best-performing mutual fund for the previous 10 years, with an average annual return above 20 percent. But the next 10 years weren't as kind to the investors in this fund. The average annual return for 1994 to 2004 was 2.87 percent, which was lower than U.S. Treasury bills during the same period. Following the old saying "What goes up, must come down," other funds have had similar stories. The Van Wagoner Emerging Growth Fund returned 291.2 percent in 1999, only to lose 59.7 percent and 64.6 percent the next two years. Similarly, the Oppenheimer Enterprise Fund gained 105.75 percent in 1999 but lost 40.6 percent in 2000, followed by two more years of double-digit losses.

Sometimes, we see proposed evidence showing that mutual fund managers collectively can beat the market. Consider 2005, when the S&P 500 gained about 3 percent. Diversified U.S. stock funds averaged 7 percent for the year, so it appears, at first glance, that mutual fund managers outperformed the market. However, in 2008, only 42 percent of all managers outperformed the market, with an average return about 1 percent lower than the market return. Over the years, the track record of the pros is relatively clear: More often than not, they underperform. In fact, based on historical averages, about 70 percent of all managers will underperform in a typical year.

The inability of the pros to consistently beat the market doesn't prove that markets are efficient. The evidence, however, does lend some credence to the semistrong form version of market efficiency. Plus, it adds to a growing body of evidence that tends to support a basic premise: While it may be possible to outperform the market for relatively short periods of time, it is very difficult to do so consistently over the long haul.

Some Common Misconceptions about the EMH

No idea in finance has attracted as much attention as that of efficient markets, and not all of the attention has been flattering. Rather than rehash the arguments here, we will be content to observe that some markets are more efficient than others. For example, financial markets on the whole are probably much more efficient than real asset markets.

Having said this, it is the case that much of the criticism of the EMH is misguided because it is based on a misunderstanding of what the hypothesis says and what it doesn't say. For example, when the notion of market efficiency was first publicized and debated in the popular financial press, it often was characterized by words to the effect that "throwing darts at the financial page will produce a portfolio that can be expected to do as well as any managed by professional security analysts."

Confusion over statements of this sort has often led to a failure to understand the implications of market efficiency. For example, sometimes it is wrongly argued that market efficiency means that it doesn't matter how you invest your money because the efficiency of the market will protect you from making a mistake. However, a random dart-thrower might wind up with all of the darts sticking into one or two high-risk stocks that deal in genetic engineering. Would you really want all of your money in two such stocks?

What efficiency does imply is that the price a firm will obtain when it sells a share of its stock is a "fair" price in the sense that it reflects the value of that stock given the information available about the firm. Shareholders do not have to worry that they are paying too much for a stock with a low dividend or some other sort of characteristic because the market already has incorporated that characteristic into the price. We sometimes say the information has been "priced in."

The concept of efficient markets can be explained further by replying to a frequent objection. It is sometimes argued that the market cannot be efficient because stock prices fluctuate from day to day. If the prices are right, the argument goes, then why do they change so much and so often? From our earlier discussion, we can see that these price movements are in no way inconsistent with efficiency. Investors are bombarded with information every day. The fact that prices fluctuate is, at least in part, a reflection of that information flow. In fact, the absence of price movements in a world that changes as rapidly as ours would suggest inefficiency.

The Forms of Market Efficiency

It is common to distinguish between three forms of market efficiency. Depending on the degree of efficiency, we say that markets are either *weak form efficient*, *semistrong form efficient*, or *strong form efficient*. The difference between these forms relates to what information is reflected in prices.

We start with the extreme case. If the market is strong form efficient, then *all* information of *every* kind is reflected in stock prices. In such a market, there is no such thing as inside information. Therefore, in our FCC example, we apparently were assuming that the market was not strong form efficient.

Casual observation, particularly in recent years, suggests that inside information does exist and it can be valuable to possess. Whether it is lawful or ethical to use that information is another issue. In any event, we conclude that private information about a particular stock may exist that is not currently reflected in the price of the stock. For example, prior knowledge of a takeover attempt could be very valuable.

The second form of efficiency, semistrong efficiency, is the most controversial. If a market is semistrong form efficient, then all *public* information is reflected in the stock price. The reason this form is controversial is that it implies that security analysts who try to identify mispriced stocks using, for example, financial statement information are wasting their time because that information is already reflected in the current price.

The third form of efficiency, weak form efficiency, suggests that, at a minimum, the current price of a stock reflects its own past prices. In other words, studying past prices in an attempt to identify mispriced securities is futile if the market is weak form efficient. While this form of efficiency might seem rather mild, it implies that searching for patterns in historical prices that are useful in identifying mispriced stocks will not work (this practice, known as "technical" analysis, is quite common).

What does capital market history say about market efficiency? Here again, there is great controversy. At the risk of going out on a limb, the evidence does seem to tell us three things. First: Prices do appear to respond very rapidly to new information, and the response is at least not grossly different from what we would expect in an efficient market. Second: The future of market prices, particularly in the short run, is very difficult to predict based on publicly available information. Third: If mispriced stocks do exist, then there is no obvious means of identifying them. Put another way: Simpleminded schemes based on public information will probably not be successful.

CONCEPT QUESTIONS

10.6a   What is an efficient market?

10.6b   What are the forms of market efficiency?

SUMMARY AND CONCLUSIONS

This chapter has explored the subject of capital market history. Such history is useful because it tells us what to expect in the way of returns from risky assets. We summed up our study of market history with two key lessons:

1. Risky assets, on average, earn a risk premium. There is a reward for bearing risk.
2. The greater the potential reward from a risky investment, the greater is the risk.

These lessons have significant implications for the financial manager. We will be considering these implications in the chapters ahead.

We also discussed the concept of market efficiency. In an efficient market, prices adjust quickly and correctly to new information. Consequently, asset prices in efficient markets are rarely too high or too low. How efficient capital markets (such as the NYSE) are is a matter of debate, but, at a minimum, they are probably much more efficient than most real asset markets.

■ connect POP QUIZ!

Can you answer the following questions? If your class is using *Connect*, log on to SmartBook to see if you know the answers to these and other questions, check out the study tools, and find out what topics require additional practice!

Section 10.1 Say you buy a share of stock for $50. Its price rises to $55, and it pays a $2 annual dividend. You do not sell the stock. What is your dividend yield for the year?

Section 10.3 What investments have the lowest historical risk premium?

Section 10.4 If Stock ABC has a mean return of 10 percent with a standard deviation of 5 percent, what is the approximate probability of earning a negative return?

Section 10.5 If you use a geometric average to project short-run wealth levels, how would you expect your results to skew?

Section 10.6 Why do stock prices fluctuate from day to day?

CHAPTER REVIEW AND SELF-TEST PROBLEMS

10.1   Recent Return History   Use Table 10.1 to calculate the average return over the years 1997–2001 for large-company stocks, long-term government bonds, and Treasury bills. (See Problem 9.)

10.2   More Recent Return History   Calculate the standard deviations using information from Problem 10.1. Which of the investments was the most volatile over this period? (See Problem 7.)

■ Answers to Chapter Review and Self-Test Problems

10.1 We calculate the averages as follows:

Year	Actual Returns and Averages		
	Large-Company Stocks	Long-Term Government Bonds	Treasury Bills
1997	.3336	.1770	.0519
1998	.2858	.1922	.0486
1999	.2104	−.1276	.0480
2000	−.0910	.2216	.0598
2001	−.1189	.0530	.0333
Average:	.1240	.1032	.0483

10.2 We first need to calculate the deviations from the average returns. Using the averages from Problem 10.1, we get:

Year	Deviations from Average Returns		
	Large-Company Stocks	Long-Term Government Bonds	Treasury Bills
1997	.2096	.0738	.0036
1998	.1618	.0890	.0003
1999	.0864	−.2308	−.0003
2000	−.2150	.1184	.0115
2001	−.2429	−.0502	−.0150
Total:	.0000	.0000	.0000

We square these deviations and calculate the variances and standard deviations:

Year	Squared Deviations from Average Returns		
	Large-Company Stocks	Long-Term Government Bonds	Treasury Bills
1997	.043941	.005441	.000013
1998	.026186	.007914	.000000
1999	.007468	.053287	.000000
2000	.046216	.014009	.000132
2001	.058991	.002524	.000226
Variance:	.0457	.0208	.0001
Standard deviation:	.2138	.1442	.0096

To calculate the variances, we added up the squared deviations and divided by 4, the number of returns less 1. Notice that the stocks had substantially greater volatility with a larger average return. Once again, such investments are risky, particularly over short periods of time.

CRITICAL THINKING AND CONCEPTS REVIEW

LO 3   **10.1 Investment Selection**   Given that Madrigal Pharmaceuticals was up by 516 percent for 2017, why didn't all investors hold Madrigal?

LO 3   **10.2 Investment Selection**   Given that Sears Holdings was down by 61 percent for 2017, why did some investors hold the stock? Why didn't they sell out before the price declined so sharply?

LO 3 **10.3 Risk and Return**   We have seen that over long periods of time, stock investments have tended to substantially outperform bond investments. However, it is not at all uncommon to observe investors with long horizons holding entirely bonds. Are such investors irrational?

LO 4 **10.4 Market Efficiency Implications**   Explain why a characteristic of an efficient market is that investments in that market have zero NPVs.

LO 4 **10.5 Efficient Markets Hypothesis**   A stock market analyst is able to identify mispriced stocks by comparing the average price for the last 10 days to the average price for the last 60 days. If this is true, what do you know about the market?

LO 4 **10.6 Semistrong Efficiency**   If a market is semistrong form efficient, is it also weak form efficient? Explain.

LO 4 **10.7 Efficient Markets Hypothesis**   What are the implications of the efficient markets hypothesis for investors who buy and sell stocks in an attempt to "beat the market"?

LO 4 **10.8 Stocks versus Gambling**   Critically evaluate the following statement: Playing the stock market is like gambling. Such speculative investing has no social value, other than the pleasure people get from this form of gambling.

LO 4 **10.9 Efficient Markets Hypothesis**   There are several celebrated investors and stock pickers frequently mentioned in the financial press who have recorded huge returns on their investments over the past two decades. Is the success of these particular investors an invalidation of the EMH? Explain.

LO 4 **10.10 Efficient Markets Hypothesis**   For each of the following scenarios, discuss whether profit opportunities exist from trading in the stock of the firm under the conditions that (1) the market is not weak form efficient, (2) the market is weak form but not semistrong form efficient, (3) the market is semistrong form but not strong form efficient, and (4) the market is strong form efficient.

   a. The stock price has risen steadily each day for the past 30 days.

   b. The financial statements for a company were released three days ago, and you believe you've uncovered some anomalies in the company's inventory and cost control reporting techniques that are causing the firm's true liquidity strength to be understated.

   c. You observe that the senior management of a company has been buying a lot of the company's stock on the open market over the past week.

QUESTIONS AND PROBLEMS

connect   Select problems are available in McGraw-Hill *Connect*. Please see the packaging options section of the Preface for more information.

BASIC (Questions 1–18)

LO 1 **1. Calculating Returns**   Suppose a stock had an initial price of $87 per share, paid a dividend of $2.15 per share during the year, and had an ending share price of $98. Compute the percentage total return. What was the dividend yield? The capital gains yield?

LO 1   **2. Calculating Returns**   Rework Problem 1 assuming the ending share price is $78.

LO 1   **3. Calculating Dollar Returns**   You purchased 250 shares of a particular stock at the beginning of the year at a price of $104.32. The stock paid a dividend of $2.34 per share, and the stock price at the end of the year was $113.65. What was your dollar return on this investment?

LO 1   **4. Calculating Returns**   Suppose you bought a bond with an annual coupon rate of 5.5 percent one year ago for $1,017. The bond sells for $1,041 today.

    a.   Assuming a $1,000 face value, what was your total dollar return on this investment over the past year?

    b.   What was your total nominal rate of return on this investment over the past year?

    c.   If the inflation rate last year was 3 percent, what was your total real rate of return on this investment?

LO 2   **5. Nominal versus Real Returns**   What was the arithmetic average annual return on large-company stocks from 1926 through 2017:

    a.   In nominal terms?

    b.   In real terms?

LO 2   **6. Bond Returns**   What is the historical real return on long-term government bonds? On long-term corporate bonds?

LO 1   **7. Calculating Returns and Variability**   Using the following returns, calculate the arithmetic average returns, the variances, and the standard deviations for X and Y.

	Returns	
Year	X	Y
1	14%	41%
2	−13	− 9
3	11	23
4	18	−13
5	8	42

LO 2   **8. Risk Premiums**   Refer to Table 10.1 in the text and look at the period from 1973 through 1978.

    a.   Calculate the arithmetic average returns for large-company stocks and T-bills over this time period.

    b.   Calculate the standard deviation of the returns for large-company stocks and T-bills over this time period.

    c.   Calculate the observed risk premium in each year for the large-company stocks versus the T-bills. What was the arithmetic average risk premium over this period? What was the standard deviation of the risk premium over this period?

    d.   Is it possible for the risk premium to be negative before an investment is undertaken? Can the risk premium be negative after the fact? Explain.

LO 1   9. **Calculating Returns and Variability**   You've observed the following returns on Yamauchi Corporation's stock over the past five years: −10 percent, 24 percent, 21 percent, 11 percent, and 8 percent.

    a. What was the arithmetic average return on the stock over this five-year period?

    b. What was the variance of the returns over this period? The standard deviation?

LO 1   10. **Calculating Real Returns and Risk Premiums**   For Problem 9, suppose the average inflation rate over this period was 3.1 percent and the average T-bill rate over the period was 4.1 percent.

    a. What was the average real return on the stock?

    b. What was the average nominal risk premium on the stock?

LO 1   11. **Calculating Real Rates**   Given the information in Problem 10, what was the average real risk-free rate over this time period? What was the average real risk premium?

LO 2
LO 3   12. **Effects of Inflation**   Look at Table 10.1 and Figure 10.7 in the text. When were T-bill rates at their highest over the period from 1926 through 2017? Why do you think they were so high during this period? What relationship underlies your answer?

LO 1   13. **Calculating Returns**   You purchased a zero-coupon bond one year ago for $267.35. The market interest rate is now 5.3 percent. If the bond had 25 years to maturity when you originally purchased it, what was your total return for the past year? Assume semiannual compounding.

LO 1   14. **Calculating Returns**   You bought a share of 4.5 percent preferred stock for $105.35 last year. The market price for your stock is now $103.18. What is your total return for last year?

LO 1   15. **Calculating Returns**   You bought a stock three months ago for $51.27 per share. The stock paid no dividends. The current share price is $55.36. What is the APR of your investment? The EAR?

LO 1   16. **Calculating Real Returns**   Refer to Table 10.1. What was the average real return for Treasury bills from 1926 through 1932?

LO 3   17. **Return Distributions**   Refer back to Figure 10.10. What range of returns would you expect to see 68 percent of the time for long-term corporate bonds? What about 95 percent of the time?

LO 3   18. **Return Distributions**   Refer back to Figure 10.10. What range of returns would you expect to see 68 percent of the time for large-company stocks? What about 95 percent of the time?

INTERMEDIATE (Questions 19–26)

LO 1   19. **Calculating Returns and Variability**   You find a certain stock that had returns of 15 percent, −17 percent, 23 percent, and 11 percent for four of the last five years. If the average return of the stock over this period was 10 percent, what was the stock's return for the missing year? What is the standard deviation of the stock's returns?

LO 1   20. **Arithmetic and Geometric Returns**   A stock has had returns of −26 percent, 12 percent, 34 percent, −8 percent, 27 percent, and 23 percent over the last six years. What are the arithmetic and geometric average returns for the stock?

LO 1

21. Arithmetic and Geometric Returns A stock has had the following year-end prices and dividends:

Year	Price	Dividend
1	$64.10	—
2	74.05	$1.10
3	67.61	1.25
4	76.25	1.45
5	82.70	1.60
6	93.15	1.75

What are the arithmetic and geometric average returns for the stock?

LO 2
LO 3

22. Calculating Returns Refer to Table 10.1 in the text and look at the period from 1973 through 1980.

a. Calculate the average return for Treasury bills and the average annual inflation rate (consumer price index) for this period.

b. Calculate the standard deviation of Treasury bill returns and inflation over this time period.

c. Calculate the real return for each year. What is the average real return for Treasury bills?

d. Many people consider Treasury bills to be risk-free. What does this tell you about the potential risks of Treasury bills?

LO 1

23. Calculating Investment Returns You bought one of Rocky Mountain Manufacturing Co.'s 5.7 percent coupon bonds one year ago for $1,032.15. These bonds make annual payments and mature nine years from now. Suppose you decide to sell your bonds today, when the required return on the bonds is 5.1 percent. If the inflation rate was 3.5 percent over the past year, what would be your total real return on the investment?

LO 1

24. Using Return Distributions Suppose the returns on long-term government bonds are normally distributed. Based on the historical record, what is the approximate probability that your return on these bonds will be less than −3.9 percent in a given year? What range of returns would you expect to see 95 percent of the time? What range would you expect to see 99 percent of the time?

LO 3

25. Using Return Distributions Assuming that the returns from holding small-company stocks are normally distributed, what is the approximate probability that your money will double in value in a single year? What about triple in value?

LO 1

26. Distributions In the previous problem, what is the probability that the return is less than −100 percent (think)? What are the implications for the distribution of returns?

CHALLENGE (Questions 27–28)

LO 3

27. Using Probability Distributions Suppose the returns on large-company stocks are normally distributed. Based on the historical record, use the NORMDIST function in Excel® to determine the probability that in any given year you will lose money by investing in large-company common stocks.

LO 3   28. **Using Probability Distributions**   Suppose the returns on long-term corporate bonds and T-bills are normally distributed. Based on the historical record, use the NORMDIST function in Excel® to answer the following questions:

a. What is the probability that in any given year, the return on long-term corporate bonds will be greater than 10 percent? Less than 0 percent?

b. What is the probability that in any given year, the return on T-bills will be greater than 10 percent? Less than 0 percent?

c. In 1979, the return on long-term corporate bonds was −4.18 percent. How likely is it that such a low return will recur at some point in the future? T-bills had a return of 10.56 percent in this same year. How likely is it that such a high return on T-bills will recur at some point in the future?

Historical Interest Rates   Go to the Federal Reserve Bank of St. Louis website at www .stlouisfed.org and find the "FRED®" link and the "Interest Rates" link. You will find a list of links for different historical interest rates. Follow the "10-Year Treasury Constant Maturity Rate" link and you will find the monthly 10-year Treasury note interest rates. Calculate the average annual 10-year Treasury interest rate for 2017 and 2018. Compare this number to the long-term government bond returns and the U.S. Treasury bill returns found in Table 10.1. How does the 10-year Treasury interest rate compare to these numbers? Do you expect this relationship to always hold? Why or why not?

WHAT'S ON THE WEB?

EXCEL *MASTER IT!* PROBLEM

As we have seen, over the 1926–2017 period, small-company stocks had the highest return and the highest risk, while U.S. Treasury bills had the lowest return and the lowest risk. While we certainly hope you have a 92-year holding period, it is likely your investment will be for fewer years. One way risk and return are examined over shorter investment periods is by using rolling returns and standard deviations. Suppose you have a series of annual returns, and you want to calculate a three-year rolling average return. You would calculate the first rolling average at Year 3 using the returns for the first three years. The next rolling average would be calculated using the returns from Years 2, 3, and 4, and so on.

a. Using the annual returns for large-company stocks and Treasury bills, calculate both the 5- and 10-year rolling average returns and standard deviations.

b. Over how many 5-year periods did Treasury bills outperform large-company stocks? How many 10-year periods?

c. Over how many 5-year periods did Treasury bills have a larger standard deviation than large-company stocks? Over how many 10-year periods?

d. Graph the rolling 5-year and 10-year average returns for large-company stocks and Treasury bills.

e. What conclusions do you draw from the preceding results?

CHAPTER CASE
A Job at S&S Air

You recently graduated from college, and your job search led you to S&S Air. Because you felt the company's business was headed skyward, you accepted the job offer. As you are finishing your employment paperwork, Chris Guthrie, who works in the finance department, stops by to inform you about the company's new 401(k) plan.

A 401(k) is a type of retirement plan offered by many companies. A 401(k) is tax deferred, which means that any deposits you make into the plan are deducted from your current income, so no current taxes are paid on the money. Assume your salary will be $40,000 per year. If you contribute $3,000 to the 401(k) plan, you will pay taxes only on $37,000 in income. No taxes will be due on any capital gains or plan income while you are invested in the plan, but you will pay taxes when you withdraw the money at retirement. You can contribute up to 15 percent of your salary to the plan. As is common, S&S Air also has a 5 percent match program. This means that the company will match your contribution dollar-for-dollar up to 5 percent of your salary, but you must contribute to get the match.

The 401(k) plan has several options for investments, most of which are mutual funds. As you know, a mutual fund is a portfolio of assets. When you purchase shares in a mutual fund, you are actually purchasing partial ownership of the fund's assets, similar to purchasing shares of stock in a company. The return of the fund is the weighted average of the return of the assets owned by the fund, minus any expenses. The largest expense is typically the management fee paid to the fund manager, who makes all of the investment decisions for the fund. S&S Air uses Arias Financial Services as its 401(k) plan administrator.

Chris Guthrie then explains that the retirement investment options offered for employees are as follows:

1. *Company stock.* One option is stock in S&S Air. The company is currently privately held. The price you would pay for the stock is based on an annual appraisal, less a 20 percent discount. When you interviewed with the owners, Mark Sexton and Todd Story, they informed you that the company stock was expected to be publicly sold in three to five years. If you needed to sell the stock before it became publicly traded, the company would buy it back at the then-current appraised value.

2. *Arias S&P 500 Index Fund.* This mutual fund tracks the S&P 500. Stocks in the fund are weighted exactly the same as they are in the S&P 500. This means that the fund's return is approximately the return of the S&P 500, minus expenses. With an index fund, the manager is not required to research stocks and make investment decisions, so fund expenses are usually low. The Arias S&P 500 Index Fund charges expenses of .20 percent of assets per year.

3. *Arias Small-Cap Fund.* This fund primarily invests in small capitalization stocks. As such, the returns of the fund are more volatile. The fund also can invest 10 percent of its assets in companies based outside the United States. This fund charges 1.70 percent of assets in expenses per year.

4. *Arias Large-Company Stock Fund.* This fund invests primarily in large capitalization stocks of companies based in the United States. The fund is managed by Melissa Arias and has outperformed the market in six of the last eight years. The fund charges 1.50 percent in expenses.

5. *Arias Bond Fund.* This fund invests in long-term corporate bonds issued by U.S.-domiciled companies. The fund is restricted to investments in bonds with an investment grade credit rating. This fund charges 1.40 percent in expenses.

6. *Arias Money Market Fund.* This fund invests in short-term, high-credit-quality debt instruments, which include Treasury bills. As such, the return on money market funds is only slightly higher than the return on Treasury bills. Because of the credit quality and short-term nature of the investments, there is only a very slight risk of negative return. The fund charges .60 percent in expenses.

QUESTIONS

1. What advantages/disadvantages do the mutual funds offer compared to company stock for your retirement investing?

2. Notice that, for every dollar you invest, S&S Air also invests a dollar. What return on your investment does this represent? What does your answer suggest about matching programs?

3. Assume you decide you should invest at least part of your money in large capitalization stocks of companies based in the United States. What are the advantages and disadvantages of choosing the Arias Large-Company Stock Fund compared to the Arias S&P 500 Index Fund?

4. The returns of the Arias Small-Cap Fund are the most volatile of all the mutual funds offered in the 401(k) plan. Why would you ever want to invest in this fund? When you examine the expenses of the mutual funds, you will notice that this fund also has the highest expenses. Will this affect your decision to invest in this fund?

5. A measure of risk-adjusted performance that often is used in practice is the Sharpe ratio. The Sharpe ratio is calculated as the risk premium of an asset divided by its standard deviation.

    The standard deviations and returns for the funds over the past 10 years are listed here. Assuming a risk-free rate of 3.1 percent, calculate the Sharpe ratio for each of these. In broad terms, what do you suppose the Sharpe ratio is intended to measure?

	10-Year Annual Return	Standard Deviation
Arias S&P 500 Index Fund	11.80%	19.35%
Arias Small-Cap Fund	15.12	27.95
Arias Large-Company Stock Fund	11.15	21.16
Arias Bond Fund	7.92	11.45

Risk and Return | 11

LEARNING OBJECTIVES

After studying this chapter, you should be able to:

LO 1 Calculate expected returns.

LO 2 Explain the impact of diversification.

LO 3 Define the systematic risk principle.

LO 4 Discuss the security market line and the risk-return trade-off.

In 2018, Hormel, Microsoft, and Okta all made major announcements. In particular, Hormel, the famed Spam manufacturer, announced that its earnings rose from $.39 per share in the first quarter of 2017 to $.44 per share in first quarter of 2018. Microsoft announced earnings of $.96 per share for the quarter, a 12 percent increase over the previous year. And Okta, which provides business identity solutions, announced that it lost $26 million in the most recent quarter.

You probably expect that these three cases represent good news for Hormel and Microsoft and bad news for Okta, and usually you would be right. But here, Hormel's stock price dropped about 1 percent, Microsoft's stock price dropped about 2 percent, and Okta's stock price jumped more than 3 percent. So when is good news really good news? The answer is fundamental to understanding risk and return, and— the good news is—this chapter explores it in detail.

This chapter continues the discussion we began in the previous chapter. We've seen pretty clearly that some investments have greater risks than others. We now begin to drill down a bit to investigate one of the most fundamental problems in finance: Just what is risk? What we will learn is that risk is not always what it seems, and the reward for bearing risk is more subtle than we have indicated so far. Understanding how risks are rewarded is important for everyone in business for the simple reason that business is risky, and only businesses that manage risk wisely will survive over the long haul.

Please visit us at essentialsofcorporatefinance.blogspot.com for the latest developments in the world of corporate finance.

In our last chapter, we learned some important lessons from capital market history. Most important, there is a reward, on average, for bearing risk. We called this reward a *risk premium*. The second lesson is that this risk premium is larger for riskier investments. This chapter explores the economic and managerial implications of this basic idea.

Thus far, we have concentrated mainly on the return behavior of a few large portfolios. We need to expand our consideration to include individual assets. Specifically, we have two tasks to accomplish. First, we have to define risk and then discuss how to measure it. We then must quantify the relationship between an asset's risk and its required return.

When we examine the risks associated with individual assets, we find there are two types of risk: systematic and unsystematic. This distinction is crucial because, as we will see, systematic risk affects almost all assets in the economy, at least to some degree, while unsystematic risk affects at most a small number of assets. We then develop the principle of diversification, which shows that highly diversified portfolios will tend to have almost no unsystematic risk.

The principle of diversification has an important implication: To a diversified investor, only systematic risk matters. It follows that in deciding whether or not to buy a particular individual asset, a diversified investor will only be concerned with that asset's systematic risk. This is a key observation, and it allows us to say a great deal about the risks and returns on individual assets. In particular, it is the basis for a famous relationship between risk and return called the *security market line*, or SML. To develop the SML, we introduce the equally famous "beta" coefficient, one of the centerpieces of modern finance. Beta and the SML are key concepts because they supply us with at least part of the answer to the question of how to go about determining the required return on an investment.

11.1 EXPECTED RETURNS AND VARIANCES

In our previous chapter, we discussed how to calculate average returns and variances using historical data. We now begin to discuss how to analyze returns and variances when the information we have concerns future possible returns and their probabilities.

Expected Return

We start with a straightforward case. Consider a single period of time, say, a year. We have two stocks, L and U, which have the following characteristics: Stock L is expected to have a return of 25 percent in the coming year. Stock U is expected to have a return of 20 percent for the same period.

In a situation like this, if all investors agreed on the expected returns, why would anyone want to hold Stock U? After all, why invest in one stock when the expectation is that another will do better? Clearly, the answer must depend on the risk of the two investments. The return on Stock L, although it is *expected* to be 25 percent, could actually turn out to be higher or lower.

Suppose the economy booms. In this case, we think Stock L will have a 70 percent return. If the economy enters a recession, we think the return will be −20 percent. In this case, we say that there are two *states of the economy*, which means that these are the only two possible situations. This setup is oversimplified, of course, but it allows us to illustrate some key ideas without a lot of computation.

Suppose we think a boom and a recession are equally likely to happen, for a 50–50 chance of each. Table 11.1 illustrates the basic information we have described and some additional information about Stock U. Notice that Stock U earns 30 percent if there is a recession and 10 percent if there is a boom.

TABLE 11.1

States of the economy and stock returns

State of Economy	Probability of State of Economy	Security Returns if State Occurs	
		Stock L	Stock U
Recession	.5	−20%	30%
Boom	.5	70	10
	1.0		

Obviously, if you buy one of these stocks, say Stock U, what you earn in any particular year depends on what the economy does during that year. However, suppose the probabilities stay the same through time. If you hold U for a number of years, you'll earn 30 percent about half the time and 10 percent the other half. In this case, we say that your **expected return** on Stock U, $E(R_U)$, is 20 percent:

expected return
Return on a risky asset expected in the future.

$$E(R_U) = .50 \times 30\% + .50 \times 10\% = 20\%$$

In other words, you should expect to earn 20 percent from this stock, on average.

For Stock L, the probabilities are the same, but the possible returns are different. Here we lose 20 percent half the time, and we gain 70 percent the other half. The expected return on L, $E(R_L)$, is thus 25 percent:

$$E(R_L) = .50 \times −20\% + .50 \times 70\% = 25\%$$

Table 11.2 illustrates these calculations.

In the previous chapter, we defined the *risk premium* as the difference between the return on a risky investment and that on a risk-free investment, and we calculated the historical risk premiums on some different investments. Using our projected returns, we can calculate the *projected*, or *expected*, *risk premium* as the difference between the expected return on a risky investment and the certain return on a risk-free investment.

Suppose risk-free investments are currently offering 8 percent. We will say that the risk-free rate, which we label as R_f, is 8 percent. Given this, what is the projected risk premium on Stock U? On Stock L? Because the expected return on Stock U, $E(R_U)$, is 20 percent, the projected risk premium is:

$$
\begin{aligned}
\text{Risk premium} &= \text{Expected return} - \text{Risk-free rate} \qquad\qquad [11.1]\\
&= E(R_U) - R_f\\
&= 20\% - 8\%\\
&= 12\%
\end{aligned}
$$

Similarly, the risk premium on Stock L is 25% − 8% = 17%.

TABLE 11.2

Calculation of expected return

(1) State of Economy	(2) Probability of State of Economy	(3) Rate of Return if State Occurs	(4) Product (2) × (3)	(5) Rate of Return if State Occurs	(6) Product (2) × (5)
		Stock L		Stock U	
Recession	.5	−.20	−.10	.30	.15
Boom	.5	.70	.35	.10	.05
	1.0		$E(R_L) = .25$		$E(R_U) = .20$

In general, the expected return on a security or other asset is equal to the sum of the possible returns multiplied by their probabilities. So, if we had 100 possible returns, we would multiply each one by its probability and then add the results. The result would be the expected return. The risk premium would then be the difference between this expected return and the risk-free rate.

EXAMPLE 11.1   **Unequal Probabilities**

Look again at Tables 11.1 and 11.2. Suppose you thought a boom would occur only 20 percent of the time instead of 50 percent. What are the expected returns on Stocks U and L in this case? If the risk-free rate is 10 percent, what are the risk premiums?

The first thing to notice is that a recession must occur 80 percent of the time $(1 - .20 = .80)$ because there are only two possibilities. With this in mind, we see that Stock U has a 30 percent return in 80 percent of the years and a 10 percent return in 20 percent of the years. To calculate the expected return, we again multiply the possibilities by the probabilities and add up the results:

$E(R_U) = .80 \times 30\% + .20 \times 10\% = 26\%$

Table 11.3 summarizes the calculations for both stocks. Notice that the expected return on L is -2 percent.

The risk premium for Stock U is $26\% - 10\% = 16\%$ in this case. The risk premium for Stock L is negative: $-2\% - 10\% = -12\%$. This is a little odd, but, for reasons we discuss later, it is not impossible.

		Stock L		Stock U		
(1) State of Economy	**(2)** Probability of State of Economy	**(3)** Rate of Return if State Occurs	**(4)** Product (2) × (3)	**(5)** Rate of Return if State Occurs	**(6)** Product (2) × (5)	
Recession	.8	−.20	−.16	.30	.24	
Boom	.2	.70	.14	.10	.02	
	1.0		$E(R_L) = -.02$		$E(R_U) = .26$	

TABLE 11.3

Calculation of expected return

Calculating the Variance

To calculate the variances of the returns on our two stocks, we first determine the squared deviations from the expected returns. We then multiply each possible squared deviation by its probability. We add these, and the result is the variance. The standard deviation, as always, is the square root of the variance.

To illustrate, Stock U from earlier has an expected return of $E(R_U) = 20\%$. In a given year, it will actually return either 30 percent or 10 percent. The possible deviations are thus $30\% - 20\% = 10\%$ and $10\% - 20\% = -10\%$. In this case, the variance is:

Variance $= \sigma_U^2 = .50 \times (.10)^2 + .50 \times (-.10)^2 = .01$

The standard deviation is the square root of this:

Standard deviation $= \sigma_U = \sqrt{.01} = .10$, **or 10%**

Table 11.4 summarizes these calculations for both stocks. Notice that Stock L has a much larger variance.

TABLE **11.4** **Calculation of variance**	**(1)** State of Economy	**(2)** Probability of State of Economy	**(3)** Return Deviation from Expected Return	**(4)** Squared Return Deviation from Expected Return	**(5)** Product (2) × (4)

(1) State of Economy	(2) Probability of State of Economy	(3) Return Deviation from Expected Return	(4) Squared Return Deviation from Expected Return	(5) Product (2) × (4)
Stock L				
Recession	.5	$-.20 - .25 = -.45$	$-.45^2 = .2025$	.10125
Boom	.5	$.70 - .25 = .45$	$.45^2 = .2025$	.10125
	1.0			$\sigma_L^2 = .2025$
Stock U				
Recession	.5	$.30 - .20 = .10$	$.10^2 = .01$	.00500
Boom	.5	$.10 - .20 = -.10$	$-.10^2 = .01$	.00500
	1.0			$\sigma_U^2 = .0100$

When we put the expected return and variability information for our two stocks together, we have:

	Stock L	Stock U
Expected return, E(R)	25%	20%
Variance, σ^2	.2025	.0100
Standard deviation, σ	45%	10%

Stock L has a higher expected return, but U has less risk. You could get a 70 percent return on your investment in L, but you could also lose 20 percent. Notice that an investment in U will always pay at least 10 percent.

Which of these two stocks should you buy? We can't really say; it depends on your personal preferences. We can be reasonably sure, however, that some investors would prefer L to U and some would prefer U to L.

You've probably noticed that the way we calculated expected returns and variances here is somewhat different from the way we did it in the last chapter. The reason is that, in Chapter 10, we were examining actual historical returns, so we estimated the average return and the variance based on some actual events. Here, we have projected future returns and their associated probabilities, so this is the information with which we must work.

EXAMPLE 11.2 **More Unequal Probabilities**

Going back to Example 11.1, what are the variances on the two stocks once we have unequal probabilities? The standard deviations?

We can summarize the needed calculations as follows:

(1) State of Economy	(2) Probability of State of Economy	(3) Return Deviation from Expected Return	(4) Squared Return Deviation from Expected Return	(5) Product (2) × (4)
Stock L				
Recession	.80	$-.20 - (-.02) = -.18$	.0324	.02592
Boom	.20	$.70 - (-.02) = .72$	.5184	.10368
				$\sigma_L^2 = .12960$
Stock U				
Recession	.80	$.30 - .26 = .04$	.0016	.00128
Boom	.20	$.10 - .26 = -.16$	.0256	.00512
				$\sigma_U^2 = .00640$

Based on these calculations, the standard deviation for L is: $\sigma_L = \sqrt{.1296} = .36$, or 36%. The standard deviation for U is much smaller: $\sigma_U = \sqrt{.0064} = .08$, or 8%.

CONCEPT QUESTIONS

11.1a   How do we calculate the expected return on a security?

11.1b   In words, how do we calculate the variance of the expected return?

11.2 PORTFOLIOS

Thus far in this chapter, we have concentrated on individual assets considered separately. However, most investors actually hold a **portfolio** of assets. All we mean by this is that investors tend to own more than just a single stock, bond, or other asset. Given that this is so, portfolio return and portfolio risk are of obvious relevance. Accordingly, we now discuss portfolio expected returns and variances.

portfolio
Group of assets such as stocks and bonds held by an investor.

Portfolio Weights

There are many equivalent ways of describing a portfolio. The most convenient approach is to list the percentages of the total portfolio's value that are invested in each portfolio asset. We call these percentages the **portfolio weights**.

For example, if we have $50 in one asset and $150 in another, then our total portfolio is worth $200. The percentage of our portfolio in the first asset is $50/$200 = .25. The percentage of our portfolio in the second asset is $150/$200, or .75. Our portfolio weights are .25 and .75. Notice that the weights have to add up to 1.00 because all of our money is invested somewhere.[1]

portfolio weight
Percentage of a portfolio's total value in a particular asset.

Portfolio Expected Returns

Let's go back to Stocks L and U. You put half your money in each. The portfolio weights are obviously .50 and .50. What is the pattern of returns on this portfolio? The expected return?

To answer these questions, suppose the economy actually enters a recession. In this case, half your money (the half in L) loses 20 percent. The other half (the half in U) gains 30 percent. Your portfolio return, R_p, in a recession will be:

$R_p = .50 \times -20\% + .50 \times 30\% = 5\%$

Table 11.5 summarizes the remaining calculations. Notice that when a boom occurs, your portfolio will return 40 percent:

$R_p = .50 \times 70\% + .50 \times 10\% = 40\%$

As indicated in Table 11.5, the expected return on your portfolio, $E(R_p)$, is 22.5 percent.

We can save ourselves some work by calculating the expected return more directly. Given these portfolio weights, we could have reasoned that we expect half of our money to

---

[1]Some of it could be in cash, of course, but we would then consider the cash to be one of the portfolio assets.

TABLE 11.5	(1) State of Economy	(2) Probability of State of Economy	(3) Portfolio Return if State Occurs	(4) Product (2) × (3)
	Recession	.50	.50 × −20% + .50 × 30% = 5%	2.5%
	Boom	.50	.50 × 70% + .50 × 10% = 40%	20
		1.00		E(R_p) = 22.5%

Expected return on an equally weighted portfolio of Stock L and Stock U

earn 25 percent (the half in L) and half of our money to earn 20 percent (the half in U). Our portfolio expected return is thus:

$$E(R_p) = .50 \times E(R_L) + .50 \times E(R_U)$$
$$= .50 \times 25\% + .50 \times 20\%$$
$$= .225, \text{ or } 22.5\%$$

This is the same portfolio expected return we had before.

This method of calculating the expected return on a portfolio works no matter how many assets there are in the portfolio. Suppose we had n assets in our portfolio, where n is any number. If we let x_i stand for the percentage of our money in Asset i, then the expected return is:

$$E(R_p) = x_1 \times E(R_1) + x_2 \times E(R_2) + \cdots + x_n \times E(R_n)$$ [11.2]

This says that the expected return on a portfolio is a straightforward combination of the expected returns on the assets in that portfolio. This seems somewhat obvious, but, as we will examine next, the obvious approach is not always the right one.

EXAMPLE 11.3   Portfolio Expected Return

Suppose we have the following projections on three stocks:

State of Economy	Probability of State	Returns Stock A	Returns Stock B	Returns Stock C
Boom	.40	10%	15%	20%
Bust	.60	8	4	0

We want to calculate portfolio expected returns in two cases. First: What would be the expected return on a portfolio with equal amounts invested in each of the three stocks? Second: What would be the expected return if half of the portfolio were in A, with the remainder equally divided between B and C?

From our earlier discussions, the expected returns on the individual stocks are (check these for practice):

$$E(R_A) = 8.8\%$$
$$E(R_B) = 8.4\%$$
$$E(R_C) = 8.0\%$$

If a portfolio has equal investments in each asset, the portfolio weights are all the same. Such a portfolio is said to be *equally weighted*. Because there are three stocks in this case, the weights are all equal to ⅓. The portfolio expected return is thus:

$$E(R_p) = \tfrac{1}{3} \times 8.8\% + \tfrac{1}{3} \times 8.4\% + \tfrac{1}{3} \times 8.0\% = 8.4\%$$

In the second case, verify that the portfolio expected return is 8.5 percent.

TABLE **11.6**

Variance on an
equally weighted
portfolio of Stock L
and Stock U

(1) State of Economy	(2) Probability of State of Economy	(3) Portfolio Return if State Occurs	(4) Squared Deviation from Expected Return	(5) Product (2) × (4)
Recession	.50	5%	$(.05 - .225)^2 = .030625$	.0153125
Boom	.50	40	$(.40 - .225)^2 = .030625$	.0153125
	1.00			$\sigma_p^2 = .030625$

$$\sigma_p = \sqrt{.030625} = .175, \text{ or } 17.5\%$$

Portfolio Variance

From our discussion above, the expected return on a portfolio that contains equal investments in Stocks U and L is 22.5 percent. What is the standard deviation of return on this portfolio? Simple intuition might suggest that half of the money has a standard deviation of 45 percent and the other half has a standard deviation of 10 percent, so the portfolio's standard deviation might be calculated as:

$$\sigma_p = .50 \times 45\% + .50 \times 10\% = 27.5\%$$

Unfortunately, this approach is completely incorrect!

Let's see what the standard deviation really is. Table 11.6 summarizes the relevant calculations. As we see, the portfolio's variance is about .031, and its standard deviation is less than we thought—it's only 17.5 percent. What is illustrated here is that the variance on a portfolio is not generally a simple combination of the variances of the assets in the portfolio.

We can illustrate this point a little more dramatically by considering a slightly different set of portfolio weights. Suppose we put $\frac{2}{11}$ (about 18 percent) in L and the other $\frac{9}{11}$ (about 82 percent) in U. If a recession occurs, this portfolio will have a return of:

$$R_p = \frac{2}{11} \times -20\% + \frac{9}{11} \times 30\% = 20.91\%$$

If a boom occurs, this portfolio will have a return of:

$$R_p = \frac{2}{11} \times 70\% + \frac{9}{11} \times 10\% = 20.91\%$$

Notice that the return is the same no matter what happens. No further calculations are needed: This portfolio has a zero variance. Apparently, combining assets into portfolios can substantially alter the risks faced by the investor. This is a crucial observation, and we will begin to explore its implications in the next section.

EXAMPLE 11.4   Portfolio Variance and Standard Deviation

In Example 11.3, what are the standard deviations on the two portfolios? To answer, we first have to calculate the portfolio returns in the two states. We will work with the second portfolio, which has 50 percent in Stock A and 25 percent in each of Stocks B and C. The relevant calculations can be summarized as follows:

State of Economy	Probability of State	Returns			
		Stock A	Stock B	Stock C	Portfolio
Boom	.40	10%	15%	20%	13.75%
Bust	.60	8	4	0	5.00

(continued)

The portfolio return when the economy booms is calculated as:

$$.50 \times 10\% + .25 \times 15\% + .25 \times 20\% = 13.75\%$$

The return when the economy goes bust is calculated the same way. The expected return on the portfolio is .085. The variance is:

$$\sigma^2 = .40 \times (.1375 - .085)^2 + .60 \times (.05 - .085)^2$$
$$= .0018375$$

The standard deviation is about 4.3 percent. For our equally weighted portfolio, verify that the standard deviation is about 5.4 percent.

CONCEPT QUESTIONS

11.2a   What is a portfolio weight?

11.2b   How do we calculate the expected return on a portfolio?

11.2c   Is there a simple relationship between the standard deviation on a portfolio and the standard deviations of the assets in the portfolio?

11.3 ANNOUNCEMENTS, SURPRISES, AND EXPECTED RETURNS

Now that we know how to construct portfolios and evaluate their returns, we begin to describe more carefully the risks and returns associated with individual securities. Thus far, we have measured volatility by looking at the difference between the actual return on an asset or portfolio, R, and the expected return, $E(R)$. We now look at why such deviations exist.

Expected and Unexpected Returns

To begin, for concreteness, we consider the return on the stock of a company called Flyers. What will determine this stock's return in, say, the coming year?

The return on any stock traded in a financial market is composed of two parts. First, the normal, or expected, return from the stock is the part of the return that shareholders in the market predict or expect. This return depends on the information shareholders have that bears on the stock, and it is based on the market's understanding today of the important factors that will influence the stock in the coming year.

The second part of the return on the stock is the uncertain, or risky, part. This is the portion that comes from unexpected information revealed within the year. A list of all possible sources of such information would be endless, but here are a few examples:

- News about research on Flyers.
- Government figures released on gross domestic product (GDP).
- The results from the latest arms control talks.
- The news that Flyers's sales figures are higher than expected.
- A sudden, unexpected drop in interest rates.

Based on this discussion, one way to express the return on Flyers's stock in the coming year would be:

Total return = Expected return + Unexpected return

$$R = E(R) + U$$

[11.3]

where R stands for the actual total return in the year, $E(R)$ stands for the expected part of the return, and U stands for the unexpected part of the return. What this says is that the actual return, R, differs from the expected return, $E(R)$, because of surprises that occur during the year. In any given year, the unexpected return will be positive or negative, but, through time, the average value of U will be zero. This means that, on average, the actual return equals the expected return.

Announcements and News

We need to be careful when we talk about the effect of news items on the return. For example, suppose Flyers's business is such that the company prospers when GDP grows at a relatively high rate and suffers when GDP is relatively stagnant. In this case, in deciding what return to expect this year from owning stock in Flyers, shareholders either implicitly or explicitly must think about what GDP is likely to be for the year.

When the government actually announces GDP figures for the year, what will happen to the value of Flyers's stock? Obviously, the answer depends on what figure is released. More to the point, however, the impact depends on how much of that figure is *new* information.

At the beginning of the year, market participants will have some idea or forecast of what the yearly GDP will be. To the extent that shareholders have predicted GDP, that prediction already will be factored into the expected part of the return on the stock, $E(R)$. On the other hand, if the announced GDP is a surprise, then the effect will be part of U, the unanticipated portion of the return.

Suppose shareholders in the market had forecast that the GDP increase this year would be .5 percent. If the actual announcement this year is exactly .5 percent, the same as the forecast, then the shareholders don't really learn anything, and the announcement isn't news. There will be no impact on the stock price as a result. This is like receiving confirmation of something that you suspected all along; it doesn't reveal anything new.

A common way of saying that an announcement isn't news is to say that the market has already "discounted" the announcement. The use of the word *discount* here is different from the use of the term in computing present values, but the spirit is the same. When we discount a dollar in the future, we say it is worth less to us because of the time value of money. When we say that we discount an announcement, or a news item, we mean that it has less of an impact on the market because the market already knew much of it.

For example, going back to Flyers, suppose the government announces that the actual GDP increase during the year has been 1.5 percent. Now shareholders have learned something, namely, that the increase is one percentage point higher than they had forecast. This difference between the actual result and the forecast, one percentage point in this example, is sometimes called the *innovation* or the *surprise*.

An announcement, then, can be broken into two parts, the anticipated, or expected, part and the surprise, or innovation:

Announcement = Expected part + Surprise

[11.4]

The expected part of any announcement is the part of the information that the market uses to form the expectation, $E(R)$, of the return on the stock. The surprise is the news that influences the unanticipated return on the stock, U.

To take another example, if shareholders knew in January that the president of the firm was going to resign, the official announcement in February would be fully expected and would be discounted by the market. Because the announcement was expected before February, its influence on the stock would have taken place before February. The announcement itself will contain no surprise, and the stock's price shouldn't change at all when it is actually made.

The fact that only the unexpected, or surprise, part of an announcement matters explains why two companies can make similar announcements but experience different stock price reactions. For example, to open the chapter, we compared Hormel, Microsoft, and Okta. In Hormel's case, even though the company's earnings had grown about 13 percent to $.44 per share, analysts' estimates for the stock pegged EPS at $.45, so the company came in below expectations. In Microsoft's case, even though the company had exceeded analysts' estimates, the company was trading at high valuations, with high PE and EV/EBITDA multiples, so the earnings "beat" was not enough to impress investors, who were expecting even better numbers. And while Okta reported a loss for the quarter, the loss was only $.09 per share, much better than the expected $.16 per share.

Our discussion of market efficiency in the previous chapter bears on this discussion. We are assuming that relevant information known today is already reflected in the expected return. This is identical to saying that the current price reflects relevant publicly available information. We are thus implicitly assuming that markets are at least reasonably efficient in the semistrong form sense.

Henceforth, when we speak of news, we will mean the surprise part of an announcement and not the portion that the market has expected and therefore already discounted.

CONCEPT QUESTIONS

11.3a   What are the two basic parts of a return?

11.3b   Under what conditions will an announcement have no effect on common stock prices?

11.4 RISK: SYSTEMATIC AND UNSYSTEMATIC

The unanticipated part of the return, that portion resulting from surprises, is the true risk of any investment. After all, if we always receive exactly what we expect, then the investment is perfectly predictable and, by definition, risk-free. In other words, the risk of owning an asset comes from surprises—unanticipated events.

There are important differences, though, among various sources of risk. Look back at our previous list of news stories. Some of these stories are directed specifically at Flyers, and some are more general. Which of the news items are of specific importance to Flyers?

Announcements about interest rates or GDP are clearly important for nearly all companies, whereas the news about Flyers's president, its research, or its sales is of specific interest to Flyers. We distinguish between these two types of events because, as we shall see, they have very different implications.

Systematic and Unsystematic Risk

The first type of surprise, the one that affects a large number of assets, we will label **systematic risk**. Because systematic risks have marketwide effects, they are sometimes called *market risks.*

   The second type of surprise we will call **unsystematic risk**. An unsystematic risk is one that affects a single asset or a small group of assets. Because these risks are unique to individual companies or assets, they are sometimes called *unique* or *asset-specific risks.* We will use these terms interchangeably.

   As we have seen, uncertainties about general economic conditions, such as GDP, interest rates, or inflation, are examples of systematic risks. These conditions affect nearly all companies to some degree. An unanticipated increase, or surprise, in inflation, for example, affects wages and the costs of the supplies that companies buy; it affects the value of the assets that companies own; and it affects the prices at which companies sell their products. Forces such as these, to which all companies are susceptible, are the essence of systematic risk.

   In contrast, the announcement of an oil strike by a company primarily will affect that company and, perhaps, a few others (such as primary competitors and suppliers). It is unlikely to have much of an effect on the world oil market, however, or on the affairs of companies not in the oil business, so this is an unsystematic event.

systematic risk
A risk that influences a large number of assets. Also *market risk.*

unsystematic risk
A risk that affects at most a small number of assets. Also *unique* or *asset-specific risk.*

Systematic and Unsystematic Components of Return

The distinction between a systematic risk and an unsystematic risk is never really as exact as we make it out to be. Even the most narrow and peculiar bit of news about a company ripples through the economy. This is true because every enterprise, no matter how tiny, is a part of the economy. It's like the tale of a kingdom that was lost because one horse lost a shoe. This is mostly hairsplitting, however. Some risks are clearly much more general than others. We'll see some evidence on this point in a moment.

   The distinction between the types of risk allows us to break down the surprise portion, U, of the return on Flyers's stock into two parts. From before, we had the actual return broken down into its expected and surprise components:

   $R = E(R) + U$

We now recognize that the total surprise for Flyers, U, has a systematic and an unsystematic component, so:

   $R = E(R) +$ **Systematic portion** $+$ **Unsystematic portion**   [11.5]

   Because it is traditional, we will use the Greek letter epsilon, ϵ, to stand for the unsystematic portion. And because systematic risks are often called market risks, we will use the letter m to stand for the systematic part of the surprise. With these symbols, we can rewrite the total return:

   $R = E(R) + U$
   $\quad = E(R) + m + \epsilon$

The important thing about the way we have broken down the total surprise, U, is that the unsystematic portion, ϵ, is more or less unique to Flyers. For this reason, it is unrelated to the unsystematic portion of the return on most other assets. To see why this is important, we need to return to the subject of portfolio risk.

CONCEPT QUESTIONS

11.4a   What are the two basic types of risk?

11.4b   What is the distinction between the two types of risk?

11.5 DIVERSIFICATION AND PORTFOLIO RISK

We saw earlier that portfolio risks, in principle, can be quite different from the risks of the assets that make up the portfolio. We now look more closely at the riskiness of an individual asset versus the risk of a portfolio of many different assets. We will examine once again some market history to get an idea of what happens with actual investments in U.S. capital markets.

The Effect of Diversification: Another Lesson from Market History

For more on risk and diversification, visit www .investopedia.com /university.

In the previous chapter, we saw that the standard deviation of the annual return on a portfolio of 500 large common stocks has historically been about 20 percent per year (see Figure 10.10, for example). Does this mean that the standard deviation of the annual return on a typical stock in that group of 500 is about 20 percent? As you might suspect by now, the answer is no. This is an extremely important observation.

To examine the relationship between portfolio size and portfolio risk, Table 11.7 illustrates typical average annual standard deviations for portfolios that contain different numbers of randomly selected NYSE securities.

TABLE **11.7**			
Standard deviations of annual portfolio returns	**(1)** Number of Stocks in Portfolio	**(2)** Average Standard Deviation of Annual Portfolio Returns	**(3)** Ratio of Portfolio Standard Deviation to Standard Deviation of a Single Stock
	1	49.24%	1.00
	2	37.36	.76
	4	29.69	.60
	6	26.64	.54
	8	24.98	.51
	10	23.93	.49
	20	21.68	.44
	30	20.87	.42
	40	20.46	.42
	50	20.20	.41
	100	19.69	.40
	200	19.42	.39
	300	19.34	.39
	400	19.29	.39
	500	19.27	.39
	1,000	19.21	.39

Sources: These figures are from Table 1 in Statman, Meir, "How Many Stocks Make a Diversified Portfolio?" *Journal of Financial and Quantitative Analysis,* vol. 22, September 1987, 353–64. They were derived from Elton, E. J. and Gruber, M. J., "Risk Reduction and Portfolio Size: An Analytical Solution," *Journal of Business,* vol. 50, October 1977, 415–37.

In Column 2 of Table 11.7, we see that the standard deviation for a "portfolio" of one security is about 49 percent. What this means is that, if you randomly selected a single NYSE stock and put all your money into it, your standard deviation of return would typically be a substantial 49 percent per year. If you were to randomly select two stocks and invest half your money in each, your standard deviation would be about 37 percent on average, and so on.

The important thing to notice in Table 11.7 is that the standard deviation declines as the number of securities is increased. By the time we have 100 randomly chosen stocks, the port-folio's standard deviation has declined by about 60 percent, from 49 percent to about 20 per-cent. With 500 securities, the standard deviation is 19.27 percent, similar to the 19.8 percent we saw in our previous chapter for the large common stock portfolio. The small difference exists because the portfolio securities and time periods examined are not identical.

The Principle of Diversification

Figure 11.1 illustrates the point we've been discussing. What we have plotted is the standard deviation of return versus the number of stocks in the portfolio. Notice in Figure 11.1 that the benefit in terms of risk reduction from adding securities drops off as we add more and more. By the time we have 10 securities, most of the effect is already realized, and by the time we get to 30 or so, there is very little remaining benefit.

Figure 11.1 illustrates two key points. First: Some of the riskiness associated with indi-vidual assets can be eliminated by forming portfolios. The process of spreading an invest-ment across assets (and thereby forming a portfolio) is called *diversification*. The **principle of diversification** tells us that spreading an investment across many assets will eliminate some of the risk. The green shaded area in Figure 11.1, labeled "diversifiable risk," is the part that can be eliminated by diversification.

principle of diversification
Spreading an investment across a number of assets will eliminate some, but not all, of the risk.

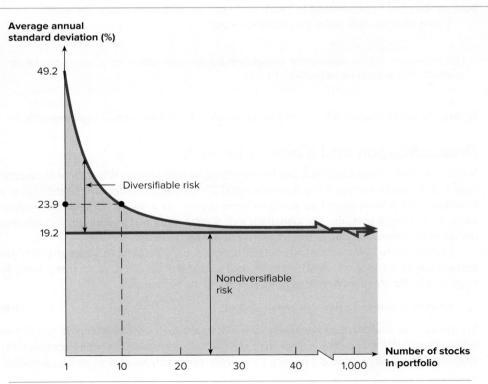

FIGURE 11.1

Portfolio diversification

The second point is equally important: There is a minimum level of risk that cannot be eliminated by diversifying. This minimum level is labeled "nondiversifiable risk" in Figure 11.1. Taken together, these two points are another important lesson from capital market history: Diversification reduces risk, but only up to a point. Put another way: Some risk is diversifiable and some is not.

Diversification and Unsystematic Risk

From our discussion of portfolio risk, we know that some of the risk associated with individual assets can be diversified away and some cannot. We are left with an obvious question: Why is this so? It turns out that the answer hinges on the distinction we made earlier between systematic and unsystematic risk.

By definition, an unsystematic risk is one that is particular to a single asset or, at most, a small group. For example, if the asset under consideration is stock in a single company, the discovery of positive NPV projects such as successful new products and innovative cost savings will tend to increase the value of the stock. Unanticipated lawsuits, industrial accidents, strikes, and similar events will tend to decrease future cash flows and thereby reduce share values.

Here is the important observation: If we only held a single stock, then the value of our investment would fluctuate because of company-specific events. If we hold a large portfolio, on the other hand, some of the stocks in the portfolio will go up in value because of positive company-specific events and some will go down in value because of negative events. The net effect on the overall value of the portfolio will be relatively small, however, as these effects will tend to cancel each other out.

Now we see why some of the variability associated with individual assets is eliminated by diversification. When we combine assets into portfolios, the unique, or unsystematic, events—both positive and negative—tend to "wash out" once we have more than a few assets.

This is an important point that bears restating:

> **Unsystematic risk is essentially eliminated by diversification, so a relatively large portfolio has almost no unsystematic risk.**

In fact, the terms *diversifiable risk* and *unsystematic risk* are often used interchangeably.

Diversification and Systematic Risk

We've seen that unsystematic risk can be eliminated by diversifying. What about systematic risk? Can it also be eliminated by diversification? The answer is no because, by definition, a systematic risk affects almost all assets to some degree. As a result, no matter how many assets we put into a portfolio, the systematic risk doesn't go away. Thus, for obvious reasons, the terms *systematic risk* and *nondiversifiable risk* are used interchangeably.

Because we have introduced so many different terms, it is useful to summarize our discussion before moving on. What we have seen is that the total risk of an investment, as measured by the standard deviation of its return, can be written as:

Total risk = Systematic risk + Unsystematic risk   [11.6]

Systematic risk is also called *nondiversifiable risk* or *market risk*. Unsystematic risk is also called *diversifiable risk*, *unique risk*, or *asset-specific risk*. For a well-diversified portfolio, the unsystematic risk is negligible. For such a portfolio, essentially all of the risk is systematic.

CONCEPT QUESTIONS

11.5a   What happens to the standard deviation of return for a portfolio if we increase the number of securities in the portfolio?

11.5b   What is the principle of diversification?

11.5c   Why is some risk diversifiable?

11.5d   Why can't systematic risk be diversified away?

11.6 SYSTEMATIC RISK AND BETA

The question that we now begin to address is this: What determines the size of the risk premium on a risky asset? Put another way: Why do some assets have a larger risk premium than other assets? The answer to these questions, as we discuss next, is also based on the distinction between systematic and unsystematic risk.

The Systematic Risk Principle

Thus far, we've seen that the total risk associated with an asset can be decomposed into two components: systematic and unsystematic risk. We also have seen that unsystematic risk can be essentially eliminated by diversification. The systematic risk present in an asset, on the other hand, cannot be eliminated by diversification.

For more on beta, see money.cnn.com.

Based on our study of capital market history, we know that there is a reward, on average, for bearing risk. However, we now need to be more precise about what we mean by risk. The **systematic risk principle** states that the reward for bearing risk depends only on the systematic risk of an investment. The underlying rationale for this principle is straightforward: Because unsystematic risk can be eliminated at virtually no cost (by diversifying), there is no reward for bearing it. Put another way: The market does not reward risks that are borne unnecessarily.

systematic risk principle
The expected return on a risky asset depends only on that asset's systematic risk.

The systematic risk principle has a remarkable and very important implication:

> **The expected return on an asset depends only on that asset's systematic risk.**

There is an obvious corollary to this principle: No matter how much total risk an asset has, only the systematic portion is relevant in determining the expected return (and the risk premium) on that asset.

Measuring Systematic Risk

Because systematic risk is the crucial determinant of an asset's expected return, we need some way of measuring the level of systematic risk for different investments. The specific measure we will use is called the **beta coefficient**, for which we will use the Greek symbol β. A beta coefficient, or beta for short, tells us how much systematic risk a particular asset has relative to an average asset. By definition, an average asset has a beta of 1.0 relative to itself. An asset with a beta of .50, therefore, has half as much systematic risk as an average asset; an asset with a beta of 2.0 has twice as much.

beta coefficient
Amount of systematic risk present in a particular risky asset relative to that in an average risky asset.

Table 11.8 contains the estimated beta coefficients for the stocks of some well-known companies. The range of betas in Table 11.8 is typical for stocks of large U.S. corporations. Betas outside this range occur, but they are less common. See our nearby *Work the Web* box to learn how to find betas online.

The important thing to remember is that the expected return, and thus the risk premium, on an asset depends only on its systematic risk. Because assets with larger betas have

W🌐RK THE WEB

Suppose you want to find the beta for a company like Sears. One way is to go to the web. We went to finance.yahoo.com and entered the ticker symbol for Sears (SHLD). Here is part of what we found:

Stock Price History	
Beta	1.44
52-Week Change [3]	-52.89%
S&P500 52-Week Change [3]	20.11%
52 Week High [3]	19.12
52 Week Low [3]	8.00

Management Effectiveness	
Return on Assets (ttm)	-8.07%
Return on Equity (ttm)	N/A

Source: finance.yahoo.com, 2018.

The reported beta for Sears is 1.44, which means that Sears has about one and one-half times the systematic risk of a typical stock. You would expect that the company is very risky and, looking at the other numbers, we agree. Sears's ROA is negative 8.07 percent, which indicates the company lost money over the past year, but the ROE is not reported. Why? If you look at the book value per share, it is negative because of the company's cumulative losses. In this case, the larger the loss, the larger the ROE! That's not good. Given this, Sears appears to be a good candidate for a high beta.

QUESTIONS

1. Has Sears's ROE "improved" since this was written? Check out the current numbers on the website to see.
2. What growth rate are analysts projecting for Sears? How does this growth rate compare to the industry?

Beta, Beta, Who's Got the Beta?

Based on what we've studied so far, you can see that beta is a pretty important topic. You might wonder, then, are all published betas created equal? Read on for a partial answer to this question.

We did some checking on betas and found some interesting results. The Value Line *Investment Survey* is one of the best-known sources for information on publicly traded companies. However, with the explosion of online investing, there has been a corresponding increase in the amount of investment information available online. We decided to compare the betas presented by Value Line to those reported by Yahoo! Finance (finance.yahoo.com) and CNN Money (money.cnn.com). What we found leads to an important note of caution.

Consider Microsoft, with its beta reported on the Internet as 1.28, which is larger than Value Line's beta of 1.00. Microsoft wasn't the only stock that showed a divergence in betas from different sources. In fact, for most of the technology companies we looked at, Value Line reported betas that were significantly lower than their online cousins. For example, the online beta for Cisco Systems was 1.22, but Value Line reported 1.05. The online beta for eBay was 1.49 versus a Value Line beta of 1.00. Value Line's betas are not always lower. For example, the online beta for Adobe (maker of the ubiquitous Acrobat software) was .80, compared to Value Line's 1.10.

We also found some unusual, and even hard-to-believe, estimates for beta. Caesars Entertainment had a very low online beta of .01, while Value Line reported Caesars's beta as 1.60. The online estimate for Southern Company was .03, compared to Value Line's .54. Perhaps the most outrageous reported betas were the online betas for SPO Global and Sunnylife Global, with betas of 155.23 and −263.53 (notice the negative sign!), respectively. Value Line did not report a beta for these companies. How do you suppose we should interpret a beta of −263.53?

There are a few lessons to be learned from all of this. First, not all betas are created equal. Some are computed using weekly returns and some using daily returns. Some are computed using 60 months of stock returns; some consider more or less. Some betas are computed by comparing the stock to the S&P 500 index, while others use alternative indices. Finally, some reporting firms (including Value Line) make adjustments to raw betas to reflect information other than the fluctuation in stock prices.

The second lesson is perhaps more subtle. We are interested in knowing what the betas of the stocks will be in the future, but betas have to be estimated using historical data. Anytime we use the past to predict the future, there is the danger of a poor estimate. As we will see later in the chapter (and in the next one), it is very unlikely that SPO Global has a beta anything like 155.23 or that Sunnylife Global has a beta of −263.53. Instead, the estimates are almost certainly poor ones. The moral of the story is that, as with any financial tool, beta is not a black box that should be taken without question.

greater systematic risks, they will have greater expected returns. Thus, from Table 11.8, an investor who buys stock in Ford, with a beta of .85, should expect to earn less, on average, than an investor who buys stock in Apple, with a beta of 1.15. To learn more about "real-world" betas, see the nearby *Finance Matters* box.

Company	Beta Coefficient (β)
Macy's	.54
Facebook	.81
Ford	.85
Pfizer	.93
Costco	1.05
Home Depot	1.06
Apple	1.15
Prudential	1.46
Amazon	1.70

TABLE 11.8

Beta coefficients for selected companies

Source: finance.yahoo.com, 2018.

EXAMPLE 11.5 | Total Risk versus Beta

Consider the following information on two securities. Which has greater total risk? Which has greater systematic risk? Greater unsystematic risk? Which asset will have a higher risk premium?

	Standard Deviation	Beta
Security A	40%	.50
Security B	20	1.50

From our discussion in this section, Security A has greater total risk, but it has substantially less systematic risk. Because total risk is the sum of systematic and unsystematic risk, Security A must have greater unsystematic risk. Finally, from the systematic risk principle, Security B will have a higher risk premium and a greater expected return, despite the fact that it has less total risk.

Portfolio Betas

Betas are easy to find on the web. Try finance .yahoo.com and money .cnn.com.

Earlier, we saw that the total riskiness of a portfolio has no simple relationship to the risks of the assets in the portfolio. A portfolio beta, however, can be calculated like a portfolio expected return. For example, looking again at Table 11.8, suppose you put half of your money in Ford and half in Prudential. What would the beta of this combination be? Because Ford has a beta of .85 and Prudential has a beta of 1.46, the portfolio's beta, β_p, would be:

$$\beta_p = .50 \times \beta_{Ford} + .50 \times \beta_{Prudential}$$
$$= .50 \times .85 + .50 \times 1.46$$
$$= 1.16$$

In general, if we had a large number of assets in a portfolio, we would multiply each asset's beta by its portfolio weight and then add the results to get the portfolio's beta.

EXAMPLE 11.6 | Portfolio Betas

Suppose we had the following investments:

Security	Amount Invested	Expected Return	Beta
Stock A	$1,000	8%	.80
Stock B	2,000	12	.95
Stock C	3,000	15	1.10
Stock D	4,000	18	1.40

What is the expected return on this portfolio? What is the beta of this portfolio? Does this portfolio have more or less systematic risk than an average asset?

To answer, we first have to calculate the portfolio weights. Notice that the total amount invested is $10,000. Of this, $1,000/$10,000 = .10, or 10% is invested in Stock A. Similarly, 20 percent is invested in Stock B, 30 percent is invested in Stock C, and 40 percent is invested in Stock D. The expected return, $E(R_p)$, is thus:

$$E(R_p) = .10 \times E(R_A) + .20 \times E(R_B) + .30 \times E(R_C) + .40 \times E(R_D)$$
$$= .10 \times 8\% + .20 \times 12\% + .30 \times 15\% + .40 \times 18\%$$
$$= 14.9\%$$

Similarly, the portfolio beta, β_P, is:

$$\beta_P = .10 \times \beta_A + .20 \times \beta_B + .30 \times \beta_C + .40 \times \beta_D$$
$$= .10 \times .80 + .20 \times .95 + .30 \times 1.10 + .40 \times 1.40$$
$$= 1.16$$

This portfolio thus has an expected return of 14.9 percent and a beta of 1.16. Because the beta is larger than 1.0, this portfolio has greater systematic risk than an average asset.

CONCEPT QUESTIONS

11.6a   What is the systematic risk principle?

11.6b   What does a beta coefficient measure?

11.6c   How do you calculate a portfolio beta?

11.6d   True or false: The expected return on a risky asset depends on that asset's total risk. Explain.

11.7 THE SECURITY MARKET LINE

We're now in a position to see how risk is rewarded in the marketplace. To begin, suppose that Asset A has an expected return of $E(R_A) = 20\%$ and a beta of $\beta_A = 1.6$. Furthermore, the risk-free rate is $R_f = 8\%$. Notice that a risk-free asset, by definition, has no systematic risk (or unsystematic risk, for that matter), so a risk-free asset has a beta of 0.

Beta and the Risk Premium

Consider a portfolio made up of Asset A and a risk-free asset. We can calculate some different possible portfolio expected returns and betas by varying the percentages invested in these two assets. For example, if 25 percent of the portfolio is invested in Asset A, then the expected return is:

$$E(R_P) = .25 \times E(R_A) + (1 - .25) \times R_f$$
$$= .25 \times 20\% + .75 \times 8\%$$
$$= 11.0\%$$

Similarly, the beta on the portfolio, β_P, would be:

$$\beta_P = .25 \times \beta_A + (1 - .25) \times 0$$
$$= .25 \times 1.6$$
$$= .40$$

Notice that, because the weights have to add up to 1, the percentage invested in the risk-free asset is equal to 1 minus the percentage invested in Asset A.

One thing that you might wonder about is whether it is possible for the percentage invested in Asset A to exceed 100 percent. The answer is yes. The way this can happen is for the investor to borrow at the risk-free rate. Suppose an investor has $100 and borrows an additional $50 at 8 percent, the risk-free rate. The total investment in Asset A would be $150, or 150 percent of the investor's wealth. The expected return in this case would be:

$$E(R_P) = 1.50 \times E(R_A) + (1 - 1.50) \times R_f$$
$$= 1.50 \times 20\% - .50 \times 8\%$$
$$= 26.0\%$$

The beta on the portfolio would be:

$$\beta_p = 1.50 \times \beta_A + (1 - 1.50) \times 0$$
$$= 1.50 \times 1.6$$
$$= 2.4$$

We can calculate some other possibilities as follows:

Percentage of Portfolio in Asset A	Portfolio Expected Return	Portfolio Beta
0%	8%	.0
25	11	.4
50	14	.8
75	17	1.2
100	20	1.6
125	23	2.0
150	26	2.4

In Figure 11.2A, these portfolio expected returns are plotted against the portfolio betas. Notice that all the combinations fall on a straight line.

The Reward-to-Risk Ratio   What is the slope of the straight line in Figure 11.2A? As always, the slope of a straight line is equal to "the rise over the run." In this case, as we move out of the risk-free asset into Asset A, the beta increases from 0 to 1.6 (a "run" of 1.6). At the same time, the expected return goes from 8 percent to 20 percent, a "rise" of 12 percent. The slope of the line is thus 12%/1.6 = 7.50%.

Notice that the slope of our line is the risk premium on Asset A, $E(R_A) - R_f$, divided by Asset A's beta, β_A:

$$Slope = \frac{E(R_A) - R_f}{\beta_A}$$
$$= \frac{20\% - 8\%}{1.6}$$
$$= 7.50\%$$

What this tells us is that Asset A offers a *reward-to-risk ratio* of 7.50 percent.[2] In other words, Asset A has a risk premium of 7.50 percent per "unit" of systematic risk.

FIGURE 11.2A

Portfolio expected returns and betas for Asset A

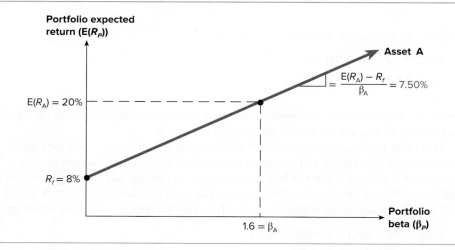

[2]This ratio is sometimes called the *Treynor index,* after one of its originators.

The Basic Argument   Now suppose we consider a second asset, Asset B. This asset has a beta of 1.2 and an expected return of 16 percent. Which investment is better, Asset A or Asset B? You might think that, once again, we really cannot say. Some investors might prefer A; some investors might prefer B. Actually, however, we can say: A is better because, as we shall demonstrate, B offers inadequate compensation for its level of systematic risk, at least relative to A.

To begin, we calculate different combinations of expected returns and betas for portfolios of Asset B and a risk-free asset as we did for Asset A. For example, if we put 25 percent in Asset B and the remaining 75 percent in the risk-free asset, the portfolio's expected return would be:

$$E(R_p) = .25 \times E(R_B) + (1 - .25) \times R_f$$
$$= .25 \times 16\% + .75 \times 8\%$$
$$= 10.0\%$$

Similarly, the beta on the portfolio, β_p, would be:

$$\beta_p = .25 \times \beta_B + (1 - .25) \times 0$$
$$= .25 \times 1.2$$
$$= .30$$

Some other possibilities are as follows:

Percentage of Portfolio in Asset B	Portfolio Expected Return	Portfolio Beta
0%	8%	.0
25	10	.3
50	12	.6
75	14	.9
100	16	1.2
125	18	1.5
150	20	1.8

When we plot these combinations of portfolio expected returns and portfolio betas in Figure 11.2B, we get a straight line as we did for Asset A.

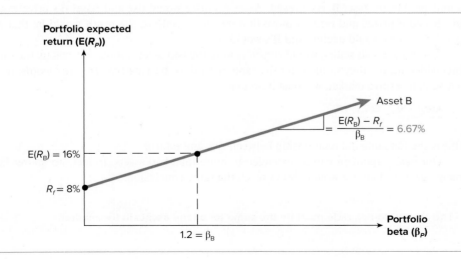

FIGURE 11.2B

Portfolio expected returns and betas for Asset B

FIGURE **11.2C**

Portfolio expected returns and betas for both assets

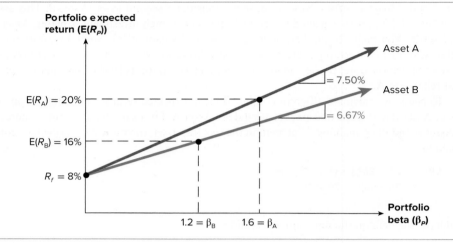

The key thing to notice is that when we compare the results for Assets A and B, as in Figure 11.2C, the line describing the combinations of expected returns and betas for Asset A is higher than the one for Asset B. What this tells us is that for any given level of systematic risk (as measured by β), some combination of Asset A and the risk-free asset always offers a larger return. This is why we were able to state that Asset A is a better investment than Asset B.

Another way of seeing that A offers a superior return for its level of risk is to note that the slope of our line for Asset B is:

$$\text{Slope} = \frac{E(R_B) - R_f}{\beta_B}$$
$$= \frac{16\% - 8\%}{1.2} = 6.67\%$$

Thus, Asset B has a reward-to-risk ratio of 6.67 percent, which is less than the 7.5 percent offered by Asset A.

The Fundamental Result   The situation we have described for Assets A and B cannot persist in a well-organized, active market because investors would be attracted to Asset A and away from Asset B. As a result, Asset A's price would rise and Asset B's price would fall. Because prices and returns move in opposite directions, the result would be that A's expected return would decline and B's would rise.

This buying and selling would continue until the two assets plotted on exactly the same line, which means they would offer the same reward for bearing risk. In other words, in an active, competitive market, we must have that:

$$\frac{E(R_A) - R_f}{\beta_A} = \frac{E(R_B) - R_f}{\beta_B}$$

This is the fundamental relationship between risk and return.

Our basic argument can be extended to more than two assets. In fact, no matter how many assets we had, we would always reach the same conclusion:

The reward-to-risk ratio must be the same for all the assets in the market.

FIGURE **11.3**

Expected returns and systematic risk

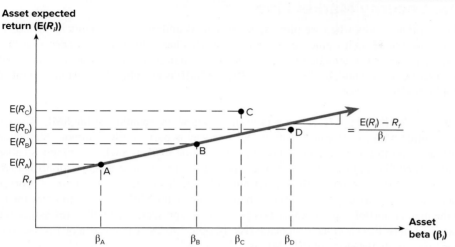

The fundamental relationship between beta and expected return is that all assets must have the same reward-to-risk ratio, $[E(R_i) - R_f]/\beta_i$. This means that they would all plot on the same straight line. Assets A and B are examples of this behavior. Asset C's expected return is too high; Asset D's is too low.

This result is really not so surprising. What it says, for example, is that, if one asset has twice as much systematic risk as another asset, its risk premium will be twice as large.

Because all of the assets in the market must have the same reward-to-risk ratio, they all must plot on the same line. This argument is illustrated in Figure 11.3. As shown, Assets A and B plot directly on the line and thus have the same reward-to-risk ratio. If an asset plotted above the line, such as C in Figure 11.3, its price would rise, and its expected return would fall until it plotted exactly on the line. Similarly, if an asset plotted below the line, such as D in Figure 11.3, its expected return would rise until it, too, plotted directly on the line.

The arguments we have presented apply to active, competitive, well-functioning markets. The financial markets, such as the NYSE, best meet these criteria. Other markets, such as real asset markets, may or may not. For this reason, these concepts are most useful in examining financial markets. We thus focus on such markets here. However, as we discuss in a later section, the information about risk and return gleaned from financial markets is crucial in evaluating the investments that a corporation makes in real assets.

EXAMPLE 11.7   Buy Low, Sell High

An asset is said to be *overvalued* if its price is too high given its expected return and risk. Suppose you observe the following situation:

Security	Expected Return	Beta
Fama Co.	14%	1.3
French Co.	10	.8

The risk-free rate is currently 6 percent. Is one of the two securities above overvalued relative to the other?

To answer, we compute the reward-to-risk ratio for both. For Fama, this ratio is (14% − 6%)/1.3 = 6.15%. For French, this ratio is 5 percent. What we conclude is that French offers an insufficient expected return for its level of risk, at least relative to Fama. Because its expected return is too low, its price is too high. In other words, French is overvalued relative to Fama, and we would expect to see its price fall relative to Fama's. Notice that we also could say Fama is *undervalued* relative to French.

The Security Market Line

The line that results when we plot expected returns and beta coefficients is obviously of some importance, so it's time we gave it a name. This line, which we use to describe the relationship between systematic risk and expected return in financial markets, is usually called the **security market line**, or **SML**. After NPV, the SML is arguably the most important concept in modern finance.

security market line (SML)
Positively sloped straight line displaying the relationship between expected return and beta.

Market Portfolios   It will be very useful to know the equation of the SML. There are many different ways we could write it, but one way is particularly common. Suppose we consider a portfolio made up of all of the assets in the market. Such a portfolio is called a market portfolio, and we will express the expected return on this market portfolio as $E(R_M)$.

Because all the assets in the market must plot on the SML, so must a market portfolio made up of those assets. To determine where it plots on the SML, we need to know the beta of the market portfolio, β_M. Because this portfolio is representative of all of the assets in the market, it must have average systematic risk. In other words, it has a beta of 1.0. We, therefore, could write the slope of the SML as:

$$\text{SML slope} = \frac{E(R_M) - R_f}{\beta_M} = \frac{E(R_M) - R_f}{1} = E(R_M) - R_f$$

market risk premium
Slope of the security market line; the difference between the expected return on a market portfolio and the risk-free rate.

The term $E(R_M) - R_f$ is often called the **market risk premium** because it is the risk premium on a market portfolio.

The Capital Asset Pricing Model   To finish up, if we let $E(R_i)$ and β_i stand for the expected return and beta, respectively, on any asset in the market, then we know that asset must plot on the SML. As a result, we know that its reward-to-risk ratio is the same as the overall market's:

$$\frac{E(R_i) - R_f}{\beta_i} = E(R_M) - R_f$$

If we rearrange this, then we can write the equation for the SML as:

$$E(R_i) = R_f + [E(R_M) - R_f] \times \beta_i \qquad \text{[11.7]}$$

capital asset pricing model (CAPM)
Equation of the security market line showing the relationship between expected return and beta.

This result is identical to the famous **capital asset pricing model (CAPM)**.

What the CAPM shows is that the expected return for a particular asset depends on three things:

1. *The pure time value of money.* As measured by the risk-free rate, R_f, this is the reward for merely waiting for your money, without taking any risk.

2. *The reward for bearing systematic risk.* As measured by the market risk premium, $[E(R_M) - R_f]$, this component is the reward the market offers for bearing an average amount of systematic risk in addition to waiting.

3. *The amount of systematic risk.* As measured by β_i, this is the amount of systematic risk present in a particular asset, relative to an average asset.

By the way, the CAPM works for portfolios of assets just as it does for individual assets. In an earlier section, we saw how to calculate a portfolio's β. To find the expected return on a portfolio, we use this β in the CAPM equation.

Figure 11.4 summarizes our discussion of the SML and the CAPM. As before, we plot expected return against beta. Now we recognize that, based on the CAPM, the slope of the SML is equal to the market risk premium, $[E(R_M) - R_f]$.

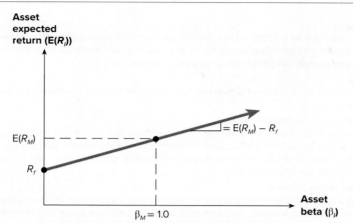

FIGURE **11.4**

The security market line, or SML

The slope of the security market line is equal to the market risk premium, i.e., the reward for bearing an average amount of systematic risk. The equation describing the SML can be written:

$$E(R_i) = R_f + [E(R_M) - R_f] \times \beta_i$$

This is the capital asset pricing model, or CAPM.

Going back to Figure 11.3, C plots above the SML and D plots below the SML. In portfolio management terms, the distance between a portfolio's actual return and the SML is often called **alpha**. When an asset plots on the SML, it earns exactly the return it should earn based on its level of risk, or beta. A positive alpha means that the asset (or portfolio) has earned a return in excess of what it should earn based on its beta. Of course, an asset can have a negative alpha, which is less than desirable.

alpha
The excess return an asset earns based on the level of risk taken.

This concludes our presentation of concepts related to the risk-return trade-off. For future reference, Table 11.9 summarizes the various concepts in the order in which we discussed them.

EXAMPLE 11.8   **Risk and Return**

Suppose the risk-free rate is 4 percent, the market risk premium is 7 percent, and a particular stock has a beta of 1.3. Based on the CAPM, what is the expected return on this stock? What would the expected return be if the beta were to double?

   With a beta of 1.3, the risk premium for the stock would be 1.3 × 7%, or 9.1 percent. The risk-free rate is 4 percent, so the expected return is 13.1 percent. If the beta doubled to 2.6, the risk premium would double to 18.2 percent, so the expected return would be 22.2 percent.

CONCEPT QUESTIONS

11.7a   What is the fundamental relationship between risk and return in well-functioning markets?

11.7b   What is the security market line? Why must all assets plot directly on it in a well-functioning market?

11.7c   What is the capital asset pricing model, or CAPM? What does it tell us about the required return on a risky investment?

TABLE 11.9

Summary of risk and return concepts

I. Total return

The *total return* on an investment has two components: the expected return and the unexpected return. The unexpected return comes about because of unanticipated events. The risk from investing stems from the possibility of an unanticipated event.

II. Total risk

The *total risk* of an investment is measured by the variance or, more commonly, the standard deviation of its return.

III. Systematic and unsystematic risks

Systematic risks (also called *market risks*) are unanticipated events that affect almost all assets to some degree because the effects are economywide. *Unsystematic risks* are unanticipated events that affect single assets or small groups of assets. Unsystematic risks are also called *unique* or *asset-specific risks*.

IV. The effect of diversification

Some, but not all, of the risk associated with a risky investment can be eliminated by diversification. The reason is that unsystematic risks, which are unique to individual assets, tend to wash out in a large portfolio, but systematic risks, which affect all of the assets in a portfolio to some extent, do not.

V. The systematic risk principle and beta

Because unsystematic risk can be freely eliminated by diversification, the *systematic risk principle* states that the reward for bearing risk depends only on the level of systematic risk. The level of systematic risk in a particular asset, relative to the average, is given by the beta of that asset.

VI. The reward-to-risk ratio and the security market line

The *reward-to-risk ratio* for Asset i is the ratio of its risk premium, $E(R_i - R_f)$, to its beta, β_i:

$$\frac{E(R_i) - R_f}{\beta_i}$$

In a well-functioning market, this ratio is the same for every asset. As a result, when asset expected returns are plotted against asset betas, all assets plot on the same straight line, called the *security market line* (SML).

VII. The capital asset pricing model

From the SML, the expected return on Asset i can be written:

$$E(R_i) = R_f + [E(R_M) - R_f] \times \beta_i$$

This is the *capital asset pricing model* (CAPM). The expected return on a risky asset thus has three components. The first is the pure time value of money, R_f; the second is the market risk premium, $[E(R_M) - R_f]$; and the third is the beta for that asset, β_i.

11.8 THE SML AND THE COST OF CAPITAL: A PREVIEW

Our goal in studying risk and return is twofold. First, risk is an extremely important consideration in almost all business decisions, so we want to discuss what risk is and how it is rewarded in the market. Our second purpose is to learn what determines the appropriate discount rate for future cash flows. We briefly discuss this second subject now; we discuss it in more detail in Chapter 12.

The Basic Idea

The security market line tells us the reward for bearing risk in financial markets. At an absolute minimum, any new investment our firm undertakes must offer an expected return that is no worse than what the financial markets offer for the same risk. The reason for this is that our shareholders always can invest for themselves in the financial markets.

The only way we benefit our shareholders is by finding investments with expected returns that are superior to what the financial markets offer for the same risk. Such an investment will have a positive NPV. So, if we ask: "What is the appropriate discount rate?" the answer is that we should use the expected return offered in financial markets on investments with the same systematic risk.

In other words, to determine whether or not an investment has a positive NPV, we essentially compare the expected return on that new investment to what the financial market offers on an investment with the same beta. This is why the SML is so important; it tells us the "going rate" for bearing risk in the economy.

The Cost of Capital

The appropriate discount rate on a new project is the minimum expected rate of return an investment must offer to be attractive. This minimum required return often is called the **cost of capital** associated with the investment. It is called this because the required return is what the firm must earn on its capital investment in a project just to break even. It thus can be interpreted as the opportunity cost associated with the firm's capital investment.

cost of capital
The minimum required return on a new investment.

Notice that when we say an investment is attractive if its expected return exceeds what is offered in financial markets for investments of the same risk, we are effectively using the internal rate of return, or IRR, criterion that we developed and discussed in Chapter 8. The only difference is that now we have a much better idea of what determines the required return on an investment. This understanding will be critical when we discuss cost of capital and capital structure in Part Seven of our book.

CONCEPT QUESTIONS

11.8a If an investment has a positive NPV, would it plot above or below the SML? Why?

11.8b What is meant by the term *cost of capital*?

SUMMARY AND CONCLUSIONS

This chapter has covered the essentials of risk. Along the way, we have introduced a number of definitions and concepts. The most important of these is the security market line, or SML. The SML is important because it tells us the reward offered in financial markets for bearing risk. Once we know this, we have a benchmark against which we compare the returns expected from real asset investments to determine if they are desirable.

Because we have covered quite a bit of ground, it's useful to summarize the basic economic logic underlying the SML as follows:

1. Based on capital market history, there is a reward for bearing risk. This reward is the risk premium on an asset.

2. The total risk associated with an asset has two parts: systematic risk and unsystematic risk. Unsystematic risk can be freely eliminated by diversification (this is the principle of diversification), so only systematic risk is rewarded. As a result, the risk premium on an asset is determined by its systematic risk. This is the systematic risk principle.

3. An asset's systematic risk, relative to the average, can be measured by its beta coefficient, β_i. The risk premium on an asset is then given by its beta coefficient multiplied by the market risk premium, $[E(R_M) - R_f] \times \beta_i$.

4. The expected return on an asset, $E(R_i)$, is equal to the risk-free rate, R_f, plus the risk premium:

$$E(R_i) = R_f + [E(R_M) - R_f] \times \beta_i$$

This is the equation of the SML, and it is often called the *capital asset pricing model*, or CAPM.

This chapter completes our discussion of risk and return and concludes Part Six of our book. Now that we have a better understanding of what determines a firm's cost of capital for an investment, the next several chapters examine more closely how firms raise the long-term capital needed for investment.

■connect POP QUIZ!

Can you answer the following questions? If your class is using *Connect*, log on to SmartBook to see if you know the answers to these and other questions, check out the study tools, and find out what topics require additional practice!

Section 11.1 What does variance measure?

Section 11.3 What is the equation for total return?

Section 11.4 What all will unsystematic risk affect?

Section 11.5 What type of risk is not reduced by diversification?

Section 11.6 By definition, what is the beta of the average asset equal to?

Section 11.7 What does the security market line show?

CHAPTER REVIEW AND SELF-TEST PROBLEMS

11.1 **Expected Return and Standard Deviation**   This problem will give you some practice calculating measures of prospective portfolio performance. There are two assets and three states of the economy:

(1) State of Economy	(2) Probability of State of Economy	(3) Stock A Rate of Return if State Occurs	(4) Stock B Rate of Return if State Occurs
Recession	.10	−.20	.30
Normal	.60	.10	.20
Boom	.30	.70	.50

What are the expected returns and standard deviations for these two stocks? (See Problem 7.)

11.2   Portfolio Risk and Return   In the previous problem, suppose you have
$20,000 total. If you put $6,000 in Stock A and the remainder in Stock B, what
will be the expected return and standard deviation on your portfolio? (See
Problem 10.)

11.3   Risk and Return   Suppose you observe the following situation:

Security	Beta	Expected Return
Cooley, Inc.	1.6	19%
Moyer Co.	1.2	16

If the risk-free rate is 8 percent, are these securities correctly priced? What would the
risk-free rate have to be if they are correctly priced? (See Problems 19 and 20.)

11.4   CAPM   Suppose the risk-free rate is 8 percent. The expected return on the market is
14 percent. If a particular stock has a beta of .60, what is its expected return based
on the CAPM? If another stock has an expected return of 20 percent, what must its
beta be? (See Problem 13.)

■ Answers to Chapter Review and Self-Test Problems

11.1   The expected returns are the possible returns multiplied by the associated
probabilities:

$$E(R_A) = .10 \times -.20 + .60 \times .10 + .30 \times .70 = .25, \text{ or } 25\%$$
$$E(R_B) = .10 \times .30 + .60 \times .20 + .30 \times .50 = .30, \text{ or } 30\%$$

The variances are given by the sums of the squared deviations from the expected
returns multiplied by their probabilities:

$$\begin{aligned}
\sigma_A^2 &= .10 \times (-.20 - .25)^2 + .60 \times (.10 - .25)^2 + .30 \times (.70 - .25)^2 \\
&= .10 \times (-.45)^2 + .60 \times (-.15)^2 + .30 \times (.45)^2 \\
&= .10 \times .2025 + .60 \times .0225 + .30 \times .2025 \\
&= .0945
\end{aligned}$$

$$\begin{aligned}
\sigma_B^2 &= .10 \times (.30 - .30)^2 + .60 \times (.20 - .30)^2 + .30 \times (.50 - .30)^2 \\
&= .10 \times (.00)^2 + .60 \times (-.10)^2 + .30 \times (.20)^2 \\
&= .10 \times .00 + .60 \times .01 + .30 \times .04 \\
&= .0180
\end{aligned}$$

The standard deviations are thus:

$$\sigma_A = \sqrt{.0945} = .3074, \text{ or } 30.74\%$$
$$\sigma_B = \sqrt{.0180} = .1342, \text{ or } 13.42\%$$

11.2   The portfolio weights are $6,000/$20,000 = .30 and $14,000/$20,000 = .70. The
expected return is thus:

$$\begin{aligned}
E(R_P) &= .30 \times E(R_A) + .70 \times E(R_B) \\
&= .30 \times 25\% + .70 \times 30\% \\
&= 28.50\%
\end{aligned}$$

Alternatively, we could calculate the portfolio's return in each of the states:

(1) State of Economy	(2) Probability of State of Economy	(3) Portfolio Return if State Occurs
Recession	.10	$.30 \times -.20 + .70 \times .30 = .15$
Normal	.60	$.30 \times .10 + .70 \times .20 = .17$
Boom	.30	$.30 \times .70 + .70 \times .50 = .56$

The portfolio's expected return is:

$$E(R_p) = .10 \times .15 + .60 \times .17 + .30 \times .56 = .2850, \text{ or } 28.50\%$$

This is the same as we had before.

The portfolio's variance is:

$$\sigma_P^2 = .10 \times (.15 - .285)^2 + .60 \times (.17 - .285)^2 + .30 \times (.56 - .285)^2$$
$$= .03245$$

So the standard deviation is $\sqrt{.03245} = .1801$, or 18.01%

11.3   If we compute the reward-to-risk ratios, we get $(19\% - 8\%)/1.6 = 6.88\%$ for Cooley versus 6.67% for Moyer. Relative to that of Cooley, Moyer's expected return is too low, so its price is too high.

   If they are correctly priced, then they must offer the same reward-to-risk ratio. The risk-free rate would have to be such that:

$$(19\% - R_f)/1.6 = (16\% - R_f)/1.2$$

With a little algebra, we find that the risk-free rate must be 7 percent:

$$(19\% - R_f) = (16\% - R_f)\,(1.6/1.2)$$
$$19\% - 16\% \times 4/3 = R_f - R_f \times 4/3$$
$$R_f = 7\%$$

11.4   Because the expected return on the market is 14 percent, the market risk premium is $14\% - 8\% = 6\%$ (the risk-free rate is 8 percent). The first stock has a beta of .60, so its expected return is $8\% + .60 \times 6\% = 11.6\%$.

   For the second stock, notice that the risk premium is $20\% - 8\% = 12\%$. Because this is twice as large as the market risk premium, the beta must be exactly equal to 2. We can verify this using the CAPM:

$$E(R_i) = R_f + [E(R_M) - R_f] \times \beta_i$$
$$20\% = 8\% + (14\% - 8\%) \times \beta_i$$
$$\beta_i = 12\%/6\% = 2.0$$

CRITICAL THINKING AND CONCEPTS REVIEW

LO 2   **11.1   Diversifiable and Nondiversifiable Risks**   In broad terms, why is some risk diversifiable? Why are some risks nondiversifiable? Does it follow that an investor can control the level of unsystematic risk in a portfolio, but not the level of systematic risk?

LO 3   **11.2   Information and Market Returns**   Suppose the government announces that, based on a just-completed survey, the growth rate in the economy is likely to be 2 percent in the coming year, as compared to 5 percent for the year just completed. Will security prices increase, decrease, or stay the same following this announcement? Does it make any difference whether or not the 2 percent figure was anticipated by the market? Explain.

LO 3   **11.3**   **Systematic versus Unsystematic Risk**   Classify the following events as mostly systematic or mostly unsystematic. Is the distinction clear in every case?

    a. Short-term interest rates increase unexpectedly.

    b. The interest rate a company pays on its short-term debt borrowing is increased by its bank.

    c. Oil prices unexpectedly decline.

    d. An oil tanker ruptures, creating a large oil spill.

    e. A manufacturer loses a multimillion-dollar product liability suit.

    f. A Supreme Court decision substantially broadens producer liability for injuries suffered by product users.

LO 3   **11.4**   **Systematic versus Unsystematic Risk**   Indicate whether the following events might cause stocks in general to change price, and whether they might cause Big Widget Corp.'s stock to change price.

    a. The government announces that inflation unexpectedly jumped by 2 percent last month.

    b. Big Widget's quarterly earnings report, just issued, generally fell in line with analysts' expectations.

    c. The government reports that economic growth last year was 3 percent, which generally agreed with most economists' forecasts.

    d. The directors of Big Widget die in a plane crash.

    e. Congress approves changes to the tax code that will increase the top marginal corporate tax rate. The legislation had been debated for the previous six months.

LO 1   **11.5**   **Expected Portfolio Returns**   If a portfolio has a positive investment in every asset, can the expected return on the portfolio be greater than that on every asset in the portfolio? Can it be less than that on every asset in the portfolio? If you answer yes to one or both of these questions, give an example to support your answer.

LO 2   **11.6**   **Diversification**   True or false: The most important characteristic in determining the expected return of a well-diversified portfolio is the variances of the individual assets in the portfolio. Explain.

LO 3   **11.7**   **Portfolio Risk**   If a portfolio has a positive investment in every asset, can the standard deviation on the portfolio be less than that on every asset in the portfolio? What about the portfolio beta?

LO 4   **11.8**   **Beta and CAPM**   Is it possible that a risky asset could have a beta of zero? Explain. Based on the CAPM, what is the expected return on such an asset? Is it possible that a risky asset could have a negative beta? What does the CAPM predict about the expected return on such an asset? Can you give an explanation for your answer?

LO 2   **11.9**   **Corporate Downsizing**   In recent years, it has been common for companies to experience significant stock price changes in reaction to announcements of massive layoffs. Critics charge that such events encourage companies to fire longtime employees and that Wall Street is cheering them on. Do you agree or disagree?

LO 1   **11.10 Earnings and Stock Returns**   As indicated by a number of examples in this chapter, earnings announcements by companies are closely followed by, and frequently result in, share price revisions. Two issues should come to mind. First: Earnings announcements concern past periods. If the market values stocks based on expectations of the future, why are numbers summarizing past performance relevant? Second: These announcements concern accounting earnings. Going back to Chapter 2, such earnings may have little to do with cash flow, so again, why are they relevant?

QUESTIONS AND PROBLEMS

connect   Select problems are available in McGraw-Hill *Connect*. Please see the packaging options section of the Preface for more information.

BASIC (Questions 1–24)

LO 1   **1. Determining Portfolio Weights**   What are the portfolio weights for a portfolio that has 185 shares of Stock A that sell for $64 per share and 115 shares of Stock B that sell for $49 per share?

LO 1   **2. Portfolio Expected Return**   You own a portfolio that has $3,140 invested in Stock A and $4,300 invested in Stock B. If the expected returns on these stocks are 9 percent and 14 percent, respectively, what is the expected return on the portfolio?

LO 1   **3. Portfolio Expected Return**   You own a portfolio that is 25 percent invested in Stock X, 35 percent in Stock Y, and 40 percent in Stock Z. The expected returns on these three stocks are 10 percent, 13 percent, and 15 percent, respectively. What is the expected return on the portfolio?

LO 1   **4. Portfolio Expected Return**   You have $10,000 to invest in a stock portfolio. Your choices are Stock X with an expected return of 12.5 percent and Stock Y with an expected return of 9.5 percent. If your goal is to create a portfolio with an expected return of 11.2 percent, how much money will you invest in Stock X? In Stock Y?

LO 1   **5. Calculating Expected Return**   Based on the following information, calculate the expected return.

State of Economy	Probability of State of Economy	Rate of Return if State Occurs
Recession	.30	−.13
Boom	.70	.21

LO 1   **6. Calculating Expected Return**   Based on the following information, calculate the expected return.

State of Economy	Probability of State of Economy	Rate of Return if State Occurs
Recession	.15	−.12
Normal	.60	.10
Boom	.25	.27

LO 1

7. **Calculating Returns and Standard Deviations**   Based on the following information, calculate the expected returns and standard deviations for the two stocks.

State of Economy	Probability of State of Economy	Rate of Return if State Occurs	
		Stock A	Stock B
Recession	.10	.02	−.30
Normal	.50	.10	.18
Boom	.40	.15	.31

LO 1

8. **Calculating Expected Returns**   A portfolio is invested 20 percent in Stock G, 35 percent in Stock J, and 45 percent in Stock K. The expected returns on these stocks are 9.6 percent, 10.9 percent, and 14.3 percent, respectively. What is the portfolio's expected return? How do you interpret your answer?

LO 1
LO 2

9. **Returns and Standard Deviations**   Consider the following information:

State of Economy	Probability of State of Economy	Rate of Return if State Occurs		
		Stock A	Stock B	Stock C
Boom	.60	.18	.04	.31
Bust	.40	.03	.16	−.11

a.   What is the expected return on an equally weighted portfolio of these three stocks?

b.   What is the variance of a portfolio invested 20 percent each in A and B and 60 percent in C?

LO 1
LO 2

10. **Returns and Standard Deviations**   Consider the following information:

State of Economy	Probability of State of Economy	Rate of Return if State Occurs		
		Stock A	Stock B	Stock C
Boom	.15	.33	.45	.33
Good	.55	.11	.10	.17
Poor	.20	.02	.02	−.05
Bust	.10	−.12	−.25	−.09

a.   Your portfolio is invested 25 percent each in A and C and 50 percent in B. What is the expected return of the portfolio?

b.   What is the variance of this portfolio? The standard deviation?

LO 3

11. **Calculating Portfolio Betas**   You own a stock portfolio invested 15 percent in Stock Q, 25 percent in Stock R, 40 percent in Stock S, and 20 percent in Stock T. The betas for these four stocks are .78, .87, 1.13, and 1.45, respectively. What is the portfolio beta?

LO 3

12. **Calculating Portfolio Betas**   You own a portfolio equally invested in a risk-free asset and two stocks. If one of the stocks has a beta of 1.29 and the total portfolio is equally as risky as the market, what must the beta be for the other stock in your portfolio?

LO 4

13. **Using CAPM**   A stock has a beta of 1.14, the expected return on the market is 10.9 percent, and the risk-free rate is 3.6 percent. What must the expected return on this stock be?

LO 4   **14. Using CAPM**   A stock has an expected return of 11.4 percent, the risk-free rate is 3.7 percent, and the market risk premium is 6.8 percent. What must the beta of this stock be?

LO 4   **15. Using CAPM**   A stock has an expected return of 10.9 percent, its beta is .90, and the risk-free rate is 2.8 percent. What must the expected return on the market be?

LO 4   **16. Using CAPM**   A stock has an expected return of 10.2 percent and a beta of .91, and the expected return on the market is 10.8 percent. What must the risk-free rate be?

LO 4   **17. Using CAPM**   A stock has a beta of 1.15 and an expected return of 11.4 percent. A risk-free asset currently earns 3.5 percent.

   a.   What is the expected return on a portfolio that is equally invested in the two assets?

   b.   If a portfolio of the two assets has a beta of .7, what are the portfolio weights?

   c.   If a portfolio of the two assets has an expected return of 9 percent, what is its beta?

   d.   If a portfolio of the two assets has a beta of 2.30, what are the portfolio weights? How do you interpret the weights for the two assets in this case? Explain.

LO 4   **18. Using the SML**   Asset W has an expected return of 11.6 percent and a beta of 1.23. If the risk-free rate is 3.15 percent, complete the following table for portfolios of Asset W and a risk-free asset. Illustrate the relationship between portfolio expected return and portfolio beta by plotting the expected returns against the betas. What is the slope of the line that results?

Percentage of Portfolio in Asset W	Portfolio Expected Return	Portfolio Beta
0%		
25		
50		
75		
100		
125		
150		

LO 4   **19. Reward-to-Risk Ratios**   Stock Y has a beta of 1.20 and an expected return of 11.4 percent. Stock Z has a beta of .80 and an expected return of 8 percent. If the risk-free rate is 2.5 percent and the market risk premium is 7 percent, are these stocks correctly priced?

LO 4   **20. Reward-to-Risk Ratios**   In the previous problem, what would the risk-free rate have to be for the two stocks to be correctly priced relative to each other?

LO 1   **21. Portfolio Returns**   Using information from Table 10.2 on capital market history, determine the return on a portfolio that was equally invested in large-company stocks and long-term corporate bonds. What was the return on a portfolio that was equally invested in small stocks and Treasury bills?

LO 1   **22. Portfolio Expected Return**   You have $250,000 to invest in a stock portfolio. Your choices are Stock H, with an expected return of 13.4 percent, and Stock L, with an expected return of 10.2 percent. If your goal is to create a portfolio with an expected return of 11.3 percent, how much money will you invest in Stock H? In Stock L?

LO 1 **23. Calculating Portfolio Weights**   Stock J has a beta of 1.23 and an expected return of 13.25 percent, while Stock K has a beta of .84 and an expected return of 10.60 percent. You want a portfolio with the same risk as the market. How much will you invest in each stock? What is the expected return of your portfolio?

LO 1 **24. Calculating Portfolio Weights and Expected Return**   You have a portfolio with the following:

Stock	Number of Shares	Price	Expected Return
W	525	$43	10%
X	780	29	15
Y	435	94	11
Z	680	51	14

What is the expected return of your portfolio?

INTERMEDIATE (Questions 25–27)

LO 1 **25. Portfolio Returns and Deviations**   Consider the following information on a
LO 2 portfolio of three stocks:

State of Economy	Probability of State of Economy	Stock A Rate of Return	Stock B Rate of Return	Stock C Rate of Return
Boom	.15	.04	.33	.55
Normal	.60	.09	.13	.19
Bust	.25	.15	−.14	−.28

a. If your portfolio is invested 40 percent each in A and B and 20 percent in C, what is the portfolio's expected return? The variance? The standard deviation?

b. If the expected T-bill rate is 3.75 percent, what is the expected risk premium on the portfolio?

LO 4 **26. CAPM**   Using the CAPM, show that the ratio of the risk premiums on two assets is equal to the ratio of their betas.

LO 2 **27. Analyzing a Portfolio**   You want to create a portfolio equally as risky as the market, and you have $500,000 to invest. Given this information, fill in the rest of the following table:

Asset	Investment	Beta
Stock A	$85,000	.80
Stock B	165,000	1.15
Stock C		1.40
Risk-free asset		

CHALLENGE (Questions 28–30)

LO 1 **28. Analyzing a Portfolio**   You have $100,000 to invest in either Stock D, Stock F, or a risk-free asset. You must invest all of your money. Your goal is to create a portfolio that has an expected return of 11.4 percent. If D has an expected return of 13.6 percent, F has an expected return of 9.7 percent, the risk-free rate is 3.8 percent, and you invest $50,000 in Stock D, how much will you invest in Stock F?

LO 4 **29. SML** Suppose you observe the following situation:

State of Economy	Probability of State	Return if State Occurs	
		Stock A	Stock B
Bust	.15	−.08	−.10
Normal	.60	.11	.09
Boom	.25	.30	.27

   a.   Calculate the expected return on each stock.

   b.   Assuming the capital asset pricing model holds and Stock A's beta is greater than Stock B's beta by .30, what is the expected market risk premium?

LO 3 **30. Systematic versus Unsystematic Risk**   Consider the following information on Stocks I and II:

State of Economy	Probability of State of Economy	Rate of Return if State Occurs	
		Stock I	Stock II
Recession	.25	.04	−.22
Normal	.60	.22	.15
Irrational exuberance	.15	.16	.45

The market risk premium is 7 percent, and the risk-free rate is 4 percent. Which stock has more systematic risk? Which one has more unsystematic risk? Which stock is "riskier"? Explain.

WHAT'S ON THE WEB?

11.1 Expected Return   You want to find the expected return for Honeywell using the CAPM. First, you need the market risk premium. Use the average large-company stock return in Table 10.3 to estimate the market risk premium. Next, go to money.cnn.com and find the current interest rate for three-month Treasury bills. Finally, go to finance.yahoo.com, enter the ticker symbol HON, and find the beta for Honeywell. What is the expected return for Honeywell using CAPM? What assumptions have you made to arrive at this number?

11.2 Portfolio Beta   You have decided to invest in an equally weighted portfolio consisting of American Express, Procter & Gamble, Home Depot, and DuPont and need to find the beta of your portfolio. Go to finance.yahoo.com and find the ticker symbols for each of these companies. Next, find the beta for each company. What is the beta for your portfolio?

11.3 Beta   Which stocks have the highest and lowest betas? Go to finance.yahoo.com and locate the Stock Screener. Enter 0 as the maximum value. How many stocks have a beta less than zero? Which stock has the lowest beta? Go back to the screener and enter 3 as the minimum value. How many stocks have a beta greater than 3? What about greater than 4? Which stock has the highest beta?

EXCEL *MASTER IT!* PROBLEM

Excel Master coverage online

The CAPM is one of the most thoroughly researched models in financial economics. When beta is estimated in practice, a variation of CAPM called the market model is often used. To derive the market model, we start with the CAPM:

$$E(R_i) = R_f + \beta[E(R_M) - R_f]$$

Because CAPM is an equation, we can subtract the risk-free rate from both sides, which gives us:

$$E(R_i) - R_f = \beta[E(R_M) - R_f]$$

This equation is deterministic, that is, exact. In a regression, we realize that there is some indeterminate error. We need to formally recognize this in the equation by adding epsilon, which represents this error:

$$E(R_i) - R_f = \beta[E(R_M) - R_f] + \varepsilon$$

Finally, think of the above equation in a regression. Because there is no intercept in the equation, the intercept is zero. However, when we estimate the regression equation, we can add an intercept term, which we will call alpha:

$$E(R_i) - R_f = \alpha_i + \beta[E(R_M) - R_f] + \varepsilon$$

This equation is often called the "market" model, though it is not the only equation with that name, which is a source of confusion. The intercept term is known as Jensen's alpha, and it represents the "excess" return. If CAPM holds exactly, this intercept should be zero. If you think of alpha in terms of the SML, if the alpha is positive, the stock plots above the SML, and if the alpha is negative, the stock plots below the SML.

a. You want to estimate the market model for an individual stock and a mutual fund. First, go to finance.yahoo.com and download the adjusted prices for the last 61 months for an individual stock, a mutual fund, and the S&P 500. Next, go to the Federal Reserve Bank of St. Louis website at www.stlouisfed.org. You should find the "FRED®" database there. Look for the "1-Month Treasury Constant Maturity Rate" and download these data. This series will be the proxy for the risk-free rate. When using this rate, you should be aware that this interest rate is the annualized interest rate. Because we are using monthly stock returns, you will need to adjust the 1-month T-bill rate. For the stock and mutual fund you select, estimate the beta and alpha using the market model. When you estimate the regression model, find the box that says "Residuals" and check this box when you do each regression. Because you are saving the residuals, you may want to save the regression output in a new worksheet.

    1. Are the alpha and beta for each regression statistically different from zero?

    2. How do you interpret the alpha and beta for the stock and the mutual fund?

    3. Which of the two regression estimates has the higher *R*-squared? Is this what you would have expected? Why?

b. In part (a), you asked Excel to return the residuals of the regression, which is the epsilon in the regression equation. If you remember back to basic statistics, the residuals are the distance from each observation to the regression line. In this context, the residuals are the part of the monthly return that is not explained by the market model estimate. The residuals can be used to calculate the appraisal ratio, which is the alpha divided by the standard deviation of the residuals.

    1. What do you think the appraisal ratio is intended to measure?

    2. Calculate the appraisal ratios for the stock and the mutual fund. Which has a better appraisal ratio?

    3. Often, the appraisal ratio is used to evaluate the performance of mutual fund managers. Why do you think the appraisal ratio is used more often for mutual funds, which are portfolios, than for individual stocks?

CHAPTER CASE
The Beta for FLIR Systems

Joey Moss, a recent finance graduate, has just begun his job with the investment firm of Covili and Wyatt. Paul Covili, one of the firm's founders, has been talking to Joey about the firm's investment portfolio.

As with any investment, Paul is concerned about the risk of the investment as well as the potential return. More specifically, because the company holds a diversified portfolio, Paul is concerned about the systematic risk of current and potential investments. One position the company currently holds is stock in FLIR Systems, Inc. (FLIR). FLIR Systems designs, manufactures, and markets thermal imaging and infrared camera systems. Although better known for its military applications, the company has divisions that design products for other applications

such as automotive night vision, commercial products that require minute temperature difference measurements, recreational marine usage, and firefighting.

Covili and Wyatt currently uses a commercial data vendor for information about its positions. Because of this, Paul is unsure exactly how the numbers provided are calculated. The data provider considers its methods proprietary, and it will not disclose how stock betas and other information are calculated. Paul is uncomfortable with not knowing exactly how these numbers are being computed and also believes that it could be less expensive to calculate the necessary statistics in-house. To explore this question, Paul has asked Joey to do the following assignments:

QUESTIONS

1. Go to finance.yahoo.com and download the ending monthly stock prices for FLIR Systems (FLIR) for the last 60 months. Be sure to use the adjusted closing price to account for any stock splits and dividend payments. Next, download the ending value of the S&P 500 index over the same period. For the historical risk-free rate, go to the Federal Reserve Bank of St. Louis website (www.stlouisfed.org) and find the three-month Treasury bill constant maturity rate. Download this file. What are the monthly returns, average monthly returns, and standard deviations for FLIR Systems stock, the three-month Treasury bill, and the S&P 500 for this period?

2. Beta is often estimated by linear regression. A model often used is called the *market model*, which is:

$$R_t - R_{ft} = \alpha_i + \beta_i [R_{Mt} - R_{ft}] + \varepsilon_t$$

In this regression, R_t is the return on the stock and R_{ft} is the risk-free rate for the same period.

R_{Mt} is the return on a stock market index such as the S&P 500 index. α_i is the regression intercept, and β_i is the slope (and the stock's estimated beta). ε_t represents the residuals for the regression. What do you think is the motivation for this particular regression? The intercept, α_i, is often called *Jensen's alpha*. What does it measure? If an asset has a positive Jensen's alpha, where would it plot with respect to the SML? What is the financial interpretation of the residuals in the regression?

3. Use the market model to estimate the beta for FLIR Systems using the last 60 months of returns (the regression procedure in Excel is one easy way to do this). Plot the monthly returns on FLIR Systems against the index and also show the fitted line.

4. Compare your beta for FLIR Systems to the beta you find on finance.yahoo.com. How similar are they? Why might they be different?

12 | Cost of Capital

With more than 115,000 employees on five continents, Germany-based BASF is a major international company. BASF operates in a variety of industries, including agriculture, oil and gas, chemicals, and plastics. In an attempt to increase value, BASF launched Vision 2020, a comprehensive plan that included all functions within the company and challenged and encouraged all employees to act in an entrepreneurial manner. The major financial component of the strategy was that the company expected to earn its weighted average cost of capital, or WACC, plus a premium. So, what exactly is the WACC?

The WACC is the minimum return a company needs to earn to satisfy all of its investors, including stockholders, bondholders, and preferred stockholders. In 2017, for example, BASF pegged its cost of capital at 10 percent, the same WACC that it used during 2016, but down slightly from the 11 percent used from 2011 to 2015. In this chapter, we learn how to compute a firm's cost of capital and find out what it means to the firm and its investors. We also will learn when to use the firm's cost of capital and, perhaps more important, when not to use it.

From our chapters on capital budgeting, we know that the discount rate, or required return, on an investment is a critical input. Thus far, however, we haven't discussed how to come up with that particular number, so it's time now to do so. This chapter brings together many of our earlier discussions dealing with stocks and bonds, capital budgeting, and risk and return. Our goal is to illustrate how firms go about determining the required return on a proposed investment. Understanding required returns is important to everyone because all proposed projects, whether they relate to marketing, management, accounting, or any other area, must offer returns in excess of their required returns to be acceptable.

LEARNING OBJECTIVES

After studying this chapter, you should be able to:

LO 1 Determine a firm's cost of equity capital.

LO 2 Determine a firm's cost of debt.

LO 3 Determine a firm's overall cost of capital.

LO 4 Identify some of the pitfalls associated with a firm's overall cost of capital and what to do about them.

Please visit us at essentialsofcorporatefinance.blogspot.com for the latest developments in the world of corporate finance.

Suppose you have just become the president of a large company and the first decision you face is whether to go ahead with a plan to renovate the company's warehouse distribution system. The plan will cost the company $50 million, and it is expected to save $12 million per year after taxes over the next six years.

This is a familiar problem in capital budgeting. To address it, you would determine the relevant cash flows, discount them, and, if the net present value is positive, take on the project; if the NPV is negative, you would scrap it. So far, so good; but what should you use as the discount rate?

From our discussion of risk and return, you know that the correct discount rate depends on the riskiness of the warehouse distribution system. In particular, the new project will have a positive NPV only if its return exceeds what the financial markets offer on investments of similar risk. We called this minimum required return the *cost of capital* associated with the project.[1]

Thus, to make the right decision as president, you must examine what the capital markets have to offer and use this information to arrive at an estimate of the project's cost of capital. Our primary purpose in this chapter is to describe how to go about doing this. There are a variety of approaches to this task, and a number of conceptual and practical issues arise.

One of the most important concepts we develop is that of the *weighted average cost of capital* (WACC). This is the cost of capital for the firm as a whole, and it can be interpreted as the required return on the overall firm. In discussing the WACC, we will recognize the fact that a firm will normally raise capital in a variety of forms and that these different forms of capital may have different costs associated with them.

We also recognize in this chapter that taxes are an important consideration in determining the required return on an investment because we are always interested in valuing the aftertax cash flows from a project. Therefore, we will discuss how to incorporate taxes explicitly into our estimates of the cost of capital.

12.1 THE COST OF CAPITAL: SOME PRELIMINARIES

In Chapter 11, we developed the security market line, or SML, and used it to explore the relationship between the expected return on a security and its systematic risk. We concentrated on how the risky returns from buying securities looked from the viewpoint of, for example, a shareholder in the firm. This helped us understand more about the alternatives available to an investor in the capital markets.

In this chapter, we turn things around a bit and look more closely at the other side of the problem, which is how these returns and securities look from the viewpoint of the companies that issue the securities. The important fact to note is that the return an investor in a security receives is the cost of that security to the company that issued it.

Required Return versus Cost of Capital

When we say that the required return on an investment is, say, 10 percent, we usually mean that the investment will have a positive NPV only if its return exceeds 10 percent. Another

---

[1]The terms *cost of money* and *hurdle rate* also are used.

way of interpreting the required return is to observe that the firm must earn 10 percent on the investment to compensate its investors for the use of the capital needed to finance the project. This is why we also could say that 10 percent is the cost of capital associated with the investment.

To illustrate the point further, imagine we are evaluating a risk-free project. In this case, how to determine the required return is obvious: We look at the capital markets and observe the current rate offered by risk-free investments, and we use this rate to discount the project's cash flows. Thus, the cost of capital for a risk-free investment is the risk-free rate.

If this project is risky, then, assuming that all the other information is unchanged, the required return is obviously higher. In other words, the cost of capital for this project, if it is risky, is greater than the risk-free rate, and the appropriate discount rate would exceed the risk-free rate.

We will henceforth use the terms *required return*, *appropriate discount rate*, and *cost of capital* more or less interchangeably because, as the discussion in this section suggests, they all mean essentially the same thing. The key fact to grasp is that the cost of capital associated with an investment depends on the risk of that investment. In other words, it's the use of the money, not the source, that matters. This is one of the most important lessons in corporate finance, so it bears repeating:

> **The cost of capital depends primarily on the use of the funds, not the source.**

It is a common error to forget this crucial point and fall into the trap of thinking that the cost of capital for an investment depends primarily on how and where the capital is raised.

Financial Policy and Cost of Capital

We know that the particular mixture of debt and equity a firm chooses to employ—its capital structure—is a managerial variable. In this chapter, we will take the firm's financial policy as given. In particular, we will assume that the firm has a fixed debt-equity ratio that it maintains. This ratio reflects the firm's *target* capital structure. How a firm might choose that ratio is the subject of a later chapter.

From our discussion above, we know that a firm's overall cost of capital will reflect the required return on the firm's assets as a whole. Given that a firm uses both debt and equity capital, this overall cost of capital will be a mixture of the returns needed to compensate its creditors and its stockholders. In other words, a firm's cost of capital will reflect both its cost of debt capital and its cost of equity capital. We discuss these costs separately in the sections that follow.

CONCEPT QUESTIONS

12.1a   What is the primary determinant of the cost of capital for an investment?

12.1b   What is the relationship between the required return on an investment and the cost of capital associated with that investment?

12.2 THE COST OF EQUITY

cost of equity
The return that equity investors require on their investment in the firm.

Excel Master
coverage online

We begin with the most difficult question on the subject of cost of capital: What is the firm's overall **cost of equity**? The reason this is a difficult question is that there is no way of directly observing the return that the firm's equity investors require on their investment. Instead, we must somehow estimate it. This section discusses two approaches to determining the cost of equity: the dividend growth model approach and the security market line, or SML, approach.

The Dividend Growth Model Approach

The easiest way to estimate the cost of equity capital is to use the dividend growth model we developed in Chapter 7. Recall that, under the assumption that the firm's dividend will grow at a constant rate, g, the price per share of the stock, P_0, can be written as:

$$P_0 = \frac{D_0 \times (1 + g)}{R_E - g} = \frac{D_1}{R_E - g}$$

where D_0 is the dividend just paid and D_1 is the next period's projected dividend. Notice that we have used the symbol R_E (the E stands for *equity*) for the required return on the stock.

As we discussed in Chapter 7, we can rearrange this to solve for R_E as follows:

$$R_E = D_1/P_0 + g \qquad\qquad [12.1]$$

Because R_E is the return that the shareholders require on the stock, it can be interpreted as the firm's cost of equity capital.

Implementing the Approach   To estimate R_E using the dividend growth model approach, we obviously need three pieces of information: P_0, D_0, and g. Of these, for a publicly traded, dividend-paying company, the first two can be observed directly, so they are easily obtained.[2] Only the third component, the expected growth rate in dividends, must be estimated.

To illustrate how we estimate R_E, suppose Greater States Public Service, a large public utility, paid a dividend of $4 per share last year. The stock currently sells for $60 per share. You estimate that the dividend will grow steadily at 6 percent per year into the indefinite future. What is the cost of equity capital for Greater States?

Using the dividend growth model, we calculate that the expected dividend for the coming year, D_1, is:

$$\begin{aligned}
D_1 &= D_0 \times (1 + g) \\
&= \$4 \times 1.06 \\
&= \$4.24
\end{aligned}$$

Given this, the cost of equity, R_E, is:

$$\begin{aligned}
R_E &= D_1/P_0 + g \\
&= \$4.24/\$60 + .06 \\
&= .1307, \text{ or } 13.07\%
\end{aligned}$$

The cost of equity is thus 13.07 percent.

Estimating g   To use the dividend growth model, we must come up with an estimate for g, the growth rate. There are essentially two ways of doing this: (1) use historical growth

---

[2] Notice that if we have D_0 and g, we can calculate D_1 by multiplying D_0 by $(1 + g)$.

rates or (2) use analysts' forecasts of future growth rates. Analysts' forecasts are available from a variety of sources. Naturally, different sources will have different estimates, so one approach might be to obtain multiple estimates and then average them.

Alternatively, we might observe dividends for the previous, say, five years; calculate the year-to-year growth rates; and average them. Suppose we observe the following for some company:

Year	Dividend
2015	$1.10
2016	1.20
2017	1.35
2018	1.40
2019	1.55

We can calculate the percentage change in the dividend for each year as follows:

Year	Dividend	Dollar Change	Percentage Change
2015	$1.10	—	—
2016	1.20	$.10	9.09%
2017	1.35	.15	12.50
2018	1.40	.05	3.70
2019	1.55	.15	10.71

Aggregate growth estimates can be found at www.zacks.com /earnings.

Notice that we calculated the change in the dividend on a year-to-year basis and then expressed the change as a percentage. Thus, in 2016, for example, the dividend rose from $1.10 to $1.20, for an increase of $.10. This represents a $.10/$1.10 = .0909, or 9.09% increase.

If we average the four growth rates, the result is $(9.09 + 12.50 + 3.70 + 10.71)/4 = .09$, or 9%, so we could use this as an estimate for the expected growth rate, g. Notice that this 9 percent growth rate we have calculated is a simple, or arithmetic, average. Going back to Chapter 10, we also could calculate a geometric growth rate. Here, the dividend grows from $1.10 to $1.55 over a four-year period. What's the compound, or geometric, growth rate? See if you don't agree that it's 8.95 percent; you can view this as a time value of money problem where $1.10 is the present value and $1.55 is the future value.

As usual, the geometric average (8.95 percent) is lower than the arithmetic average (9.00 percent), but the difference here is not likely to be of any practical significance. In general, if the dividend has grown at a relatively steady rate, as we assume when we use this approach, then it can't make much difference which way we calculate the average dividend growth rate.

Advantages and Disadvantages of the Approach

The primary advantage of the dividend growth model approach is its simplicity. It is both easy to understand and easy to use. However, there are a number of associated practical problems and disadvantages.

First and foremost, the dividend growth model is obviously only applicable to companies that pay dividends. This means that the approach is useless in many cases. Furthermore, even for companies that do pay dividends, the key underlying assumption is that the dividend grows at a constant rate. As our example above illustrates, this will never be *exactly* the case. More generally, the model is really only applicable to cases in which reasonably steady growth is likely to occur.

A second problem is that the estimated cost of equity is very sensitive to the estimated growth rate. For a given stock price, an upward revision of g by just one percentage point, for example, increases the estimated cost of equity by at least a full percentage point. Because D_1 will probably be revised upward as well, the increase will actually be somewhat larger than that.

Finally, this approach really does not explicitly consider risk. Unlike the SML approach (which we consider next), this one has no direct adjustment for the riskiness of the investment. For example, there is no allowance for the degree of certainty or uncertainty surrounding the estimated growth rate in dividends. As a result, it is difficult to say whether or not the estimated return is commensurate with the level of risk.[3]

The SML Approach

In Chapter 11, we discussed the security market line, or SML. Our primary conclusion was that the required or expected return on a risky investment depends on three things:

1. The risk-free rate, R_f
2. The market risk premium, $E(R_M) - R_f$
3. The systematic risk of the asset relative to that in an average risky asset, which we called its beta coefficient, β

Using the SML, we can write the expected return on the company's equity, $E(R_E)$, as:

$$E(R_E) = R_f + \beta_E \times [E(R_M) - R_f]$$

where β_E is the estimated beta for the equity. To make the SML approach consistent with the dividend growth model, we will drop the Es denoting expectations and henceforth write the required return from the SML, R_E, as:

$$R_E = R_f + \beta_E \times (R_M - R_f) \tag{12.2}$$

Implementing the Approach   To use the SML approach, we need a risk-free rate, R_f; an estimate of the market risk premium, $R_M - R_f$; and an estimate of the relevant beta, β_E. In Chapter 10, we saw that one estimate of the market risk premium is about 7 percent. U.S. Treasury bills are paying about 1.90 percent as this is being written, so we will use this as our risk-free rate. Beta coefficients for publicly traded companies are widely available.[4]

To illustrate, in Chapter 11, we saw that Apple had an estimated beta of 1.15 (Table 11.8). We could thus estimate Apple's cost of equity as:

$$R_{Apple} = R_f + \beta_{Apple} \times (R_M - R_f)$$
$$= 1.90\% + 1.15 \times 7\%$$
$$= 9.95\%$$

Thus, using the SML approach, Apple's cost of equity is about 10 percent.

Both betas and T-bill rates can be found at www.bloomberg.com.

---

[3]There is an implicit adjustment for risk because the current stock price is used. All other things being equal, the higher the risk, the lower is the stock price. Further, the lower the stock price, the greater is the cost of equity, again assuming that all the other information is the same.

[4]Beta coefficients can be estimated directly by using historical data. For a discussion of how to do this, see Chapters 10, 11, and 12 in S. A. Ross, R. W. Westerfield, J. F. Jaffe, and B. D. Jordan, *Corporate Finance*, 12th ed. (Chicago, IL: McGraw-Hill Education, 2019).

Advantages and Disadvantages of the Approach   The SML approach has two primary advantages. First: It explicitly adjusts for risk. Second: It is applicable to companies other than those with steady dividend growth. Thus, it may be useful in a wider variety of circumstances.

There are drawbacks, of course. The SML approach requires that two things be estimated: the market risk premium and the beta coefficient. To the extent that our estimates are poor, the resulting cost of equity will be inaccurate. For example, our estimate of the market risk premium, 7 percent, is based on about 100 years of returns on a particular portfolio of stocks. Using different time periods or different stocks could result in very different estimates.

Finally, as with the dividend growth model, we essentially rely on the past to predict the future when we use the SML approach. Economic conditions can change very quickly, so, as always, the past may not be a good guide to the future. In the best of all worlds, both approaches (dividend growth model and SML) are applicable and result in similar answers. If this happens, we might have some confidence in our estimates. We also might wish to compare the results to those for other, similar companies as a reality check.

EXAMPLE 12.1   **The Cost of Equity**

Suppose stock in Alpha Air Freight has a beta of 1.2. The market risk premium is 8 percent, and the risk-free rate is 6 percent. Alpha's last dividend was $2 per share, and the dividend is expected to grow at 8 percent indefinitely. The stock currently sells for $30. What is Alpha's cost of equity capital?

We can start off by using the SML. Doing this, we find that the expected return on the common stock of Alpha Air Freight is:

$$R_E = R_f + \beta_E \times (R_M - R_f)$$
$$= 6\% + 1.2 \times 8\%$$
$$= 15.6\%$$

This suggests that 15.6 percent is Alpha's cost of equity. We next use the dividend growth model. The projected dividend is $D_0 \times (1 + g) = \$2 \times 1.08 = \$2.16$, so the expected return using this approach is:

$$R_E = D_1/P_0 + g$$
$$= \$2.16/\$30 + .08$$
$$= 15.2\%$$

Our two estimates are reasonably close, so we might average them to find that Alpha's cost of equity is approximately 15.4 percent.

CONCEPT QUESTIONS

12.2a What do we mean when we say that a corporation's cost of equity capital is 16 percent?

12.2b What are two approaches to estimating the cost of equity capital?

12.3 THE COSTS OF DEBT AND PREFERRED STOCK

In addition to ordinary equity, firms use debt and, to a lesser extent, preferred stock to finance their investments. As we discuss next, determining the costs of capital associated with these sources of financing is much easier than determining the cost of equity.

Excel Master
coverage online

The Cost of Debt

cost of debt
The return that lenders require on the firm's debt.

The **cost of debt** is the return that the firm's creditors demand on new borrowing. In principle, we could determine the beta for the firm's debt and then use the SML to estimate the required return on debt just as we estimate the required return on equity. This isn't really necessary, however.

Unlike a firm's cost of equity, its cost of debt normally can be observed either directly or indirectly because the cost of debt is the interest rate the firm must pay on new borrowing, and we can observe interest rates in the financial markets. For example, if the firm already has bonds outstanding, then the yield to maturity on those bonds is the market-required rate on the firm's debt.

Alternatively, if we knew that the firm's bonds were rated, say, AA, then we could find out what the interest rate was on newly issued AA-rated bonds. Either way, there is no need to actually estimate a beta for the debt because we can directly observe the rate we want to know.

There is one thing to be careful about, though. The coupon rate on the firm's outstanding debt is irrelevant here. That tells us roughly what the firm's cost of debt was back when the bonds were issued, not what the cost of debt is today.[5] This is why we have to look at the yield on the debt in today's marketplace. For consistency with our other notation, we will use the symbol R_D for the cost of debt.

EXAMPLE 12.2   **The Cost of Debt**

Suppose the General Tool Company issued a 30-year, 7 percent bond eight years ago. The bond is currently selling for 96 percent of its face value, or $960. What is General Tool's cost of debt?

Going back to Chapter 6, we need to calculate the yield to maturity on this bond. Because the bond is selling at a discount, the yield is apparently greater than 7 percent, but not much greater because the discount is fairly small. You can verify that the yield to maturity is about 7.37 percent, assuming semiannual coupons. General Tool's cost of debt, R_D, is thus 7.37 percent.

The Cost of Preferred Stock

Determining the *cost of preferred stock* is quite straightforward. As we discussed in Chapters 6 and 7, preferred stock has a fixed dividend paid every period forever, so a share of preferred stock is essentially a perpetuity. The cost of preferred stock, R_p, is thus:

$$R_P = D/P_0 \qquad \text{[12.3]}$$

where D is the fixed dividend and P_0 is the current price per share of the preferred stock. Notice that the cost of preferred stock is equal to the dividend yield on the preferred stock. Alternatively, preferred stocks are rated in much the same way as bonds, so the cost of preferred stock can be estimated by observing the required returns on other, similarly rated shares of preferred stock.

---

[5]The firm's cost of debt based on its historic borrowing is sometimes called the *embedded debt cost*.

EXAMPLE 12.3   **Alabama Power's Cost of Preferred Stock**

In 2018, Alabama Power had an issue of preferred stock that traded on the NYSE. The stock paid $1.25 annually per share and sold for $25.85 per share. What was Alabama Power's cost of preferred stock?

Using Equation 12.3, the cost of preferred stock was:

$$R_P = D/P_0$$
$$= \$1.25/\$25.85$$
$$= .0484, \text{ or } 4.84\%$$

So, Alabama Power's cost of preferred stock appears to have been just under 5 percent.

CONCEPT QUESTIONS

12.3a   How can the cost of debt be calculated?

12.3b   How can the cost of preferred stock be calculated?

12.3c   Why is the coupon rate a bad estimate of a firm's cost of debt?

12.4 THE WEIGHTED AVERAGE COST OF CAPITAL

Now that we have the costs associated with the main sources of capital the firm employs, we need to worry about the specific mix. As we mentioned above, we will take this mix, which is the firm's capital structure, as given for now. Also, we will focus mostly on debt and ordinary equity in this discussion.

Excel Master
coverage online

The Capital Structure Weights

We will use the symbol E (for *equity*) to stand for the *market* value of the firm's equity. We calculate this by taking the number of shares outstanding and multiplying it by the price per share. Similarly, we will use the symbol D (for *debt*) to stand for the *market* value of the firm's debt. For long-term debt, we calculate this by multiplying the market price of a single bond by the number of bonds outstanding.

If there are multiple bond issues (as there normally would be), we repeat this calculation for each and then add the results. If there is debt that is not publicly traded (because it is held by a life insurance company, for example), we must observe the yield on similar, publicly traded debt and then estimate the market value of the privately held debt using this yield as the discount rate. For short-term debt, the book (accounting) values and market values should be somewhat similar, so we might use the book values as estimates of the market values.

Finally, we will use the symbol V (for *value*) to stand for the combined market value of the debt and equity:

$$V = E + D \tag{12.4}$$

If we divide both sides by V, we can calculate the percentages of the total capital represented by the debt and equity:

$$100\% = E/V + D/V \tag{12.5}$$

These percentages can be interpreted like portfolio weights, and they often are called the *capital structure weights.*

For example, if the total market value of a company's stock was calculated as $200 million and the total market value of the company's debt was calculated as $50 million, then the combined value would be $250 million. Of this total, $E/V = \$200/\$250 = .80$, so 80 percent of the firm's financing would be equity and the remaining 20 percent would be debt.

We emphasize here that the correct way to proceed is to use the *market* values of the debt and equity. Under certain circumstances, such as when considering a privately owned company, it may not be possible to get reliable estimates of these quantities. In this case, we might go ahead and use the accounting values for debt and equity. While this would probably be better than nothing, we would have to take the answer with a grain of salt.

Taxes and the Weighted Average Cost of Capital

There is one final issue we need to discuss. Recall that we are always concerned with after-tax cash flows. If we are determining the discount rate appropriate to those cash flows, then the discount rate also needs to be expressed on an aftertax basis.

As we discussed previously in various places in this book (and as we will discuss later), the interest paid by a corporation is deductible for tax purposes. Payments to stockholders, such as dividends, are not. What this means, effectively, is that the government pays some of the interest. Thus, in determining an aftertax discount rate, we need to distinguish between the pretax and the aftertax cost of debt.

To illustrate, suppose a firm borrows $1 million at 9 percent interest. The corporate tax rate is 21 percent. What is the aftertax interest rate on this loan? The total interest bill will be $90,000 per year. This amount is tax deductible, however, so the $90,000 interest reduces our tax bill by $.21 \times \$90,000 = \$18,900$. The aftertax interest bill is thus $\$90,000 - 18,900 = \$71,100$. The aftertax interest rate is thus $\$71,100/\$1$ million $= .0711$, or 7.11%.

Notice that, in general, the aftertax interest rate is equal to the pretax rate multiplied by 1 minus the tax rate. Thus, if we use the symbol T_C to stand for the corporate tax rate, then the aftertax rate that we use for the cost of debt can be written as $R_D \times (1 - T_C)$. For example, using the numbers above, we find that the aftertax interest rate is $9\% \times (1 - .21) = 7.11\%$.

Collecting the various topics we have discussed in this chapter, we now have the capital structure weights along with the cost of equity and the aftertax cost of debt. To calculate the firm's overall cost of capital, we multiply the capital structure weights by the associated costs and add the pieces. The result is the **weighted average cost of capital**, or **WACC**.

weighted average cost of capital (WACC)

The WACC is the overall return the firm must earn on its existing assets to maintain the value of its stock.

$$\text{WACC} = (E/V) \times R_E + (D/V) \times R_D \times (1 - T_C) \qquad \text{[12.6]}$$

This WACC has a very straightforward interpretation. It is the overall return the firm must earn on its existing assets to maintain the value of its stock. This is an important point, so it bears repeating:

> **The WACC is the overall return the firm must earn on its existing assets to maintain the value of its stock.**

The WACC is also the required return on any investments by the firm that have essentially the same risks as existing operations. So, if we were evaluating the cash flows

EVA: An Old Idea Moves into the Modern Age

You might not think of Briggs and Stratton, Coca-Cola, and Microsoft as having much in common. However, all three have linked their fortunes to a way of managing and measuring corporate performance that depends critically on the cost of capital. It goes by many names, but consulting firm Stern Stewart & Co., a well-known advocate, calls its particular flavor "economic value added," or EVA. Stockholder value added (SVA) is a common variant. Whatever the name, EVA and its cousins have become an important tool for corporate management since the mid-1990s.

Briefly stated, EVA is a method of measuring financial performance. To compute EVA, you must calculate your overall cost of capital. Then, you identify how much capital is tied up in your business. Next, you multiply the amount of capital by the cost of capital. The result is the amount, in dollars, you should be providing to your investors. Subtract out your actual operating cash flow, and the difference is a measure of EVA. A positive value means that you earned more than your cost of capital, thereby creating value, and vice versa (this is a quick overview; for more detail, visit www.eva.com).

Each year, Stern Stewart & Co. prepares the Stern Stewart 1000, a ranking of the 1,000 largest U.S. companies based on their respective EVAs. Over the history of the Stern Stewart 1000, several companies have shown consistently strong performances. For example, Microsoft, Intel, and ExxonMobil often appear near the top of the list. The list also has perennial poor performers, and some of the names may surprise you, for example, General Motors, Time Warner, and Goodyear Tire & Rubber. Evidently, a well-known brand name does not always result in shareholder wealth.

One thing the Stern Stewart 1000 has done is to show the changing face of the economy. For instance, Intel, Cisco Systems, and eBay all have ranked rather well on the list. Consider that Intel is the oldest of these companies, having been publicly traded since 1971, while eBay has been publicly traded only since 1998. This highlights the dramatic impact of technology companies on the economy. Of course, not all technology-related companies have performed as well.

According to Bennett Stewart, one of the cofounders of Stern Stewart, EVA shows an important distinction between accounting income and economic profit. Accounting rules dictate that the interest expense a company incurs must be deducted from its reported profit, but those same rules forbid deducting a charge for the shareholders' funds used by a firm. In economic terms, equity capital is in fact a very costly financing source because shareholders bear the risk of being paid last, after all other stakeholders and investors are paid. But according to accountants, shareholder equity is essentially free. This oversight has dire practical consequences. For instance, it means that the profit figure accountants certify to be correct can conflict with the net present value decision rule. This conflict occurs when accounting rules lead to a focus on the accountant's bottom line rather than the more important question of whether a project's projected return exceeds its required return.

While EVA and its variants are sound in principle, they still have shortcomings. For one thing, they are typically computed using asset book values instead of market values. For another, they sometimes are based on accounting measures of income when cash flow would be a better choice. Nonetheless, potential problems aside, the concept of EVA focuses management attention on creating wealth for investors. That, in itself, makes EVA a worthwhile tool.

---

from a proposed expansion of our existing operations, this is the discount rate we would use.

If a firm uses preferred stock in its capital structure, then our expression for the WACC needs a simple extension. If we define P/V as the percentage of the firm's financing that comes from preferred stock, then the WACC is:

$$\text{WACC} = (E/V) \times R_E + (P/V) \times R_P + (D/V) \times R_D \times (1 - T_C) \qquad [12.7]$$

where R_p is the cost of preferred stock.

The WACC is increasingly being used by corporations to evaluate financial performance. The accompanying *Finance Matters* box provides some details on how this is being done.

EXAMPLE 12.4   **Calculating the WACC**

The B. B. Lean Co. has 1.4 million shares of stock outstanding. The stock currently sells for $20 per share. The firm's debt is publicly traded and was recently quoted at 93 percent of face value. It has a total face value of $5 million, and it is currently priced to yield 11 percent. The risk-free rate is 8 percent, and the market risk premium is 7 percent. You've estimated that Lean has a beta of .74. If the corporate tax rate is 21 percent, what is the WACC of Lean Co.?

We first can determine the cost of equity and the cost of debt. From the SML, the cost of equity is 8% + .74 × 7% = 13.18%. The total value of the equity is 1.4 million × $20 = $28 million. The pretax cost of debt is the current yield to maturity on the outstanding debt, 11 percent. The debt sells for 93 percent of its face value, so its current market value is .93 × $5 million = $4.65 million. The total market value of the equity and debt together is $28 + 4.65 = $32.65 million.

From here, we can calculate the WACC easily enough. The percentage of equity used by Lean to finance its operations is $28/$32.65 = .8576, or 85.76%. Because the weights have to add up to 1.0, the percentage of debt is 1.0 − .8576 = .1424, or 14.24%. The WACC is thus:

$$\text{WACC} = (E/V) \times R_E + (D/V) \times R_D \times (1 - T_C)$$
$$= .8576 \times 13.18\% + .1424 \times 11\% \times (1 - .21)$$
$$= 12.54\%$$

B. B. Lean thus has an overall weighted average cost of capital of 12.54 percent.

Solving the Warehouse Problem and Similar Capital Budgeting Problems

Now we can use the WACC to solve the warehouse problem we posed at the beginning of the chapter. However, before we rush to discount the cash flows at the WACC to estimate NPV, we need to first make sure we are doing the right thing.

Going back to first principles, we need to find an alternative in the financial markets that is comparable to the warehouse renovation. To be comparable, an alternative must be of the same risk as the warehouse project. Projects that have the same risk are said to be in the same risk class.

The WACC for a firm reflects the risk and the target capital structure of the firm's existing assets as a whole. As a result, strictly speaking, the firm's WACC is the appropriate discount rate only if the proposed investment is a replica of the firm's existing operating activities.

In broader terms, whether or not we can use the firm's WACC to value the warehouse project depends on whether the warehouse project is in the same risk class as the firm. We will assume that this project is an integral part of the overall business of the firm. In such cases, it is natural to think that the cost savings will be as risky as the general cash flows of the firm, and the project thus will be in the same risk class as the overall firm. More generally, projects like the warehouse renovation that are intimately related to the firm's existing operations often are viewed as being in the same risk class as the overall firm.

We now can see what the president should do. Suppose the firm has a target debt-equity ratio of $1/3$. From Chapter 3, we know that a debt-equity ratio of $D/E = 1/3$ implies that E/V is .75 and D/V is .25. Further suppose the cost of debt is 10 percent and the cost of equity is 20 percent. Assuming a 21 percent tax rate, the WACC will then be:

$$\textbf{WACC} = (E/V) \times R_E + (D/V) \times R_D \times (1 - T_C)$$
$$= .75 \times 20\% + .25 \times 10\% \times (1 - .21)$$
$$= 16.98\%$$

Recall that the warehouse project had a cost of $50 million and expected aftertax cash flows (the cost savings) of $12 million per year for six years. The NPV is thus:

$$\text{NPV} = -\$50 + \frac{12}{(1+\text{WACC})^1} + \cdots + \frac{12}{(1+\text{WACC})^6}$$

Because the cash flows are in the form of an ordinary annuity, we can calculate this NPV using 16.98 percent (the WACC) as the discount rate as follows:

$$\text{NPV} = -\$50 + 12 \times \frac{1 - \left[1/(1+.1698)^6\right]}{.1698}$$

$$= -\$50 + 12 \times 3.5915$$

$$= -\$6.90 \text{ million}$$

Should the firm take on the warehouse renovation? The project has a negative NPV using the firm's WACC. This means that the financial markets offer superior projects in the same risk class (namely, the firm itself). The answer is clear: The project should be rejected. For future reference, our discussion of the WACC is summarized in Table 12.1. Our upcoming *Finance Matters* box discusses a different use of the WACC.

You can find the WACC for many companies at www.thatswacc.com.

Calculating the WACC for Eastman Chemical

In this section, we illustrate how to calculate the WACC for Eastman Chemical, a well-known chemical, plastics, and fiber producer. Our goal is to take you through, on a step-by-step basis, the process of finding and using the information needed using online sources. As you will see, there is a fair amount of detail involved, but the necessary information is, for the most part, readily available.

TABLE 12.1

Summary of capital cost calculations

I.   **The cost of equity, R_E**

   A.   Dividend growth model approach (from Chapter 7):

   $$R_E = D_1/P_0 + g$$

   where D_1 is the expected dividend in one period, g is the dividend growth rate, and P_0 is the current stock price.

   B.   SML approach (from Chapter 11):

   $$R_E = R_f + \beta_E \times (R_M - R_f)$$

   where R_f is the risk-free rate, R_M is the expected return on the overall market, and β_E is the systematic risk of the equity.

II. **The cost of debt, R_D**

   A.   For a firm with publicly held debt, the cost of debt can be measured as the yield to maturity on the outstanding debt. The coupon rate is irrelevant. Yield to maturity is covered in Chapter 6.

   B.   If the firm has no publicly traded debt, then the cost of debt can be measured as the yield to maturity on similarly rated bonds (bond ratings are discussed in Chapter 6).

III. **The weighted average cost of capital, WACC**

   A.   The firm's WACC is the overall required return on the firm as a whole. It is the appropriate discount rate to use for cash flows similar in risk to the overall firm.

   B.   The WACC is calculated as:

   $$\text{WACC} = (E/V) \times R_E + (D/V) \times R_D \times (1 - T_C)$$

   where T_C is the corporate tax rate, E is the *market* value of the firm's equity, D is the *market* value of the firm's debt, and $V = E + D$. Note that E/V is the percentage of the firm's financing (in market value terms) that is equity and D/V is the percentage that is debt.

The Cost of Capital, Texas Style

We have seen how the WACC is used in the corporate world. It also is used by state governments to value property for tax purposes. Property valuation can be tricky. The value of a home depends on what it could be sold for, which is not too hard to estimate, but how do you value an oil or gas field? For the Texas Comptroller of Public Accounts, the answer is to estimate the present value of the future cash flows of the property. As you know by now, the cost of capital depends on the use of funds, not the source of funds. So, Texas calculates the WACC for companies in the oil industry and adjusts the industry average WACC for company-specific factors. The table below shows the state's calculations for integrated oil companies.

TABLE 1
Petroleum Companies' Financial Information Used for WACC Method

Company Name	Total Capital	Total Equity	Total Convertible Preferred Stock	Total Long-Term Debt	Equity % Of Capital	Convertible Preferred Stock % Of Capital	Long-Term Debt % Of Capital	Beta Factor	After Income Tax Cost of Equity, %	Before Income Tax Cost of Equity, %	Cost Of Convertible Preferred Stock %	Cost Of Debt %	Before Income Tax WACC %
Anadarko	$53,716,176,000	$38,435,176,000	$0	$15,281,000,000	71.55	0.000	28.45	1.55	12.12	18.65	0.00	4.78	14.68
Apache	$32,627,036,236	$24,083,036,236	$0	$8,544,000,000	73.81	0.000	26.19	1.45	11.52	17.73	0.00	4.22	14.19
Cabot	$12,386,434,280	$10,865,904,280	$0	$1,520,530,000	87.72	0.000	12.28	1.05	9.12	14.04	0.00	3.62	13.00
Chevron	$257,916,305,869	$222,630,305,869	$0	$35,286,000,000	86.32	0.000	13.68	1.15	9.72	14.96	0.00	3.01	13.32
Cimarex	$14,224,978,998	$12,737,039,998	$0	$1,487,939,000	89.54	0.000	10.46	1.50	11.82	18.19	0.00	4.37	16.74
Conoco Phillips	$88,222,684,507	$62,036,684,507	$0	$26,186,000,000	70.32	0.000	29.68	1.35	10.92	16.81	0.00	4.50	13.15
Devon	$34,039,410,000	$23,885,410,000	$0	$10,154,000,000	70.17	0.000	29.83	1.65	12.72	19.57	0.00	4.65	15.12
Encana	$15,621,000,000	$11,423,020,000	$0	$4,198,000,000	73.13	0.000	26.87	1.65	12.72	19.57	0.00	5.20	15.71
Energen	$6,122,187,439	$5,594,744,439	$0	$527,443,000	91.38	0.000	8.62	1.60	12.42	19.11	0.00	5.15	17.91
EOG	$65,284,160,829	$58,304,381,829	$0	$6,979,779,000	89.31	0.000	10.69	1.45	11.52	17.73	0.00	3.37	16.19
Exxon Mobil	$403,330,480,000	$374,398,480,000	$0	$28,932,000,000	92.83	0.000	7.17	0.95	8.52	13.11	0.00	3.27	12.41
Hess	$26,451,230,128	$19,716,230,128	$41,000,000	$6,694,000,000	74.54	0.002	25.31	1.60	12.42	19.11	7.13	5.62	15.68
Marathon	$71,250,570,000	$14,661,570,000	$0	$6,589,000,000	68.99	0.000	31.01	1.75	13.32	20.50	0.00	4.95	15.68
Murphy	$7,783,403,770	$5,360,653,770	$0	$2,422,750,000	68.87	0.000	31.13	1.55	12.12	18.65	0.00	5.34	14.51
Noble	$23,506,170,165	$16,495,170,165	$0	$7,011,000,000	70.17	0.000	29.83	1.40	11.22	17.27	0.00	4.48	13.45
Occidental	$64,255,622,737	$54,436,622,737	$0	$9,819,000,000	84.72	0.000	15.28	1.15	9.72	14.96	0.00	3.71	13.16
Pioneer	$33,290,219,227	$30,562,219,227	$0	$2,728,000,000	91.81	0.000	8.19	1.45	11.52	17.73	0.00	3.78	16.58
Range	$12,300,692,072	$8,491,880,072	$0	$3,808,812,000	69.04	0.000	30.96	1.15	9.72	14.96	0.00	5.56	12.85
TOTAL	$1,172,328,782,256	$994,118,529,256	$41,000,000	$178,169,253,000	1,424.22	0.002	375.62	25.40	208.22	312.65	7.13	80.92	263.55
ENTRIES					18	1	18	18	18	18	1	18	18
AVERAGE					79.12	0.002	20.87	1.41	11.29	17.37	7.13	4.50	14.64
STANDARD DEVIATION					8.57	0.000	8.57	0.23	1.38	2.13	1.68	0.87	1.66

As you can see, the 2017 WACC numbers for the companies are similar. Range has the lowest WACC at 12.05 percent and Energen has the highest at 17.91 percent, but most other companies are in the 14 to 16 percent range. The average WACC for a company in this industry is 14.64 percent, with a standard deviation of 1.66 percent. When Texas uses this calculation, a 2 percent adjustment factor is added, plus any property-specific risk adjustment.

Notice that the Texas Comptroller of Public Accounts calculated these numbers on a pretax, rather than aftertax, basis. In other words, the state did not account for the tax deductibility of interest payments in this calculation. The reason is that the state adjusts the cost of capital for taxes on a company-by-company basis.

Eastman's Cost of Equity   Our first stop is the stock price for Eastman, available at finance.yahoo.com (ticker: "EMN"). As of mid-2018, here's what the screen looked like:

Source: **finance.yahoo.com**

We next looked under the "Statistics" link. Here is what we found:

Trading Information		Balance Sheet	
Stock Price History		Total Cash (mrq)	194M
Beta	0.98	Total Cash Per Share (mrq)	1.36
52-Week Change [3]	19.02%	Total Debt (mrq)	6.9B
S&P500 52-Week Change [3]	12.09%	Total Debt/Equity (mrq)	122.78
52 Week High [3]	112.45	Current Ratio (mrq)	1.72
52 Week Low [3]	81.91	Book Value Per Share (mrq)	38.88
50-Day Moving Average [3]	105.67		
200-Day Moving Average [3]	102.56	**Dividends & Splits**	
Share Statistics		Forward Annual Dividend Rate [4]	2.24
Avg Vol (3 month) [3]	990.61k	Forward Annual Dividend Yield [4]	2.22%
Avg Vol (10 day) [3]	1.11M	Trailing Annual Dividend Rate [3]	2.14
Shares Outstanding [5]	142.76M	Trailing Annual Dividend Yield [3]	2.15%
Float	141.86M	5 Year Average Dividend Yield [4]	2.08
% Held by Insiders [1]	0.42%	Payout Ratio [4]	22.34%
% Held by Institutions [1]	88.02%	Dividend Date [3]	Jul 6, 2018
Shares Short [3]	4.31M	Ex-Dividend Date [4]	Jun 14, 2018
Short Ratio [3]	4.47	Last Split Factor (new per old) [2]	2/1
Short % of Float [3]	3.02%	Last Split Date [3]	Oct 4, 2011
Shares Short (prior month) [3]	3.36M		

According to this screen, Eastman has 142.76 million shares of stock outstanding. The book value per share is $38.88, but the stock sells for $98.53. Total equity is therefore about $5.551 billion on a book value basis, but it is closer to $14.066 billion on a market value basis.

To estimate Eastman's cost of equity, we will assume a market risk premium of 7 percent, similar to what we saw in Chapter 10. Eastman's beta on Yahoo! is .98, which is about the same as the beta of the average stock. To confirm this, we look at the beta reported in Value Line. The beta there was 1.20, while the beta reported at www.reuters.com was 1.37. Because we have three different betas for the stock, we decided to go with the Value Line beta of 1.20, which is about the average. According to the bond section of finance.yahoo.com, T-bills were paying about 1.98 percent. Using the CAPM to estimate the cost of equity, we find:

$$R_E = .0198 + 1.20(.07) = .1038, \text{ or } 10.38\%$$

Eastman only has paid dividends for a few years, so calculating the future growth rate for the dividend discount model is problematic. However, under the "Analysis" link at finance.yahoo.com, we found the following:

Growth Estimates	EMN	Industry	Sector	S&P 500
Current Qtr.	11.60%	N/A	N/A	0.42
Next Qtr.	5.50%	N/A	N/A	0.47
Current Year	12.50%	N/A	N/A	0.22
Next Year	9.00%	N/A	N/A	0.10
Next 5 Years (per annum)	10.47%	N/A	N/A	0.11
Past 5 Years (per annum)	3.30%	N/A	N/A	N/A

Analysts estimate the growth in earnings per share for the company will be 10.47 percent for the next five years. The link between earnings growth and dividends is discussed in a later chapter, but this would be a very high long-run growth rate for dividends. The dividend growth rate estimate reported by Value Line was a more plausible 6.5 percent, so we will use that instead. The estimated cost of equity using the dividend discount model is thus:

$$R_E = \left(\frac{\$2.24}{\$98.53}\right) + .065 = .0877, \text{ or } 8.77\%$$

Notice that the estimates for the cost of equity are similar in this case. In broader terms, remember that each method of estimating the cost of equity relies on different assumptions, so different estimates should not surprise us. If the estimates are different, there are two simple solutions. First, we could ignore one of the estimates. We would look at each estimate to see if one of them seemed too high or too low to be reasonable. Second, we could average the two estimates. Averaging the two estimates for Eastman's cost of equity gives us a cost of equity of 9.58 percent. Because this seems like a reasonable number, we will use it in calculating the cost of capital.

Eastman's Cost of Debt   Eastman has 11 long-term bond issues that account for essentially all of its long-term debt. To calculate the cost of debt, we will have to combine these 11 issues. What we will do is compute a weighted average. We went to finra-markets.morningstar.com/BondCenter/ to find quotes on the bonds. We should note here that finding the yield to maturity for all of a company's outstanding bond issues on a single day is unusual. If you remember our previous discussion on bonds, the bond market is not as liquid as the stock market, and, on many days, individual bond issues may not trade. To find the book value of the bonds, we went to www.sec.gov and found the 10-Q report dated March 31, 2018, and filed with the SEC on May 7, 2018. The basic information is as follows:

Coupon Rate	Maturity	Book Value (face value, in $ millions)	Price (% of par)	Yield to Maturity
5.50%	2019	$250	103.354%	2.974%
2.70	2020	798	99.373	3.124
4.50	2021	192	102.220	3.487
3.60	2022	753	99.691	3.681
1.25	2023	920	88.846	3.715
7.25	2024	197	117.005	3.850
7.625	2024	43	116.540	4.447
3.80	2025	689	98.998	3.971
7.60	2027	195	124.517	4.200
4.80	2042	493	99.498	4.835
4.65	2044	871	98.030	4.782
		$5,401		

To calculate the weighted average cost of debt, we take the percentage of the total debt represented by each issue and multiply by the yield on the issue. We then add to get the overall weighted average debt cost. We use both book values and market values here for comparison. The results of the calculations are as follows:

Coupon Rate	Book Value (in millions)	Percentage of Total	Market Value (in millions)	Percentage of Total	Yield to Maturity	Book Values	Market Values
5.50%	$250	.05	$258.39	.05	2.97%	.14%	.14%
2.70	798	.15	793.00	.15	3.12	.46	.46
4.50	192	.04	192.26	.04	3.49	.12	.13
3.60	753	.14	750.67	.14	3.68	.51	.51
1.25	920	.17	817.38	.15	3.72	.63	.57
7.25	197	.04	230.50	.04	3.85	.14	.17
7.625	43	.01	50.11	.01	4.45	.04	.04
3.80	689	.13	682.10	.13	3.97	.51	.50
7.60	195	.04	242.81	.05	4.20	.15	.19
4.80	493	.09	490.53	.09	4.84	.44	.44
4.65	871	.16	853.84	.16	4.78	.77	.76
	$5,401	1.00	$5,365.58	1.00		3.92%	3.92%

As these calculations show, Eastman's cost of debt is 3.92 percent on a book value basis and 3.92 percent on a market value basis. Thus, for Eastman, whether market values or book values are used makes no difference. The reason is that the market values and book values are similar. This often will be the case and explains why companies frequently use book values for debt in WACC calculations. Also, Eastman has no preferred stock, so we don't need to consider the cost of preferred.

W🌐RK THE WEB

So how does our estimate of the WACC for Eastman compare to others? One place to find estimates for WACC is www.valuepro.net. We went there and found the following information for Eastman.

Online Valuation for EMN – 7 / 3 / 2018

Intrinsic Stock Value | 125.8 | Recalculate | Value Another Stock |

Excess Return Period (yrs)	10	Depreciation Rate (% of Rev)	4.44
Revenues ($mil)	8588	Investment Rate (% of Rev)	5.8
Growth Rate (%)	11.5	Working Capital (% of Rev)	9.21
Net Oper. Profit Margin (%)	14.68	Short-Term Assets ($mil)	2737
Tax Rate (%)	32.583	Short-Term Liab. ($mil)	1335
Stock Price ($)	88.82	Equity Risk Premium (%)	3
Shares Outstanding (mil)	154.8	Company Beta	1.365
10-Yr Treasury Yield (%)	5	Value Debt Out. ($mil)	4779
Bond Spread Treasury (%)	1.5	Value Pref. Stock Out. ($mil)	0
Preferred Stock Yield (%)	7.5	Company WACC (%)	7.88

Source: **valuepro.net**

As you can see, ValuePro estimates the WACC for Eastman as 7.88 percent, which is almost identical to our estimate of 7.79 percent. The methods used by this site are not identical to ours, but they are similar in the most important regards. However, notice that several important estimates differ. For example, ValuePro uses a market risk premium of 3 percent, while our estimate was 7 percent. Using our estimate of the market risk premium in the ValuePro website results in a WACC estimate of 11.93 percent, which is higher than our estimate. Visit the site to learn more if you are so inclined.

Eastman's WACC   We now have the various pieces necessary to estimate Eastman's WACC. First, we need to calculate the capital structure weights. On a book value basis, Eastman's equity and debt are worth $5.551 billion and $5.401 billion, respectively. The total value is $10.952 billion, so the equity and debt percentages are $5.551 billion/$10.952 billion = .51 and $5.401 billion/$10.952 billion = .49, respectively. Assuming a tax rate of 21 percent, Eastman's WACC is:

$$\text{WACC} = .51 \times 9.58\% + .49 \times 3.92\% \times (1 - .21)$$
$$= 6.38\%$$

Thus, using book value capital structure weights, we get about 6.38 percent for Eastman's WACC.

If we use market value weights, however, the WACC will be higher. To see why, notice that on a market value basis, Eastman's equity and debt are worth $14.066 billion and $5.366 billion, respectively. The capital structure weights are therefore $14.066 billion/$19.432 billion = .72 for equity and $5.366 billion/$19.432 billion = .28 for debt, so the equity percentage is much higher. With these weights, Eastman's WACC is:

$$\text{WACC} = .72 \times 9.58\% + .28 \times 3.92\% \times (1 - .21)$$
$$= 7.79\%$$

Thus, using market value weights, we get 7.79 percent for Eastman's WACC, which is noticeably higher than the 6.38 percent WACC we got using book value weights.

As this example illustrates, using book values can lead to trouble, particularly if equity book values are used. Going back to Chapter 3, recall that we discussed the market-to-book ratio (the ratio of market value per share to book value per share). This ratio is often substantially bigger than 1. For Eastman, for example, verify that it's about 2.53, so book values significantly overstate the percentage of Eastman's financing that comes from debt. In addition, if we were computing a WACC for a company that did not have publicly traded stock, we would try to come up with a suitable market-to-book ratio by looking at publicly traded companies, and we would then use this ratio to adjust the book value of the company under consideration. As we have seen, failure to do so can lead to significant underestimation of the WACC. See our nearby *Work the Web* box for more on the WACC.

CONCEPT QUESTIONS

12.4a How is the WACC calculated?

12.4b Why do we multiply the cost of debt by $(1 - T_c)$ when we compute the WACC?

12.4c Under what conditions is it correct to use the WACC to determine NPV?

12.5 DIVISIONAL AND PROJECT COSTS OF CAPITAL

As we have seen, using the WACC as the discount rate for future cash flows is only appropriate when the proposed investment is similar to the firm's existing activities. This is not as restrictive as it sounds. If we were in the pizza business, for example, and we were thinking of opening a new location, then the WACC would be the discount rate to use. The same would be true of a retailer thinking of a new store, a manufacturer thinking of expanding production, or a consumer products company thinking of expanding its markets.

FIGURE **12.1**

The security market line, SML, and the weighted average cost of capital, WACC

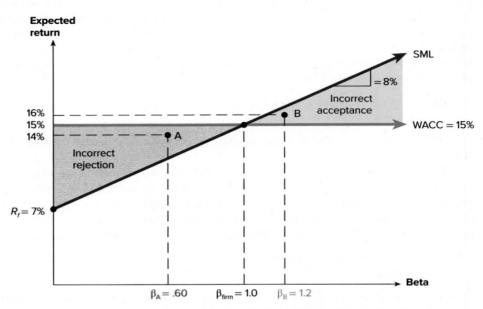

If a firm uses its WACC to make accept-reject decisions for all types of projects, it will have a tendency toward incorrectly accepting risky projects and incorrectly rejecting less risky projects.

Nonetheless, despite the usefulness of the WACC as a benchmark, there will clearly be situations where the cash flows under consideration have risks distinctly different from those of the overall firm. We consider how to cope with this problem next.

The SML and the WACC

When we are evaluating investments with risks that are substantially different from those of the overall firm, the use of the WACC will potentially lead to poor decisions. Figure 12.1 illustrates why.

In Figure 12.1, we have plotted an SML corresponding to a risk-free rate of 7 percent and a market risk premium of 8 percent. To keep things simple, we consider an all-equity company with a beta of 1. As we have indicated, the WACC and the cost of equity are exactly equal to 15 percent for this company because there is no debt.

Suppose our firm uses its WACC to evaluate all investments. This means that any investment with a return of greater than 15 percent will be accepted and any investment with a return of less than 15 percent will be rejected. We know from our study of risk and return, however, that a desirable investment is one that plots above the SML. As Figure 12.1 illustrates, using the WACC for all types of projects can result in the firm's incorrectly accepting relatively risky projects and incorrectly rejecting relatively safe ones.

For example, consider Point A. This project has a beta of $\beta_A = .60$ compared to the firm's beta of 1.0. It has an expected return of 14 percent. Is this a desirable investment? The answer is yes because its required return is only:

$$\text{Required return} = R_f + \beta_A \times (R_M - R_f)$$
$$= 7\% + .60 \times 8\%$$
$$= 11.8\%$$

However, if we use the WACC as a cutoff, then this project will be rejected because its return is less than 15 percent. This example illustrates that a firm that uses its WACC as a cutoff will tend to reject profitable projects with risks less than those of the overall firm.

At the other extreme, consider Point B. This project has a beta of $\beta_B = 1.2$. It offers a 16 percent return, which exceeds the firm's cost of capital. This is not a good investment, however, because, given its level of systematic risk, its return is inadequate. Nonetheless, if we use the WACC to evaluate it, it will appear to be attractive. So the second error that will arise if we use the WACC as a cutoff is that we will tend to make unprofitable investments with risks greater than those of the overall firm. As a consequence, through time, a firm that uses its WACC to evaluate all projects will have a tendency to both accept unprofitable investments and become increasingly risky.

Divisional Cost of Capital

The same type of problem with the WACC can arise in a corporation with more than one line of business. Suppose a corporation has two divisions, a regulated electric company and an electronics manufacturing operation. The first of these (the electric operation) has relatively low risk; the second has relatively high risk.

In this case, the firm's overall cost of capital is really a mixture of two different costs of capital, one for each division. If the two divisions were competing for resources, and the firm used a single WACC as a cutoff, which division would tend to be awarded greater funds for investment?

The answer is that the riskier division would tend to have greater returns (ignoring the greater risk), so it would tend to be the "winner." The less glamorous operation might have great profit potential that would end up being ignored. Large corporations in the United States are aware of this problem, and many work to develop separate divisional costs of capital.

The Pure Play Approach

We've seen that using the firm's WACC inappropriately can lead to problems. How can we come up with the appropriate discount rates in such circumstances? Because we cannot observe the returns on these investments, there generally is no direct way of coming up with a beta, for example. Instead, what we must do is examine other investments outside the firm that are in the same risk class as the one we are considering and use the market-required returns on these investments as the discount rate. In other words, we will try to determine what the cost of capital is for such investments by trying to locate some similar investments in the marketplace.

For example, going back to our electric division, suppose we want to come up with a discount rate to use for that division. What we can do is identify several other electric companies that have publicly traded securities. We might find that a typical electric company has a beta of .80, AA-rated debt, and a capital structure that is about 80 percent debt and 20 percent equity. Using this information, we could develop a WACC for a typical electric company and use this as our discount rate.

Alternatively, if we were thinking of entering a new line of business, we would try to develop the appropriate cost of capital by looking at the market-required returns on companies already in that business. In the language of Wall Street, a company that focuses only on a single line of business is called a *pure play*. For example, if you wanted to bet on the price of crude oil by purchasing common stocks, you would try to identify companies that dealt exclusively with this product because they would be the most affected by changes in the price of crude oil. Such companies would be called *pure plays* on the price of crude oil.

pure play approach
Use of a weighted
average cost of capital
that is unique to a
particular project, based
on companies in similar
lines of business.

What we try to do here is to find companies that focus as exclusively as possible on the type of project in which we are interested. Our approach, therefore, is called the **pure play approach** to estimating the required return on an investment. To illustrate, suppose McDonald's decides to enter the hotel business with a line of hotels called McRooms. The risks involved are quite different from those in the fast-food business. As a result, McDonald's would need to look at companies already in the hotel business to compute a cost of capital for the new division. An obvious "pure play" candidate would be La Quinta, which is predominately in this line of business. Marriott may not be as good a choice as it operates high-end motels and resorts, residential properties, and timeshares.

In Chapter 3, we discussed the subject of identifying similar companies for comparison purposes. The same problems we described there come up here. The most obvious one is that we may not be able to find any suitable companies. In this case, how to objectively determine a discount rate becomes a very difficult question. Even so, the important thing is to be aware of the issue so that we at least reduce the possibility of the kinds of mistakes that can arise when the WACC is used as a cutoff on all investments.

The Subjective Approach

Because of the difficulties that exist in objectively establishing discount rates for individual projects, firms often adopt an approach that involves making subjective adjustments to the overall WACC. To illustrate, suppose a firm has an overall WACC of 14 percent. It places all proposed projects into four categories as follows:

Category	Examples	Adjustment Factor	Discount Rate
High risk	New products	+6%	20%
Moderate risk	Cost savings, expansion of existing lines	+0	14
Low risk	Replacement of existing equipment	−4	10
Mandatory	Pollution control equipment	n/a	n/a

n/a = Not applicable.

The effect of this crude partitioning is to assume that all projects either fall into one of three risk classes or else are mandatory. In this last case, the cost of capital is irrelevant because the project must be taken. Of course, the firm's WACC may change through time as economic conditions change. As this happens, the discount rates for the different types of projects also will change.

Within each risk class, some projects will presumably have more risk than others, and the danger of incorrect decisions still will exist. Figure 12.2 illustrates this point. Comparing Figures 12.1 and 12.2, we see that similar problems exist, but the magnitude of the potential error is less with the subjective approach. For example, the project labeled "A" would be accepted if the WACC were used, but it is rejected once it is classified as a high-risk investment. What this illustrates is that some risk adjustment, even if it is subjective, is probably better than no risk adjustment.

It would be better, in principle, to objectively determine the required return for each project separately. However, as a practical matter, it may not be possible to go much beyond subjective adjustments because either the necessary information is unavailable or else the cost and effort required are not worthwhile.

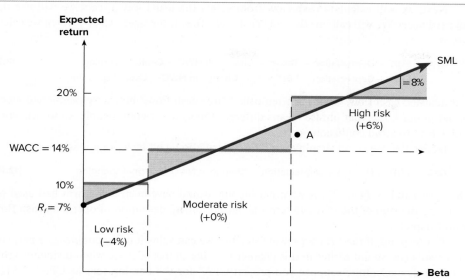

FIGURE **12.2**

The security market line, SML, and the subjective approach

With the subjective approach, the firm places projects into one of several risk classes. The discount rate used to value the project is then determined by adding (for high risk) or subtracting (for low risk) an adjustment factor to or from the firm's WACC. This results in fewer incorrect decisions than if the firm used the WACC to make the decisions.

CONCEPT QUESTIONS

12.5a   What are the likely consequences if a firm uses its WACC to evaluate all proposed investments?

12.5b   What is the pure play approach to determining the appropriate discount rate? When might it be used?

12.6   COMPANY VALUATION WITH THE WACC

When valuing a company, our approach is the same as the one we used for individual capital projects like the warehouse renovation, but there is one issue we have to deal with. When we look at an entire company, we often will see an interest deduction because the company has borrowed money. But as we have consistently emphasized, interest paid is a financing cost, not an operating cost. However, because interest paid is a tax-deductible expense, a company's tax bill is lower than it would have been had the company not used debt financing. We will have much more to say about this in a later chapter.

For now, to calculate cash flow from assets, we need to first calculate what the firm's tax bill would have been if it had not used debt financing. To do that, we take earnings before interest and taxes (EBIT) and multiply it by the firm's tax rate (T_c) to get the firm's "would-have-been" tax bill, which we will call the "adjusted" taxes and label Taxes*:

$$\text{Taxes*} = \text{EBIT} \times T_c \qquad [12.8]$$

Next, we will calculate cash flow from assets the usual way, except we will use the adjusted taxes. We will call this the "adjusted" cash flow from assets, CFA*, which we calculate as:

$$\text{CFA* = EBIT + Depreciation − Taxes* − Change in NWC − Capital spending} \quad [12.9]$$
$$\text{= EBIT + Depreciation − EBIT} \times T_c \text{ − Change in NWC − Capital spending}$$

Our adjusted cash flow, CFA*, is often called "free cash flow," but as we mentioned much earlier in our book, that phrase means different things to different people, so we will stick with CFA* to avoid confusion.

Notice that we could simplify our CFA* calculation a bit by writing it as:

$$\text{CFA* = EBIT} \times (1 − T_c) \text{ + Depreciation − Change in NWC − Capital spending} \quad [12.10]$$

The term EBIT $\times$ $(1 − T_c)$ is what net income would have been if the firm had used no debt, and the sum of the first two terms is our bottom-up definition of operating cash flow from Chapter 9.

At this point, if the firm is growing steadily, we can value it using our growing perpetuity formula (as we did earlier in this chapter to value shares of stock when dividends grow steadily). For example, suppose you project CFA* for the coming year as $CFA_1^* = \$120$ million. You think this amount will grow indefinitely at $g = 5$ percent per year. You've estimated the firm's WACC to be 9 percent, so the value of the firm today (V_0) is:

$$\text{Firm value today} = V_0 = \frac{\text{CFA}_1^*}{\text{WACC} − g} = \frac{\$120}{.09 − .05} = \$3 \text{ billion}$$

In sum, valuing a firm is no different from valuing a project, except for the fact that we have to adjust the taxes to remove the effect of any debt financing.

We also can consider the impact of nonconstant growth (as we did in an earlier chapter on stock valuation using the dividend growth model). In this case, we assume that constant growth begins at Time t in the future. In that case, we can write the value of the firm today as:

$$V_0 = \frac{\text{CFA}_1^*}{1 + \text{WACC}} + \frac{\text{CFA}_2^*}{(1 + \text{WACC})^2} + \frac{\text{CFA}_3^*}{(1 + \text{WACC})^3} + \cdots + \frac{\text{CFA}_t^* + V_t}{1 + \text{WACC}} \quad [12.11]$$

Here, V_t is value of the firm at Time t, which we again calculate using the growing perpetuity formula:

$$V_t = \frac{\text{CFA}_{t+1}^*}{\text{WACC} − g} \quad [12.12]$$

As always, notice that the tricky part is that to get the value at Time t, we have to use the cash flow that occurs at the end of that period at Time $t + 1$. Also, the value of the firm in the future, V_t, often is referred to as the "terminal value."

EXAMPLE 12.5 **Valuing Feline Fancy**

A guest on the popular show *Great White Tank* is attempting to raise money for her new company, Feline Fancy, which makes cat toys. The potential investor wants to value the company, which is privately held. Because of this, he uses the pure play approach to determine that the appropriate WACC for the company is 8 percent. The relevant tax rate is 21 percent.

Feline Fancy currently has $40 million in debt and 3.5 million shares outstanding. Sales this coming year are expected to be $30 million, and that amount is expected to grow at 15 percent per year for the following four years. After that, sales are expected to grow at 2 percent indefinitely. EBIT this coming year will be $10 million. EBIT, depreciation, capital spending, and the change in net working capital will grow at the same rate as sales. What value would you assign to Feline Fancy as a whole? What price per share would you assign?

To value the company, we begin by estimating the adjusted cash flow from assets (CFA*) for the next five years. The Year 1 values are the projections in millions for next year:

	Year 1	Year 2	Year 3	Year 4	Year 5
EBIT	$10.00	$11.50	$13.23	$15.21	$17.49
Depreciation	1.50	1.73	1.98	2.28	2.62
Taxes*	2.10	2.42	2.78	3.19	3.67
Change in NWC	.80	.92	1.06	1.22	1.40
Capital spending	2.40	2.76	3.17	3.65	4.20
CFA*	$6.20	$7.13	$8.20	$9.43	$10.84

Because the CFA* will grow at 2 percent after Year 5, the terminal value of the company in Year 5 will be:

$$V_5 = \frac{\$10.84(1 + .02)}{.08 - .02} = \$184.35 \text{ million}$$

We now can find the value of the company today by discounting the first five CFA* values and the terminal value back to the present using the WACC. Doing so, we find:

$$V_0 = \frac{\$6.20}{1.08} + \frac{\$7.13}{1.08^2} + \frac{\$8.20}{1.08^3} + \frac{\$9.43}{1.08^4} + \frac{\$10.84 + 184.35}{1.08^5} = \$158.14 \text{ million}$$

To find the value of equity, we subtract the $40 million in debt, resulting in a total equity value of $118.14 million. To find the share price, we divide this by the number of shares (3.5 million), which gives us a share price of:

Price per share = $118.14/3.5 = $33.75

Another common way to calculate the terminal value is to use a target ratio, similar to the way we used the PE and price-sales ratios in Chapter 7. For example, suppose the potential investor believes the appropriate price-sales ratio when the company's growth rate slows is 3 times. Sales in Year 5 are projected at $30 million × 1.15⁴ = $52.47 million (notice that we compounded the $30 million forward four years because $30 million is sales by the end of Year 1, not sales from last year). So, the new estimated terminal value is:

$$V_5 = 3 \times \$52.47 \text{ million} = \$157.41 \text{ million}$$

So, with this new terminal value, the value of the company today will be:

$$V_0 = \frac{\$6.20}{1.08} + \frac{\$7.13}{1.08^2} + \frac{\$8.20}{1.08^3} + \frac{\$9.43}{1.08^4} + \frac{\$10.84 + 157.41}{1.08^5} = \$139.80 \text{ million}$$

See for yourself if you don't agree that using this terminal value will result in an estimated per share value of $28.52.

CONCEPT QUESTIONS

12.6a Why do we adjust a firm's taxes when we do a firm valuation?

12.6b Why do you think we might prefer to use a ratio when calculating the terminal value when we value a firm?

SUMMARY AND CONCLUSIONS

This chapter has discussed cost of capital. The most important concept is the weighted average cost of capital, or WACC, which we interpreted as the required rate of return on the overall firm. It is also the discount rate appropriate for cash flows that are similar in risk to the overall firm. We described how the WACC can be calculated, and we illustrated how it can be used in certain types of analysis.

We also pointed out situations in which it is inappropriate to use the WACC as the discount rate. To handle such cases, we described some alternative approaches to developing discount rates, such as the pure play approach.

connect POP QUIZ!

Can you answer the following questions? If your class is using *Connect*, log on to SmartBook to see if you know the answers to these and other questions, check out the study tools, and find out what topics require additional practice!

Section 12.1 What are the components used to construct the WACC?

Section 12.2 What is the required return on a stock, according to the constant dividend growth model, if the growth rate is zero?

Section 12.3 What is the equation for finding the cost of preferred stock?

Section 12.4 A company has a borrowing rate of 15 percent and a tax rate of 21 percent. What is its aftertax cost of debt?

Section 12.5 True or False: Projects should always be discounted at the firm's overall cost of capital.

CHAPTER REVIEW AND SELF-TEST PROBLEMS

12.1 Calculating the Cost of Equity   Suppose stock in Boone Corporation has a beta of .90. The market risk premium is 7 percent, and the risk-free rate is 8 percent. Boone's last dividend was $1.80 per share, and the dividend is expected to grow at 7 percent indefinitely. The stock currently sells for $25. What is Boone's cost of equity capital? (See Problem 1.)

12.2 Calculating the WACC   In addition to the information in the previous problem, suppose Boone has a target debt-equity ratio of 50 percent. Its cost of debt is 8 percent, before taxes. If the tax rate is 21 percent, what is the WACC? (See Problem 9.)

■ Answers to Chapter Review and Self-Test Problems

12.1   We start off with the SML approach. Based on the information given, the expected return on Boone's common stock is:

$$R_E = R_f + \beta_E \times (R_M - R_f)$$
$$= 8\% + .9 \times 7\%$$
$$= 14.3\%$$

We now use the dividend growth model. The projected dividend is $D_0 \times (1 + g) =$ $\$1.80 \times 1.07 = \$1.926$, so the expected return using this approach is:

$$R_E = D_1/P_0 + g$$
$$= \$1.926/\$25 + .07$$
$$= .14704, \text{ or } 14.704\%$$

Because these two estimates, 14.3 percent and 14.7 percent, are fairly close, we will average them. Boone's cost of equity is approximately 14.5 percent.

12.2 Because the target debt-equity ratio is .50, Boone uses $.50 in debt for every $1.00 in equity. In other words, Boone's target capital structure is ⅓ debt and ⅔ equity. The WACC is thus:

$$\text{WACC} = (E/V) \times R_E + (D/V) \times R_D \times (1 - T_C)$$
$$= \tfrac{2}{3} \times 14.5\% + \tfrac{1}{3} \times 8\% \times (1 - .21)$$
$$= 11.775\%$$

CRITICAL THINKING AND CONCEPTS REVIEW

LO 3 12.1 **WACC**   On the most basic level, if a firm's WACC is 12 percent, what does this mean?

LO 3 12.2 **Book Values versus Market Values**   In calculating the WACC, if you had to use book values for either debt or equity, which would you choose? Why?

LO 4 12.3 **Project Risk**   If you can borrow all the money you need for a project at 6 percent, doesn't it follow that 6 percent is your cost of capital for the project?

LO 4 12.4 **WACC and Taxes**   Why do we use an aftertax figure for cost of debt but not for cost of equity?

LO 1 12.5 **DGM Cost of Equity Estimation**   What are the advantages of using the dividend growth model (DGM) for determining the cost of equity capital? What are the disadvantages? What specific piece of information do you need to find the cost of equity using this model? What are some of the ways in which you could get an estimate of this number?

LO 1 12.6 **SML Cost of Equity Estimation**   What are the advantages of using the SML approach to finding the cost of equity capital? What are the disadvantages? What are the specific pieces of information needed to use this method? Are all of these variables observable, or do they need to be estimated? What are some of the ways in which you could get these estimates?

LO 2 12.7 **Cost of Debt Estimation**   How do you determine the appropriate cost of debt for a company? Does it make a difference if the company's debt is privately placed as opposed to being publicly traded? How would you estimate the cost of debt for a firm whose only debt issues are privately held by institutional investors?

LO 4 12.8 **Cost of Capital**   Suppose Tom O'Bedlam, president of Bedlam Products, Inc., has hired you to determine the firm's cost of debt and cost of equity capital.

  a. The stock currently sells for $50 per share, and the dividend per share will probably be about $5. Tom argues, "It will cost us $5 per share to use the stockholders' money this year, so the cost of equity is equal to 10 percent (= $5/$50)." What's wrong with this conclusion?

b. Based on the most recent financial statements, Bedlam Products' total liabilities are $8 million. Total interest expense for the coming year will be about $1 million. Tom therefore reasons, "We owe $8 million, and we will pay $1 million interest. Therefore, our cost of debt is obviously $1 million/$8 million = .125, or 12.5%." What's wrong with this conclusion?

c. Based on his own analysis, Tom is recommending that the company increase its use of equity financing, because "Debt costs 12.5 percent, but equity only costs 10 percent; thus equity is cheaper." Ignoring all the other issues, what do you think about the conclusion that the cost of equity is less than the cost of debt?

LO 4 **12.9 Company Risk versus Project Risk** Both Dow Chemical Company, a large natural gas user, and Superior Oil, a major natural gas producer, are thinking of investing in natural gas wells near Houston. Both are all-equity-financed companies. Dow and Superior are looking at identical projects. They've analyzed their respective investments, which would involve a negative cash flow now and positive expected cash flows in the future. These cash flows would be the same for both firms. No debt would be used to finance the projects. Each company estimates that its project would have a net present value of $1 million at an 18 percent discount rate and a −$1.1 million NPV at a 22 percent discount rate. Dow has a beta of 1.25, whereas Superior has a beta of .75. The expected risk premium on the market is 8 percent, and risk-free bonds are yielding 12 percent. Should either company proceed? Should both? Explain.

LO 4 **12.10 Divisional Cost of Capital** Under what circumstances would it be appropriate for a firm to use different costs of capital for its different operating divisions? If the overall firm WACC was used as the hurdle rate for all divisions, would the riskier divisions or the more conservative divisions tend to get most of the investment projects? Why? If you were to try to estimate the appropriate cost of capital for different divisions, what problems might you encounter? What are two techniques you could use to develop a rough estimate for each division's cost of capital?

QUESTIONS AND PROBLEMS

Mc Graw Hill Education **connect** Select problems are available in McGraw-Hill *Connect*. Please see the packaging options section of the Preface for more information.

BASIC (Questions 1–19)

LO 1 **1. Calculating Cost of Equity** The Pierce Co. just issued a dividend of $2.35 per share on its common stock. The company is expected to maintain a constant 5 percent growth rate in its dividends indefinitely. If the stock sells for $44 a share, what is the company's cost of equity?

LO 1 **2. Calculating Cost of Equity** Hoolahan Corporation's common stock has a beta of .87. If the risk-free rate is 3.6 percent and the expected return on the market is 11 percent, what is the company's cost of equity capital?

LO 1 3. **Estimating the DCF Growth Rate** Suppose Potter Ltd. just issued a dividend of $1.82 per share on its common stock. The company paid dividends of $1.36, $1.46, $1.53, and $1.68 per share in the last four years, respectively. If the stock currently sells for $55, what is your best estimate of the company's cost of equity capital using arithmetic and geometric growth rates?

LO 1 4. **Calculating Cost of Preferred Stock** Sixth Fourth Bank has an issue of preferred stock with a $3.80 stated dividend that just sold for $89 per share. What is the bank's cost of preferred stock?

LO 2 5. **Calculating Cost of Debt** ICU Window, Inc., is trying to determine its cost of debt. The firm has a debt issue outstanding with seven years to maturity that is quoted at 103 percent of face value. The issue makes semiannual payments and has an embedded cost of 5.1 percent annually. What is the company's pretax cost of debt? If the tax rate is 21 percent, what is the aftertax cost of debt?

LO 2 6. **Calculating Cost of Debt** Jiminy's Cricket Farm issued a 30-year, 6.3 percent semiannual bond eight years ago. The bond currently sells for 110 percent of its face value. The company's tax rate is 22 percent.
   a.   What is the pretax cost of debt?
   b.   What is the aftertax cost of debt?
   c.   Which is more relevant, the pretax or the aftertax cost of debt? Why?

LO 2 7. **Calculating Cost of Debt** For the firm in Problem 6, suppose the book value of the debt issue is $135 million. In addition, the company has a second debt issue, a zero coupon bond with 12 years left to maturity; the book value of this issue is $65 million, and it sells for 64.3 percent of par. What is the total book value of debt? The total market value? What is the aftertax cost of debt now?

LO 3 8. **Calculating WACC** Baron Corporation has a target capital structure of 75 percent common stock, 5 percent preferred stock, and 20 percent debt. Its cost of equity is 11.3 percent, the cost of preferred stock is 4.9 percent, and the pretax cost of debt is 5.8 percent. The relevant tax rate is 23 percent.
   a.   What is the company's WACC?
   b.   The company president has approached you about the company's capital structure. He wants to know why the company doesn't use more preferred stock financing because it costs less than debt. What would you tell the president?

LO 3 9. **Taxes and WACC** Caddie Manufacturing has a target debt-equity ratio of .45. Its cost of equity is 10.3 percent, and its pretax cost of debt is 6.4 percent. If the tax rate is 21 percent, what is the company's WACC?

LO 3 10. **Finding the Target Capital Structure** Fama's Llamas has a WACC of 8.95 percent. The company's cost of equity is 10.4 percent, and its pretax cost of debt is 5.3 percent. The tax rate is 21 percent. What is the company's target debt-equity ratio?

LO 4 11. **Book Value versus Market Value** Masterson, Inc., has 4.1 million shares of common stock outstanding. The current share price is $84, and the book value per share is $11. The company also has two bond issues outstanding. The first bond issue has a face value of $70 million, has a coupon rate of

5.1 percent, and sells for 98 percent of par. The second issue has a face value of $50 million, has a coupon rate of 5.60 percent, and sells for 108 percent of par. The first issue matures in 20 years, the second in 12 years.

a. What are the company's capital structure weights on a book value basis?

b. What are the company's capital structure weights on a market value basis?

c. Which are more relevant, the book or market value weights? Why?

12. Calculating the WACC In Problem 11, suppose the most recent dividend was $3.95 and the dividend growth rate is 5 percent. Assume that the overall cost of debt is the weighted average of that implied by the two outstanding debt issues. Both bonds make semiannual payments. The tax rate is 21 percent. What is the company's WACC?

13. WACC Clifford, Inc., has a target debt-equity ratio of .65. Its WACC is 8.1 percent, and the tax rate is 23 percent.

a. If the company's cost of equity is 11 percent, what is its pretax cost of debt?

b. If the aftertax cost of debt is 3.8 percent, what is the cost of equity?

14. Finding the WACC Given the following information for Lightning Power Co., find the WACC. Assume the company's tax rate is 21 percent.

Debt:	16,000 6.2 percent coupon bonds outstanding, $1,000 par value, 25 years to maturity, selling for 108 percent of par; the bonds make semiannual payments.
Common stock:	535,000 shares outstanding, selling for $81 per share; beta is 1.20.
Preferred stock:	20,000 shares of 4.2 percent preferred stock outstanding, currently selling for $92 per share. The par value is $100.
Market:	7 percent market risk premium and 3.1 percent risk-free rate.

15. Finding the WACC Hankins Corporation has 5.4 million shares of common stock outstanding; 290,000 shares of 5.2 percent preferred stock outstanding, par value of $100; and 125,000 5.7 percent semiannual bonds outstanding, par value $1,000 each. The common stock currently sells for $72 per share and has a beta of 1.13, the preferred stock currently sells for $103 per share, and the bonds have 20 years to maturity and sell for 103 percent of par. The market risk premium is 6.8 percent, T-bills are yielding 4.3 percent, and the firm's tax rate is 23 percent.

a. What is the firm's market value capital structure?

b. If the firm is evaluating a new investment project that has the same risk as the firm's typical project, what rate should the firm use to discount the project's cash flows?

16. SML and WACC An all-equity firm is considering the following projects:

Project	Beta	IRR
W	.80	9.3%
X	.90	11.4
Y	1.10	12.1
Z	1.35	15.1

The T-bill rate is 4 percent, and the expected return on the market is 12 percent.

a. Which projects have a higher expected return than the firm's 12 percent cost of capital?

b. Which projects should be accepted?

c. Which projects will be incorrectly accepted or rejected if the firm's overall cost of capital were used as a hurdle rate?

LO 3 **17. Calculating the WACC** You are given the following information concerning Parrothead Enterprises:

Debt:	13,000 6.4 percent coupon bonds outstanding, with 15 years to maturity and a quoted price of 107. These bonds pay interest semiannually.
Common stock:	345,000 shares of common stock selling for $76.50 per share. The stock has a beta of .90 and will pay a dividend of $3.80 next year. The dividend is expected to grow by 5 percent per year indefinitely.
Preferred stock:	10,000 shares of 4.4 percent preferred stock selling at $86 per share.
Market:	11 percent expected return, risk-free rate of 3.6 percent, and a 22 percent tax rate.

Calculate the company's WACC.

LO 3 **18. Calculating Capital Structure Weights** Ace Industrial Machines issued 195,000 zero coupon bonds four years ago. The bonds originally had 30 years to maturity with a yield to maturity of 5.2 percent. Interest rates have recently decreased, and the bonds now have a yield to maturity of 4.9 percent. If the company has a $73 million market value of equity, what weight should it use for debt when calculating the cost of capital?

LO 3 **19. Calculating the WACC** Gnomes R Us is considering a new project. The company has a debt-equity ratio of .62. The company's cost of equity is 11.8 percent, and the aftertax cost of debt is 4.9 percent. The firm feels that the project is riskier than the company as a whole and that it should use an adjustment factor of +3 percent. What is the WACC it should use for the project?

INTERMEDIATE (Questions 20–26)

LO 2 **20. Calculating Cost of Equity** Stock in CDB Industries has a beta of 1.10. The market risk premium is 7.2 percent, and T-bills are currently yielding 4.1 percent. The most recent dividend was $2.56 per share, and dividends are expected to grow at an annual rate of 5 percent indefinitely. If the stock sells for $45 per share, what is your best estimate of the company's cost of equity?

LO 4 **21. WACC and NPV** Hankins, Inc., is considering a project that will result in initial aftertax cash savings of $4.3 million at the end of the first year, and these savings will grow at a rate of 1.9 percent per year indefinitely. The firm has a target debt-equity ratio of .40, a cost of equity of 10.8 percent, and an aftertax cost of debt of 3.2 percent. The cost-saving proposal is somewhat riskier than the usual project the firm undertakes; management uses the subjective approach and applies an adjustment factor of +2 percent to the cost of capital for such risky projects. Under what circumstances should the company take on the project?

LO 2 22. **Calculating the Cost of Debt** Ying Import has several bond issues outstanding, each making semiannual interest payments. The bonds are listed in the table below. If the corporate tax rate is 24 percent, what is the aftertax cost of the company's debt?

Bond	Coupon Rate	Price Quote	Maturity	Face Value
1	6.5%	109.0	5 years	$30,000,000
2	5.3	97.4	8 years	50,000,000
3	6.9	110.5	15½ years	65,000,000
4	7.3	109.8	25 years	85,000,000

LO 1 23. **Calculating the Cost of Equity** Gabriel Industries stock has a beta of 1.12. The company just paid a dividend of $1.15, and the dividends are expected to grow at 4 percent. The expected return on the market is 11.4 percent, and Treasury bills are yielding 3.8 percent. The most recent stock price is $85.

    a. Calculate the cost of equity using the dividend growth model method.

    b. Calculate the cost of equity using the SML method.

    c. Why do you think your estimates in (a) and (b) are so different?

LO 3 24. **Adjusted Cash Flow from Assets** Dewey Corp. is expected to have an EBIT of $2.45 million next year. Depreciation, the increase in net working capital, and capital spending are expected to be $180,000, $85,000, and $185,000, respectively. All are expected to grow at 18 percent per year for four years. The company currently has $13 million in debt and 800,000 shares outstanding. After Year 5, the adjusted cash flow from assets is expected to grow at 2.5 percent indefinitely. The company's WACC is 9.1 percent and the tax rate is 21 percent. What is the price per share of the company's stock?

LO 3 25. **Adjusted Cash Flow from Assets** In the previous problem, instead of a perpetual growth rate in adjusted cash flow from assets, you decide to calculate the terminal value of the company with the price-sales ratio. You believe that Year 5 sales will be $27.4 million and the appropriate price-sales ratio is 1.9. What is your new estimate of the current share price?

LO 3 26. **Adjusted Cash Flow from Assets** You have looked at the current financial statements for Reigle Homes, Co. The company has an EBIT of $3.25 million this year. Depreciation, the increase in net working capital, and capital spending were $245,000, $115,000, and $495,000, respectively. You expect that over the next five years, EBIT will grow at 15 percent per year, depreciation and capital spending will grow at 20 percent per year, and NWC will grow at 10 percent per year. The company has $19.5 million in debt and 400,000 shares outstanding. After Year 5, the adjusted cash flow from assets is expected to grow at 3.2 percent indefinitely. The company's WACC is 9.25 percent, and the tax rate is 21 percent. What is the price per share of the company's stock?

CHALLENGE (Questions 27–28)

LO 3 27. **WACC and NPV** Photochronograph Corporation (PC) manufactures time series photographic equipment. It is currently at its target debt-equity ratio of .35. It's considering building a new $37 million manufacturing facility.

This new plant is expected to generate aftertax cash flows of $5.1 million in perpetuity. There are three financing options:

a. *A new issue of common stock:* The required return on the company's new equity is 15 percent.

b. *A new issue of 20-year bonds:* If the company issues these new bonds at an annual coupon rate of 7 percent, they will sell at par.

c. *Increased use of accounts payable financing:* Because this financing is part of the company's ongoing daily business, the company assigns it a cost that is the same as the overall firm WACC. Management has a target ratio of accounts payable to long-term debt of .15. (Assume there is no difference between the pretax and aftertax accounts payable cost.)

What is the NPV of the new plant? Assume that the company has a 21 percent tax rate.

LO 3   **28. Project Evaluation**   This is a comprehensive project evaluation problem bringing together much of what you have learned in this and previous chapters. Suppose you have been hired as a financial consultant to Defense Electronics, Inc. (DEI), a large, publicly traded firm that is the market share leader in radar detection systems (RDSs). The company is looking at setting up a manufacturing plant overseas to produce a new line of RDSs. This will be a five-year project. The company bought some land three years ago for $4.5 million in anticipation of using it as a toxic dump site for waste chemicals, but it built a piping system to safely discard the chemicals instead. If the land were sold today, the net proceeds would be $5.5 million after taxes. In five years, the land will be worth $5.8 million after taxes. The company wants to build its new manufacturing plant on this land; the plant will cost $21.2 million to build. The following market data on DEI's securities are current:

Debt:	60,000 6.2 percent coupon bonds outstanding, 25 years to maturity, selling for 98 percent of par; the bonds have a $1,000 par value each and make semiannual payments.
Common stock:	1,350,000 shares outstanding, selling for $97 per share; the beta is 1.15.
Preferred stock:	90,000 shares of 5.7 percent preferred stock outstanding, par value of $100, selling for $95 per share.
Market:	7 percent expected market risk premium; 3.8 percent risk-free rate.

DEI's tax rate is 25 percent. The project requires $825,000 in initial net working capital investment to get operational.

a. Calculate the project's Time 0 cash flow, taking into account all side effects.

b. The new RDS project is somewhat riskier than a typical project for DEI, primarily because the plant is being located overseas. Management has told you to use an adjustment factor of +2 percent to account for this increased riskiness. Calculate the appropriate discount rate to use when evaluating DEI's project.

c. The manufacturing plant has an eight-year tax life, and DEI uses straight-line depreciation. At the end of the project (i.e., the end of Year 5), the plant can be scrapped for $2.4 million. What is the aftertax salvage value of this manufacturing plant?

d. The company will incur $3.6 million in annual fixed costs. The plan is to manufacture 13,500 RDSs per year and sell them at $10,800 per machine; the variable production costs are $9,900 per RDS. What is the annual operating cash flow, OCF, from this project?

e. Finally, DEI's president wants you to throw all your calculations, all your assumptions, and everything else into a report for the chief financial officer; all he wants to know is what the RDS project's internal rate of return, IRR, and net present value, NPV, are. What will you report?

WHAT'S ON THE WEB?

12.1 Cost of Equity   Go to finance.yahoo.com and look up the information for Activision Blizzard (ATVI), a video game company in the S&P 500. You want to estimate the cost of equity for the company. First, find the current Treasury bill rate. Next, find the beta for ATVI. Using the historical market risk premium, what is the estimated cost of equity for ATVI using the CAPM? Now find the analysts' growth rate estimates for the next five years for the company. Using this growth rate in the dividend growth model, what is the estimated cost of equity? Now find the dividends paid by the company over the past five years and calculate the arithmetic and geometric growth rates in dividends. Using these growth rates, what is the estimated cost of equity? Looking at these four estimates, what cost of equity would you use for the company?

12.2 Cost of Debt   Go to finra-markets.morningstar.com/BondCenter/ and look up the outstanding bonds for Nike. Record the most recent price and YTM of each bond issue. Now go to www.sec.gov and find the most recent 10-Q or 10-K report filed by the company and find the book value of each bond issue. Assuming Nike's tax rate is 21 percent, what is the cost of debt using book value weights? What is the cost of debt using market value weights? Which of these numbers is more relevant?

EXCEL *MASTER IT!* PROBLEM

Excel
Master
coverage online

You want to calculate the WACC for auto parts retailer AutoZone (AZO). Complete the following steps to construct a spreadsheet that can be updated.

a. Using an input for the ticker symbol, create hyperlinks to the web pages that you will need to find all of the information necessary to calculate the cost of equity. Use a market risk premium of 7 percent when using CAPM.

b. Create hyperlinks to go to the FINRA bond quote website and the SEC EDGAR database and find the information for the company's bonds. Create a table that calculates the cost of debt for the company. Assume the tax rate is 21 percent.

c. Finally, calculate the market value weights for debt and equity. What is the WACC for AutoZone?

CHAPTER CASE
Cost of Capital for Layton Motors

You have recently been hired by Layton Motors, Inc. (LMI), in its relatively new treasury management department. LMI was founded eight years ago by Rachel Layton. Rachel found a method to manufacture a cheaper battery that will hold a larger charge, giving a car powered by the battery a range of 700 miles before requiring a recharge. The cars manufactured by LMI are midsized and carry a price that allows the company to compete with other mainstream auto manufacturers. The company is privately owned by Rachel and her family, and it had sales of $197 million last year.

LMI primarily sells to customers who buy the cars online, although it does have a limited number of company-owned dealerships. The customer selects any customization and makes a deposit of 20 percent of the purchase price. After the order is taken, the car is made to order, typically within 45 days. LMI's growth to date has come from its profits. When the company had sufficient capital, it would expand production. Relatively little formal analysis has been used in its capital budgeting process. Rachel has just read about capital budgeting techniques and has come to you for help. For starters, the company has never attempted to determine its cost of capital, and Rachel would like you to perform the analysis. Because the company is privately owned, it is difficult to determine the cost of equity for the company. Rachel wants you to use the pure play approach to estimate the cost of capital for LMI, and she has chosen Tesla Motors as a representative company. The following questions will lead you through the steps to calculate this estimate.

QUESTIONS

1. Most publicly traded corporations are required to submit quarterly (10-Q) and annual (10-K) reports to the SEC detailing the financial operations of the company over the past quarter or year, respectively. These corporate filings are available on the SEC website at www.sec.gov. Go to the SEC website and search for SEC filings made by Tesla Motors (TSLA). Find the most recent 10-Q or 10-K, and download the form. Look on the balance sheet to find the book value of debt and the book value of equity.

2. To estimate the cost of equity for TSLA, go to finance.yahoo.com and enter the ticker symbol TSLA. Follow the links to answer the following questions: What is the most recent stock price listed for TSLA? What is the market value of equity, or market capitalization? How many shares of stock does TSLA have outstanding? What is the most recent annual dividend? Can you use the dividend discount model in this case? What is the beta for TSLA? Now go back to finance.yahoo.com and find the current U.S. Treasury bond rates. What is the yield on three-month Treasury bills? Using the historical market risk premium, what is the cost of equity for TSLA using CAPM?

3. You now need to calculate the cost of debt for TSLA. Go to finra-markets.morningstar.com/Bond-Center/, enter TSLA as the company, and find the yield to maturity for each of TSLA's bonds. What is the weighted average cost of debt for TSLA using the book value weights and using the market value weights? Does it make a difference in this case if you use book value weights or market value weights?

4. You now have all the necessary information to calculate the weighted average cost of capital for TSLA. Calculate this using book value weights and market value weights, assuming TSLA has a 21 percent marginal tax rate. Which number is more relevant?

5. You used TSLA as a pure play company to estimate the cost of capital for LMI. Are there any potential problems with this approach in this situation?

Leverage and Capital Structure | 13

LEARNING OBJECTIVES

After studying this chapter, you should be able to:

LO 1 Discuss the effect of financial leverage.

LO 2 Analyze the impact of taxes and bankruptcy on capital structure choice.

LO 3 Identify the essentials of the bankruptcy process.

In addition to lowering the corporate tax rate from 35 percent to 21 percent, the Tax Cuts and Jobs Act of 2017, which was passed in December of that year, limited the tax deductibility of interest expense. The deduction of interest expense is now limited to 30 percent of "adjustable tax income," roughly equivalent to earnings before interest and taxes. Earlier in 2017, with the new law being discussed, corporations responded. For example, BHP announced plans to repurchase $2.5 billion of its bonds, Walmart repurchased $8.5 billion of its debt, and Sprint repurchased $1 billion of its debt. In fact, through the middle of October 2017, U.S. corporations announced plans to repurchase $178.5 billion in debt, more than double the $80 billion of repurchases for the same period in 2016, and way more than the $18 billion in 2014.

A firm's choice of how much debt it should have relative to equity is known as a capital structure decision. Such a choice has many implications for a firm and is far from being a settled issue in either theory or practice. In this chapter, we discuss the basic ideas underlying capital structures and how firms choose them.

A firm's capital structure is really a reflection of its borrowing policy. Should we borrow a lot of money or a little? At first glance, it probably seems that debt is something to be avoided. After all, the more debt a firm has, the greater is the risk of bankruptcy. What we learn is that debt is really a double-edged sword, and, properly used, debt can be enormously beneficial to the firm.

A good understanding of the effects of debt financing is important because the role of debt is so misunderstood, and many firms (and individuals) are far too conservative in their use of debt. Having said this, we also can say that firms sometimes err in the opposite direction, becoming much too heavily indebted, with bankruptcy as the unfortunate consequence. Striking the right balance is what the capital structure issue is all about.

Please visit us at essentialsofcorporatefinance.blogspot.com for the latest developments in the world of corporate finance.

Thus far, we have taken the firm's capital structure as given. Debt-equity ratios don't drop on firms from the sky, of course, so now it's time to wonder where they do come from. Going back to Chapter 1, we call decisions about a firm's debt-equity ratio *capital structure decisions.*[1]

For the most part, a firm can choose any capital structure that it wants. If management so desired, a firm could issue bonds and use the proceeds to buy back some stock, thereby increasing the debt-equity ratio. Alternatively, it could issue stock and use the money to pay off some debt, thereby reducing the debt-equity ratio. Activities such as these that alter the firm's existing capital structure are called capital *restructurings.* In general, such restructurings take place whenever the firm substitutes one capital structure for another while leaving the firm's assets unchanged.

Because the assets of a firm are not directly affected by a capital restructuring, we can examine the firm's capital structure decision separately from its other activities. This means that a firm can consider capital restructuring decisions in isolation from its investment decisions. In this chapter, then, we will ignore investment decisions and focus on the long-term financing, or capital structure, question.

What we will see in this chapter is that capital structure decisions can have important implications for the value of the firm and its cost of capital. We also will find that important elements of the capital structure decision are easy to identify, but precise measures of these elements are generally not obtainable. As a result, we are only able to give an incomplete answer to the question of what the best capital structure might be for a particular firm at a particular time.

13.1 THE CAPITAL STRUCTURE QUESTION

How should a firm go about choosing its debt-equity ratio? Here, as always, we assume that the guiding principle is to choose the course of action that maximizes the value of a share of stock. However, when it comes to capital structure decisions, this is essentially the same thing as maximizing the value of the whole firm, and, for convenience, we will tend to frame our discussion in terms of firm value.

In Chapter 12, we discussed the concept of the firm's weighted average cost of capital, or WACC. You may recall that the WACC tells us that the firm's overall cost of capital is a weighted average of the costs of the various components of the firm's capital structure. When we described the WACC, we took the firm's capital structure as given. Thus, one important issue that we will want to explore in this chapter is what happens to the cost of capital when we vary the amount of debt financing, or the debt-equity ratio.

A primary reason for studying the WACC is that the value of the firm is maximized when the WACC is minimized. To see this, recall that the WACC is the discount rate appropriate for the firm's overall cash flows. Because values and discount rates move in opposite directions, minimizing the WACC will maximize the value of the firm's cash flows.

Thus, we will want to choose the firm's capital structure so that the WACC is minimized. For this reason, we will say that one capital structure is better than another if it results in a lower weighted average cost of capital. Further, we say that a particular debt-equity ratio represents the *optimal capital structure* if it results in the lowest possible WACC. This optimal capital structure is sometimes called the firm's *target* capital structure as well.

---

[1]It is conventional to refer to decisions regarding debt and equity as *capital structure decisions.* However, the term *financial structure* would be more accurate, and we use the terms interchangeably.

CONCEPT QUESTIONS

13.1a   What is the relationship between the WACC and the value of the firm?

13.1b   What is an optimal capital structure?

13.2 THE EFFECT OF FINANCIAL LEVERAGE

Excel
Master
coverage online

In this section, we examine the impact of financial leverage on the payoffs to stockholders. As you may recall, financial leverage refers to the extent to which a firm relies on debt. The more debt financing a firm uses in its capital structure, the more financial leverage it employs.

As we describe, financial leverage can dramatically alter the payoffs to shareholders in the firm. Remarkably, however, financial leverage may not affect the overall cost of capital. If this is true, then a firm's capital structure is irrelevant because changes in capital structure won't affect the value of the firm. We return to this issue a little later.

The Impact of Financial Leverage

We start by illustrating how financial leverage works. For now, we ignore the impact of taxes. Also, for ease of presentation, we describe the impact of leverage in terms of its effects on earnings per share, EPS, and return on equity, ROE. These are, of course, accounting numbers and, as such, are not our primary concern. Using cash flows instead of these accounting numbers would lead to precisely the same conclusions, but a little more work would be needed. We discuss the impact of leverage on market values in a subsequent section.

Financial Leverage, EPS, and ROE: An Example   The Trans Am Corporation currently has no debt in its capital structure. The CFO, Ms. Morris, is considering a restructuring that would involve issuing debt and using the proceeds to buy back some of the outstanding equity. Table 13.1 presents both the current and proposed capital structures. As shown, the firm's assets have a market value of $8 million, and there are 400,000 shares outstanding. Because Trans Am is an all-equity firm, the price per share is $20.

The proposed debt issue would raise $4 million; the interest rate would be 10 percent. The stock sells for $20 per share, so the $4 million in new debt would be used to purchase $4 million/$20 = 200,000 shares, leaving 200,000 outstanding. After the restructuring, Trans Am would have a capital structure that was 50 percent debt, so the debt-equity ratio would be 1. Notice that, for now, we assume that the stock price will remain at $20.

TABLE **13.1**		Current	Proposed
Current and proposed capital structures for the Trans Am Corporation	Assets	$8,000,000	$8,000,000
	Debt	$ 0	$4,000,000
	Equity	$8,000,000	$4,000,000
	Debt-equity ratio	0	1
	Share price	$20	$20
	Shares outstanding	400,000	200,000
	Interest rate	10%	10%

TABLE **13.2**

Capital structure
scenarios for the
Trans Am
Corporation

Current Capital Structure: No Debt		
	Recession	Expected	Expansion
EBIT	$500,000	$1,000,000	$1,500,000
Interest	0	0	0
Net income	$500,000	$1,000,000	$1,500,000
ROE	6.25%	12.50%	18.75%
EPS	$1.25	$2.50	$3.75

Proposed Capital Structure: Debt = $4 million		
	Recession	Expected	Expansion
EBIT	$500,000	$1,000,000	$1,500,000
Interest	400,000	400,000	400,000
Net income	$100,000	$ 600,000	$1,100,000
ROE	2.50%	15.00%	27.50%
EPS	$.50	$3.00	$5.50

To investigate the impact of the proposed restructuring, Ms. Morris has prepared Table 13.2, which compares the firm's current capital structure to the proposed capital structure under three scenarios. The scenarios reflect different assumptions about the firm's EBIT. Under the expected scenario, EBIT is $1 million. In the recession scenario, EBIT falls to $500,000. In the expansion scenario, it rises to $1.5 million.

To illustrate some of the calculations in Table 13.2, consider the expansion case. EBIT is $1.5 million. With no debt (the current capital structure) and no taxes, net income is also $1.5 million. In this case, there are 400,000 shares worth $8 million total. EPS is therefore $1.5 million/400,000 = $3.75 per share. Also, because accounting return on equity, ROE, is net income divided by total equity, ROE is $1.5 million/$8 million = .1875, or 18.75 percent.[2]

With $4 million in debt (the proposed capital structure), things are somewhat different. Because the interest rate is 10 percent, the interest bill is $400,000. With EBIT of $1.5 million, interest of $400,000, and no taxes, net income is $1.1 million. Now there are only 200,000 shares worth $4 million total. EPS is therefore $1.1 million/200,000 = $5.50 per share versus the $3.75 per share that we calculated above. Furthermore, ROE is $1.1 million/$4 million = .275, or 27.5 percent. This is well above the 18.75 percent we calculated for the current capital structure.

EPS versus EBIT   The impact of leverage is evident in Table 13.2 when the effect of the restructuring on EPS and ROE is examined. In particular, the variability in both EPS and ROE is much larger under the proposed capital structure. This illustrates how financial leverage acts to magnify gains and losses to shareholders.

In Figure 13.1, we take a closer look at the effect of the proposed restructuring. This figure plots earnings per share, EPS, against earnings before interest and taxes, EBIT, for the current and proposed capital structures. The first line, labeled "No debt," represents the case of no leverage. This line begins at the origin, indicating that EPS would be zero if EBIT were zero. From there, every $400,000 increase in EBIT increases EPS by $1 (because there are 400,000 shares outstanding).

---

[2]ROE is discussed in some detail in Chapter 3.

Financial leverage: EPS and EBIT for the Trans Am Corporation

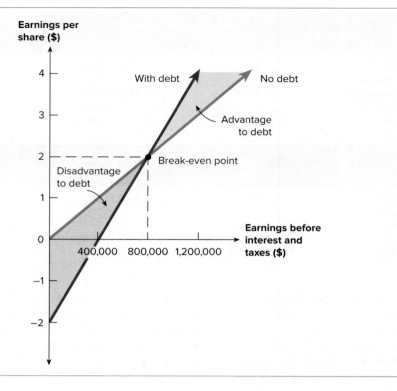

The second line represents the proposed capital structure. Here, EPS is negative if EBIT is zero. This follows because $400,000 of interest must be paid regardless of the firm's profits. Because there are 200,000 shares in this case, EPS is −$2 per share as shown. Similarly, if EBIT were $400,000, EPS would be exactly zero.

The important thing to notice in Figure 13.1 is that the slope of the line in this second case is steeper. In fact, for every $400,000 increase in EBIT, EPS rises by $2, so the line is twice as steep. This tells us that EPS is twice as sensitive to changes in EBIT because of the financial leverage employed.

Another observation to make in Figure 13.1 is that the lines intersect. At that point, EPS is exactly the same for both capital structures. To find this point, note that EPS is equal to EBIT/400,000 in the no-debt case. In the with-debt case, EPS is (EBIT − $400,000)/200,000. If we set these equal to each other, EBIT is:

$$\text{EBIT}/400,000 = (\text{EBIT} - \$400,000)/200,000$$
$$\text{EBIT} = 2 \times (\text{EBIT} - \$400,000)$$
$$\text{EBIT} = \$800,000$$

When EBIT is $800,000, EPS is $2 per share under either capital structure. This is labeled as the break-even point in Figure 13.1; we also could call it the indifference point. If EBIT is above this level, leverage is beneficial; if it is below this point, it is not.

There is another, more intuitive, way of seeing why the break-even point is $800,000. Notice that if the firm has no debt and its EBIT is $800,000, its net income is also $800,000. In this case, the ROE is $800,000/$8,000,000 = .10, or 10 percent. This is precisely the same as the interest rate on the debt, so the firm earns a return that is just sufficient to pay the interest.

EXAMPLE 13.1   **Break-Even EBIT**

The MPD Corporation has decided in favor of a capital restructuring. Currently, MPD uses no debt financing. Following the restructuring, however, debt will be $1 million. The interest rate on the debt will be 9 percent. MPD currently has 200,000 shares outstanding, and the price per share is $20. If the restructuring is expected to increase EPS, what is the minimum level for EBIT that MPD's management must be expecting? Ignore taxes in answering.

To answer, we calculate the break-even EBIT. At any EBIT above this, the increased financial leverage will increase EPS, so this will tell us the minimum level for EBIT. Under the old capital structure, EPS is EBIT/200,000. Under the new capital structure, the interest expense will be $1 million × .09 = $90,000. Furthermore, with the $1 million proceeds, MPD will repurchase $1 million/20 = 50,000 shares of stock, leaving 150,000 outstanding. EPS is thus (EBIT − $90,000)/150,000.

Now that we know how to calculate EPS under both scenarios, we set the two expressions for EPS equal to each other and solve for the break-even EBIT:

$$\text{EBIT}/200{,}000 = (\text{EBIT} - \$90{,}000)/150{,}000$$
$$\text{EBIT} = (4/3) \times (\text{EBIT} - \$90{,}000)$$
$$\text{EBIT} = \$360{,}000$$

Verify that, in either case, EPS is $1.80 when EBIT is $360,000. Management at MPD is apparently of the opinion that EPS will exceed $1.80.

Corporate Borrowing and Homemade Leverage

Based on Tables 13.1 and 13.2 and Figure 13.1, Ms. Morris draws the following conclusions:

1. The effect of financial leverage depends on the company's EBIT. When EBIT is relatively high, leverage is beneficial.

2. Under the expected scenario, leverage increases the returns to shareholders, as measured by both ROE and EPS.

3. Shareholders are exposed to more risk under the proposed capital structure because the EPS and ROE are much more sensitive to changes in EBIT in this case.

4. Because of the impact that financial leverage has on both the expected return to stockholders and the riskiness of the stock, capital structure is an important consideration.

The first three of these conclusions are clearly correct. Does the last conclusion necessarily follow? Surprisingly, the answer is no. As we discuss next, the reason is that shareholders can adjust the amount of financial leverage by borrowing and lending on their own. This use of personal borrowing to alter the degree of financial leverage is called **homemade leverage**.

We now will illustrate that it actually makes no difference whether or not Trans Am adopts the proposed capital structure because any stockholder who prefers the proposed capital structure can create it using homemade leverage. To begin, the first part of Table 13.3 shows what will happen to an investor who buys $2,000 worth of Trans Am stock if the proposed capital structure is adopted. This investor purchases 100 shares of stock. From Table 13.2, EPS will be either $.50, $3, or $5.50, so the total earnings for 100 shares will either be $50, $300, or $550 under the proposed capital structure.

Now, suppose Trans Am does not adopt the proposed capital structure. In this case, EPS will be $1.25, $2.50, or $3.75. The second part of Table 13.3 demonstrates how a stockholder who prefers the payoffs under the proposed structure can create them using

homemade leverage
The use of personal borrowing to change the overall amount of financial leverage to which an individual is exposed.

<table>
<tr><td>TABLE 13.3</td><td colspan="4">Proposed Capital Structure</td></tr>
</table>

TABLE 13.3	Proposed Capital Structure		
	Recession	**Expected**	**Expansion**

Proposed capital structure versus original capital structure with homemade leverage

	Recession	**Expected**	**Expansion**
EPS	$ .50	$ 3.00	$ 5.50
Earnings for 100 shares	50.00	300.00	550.00

Net cost = 100 shares at $20 = $2,000

Original Capital Structure and Homemade Leverage			
	Recession	**Expected**	**Expansion**
EPS	$ 1.25	$ 2.50	$ 3.75
Earnings for 200 shares	250.00	500.00	750.00
Less: Interest on $2,000 at 10%	200.00	200.00	200.00
Net earnings	$ 50.00	$300.00	$550.00

Net cost = 200 shares at $20 − Amount borrowed = $4,000 − 2,000 = $2,000

personal borrowing. To do this, the stockholder borrows $2,000 at 10 percent on his or her own. Our investor uses this amount, along with the original $2,000, to buy 200 shares of stock. As shown, the net payoffs are exactly the same as those for the proposed capital structure.

How did we know to borrow $2,000 to create the right payoffs? We are trying to replicate Trans Am's proposed capital structure at the personal level. The proposed capital structure results in a debt-equity ratio of 1. To replicate this capital structure at the personal level, the stockholder must borrow enough to create this same debt-equity ratio. Because the stockholder has $2,000 in equity invested, borrowing another $2,000 will create a personal debt-equity ratio of 1.

This example demonstrates that investors always can increase financial leverage themselves to create a different pattern of payoffs. It thus makes no difference whether or not Trans Am chooses the proposed capital structure.

EXAMPLE 13.2   Unlevering the Stock

In our Trans Am example, suppose management adopted the proposed capital structure. Further, suppose that an investor who owned 100 shares preferred the original capital structure. Show how this investor could "unlever" the stock to recreate the original payoffs.

To create leverage, investors borrow on their own. To undo leverage, investors must loan out money. For Trans Am, the corporation borrowed an amount equal to half its value. The investor can unlever the stock by loaning out money in the same proportion. In this case, the investor sells 50 shares for $1,000 total and then loans out the $1,000 at 10 percent. The payoffs are calculated in the following table.

	Recession	Expected	Expansion
EPS (proposed structure)	$ .50	$ 3.00	$ 5.50
Earnings for 50 shares	25.00	150.00	275.00
Plus: Interest on $1,000 @ 10%	100.00	100.00	100.00
Total payoff	$125.00	$250.00	$375.00

These are precisely the payoffs the investor would have experienced under the original capital structure.

CONCEPT QUESTIONS

13.2a   What is the impact of financial leverage on stockholders?

13.2b   What is homemade leverage?

13.2c   Why is Trans Am's capital structure irrelevant?

13.3 CAPITAL STRUCTURE AND THE COST OF EQUITY CAPITAL

Excel Master coverage online

We have seen that there is nothing special about corporate borrowing because investors can borrow or lend on their own. As a result, whichever capital structure Trans Am chooses, the stock price will be the same. Trans Am's capital structure is thus irrelevant, at least in the simple world we have examined.

Our Trans Am example is based on a famous argument advanced by two Nobel laureates, Franco Modigliani and Merton Miller, whom we will henceforth call M&M. What we illustrated for the Trans Am Corporation is a special case of **M&M Proposition I**. M&M Proposition I states that it is completely irrelevant how a firm chooses to arrange its finances.

M&M Proposition I
The value of a firm is independent of its capital structure.

M&M Proposition I: The Pie Model

One way to illustrate M&M Proposition I is to imagine two firms that are identical on the left-hand side of the balance sheet. Their assets and operations are exactly the same. The right-hand sides are different because the two firms finance their operations differently. In this case, we can view the capital structure question in terms of a "pie" model. Why we choose this name is apparent in Figure 13.2. Figure 13.2 gives two possible ways of cutting up this pie between the equity slice, E, and the debt slice, D: 40%–60% and 60%–40%. However, the size of the pie in Figure 13.2 is the same for both firms because the value of the assets is the same. This is precisely what M&M Proposition I states: The size of the pie doesn't depend on how it is sliced.

The Cost of Equity and Financial Leverage: M&M Proposition II

Although changing the capital structure of the firm may not change the firm's *total* value, it does cause important changes in the firm's debt and equity. We now examine what

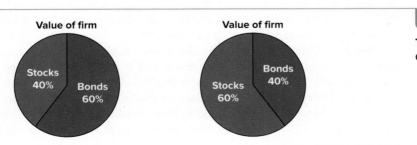

Value of firm

Stocks 40%   Bonds 60%

Value of firm

Stocks 60%   Bonds 40%

FIGURE 13.2

Two pie models of capital structure

FIGURE **13.3**

The cost of equity and the WACC: M&M Propositions I and II with no taxes

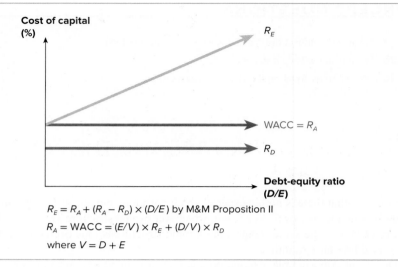

$$R_E = R_A + (R_A - R_D) \times (D/E) \text{ by M\&M Proposition II}$$
$$R_A = \text{WACC} = (E/V) \times R_E + (D/V) \times R_D$$
$$\text{where } V = D + E$$

happens to a firm financed with debt and equity when the debt-equity ratio is changed. To simplify our analysis, we will continue to ignore taxes.

Based on our discussion in Chapter 12, if we ignore taxes, the weighted average cost of capital, WACC, is:

$$\textbf{WACC} = \textbf{(\textit{E}/\textit{V})} \times \textbf{\textit{R}}_\textbf{\textit{E}} + \textbf{(\textit{D}/\textit{V})} \times \textbf{\textit{R}}_\textbf{\textit{D}}$$

where $V = E + D$. We also saw that one way of interpreting the WACC is as the required return on the firm's overall assets. To remind us of this, we use the symbol R_A to stand for the WACC and write:

$$\textbf{\textit{R}}_\textbf{\textit{A}} = \textbf{(\textit{E}/\textit{V})} \times \textbf{\textit{R}}_\textbf{\textit{E}} + \textbf{(\textit{D}/\textit{V})} \times \textbf{\textit{R}}_\textbf{\textit{D}}$$

If we rearrange this to solve for the cost of equity capital, we see that:

$$\textbf{\textit{R}}_\textbf{\textit{E}} = \textbf{\textit{R}}_\textbf{\textit{A}} + \textbf{(\textit{R}}_\textbf{\textit{A}} - \textbf{\textit{R}}_\textbf{\textit{D}}\textbf{)} \times \textbf{(\textit{D}/\textit{E})} \qquad [13.1]$$

M&M Proposition II
A firm's cost of equity capital is a positive linear function of its capital structure.

This is the famous **M&M Proposition II**, which tells us that the cost of equity depends on three things: the required rate of return on the firm's assets, R_A; the firm's cost of debt, R_D; and the firm's debt-equity ratio, D/E.

Figure 13.3 summarizes our discussion thus far by plotting the cost of equity capital, R_E, against the debt-equity ratio. As shown, M&M Proposition II indicates that the cost of equity, R_E, is given by a straight line with a slope of $(R_A - R_D)$. The y-intercept corresponds to a firm with a debt-equity ratio of zero, so $R_A = R_E$ in that case. Figure 13.3 shows that, as the firm raises its debt-equity ratio, the increase in leverage raises the risk of the equity and therefore the required return, or cost of equity (R_E).

Notice in Figure 13.3 that the WACC doesn't depend on the debt-equity ratio; it's the same no matter what the debt-equity ratio is. This is another way of stating M&M Proposition I: The firm's overall cost of capital is unaffected by its capital structure. As illustrated, the fact that the cost of debt is lower than the cost of equity is exactly offset by the increase in the cost of equity from borrowing. In other words, the change in the capital structure weights (E/V and D/V) is exactly offset by the change in the cost of equity (R_E), so the WACC stays the same.

EXAMPLE 13.3   The Cost of Equity Capital

The Ricardo Corporation has a weighted average cost of capital (ignoring taxes) of 12 percent. It can borrow at 8 percent. Assuming that Ricardo has a target capital structure of 80 percent equity and 20 percent debt, what is its cost of equity? What is the cost of equity if the target capital structure is 50 percent equity? Calculate the WACC, using your answers to verify that it is the same in both cases.

According to M&M Proposition II, the cost of equity, R_E, is:

$$R_E = R_A + (R_A - R_D) \times (D/E)$$

In the first case, the debt-equity ratio is $.2/.8 = .25$, so the cost of the equity is:

$$R_E = 12\% + (12\% - 8\%) \times .25$$
$$= 13\%$$

In the second case, verify that the debt-equity ratio is 1.0, so the cost of equity is 16 percent.

We can now calculate the WACC assuming that the percentage of equity financing is 80 percent, the cost of equity is 13 percent, and the tax rate is zero:

$$WACC = (E/V) \times R_E + (D/V) \times R_D$$
$$= .80 \times 13\% + .20 \times 8\%$$
$$= 12\%$$

In the second case, the percentage of equity financing is 50 percent and the cost of equity is 16 percent. The WACC is:

$$WACC = (E/V) \times R_E + (D/V) \times R_D$$
$$= .50 \times 16\% + .50 \times 8\%$$
$$= 12\%$$

As we calculated, the WACC is 12 percent in both cases.

Business and Financial Risk

M&M Proposition II shows that the firm's cost of equity can be broken down into two components. The first component, R_A, is the required return on the firm's overall assets, and it depends on the nature of the firm's operating activities. The risk inherent in a firm's operations is called the **business risk** of the firm's equity. Referring back to Chapter 11, we see that this business risk depends on the systematic risk of the firm's assets. The greater a firm's business risk, the greater R_A will be, and, all other things being the same, the greater will be the firm's cost of equity.

The second component in the cost of equity, $(R_A - R_D) \times (D/E)$, is determined by the firm's financial structure. For an all-equity firm, this component is zero. As the firm begins to rely on debt financing, the required return on equity rises. This occurs because the debt financing increases the risks borne by the stockholders. This extra risk that arises from the use of debt financing is called the **financial risk** of the firm's equity.

The total systematic risk of the firm's equity thus has two parts: business risk and financial risk. The first part (the business risk) depends on the firm's assets and operations and is not affected by capital structure. Given the firm's business risk (and its cost of debt), the second part (the financial risk) is completely determined by financial policy. As we have illustrated, the firm's cost of equity rises when it increases its use of financial leverage because the financial risk of the equity increases while the business risk remains the same.

business risk
The equity risk that comes from the nature of the firm's operating activities.

financial risk
The equity risk that comes from the financial policy (i.e., capital structure) of the firm.

CONCEPT QUESTIONS

13.3a What does M&M Proposition I state?

13.3b What are the three determinants of a firm's cost of equity?

13.3c The total systematic risk of a firm's equity has two parts. What are they?

13.4 CORPORATE TAXES AND CAPITAL STRUCTURE

Debt has two distinguishing features that we have not taken into proper account. First, as we have mentioned in a number of places, interest paid on debt is tax deductible. This is good for the firm, and it may be an added benefit to debt financing. Second, failure to meet debt obligations can result in bankruptcy. This is not good for the firm, and it may be an added cost of debt financing. Because we haven't explicitly considered either of these two features of debt, we may get a different answer about capital structure once we do. Accordingly, we consider taxes in this section and bankruptcy in the next one.

Our discussion here will assume that all interest paid is tax deductible. In reality, however, the Tax Cuts and Jobs Act of 2017 placed limits on the amount of interest that can be deducted. Specifically, for 2018 through 2021, the net interest deduction is limited to at most 30 percent of EBITDA. After 2021, it drops to 30 percent of EBIT. The term "net interest" means interest paid less interest earned (if any). Also, the limits aren't exactly based on EBITDA and EBIT because of some adjustments, but the differences will be minor in most cases. Importantly, any interest that can't be deducted in a particular year can be carried forward and deducted later. Thus, the tax deductibility isn't lost; it is deferred.

We can start by considering what happens when we consider the effect of corporate taxes. To do this, we will examine two firms, Firm U (unlevered) and Firm L (levered). These two firms are identical on the left-hand side of the balance sheet, so their assets and operations are the same.

We assume that EBIT is expected to be $1,000 every year forever for both firms. The difference between the two firms is that Firm L has issued $1,000 worth of perpetual bonds on which it pays 8 percent interest each year. The interest bill is thus .08 × $1,000 = $80 every year forever. Also, we assume that the corporate tax rate is 21 percent.

For our two firms, U and L, we can now calculate the following:

	Firm U	Firm L
EBIT	$1,000	$1,000.00
Interest	0	80.00
Taxable income	$1,000	$ 920.00
Taxes (21%)	210	193.20
Net income	$ 790	$ 726.80

The Interest Tax Shield

To simplify things, we will assume that depreciation is zero. We also will assume that capital spending is zero and that there are no additions to NWC. In this case, cash flow from assets is equal to EBIT − Taxes. For Firms U and L, we thus have:

Cash Flow from Assets	Firm U	Firm L
EBIT	$1,000	$1,000.00
−Taxes	210	193.20
Total	$ 790	$ 806.80

We immediately see that capital structure is now having some effect because the cash flows from U and L are not the same even though the two firms have identical assets.

To see what's going on, we can compute the cash flow to stockholders and bondholders.

Cash Flow	Firm U	Firm L
To stockholders	$ 790	$ 726.80
To bondholders	0	80.00
Total	$ 790	$ 806.80

What we are seeing is that the total cash flow to L is $16.80 more. This occurs because L's tax bill (which is a cash outflow) is $16.80 less. The fact that interest is deductible for tax purposes has generated a tax saving equal to the interest payment ($80) multiplied by the corporate tax rate (21 percent): $80 × .21 = $16.80. We call this tax saving the **interest tax shield**.

interest tax shield
The tax saving attained by a firm from the tax deductibility of interest expense.

Taxes and M&M Proposition I

Because the debt is perpetual, the same $16.80 shield will be generated every year forever. The aftertax cash flow to L will thus be the same $790 that U earns plus the $16.80 tax shield. Because L's cash flow is always $16.80 greater, Firm L is worth more than Firm U by the value of this $16.80 perpetuity.

Because the tax shield is generated by paying interest, it has the same risk as the debt, and 8 percent (the cost of debt) is, therefore, the appropriate discount rate. The value of the tax shield is thus:

$$PV = \frac{\$16.80}{.08} = \frac{.21 \times \$1{,}000 \times .08}{.08} = .21 \times \$1{,}000 = \$210$$

As our example illustrates, the present value of the interest tax shield can be written as:

$$\text{Present value of the interest tax shield} = (T_c \times D \times R_D)/R_D$$
$$= T_c \times D \qquad [13.2]$$

We have now come up with another famous result, M&M Proposition I with corporate taxes. We have seen that the value of Firm L, V_L, exceeds the value of Firm U, V_U, by the present value of the interest tax shield, $T_c \times D$. M&M Proposition I with taxes therefore states that:

$$V_L = V_U + T_c \times D \qquad [13.3]$$

The effect of borrowing in this case is illustrated in Figure 13.4. We have plotted the value of the levered firm, V_L, against the amount of debt, D. M&M Proposition I with corporate taxes implies that the relationship is given by a straight line with a slope of T_c.

In Figure 13.4, we also have drawn a horizontal line representing V_U. As is shown, the distance between the two lines is $T_c \times D$, the present value of the tax shield.

As Figure 13.4 indicates, the value of the firm goes up by $.21 for every $1 in debt. In other words, the NPV *per dollar* of debt is $.21. It is difficult to imagine why any corporation would not borrow to the absolute maximum under these circumstances.

Conclusion

The result of our analysis in this section is that, once we include taxes, capital structure definitely matters. However, we immediately reach the illogical conclusion that the optimal capital structure is 100 percent debt. Of course, we have not yet considered the impact of bankruptcy, so our story may change. For future reference, Table 13.4 contains a summary of the various M&M calculations and conclusions.

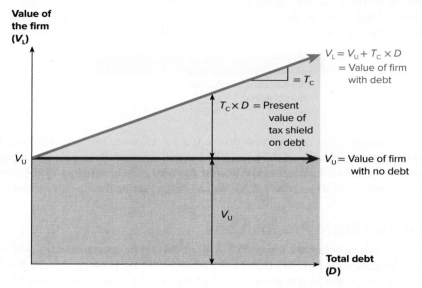

$V_L = V_U + T_C \times D$
= Value of firm with debt

$T_C \times D$ = Present value of tax shield on debt

V_U = Value of firm with no debt

The value of the firm increases as total debt increases because of the interest tax shield. This is the basis of M&M Proposition I with taxes.

I. **The no-tax case**

A. **Proposition I:** The value of the leveraged firm (V_L) is equal to the value of the unleveraged firm (V_U):
$$V_L = V_U$$

B. **Implications of Proposition I:**

  1. A firm's capital structure is irrelevant.
  2. A firm's weighted average cost of capital, WACC, is the same no matter what mixture of debt and equity is used to finance the firm.

C. **Proposition II:** The cost of equity, R_E, is:
$$R_E = R_A + (R_A - R_D) \times D/E$$
where R_A is the WACC, R_D is the cost of debt, and D/E is the debt-equity ratio.

D. **Implications of Proposition II:**

  1. The cost of equity rises as the firm increases its use of debt financing.
  2. The risk of the equity depends on two things: the riskiness of the firm's operations (*business risk*) and the degree of financial leverage (*financial risk*). Business risk determines R_A; financial risk is determined by D/E.

II. **The tax case**

A. **Proposition I with taxes:** The value of the leveraged firm (V_L) is equal to the value of the unleveraged firm (V_U) plus the present value of the interest tax shield:
$$V_L = V_U + T_C \times D$$
where T_C is the corporate tax rate and D is the amount of debt.

B. **Implications of Proposition I with taxes:**

  1. Debt financing is highly advantageous, and, in the extreme, a firm's optimal capital structure is 100 percent debt.
  2. A firm's weighted average cost of capital, WACC, decreases as the firm relies more heavily on debt financing.

CONCEPT QUESTIONS

13.4a What is the relationship between the value of an unlevered firm and the value of a levered firm once we consider the effect of corporate taxes?

13.4b If we only consider the effect of taxes, what is the optimum capital structure?

13.5 BANKRUPTCY COSTS

One limit to the amount of debt a firm might use comes in the form of *bankruptcy costs.* As the debt-equity ratio rises, so too does the probability that the firm will be unable to pay its bondholders what was promised to them. When this happens, ownership of the firm's assets ultimately is transferred from the stockholders to the bondholders.

In principle, a firm becomes bankrupt when the value of its assets equals the value of its debt. When this occurs, the value of equity is zero, and the stockholders turn over control of the firm to the bondholders. At this point, the bondholders hold assets whose value is exactly equal to what is owed on the debt. In a perfect world, there are no costs associated with this transfer of ownership, and the bondholders don't lose anything.

This idealized view of bankruptcy is not, of course, what happens in the real world. Ironically, it is expensive to go bankrupt. As we discuss, the costs associated with bankruptcy eventually may offset the tax-related gains from leverage.

Direct Bankruptcy Costs

When the value of a firm's assets equals the value of its debt, then the firm is economically bankrupt in the sense that the equity has no value. However, the formal turning over of the assets to the bondholders is a legal process, not an economic one. There are legal and administrative costs to bankruptcy, and it has been remarked that bankruptcies are to lawyers what blood is to sharks.

Because of the expenses associated with bankruptcy, bondholders won't get all that they are owed. Some fraction of the firm's assets will "disappear" in the legal process of going bankrupt. These are the legal and administrative expenses associated with the bankruptcy proceeding. We call these costs direct bankruptcy costs.

direct bankruptcy costs
The costs that are directly associated with bankruptcy, such as legal and administrative expenses.

Indirect Bankruptcy Costs

Because it is expensive to go bankrupt, a firm will spend resources to avoid doing so. When a firm is having significant problems in meeting its debt obligations, we say that it is experiencing financial distress. Some financially distressed firms ultimately file for bankruptcy, but most do not because they are able to recover or otherwise survive.

The costs of avoiding a bankruptcy filing incurred by a financially distressed firm are called indirect bankruptcy costs. We use the term financial distress costs to refer generically to the direct and indirect costs associated with going bankrupt and/or avoiding a bankruptcy filing.

The problems that come up in financial distress are particularly severe, and the financial distress costs are thus larger, when the stockholders and the bondholders are different groups. Until the firm is legally bankrupt, the stockholders control it. They, of course, will take actions in their own economic interests. Because the stockholders can be wiped out in a legal bankruptcy, they have a very strong incentive to avoid a bankruptcy filing.

The bondholders, on the other hand, are primarily concerned with protecting the value of the firm's assets and will try to take control away from the stockholders. They have a

indirect bankruptcy costs
The costs of avoiding a bankruptcy filing incurred by a financially distressed firm.

financial distress costs
The direct and indirect costs associated with going bankrupt or experiencing financial distress.

strong incentive to seek bankruptcy to protect their interests and keep stockholders from further dissipating the assets of the firm. The net effect of all this fighting is that a long, drawn-out, and potentially quite expensive legal battle gets started.

Meanwhile, as the wheels of justice turn in their ponderous way, the assets of the firm lose value because management is busy trying to avoid bankruptcy instead of running the business. Normal operations are disrupted, and sales are lost. Valuable employees leave, potentially fruitful programs are dropped to preserve cash, and otherwise profitable investments are not taken.

These are all indirect bankruptcy costs, or costs of financial distress. Whether or not the firm ultimately goes bankrupt, the net effect is a loss of value because the firm chose to use debt in its capital structure. It is this possibility of loss that limits the amount of debt that a firm will choose to use.

CONCEPT QUESTIONS

13.5a What are direct bankruptcy costs?

13.5b What are indirect bankruptcy costs?

13.6 OPTIMAL CAPITAL STRUCTURE

Our previous two sections have established the basis for an optimal capital structure. A firm will borrow because the interest tax shield is valuable. At relatively low debt levels, the probability of bankruptcy and financial distress is low, and the benefit from debt outweighs the cost. At very high debt levels, the possibility of financial distress is a chronic, ongoing problem for the firm, so the benefit from debt financing may be more than offset by the financial distress costs. Based on our discussion, it would appear that an optimal capital structure exists somewhere in between these extremes.

The Static Theory of Capital Structure

static theory of capital structure
Theory that a firm borrows up to the point where the tax benefit from an extra dollar in debt is exactly equal to the cost that comes from the increased probability of financial distress.

The theory of capital structure that we have outlined is called the **static theory of capital structure**. It says that firms borrow up to the point where the tax benefit from an extra dollar in debt is exactly equal to the cost that comes from the increased probability of financial distress. We call this the static theory because it assumes that the firm is fixed in terms of its assets and operations, and it only considers possible changes in the debt-equity ratio.

The static theory is illustrated in Figure 13.5, which plots the value of the firm, V_L, against the amount of debt, D. In Figure 13.5, we have drawn lines corresponding to three different stories. The first is M&M Proposition I with no taxes. This is the horizontal line extending from V_U, and it indicates that the value of the firm is unaffected by its capital structure. The second case, M&M Proposition I with corporate taxes, is given by the upward-sloping straight line. These two cases are exactly the same as the ones we previously illustrated in Figure 13.4.

The third case in Figure 13.5 illustrates our current discussion: The value of the firm rises to a maximum and then declines beyond that point. This is the picture that we get from our static theory. The maximum value of the firm, V_L^*, is reached at a debt level of D^*, so this is the optimal amount of borrowing. Put another way, the firm's optimal capital structure is composed of D^*/V_L^* in debt and $(1 - D^*/V_L^*)$ in equity.

The final thing to notice in Figure 13.5 is that the difference between the value of the firm in our static theory and the M&M value of the firm with taxes is the loss in

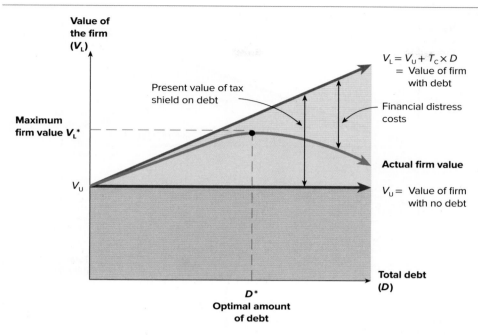

FIGURE **13.5**

The static theory of capital structure: The optimal capital structure and the value of the firm

According to the static theory, the gain from the tax shield on debt is offset by financial distress costs. An optimal capital structure exists that balances the additional gain from leverage against the added financial distress costs.

value from the possibility of financial distress. Also, the difference between the static theory value of the firm and the M&M value with no taxes is the gain from leverage, net of distress costs.

Optimal Capital Structure and the Cost of Capital

As we discussed earlier, the capital structure that maximizes the value of the firm is also the one that minimizes the cost of capital. With the help of Figure 13.6, we can illustrate this point and tie together our discussion of capital structure and cost of capital. As we have seen, there are essentially three cases. We will use the simplest of the three cases as a starting point and then build up to the static theory of capital structure. Along the way, we will pay particular attention to the connection between capital structure, firm value, and cost of capital.

Figure 13.6 illustrates the original M&M, no-tax, no-bankruptcy argument in Case I. This is the most basic case. In the top part, we have plotted the value of the firm, V_L, against total debt, D. When there are no taxes, bankruptcy costs, or other real-world imperfections, we know that the total value of the firm is not affected by its debt policy, so V_L is constant. The bottom part of Figure 13.6 tells the same story in terms of the cost of capital. Here, the weighted average cost of capital, WACC, is plotted against the debt-equity ratio, D/E. As with total firm value, the overall cost of capital is not affected by debt policy in this basic case, so the WACC is constant.

Next, we consider what happens to the original M&M arguments once taxes are introduced. As Case II illustrates, the firm's value now critically depends on its debt policy. The more the firm borrows, the more it is worth. From our earlier discussion, we know that this

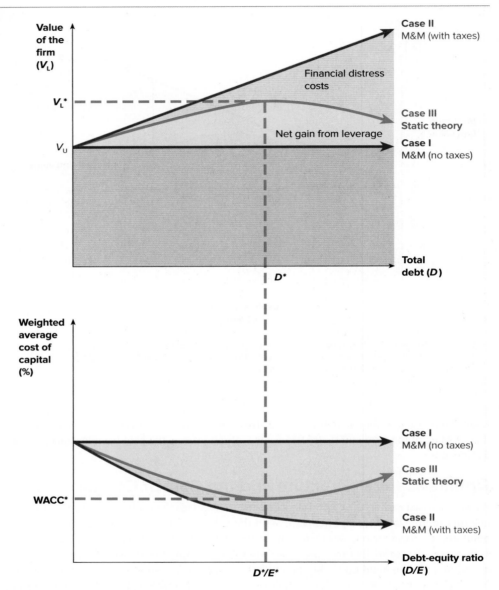

FIGURE **13.6**

The capital structure question

Case I
With no taxes or bankruptcy costs, the value of the firm and its weighted average cost of capital are not affected by capital structures.

Case II
With corporate taxes and no bankruptcy costs, the value of the firm increases and the weighted average cost of capital decreases as the amount of debt goes up.

Case III
With corporate taxes and bankruptcy costs, the value of the firm, V_L, reaches a maximum at D^*, the optimal amount of borrowing. At the same time, the weighted average cost of capital, WACC, is minimized at D^*/E^*.

happens because interest payments are tax deductible, and the gain in firm value is equal to the present value of the interest tax shield.

In the bottom part of Figure 13.6, notice how the WACC declines as the firm uses more and more debt financing. As the firm increases its financial leverage, the cost of equity does increase, but this increase is more than offset by the tax break associated with debt financing. As a result, the firm's overall cost of capital declines.

To finish our story, we include the impact of bankruptcy, or financial distress, costs to get Case III. As is shown in the top part of Figure 13.6, the value of the firm will not be as large as we previously indicated. The reason is that the firm's value is reduced by the present value of the potential future bankruptcy costs. These costs grow as the firm borrows more and more, and they eventually overwhelm the tax advantage of debt financing. The optimal capital structure occurs at D^*, the point at which the tax saving from an additional dollar in debt financing is exactly balanced by the increased bankruptcy costs associated with the additional borrowing. This is the essence of the static theory of capital structure.

The bottom part of Figure 13.6 presents the optimal capital structure in terms of the cost of capital. Corresponding to D^*, the optimal debt level, is the optimal debt-to-equity ratio, D^*/E^*. At this level of debt financing, the lowest possible weighted average cost of capital, **WACC***, occurs.

Capital Structure: Some Managerial Recommendations

The static model that we have described is not capable of identifying a precise optimal capital structure, but it does point out two of the more relevant factors: taxes and financial distress. We can draw some limited conclusions concerning these.

Taxes   First of all, the tax benefit from leverage is obviously only important to firms that are in a tax-paying position. Firms with substantial accumulated losses will get little value from the interest tax shield. Furthermore, firms that have substantial tax shields from other sources, such as depreciation, will get less benefit from leverage.

Also, not all firms have the same tax rate. The higher the tax rate, the greater the incentive to borrow.

Financial Distress   Firms with a greater risk of experiencing financial distress will borrow less than firms with a lower risk of financial distress. For example, all other things being equal, the greater the volatility in EBIT, the less a firm should borrow.

In addition, financial distress is more costly for some firms than for others. The costs of financial distress depend primarily on the firm's assets. In particular, financial distress costs will be determined by how easily ownership of those assets can be transferred.

For example, a firm with mostly tangible assets that can be sold without great loss in value will have an incentive to borrow more. For firms that rely heavily on intangibles, such as employee talent or growth opportunities, debt will be less attractive since these assets effectively cannot be sold.

CONCEPT QUESTIONS

13.6a   Can you describe the trade-off that defines the static theory of capital structure?

13.6b   What are the important factors in making capital structure decisions?

13.7 OBSERVED CAPITAL STRUCTURES

No two firms have identical capital structures. Nonetheless, there are some regular elements that we see when we start looking at actual capital structures. We discuss a few of these next.

The most striking thing we observe about capital structures, particularly in the United States, is that most corporations seem to have relatively low debt-equity ratios. In fact, most corporations use much less debt financing than equity financing. To illustrate, Table 13.5 presents median debt ratios and debt-equity ratios for various U.S. industries classified by SIC code (we discussed such codes in Chapter 3).

In Table 13.5, what is most striking is the wide variation across industries, ranging from essentially no debt for drug and computer companies to relatively heavy debt usage in the airline and cable television industries. Notice that these last two industries are the only ones for which more debt is used than equity, and most of the other industries rely far more heavily on equity than debt. This is true even though many of the companies in these industries pay substantial taxes. Table 13.5 makes it clear that corporations, in general, have not issued debt up to the point that tax shelters have been completely used up, and we conclude that there must be limits to the amount of debt corporations can use. Take a look at our nearby *Work the Web* box for more on actual capital structures.

Different industries have different operating characteristics in terms of, for example, EBIT volatility and asset types, and there does appear to be some connection between these characteristics and capital structure. Our story involving tax savings and financial distress costs undoubtedly supplies part of the reason, but, to date, there is no fully satisfactory theory that explains these regularities in capital structures.

TABLE 13.5

Capital structures for U.S. industries

Industry	Ratio of Debt to Total Capital (%)*	Ratio of Debt to Equity (%)	Number of Companies	SIC Code	Representative Companies
Electric utilities	48.54	94.31	33	491	American Electric Power, Southern Co.
Computer equipment	9.09	10.02	48	357	Apple, Cisco
Paper	27.75	38.40	24	26	Avery Dennison, Weyerhaeuser
Petroleum refining	32.27	47.65	18	29	Chevron, Sunoco
Airlines	63.92	177.19	10	4512	Delta, Southwest
Pay television	63.56	193.88	5	484	Dish Network, TiVo
Motor vehicles	17.77	21.60	25	371	Ford, Winnebago
Fabric apparel	15.86	18.84	14	23	Guess, Jones Apparel
Department stores	27.40	37.73	8	531	JCPenney, Macy's
Eating places	23.40	30.54	42	5812	McDonald's, Papa John's
Drugs	7.80	8.46	194	283	Merck, Pfizer
Steel works	19.96	24.95	9	331	Nucor, U.S. Steel

*Debt is the book value of preferred stock and long-term debt, including amounts due in one year. Equity is the market value of outstanding shares. Total capital is the sum of debt and equity. Median values are shown.

Source: Cost of Capital, 2010 Yearbook (Chicago: Morningstar, 2010).

W🌐RK THE WEB

When it comes to capital structure, all companies (and industries) are not created equal. To illustrate, we looked up some capital structure information on American Electric Power (AEP) and Johnson & Johnson (JNJ) using the "Financials" area of www.reuters.com. American Electric Power's capital structure looks like this (note that leverage ratios are expressed as percentages on this site):

FINANCIAL STRENGTH

	Company	industry	sector
Quick Ratio (MRQ)	0.34	1.18	1.73
Current Ratio (MRQ)	0.45	1.25	1.85
LT Debt to Equity (MRQ)	94.21	132.02	103.81
Total Debt to Equity (MRQ)	120.05	156.69	119.66
Interest Coverage (TTM)	4.30	4.10	6.44

For every dollar of equity, American Electric Power has long-term debt of $.9421 and total debt of $1.2005. Compare this result to Johnson & Johnson:

FINANCIAL STRENGTH

	Company	industry	sector
Quick Ratio (MRQ)	1.01	2.15	2.22
Current Ratio (MRQ)	1.34	2.94	3.03
LT Debt to Equity (MRQ)	38.05	10.03	12.39
Total Debt to Equity (MRQ)	48.07	14.07	16.72
Interest Coverage (TTM)	69.04	35.78	32.64

For every dollar of equity, Johnson & Johnson has only $.3805 of long-term debt and total debt of $.4807. When we examine the industry and sector averages, the differences are again apparent. The electric utility industry on average has $1.3202 of long-term debt and $1.5669 of total debt for every dollar of equity. By comparison, the healthcare industry on average has only $.1003 of long-term debt and $.1407 of total debt for every dollar of equity. Thus, we see that choice of capital structure is a management decision, but it also clearly is influenced by industry characteristics.

QUESTIONS

1. *The ratios shown for these companies are based on July 2018 figures. Go to www .reuters.com and find the current long-term debt-to-equity and total debt-to-equity ratios for both American Electric Power (AEP) and Johnson & Johnson (JNJ). How have these ratios changed over this time?*

2. *Go to www.reuters.com and find the long-term debt-to-equity and total debt-to-equity ratios for Bank of America (BAC), Tesla (TSLA), and Chevron (CVX). Why do you think these three companies use such differing amounts of debt?*

CONCEPT QUESTIONS

13.7a   Do U.S. corporations rely heavily on debt financing?

13.7b   What regularities do we observe in capital structures?

13.8 A QUICK LOOK AT THE BANKRUPTCY PROCESS

As we have discussed, one of the consequences of using debt is the possibility of financial distress, which can be defined in several ways:

1. *Business failure.* This term is usually used to refer to a situation in which a business has terminated with a loss to creditors, but even an all-equity firm can fail.
2. *Legal bankruptcy.* Firms or creditors bring petitions to a federal court for bankruptcy. **Bankruptcy** is a legal proceeding for liquidating or reorganizing a business.
3. *Technical insolvency.* Technical insolvency occurs when a firm is unable to meet its financial obligations.
4. *Accounting insolvency.* Firms with negative net worth are insolvent on the books. This happens when the total book liabilities exceed the book value of the total assets.

We now very briefly discuss some of the terms and more relevant issues associated with bankruptcy and financial distress.

bankruptcy
A legal proceeding for liquidating or reorganizing a business. Also, the transfer of some or all of a firm's assets to its creditors.

The SEC has a good overview of the bankruptcy process in its "Investor Reports/ Publications" link of www.sec.gov.

liquidation
Termination of the firm as a going concern.

reorganization
Financial restructuring of a failing firm to attempt to continue operations as a going concern.

Liquidation and Reorganization

Firms that cannot or choose not to make contractually required payments to creditors have two basic options: liquidation or reorganization. **Liquidation** means termination of the firm as a going concern, and it involves selling off the assets of the firm. The proceeds, net of selling costs, are distributed to creditors in order of established priority. **Reorganization** is the option of keeping the firm a going concern; it often involves issuing new securities to replace old securities. Liquidation or reorganization is the result of a bankruptcy proceeding. Which occurs depends on whether the firm is worth more "dead or alive."

Bankruptcy Liquidation   Chapter 7 of the Federal Bankruptcy Reform Act of 1978 deals with "straight" liquidation. The following sequence of events is typical:

1. A petition is filed in a federal court. A corporation may file a voluntary petition, or involuntary petitions may be filed against the corporation by several of its creditors.
2. A trustee-in-bankruptcy is elected by the creditors to take over the assets of the debtor corporation. The trustee will attempt to liquidate the assets.
3. When the assets are liquidated, after payment of the bankruptcy administration costs, the proceeds are distributed among the creditors.
4. If any proceeds remain, after expenses and payments to creditors, they are distributed to the shareholders.

The distribution of the proceeds of the liquidation occurs according to the following priority list:

1. Administrative expenses associated with the bankruptcy.
2. Other expenses arising after the filing of an involuntary bankruptcy petition but before the appointment of a trustee.

3. Wages, salaries, and commissions.
4. Contributions to employee benefit plans.
5. Consumer claims.
6. Government tax claims.
7. Payment to unsecured creditors.
8. Payment to preferred stockholders.
9. Payment to common stockholders.

This priority list for liquidation is a reflection of the **absolute priority rule (APR)**. The higher a claim is on this list, the more likely it is to be paid. In many of these categories, there are various limitations and qualifications that we omit for the sake of brevity.

    Two qualifications to this list are in order. The first concerns secured creditors. Such creditors are entitled to the proceeds from the sale of the security and are outside this ordering. However, if the secured property is liquidated and provides cash insufficient to cover the amount owed, the secured creditors join with unsecured creditors in dividing the remaining liquidated value. In contrast, if the secured property is liquidated for proceeds greater than the secured claim, the net proceeds are used to pay unsecured creditors and others. The second qualification to the APR is that, in reality, what happens, and who gets what in the event of bankruptcy, is subject to much negotiation, and, as a result, the APR is frequently not followed.

> **absolute priority rule (APR)**
> The rule establishing priority of claims in liquidation.

Bankruptcy Reorganization   Corporate reorganization takes place under Chapter 11 of the Federal Bankruptcy Reform Act of 1978. The general objective of a proceeding under Chapter 11 is to plan to restructure the corporation with some provision for repayment of creditors. A typical sequence of events follows:

> The American Bankruptcy Institute provides extensive information on bankruptcy. See www .abi.org.

1. A voluntary petition can be filed by the corporation, or an involuntary petition can be filed by creditors.
2. A federal judge either approves or denies the petition. If the petition is approved, a time for filing proofs of claims is set.
3. In most cases, the corporation (the "debtor in possession") continues to run the business.
4. The corporation (and, in certain cases, the creditors) submits a reorganization plan.
5. Creditors and shareholders are divided into classes. A class of creditors accepts the plan if a majority of the class agrees to the plan.
6. After its acceptance by creditors, the plan is confirmed by the court.
7. Payments in cash, property, and securities are made to creditors and shareholders. The plan may provide for the issuance of new securities.
8. For some fixed length of time, the firm operates according to the provisions of the reorganization plan.

The corporation may wish to allow the old stockholders to retain some participation in the firm. Needless to say, this may involve some protest by the holders of unsecured debt.

    To give you some idea of the costs associated with a bankruptcy, consider the case of Lehman Brothers, which filed for bankruptcy in September 2008. The company wanted to reorganize through the bankruptcy process, but complications arose almost from the bankruptcy filing date. Because of the complexity of many of Lehman's assets, unwinding and selling them was difficult and time-consuming. Eventually, Lehman exited bankruptcy about three and a half years later in March 2012. Some of the firms that were involved in the Lehman bankruptcy were Alvarez & Marsal, which billed about $512 million in fees; Weil, Gotshal, & Manges, which billed $383 million; and Milbank, Tweed, Hadley, & McCloy, which billed $133 million. In all, Lehman's bankruptcy costs were $2.2 *billion* in fees. The next-largest bankruptcy fees appear to have been paid to those involved in energy giant Enron's bankruptcy. The fees in that case reached a mere $1 billion.

So-called prepackaged bankruptcies are a relatively new phenomenon. What happens is that the corporation secures the necessary approval of a bankruptcy plan from a majority of its creditors first, and then it files for bankruptcy. As a result, the company enters bankruptcy and reemerges almost immediately.

In some cases, the bankruptcy procedure is needed to invoke the "cram-down" power of the bankruptcy court. Under certain circumstances, a class of creditors can be forced to accept a bankruptcy plan even if they vote not to approve it, hence the remarkably apt description "cram down."

In 2005, Congress passed the most significant overhaul of U.S. bankruptcy laws in the last 25 years, the Bankruptcy Abuse Prevention and Consumer Protection Act of 2005 (BAPCPA). Most of the changes were aimed at individual debtors, but corporations also were affected. Before BAPCPA, a bankrupt company had the exclusive right to submit reorganization plans to the bankruptcy court. It has been argued that this exclusivity is one reason some companies have remained in bankruptcy for so long. Under the new law, after 18 months, creditors can submit their own plan for the court's consideration. This change is likely to speed up bankruptcies and also lead to more "prepacks" (to learn about prepacks, see our nearby *Finance Matters* box).

One controversial change made by BAPCPA has to do with so-called key employee retention plans, or KERPs. Strange as it may sound, bankrupt companies routinely give bonus payments to executives, even though the executives may be the same ones who led the company into bankruptcy in the first place. Such bonuses are intended to keep valuable employees from moving to more successful firms, but critics have argued they often are abused. The new law permits KERPs only if the employee in question actually has a job offer from another company.

Recently, Section 363 of the bankruptcy code has been in the news. In a traditional Chapter 11 filing, the bankruptcy plan is described to creditors and shareholders in a prospectus-like disclosure. The plan then must be approved by a vote involving the interested parties. A Section 363 bankruptcy is more like an auction. An initial bidder, known as a *stalking horse*, bids on all or part of the bankrupt company's assets. Other bidders are then invited into the process to determine the highest bid for the company's assets. The main advantage of a Section 363 bankruptcy is speed. Because a traditional bankruptcy requires the approval of interested parties, it is not uncommon for the process to take several years, while a Section 363 bankruptcy is generally much quicker. For example, in the middle of 2009, both General Motors and Chrysler sped through the bankruptcy process in less than 45 days with the help of Section 363 sales.

Financial Management and the Bankruptcy Process

Get the latest on bankruptcy at www .bankruptcydata.com.

It may seem a little odd, but the right to go bankrupt is very valuable. There are several reasons this is true. First of all, from an operational standpoint, when a firm files for bankruptcy, there is an immediate "stay" on creditors, usually meaning that payments to

Bankruptcy, "Prepack" Style

On March 21, 2018, Southeastern Grocers, owner of Winn-Dixie and Bi-Lo grocery stores, filed for Chapter 11 reorganization under the U.S. bankruptcy code. A firm in this situation reasonably could be expected to spend a year or more in bankruptcy. Not so with Southeastern Grocers. The company exited bankruptcy in May 2018, about two months later. In this case, the company's debt was reduced to $600 million, and creditors were given an equity stake in the company. Even though Southeastern Grocers had a brief stay in bankruptcy, the all-time record belongs to Blue Bird, maker of the iconic yellow school buses. Blue Bird's stay in bankruptcy was *one day*!

Firms typically file for bankruptcy to seek protection from their creditors, essentially admitting that they cannot meet their financial obligations as they are then structured. Once in bankruptcy, the firm attempts to reorganize its operations and finances so that it can survive. A key to this process is that most of the creditors ultimately must give their approval to the restructuring plan. The time a firm spends in Chapter 11 depends on many things, but it usually depends most on the time it takes to get creditors to agree to a plan of reorganization.

Blue Bird was able to expedite its bankruptcy by filing a presolicited, or prepackaged, bankruptcy, often called a *prepack*. The idea is simple. Before filing for bankruptcy, the firm approaches its creditors with a plan for reorganization. The two sides negotiate a settlement and agree on the details of how the firm's finances will be restructured. Then, the firm puts together the necessary paperwork for the bankruptcy court before filing for bankruptcy. A filing is a prepack if the firm essentially walks into court and, at the same time, files a reorganization plan complete with the documentation of its creditors' approval, which is exactly what Blue Bird did.

The key to the prepackaged reorganization process is that both sides have something to gain and something to lose. If bankruptcy is imminent, it may make sense for the creditors to expedite the process even though they are likely to take a financial loss in the restructuring. Blue Bird's bankruptcy was relatively painless for most of its creditors. Several different classes of creditors were involved. Bank loans were converted into senior secured notes, and senior bondholders exchanged their bonds for new bonds with the same face value and terms. Of course, the old stockholders received nothing, and, in fact, had their shares canceled.

For a firm, operating in bankruptcy can be a difficult process. The bankruptcy court typically has a great deal of oversight over the firm's day-to-day operations, and putting together a reorganization plan to emerge from bankruptcy can be a tremendous drain on management time, time that would be better spent making the firm profitable again. Also, news that a firm is in bankruptcy can make skittish customers turn to competitors, endangering the future health of the firm. A prepack can't completely eliminate these problems, but by speeding up the bankruptcy process, it can reduce the headaches involved.

creditors will cease, and creditors will have to await the outcome of the bankruptcy process to find out if and how much they will be paid. This stay gives the firm time to evaluate its options, and it prevents what is usually termed a "race to the courthouse steps" by creditors and others.

Beyond this, some bankruptcy filings are actually strategic actions intended to improve a firm's competitive position, and firms have filed for bankruptcy even though they were not insolvent at the time. Probably the most famous example is Continental Airlines. In 1983, following deregulation of the airline industry, Continental found itself competing with newly established airlines that had much lower labor costs. In response, Continental filed for reorganization under Chapter 11 even though it was not insolvent.

Continental argued that, based on pro forma data, it would become insolvent in the future, and a reorganization was therefore necessary. By filing for bankruptcy, Continental was able to terminate its existing labor agreements, lay off large numbers of workers, and slash wages for the remaining employees. In other words, at least in the eyes of critics, Continental essentially used the bankruptcy process as a vehicle for reducing labor costs. Congress has subsequently modified bankruptcy laws to make it more difficult, though not

TABLE 13.6	Company	Date of Filing	Liabilities ($ millions)
	Lehman Brothers Holdings, Inc.	September 15, 2008	$613,000
	General Motors Corp.	June 1, 2009	172,810
	CIT Group, Inc.	November 1, 2009	64,901
	Chrysler, LLC	April 30, 2009	55,200
	Energy Future Holdings Corp.	April 29, 2014	49,701
	MF Global Holdings Ltd.	October 31, 2011	39,684
	AMR Corp.	November 29, 2011	29,552
	General Growth Properties, Inc.	April 22, 2009	27,294
	Thornburg Mortgage, Inc.	May 1, 2009	24,700
	Charter Ccommunications, Inc.	March 27, 2009	24,186

Ten largest U.S. bankruptcy filings

Source: Edward I. Altman, NYU Salomon Center, Stern School of Business.

impossible, for companies to abrogate a labor contract through the bankruptcy process. For example, Delta Air Lines filed for bankruptcy in 2005, in part to renegotiate the contracts with its union employees.

Other famous examples of strategic bankruptcies exist. For example, Manville (then known as Johns-Manville) and Dow Corning filed for bankruptcies because of expected future losses resulting from litigations associated with asbestos and silicone breast implants, respectively. Similarly, in the then-largest-ever bankruptcy, Texaco filed in 1987 after Pennzoil was awarded a $10.3 billion judgment against the company. Texaco later settled for $3.5 billion and emerged from bankruptcy.

The 2008 recession shows how an economic downturn can result in bankruptcy for levered firms. Table 13.6 contains the ten largest bankruptcy filings in the United States from 2008 through mid-2018. As you can see, seven of the ten occurred immediately after the recession. At the top of the list, the Lehman Brothers collapse was the largest in U.S. history, but the 2003 bankruptcy filing of Italian dairy company Parmalat may have topped them all in terms of relative importance. This company, by itself, represented 1.5 percent of the Italian gross national product!

Agreements to Avoid Bankruptcy

When a firm defaults on an obligation, it can avoid a bankruptcy filing. Because the legal process of bankruptcy can be lengthy and expensive, it is often in everyone's best interest to devise a "workout" that avoids a bankruptcy filing. Much of the time, creditors can work with the management of a company that has defaulted on a loan contract. Voluntary arrangements to restructure, or "reschedule," the company's debt can be and often are made. This may involve *extension*, which postpones the date of payment, or *composition*, which allows a reduced payment.

CONCEPT QUESTIONS

13.8a What is the APR (in connection with bankruptcy proceedings)?
13.8b What is the difference between liquidation and reorganization?

SUMMARY AND CONCLUSIONS

The ideal mixture of debt and equity for a firm—its optimal capital structure—is the one that maximizes the value of the firm and minimizes the overall cost of capital. If we ignore taxes, financial distress costs, and any other imperfections, we find that there is no ideal mixture. Under these circumstances, the firm's capital structure is irrelevant.

If we consider the effect of corporate taxes, we find that capital structure matters a great deal. This conclusion is based on the fact that interest is tax deductible and thus generates a valuable tax shield. Unfortunately, we also find that the optimal capital structure is 100 percent debt, which is not something we observe in healthy firms.

We next introduced costs associated with bankruptcy, or, more generally, financial distress. These costs reduce the attractiveness of debt financing. We concluded that an optimal capital structure exists when the net tax saving from an additional dollar in interest just equals the increase in expected financial distress costs. This is the essence of the static theory of capital structure.

When we examine actual capital structures, we find two regularities. First, firms in the United States typically do not use great amounts of debt, but they pay substantial taxes. This suggests that there is a limit to the use of debt financing to generate tax shields. Second, there is wide variation in the use of debt across industries, suggesting that the nature of a firm's assets and operations is an important determinant of its capital structure.

 connect POP QUIZ!

Can you answer the following questions? If your class is using *Connect*, log on to SmartBook to see if you know the answers to these and other questions, check out the study tools, and find out what topics require additional practice!

Section 13.3 What assumptions are necessary for M&M Proposition I to hold?

Section 13.5 What are indirect costs of bankruptcy?

Section 13.6 The static theory of capital structure is based on the theory that firms use leverage up to the point where the marginal value of what two things are equal?

Section 13.7 What would generally receive the lowest priority when the assets of a Chapter 7 bankruptcy firm are distributed?

CHAPTER REVIEW AND SELF-TEST PROBLEMS

13.1 EBIT and EPS Suppose the GNR Corporation has decided in favor of a capital restructuring that involves increasing its existing $5 million in debt to $25 million. The interest rate on the debt is 12 percent and is not expected to change. The firm currently has 1 million shares outstanding, and the price per share is $40. If the restructuring is expected to increase the ROE, what is the minimum level for EBIT that GNR's management must be expecting? Ignore taxes in your answer. (See Problem 4.)

13.2 **M&M Proposition II (no taxes)** The Pro Bono Corporation has a WACC of 20 percent. Its cost of debt is 12 percent. If Pro Bono's debt-equity ratio is 2, what is its cost of equity capital? Ignore taxes in your answer. (See Problem 10.)

13.3 **M&M Proposition I (with corporate taxes)** Suppose TransGlobal Co. currently has no debt and its equity is worth $20,000. If the corporate tax rate is 21 percent, what will the value of the firm be if TransGlobal borrows $6,000 and uses the proceeds to buy up stock? (See Problem 14.)

■ **Answers to Chapter Review and Self-Test Problems**

13.1 To answer, we can calculate the break-even EBIT. At any EBIT above this, the increased financial leverage will increase EPS. Under the old capital structure, the interest bill is $5 million × .12 = $600,000. There are 1 million shares of stock, so, ignoring taxes, EPS is (EBIT − $600,000)/1 million.

Under the new capital structure, the interest expense will be $25 million × .12 = $3 million. Furthermore, the debt rises by $20 million. This amount is sufficient to repurchase $20 million/40 = 500,000 shares of stock, leaving 500,000 outstanding. EPS is thus (EBIT − $3 million)/500,000.

Now that we know how to calculate EPS under both scenarios, we set the two expressions for EPS equal to each other and solve for the break-even EBIT:

$$(EBIT − \$600{,}000)/1 \text{ million} = (EBIT − \$3 \text{ million})/500{,}000$$
$$EBIT − \$600{,}000 = 2 × (EBIT − \$3 \text{ million})$$
$$EBIT = \$5{,}400{,}000$$

Verify that, in either case, EPS is $4.80 when EBIT is $5.4 million.

13.2 According to M&M Proposition II (no taxes), the cost of equity is:

$$R_E = R_A + (R_A − R_D) × (D/E)$$
$$= 20\% + (20\% − 12\%) × 2$$
$$= 36\%$$

13.3 After the debt issue, TransGlobal will be worth the original $20,000 plus the present value of the tax shield. According to M&M Proposition I with taxes, the present value of the tax shield is $T_c × D$, or .21 × $6,000 = $1,260, so the firm is worth $20,000 + 1,260 = $21,260.

CRITICAL THINKING AND CONCEPTS REVIEW

LO 1 13.1 **Business Risk versus Financial Risk** Explain what is meant by business and financial risk. Suppose Firm A has greater business risk than Firm B. Is it true that Firm A also has a higher cost of equity capital? Explain.

LO 1 13.2 **M&M Propositions** How would you answer in the following debate?
Q: Isn't it true that the riskiness of a firm's equity will rise if the firm increases its use of debt financing?
A: Yes, that's the essence of M&M Proposition II.
Q: And isn't it true that, as a firm increases its use of borrowing, the likelihood of default increases, which increases the risk of the firm's debt?
A: Yes.

Q: In other words, increased borrowing increases the risk of the equity and the debt?

A: That's right.

Q: Well, given that the firm uses only debt and equity financing, and given that the risk of both is increased by increased borrowing, does it not follow that increasing debt increases the overall risk of the firm and therefore decreases the value of the firm?

A: ??

LO 1   **13.3   Optimal Capital Structure**   Is there an easily identifiable debt-equity ratio that will maximize the value of a firm? Why or why not?

LO 1   **13.4   Observed Capital Structures**   Refer to the observed capital structures given in Table 13.5 of the text. What do you notice about the types of industries with respect to their average debt-equity ratios? Are certain types of industries more likely to be highly leveraged than others? What are some possible reasons for this observed segmentation? Do the operating results and tax history of the firms play a role? How about their future earnings prospects? Explain.

LO 1   **13.5   Financial Leverage**   Why is the use of debt financing referred to as using financial "leverage"?

LO 1   **13.6   Homemade Leverage**   What is homemade leverage?

LO 3   **13.7   Bankruptcy and Corporate Ethics**   As mentioned in the text, some firms have filed for bankruptcy because of actual or likely litigation-related losses. Is this a proper use of the bankruptcy process?

LO 3   **13.8   Bankruptcy and Corporate Ethics**   Firms sometimes use the threat of a bankruptcy filing to force creditors to renegotiate terms. Critics argue that in such cases, the firm is using bankruptcy laws "as a sword rather than a shield." Is this an ethical tactic?

LO 3   **13.9   Bankruptcy and Corporate Ethics**   As mentioned in the text, Continental Airlines filed for bankruptcy, at least in part as a means of reducing labor costs. Whether this move was ethical, or proper, was hotly debated. Give both sides of the argument.

LO 1   **13.10   Capital Structure Goal**   What is the basic goal of financial management with regard to capital structure?

QUESTIONS AND PROBLEMS

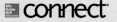   Select problems are available in McGraw-Hill *Connect*. Please see the packaging options section of the Preface for more information.

BASIC (Questions 1–13)

LO 1   **1. EBIT and Leverage**   Minion, Inc., has no debt outstanding and a total market value of $211,875. Earnings before interest and taxes, EBIT, are projected to be $14,300 if economic conditions are normal. If there is strong expansion in the economy, then EBIT will be 20 percent higher. If there is a recession, then EBIT will be 35 percent lower. The company is considering a $33,900 debt issue with an interest rate of 6 percent. The proceeds will be used to repurchase shares of stock. There are currently 7,500 shares outstanding. Ignore taxes for this problem.

a. Calculate earnings per share, EPS, under each of the three economic scenarios before any debt is issued. Also, calculate the percentage changes in EPS when the economy expands or enters a recession.

b. Repeat part (a) assuming that the company goes through with recapitalization. What do you observe? Assume the stock price remains constant.

LO 2   **2. EBIT, Taxes, and Leverage**   Repeat parts (a) and (b) in Problem 1 assuming the company has a tax rate of 21 percent.

LO 1
LO 2   **3. ROE and Leverage**   Suppose the company in Problem 1 has a market-to-book ratio of 1.0 and the stock price remains constant.

a. Calculate return on equity, ROE, under each of the three economic scenarios before any debt is issued. Also, calculate the percentage changes in ROE for economic expansion and recession, assuming no taxes.

b. Repeat part (a) assuming the firm goes through with the proposed recapitalization.

c. Repeat parts (a) and (b) of this problem assuming the firm has a tax rate of 21 percent.

LO 1   **4. Break-Even EBIT**   Trapper Corporation is comparing two different capital structures, an all-equity plan (Plan I) and a levered plan (Plan II). Under Plan I, the company would have 320,000 shares of stock outstanding. Under Plan II, there would be 240,000 shares of stock outstanding and $2,272,000 in debt outstanding. The interest rate on the debt is 10 percent, and there are no taxes.

a. If EBIT is $700,000, which plan will result in the higher EPS?

b. If EBIT is $950,000, which plan will result in the higher EPS?

c. What is the break-even EBIT?

LO 1   **5. M&M and Stock Value**   In Problem 4, use M&M Proposition I to find the price per share of equity under each of the two proposed plans. What is the value of the firm?

LO 1
LO 2   **6. Break-Even EBIT and Leverage**   Honeycutt Co. is comparing two different capital structures. Plan I would result in 12,700 shares of stock and $109,250 in debt. Plan II would result in 9,800 shares of stock and $247,000 in debt. The interest rate on the debt is 10 percent.

a. Ignoring taxes, compare both of these plans to an all-equity plan assuming that EBIT will be $79,000. The all-equity plan would result in 15,000 shares of stock outstanding. Which of the three plans has the highest EPS? The lowest?

b. In part (a), what are the break-even levels of EBIT for each plan as compared to that for an all-equity plan? Is one higher than the other? Why?

c. Ignoring taxes, when will EPS be identical for Plans I and II?

d. Repeat parts (a), (b), and (c) assuming that the corporate tax rate is 21 percent. Are the break-even levels of EBIT different from before? Why or why not?

LO 1   **7. Leverage and Stock Value**   Ignoring taxes in Problem 6, what is the price per share of equity under Plan I? Plan II? What principle is illustrated by your answers?

LO 1   **8. Homemade Leverage**   FCOJ, Inc., a prominent consumer products firm, is debating whether or not to convert its all-equity capital structure to one that is 30 percent debt. Currently, there are 7,400 shares outstanding and the price per share is $55. EBIT is expected to remain at $20,900 per year forever. The interest rate on new debt is 8 percent, and there are no taxes.

   a. Melanie, a shareholder of the firm, owns 100 shares of stock. What is her cash flow under the current capital structure, assuming the firm has a dividend payout rate of 100 percent?

   b. What will Melanie's cash flow be under the proposed capital structure of the firm? Assume that she keeps all 100 of her shares.

   c. Suppose FCOJ does convert, but Melanie prefers the current all-equity capital structure. Show how she could unlever her shares of stock to recreate the original capital structure.

   d. Using your answer to part (c), explain why FCOJ's choice of capital structure is irrelevant.

LO 1   **9. Homemade Leverage**   Pagemaster Enterprises is considering a change from its current capital structure. The company currently has an all-equity capital structure and is considering a capital structure with 25 percent debt. There are currently 8,100 shares outstanding at a price per share of $50. EBIT is expected to remain constant at $44,000. The interest rate on new debt is 7 percent and there are no taxes.

   a. Rebecca owns $17,000 worth of stock in the company. If the firm has a 100 percent payout, what is her cash flow?

   b. What would her cash flow be under the new capital structure assuming that she keeps all of her shares?

   c. Suppose the company does convert to the new capital structure. Show how Rebecca can maintain her current cash flow.

   d. Under your answer to part (c), explain why the company's choice of capital structure is irrelevant.

LO 1   **10. Calculating WACC**   Brown Industries has a debt-equity ratio of 1.5. Its WACC is 9.6 percent, and its cost of debt is 5.7 percent. There is no corporate tax.

   a. What is the company's cost of equity capital?

   b. What would the cost of equity be if the debt-equity ratio were 2.0? What if it were .5? What if it were zero?

LO 1   **11. Calculating WACC**   Irving Corp. has no debt but can borrow at 6.4 percent. The firm's WACC is currently 10.9 percent, and there is no corporate tax.

   a. What is the company's cost of equity?

   b. If the firm converts to 30 percent debt, what will its cost of equity be?

   c. If the firm converts to 60 percent debt, what will its cost of equity be?

   d. What is the company's WACC in part (b)? In part (c)?

LO 2 **12. M&M and Taxes**   Tatum can borrow at 6.7 percent. The company currently has no debt, and the cost of equity is 12.9 percent. The current value of the firm is $595,000. What will the value be if the company borrows $310,000 and uses the proceeds to repurchase shares? The corporate tax rate is 21 percent.

LO 2 **13. Interest Tax Shield**   Hayward Co. has a 22 percent tax rate. Its total interest payment for the year just ended was $14.3 million. What is the interest tax shield? How do you interpret this amount?

INTERMEDIATE (Questions 14–16)

LO 1 **14. M&M**   Bird Enterprises has no debt. Its current total value is $47 million. Ignoring taxes, what will the company's value be if it sells $18.4 million in debt? Suppose now that the company's tax rate is 23 percent. What will its overall value be if it sells $18.4 million in debt? Assume debt proceeds are used to repurchase equity.

LO 1 **15. M&M**   In the previous question, what is the debt-equity ratio in both cases?

LO 1 **16. M&M**   Horford Co. has no debt. Its cost of capital is 8.9 percent. Suppose the company converts to a debt-equity ratio of 1.0. The interest rate on the debt is 5.7 percent. Ignoring taxes, what is the company's new cost of equity? What is its new WACC?

CHALLENGE (Questions 17–20)

LO 2 **17. Firm Value**   Calvert Corporation expects an EBIT of $22,300 every year forever. The company currently has no debt, and its cost of equity is 15 percent.

   a. What is the current value of the company?

   b. Suppose the company can borrow at 10 percent. If the corporate tax rate is 21 percent, what will the value of the firm be if the company takes on debt equal to 50 percent of its unlevered value? What if it takes on debt equal to 100 percent of its unlevered value?

   c. What will the value of the firm be if the company takes on debt equal to 50 percent of its levered value? What if the company takes on debt equal to 100 percent of its levered value?

LO 2 **18. Firm Value**   What is the cost of capital for a firm that is 100 percent debt financed? What is the value of the firm?

LO 2 **19. Cost of Equity and Leverage**   Assuming a world of corporate taxes only, show that the cost of equity, R_E, is as follows: $R_E = R_U + (R_U - R_D) \times (D/E) \times (1 - T_C)$.

LO 2 **20. Business and Financial Risk**   Assume a firm's debt is risk-free, so that the cost of debt equals the risk-free rate, R_f. Define β_A as the firm's *asset* beta— that is, the systematic risk of the firm's assets. Define β_E to be the beta of the firm's equity. Use the capital asset pricing model (CAPM) along with M&M Proposition II to show that $\beta_E = \beta_A \times (1 + D/E)$, where D/E is the debt-equity ratio. Assume the tax rate is zero.

WHAT'S ON THE WEB?

13.1 Capital Structure   Go to www.reuters.com and enter the ticker symbol AMGN for Amgen, a biotechnology company. Find the long-term debt-equity and total debt-equity ratios. How does Amgen compare to the industry, sector, and S&P 500 in these areas? Now answer the same question for Edison International (EIX), the parent company of Southern California Edison, a utility company. How do the capital structures of Amgen and Edison International compare? Can you think of possible explanations for the difference between these two companies?

13.2 Capital Structure   Go to finance.yahoo.com and find the stock screener. Use the stock screener to answer the following questions. How many companies have debt-equity ratios greater than 2? Greater than 5? Greater than 10? What company has the highest debt-equity ratio? What is the ratio? Now find how many companies have a negative debt-equity ratio. What is the lowest debt-equity ratio? What does it mean if a company has a negative debt-equity ratio?

EXCEL *MASTER IT!* PROBLEM

The TL Corporation currently has no debt outstanding. Josh Culberson, the CFO, is considering restructuring the company by issuing debt and using the proceeds to repurchase outstanding equity. The company's assets are worth $40 million, the stock price is $25 per share, and there are 1,600,000 shares outstanding. In the expected state of the economy, EBIT is expected to be $3 million. If there is a recession, EBIT would fall to $1.8 million; in an expansion, EBIT would increase to $4.3 million. If the company issues debt, it will issue a combination of short-term debt and long-term debt. The ratio of short-term debt to long-term debt will be .20. The short-term debt will have an interest rate of 3 percent and the long-term debt will have an interest rate of 8 percent.

a. On the applicable worksheet, fill in the values in each table. For the debt-equity ratio, create a spinner that changes the debt-equity ratio. The resulting debt-equity ratio should range from 0 to 10 at increments of .1.

b. Graph the EBIT and EPS for the TL Corporation on the same graph using a scatter plot.

c. What is the break-even EBIT between the current capital structure and the new capital structure?

d. To illustrate the new capital structure, you would like to create a pie chart. One type of pie chart that is available is the pie-in-pie chart. Using the pie-in-pie chart, graph the equity and total debt in the main pie chart and the short-term debt and long-term debt in the secondary pie chart. Note, if you right-click on a data series in the chart and select Format Data Series, the Series Options will permit you to display the series by a customized choice. In the customization, you can select which data series you want displayed in the primary pie chart and the secondary pie chart.

CHAPTER CASE
Stephenson Real Estate Recapitalization

Stephenson Real Estate Company was founded 25 years ago by the current CEO, Robert Stephenson. The company purchases real estate, including land and buildings, and rents the property to tenants. The company has shown a profit every year for the past 18 years, and the shareholders are satisfied with the company's management. Prior to founding Stephenson Real Estate, Robert was the founder and CEO of a failed alpaca farming operation. The resulting bankruptcy made him extremely averse to debt financing. As a result, the company is entirely equity financed, with 8.5 million shares of common stock outstanding. The stock currently trades at $44.50 per share.

Stephenson is evaluating a plan to purchase a huge tract of land in the southeastern United States for $50 million. The land will subsequently be leased to tenant farmers. This purchase is expected to increase Stephenson's annual pretax earnings by $11 million in perpetuity. Kim Weyand, the company's new CFO, has been put in charge of the project. Kim has determined that the company's current cost of capital is 12.5 percent. She feels that the company would be more valuable if it included debt in its capital structure, so she is evaluating whether the company should issue debt to entirely finance the project. Based on some conversations with investment banks, she thinks that the company can issue bonds at par value with a coupon rate of 8 percent. From her analysis, she also believes that a capital structure in the range of 70 percent equity/30 percent debt would be optimal. If the company goes beyond 30 percent debt, its bonds would carry a lower rating and a much higher coupon because the possibility of financial distress and the associated costs would rise sharply. Stephenson has a 21 percent corporate tax rate (state and federal).

QUESTIONS

1. If Stephenson wishes to maximize its total market value, would you recommend that it issue debt or equity to finance the land purchase? Explain.

2. Construct Stephenson's market value balance sheet before it announces the purchase.

3. Suppose Stephenson decides to issue equity to finance the purchase.

   a. What is the net present value of the project?

   b. Construct Stephenson's market value balance sheet after it announces that the firm will finance the purchase using equity. What would be the new price per share of the firm's stock? How many shares will Stephenson need to issue to finance the purchase?

   c. Construct Stephenson's market value balance sheet after the equity issue but before the purchase has been made.

   How many shares of common stock does Stephenson have outstanding? What is the price per share of the firm's stock?

   d. Construct Stephenson's market value balance sheet after the purchase has been made.

4. Suppose Stephenson decides to issue debt to finance the purchase.

   a. What will the market value of the Stephenson Company be if the purchase is financed with debt?

   b. Construct Stephenson's market value balance sheet after both the debt issue and the land purchase. What is the price per share of the firm's stock?

5. Which method of financing maximizes the per-share stock price of Stephenson's equity?

14 Dividends and Dividend Policy

On May 1, 2018, Apple announced a broad plan to reward stockholders for the recent success of the firm's business. Under the plan, Apple would (1) boost its annual dividend by 16 percent, from 63 cents per share to 73 cents per share, and (2) repurchase about $100 billion of its common stock. Investors cheered, bidding up the stock price by about 2.3 percent on the announcement. Why were investors pleased? To find out, this chapter explores these actions and their implications for shareholders.

This chapter is about dividend policy. In Chapter 7, we saw that the value of a share of stock depends on all the future dividends that will be paid to shareholders. In that analysis, we took the future stream of dividends as given. What we now examine is how corporations decide on the size and timing of dividend payments. What we would like to find out is how to establish an optimal dividend policy, meaning a dividend policy that maximizes the stock price. What we discover, among other things, is that it is not at all clear how to do this, or even if there is such a thing as an optimal dividend policy!

Please visit us at essentialsofcorporatefinance.blogspot.com for the latest developments in the world of corporate finance.

Dividend policy is an important subject in corporate finance, and dividends are a major cash outlay for many corporations. At first glance, it may seem obvious that a firm would always want to give as much as possible back to its shareholders by paying dividends. It might seem equally obvious, however, that a firm always can invest the money for its shareholders instead of paying it out. The heart of the dividend policy question is just this: Should the firm pay out money to its shareholders, or should the firm take that money and invest it for its shareholders?

It may seem surprising, but much research and economic logic suggest that dividend policy doesn't matter. In fact, it turns out that the dividend policy issue is much like the capital structure question. The important elements are not difficult to identify, but the interactions between those elements are complex, and no easy answer exists.

Dividend policy is controversial. Many implausible reasons are given for why dividend policy might be important, and many of the claims made about dividend policy are economically illogical. Even so, in the real world of corporate finance, determining the most appropriate dividend policy is considered an important issue. It could be that financial managers who worry about dividend policy are wasting time, but it also could be true that we are missing something important in our discussions.

In part, all discussions of dividends are plagued by the "two-handed lawyer" problem. President Truman, while discussing the legal implications of a possible presidential decision, asked his staff to set up a meeting with a lawyer. Supposedly, Mr. Truman said, "But I don't want one of those two-handed lawyers." When asked what a two-handed lawyer was, he replied, "You know, a lawyer who says, 'On the one hand I recommend you do so and so because of the following reasons, but on the other hand I recommend that you don't do it because of these other reasons.'"

Unfortunately, any sensible treatment of dividend policy will appear to have been written by a two-handed lawyer (or, in fairness, several two-handed financial economists). On the one hand, there are many good reasons for corporations to pay high dividends, but, on the other hand, there are also many good reasons to pay low dividends.

We cover three broad topics that relate to dividends and dividend policy in this chapter. First, we describe the various kinds of dividends and how dividends are paid. Second, we consider an idealized case in which dividend policy doesn't matter. We then discuss the limitations of this case and present some real-world arguments for both high- and low-dividend payouts. Finally, we conclude the chapter by looking at some strategies that corporations might employ to implement a dividend policy, and we discuss share repurchases as an alternative to dividends.

14.1 CASH DIVIDENDS AND DIVIDEND PAYMENT

dividend
Payment made out of a firm's earnings to its owners, in the form of either cash or stock.

distribution
Payment made by a firm to its owners from sources other than current or accumulated retained earnings.

The term **dividend** usually refers to cash paid out of earnings. If a payment is made from sources other than current or accumulated retained earnings, the term **distribution**, rather than *dividend*, is used. However, it is acceptable to refer to a distribution from earnings as a dividend and a distribution from capital as a liquidating dividend. More generally, any direct payment by the corporation to the shareholders may be considered a dividend or a part of dividend policy.

Dividends come in several different forms. The basic types of cash dividends are:

1. Regular cash dividends
2. Extra dividends
3. Special dividends
4. Liquidating dividends

Later in the chapter, we discuss dividends paid in stock instead of cash, and we also consider an alternative to cash dividends, a stock repurchase.

Cash Dividends

regular cash dividend
Cash payment made by a firm to its owners in the normal course of business, usually quarterly.

The most common type of dividend is a cash dividend. Commonly, public companies pay **regular cash dividends** four times a year. As the name suggests, these are cash payments made directly to shareholders, and they are made in the regular course of business. In other words, management sees nothing unusual about the dividend and no reason why it won't be continued.

Sometimes firms will pay a regular cash dividend and an *extra cash dividend.* By calling part of the payment "extra," management is indicating that that part may or may not be repeated in the future. A *special dividend* is similar, but the name usually indicates that this dividend is viewed as a truly unusual or one-time event and it won't be repeated. Finally, the payment of a *liquidating dividend* usually means that some or all of the business has been liquidated, that is, sold off.

However it is labeled, a cash dividend payment reduces corporate cash and retained earnings, except in the case of a liquidating dividend (where paid-in capital may be reduced).

Of course, there are other types of dividends. Companies listed on the Japanese Nikkei stock market have given shareholders alternative dividends in the form of food items, prepaid phone cards, and so forth. For example, McDonald's Holdings Company (Japan) gave its shareholders coupon books for free hamburgers.

Standard Method of Cash Dividend Payment

The decision to pay a dividend rests in the hands of the board of directors of the corporation. When a dividend has been declared, it becomes a liability of the firm and cannot be rescinded easily. Sometime after it has been declared, a dividend is distributed to all shareholders as of some specific date.

Commonly, the amount of the cash dividend is expressed in terms of dollars per share (*dividends per share*). As we have seen in other chapters, it is also expressed as a percentage of the market price (*the dividend yield*) or as a percentage of net income or earnings per share (*the dividend payout*).

Dividend Payment: A Chronology

The mechanics of a cash dividend payment can be illustrated by the example in Figure 14.1 and the following description:

1. **Declaration date.** On January 15, the board of directors passes a resolution to pay a dividend of $1 per share on February 16 to all holders of record as of January 30.

2. **Ex-dividend date.** To make sure that dividend checks go to the right people, brokerage firms and stock exchanges establish an *ex-dividend date.* This date is two business days before the date of record (discussed next). If you buy the stock before this date, then you are entitled to the dividend. If you buy on this date or after, then the previous owner will get the dividend.

declaration date
Date on which the board of directors passes a resolution to pay a dividend.

ex-dividend date
Date two business days before the date of record, establishing those individuals entitled to a dividend.

FIGURE 14.1

Example of the procedure for dividend payment

1. *Declaration date:* The board of directors declares a payment of dividends.
2. *Ex-dividend date:* A share of stock goes ex dividend on the date the seller is entitled to keep the dividend; under NYSE rules, shares are traded ex dividend on and after the second business day before the record date.
3. *Record date:* The declared dividends are distributable to those who are shareholders of record as of this specific date.
4. *Payment date:* The dividend checks are mailed to shareholders of record.

In Figure 14.1, Wednesday, January 28, is the ex-dividend date. Before this date, the stock is said to trade "with dividend," or "cum dividend." Afterwards, the stock trades "ex dividend."

The ex-dividend date convention removes any ambiguity about who is entitled to the dividend. Because the dividend is valuable, the stock price will be affected when the stock goes "ex." We examine this effect below.

date of record

Date by which holders must be on record to receive a dividend.

3. **Date of record.** Based on its records, the corporation prepares a list on January 30 of all individuals believed to be stockholders. These are the *holders of record*, and January 30 is the *date of record* (or record date). The word *believed* is important here. If you bought the stock just before this date, the corporation's records might not reflect that fact because of mailing or other delays. Without some modification, some of the dividend checks would get mailed to the wrong people. This is the reason for the ex-dividend day convention.

date of payment

Date that the dividend checks are mailed.

4. **Date of payment.** The dividend checks are mailed on February 16.

More on the Ex-Dividend Date

The ex-dividend date is important and is a common source of confusion. We examine what happens to the stock when it goes ex, meaning that the ex-dividend date arrives. To illustrate, suppose we have a stock that sells for $10 per share. The board of directors declares a dividend of $1 per share, and the record date is Tuesday, June 12. Based on our discussion above, we know that the ex date will be two business (not calendar) days earlier, on Friday, June 8.

If you buy the stock on Thursday, June 7, right as the market closes, you'll get the $1 dividend because the stock is trading cum dividend. If you wait and buy the stock right as the market opens on Friday, you won't get the $1 dividend. What will happen to the value of the stock overnight?

If you think about it, the stock is obviously worth about $1 less on Friday morning, so its price will drop by this amount between close of business on Thursday and the Friday opening. In general, we expect that the value of a share of stock will go down by about the dividend amount when the stock goes ex dividend. The key word here is *about*. Because dividends are taxed, the actual price drop might be closer to some measure of the aftertax value of the dividend. Determining this value is complicated because of the different tax rates and tax rules that apply for different buyers. The series of events described here is illustrated in Figure 14.2.

FIGURE 14.2

Price behavior around the ex-dividend date for a $1 cash dividend

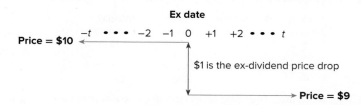

The stock price will fall by the amount of the dividend on the ex date (Time 0). If the dividend is $1 per share, the price will be equal to $10 − 1 = $9 on the ex date.

Before ex date (Time −1)	Dividend = $0	Price = $10
On ex date (Time 0)	Dividend = $1	Price = $ 9

As an example of the price drop on the ex-dividend date, we examine the large dividend paid by Warrior Met Coal, operator of coal mines in Alabama, in November 2017. The dividend was $11.21 per share at a time when the stock price was around $30, so the dividend was about 40 percent of the total stock price, a truly special dividend.

The stock went ex dividend on November 24, 2017. The stock price chart here shows the change in Warrior stock four days prior to the ex-dividend date and on the ex-dividend date.

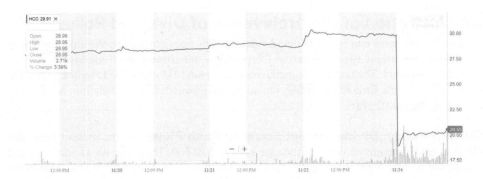

The stock closed at $29.90 on November 22 (November 23 was a holiday) and opened at $18.65 on November 24—a drop of $11.25. With a 20 percent tax rate on dividends, we would have expected a drop of about $9, so the actual price dropped more than we would have expected. We discuss dividends and taxes in more detail in a subsequent section.

EXAMPLE 14.1   **"Ex" Marks the Day**

The board of directors of Divided Airlines has declared a dividend of $2.50 per share payable on Tuesday, May 30, to shareholders of record as of Tuesday, May 9. Cal Icon buys 100 shares of Divided on Tuesday, May 2, for $150 per share. What is the ex date? Describe the events that will occur with regard to the cash dividend and the stock price.

The ex date is two business days before the date of record, Tuesday, May 9, so the stock will go ex on Friday, May 5. Cal buys the stock on Tuesday, May 2, so Cal purchases the stock cum dividend. In other words, Cal will get $2.50 × 100 = $250 in dividends. The check will be mailed on Tuesday, May 30. When the stock does go ex on Friday, its value will drop overnight by about $2.50 per share.

CONCEPT QUESTIONS

14.1a   What are the different types of cash dividends?

14.1b   What are the mechanics of the cash dividend payment?

14.1c   How should the price of a stock change when the stock goes ex dividend?

14.2 DOES DIVIDEND POLICY MATTER?

To decide whether or not dividend policy matters, we first have to define what we mean by dividend *policy*. All other things being the same, of course dividends matter. Dividends are paid in cash, and cash is something that everybody likes. The question we will be discussing here is whether the firm should pay out cash now or invest the cash and pay it out later. Dividend policy, therefore, is the time pattern of dividend payout. In particular, should the firm pay out a large percentage of its earnings now or a small (or even zero) percentage? This is the dividend policy question.

An Illustration of the Irrelevance of Dividend Policy

A powerful argument can be made that dividend policy does not matter. We illustrate this by considering the simple case of Wharton Corporation. Wharton is an all-equity firm that has existed for 10 years. The current financial managers plan to dissolve the firm in 2 years. The total cash flows the firm will generate, including the proceeds from liquidation, are $10,000 in each of the next 2 years.

Current Policy: Dividends Set Equal to Cash Flow At the present time, dividends at each date are set equal to the cash flow of $10,000. There are 100 shares outstanding, so the dividend per share will be $100. In Chapter 7, we showed that the value of the stock is equal to the present value of the future dividends. Assuming a 10 percent required return, the value of a share of stock today, P_0, is:

$$P_0 = \frac{D_1}{(1+R)^1} + \frac{D_2}{(1+R)^2}$$
$$= \frac{\$100}{1.10} + \frac{\$100}{1.10^2}$$
$$= \$173.55$$

The firm as a whole is thus worth: $100 \times \$173.55 = \$17,355$.

Several members of the board of Wharton have expressed dissatisfaction with the current dividend policy and have asked you to analyze an alternative policy.

Alternative Policy: Initial Dividend Greater Than Cash Flow Another policy is for the firm to pay a dividend of $110 per share on the first date (Date 1), which is, of course, a total dividend of $11,000. Because the cash flow is only $10,000, an extra $1,000 must somehow be raised. One way to do this is to issue $1,000 worth of bonds or stock at Date 1. Assume that stock is issued. The new stockholders will desire enough cash flow at Date 2 so that they earn the required 10 percent return on their Date 1 investment.

What is the value of the firm with this new dividend policy? The new stockholders invest $1,000. They require a 10 percent return, so they will demand $1,000 \times 1.10 = $1,100 of the Date 2 cash flow, leaving only $8,900 to the old stockholders. The dividends to the old stockholders will be:

	Date 1	Date 2
Aggregate dividends to old stockholders	$11,000	$8,900
Dividends per share	110	89

The present value of the dividends per share is therefore:

$$P_0 = \frac{\$110}{1.10} + \frac{\$89}{1.10^2} = \$173.55$$

This is the same value we had before.

The value of the stock is unaffected by this switch in dividend policy even though we had to sell some new stock to finance the dividend. In fact, no matter what pattern of dividend payout the firm chooses, the value of the stock will always be the same in this example. In other words, for the Wharton Corporation, dividend policy makes no difference. The reason is simple: Any increase in a dividend at some point in time is exactly offset by a decrease somewhere else, so the net effect, once we account for time value, is zero.

A Test

Our discussion to this point can be summarized by considering the following true-false test questions:

1. True or false: Dividends are irrelevant.
2. True or false: Dividend policy is irrelevant.

The first statement is surely false, and the reason follows from common sense. Clearly, investors prefer higher dividends to lower dividends at any single date if the dividend level is held constant at every other date. To be more precise regarding the first question, if the dividend per share at a given date is raised, while the dividend per share at every other date is held constant, the stock price will rise. The reason is that the present value of the future dividends must go up if this occurs. This action can be accomplished by management decisions that improve productivity, increase tax savings, strengthen product marketing, or otherwise improve cash flow.

The second statement is true, at least in the simple case we have been examining. Dividend policy by itself cannot raise the dividend at one date while keeping it the same at all other dates. Rather, dividend policy merely establishes the trade-off between dividends at one date and dividends at another date. Once we allow for time value, the present value of the dividend stream is unchanged. Thus, in this simple world, dividend policy does not matter because managers choosing either to raise or to lower the current dividend do not affect the current value of their firm. However, we have ignored several real-world factors that might lead us to change our minds; we pursue some of these in subsequent sections.

Some Real-World Factors Favoring a Low Payout

The example we used to illustrate the irrelevance of dividend policy ignored taxes and flotation costs. We will now see that these factors might lead us to prefer a low-dividend payout.

Taxes   U.S. tax laws are complex, and they affect dividend policy in a number of ways. The key tax feature has to do with the taxation of dividend income and capital gains. For individual shareholders, *effective* tax rates on dividend income are higher than the tax rates on capital gains. Historically, dividends received have been taxed as ordinary income. Capital gains have been taxed at somewhat lower rates, and the tax on a capital gain is deferred until the stock is sold. This second aspect of capital gains taxation makes the effective tax rate much lower because the present value of the tax is less.[1]

A firm that adopts a low-dividend payout will reinvest the money instead of paying it out. This reinvestment increases the value of the firm and of the equity. All other things being equal, the net effect is that the expected capital gains portion of the return will be higher in the future. So the fact that capital gains are taxed favorably may lead us to prefer this approach.

Recent tax law changes have led to a renewed interest in the effect of taxes on corporate dividend policies. As we previously noted, historically, dividends have been taxed as ordinary income (at ordinary income tax rates). In 2003, this changed dramatically. The maximum tax rate on dividends was lowered from the 35–39 percent range to 15 percent, giving corporations a much larger tax incentive to pay dividends. In 2018, the tax rate on dividends was 0 percent, 15 percent, or 20 percent, depending on the individual's income.

Flotation Costs   In our example illustrating that dividend policy doesn't matter, we saw that the firm could sell some new stock if necessary to pay a dividend. As we discuss in our next chapter, selling new stock can be very expensive. If we include the costs of selling stock ("flotation" costs) in our argument, then we will find that the value of the stock decreases if we sell new stock.

More generally, imagine two firms identical in every way except that one pays out a greater percentage of its cash flow in the form of dividends. Because the other firm plows back more, its equity grows faster. If these two firms are to remain identical, then the one with the higher payout will have to periodically sell some stock to catch up. Because this is expensive, a firm might be inclined to have a low payout.

Dividend Restrictions   In some cases, a corporation may face restrictions on its ability to pay dividends. For example, as we discussed in Chapter 6, a common feature of a bond indenture is a covenant prohibiting dividend payments above some level. Also, a corporation may be prohibited by state law from paying dividends if the dividend amount exceeds the firm's retained earnings.

Some Real-World Factors Favoring a High Payout

In this section, we consider reasons a firm might pay its shareholders higher dividends even if it means the firm must issue more shares of stock to finance the dividend payments.

Desire for Current Income   It has been argued that many individuals desire current income. The classic example is the group of retired people and others living on a fixed income, the proverbial "widows and orphans." It is argued that this group is willing to pay a premium to get a higher dividend yield.

---

[1]In fact, capital gains taxes can sometimes be avoided altogether. Although we do not recommend this particular tax-avoidance strategy, the capital gains tax may be avoided by dying. Your heirs are not considered to have a capital gain, so the tax liability dies when you do. In this instance, you can take it with you.

It is easy to see, however, that this argument is irrelevant in our simple case. An individual preferring high current cash flow but holding low-dividend securities easily could sell off shares to provide the necessary funds. Similarly, an individual desiring a low current cash flow but holding high-dividend securities could reinvest the dividends. Thus, in a world of no transaction costs, a policy of high current dividends would be of no value to the stockholder.

The current-income argument may have relevance in the real world. Here, the sale of low-dividend stocks would involve brokerage fees and other transaction costs. Such a sale also might trigger capital gains taxes. These direct cash expenses could be avoided by an investment in high-dividend securities. In addition, the expenditure of the stockholder's own time when selling securities and the natural (though not necessarily rational) fear of consuming out of principal might further lead many investors to buy high-dividend securities.

Tax and Legal Benefits from High Dividends   Earlier we saw that dividends were taxed unfavorably for individual investors. This fact is a powerful argument for a low payout. However, there are a number of other investors who do not receive unfavorable tax treatment from holding high-dividend yield, rather than low-dividend yield, securities.

Corporate investors   A significant tax break on dividends occurs when a corporation owns stock in another corporation. A corporate stockholder receiving either common or preferred dividends is granted a 50 percent (or more) dividend exclusion. The 50 percent exclusion does not apply to capital gains, so this group is taxed unfavorably on capital gains.

As a result of the dividend exclusion, high-dividend, low-capital-gains stocks may be more appropriate for corporations to hold. In fact, this is why corporations hold a substantial percentage of the outstanding preferred stock in the economy. This tax advantage of dividends also leads some corporations to hold high-yielding stocks instead of long-term bonds because there is no similar tax exclusion of interest payments to corporate bondholders.

Tax-exempt investors   We have pointed out both the tax advantages and the tax disadvantages of a low-dividend payout. Of course, this discussion is irrelevant to those in zero tax brackets. This group includes some of the largest investors in the economy, such as pension funds, endowment funds, and trust funds.

There are some legal reasons for large institutions to favor high-dividend yields. First, institutions such as pension funds and trust funds are often set up to manage money for the benefit of others. The managers of such institutions have a *fiduciary responsibility* to invest the money prudently. It has been considered imprudent in courts of law to buy stock in companies with no established dividend record.

Second, institutions such as university endowment funds and trust funds are frequently prohibited from spending any of the principal. Such institutions therefore might prefer high-dividend-yield stocks so they have some ability to spend. Like widows and orphans, this group thus prefers current income. Unlike widows and orphans, this group is very large in terms of the amount of stock owned.

Overall, individual investors (for whatever reason) may have a desire for current income and thus may be willing to pay the dividend tax. In addition, some very large investors such as corporations and tax-free institutions may have a very strong preference for high-dividend payouts.

Clientele Effects: A Resolution of Real-World Factors?

In our earlier discussion, we saw that some groups (wealthy individuals, for example) have an incentive to pursue low-payout (or zero-payout) stocks. Other groups (corporations, for example) have an incentive to pursue high-payout stocks. Companies with high payouts thus will attract one group, and low-payout companies will attract another.

clientele effect
Argument that stocks attract particular groups based on dividend yield and the resulting tax effects.

These different groups are called *clienteles*, and what we have described is a **clientele effect**. The clientele effect argument states that different groups of investors desire different levels of dividends. When a firm chooses a particular dividend policy, the only effect is to attract a particular clientele. If a firm changes its dividend policy, then it attracts a different clientele.

What we are left with is a simple supply and demand argument. Suppose 40 percent of all investors prefer high dividends, but only 20 percent of the firms pay high dividends. Here, the high-dividend firms will be in short supply; thus, their stock prices will rise. Consequently, low-dividend firms will find it advantageous to switch policies until 40 percent of all firms have high payouts. At this point, the *dividend market* is in equilibrium. Further changes in dividend policy are pointless because all of the clienteles are satisfied. The dividend policy for any individual firm is now irrelevant.

To see if you understand the clientele effect, consider the following statement: In spite of the theoretical argument that dividend policy is irrelevant or that firms should not pay dividends, many investors like high dividends; because of this fact, a firm can boost its share price by having a higher dividend payout ratio. True or false?

The answer is "false" if clienteles exist. As long as enough high-dividend firms satisfy the dividend-loving investors, a firm won't be able to boost its share price by paying high dividends. An unsatisfied clientele must exist for this to happen, and there is no evidence that this is the case.

CONCEPT QUESTIONS

14.2a Are dividends irrelevant?

14.2b What are some of the reasons for a low payout?

14.2c What are the implications of dividend clienteles for payout policies?

14.3 STOCK REPURCHASES: AN ALTERNATIVE TO CASH DIVIDENDS

repurchase
Refers to a firm's purchase of its own stock; an alternative to a cash dividend. Also called *stock repurchase*.

Thus far in our chapter, we have considered cash dividends. However, cash dividends are not the only way corporations distribute cash. Instead, a company can **repurchase** its own stock. Repurchases (or *buybacks*) have become an increasingly popular tool, and the amount spent on repurchases has become huge. For example, in 2017, $519 billion of stock was repurchased by S&P 500 companies, a tremendous increase from the recent low of $138 billion in 2009.

Another way to see how important repurchases have become is to compare them to cash dividends. Consider Figure 14.3, which shows aggregate real (inflation-adjusted) dividends and stock repurchases by publicly held U.S. industrial firms for the period 1971–2017, along with the combined total. Aggregate real dividends have grown relatively

FIGURE 14.3

FIGURE 14.3 **Aggregate real (2012) dividends and stock repurchases by publicly held U.S. industrial firms: 1971–2017**

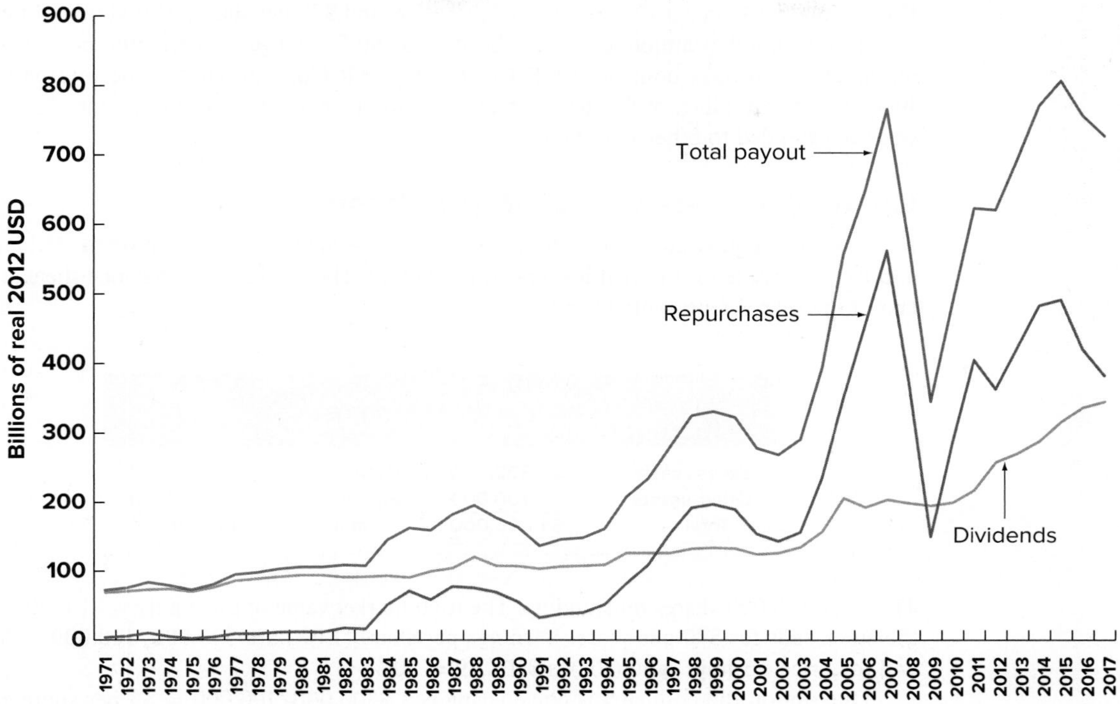

Source: **Redrawn by authors using Compustat data, following Farre-Mensa, Michaely, and Schmalz, "Payout Policy,"** *Annual Review of Financial Economics*, **vol. 6, 2014, 75–134. Updated by authors.**

steadily through time, but repurchases have exploded in the last two decades. They reached a peak of $563 billion in 2007, or about 2.75 times the size of aggregate dividends. Repurchases plunged in the 2008–2009 recession as firms conserved cash, but they rebounded in 2010.

Share repurchases are typically accomplished in one of three ways. First, companies may purchase their own stock, just as anyone would buy shares of a particular stock. In these *open market purchases*, the firm does not reveal itself as the buyer. Thus, the seller does not know whether the shares were sold back to the firm or to another investor.

Second, the firm could institute a *tender offer*. Here, the firm announces to all of its stockholders that it is willing to buy a fixed number of shares at a specific price. For example, suppose Arts and Crafts (A&C), Inc., has 1 million shares of stock outstanding, with a stock price of $50 per share. The firm makes a tender offer to buy back 300,000 shares at $60 per share. A&C chooses a price above $50 to induce shareholders to sell, that is, tender, their shares. In fact, if the tender price is set high enough, shareholders very well may want to sell more than the 300,000 shares. In the extreme case where all outstanding shares are tendered, A&C will buy back 3 out of every 10 shares that a shareholder has.

Finally, firms may repurchase shares from specific individual stockholders. This procedure has been called a *targeted repurchase*. For example, suppose the International Biotechnology Corporation purchased approximately 10 percent of the outstanding stock of the Prime Robotics Company (P-R Co.) in April at around $38 per share. At that time, International Biotechnology announced to the Securities and Exchange Commission that it eventually might try to take control of P-R Co. In May, P-R Co. repurchased the International Biotechnology holdings at $48 per share, well above the market price at that time. This offer was not extended to other shareholders.

Cash Dividends versus Repurchase

Imagine an all-equity company with excess cash of $300,000. The firm pays no dividends, and its net income for the year just ended is $49,000. The market value balance sheet at the end of the year is represented here:

Market Value Balance Sheet (before paying out excess cash)			
Excess cash	$ 300,000	Debt	$ 0
Other assets	700,000	Equity	1,000,000
Total	$1,000,000	Total	$1,000,000

There are 100,000 shares outstanding. The total market value of the equity is $1 million, so the stock sells for $10 per share. Earnings per share (EPS) are $49,000/100,000 = $.49, and the price-earnings ratio (PE) is $10/.49 = 20.4.

One option the company is considering is a $300,000/100,000 = $3 per share extra cash dividend. Alternatively, the company is thinking of using the money to repurchase $300,000/$10 = 30,000 shares of stock.

If commissions, taxes, and other imperfections are ignored in our example, the stockholders shouldn't care which option is chosen. Does this seem surprising? It shouldn't, really. What is happening here is that the firm is paying out $300,000 in cash. The new balance sheet is represented here:

Market Value Balance Sheet (after paying out excess cash)			
Excess cash	$ 0	Debt	$ 0
Other assets	700,000	Equity	700,000
Total	$700,000	Total	$700,000

If the cash is paid out as a dividend, there are still 100,000 shares outstanding, so each is worth $7.

The fact that the per-share value fell from $10 to $7 is not a cause for concern. Consider a stockholder who owns 100 shares. At $10 per share before the dividend, the total value is $1,000.

After the $3 dividend, this same stockholder has 100 shares worth $7 each, for a total of $700, plus 100 × $3 = $300 in cash, for a combined total of $1,000. This illustrates what we saw early on: A cash dividend doesn't affect a stockholder's wealth if there are no imperfections. In this case, the stock price fell by $3 when the stock went ex dividend.

Also, because total earnings and the number of shares outstanding haven't changed, EPS is still 49 cents. The price-earnings ratio, however, falls to $7/.49 = 14.3$. Why we are looking at accounting earnings and PE ratios will be apparent in a moment.

Alternatively, if the company repurchases 30,000 shares, there are 70,000 left outstanding. The balance sheet looks the same:

Market Value Balance Sheet (after share repurchase)			
Excess cash	$ 0	Debt	$ 0
Other assets	700,000	Equity	700,000
Total	$700,000	Total	$700,000

The company is worth $700,000 again, so each remaining share is worth $700,000/70,000 = \$10$. Our stockholder with 100 shares is obviously unaffected. For example, if she was so inclined, she could sell 30 shares and end up with $300 in cash and $700 in stock, as she has if the firm pays the cash dividend. This is an example of a homemade dividend.

In this second case, EPS goes up because total earnings remain the same while the number of shares goes down. The new EPS is $49,000/70,000 = \$.70$. However, the important thing to notice is that the PE ratio is $10/.70 = 14.3$, the same as it was following the dividend.

This example illustrates the important point that, if there are no imperfections, a cash dividend and a share repurchase are essentially the same thing. This is another illustration of dividend policy irrelevance when there are no taxes or other imperfections.

Real-World Considerations in a Repurchase

The example we have described shows that a repurchase and a cash dividend are the same thing in a world without taxes and transaction costs. In the real world, there are some accounting differences between a share repurchase and a cash dividend, but the most important difference is in the tax treatment.

Under current tax law, a repurchase has a significant tax advantage over a cash dividend. A dividend is taxed, and a shareholder has no choice about whether or not to receive the dividend. In a repurchase, a shareholder pays taxes only if (1) the shareholder actually chooses to sell and (2) the shareholder has a capital gain on the sale.

Suppose a dividend of $1 per share is taxed at ordinary rates. Investors in the 28 percent tax bracket who own 100 shares of the security pay $100 × .28 = \$28$ in taxes. Selling shareholders would pay far lower taxes if $100 worth of stock were repurchased. This is because taxes are paid only on the profit from a sale. Thus, the gain on a sale would be only $40 if shares sold at $100 were originally purchased at $60. The capital gains tax would be $.28 × \$40 = \$11.20$. Note that the recent reductions in dividend and capital gains tax rates do not change the fact that a repurchase has a potentially large tax edge.

To give a few examples of recent activity, as we mentioned in the chapter opener, Apple announced a $100 billion buyback in 2018. This purchase came after the company said in May 2017 that it had completed $211 billion of its then-current $250 billion buyback program. And IBM is well known for its aggressive buyback policies. In late 2017, the company announced it would repurchase about $3 billion of its stock during 2018. This amount was much lower than the more than $50 billion it spent from 2010 through 2015. So how much of its stock has IBM repurchased? In 1995, the company had about 2.2 billion shares of stock outstanding. At the end of 2017, there were only about 918 million

Stock Buybacks: No End in Sight

Although the recent recession slowed stock buybacks, recently buybacks have begun to grow again. In fact, for the past several years, share repurchases have been so large that U.S. corporations bought back more shares than they sold. In other words, aggregate net equity raised by U.S. corporations has been negative. For example, during 2017, S&P 500 companies repurchased about $519 billion of stock, while at the same time new equity issuance was only $140 billion.

Some companies appear to have become serial repurchasers. For example, ExxonMobil had suspended its repurchase program in late 2017. However, from 2008 to 2017, ExxonMobil repurchased about $180 billion of its stock. Microsoft is another serial repurchaser. During its 2014 fiscal year, the company repurchased about $6.4 billion of its stock and had repurchased about $117 billion over the 2008–2017 period. And Microsoft still had plans to complete its announced $40 billion repurchase.

Stock buybacks have evolved to the point where they are used for other purposes. For example, in January 2005, consumer products giant Procter & Gamble (P&G) announced that it was purchasing razor manufacturer Gillette for $54 billion. The purchase was paid for entirely with stock in P&G. This is important because if a company acquires another company for cash, the shareholders of the acquired company may be forced to pay taxes. If shareholders receive stock, no taxes are due. What made the deal unique was that P&G announced at the same time that it would repurchase from $18 to $22 billion in stock. Thus, P&G essentially paid about 60 percent in stock and 40 percent in cash, but the way the deal was structured made it look like a 100 percent stock acquisition to Gillette's stockholders.

Stock buybacks can be a large percentage of a company's equity. For example, in May 2018, Micron Technology announced plans to buy back $10 billion of its stock. While this amount is not as large as many other buybacks, it represented about 17 percent of the company's stock. Another example in the same month is Qualcomm, which spent about $12 billion on buybacks, or about 15 percent of the company's value. And MGM Resorts announced plans to repurchase $2 billion of its stock, which would account for about 13 percent of the company's value.

We haven't discussed what happens to the stock when a company does a buyback. There are actually several things the company can do. Many companies keep the stock and use the shares for employee stock option plans. When employee stock options are exercised by the employees, new shares are created, which increases the number of shares of stock outstanding. By using the repurchased shares, the company does not need to issue any new shares. A company also can keep the repurchased stock for itself as Treasury stock. Finally, the company can cancel the stock completely. In essence, it destroys the shares repurchased, which reduces the number of shares outstanding.

shares outstanding, so over a 22-year period, the company had repurchased more than half its stock!

One cautionary note is in order concerning share repurchases, or buybacks. A company announcing plans to buy back some of its stock has no legal obligation to actually do it, and it turns out that many announced repurchases are never completed. Our nearby *Finance Matters* discusses some recent events in stock buybacks.

Share Repurchase and EPS

You may read in the popular financial press that a share repurchase is beneficial because it causes earnings per share to increase. As we have seen, this will happen. The reason is that a share repurchase reduces the number of outstanding shares, but it has no effect on total earnings. As a result, EPS rises.

However, the financial press may place undue emphasis on EPS figures in a repurchase agreement. In our preceding example, we saw that the value of the stock wasn't affected by the EPS change. In fact, the PE ratio was exactly the same when we compared a cash dividend to a repurchase.

CONCEPT QUESTIONS

14.3a Why might a stock repurchase make more sense than an extra cash dividend?

14.3b What is the effect of a stock repurchase on a firm's EPS? Its PE?

14.4 WHAT WE KNOW AND DO NOT KNOW ABOUT DIVIDEND AND PAYOUT POLICIES

Dividends and Dividend Payers

As we have discussed, there are numerous good reasons favoring a dividend policy of low (or no) payout. Nonetheless, as we showed earlier in Figure 14.3, in the United States, aggregate dividends paid are quite large. For example, in 1978, U.S. industrial firms listed on the major exchanges paid $32 billion in total dividends. By 2010, that number had risen to $199 billion (unadjusted for inflation), an increase of more than 500 percent (after adjusting for inflation, the increase is smaller, 84 percent, but still substantial).

While we know dividends are large in the aggregate, we also know that the number of companies that pay dividends has declined. Over the same 1978–2010 period, the number of industrial companies paying dividends declined from more than 2,000 to 855, and the percentage of these firms paying dividends declined 50 percent, to just under 30 percent.[2]

The fact that aggregate dividends grew while the number of payers fell so sharply seems a bit paradoxical, but the explanation is straightforward. Dividend payments are heavily concentrated in a relatively small set of large firms. In 2010, for example, more than 80 percent of aggregate dividends were paid by just 100 firms. The top 25 payers, which included such well-known giants as ExxonMobil and General Electric, collectively paid about 54 percent of all dividends. Thus, the reason that dividends grew while dividend payers shrank is that the decline in dividend payers is almost entirely due to smaller firms, which tend to pay smaller dividends in the first place.

One important reason that the percentage of dividend-paying firms has declined is that the population of firms has changed. There has been a huge increase in the number of newly listed firms over the last 25 or so years. Newly listed firms tend to be younger and less profitable. Such firms need their internally generated cash to fund growth and typically do not pay dividends.

Another factor at work is that firms appear to be more likely to begin making payouts using share repurchases, which are flexible, rather than committing to making cash distributions. Such a policy seems quite sensible. However, after controlling for the changing mix of firms and the increase in share repurchasing activity, there still appears to be a decreased propensity to pay dividends among certain types of older, better-established firms, though further research is needed on this subject.

The fact that the number of dividend-paying firms has declined so sharply is an interesting phenomenon. Making matters even more interesting is evidence showing that the trend may have begun to reverse itself. Take a look at Figure 14.4, which shows the percentage of industrial firms paying dividends over the period 1971–2017, along with the percentage of (1) firms doing repurchases and (2) firms with a positive payout of one type or the other

---

[2]These figures and those in the following two paragraphs are from H. DeAngelo, L. DeAngelo, and D. Skinner, "Corporate Payout Policy," *Foundations and Trends in Finance* 3 (2009), as updated by the authors.

FIGURE 14.4   **Proportion of dividend payers, repurchasers, and firms with positive total payout among all publicly held U.S. industrial firms: 1971–2017**

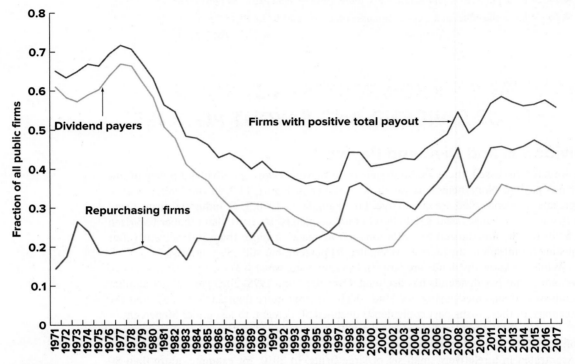

Source: Redrawn by authors, using Compustat data, following Farre-Mensa, J., Michaely, R. and Schmalz, M. C., "Payout Policy," *Annual Review of Financial Economics*, vol. 6, 2014, 75–134. Update by authors.

(or both). As shown, there is a pronounced downward trend of dividend payers, but that trend appears to bottom out in 2000 and then reverse somewhat in 2002. So what's going on?

Part of the apparent rebound in Figure 14.4 is probably an illusion. The number of firms listed on the major stock markets dropped sharply, from over 5,000 to under 4,000, during the period 2000–2005. About 2,000 firms delisted over this period, 98 percent of which were not dividend payers. Thus, the percentage of firms paying dividends rose because nonpayers dropped out in large numbers.[3] By 2017, the number of listed firms had declined to below 3,000, and the percentage of dividend payers reached 34 percent.

However, once we control for the dropout problem, there is still an increase in the proportion of dividend payers, but it happens in 2003. As shown in Figure 14.5, the uptick is concentrated in the months following May 2003. What is so special about this month? The answer is that in May 2003, top personal tax rates on dividends were slashed from about 38 to 15 percent. Thus, consistent with our earlier tax arguments, a reduction in personal tax rates led to increases in dividends.

However, it is important not to read too much into Figure 14.5. It seems clear that the reduction in tax rates did have an effect, but, on balance, what we see is a few hundred firms initiating dividends. There are still thousands of firms that did not initiate dividends, even

[3]These numbers and this explanation are from R. Chetty and E. Saez, "The Effects of the 2003 Dividend Tax Cut on Corporate Behavior: Interpreting the Evidence," *American Economic Review Papers and Proceedings* 96 (2006).

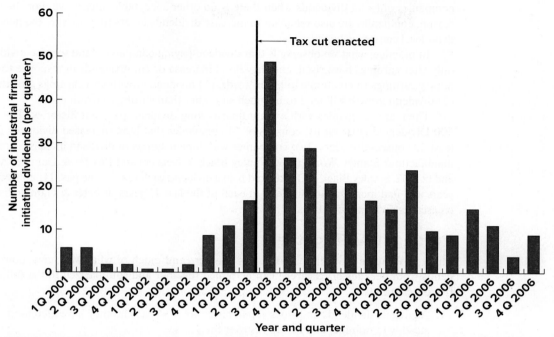

FIGURE **14.5**   Regular dividend initiations, 2001–2006

Source: Brav, A., Graham, J. R., Harvey, C. R. and Michaely, R., "Managerial Response to the May 2003 Dividend Tax Cut," *Financial Management*, vol. 37, 2008.

though the tax rate reduction was very large. Thus, the evidence suggests that tax rates matter, but they are not a primary determinant of dividend policy. This interpretation is consistent with the results of a 2005 survey of financial executives, more than ⅔ of whom said that the tax rate cut probably or definitely would not affect their dividend policies.[4]

A second force that may be at work over time is the maturing of many of the (surviving) newly listed firms we mentioned earlier. As these firms have become better established, their profitability has increased (and, potentially, their investment opportunities have decreased), and they have begun to pay dividends.

A third factor that may be contributing to the increase in the number of dividend payers is a little more subtle. The technology-heavy NASDAQ index plummeted in the spring of 2000 (due to the "dot-com" crash), and it became clear that many newly listed companies were likely to fail. Shortly thereafter, major accounting scandals at companies such as Enron and WorldCom left investors unsure of the trustworthiness of reported earnings. In such an environment, companies may have chosen to initiate dividends in an attempt to signal to investors that they had the cash to make dividend payments now and in the future.

The apparent reversal in the decline of dividend payers is a recent phenomenon, so its significance remains to be seen. It may prove to be just a transient event in the middle of a long decline. We will have to wait and see.

---

[4]See A. Brav, J. R. Graham, C. R. Harvey, and R. Michaely, "Managerial Response to the May 2003 Dividend Tax Cut," *Financial Management* 37 (2008).

Corporations Smooth Dividends

Dividend cuts are frequently viewed as very bad news by market participants. As a result, companies only cut dividends when there is no other acceptable alternative. For the same reason, companies are also reluctant to increase dividends unless they are sure the new dividend level can be sustained.

In practice, what we observe is that dividend-paying companies tend to raise dividends only after earnings have risen, and they don't increase or cut dividends in response to temporary earnings fluctuations. In other words, (1) dividend growth lags earnings growth and (2) dividend growth will tend to be much smoother than earnings growth.

There are companies with extraordinarily long dividend payment histories. The S&P 500 Dividend Aristocrat list consists of 54 companies that have increased dividends for at least 25 consecutive years. Two companies with long histories of dividend increases are tool manufacturer Stanley Works (now Stanley Black & Decker) and Procter & Gamble. At the end of 2017, Stanley Black & Decker had paid a dividend each year for the past 141 consecutive years and had increased its dividend in each of the last 47 years. Procter & Gamble had increased its dividend for 61 years.

Putting It All Together

Much of what we have discussed in this chapter (and much of what we know about dividends from decades of research) can be pulled together and summarized in the following five observations:[5]

1. Aggregate dividends and stock repurchases are massive, and they have increased steadily in nominal and real terms over the years.

2. Dividends are heavily concentrated among a relatively small number of large, mature firms.

3. Managers are very reluctant to cut dividends, normally doing so only due to firm-specific problems.

4. Managers smooth dividends, raising them slowly and incrementally as earnings grow.

5. Stock prices react to unanticipated changes in dividends.

The challenge now is to fit these five pieces into a reasonably coherent picture. With regard to payouts in general, meaning the combination of stock repurchases and cash dividends, a simple life-cycle theory fits Points 1 and 2. The key ideas are straightforward. First, relatively young and less-profitable firms generally should not make cash distributions. They need the cash to fund investments (and flotation costs discourage the raising of outside cash).

However, as a firm matures, it begins to generate free cash flow (which, you will recall, is internally generated cash flow beyond that needed to fund profitable investment activities). Significant free cash flow can lead to agency problems if it is not distributed. Managers may become tempted to pursue empire building or otherwise spend the excess cash in ways not in the shareholders' best interests. Thus, firms come under pressure to make distributions rather than hoard cash. And, consistent with what we observe, we expect large firms with a history of profitability to make large distributions.

Thus, the life-cycle theory says that firms trade off the agency costs of excess cash retention against the potential future costs of external equity financing. A firm should begin making distributions when it generates sufficient internal cash flow to fund its investment needs now and into the foreseeable future.

---

[5]This list is distilled in part from a longer list in DeAngelo, H. and DeAngelo, L., "Payout Policy Pedagogy: What Matters and Why," *European Financial Management*, vol. 13, 2007.

The more complex issue concerns the type of distribution, cash dividends versus repurchases. The tax argument in favor of repurchases is a clear and strong one. Further, repurchases are a much more flexible option (and managers greatly value financial flexibility), so the question is: Why would firms ever choose a cash dividend?

If we are to answer this question, we have to ask a different question. What can a cash dividend accomplish that a share repurchase cannot? One answer is that when a firm makes a commitment to pay a cash dividend now and into the future, it sends a two-part signal to the markets. As we already have discussed, one signal is that the firm anticipates being profitable, with the ability to make the payments on an ongoing basis. Note that a firm cannot benefit by trying to fool the market in this regard because the firm would ultimately be punished when it couldn't make the dividend payment (or couldn't make it without relying on external financing). Thus, a cash dividend may let a firm distinguish itself from less-profitable rivals.

A second, and more subtle, signal takes us back to the agency problem of free cash flow. By committing to pay cash dividends now and in the future, the firm signals that it won't be hoarding cash (or at least not as much cash), thereby reducing agency costs and enhancing shareholder wealth.

This two-part signaling story is consistent with Points 3–5 above, but an obvious objection remains. Why don't firms just commit to a policy of setting aside whatever money would be used to pay dividends and use it instead to buy back shares? After all, either way, a firm is committing to pay out cash to shareholders.

A fixed repurchase strategy suffers from two drawbacks. The first is verifiability. A firm could announce an open market repurchase and then not do it. By suitably fudging its books, it would be some time before the deception was discovered. Thus, it would be necessary for shareholders to develop a monitoring mechanism, meaning some sort of way for stockholders to know for sure that the repurchase in fact was done. Such a mechanism wouldn't be difficult to build (it could be a simple trustee relationship such as we observe in the bond markets), but it currently does not exist. Of course, a tender offer repurchase needs little or no verification, but such offers have expenses associated with them. The beauty of a cash dividend is that it needs no monitoring. A firm is forced to cut and mail checks four times a year, year in and year out.

A second objection to a fixed repurchase strategy is more controversial. Suppose managers, as insiders, are better able than stockholders to judge whether their stock price is too high or too low. (Note that this idea does not conflict with semistrong market efficiency if inside information is the reason.) In this case, a fixed repurchase commitment forces management to buy back stock even in circumstances when the stock is overvalued. In other words, it forces management into making negative NPV investments.

More research on the cash dividend versus share repurchase question is needed, but the historical trend seems to be favoring continued growth in repurchases relative to dividends. Total corporate payouts seem to be relatively stable over time at roughly 20 percent of aggregate earnings, but repurchases are becoming a larger portion of that total. The split reached about 50–50 in the latter part of the 1990s, but it looks like aggregate repurchases have recently passed aggregate dividends.

One aspect of aggregate cash dividends that has not received much attention is that there may be a strong legacy effect. Before 1982, the regulatory status of stock repurchases was somewhat murky, creating a significant disincentive. In 1982, the SEC, after years of debate, created a clear set of guidelines for firms to follow, thereby making repurchases much more attractive. The impact of this change is clear in Figure 14.3. Repurchases immediately began growing in 1983–1984.

The legacy effect arises because many of the giant firms that pay such a large portion of aggregate dividends were paying dividends before (and perhaps long before) 1982. To the extent that these firms are unwilling to cut their dividends, aggregate cash dividends will be large, but only because of a "lock-in" effect for older firms. If locked-in, legacy payers account for much of the aggregate dividend, what we should observe is (1) a sharply reduced tendency for maturing firms to initiate dividends and (2) a growth in repurchases relative to cash dividends over time. We actually do see evidence of both of these trends; however, legacy effects alone can't account for all cash dividend payers.

THE PROS AND CONS OF PAYING DIVIDENDS	
Pros	**Cons**
1. Cash dividends can underscore good results and provide support to the stock price.	1. Dividends are taxed to recipients.
2. Dividends may attract institutional investors who prefer some return in the form of dividends. A mix of institutional and individual investors may allow a firm to raise capital at a lower cost because of the ability of the firm to reach a wider market.	2. Dividends can reduce internal sources of financing. Dividends may force the firm to forgo positive NPV projects or to rely on costly external equity financing.
3. Stock price usually increases with the announcement of a new or increased dividend.	3. Once established, dividend cuts are hard to make without adversely affecting a firm's stock price.
4. Dividends absorb excess cash flow and may reduce agency costs that arise from conflicts between management and shareholders.	

Some Survey Evidence on Dividends

A recent study surveyed a large number of financial executives regarding dividend policy. One of the questions asked was, "Do these statements describe factors that affect your company's dividend decisions?" Table 14.1 shows some of the results.

As shown in Table 14.1, financial managers are very disinclined to cut dividends. Moreover, they are very conscious of their previous dividends and desire to maintain a relatively steady dividend. In contrast, the cost of external capital and the desire to attract "prudent man" investors (those with fiduciary duties) are less important.

TABLE 14.1 Survey responses on dividend decisions*	Policy Statements	Percent Who Agree or Strongly Agree
	1. We try to avoid reducing dividends per share.	93.8%
	2. We try to maintain a smooth dividend from year to year.	89.6
	3. We consider the level of dividends per share that we have paid in recent quarters.	88.2
	4. We are reluctant to make dividend changes that might have to be reversed in the future.	77.9
	5. We consider the change or growth in dividends per share.	66.7
	6. We consider the cost of raising external capital to be smaller than the cost of cutting dividends.	42.8
	7. We pay dividends to attract investors subject to "prudent man" investment restrictions.	41.7

*Survey respondents were asked the question, "Do these statements describe factors that affect your company's dividend decisions?"

Source: Adapted from Table 4 of Brav, A., Graham, J. R., Harvey, C. R., and Michaely, R., "Payout Policy in the 21st Century," *Journal of Financial Economics*, Elsevier, 2005.

Policy Statements	Percent Who Think This Is Important or Very Important
1. Maintaining consistency with our historic dividend policy.	84.1%
2. Stability of future earnings.	71.9
3. A sustainable change in earnings.	67.1
4. Attracting institutional investors to purchase our stock.	52.5
5. The availability of good investment opportunities for our firm to pursue.	47.6
6. Attracting retail investors to purchase our stock.	44.5
7. Personal taxes our stockholders pay when receiving dividends.	21.1
8. Flotation costs to issuing new equity.	9.3

TABLE 14.2

Survey responses on dividend decisions*

*Survey respondents were asked the question, "How important are the following factors to your company's dividend decision?"

Source: Adapted from Table 5 of Brav, A., Graham, J. R., Harvey, C. R., and Michaely, R., "Payout Policy in the 21st Century," *Journal of Financial Economics*, Elsevier, 2005. Used with permission.

Table 14.2 is drawn from the same survey, but here the responses are to the question, "How important are the following factors to your company's dividend decision?" Not surprisingly, given the responses in Table 14.1 and our earlier discussion, the highest priority is maintaining a consistent dividend policy. The next several items are also consistent with our previous analysis. Financial managers are very concerned about earnings stability and future earnings levels in making dividend decisions, and they consider the availability of good investment opportunities. Survey respondents also believed that attracting both institutional and individual (retail) investors was relatively important.

In contrast to our discussion of taxes and flotation costs in the earlier part of this chapter, the financial managers in this survey did not think that personal taxes paid on dividends by shareholders are very important. And even fewer think that equity flotation costs are relevant.

14.5 STOCK DIVIDENDS AND STOCK SPLITS

Another type of dividend is paid out in shares of stock. This type of dividend is called a **stock dividend**. A stock dividend is not a true dividend because it is not paid in cash. The effect of a stock dividend is to increase the number of shares that each owner holds. Because there are more shares outstanding, each is worth less.

A stock dividend is commonly expressed as a percentage; for example, a 20 percent stock dividend means that a shareholder receives one new share for every five currently owned (a 20 percent increase). Because every shareholder owns 20 percent more stock, the total number of shares outstanding rises by 20 percent. As we will see in a moment, the result is that each share of stock is worth about 20 percent less.

A **stock split** is essentially the same thing as a stock dividend, except that a split is expressed as a ratio instead of a percentage. When a split is declared, each share is split up to create additional shares. For example, in a three-for-one stock split, each old share is split into three new shares. As a result, the par value of each share would be reduced to one-third of the presplit value.

By convention, stock dividends of less than 20 to 25 percent are called *small stock dividends*. A stock dividend greater than this 20 to 25 percent is called a *large stock dividend*. For

stock dividend
Payment made by a firm to its owners in the form of stock, diluting the value of each share outstanding.

stock split
An increase in a firm's shares outstanding without any change in owners' equity.

example, in March 2018, Aflac, known for its "spokesduck," completed a two-for-one stock split in the form of a stock dividend. In June 2018, Trex Company, manufacturer of decking materials, announced its 100 percent stock dividend in the form of a two-for-one stock split. Except for some relatively minor accounting differences, a stock dividend has the same effect as a stock split. In fact, you can see the relationship between the two because both companies announced the stock dividend in the same way a stock split would be announced.

Value of Stock Splits and Stock Dividends

The laws of logic tell us that stock splits and stock dividends can (1) leave the value of the firm unaffected, (2) increase its value, or (3) decrease its value. Unfortunately, the issues are complex enough that one cannot easily determine which of the three relationships holds.

Information on upcoming stock splits is available on the splits calendar at investmenthouse.com/splits.htm and finance.yahoo.com.

The Benchmark Case   A strong case can be made that stock dividends and splits do not change either the wealth of any shareholder or the wealth of the firm as a whole. The reason is that they are just paper transactions and alter the number of shares outstanding. For example, if a firm declares a two-for-one split, all that happens is that the number of shares is doubled, with the result that each share is worth half as much. The total value is not affected.

Although this simple conclusion is relatively obvious, there are reasons that often are given to suggest that there may be some benefits to these actions. The typical financial manager is aware of many real-world complexities, and, for that reason, the stock split or stock dividend decision is not treated lightly in practice.

trading range
Price range between highest and lowest prices at which a stock is typically traded.

Popular Trading Range   Proponents of stock dividends and stock splits frequently argue that a security has a proper **trading range**. When the security is priced above this level, many investors do not have the funds to buy the common trading unit of 100 shares, called a *round lot*. Thus, firms will split the stock to keep the price in this trading range.

Although this argument is a popular one, its validity is questionable for a number of reasons. Mutual funds, pension funds, and other institutions have steadily increased their trading activity since World War II and now handle a sizable percentage of total trading volume (e.g., on the order of 80 percent of NYSE trading volume). Because these institutions buy and sell in huge amounts, the individual share price is of little concern.

Furthermore, we sometimes observe share prices that are quite large without appearing to cause problems. For example, consider the Swiss chocolatier Lindt. In July 2018, Lindt shares were selling for around 77,000 Swiss francs each, or about $77,600. A round lot would have cost a cool $7.76 million. This is fairly expensive, but not compared to Berkshire Hathaway, the U.S. company run by legendary investor Warren Buffett. In July 2018, each share of the company's Class A stock sold for about $285,000, down from a high of $326,000 in January 2018 (the Class B stock was much cheaper at $186 per share).

Finally, there is evidence that stock splits actually may decrease the liquidity of the company's shares. Following a two-for-one split, the number of shares traded should more than double if liquidity is increased by the split. This doesn't appear to happen, and the opposite is sometimes observed.

Reverse Splits

reverse split
Stock split under which a firm's number of shares outstanding is reduced.

A less frequently encountered financial maneuver is the **reverse split**. For example, in May 2018, shopping center owner DDR Corporation underwent a one-for-two reverse stock split, and, in February 2018, Tenax Therapeutics, a specialty pharmaceutical company, underwent a 1-for-20 reverse stock split. In a 1-for-20 reverse split, each investor exchanges 20 old shares for 1 new share. The par value is increased by a factor of 20 in the process. For small companies, reverse splits can become quite large. In February 2018, dry bulk transportation company FreeSeas, Inc., completed a whopper, a 1-for-5,000 reverse split.

Given real-world imperfections, three related reasons are cited for reverse splits. First, transaction costs to shareholders may be less after the reverse split. Second, the liquidity and marketability of a company's stock might be improved when its price is raised to the popular trading range. Third, stocks selling at prices below a certain level are not considered respectable, meaning that investors underestimate these firms' earnings, cash flow, growth, and stability. Some financial analysts argue that a reverse split can help achieve instant respectability. As was the case with stock splits, none of these reasons is particularly compelling, especially not the third one.

There are two other reasons for reverse splits. First, stock exchanges have minimum price per share requirements. A reverse split may bring the stock price up to such a minimum. For example, NASDAQ begins the delisting process for companies whose stock price drops below $1 per share for 30 days. Following the collapse of the Internet boom in 2001–2002, a large number of Internet-related companies found themselves in danger of being delisted and used reverse splits to boost their stock prices. Second, companies sometimes perform reverse splits and, at the same time, buy out any stockholders who end up with less than a certain number of shares.

For example, in February 2017, Lime Energy completed a reverse/forward split. In this case, the company first did a 1-for-300 reverse stock split. The company repurchased all shares held by stockholders with less than one share of stock, thereby eliminating small shareholders (and reducing the total number of shareholders). The purpose of the reverse split was to allow the company to save on administrative expenses related to shareholder relations. What made the proposal especially imaginative was that immediately after the reverse split, the company did a 300-for-1 ordinary split to restore the stock to its original cost!

CONCEPT QUESTIONS

14.5a What is the effect of a stock split on stockholder wealth?
14.5b What is a reverse split?

SUMMARY AND CONCLUSIONS

In this chapter, we first discussed the types of dividends and how they are paid. We then defined dividend policy and examined whether or not dividend policy matters. Next, we illustrated how a firm might establish a dividend policy and described an important alternative to cash dividends, a share repurchase.

In covering these subjects, we saw that:

1. Dividend policy is irrelevant when there are no taxes or other imperfections.
2. Individual shareholder income taxes and new issue flotation costs are real-world considerations that favor a low-dividend payout. With taxes and new issue costs, the firm should pay out dividends only after all positive NPV projects have been fully financed.

3. There are groups in the economy that may favor a high payout. These include many large institutions such as pension plans. Recognizing that some groups prefer a high payout and some prefer a low payout, the clientele effect supports the idea that dividend policy responds to the needs of stockholders. For example, if 40 percent of the stockholders prefer low dividends and 60 percent of the stockholders prefer high dividends, approximately 40 percent of companies will have a low-dividend payout, while 60 percent will have a high payout. This sharply reduces the impact of any individual firm's dividend policy on its market price.

4. Dividend stability is usually viewed as highly desirable. We therefore discussed a compromise strategy that provides for a stable dividend and appears to be quite similar to the dividend policies many firms follow in practice.

5. A stock repurchase acts much like a cash dividend but has a significant tax advantage. Stock repurchases are therefore a very useful part of overall dividend policy.

To close out our discussion of dividends, we emphasize one last time the difference between dividends and dividend policy. Dividends are important because the value of a share of stock is ultimately determined by the dividends that will be paid. What is less clear is whether or not the time pattern of dividends (more now versus more later) matters. This is the dividend policy question, and it is not easy to give a definitive answer to it.

⬛connect· POP QUIZ!

Can you answer the following questions? If your class is using *Connect*, log on to SmartBook to see if you know the answers to these and other questions, check out the study tools, and find out what topics require additional practice!

Section 14.1 What are the forms of cash dividends?

Section 14.2 According to the clientele effect, can a firm boost its share price by raising dividends?

Section 14.3 When a firm authorizes a trustee to repurchase shares as they become available, what purchase technique is it using?

Section 14.4 What is a firm paying cash dividends signaling?

Section 14.5 Why is a stock dividend not a true dividend?

CHAPTER REVIEW AND SELF-TEST PROBLEM

14.1 Repurchase versus Cash Dividend Trantor Corporation is deciding whether to pay out $300 in excess cash in the form of an extra dividend or a share repurchase. Current earnings are $1.50 per share, and the stock sells for $15. The market value balance sheet before paying out the $300 is as follows:

Market Value Balance Sheet
(before paying out excess cash)

Excess cash	$ 300	Debt	$ 400
Other assets	1,600	Equity	1,500
Total	$1,900	Total	$1,900

Evaluate the two alternatives in terms of the effect on the price per share of the stock, the EPS, and the PE ratio. (See Problem 12.)

■ Answer to Chapter Review and Self-Test Problem

14.1   The market value of the equity is $1,500. The price per share is $15, so there are 100 shares outstanding. The cash dividend would amount to $300/100 = $3 per share. When the stock goes ex dividend, the price will drop by $3 per share to $12. Put another way, the total assets decrease by $300, so the equity value goes down by this amount to $1,200. With 100 shares, the new stock price is $12 per share. After the dividend, EPS will be the same, $1.50, but the PE ratio will be $12/$1.50 = 8 times.

  With a repurchase, $300/15 = 20 shares will be bought up, leaving 80. The equity will again be worth $1,200 total. With 80 shares, this is $1,200/80 = $15 per share, so the price doesn't change. Total earnings for Trantor must be $1.50 × 100 = $150. After the repurchase, EPS will be higher at $150/80 = $1.875. The PE ratio, however, still will be $15/$1.875 = 8 times.

CRITICAL THINKING AND CONCEPTS REVIEW

LO 2   **14.1   Dividend Policy Irrelevance**   How is it possible that dividends are so important, but, at the same time, dividend policy is irrelevant?

LO 4   **14.2   Stock Repurchases**   What is the impact of a stock repurchase on a company's debt ratio? Does this suggest another use for excess cash?

LO 1   **14.3   Life Cycle Theory of Dividends**   Explain the life cycle theory of dividend payments. How does it explain corporate dividend payments that are seen in the stock market?

LO 1   **14.4   Dividend Chronology**   On Friday, December 8, Hometown Power Co.'s board of directors declares a dividend of 75 cents per share payable on Wednesday, January 17, to shareholders of record as of Wednesday, January 3. When is the ex-dividend date? If a shareholder buys stock before that date, who gets the dividends on those shares, the buyer or the seller?

LO 1   **14.5   Alternative Dividends**   Some corporations, like one British company that offers its large shareholders free crematorium use, pay dividends in kind (i.e., offer their services to shareholders at below-market cost). Should mutual funds invest in stocks that pay these dividends in kind? (The fundholders do not receive these services.)

LO 2   **14.6   Dividends and Stock Price**   If increases in dividends tend to be followed by (immediate) increases in share prices, how can it be said that dividend policy is irrelevant?

LO 2   **14.7   Dividends and Stock Price**   Last month, Central Virginia Power Company, which had been having trouble with cost overruns on a nuclear power plant that it had been building, announced that it was "temporarily suspending dividend payments due to the cash flow crunch associated with its investment program." The company's stock price dropped from $28.50 to $25 when this announcement was made. How would you interpret this change in the stock price (i.e., what would you say caused it)?

LO 1   **14.8   Dividend Reinvestment Plans**   The DRK Corporation recently has developed a dividend reinvestment plan (DRIP). The plan allows investors to reinvest cash dividends automatically in DRK in exchange for new shares of stock. Over time, investors in DRK will be able to build their holdings by reinvesting dividends to purchase additional shares of the company.

Over 1,000 companies offer dividend reinvestment plans. Most companies with DRIPs charge no brokerage or service fees. In fact, the shares of DRK will be purchased at a 10 percent discount from the market price.

A consultant for DRK estimates that about 75 percent of DRK's shareholders will take part in this plan. This is somewhat higher than the average.

Evaluate DRK's dividend reinvestment plan. Will it increase shareholder wealth? Discuss the advantages and disadvantages involved here.

LO 2 **14.9 Dividend Policy** During 2017, 108 companies went public with common stock offerings, raising a combined total of $24.5 billion. Relatively few of these 108 companies involved paid cash dividends. Why do you think most chose not to pay dividends?

LO 1 **14.10 Investment and Dividends** The Phew Charitable Trust pays no taxes on its capital gains or on its dividend income or interest income. Would it be irrational for it to have low-dividend, high-growth stocks in its portfolio? Would it be irrational for it to have municipal bonds in its portfolio? Explain.

QUESTIONS AND PROBLEMS

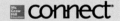 **connect** Select problems are available in McGraw-Hill *Connect*. Please see the packaging options section of the Preface for more information.

BASIC (Questions 1–11)

LO 2 **1. Dividends and Stock Prices** Your portfolio is 200 shares of Callahan, Inc. The stock currently sells for $93 per share. The company has announced a dividend of $1.43 per share with an ex-dividend date of April 19. Assuming no taxes, how much will your stock be worth on April 19?

LO 2 **2. Dividends and Stock Prices** It is April 19. Using the information in the previous problem, what is your total portfolio value?

LO 2 **3. Dividends and Taxes** Estes Park, Inc., has declared a dividend of $8.40 per share. Suppose capital gains are not taxed, but dividends are taxed at 15 percent. New IRS regulations require that taxes be withheld at the time the dividend is paid. The company's stock sells for $87 per share, and the stock is about to go ex dividend. What do you think the ex-dividend price will be?

LO 3 **4. Stock Dividends** The owners' equity accounts for Masterson International are shown here:

Common stock ($1 par value)	$ 45,000
Capital surplus	157,000
Retained earnings	603,000
Total owners' equity	$805,000

a. If the company's stock currently sells for $42 per share and a 10 percent stock dividend is declared, how many new shares will be distributed? Show how the equity accounts would change.

b. If the company declared a 25 percent stock dividend, how would the accounts change?

LO 3   **5. Stock Splits**   For the company in Problem 4, show how the equity accounts will change if:

    a.   The company declares a two-for-one stock split. How many shares are outstanding now? What is the new par value per share?

    b.   The company declares a one-for-five reverse stock split. How many shares are outstanding now? What is the new par value per share?

LO 3   **6. Stock Splits and Stock Dividends**   Bermuda Triangle Corporation (BTC) currently has 395,000 shares of stock outstanding that sell for $83 per share. Assuming no market imperfections or tax effects exist, what will the share price be after:

    a.   BTC has a five-for-three stock split?

    b.   BTC has a 15 percent stock dividend?

    c.   BTC has a 42.5 percent stock dividend?

    d.   BTC has a four-for-seven reverse stock split?

    e.   Determine the new number of shares outstanding in parts (a) through (d).

LO 1   **7. Regular Dividends**   The balance sheet for Tempest, Inc., is shown here in market value terms. There are 19,000 shares of stock outstanding.

Market Value Balance Sheet

Cash	$120,000		
Fixed assets	476,600	Equity	$596,600
Total	$596,600	Total	$596,600

The company has declared a dividend of $1.15 per share. The stock goes ex dividend tomorrow. Ignoring any tax effects, what is the stock selling for today? What will it sell for tomorrow? What will the balance sheet look like after the dividends are paid?

LO 4   **8. Share Repurchase**   In the previous problem, suppose the company has announced it is going to repurchase $21,850 worth of stock instead of paying a dividend. What effect will this transaction have on the equity of the firm? How many shares will be outstanding? What will the price per share be after the repurchase? Ignoring tax effects, show how the share repurchase is effectively the same as a cash dividend.

LO 3   **9. Stock Dividends**   The market value balance sheet for Briggs Manufacturing is shown here. The company has declared a 20 percent stock dividend. The stock goes ex dividend tomorrow (the chronology for a stock dividend is similar to that for a cash dividend). There are 21,000 shares of stock outstanding. What will the ex-dividend price be?

Market Value Balance Sheet

Cash	$135,000	Debt	$215,000
Fixed assets	730,000	Equity	650,000
Total	$865,000	Total	$865,000

LO 3   **10. Stock Dividends**   The company with the common equity accounts shown here has declared a 10 percent stock dividend at a time when the market

value of its stock is $48 per share. What effects on the equity accounts will the distribution of the stock dividend have?

Common stock ($1 par value)	$ 225,000
Capital surplus	1,070,000
Retained earnings	2,543,000
Total owners' equity	$3,838,000

LO 3 **11. Stock Splits** In the previous problem, suppose the company instead decides on a two-for-one stock split. The firm's 67-cent-per-share cash dividend on the new (postsplit) shares represents an increase of 10 percent over last year's dividend on the presplit stock. What effect does this have on the equity accounts? What was last year's dividend per share?

INTERMEDIATE (Questions 12–13)

LO 4 **12. Stock Repurchase** Taco Time Corporation is evaluating an extra dividend versus a share repurchase. In either case, $7,095 would be spent. Current earnings are $2.70 per share, and the stock currently sells for $59 per share. There are 4,300 shares outstanding. Ignore taxes and other imperfections in answering the first two questions.

    a. Evaluate the two alternatives in terms of the effect on the price per share of the stock and shareholder wealth.

    b. What will be the effect on the company's EPS and PE ratio under the two different scenarios?

    c. In the real world, which of these actions would you recommend? Why?

LO 2 **13. Dividend Policy** The Quick Buck Company is an all-equity firm that has been in existence for the past three years. Company management expects that the company will last for two more years and then be dissolved. The firm will generate cash flows of $450,000 next year and $790,000 in two years, including the proceeds from the liquidation. There are 20,000 shares of stock outstanding and shareholders require a return of 12 percent.

    a. What is the current price per share of the stock?

    b. The board of directors is dissatisfied with the current dividend policy and proposes that a dividend of $580,000 be paid next year. To raise the cash necessary for the increased dividend, the company will sell new shares of stock. How many shares of stock must be sold? What is the new price per share of the existing shares of stock?

CHALLENGE (Questions 14–15)

LO 2 **14. Expected Return, Dividends, and Taxes** The Gecko Company and the Gordon Company are two firms whose business risk is the same while having different dividend policies. Gecko pays no dividend, whereas Gordon has an expected dividend yield of 3.5 percent. Suppose the capital gains tax rate is zero, whereas the income tax rate is 28 percent. Gecko has an expected earnings growth rate of 12 percent annually, and its stock price is expected to grow at this same rate. If the aftertax expected returns on the two stocks are equal (because they are in the same risk class), what is the pretax required return on Gordon's stock?

LO 2

15. Dividends and Taxes As discussed in the text, in the absence of market imperfections and tax effects, we would expect the share price to decline by the amount of the dividend payment when the stock goes ex dividend. Once we consider the role of taxes, however, this is not necessarily true. One model has been proposed that incorporates tax effects into determining the ex-dividend price:[6]

$$(P_0 - P_x)/D = (1 - T_P)/(1 - T_G)$$

where P_0 is the price just before the stock goes ex, P_x is the ex-dividend share price, D is the amount of the dividend per share, T_P is the relevant marginal personal tax rate on dividends, and T_G is the effective marginal tax rate on capital gains.

a. If $T_P = T_G = 0$, how much will the share price fall when the stock goes ex?

b. If $T_P = 15$ percent and $T_G = 0$, how much will the share price fall?

c. If $T_P = 15$ percent and $T_G = 30$ percent, how much will the share price fall?

d. Suppose the only owners of stock are corporations. Recall that corporations get at least an 80 percent exemption from taxation on the dividend income they receive, but they do not get such an exemption on capital gains. If the corporation's income and capital gains tax rates are both 21 percent, what does this model predict the ex-dividend share price will be?

e. What does this problem tell you about real-world tax considerations and the dividend policy of the firm?

WHAT'S ON THE WEB?

14.1 Dividend Reinvestment Plans Dividend reinvestment plans (DRIPs) permit shareholders to automatically reinvest cash dividends in the company. To find out more about DRIPs, go to www.fool.com and answer the following questions. What are the advantages Motley Fool lists for DRIPs? What are the different types of DRIPs? What is a direct purchase plan? How does a direct purchase plan differ from a DRIP?

14.2 Dividends Go to www.thestreet.com/dividends and find the list of dividends. How many companies went ex dividend today? What is the largest declared dividend? For the stocks going ex today, what is the longest time until the payable date?

14.3 Stock Splits Go to www.stocksplits.net and find the stock splits. How many stock splits are listed? How many are reverse splits? What is the largest split and the largest reverse split in terms of shares? Pick a company and follow the link. What type of information do you find?

14.4 Stock Splits How many times has Procter & Gamble stock split? Go to P&G's webpage at www.pg.com and find the history of the company's stock splits. When did Procter & Gamble stock first split? What was the split? When was the most recent stock split? If you owned 100 shares of Procter & Gamble on January 1, 1950, and never sold any shares, how many shares would you own today?

---

[6]N. Elton and M. Gruber, "Marginal Stockholder Tax Rates and the Clientele Effect," *Review of Economics and Statistics* 52 (February 1970).

CHAPTER CASE
Electronic Timing, Inc.

Electronic Timing, Inc. (ETI), is a small company founded 15 years ago by electronics engineers Tom Miller and Jessica Kerr. ETI manufactures integrated circuits to capitalize on the complex mixed-signal design technology and recently has entered the market for frequency timing generators, or silicon timing devices, which provide the timing signals or "clocks" necessary to synchronize electronic systems. Its clock products originally were used in PC video graphics applications, but the market subsequently expanded to include motherboards, PC peripheral devices, and other digital consumer electronics, such as digital television boxes and game consoles. ETI also designs and markets custom application-specific integrated circuits (ASICs) for industrial customers. The ASIC's design combines analog and digital, or mixed-signal, technology. In addition to Tom and Jessica, Nolan Pittman,

who provided capital for the company, is the third primary owner. Each owns 25 percent of the 1 million shares outstanding. The company has several other individuals, including current employees, who own the remaining shares.

Recently, the company designed a new computer motherboard. The company's design is both more efficient and less expensive to manufacture, and the ETI design is expected to become standard in many personal computers. After investigating the possibility of manufacturing the new motherboard, ETI determined that the costs involved in building a new plant would be prohibitive. The owners also decided that they were unwilling to bring in another large outside owner. Instead, ETI sold the design to an outside firm. The sale of the motherboard design was completed for an aftertax payment of $30 million.

QUESTIONS

1. Tom believes the company should use the extra cash to pay a special one-time dividend. How will this proposal affect the stock price? How will it affect the value of the company?

2. Jessica believes the company should use the extra cash to pay off debt and upgrade and expand its existing manufacturing capability. How would Jessica's proposals affect the company?

3. Nolan favors a share repurchase. He argues that a repurchase will increase the company's PE ratio, return on assets, and return on equity. Are his arguments correct? How will a share repurchase affect the value of the company?

4. Another option discussed by Tom, Jessica, and Nolan would be to begin a regular dividend payment to shareholders. How would you evaluate this proposal?

5. One way to value a share of stock is the dividend growth, or growing perpetuity, model. Consider

the following: The dividend payout ratio is $1 - b$, where b is the "retention" or "plowback" ratio. So, the dividend next year will be the earnings next year, E_1, times $(1 - b)$. The most commonly used equation to calculate the sustainable growth rate is the return on equity times the retention ratio. Substituting these relationships into the dividend growth model, we get the following equation to calculate the price of a share of stock today:

$$P_0 = \frac{E_1(1 - b)}{R_S - \text{ROE} \times b}$$

What are the implications of this result in terms of whether the company should pay a dividend or upgrade and expand its manufacturing capability? Explain.

6. Does the question of whether the company should pay a dividend depend on whether the company is organized as a corporation or an LLC?

15 | Raising Capital

On March 23, 2018, online backup and collaboration company Dropbox went public. Assisted by the investment banks Goldman Sachs and JPMorgan, along with a syndicate of 10 other banks, Dropbox sold about 26.8 million shares of stock to the public at a price of $21. The stock price opened trading at $29 before reaching a high for the day of $31.60. At the end of the day, the stock closed at $28.48. The Dropbox IPO raised $563 million, not an extremely large amount for an IPO. However, company insiders still held about 26 percent of the company's stock. In this chapter, we examine the process by which companies such as Dropbox sell stock to the public, the costs of doing so, and the role of investment banks in the process.

Businesses large and small have one thing in common: They need long-term capital. This chapter describes how they get it. We pay particular attention to what is probably the most important stage in a company's financial life cycle, the initial public offering. Such offerings are the process by which companies convert from being privately owned to being publicly owned. For many, starting a company, growing it, and taking it public is the ultimate entrepreneurial dream.

LEARNING OBJECTIVES

After studying this chapter, you should be able to:

LO 1 Explain the venture capital market and its role in the financing of new, high-risk ventures.

LO 2 Describe how securities are sold to the public and the role of investment banks in the process.

LO 3 Explain initial public offerings, and identify some of the costs of going public.

Please visit us at essentialsofcorporatefinance.blogspot.com for the latest developments in the world of corporate finance.

All firms, at varying times, must obtain capital. To do so, a firm must either borrow the money (debt financing), sell a portion of the firm (equity financing), or both. How a firm raises capital depends a great deal on the size of the firm, its life-cycle stage, and its growth prospects.

In this chapter, we examine some of the ways in which firms actually raise capital. We begin by looking at companies in the early stages of their lives and the importance of venture capital for such firms. We then look at the process of going public and the role of investment banks. Along the way, we discuss many of the issues associated with selling securities to the public and their implications for all types of firms. We close the chapter with a discussion of sources of debt capital.[1]

15.1 THE FINANCING LIFE CYCLE OF A FIRM: EARLY-STAGE FINANCING AND VENTURE CAPITAL

One day, you and a friend have a great idea for a new computer software product that helps users communicate using the next generation Meganet. Filled with entrepreneurial zeal, you christen the product MegaComm and set about bringing it to market.

Working nights and weekends, you are able to create a prototype of your product. It doesn't actually work, but at least you can show it around to illustrate your idea. To actually develop the product, you need to hire programmers, buy computers, rent office space, and so on. Unfortunately, because you are both college students, your combined assets are not sufficient to fund a pizza party, much less a start-up company. You need what is often referred to as OPM—other people's money.

Your first thought might be to approach a bank for a loan. You would probably discover, however, that banks are generally not interested in making loans to start-up companies with no assets (other than an idea) run by fledgling entrepreneurs with no track record. Instead, your search for capital would very likely lead you to the **venture capital (VC)** market.

venture capital (VC)
Financing for new, often high-risk, ventures.

Venture Capital

The term *venture capital* does not have a precise meaning, but it generally refers to financing for new, often high-risk, ventures. For example, before it went public, Internet auctioneer eBay was venture capital-financed. Individual venture capitalists invest their own money, whereas venture capital firms specialize in pooling funds from various sources and investing them. The underlying sources of funds for such firms include individuals, pension funds, insurance companies, large corporations, and even university endowment funds. The broad term *private equity* often is used to label the rapidly growing area of equity financing for nonpublic companies.[2]

Venture capitalists and venture capital firms recognize that many, or even most, new ventures will not fly, but the occasional one will. The potential profits are enormous in such cases. To limit their risk, venture capitalists generally provide financing in stages. At each stage, enough money is invested to reach the next milestone or planning stage. For example, the *first-stage* (or first "round") *financing* might be enough to get a prototype built and a manufacturing plan completed. Based on the results, the *second-stage financing* might be a major investment needed to actually begin manufacturing, marketing, and distribution. There might be many such stages, each of which represents a key step in the process of growing the company.

Venture capital firms often specialize in different stages. Some specialize in very early "seed money," or ground floor, financing. In contrast, financing in the later stages might

---

[1]We are indebted to Jay R. Ritter of the University of Florida and M. Shane Hadden of *The Currency Report* (www.globalcurrencyreport.com) for helpful comments and suggestions on this chapter.
[2]So-called vulture capitalists specialize in high-risk investments in established, but financially distressed, firms.

come from venture capitalists specializing in so-called mezzanine level financing, where *mezzanine level* refers to the level just above the ground floor.

The fact that financing is available in stages and is contingent on specified goals being met is a powerful motivating force for the firm's founders. Often, the founders receive relatively little in the way of salary and have substantial portions of their personal assets tied up in the business. At each stage of financing, the value of the founders' stake grows and the probability of success rises. If goals are not met, the venture capitalist will withhold further financing, thereby limiting future losses.

In addition to providing financing, venture capitalists generally will actively participate in running the firm, providing the benefit of experience with previous start-ups as well as general business expertise. This is especially true when the firm's founders have little or no hands-on experience running a company.

Some Venture Capital Realities

Although there is a large venture capital market, the truth is that access to venture capital is really very limited. Venture capital companies receive huge numbers of unsolicited proposals, the vast majority of which end up in the circular file (the waste basket). Venture capitalists rely heavily on informal networks of engineers, scientists, lawyers, accountants, bankers, and other venture capitalists to help identify potential investments. As a result, personal contacts are important in gaining access to the venture capital market; it is very much an "introduction" market.

Another simple fact about venture capital is that it is incredibly expensive. In a typical deal, the venture capitalist will demand (and get) 40 percent or more of the equity in the company. The venture capitalist frequently will hold voting convertible preferred stock, which gives various priorities in the event that the company is sold or liquidated. The venture capitalist typically will demand (and get) several seats on the company's board of directors and even may appoint one or more members of senior management.

Choosing a Venture Capitalist

Some start-up companies, particularly those headed by experienced, previously successful entrepreneurs, will be in such demand that they will have the luxury of looking beyond the money in choosing a venture capitalist. There are some key considerations in such a case, some of which can be summarized as follows:

1. *Financial strength is important.* The venture capitalist needs to have the resources and financial reserves for additional financing stages should they become necessary. This doesn't mean that bigger is necessarily better, however, because of our next consideration.

2. *Style is important.* Some venture capitalists will wish to be very much involved in day-to-day operations and decision making, whereas others will be content with monthly reports. Which is better depends on the firm and also on the venture capitalists' business skills. In addition, a large venture capital firm may be less flexible and more bureaucratic than a smaller "boutique" firm.

3. *References are important.* Has the venture capitalist been successful with similar firms? Of equal importance, how has the venture capitalist dealt with situations that didn't work out?

4. *Contacts are important.* A venture capitalist may be able to help the business in ways other than helping with financing and management by providing introductions to potentially important customers, suppliers, and other industry contacts. Venture

capitalist firms frequently specialize in a few particular industries, and such specialization could prove quite valuable.

5. *Exit strategy is important.* Venture capitalists are generally not long-term investors. How and under what circumstances the venture capitalist will "cash out" of the business should be carefully evaluated.

Conclusion

If a start-up succeeds, the big payoff frequently comes when the company is sold to another company or goes public. Either way, investment bankers often are involved in the process.

CONCEPT QUESTIONS

15.1a   What is venture capital?

15.1b   Why is venture capital often provided in stages?

15.2 SELLING SECURITIES TO THE PUBLIC: THE BASIC PROCEDURE

We discuss the process of selling securities to the public in the next several sections, paying particular attention to the process of going public.

Find out what firms are going public this week at marketwatch.com.

There are many rules and regulations surrounding the process of selling securities. The Securities Act of 1933 is the origin of federal regulations for all new interstate securities issues. The Securities Exchange Act of 1934 is the basis for regulating securities already outstanding. The Securities and Exchange Commission, or SEC, administers both acts.

There are a series of steps involved in issuing securities to the public. In general terms, the basic procedure is as follows:

1. Management's first step in issuing any securities to the public is to obtain approval from the board of directors. In some cases, the number of authorized shares of common stock must be increased. This requires a vote of the shareholders.

registration statement
A statement filed with the SEC that discloses all material information concerning the corporation making a public offering.

2. The firm must prepare a **registration statement** and file it with the SEC. With a few exceptions, the registration statement is required for all public, interstate issues of securities.

   Normally, a registration statement contains many pages of financial information, including a financial history, details of the existing business, proposed financing, and plans for the future.

prospectus
A legal document describing details of the issuing corporation and the proposed offering to potential investors.

3. The SEC examines the registration statement during a waiting period. During this time, the firm may distribute copies of a preliminary **prospectus**. The prospectus contains much of the information put into the registration statement, and it is given to potential investors by the firm. The preliminary prospectus is sometimes called a **red herring**, in part because bold red letters are printed on the cover.

red herring
A preliminary prospectus distributed to prospective investors in a new issue of securities.

A registration statement becomes effective on the 20th day after its filing unless the SEC sends a *letter of comment* suggesting changes. In that case, after the changes are made, the 20-day waiting period starts again. It is important to note that the SEC does not consider the economic merits of the proposed sale; it merely makes sure that various rules and regulations are followed. Also, the SEC generally does not check the accuracy or truthfulness of information in the prospectus.

The registration statement does not initially contain the price of the new issue. Usually, a price amendment is filed at or near the end of the waiting period, and the registration becomes effective.

4. The company cannot sell the securities during the waiting period. However, oral offers can be made.

5. On the effective date of the registration statement, a price is determined and a full-fledged selling effort gets under way. A final prospectus must accompany the delivery of securities or confirmation of sale, whichever comes first.

Tombstone advertisements (or *tombstones*) are used by underwriters after the waiting period. An example is reproduced in Figure 15.1. The tombstone contains the name of the issuer (the World Wrestling Federation, or WWF, in this case). It provides some information about the issue, and it lists the investment banks (the underwriters) that are involved with selling the issue. The role of the investment banks in selling securities is discussed more fully in the following pages.

tombstone
An advertisement announcing a public offering.

The investment banks are divided into groups called *brackets* on the tombstone, based on their participation in the issue, and the names of the banks are listed alphabetically within each bracket. The brackets often are viewed as a kind of pecking order. In general, the higher the bracket, the greater is the underwriter's prestige.

Crowdfunding

On April 5, 2012, the JOBS Act was signed into law. A provision of this act allowed companies to raise money through crowdfunding, which is the practice of raising small amounts of capital from a large number of people, typically via the Internet. Crowdfunding was first used to underwrite the U.S. tour of British rock band Marillion, but the JOBS Act allows companies to sell regular equity by crowdfunding. Originally, the JOBS Act allowed a company to issue up to $1 million in securities in a 12-month period, although this limit was raised to $5 million in 2015.

We should make an important distinction about two types of crowdfunding—*project crowdfunding* and *equity crowdfunding*. As an example of project crowdfunding, consider the card game Exploding Kittens, which exploded on the crowdfunding website Kickstarter and raised $8.8 million from about 220,000 backers. During the crowdfunding campaign, the company presold card decks. Every backer was shipped a deck of cards for the game, beginning about six months after the campaign ended. In this case, the backers were purchasers, not investors. This type of crowdfunding also has become a popular way to raise money for charitable causes. In contrast, with equity crowdfunding, the backers receive equity in the company.

In May 2016, Regulation CF (also known as Title III of the JOBS Act) kicked in, which allows small investors access to new crowdfunding "portals." Previously, investors in crowdfunding had to be "accredited." For an individual, this requirement translates to more than $1 million in net worth or more than $200,000 in income for two of the past three years. Regulation CF allows investors with less than $100,000 in income or assets to invest at least $2,000 per year, up to a maximum of $5,000.

Check out two of the more well-known project and charitable crowdfunding websites at www.kickstarter.com and www.gofundme.com.

To sell securities through Regulation CF, a company must file a form with the SEC. This filing makes the company eligible to list its securities on a crowdfunding portal that is approved by FINRA (the Financial Industry Regulatory Authority), the same agency we mentioned earlier in the textbook for bond price reporting. Crowdfunding portals are already specializing. For example, there are portals that specialize in only accredited investors, all investors, or real estate, to name just a few.

FIGURE **15.1**

An example of a
tombstone
advertisement

This announcement is neither an offer to sell nor a solicitation of an offer to buy any of these securities.
The offering is made only by the Prospectus.

New Issue

11,500,000 Shares

World Wrestling Federation Entertainment, Inc.

Class A Common Stock

Price $17.00 Per Share

Copies of the Prospectus may be obtained in any State in which this announcement
is circulated from only such of the Underwriters, including the undersigned,
as may lawfully offer these securities in such State.

U.S. Offering

9,200,000 Shares

This portion of the underwriting is being offered in the United States and Canada.

Bear, Stearns & Co. Inc.

Credit Suisse First Boston

Merrill Lynch & Co.

Wit Capital Corporation

Allen & Company _{Incorporated}	Banc of America Securities LLC	Deutsche Banc Alex. Brown
Donaldson, Lufkin & Jenrette	A.G. Edwards & Sons, Inc.	Hambrecht & Quist — ING Barings
Prudential Securities — SG Cowen	Wassertein Perella Securities, Inc.	Advest, Inc.
Axiom Capital Management, Inc.	Blackford Securities Corp.	J.C. Bradford & Co.
Joseph Charles & Assoc., Inc.	Chatsworth Securities LLC	Gabelli & Company, Inc.
Gaines, Berland Inc. — Jefferies & Company, Inc.	Josephthal & Co. Inc.	Neuberger Berman, LLC
Raymond James & Associates, Inc.		Sanders Morris Mundy
Tucker Anthony Cleary Gull		Wachovia Securities, Inc.

International Offering

2,300,000 Shares

This portion of the underwriting is being offered outside of the United States and Canada.

Bear, Stearns International Limited

Credit Suisse First Boston

Merrill Lynch International

Initial Coin Offerings

In addition to sales of traditional debt and equity, a company can raise funds by selling *tokens*. These tokens often grant the holder the right to use the company's service in the future. For example, a company building a railroad may issue a token that can be used as a train ticket after the railroad is built.

See upcoming ICOs at tokenmarket.net /ico-calendar.

Token sales occur on digital currency platforms and easily can be transferred on the platform or converted to U.S. dollars on specialized token exchanges. This liquidity has made tokens a popular means of funding since their introduction in 2015. Tokens are now purchased by both customers and investors, who may never use the token for the service being offered.

The initial sale of a token on a digital currency platform is often called an *initial coin offering* or *ICO* (to sound like IPO). Many start-up companies are now choosing to raise funding through an ICO rather than the traditional venture capital channels. The most common platform for issuing new tokens is Ethereum, but there are many competitors. In 2017, there were 234 ICOs with a total value of about $3.7 billion.

The SEC has some warnings on ICOs at www .sec.gov/news/public -statement/statement -clayton-2017-12-11.

Token sales are most popular among companies that are building services based on blockchain technology. This technology is at the heart of bitcoin and other cryptocurrencies. A blockchain is a timestamped ledger of transactions that is kept among a network of users without centralized control. It is similar to a traditional database, except that cryptography is used to make it infeasible to change the data once they are added to the chain. Many industries, including finance, are now updating their recordkeeping infrastructure with blockchain technology.

Token sales also can serve as an effective marketing tool. This is especially true if the business benefits from network effects as the potential for price appreciation in the tokens attracts new customers. The increase in customers increases the value of the service, which in turn increases the value of the tokens. For example, Civic is building a blockchain-based identity platform and its currency is used to purchase identity verification services from trusted parties. The company raised $33 million in June 2017 through an ICO of the CVC token. The total value of the tokens at the end of 2017 was $224 million, although in an indication of the volatility of tokens, the value dropped to less than $70 million by the middle of 2018.

See the market value of tokens at https://coin marketcap.com.

CONCEPT QUESTIONS

15.2a What are the basic procedures in selling a new issue?

15.2b What is a registration statement?

15.3 ALTERNATIVE ISSUE METHODS

When a company decides to issue a new security, it can sell it as a public issue or a private issue. In the case of a public issue, the firm is required to register the issue with the SEC. However, if the issue is to be sold to fewer than 35 investors, the sale can be carried out privately. In this case, a registration statement is not required.[3]

---

[3]A variety of different arrangements can be made for private equity issues. Selling unregistered securities avoids the costs of complying with the Securities Exchange Act of 1934. Regulation significantly restricts the resale of unregistered equity securities. For example, the purchaser may be required to hold the securities for at least two years. Many of the restrictions were significantly eased in 1990 for very large institutional investors, however. The private placement of bonds is discussed in a later section.

TABLE 15.1

The methods of issuing new securities

Method	Type	Definition
Public		
Traditional negotiated cash offer	Firm commitment cash offer	Company negotiates an agreement with an investment banker to underwrite and distribute the new shares. A specified number of shares are bought by underwriters and sold at a higher price.
	Best efforts cash offer	Company has investment bankers sell as many of the new shares as possible at the agreed-upon price. There is no guarantee concerning how much cash will be raised. Some best efforts offerings do not use an underwriter.
	Dutch auction cash offer	Company has investment bankers auction shares to determine the highest offer price obtainable for a given number of shares to be sold.
Privileged subscription	Direct rights offer	Company offers the new stock directly to its existing shareholders.
	Standby rights offer	Like the direct rights offer, this contains a privileged subscription arrangement with existing shareholders. The net proceeds are guaranteed by the underwriters.
Nontraditional cash offer	Shelf cash offer	Qualifying companies can authorize all the shares they expect to sell over a two-year period and sell them when needed.
	Competitive firm cash offer	Company can elect to award the underwriting contract through a public auction instead of negotiation.
Private	Direct placement	Securities are sold directly to the purchaser, who, at least until recently, generally could not resell the securities for at least two years.

general cash offer
An issue of securities offered for sale to the general public on a cash basis.

rights offer
A public issue of securities in which securities are first offered to existing shareholders. Also known as *rights offering.*

initial public offering (IPO)
A company's first equity issue made available to the public. Also *unseasoned new issue.*

seasoned equity offering (SEO)
A new equity issue of securities by a company that has previously issued securities to the public.

For equity sales, there are two kinds of public issues: a **general cash offer** and a **rights offer** (or *rights offering*). With a cash offer, securities are offered to the general public on a "first come, first served" basis. With a rights offer, securities are initially offered only to existing owners. Rights offers are fairly common in other countries, but they are relatively rare in the United States, particularly in recent years. We therefore focus on cash offers in this chapter.

The first public equity issue that is made by a company is referred to as an **initial public offering (IPO)**, or an *unseasoned new issue.* This issue occurs when a company decides to go public. Obviously, all initial public offerings are cash offers. If the firm's existing shareholders wanted to buy the shares, the firm wouldn't have to sell them publicly in the first place.

A **seasoned equity offering (SEO)** is a new issue for a company with securities that have been previously issued. The terms *secondary* and *follow-on offering* also are commonly used. A seasoned equity offering of common stock can be made by using a cash offer or a rights offer.

These methods of issuing new securities are shown in Table 15.1. They are discussed beginning in Section 15.4.

CONCEPT QUESTIONS

15.3a   Why is an initial public offering necessarily a cash offer?

15.3b   What is the difference between a rights offer and a cash offer?

15.4 UNDERWRITERS

If the public issue of securities is a cash offer, **underwriters** are usually involved. Underwriting is an important line of business for large investment firms such as Merrill Lynch. Underwriters perform services such as the following for corporate issuers:

1. Formulating the method used to issue the securities.
2. Pricing the new securities.
3. Selling the new securities.

Typically, the underwriter buys the securities for less than the offering price and accepts the risk of not being able to sell them. The difference between the underwriter's buying price and the offering price is called the **spread**, or discount. It is the basic compensation received by the underwriter. Sometimes the underwriter will get noncash compensation in the form of warrants and stock in addition to the spread.[4]

Underwriters combine to form an underwriting group called a **syndicate** to share the risk and to help sell the issue. In a syndicate, one or more managers arrange the offering. This manager is designated as the lead manager, or principal manager. The lead manager typically has the responsibility of pricing the securities. The other underwriters in the syndicate serve primarily to distribute the issue.

Choosing an Underwriter

A firm can offer its securities to the highest bidding underwriter on a *competitive offer* basis, or it can negotiate directly with an underwriter. In most cases, companies usually do new issues of debt and equity on a *negotiated offer* basis.

There is evidence that competitive underwriting is cheaper to use than negotiated underwriting, and the underlying reasons for the dominance of negotiated underwriting in the United States are the subject of ongoing debate.

Types of Underwriting

Two basic types of underwriting are involved in a cash offer: firm commitment and best efforts.

Firm Commitment Underwriting In **firm commitment underwriting**, the issuer sells the entire issue to the underwriters, who then attempt to resell it. This is the most prevalent type of underwriting in the United States. This is really a purchase-resale arrangement, and the underwriter's fee is the spread. For a new issue of seasoned equity, the underwriters can look at the market price to determine what the issue should sell for, and 95 percent of all such new issues are firm commitments.

If the underwriter cannot sell all of the issue at the agreed-upon offering price, it may have to lower the price on the unsold shares. Nonetheless, with firm commitment underwriting, the issuer receives the agreed-upon amount, and all the risk associated with selling the issue is transferred to the underwriter.

Because the offering price usually isn't set until the underwriters have investigated how receptive the market is to the issue, this risk is usually minimal. Also, because the offering price usually is not set until just before selling commences, the issuer doesn't know precisely what its net proceeds will be until that time.

underwriters
Investment firms that act as intermediaries between a company selling securities and the investing public.

spread
Compensation to the underwriter, determined by the difference between the underwriter's buying price and offering price.

syndicate
A group of underwriters formed to share the risk and to help sell an issue.

firm commitment underwriting
The underwriter buys the entire issue, assuming full financial responsibility for any unsold shares.

---

[4]Warrants are essentially options to buy stock at a fixed price for some fixed period of time.

To determine the offering price, the underwriter will meet with potential buyers, typically large institutional buyers such as mutual funds. Often, the underwriter and company management will do presentations in multiple cities, pitching the stock in what is known as a *road show*. Potential buyers provide information on the price they would be willing to pay and the number of shares they would purchase at a particular price. This process of soliciting information about buyers and the prices and quantities they would demand is known as *book building*. As we will see, despite the book building process, underwriters frequently get the price wrong, or so it seems.

best efforts underwriting
The underwriter sells as much of the issue as possible but can return any unsold shares to the issuer without financial responsibility.

Dutch auction underwriting
The type of underwriting in which the offer price is set based on competitive bidding by investors. Also known as a *uniform price auction*.

Best Efforts Underwriting In **best efforts underwriting**, the underwriter is legally bound to use "best efforts" to sell the securities at the agreed-upon offering price. Beyond this, the underwriter does not guarantee any particular amount of money to the issuer. This form of underwriting has become very uncommon; firm commitments are the dominant form.

Dutch Auction Underwriting With **Dutch auction underwriting**, the underwriter does not set a fixed price for the shares to be sold. Instead, the underwriter conducts an auction in which investors bid for shares. The offer price is determined based on the submitted bids. A Dutch auction also is known by the more descriptive name *uniform price auction*. This approach to selling securities to the public is relatively new in the IPO market and has not been widely used there, but it is very common in the bond markets. For example, it is the sole procedure used by the U.S. Treasury to sell enormous quantities of notes, bonds, and bills to the public.

Dutch auction underwriting was much in the news in 2004 because the web search company Google (now known as Alphabet) elected to use this approach. The best way to understand a Dutch or uniform price auction is to consider a simple example. Suppose the Rial Company wants to sell 400 shares to the public. The company receives five bids as follows:

Bidder	Quantity	Price
A	100 shares	$16
B	100 shares	14
C	200 shares	12
D	100 shares	12
E	200 shares	10

Learn all about Dutch auction IPOs at www.wrhambrecht.com.

Thus, Bidder A is willing to buy 100 shares at $16 each, Bidder B is willing to buy 100 shares at $14, and so on. The Rial Company examines the bids to determine the highest price that will result in all 400 shares being sold. So, for example, at $14, A and B would buy only 200 shares, so that price is too high. Working our way down, all 400 shares won't be sold until we hit a price of $12, so $12 will be the offer price in the IPO. Bidders A through D will receive shares; Bidder E will not.

There are two additional important points to observe in our example: First, all the winning bidders will pay $12, even Bidders A and B, who actually bid a higher price. The fact that all successful bidders pay the same price is the reason for the name "uniform price auction." The idea in such an auction is to encourage bidders to bid aggressively by providing some protection against bidding a price that is too high.

Second, notice that at the $12 offer price, there are actually bids for 500 shares, which exceeds the 400 shares Rial wants to sell. Thus, there has to be some sort of allocation. How this is done varies a bit, but, in the IPO market, the approach has been to compute the ratio of shares offered to shares bid at the offer price or better, which, in our example, is 400/500 = .8, and allocate bidders that percentage of their bids. In other words, Bidders A through D would each receive 80 percent of the shares they bid at a price of $12 per share.

The Green Shoe Provision

Many underwriting contracts contain a **Green Shoe provision** (sometimes called the *overallotment option*), which gives the members of the underwriting group the option to purchase additional shares from the issuer at the offering price.[5] Essentially, all IPOs and SEOs include this provision, but ordinary debt offerings generally do not. The stated reason for the Green Shoe option is to cover excess demand and oversubscriptions. Green Shoe options usually last for about 30 days and involve no more than 15 percent of the newly issued shares.

Green Shoe provision
A contract provision giving the underwriter the option to purchase additional shares from the issuer at the offering price. Also *overallotment option*.

The Aftermarket

The period after a new issue is initially sold to the public is referred to as the *aftermarket*. The lead underwriter frequently will "stabilize," or support, the market price for a relatively short time following the offering. This is done by actually selling 115 percent of the issue. If the price rises in the aftermarket, the underwriter will exercise the Green Shoe option to purchase the extra 15 percent needed. If the price declines, however, the underwriter will step in and buy the stock in the open market, thereby supporting the price. In this second case, the underwriter allows the Green Shoe option to expire.[6] This happened in the May 2012 IPO of Facebook when lead underwriter Morgan Stanley was forced to step in and stabilize the stock price. Even though the stock opened at $42.05, it quickly fell to $38 less than an hour after trading on the stock began. At that point, Morgan Stanley stepped in and began buying shares of the stock to create a floor of $38 per share.

Lockup Agreements

Although they are not required by law, almost all underwriting contracts contain so-called **lockup agreements**. Such agreements specify how long insiders must wait after an IPO before they can sell some or all of their stock. Lockup periods have become fairly standardized in recent years at 180 days. Thus, following an IPO, insiders can't cash out until six months have gone by, which ensures that they maintain a significant economic interest in the company going public.

Lockup periods are also important because it is not unusual for the number of locked-up shares to exceed the number of shares held by the public, sometimes by a substantial multiple. On the day the lockup period expires, there is the possibility that a large number of shares will hit the market on the same day and thereby depress values. The evidence suggests that, on average, venture capital-backed companies are particularly likely to experience a loss in value on the lockup expiration day.

lockup agreement
The part of the underwriting contract that specifies how long insiders must wait after an IPO before they can sell stock.

Learn more about investment banks at Merrill Lynch's website: www.ml .com.

---

[5]The term *Green Shoe provision* sounds quite exotic, but the origin is relatively mundane. The term comes from the name of the Green Shoe Manufacturing Company, which, in 1963, was the first issuer to grant such an option.
[6]Occasionally, the price of a security falls dramatically when the underwriter ceases to stabilize the price. In such cases, Wall Street humorists (the ones who didn't buy any of the stock) have referred to the period following the aftermarket as the *aftermath*.

The Quiet Period

From the time a company begins to seriously consider an IPO until 40 calendar days following an IPO, the SEC requires that a firm and its managing underwriters observe a "quiet period." This means that all communications with the public must be limited to ordinary announcements and other purely factual matters. The SEC's logic is that all relevant information should be contained in the prospectus. An important result of this requirement is that the underwriters' analysts are prohibited from making recommendations to investors. As soon as the quiet period ends, however, the managing underwriters typically publish research reports, usually accompanied by a favorable "buy" recommendation.

Firms that don't stay quiet can have their IPOs delayed. For example, just before Google's IPO, an interview with cofounders Sergey Brin and Larry Page appeared in *Playboy*. The interview almost caused a postponement of the IPO, but Google was able to amend its prospectus in time (by including the article!). However, in May 2004, Salesforce.com's IPO was delayed because an interview with CEO Marc Benioff appeared in *The New York Times*. Salesforce.com finally went public two months later.

Direct Listing

direct listing
A security offering in which the company offers securities directly to investors, bypassing underwriters.

While firms usually use underwriters to help their stock become publicly traded, it is not required. If it wishes to do so, and it meets the requirements of the stock exchange, a company can do a **direct listing**. In this case, the firm arranges for its stock to be listed on the exchange without marketing and other help from an underwriter. Direct listings are uncommon for large firms, but music-streaming giant Spotify, with a valuation well into the billions of dollars, completed one on the NYSE in 2018. Among other things, a direct listing is much less expensive because there are no underwriting fees and other associated costs. Such fees are discussed in detail in a subsequent section, and they can be substantial.

CONCEPT QUESTIONS

15.4a What do underwriters do?

15.4b What is the Green Shoe provision?

15.5 IPOs AND UNDERPRICING

Determining the correct offering price is the most difficult thing an underwriter must do for an initial public offering. The issuing firm faces a potential cost if the offering price is set too high or too low. If the issue is priced too high, it may be unsuccessful and have to be withdrawn. If the issue is priced below the true market value, the issuer's existing shareholders will experience an opportunity loss when they sell their shares for less than they are worth.

Underpricing is fairly common. It obviously helps new shareholders earn a higher return on the shares they buy. However, the existing shareholders of the issuing firm are not helped by underpricing. To them, it is an indirect cost of issuing new securities. For example, consider Chinese online retailer Alibaba's IPO in September 2014. The stock was priced at $68 in the IPO and rose to a first-day high of $99.70 before closing at $93.89, a gain of about 38.1 percent. Based on these numbers, Alibaba was underpriced by about $25.89 per share. Because Alibaba sold 320.1 million shares, the company missed out on an additional $8.3 billion, a record amount "left on the table." The previous record of $5.1 billion was held by Visa, set in its 2008 IPO.

Dutch auctions are supposed to eliminate this kind of "pop" in first-day prices. As we previously discussed, Google sold 19.6 million shares at a price of $85 in a Dutch auction IPO. However, the stock closed at $100.34 on the first day, an increase of 18 percent, so Google missed out on an additional $300 million.

One of the largest dollar amounts "left on the table" occurred in 1999 when eToys went public, offering 8.2 million shares. The stock jumped $57 above the offer price on the first day, which meant eToys left about half a billion dollars on the table. eToys could have used the money; it filed for bankruptcy less than two years later. In May 2002, the company sued its lead underwriter, claiming the offer price was deliberately set too low.

Of course, not all IPOs increase in price on the first day. For example, security company ADT went public on January 19, 2018, at a price of $14. The company's stock opened at $12.65, dropped to $12.00, before closing at $12.29 by the end of the day, a drop of about 12 percent from the IPO price.

A worse fate awaited BATS Global Markets. BATS, which stands for Better Alternative Trading System, was an electronic stock market that handled about 11 percent of the trading on the U.S. markets. On March 23, 2012, the company went public, selling 6.3 million shares at a price of $16 each. The IPO was the first IPO to take place on the BATS market, an important step toward attracting other new IPOs. However, shortly after trading on BATS stock began, things turned sour. Trades were executed at $15.25, below the initial offering price. Less than nine seconds later, the stock price dropped to .0002 *cent*! Less than 30 seconds later, trading on BATS stock was halted, all trades in the stock were canceled, and the IPO was withdrawn.

> IPO information is ubiquitous on the World Wide Web. Two sites of interest are www.rena issancecapital.com and IPO Monitor at www .ipomonitor.com.

Evidence on Underpricing

Figure 15.2 provides a more general illustration of the underpricing phenomenon. What is shown is the month-by-month history of underpricing for SEC-registered IPOs.[7] The period

FIGURE 15.2 **Average initial returns by month for SEC-registered initial public offerings: 1960–2017**

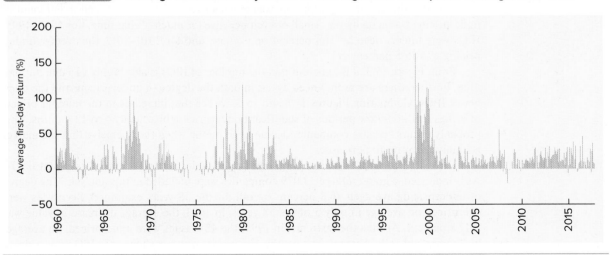

Source: Ibbotson, R. G., Sindelar, J. L. and Ritter, J. R., "The Market's Problems with the Pricing of Initial Public Offerings," *Journal of Applied Corporate Finance,* vol. 7, Spring 1994, as updated by the authors.

---

[7]The discussion in this section draws on Jay R. Ritter, "Initial Public Offerings," *Contemporary Finance Digest* 2 (Spring 1998).

Number of offerings by month for SEC-registered initial public offerings: 1960–2017

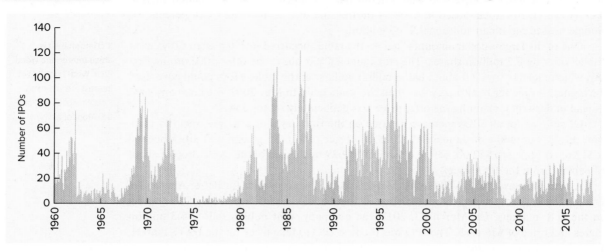

Source: Ibbotson, R. G., Sindelar, J. L. and Ritter, J. R., "The Market's Problems with the Pricing of Initial Public Offerings," *Journal of Applied Corporate Finance,* vol. 7, Spring 1994, as updated by the authors.

covered is 1960 through 2017. Figure 15.3 presents the number of offerings in each month for the same period.

Figure 15.2 shows that underpricing can be quite dramatic, exceeding 100 percent in some months. In such months, the average IPO more than doubled in value, sometimes in a matter of hours. Also, the degree of underpricing varies through time, and periods of severe underpricing ("hot issue" markets) are followed by periods of little underpricing ("cold issue" markets). For example, in the 1960s, the average IPO was underpriced by 21.2 percent. In the 1970s, the average underpricing was much smaller (7.2 percent), and the amount of underpricing was actually very small or even negative for much of that time. For 1990–1999, IPOs were underpriced by 21.4 percent on average, and for 2010–2017, the average underpricing was 15.5 percent.

From Figure 15.3, it is apparent that the number of IPOs is also highly variable through time. Further, there are pronounced cycles in both the degree of underpricing and the number of IPOs. Comparing Figures 15.2 and 15.3, we see that increases in the number of new offerings tend to follow periods of significant underpricing by roughly 6 to 12 months. This probably occurs because companies decide to go public when they perceive that the market is highly receptive to new issues.

Table 15.2 contains a year-by-year summary of underpricing for the years 1960 to 2017. As is indicated, a grand total of 13,079 companies were included in this analysis. The degree of underpricing averaged 16.8 percent overall for the 58 years examined. Securities were overpriced on average in only 5 of the 58 years; in 1973, the average decrease in value was −17.8 percent. At the other extreme, in 1999, the 484 issues were underpriced, on average, by a remarkable 69.7 percent. The nearby *Finance Matters* box shows that IPO underpricing is not confined to the United States; instead, it seems to be a global phenomenon.

IPO Underpricing: The 1999–2000 Experience

Table 15.2, along with Figures 15.2 and 15.3, show that 1999 and 2000 were extraordinary years in the IPO market. During these two years, 866 companies went public, and the

TABLE 15.2 Number of offerings, average first-day returns, and gross proceeds of initial public offerings: 1960–2017

Year	Number of Offerings*	Average First-Day Return, %[†]	Gross Proceeds, $ Millions[‡]	Year	Number of Offerings*	Average First-Day Return, %[†]	Gross Proceeds, $ Millions[‡]
1960	269	17.8	553	1993	527	12.7	31,756
1961	435	34.1	1,243	1994	410	9.8	17,418
1962	298	−1.6	431	1995	464	21.1	28,017
1963	83	3.9	246	1996	689	17.3	42,428
1964	97	5.3	380	1997	485	13.9	32,547
1965	146	12.7	409	1998	308	20.3	34,400
1966	85	7.1	275	1999	484	69.7	64,809
1967	100	37.7	641	2000	382	56.2	64,931
1968	368	55.9	1,205	2001	79	14.2	34,241
1969	780	12.5	2,605	2002	70	8.6	22,136
1970	358	−.7	780	2003	68	11.9	10,075
1971	391	21.2	1,655	2004	181	12.3	31,663
1972	562	7.5	2,724	2005	167	10.1	28,577
1973	105	−17.8	330	2006	162	11.9	30,648
1974	9	−7.0	51	2007	160	14.0	35,704
1975	12	−.2	261	2008	21	5.7	22,762
1976	26	1.9	214	2009	42	10.6	13,296
1977	15	3.6	128	2010	100	9.2	30,708
1978	19	12.6	207	2011	82	13.2	27,750
1979	39	8.5	313	2012	105	17.1	32,074
1980	71	13.9	905	2013	162	20.9	39,093
1981	193	6.2	2,313	2014	225	14.9	46,967
1982	79	10.5	1,012	2015	122	18.1	22,020
1983	521	8.9	11,418	2016	78	14.4	12,843
1984	213	2.8	2,608	2017	119	12.4	25,596
1985	217	6.5	4,848	1960–1969	2,661	21.2	7,988
1986	478	6.1	15,549	1970–1979	1,536	7.2	6,663
1987	337	5.7	12,623	1980–1989	2,365	6.9	61,271
1988	132	5.4	4,089	1990–1999	4,192	21.4	294,890
1989	124	7.8	5,906	2000–2009	1,332	24.5	294,033
1990	116	10.4	4,334	2010–2017	993	15.5	237,051
1991	293	11.8	16,431	1960–2017	13,079	16.8	901,896
1992	416	10.2	22,750				

*The number of offerings excludes IPOs with an offer price of less than $5.00, ADRs, best efforts, units, Regulation A offers (small issues, raising less than $1.5 million during the 1980s), real estate investment trusts (REITs), partnerships, and closed-end funds. Banks and S&Ls and non-CRSP-listed IPOs are included.

[†]First-day returns are computed as the percentage return from the offering price to the first closing market price.

[‡]Gross proceeds exclude overallotment options but include the international tranche, if any. No adjustments for inflation have been made.

Source: Data from 1960–1974 is taken from Table 1 of Ibbotson, R., Sindelar, J. and Ritter, J. R., *Journal of Applied Corporate Finance* article, "The Market's Problems with the Pricing of Initial Public Offerings," vol. 7, no. 1, Spring 1994, 66–74; Data from 1975–2017 is compiled by Ritter, Jay R. using Thomson Financial, Dealogic, and other sources. The 1975–1992 numbers are different from those reported in the *JACF* article because the published article included IPOs that did not qualify for listing on Nasdaq, the Amex, or NYSE (mainly penny stocks).

average first-day return across the two years was about 65 percent. During this time, 194 IPOs doubled, or more than doubled, in value on the first day. In contrast, only 39 did so in the preceding 24 years combined. One company, VA Linux, shot up 698 percent!

The dollar amount raised in 2000, $64.9 billion, was a record, followed closely by 1999. The underpricing was so severe in 1999 that companies left another $36 billion "on the table," which was substantially more than in 1990 through 1998 combined, and, in 2000, the

IPO Underpricing around the World

The United States is not the only country in which initial public offerings (IPOs) of common stock are underpriced. The phenomenon exists in every country with a stock market, although the extent of underpricing varies from country to country.

In general, countries with developed capital markets have more moderate underpricing than in emerging markets. During the Internet bubble of 1999–2000, however, underpricing in the developed capital markets increased dramatically. In the United States, for example, the average first-day return during 1999–2000 was 65 percent. At the same time that underpricing in the developed capital markets increased, the underpricing of IPOs sold to residents of China moderated. The Chinese average has come down to a mere 118 percent, which is lower than it had been in the early and mid-1990s. After the bursting of the Internet bubble in mid-2000, the level of underpricing in the United States, Germany, and other developed capital markets has returned to more traditional levels.

The accompanying table gives a summary of the average first-day returns on IPOs in a number of countries around the world, with the figures collected from a number of studies by various authors.

Country	Sample Size	Time Period	Average Initial Return (%)	Country	Sample Size	Time Period	Average Initial Return (%)
Argentina	26	1991–2013	4.2%	Malaysia	474	1980–2013	56.2%
Australia	1,562	1976–2011	21.8	Mauritius	40	1989–2005	15.2
Austria	103	1971–2013	6.4	Mexico	123	1987–2012	11.6
Belgium	114	1984–2006	13.5	Morocco	33	2004–2011	33.3
Brazil	275	1979–2011	33.1	Netherlands	181	1982–2006	10.2
Bulgaria	9	2004–2007	36.5	New Zealand	242	1979–2013	18.6
Canada	743	1971–2016	6.5	Nigeria	122	1989–2013	13.1
Chile	81	1982–2013	7.4	Norway	209	1984–2013	8.1
China	3,116	1990–2016	145.4	Pakistan	80	2000–2013	22.1
Cyprus	73	1997–2012	20.3	Philippines	155	1987–2013	18.1
Denmark	164	1984–2011	7.4	Poland	309	1991–2012	13.3
Egypt	62	1990–2010	10.4	Portugal	32	1992–2013	11.9
Finland	168	1971–2013	16.9	Russia	64	1999–2013	3.3
France	697	1983–2010	10.5	Saudi Arabia	80	2003–2011	239.8
Germany	779	1978–2014	23.0	Singapore	609	1973–2013	25.81
Greece	373	1976–2013	50.8	South Africa	316	1980–2013	17.4
Hong Kong	1,486	1980–2013	15.8	South Korea	1,758	1980–2014	58.8
India	2,983	1990–2014	88.0	Spain	143	1986–2013	10.3
Indonesia	464	1990–2014	24.9	Sri Lanka	105	1987–2008	33.5
Iran	279	1991–2004	22.4	Sweden	405	1980–2015	25.9
Ireland	38	1991–2013	21.6	Switzerland	164	1983–2013	27.3
Israel	348	1990–2006	13.8	Taiwan	1,620	1980–2013	38.1
Italy	312	1985–2013	15.2	Thailand	500	1987–2012	35.1
Japan	3,488	1970–2016	44.7	Turkey	355	1990–2011	10.3
Jordan	53	1999–2008	149.0	United Kingdom	4,932	1959–2012	16.0
Korea	1,720	1980–2013	59.3	United States	13,079	1960–2017	16.8

Source: **Professor Jay R. Ritter, the Joseph B. Cordell Professor of Finance at the University of Florida. An outstanding scholar, he is well known for his insightful analyses of new issues and going public.**

amount was at least $27 billion. In other words, over the two-year period, companies missed out on $63 billion because of underpricing.

October 19, 1999, was one of the more memorable days during this time. The World Wrestling Federation (WWF) (now known as World Wrestling Entertainment, or WWE) and Martha Stewart Omnimedia both went public, so it was Martha Stewart versus "Stone Cold" Steve Austin in a Wall Street version of MTV's *Celebrity Deathmatch*. When the closing bell rang, it was a clear smackdown as Martha Stewart gained 98 percent on the first day compared to 48 percent for the WWF. If you're interested in finding out how IPOs have done recently, check out our nearby *Work the Web* box.

The IPO market cooled off considerably in 2001. Many observers now refer to the 1999–2000 period as the Internet "bubble" period. The word *bubble* in this context refers to a situation in which prices are bid up to irrational, and unsustainable, levels. During 1999, for example, 323 of the companies that went public were considered Internet IPOs, meaning companies that did most (or all) of their business on the Internet, or companies whose products were used for computers or networks. By April 2001, of the 1999 internet IPOs, only 12, or 4 percent, were trading above their offer price, and only 4, or 1 percent, were trading above their first-day close. Was it really a bubble? Let us say that, at a minimum, there were instances of valuations that are very hard to reconcile with economic reality. A nearby *Finance Matters* box discusses one of the most notorious, the case of Palm, Inc., maker of handheld computers.

WORK THE WEB

So, do the high returns IPOs sometimes earn have you excited? Do you wonder how recent NASDAQ IPOs have performed? You can find out at www.nasdaq.com/markets/ipos/performance.aspx. On the website, you can sort by 1-day, 30-day, 60-day, and 6-month performance after the IPO. We went to the website and here is part of what we found:

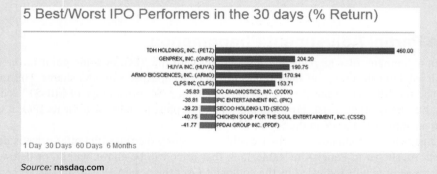

5 Best/Worst IPO Performers in the 30 days (% Return)

Company	% Return
TDH HOLDINGS, INC. (PETZ)	460.00
GENPREX, INC. (GNPX)	204.20
HUYA INC. (HUYA)	190.75
ARMO BIOSCIENCES, INC. (ARMO)	170.94
CLPS INC (CLPS)	153.71
CO-DIAGNOSTICS, INC. (CODX)	-35.83
PIC ENTERTAINMENT INC. (PIC)	-38.81
SECOO HOLDING LTD (SECO)	-39.23
CHICKEN SOUP FOR THE SOUL ENTERTAINMENT, INC. (CSSE)	-40.75
PPDAI GROUP INC. (PPDF)	-41.77

1 Day 30 Days 60 Days 6 Months

Source: **nasdaq.com**

As you can see, TDH Holdings was up 460 percent in the 30 days after its IPO, and Genprex was up about 204 percent in the first 30 days of trading.

QUESTIONS

1. *Go to www.nasdaq.com/markets/ipos/performance.aspx and find the companies that have had the best 1-day, 30-day, 60-day, and 6-month performances. How do the most recent gains compare with the gains shown above? Which companies had the biggest first-day drops?*

2. *Go to www.ipomonitor.com and find out which companies have filed for an IPO but have yet to start trading.*

The (Mis)pricing of Palm, Inc.

At one time, Palm was entirely owned by 3Com, Inc., a profitable provider of computer networking products and services. On March 2, 2000, 3Com sold 5 percent of its stake in Palm to the public via an IPO. This type of IPO, in which a company sells a part of its stock (usually a minority share) in a subsidiary, is called an equity "carve-out," and such carve-outs are not uncommon events.

At some point following a carve-out, the parent company often will distribute the remaining shares in the subsidiary to its stockholders. This transaction is called a *spin-off*. In Palm's case, 3Com planned to spin off its remaining shares to 3Com's shareholders before the end of the year. Under the plan, 3Com shareholders would receive about 1.5 shares of Palm for every share of 3Com that they owned. Thus, after the IPO, investors could buy shares in Palm directly, or they could buy shares indirectly by purchasing stock in 3Com and waiting a little while.

Here is where it gets interesting. Because the owner of a share of 3Com will ultimately get 1.5 shares of Palm, each share of 3Com has to be worth at least as much as 1.5 shares of Palm, right? In fact, given that 3Com's other businesses were profitable, 3Com's stock price should be well above 1.5 times that of Palm.

It didn't happen that way. The day before the Palm IPO, 3Com closed at $104.13 per share. After the first day of trading, Palm closed at $95.06 per share, implying that the price of 3Com should have jumped to at least $145. Instead, 3Com fell to $81.81. The next day, the wacky pricing was prominently discussed in *The Wall Street Journal* and elsewhere, so it wasn't a secret. It was easy to see, yet it persisted for months.

Based on these prices, the stock market was placing a negative value on 3Com's non-Palm businesses. Because the stock sold for about $82 per share when it should have sold for at least $145, the market was valuing all of 3Com's non-Palm operations at $82 − 145 = −$63 per share, or about −$22 billion in all! Of course, stock prices can't be negative, so a reasonable interpretation would be that Palm's stock price was far too high relative to 3Com's.

Episodes like that of Palm are rare, but there were at least five other cases of clear negative valuations in roughly the same time period as Palm's IPO. In all cases, the negative values gradually disappeared, so the misvaluations were corrected, but it took time in each case.

The Partial Adjustment Phenomenon

When a company files its registration statement with the SEC, at some point in the process it will indicate a range of stock prices within which it expects to offer shares. This range is called the "file price range," or words to that effect. A file price range of $10–$12 is common, but many others exist. For example, when Dropbox initially filed for its IPO, it indicated an anticipated price in the $16 to $18 range.

Just before a company's shares are sold to investors, the final IPO offer price is determined. As shown in Panel A of Table 15.3, that price can be above, within, or below the price range originally indicated by the company. Over the period 1980–2017, 48 percent of IPOs were within the file range, with 29 percent below and 23 percent above.

Panel B of Table 15.3 illustrates an interesting and very clear pattern. IPO underpricing is much more severe when an offer is priced above the file range. Again over the 1980–2017 period, IPOs that priced above the file range were underpriced by 50 percent, on average, compared to only 3 percent for firms priced below it. The 1999–2000 period again stands out. Issues that "went off" above the file range were underpriced, on average, by 122 percent!

This pattern is known as the "partial adjustment" phenomenon. The name refers to the fact that when firms raise their IPO offer prices, they only do so partially, meaning that they don't move the price high enough. In Dropbox's case, the final offer price was $21, much higher than the original file range, but not high enough: The stock jumped to $31.60 on the first day of trading on March 23, 2018, when it closed at $28.48.

A. Percentage of IPOs Relative to File Price Range			
	Below	Within	Above
1980–1989	30%	57%	13%
1990–1998	27	49	24
1999–2000	18	38	44
2001–2017	35	44	21
1980–2017	29	48	23

B. Average First-Day Returns Relative to File Price Range			
	Below	Within	Above
1980–1989	0%	6%	20%
1990–1998	4	11	31
1999–2000	8	26	122
2001–2017	3	11	37
1980–2017	3	11	50

TABLE 15.3

IPO underpricing and file price range

Source: **Professor Jay R. Ritter, University of Florida.**

Why does the partial adjustment phenomenon exist? The answer is unknown. The question is related to the broader question of why IPO underpricing exists, which we consider next.

Why Does Underpricing Exist?

Based on the evidence we've examined, an obvious question is why does underpricing continue to exist? As we discuss, there are various explanations, but, to date, there is a lack of complete agreement among researchers as to which is correct.

We present some pieces of the underpricing puzzle by stressing two important caveats to our preceding discussion. First, the average figures we have examined tend to obscure the fact that much of the apparent underpricing is attributable to the smaller, more highly speculative issues. This point is illustrated in Table 15.4, which shows the extent of

TABLE 15.4   Average first-day returns, categorized by sales, for IPOs: 1980–2017*

Annual Sales of Issuing Firms	1980–1989		1990–1998		1999–2000		2001–2017	
	Number of Firms	First-Day Average Return	Number of Firms	First-Day Average Return	Number of Firms	First-Day Average Return	Number of Firms	First-Day Average Return
$0 ≤ sales ≤ $10m	425	10.3%	741	17.2%	331	68.9%	372	9.6%
$10m ≤ sales ≤ $20m	242	8.6	393	18.5	138	81.4	82	13.6
$20m ≤ sales ≤ $50m	501	7.8	789	18.8	154	75.5	217	14.8
$50m ≤ sales ≤ $100m	356	6.3	590	12.8	86	62.2	284	20.5
$100m ≤ sales ≤ $200m	234	5.1	454	11.8	56	35.8	241	17.9
$200m ≤ sales	290	3.4	646	8.7	91	25.0	647	11.8
All	2,048	7.2	3,613	14.8	856	64.6	1,843	13.9

*Sales, measured in millions, are for the last 12 months prior to going public. All sales have been converted into dollars of 2003 purchasing power, using the Consumer Price Index. There are 8,360 IPOs, after excluding IPOs with an offer price of less than $5.00 per share. The average first-day return is 17.8 percent.

Source: **Professor Jay R. Ritter, University of Florida.**

underpricing for 8,360 firms over the period from 1980 through 2017. Here, the firms are grouped based on their total sales in the 12 months prior to the IPO.

As illustrated in Table 15.4, there is a tendency for underpricing to be more pronounced for firms with relatively small pre-IPO sales. These firms tend to be young firms, and such young firms can be very risky investments. Arguably, they must be significantly underpriced, on average, to attract investors, and this is one explanation for the underpricing phenomenon.

The second caveat is that relatively few IPO buyers actually will get the initial high average returns observed in IPOs, and many actually will lose money. Although it is true that, on average, IPOs have positive initial returns, a significant fraction of them have price drops. Furthermore, when the price is too low, the issue is often "oversubscribed." This means investors will not be able to buy all of the shares they want, and the underwriters will allocate the shares among investors.

The average investor will find it difficult to get shares in a "successful" offering (one in which the price increases) because there will not be enough shares to go around. On the other hand, an investor blindly submitting orders for IPOs tends to get more shares in issues that go down in price.

To illustrate, consider this tale of two investors. Smith knows very accurately what the Bonanza Corporation is worth when its shares are offered. She is confident that the shares are underpriced. Jones knows only that IPOs are usually underpriced. Armed with this information, Jones decides to buy 1,000 shares of every IPO. Does he actually earn an abnormally high return on the initial offering?

The answer is no, and at least one reason is Smith. Knowing about the Bonanza Corporation, Smith invests all her money in its IPO. When the issue is oversubscribed, the underwriters have to somehow allocate the shares between Smith and Jones. The net result is that when an issue is underpriced, Jones doesn't get to buy as much of it as he wanted.

Smith also knows that the Blue Sky Corporation IPO is overpriced. In this case, she avoids its IPO altogether, and Jones ends up with a full 1,000 shares. To summarize this tale, Jones gets fewer shares when more knowledgeable investors swarm to buy an underpriced issue and gets all he wants when the smart money avoids the issue.

This is an example of a "winner's curse," and it is thought to be another reason why IPOs have such a large average return. When the average investor "wins" and gets the entire allocation, it may be because those who knew better avoided the issue. The only way underwriters can counteract the winner's curse and attract the average investor is to underprice new issues (on average) so that the average investor still makes a profit.

A final reason for underpricing is that the underpricing is a kind of insurance for the investment banks. Conceivably, an investment bank could be sued successfully by angry customers if it consistently overpriced securities. Underpricing guarantees that, at least on average, customers will come out ahead.

CONCEPT QUESTIONS

15.5a Why is underpricing a cost to the issuing firm?

15.5b Suppose a stockbroker calls you up out of the blue and offers to sell you "all the shares you want" of a new issue. Do you think the issue will be more, or less, underpriced than average?

15.6 NEW EQUITY SALES AND THE VALUE OF THE FIRM

We now turn to a consideration of seasoned equity offerings (SEOs), which, as we discussed earlier, are offerings by firms that already have outstanding securities. It seems reasonable to believe that new long-term financing is arranged by firms after positive net present value projects are put together. As a consequence, when the announcement of external financing is made, the firm's market value should go up. Interestingly, this is not what happens. Stock prices tend to decline following the announcement of a new equity issue, although they tend to not change much following a debt announcement. A number of researchers have studied this issue. Plausible reasons for this strange result include the following:

1. *Managerial information.* If management has superior information about the market value of the firm, it may know when the firm is overvalued. If it does, it will attempt to issue new shares of stock when the market value exceeds the correct value. This will benefit existing shareholders. However, the potential new shareholders are not stupid, and they will anticipate this superior information and discount it in lower market prices at the new issue date.

2. *Debt usage.* A company's issuing new equity may reveal that the company has too much debt or too little liquidity. One version of this argument says that the equity issue is a bad signal to the market. After all, if the new projects are favorable ones, why should the firm let new shareholders in on them? It could just issue debt and let the existing shareholders have all the gain.

3. *Issue costs.* As we discuss next, there are substantial costs associated with selling securities.

The drop in value of the existing stock following the announcement of a new issue is an example of an indirect cost of selling securities. This drop typically might be on the order of 3 percent for an industrial corporation (and somewhat smaller for a public utility), so, for a large company, it can represent a substantial amount of money. We label this drop the *abnormal return* in our discussion of the costs of new issues that follows.

CONCEPT QUESTIONS

15.6a What are some possible reasons the price of a stock drops on the announcement of a new equity issue?

15.6b Explain why we might expect a firm with a positive NPV investment to finance it with debt instead of equity.

15.7 THE COST OF ISSUING SECURITIES

Issuing securities to the public isn't free, and the costs of different methods are important determinants of which is used. These costs associated with *floating* a new issue are generically called *flotation costs.* In this section, we take a closer look at the flotation costs associated with equity sales to the public.

The costs of selling stock are classified in the following table and fall into six categories: (1) the spread, (2) other direct expenses, (3) indirect expenses, (4) abnormal returns (discussed previously), (5) underpricing, and (6) the Green Shoe option.

The Costs of Issuing Securities	
1. Spread	The spread consists of direct fees paid by the issuer to the underwriting syndicate—the difference between the price the issuer receives and the offer price.
2. Other direct expenses	These are direct costs incurred by the issuer that are not part of the compensation to underwriters. These costs include filing fees, legal fees, and taxes—all reported on the prospectus.
3. Indirect expenses	These costs are not reported on the prospectus and include the cost of management time spent working on the new issue.
4. Abnormal returns	In a seasoned issue of stock, the price of the existing stock drops on average by 3 percent upon the announcement of the issue. This drop is called the abnormal return.
5. Underpricing	For initial public offerings, losses arise from selling the stock below the true value.
6. Green Shoe option	The Green Shoe option gives the underwriters the right to buy additional shares at the offer price to cover overallotments.

Table 15.5 reports direct costs as a percentage of the gross amount raised for IPOs, SEOs, straight (ordinary) bonds, and convertible bonds sold by U.S. companies over the 19-year period from 1990 through 2008. These are direct costs only. Not included are indirect expenses, the cost of the Green Shoe provision, underpricing (for IPOs), and abnormal returns (for SEOs).

As Table 15.5 shows, the direct costs alone can be very large, particularly for smaller issues (less than $10 million). On a smaller IPO, for example, the total direct costs amount to 25.22 percent of the amount raised. This means that if a company sells $10 million in stock, it will net only about $7.5 million; the other $2.5 million goes to cover the underwriter spread and other direct expenses. Typical underwriter spreads on an IPO range from about 5 percent for large offerings to 10 percent for small offerings, but, for about half of the IPOs in Table 15.5, the spread is exactly 7 percent, so this is, by far, the most common spread. The nearby *Finance Matters* box provides a detailed example for a particular company.

Overall, four clear patterns emerge from Table 15.5. First of all, with the possible exception of straight debt offerings (about which we will have more to say later), there are substantial economies of scale. The underwriter spreads are smaller on larger issues, and the other direct costs fall sharply as a percentage of the amount raised, a reflection of the mostly fixed nature of such costs. Second, the costs associated with selling debt are substantially less than the costs of selling equity. Third, IPOs have higher expenses than SEOs, but the difference is not as great as might originally be guessed. Finally, straight bonds are cheaper to float than convertible bonds.

As we have discussed, the underpricing of IPOs is an additional cost to the issuer. To give a better idea of the total cost of going public, Table 15.6 combines the information in Table 15.5 for IPOs with data on the underpricing experienced by these firms. Comparing the total direct costs (in the fifth column) to the underpricing (in the sixth column), we see that they tend to be similar in size, so the direct costs are only about half of the total for small issues. Overall, across all size groups, the total direct costs amount to 10 percent of the amount raised and the underpricing amounts to 19 percent.

TABLE 15.5	Direct costs as a percentage of gross proceeds for equity (IPOs and SEOs) and straight and convertible bonds offered by domestic operating companies: 1990–2008

Proceeds ($ millions)	IPOs				SEOs			
	Number of Issues	Gross Spread	Other Direct Expense	Total Direct Cost	Number of Issues	Gross Spread	Other Direct Expense	Total Direct Cost
2.00–9.99	1,007	9.40%	15.82%	25.22%	515	8.11%	26.99%	35.11%
10.00–19.99	810	7.39	7.30	14.69	726	6.11	7.76	13.86
20.00–39.99	1,422	6.96	7.06	14.03	1,393	5.44	4.10	9.54
40.00–59.99	880	6.89	2.87	9.77	1,129	5.03	8.93	13.96
60.00–79.99	522	6.79	2.16	8.94	841	4.88	1.98	6.85
80.00–99.99	327	6.71	1.84	8.55	536	4.67	2.05	6.72
100.00–199.99	702	6.39	1.57	7.96	1,372	4.34	.89	5.23
200.00–499.99	440	5.81	1.03	6.84	811	3.72	1.22	4.94
500.00 and up	155	5.01	.49	5.50	264	3.10	.27	3.37
Total/Average	**6,265**	**7.19**	**3.18**	**10.37**	**7,587**	**5.02**	**2.68**	**7.69**

Proceeds ($ millions)	Straight Bonds				Convertible Bonds			
	Number of Issues	Gross Spread	Other Direct Expense	Total Direct Cost	Number of Issues	Gross Spread	Other Direct Expense	Total Direct Cost
2.00–9.99	3,962	1.64	2.40	4.03	14	6.39	3.43	9.82
10.00–19.99	3,400	1.50	1.71	3.20	23	5.52	3.09	8.61
20.00–39.99	2,690	1.25	.92	2.17	30	4.63	1.67	6.30
40.00–59.99	3,345	.81	.79	1.59	35	3.49	1.04	4.54
60.00–79.99	891	1.65	.80	2.44	60	2.79	.62	3.41
80.00–99.99	465	1.41	.57	1.98	16	2.30	.62	2.92
100.00–199.99	4,949	1.61	.52	2.14	82	2.66	.42	3.08
200.00–499.99	3,305	1.38	.33	1.71	46	2.65	.33	2.99
500.00 and up	1,261	.61	.15	.76	7	2.16	.13	2.29
Total/Average	**24,268**	**1.38**	**.61**	**2.00**	**313**	**3.07**	**.85**	**3.92**

Source: Lee, I., Lochhead, S., Ritter, J. and Zhao, Quanshui, "The Costs of Raising Capital," *Journal of Financial Research*, vol. 1, Spring 1996, calculations and updates by the authors.

Anatomy of an IPO

On June 29, 2018, Domo, Inc., the corporate communications company based in American Fork, Utah, went public via an IPO. Domo issued 9.2 million shares of stock at a price of $21 each. The lead underwriters on the IPO were JMP Securities and William Blair & Company, assisted by a syndicate of other investment banks. Even though the IPO raised a gross sum of $193.2 million, Domo got to keep only about $175.7 million after expenses. The biggest expense was the 7 percent underwriter spread, which is ordinary for an offering of this size. Domo sold each of the 9.2 million shares to the underwriters for $19.53, and the underwriters in turn sold the shares to the public for $21.00 each.

But wait—there's more. Domo spent $28,979 in SEC registration fees, $35,414 in other filing fees, and $152,500 to be listed on the NASDAQ Global Market. The company also spent $1.8 million in legal fees, $1.575 million on accounting to obtain the necessary audits, $4,000 for a transfer agent to physically transfer the shares and maintain a list of shareholders, $185,000 for printing and engraving expenses, and, finally, $200,000 in miscellaneous expenses.

As Domo's outlays show, an IPO can be a costly undertaking! In the end, Domo's expenses totaled about $17.5 million, of which $13.52 million went to the underwriters and $3.98 million went to other parties. All told, the total direct cost to Domo was 9.7 percent of the issue proceeds raised by the company. This amount doesn't include the indirect cost of the first-day price pop. Domo's stock closed at $27.30 on the first day of trading, so the company left about $60 million on the table.

Finally, with regard to debt offerings, there is a general pattern in issue costs that is somewhat obscured in Table 15.5. Recall from Chapter 6 that bonds carry different credit ratings. Higher-rated bonds are said to be investment grade, whereas lower-rated bonds are noninvestment grade. Table 15.7 contains a breakdown of direct costs for bond issues after the investment and noninvestment grades have been separated.

Table 15.7 clarifies three things regarding debt issues. First, there are substantial economies of scale here as well. Second, investment-grade issues have much lower direct costs, particularly for straight bonds. Finally, there are relatively few noninvestment-grade issues in the smaller size categories, reflecting the fact that such issues are more commonly handled as private placements, which we discuss in our next section.

TABLE 15.6	Proceeds ($ in millions)	Number of Issues	Gross Spread	Other Direct Expense	Total Direct Cost	Underpricing
Direct and indirect costs, in percentages, of equity IPOs: 1990–2008	2.00–9.99	1,007	9.40%	15.82%	25.22%	20.42%
	10.00–19.99	810	7.39	7.30	14.69	10.33
	20.00–39.99	1,422	6.96	7.06	14.03	17.03
	40.00–59.99	880	6.89	2.87	9.77	28.26
	60.00–79.99	522	6.79	2.16	8.94	28.36
	80.00–99.99	327	6.71	1.84	8.55	32.92
	100.00–199.99	702	6.39	1.57	7.96	21.55
	200.00–499.99	440	5.81	1.03	6.84	6.19
	500.00 and up	155	5.01	.49	5.50	6.64
	Total/Average	6,265	7.19	3.18	10.37	19.34

Source: Inmoo Lee, Inmoo, Lochhead, Scott, Ritter, Jay and Zhao, Quanshui, "The Costs of Raising Capital," *Journal of Financial Research*, vol. 1, Spring 1996, calculations and updates by the authors.

TABLE 15.7 Average gross spreads and total direct costs for domestic debt issues: 1990–2008

Convertible Bonds

Proceeds ($ millions)	Investment Grade				Junk or Not Rated			
	Number of Issues	Gross Spread	Other Direct Expense	Total Direct Cost	Number of Issues	Gross Spread	Other Direct Expense	Total Direct Cost
2.00–9.99	—	—	—	—	14	6.39%	3.43%	9.82%
10.00–19.99	1	14.12%	1.87%	15.98%	23	5.52	3.09	8.61
20.00–39.99	—	—	—	—	30	4.63	1.67	6.30
40.00–59.99	3	1.92	.51	2.43	35	3.49	1.04	4.54
60.00–79.99	6	1.65	.44	2.09	60	2.79	.62	3.41
80.00–99.99	4	.89	.27	1.16	16	2.30	.62	2.92
100.00–199.99	27	2.22	.33	2.55	82	2.66	.42	3.08
200.00–499.99	27	2.03	.19	2.22	46	2.65	.33	2.99
500.00 and up	11	1.94	.13	2.06	7	2.16	.13	2.29
Total/Average	79	2.15	.29	2.44	313	3.31	.98	4.29

Straight Bonds

Proceeds ($ millions)	Investment Grade				Junk or Not Rated			
	Number of Issues	Gross Spread	Other Direct Expense	Total Direct Cost	Number of Issues	Gross Spread	Other Direct Expense	Total Direct Cost
2.00–9.99	2,709	.62%	1.28%	1.90%	1,253	2.77%	2.50%	5.27%
10.00–19.99	2,564	.59	1.17	1.76	836	3.15	1.97	5.12
20.00–39.99	2,400	.63	.74	1.37	290	3.07	1.13	4.20
40.00–59.99	3,146	.40	.52	.92	199	2.93	1.20	4.14
60.00–79.99	792	.58	.38	.96	99	3.12	1.16	4.28
80.00–99.99	385	.66	.29	.96	80	2.73	.93	3.66
100.00–199.99	4,427	.54	.25	.79	522	2.73	.68	3.41
200.00–499.99	3,031	.52	.25	.76	274	2.59	.39	2.98
500.00 and up	1,207	.31	.08	.39	54	2.38	.25	2.63
Total/Average	20,661	.52	.35	.87	3,607	2.76	.81	3.57

Source: Lee, Inmoo, Lochhead, Scott, Ritter, Jay and Zhao, Quanshui, "The Costs of Raising Capital," *Journal of Financial Research*, vol. 1, Spring 1996, calculations and updates by the authors.

> ### EXAMPLE 15.1   How Much Does That IPO Cost?
>
> The Faulk Co. has just gone public under a firm commitment agreement. Faulk received $32 for each of the 4.1 million shares sold. The initial offering price was $34.40 per share, and the stock rose to $41 per share in the first few minutes of trading. Faulk paid $905,000 in legal and other direct costs and $250,000 in indirect costs. What was the flotation cost as a percentage of funds raised?
>
> The net amount raised is the number of shares offered times the price received by the company, minus the costs associated with the offer, so:
>
> > Net amount raised = (4,100,000 shares)($32) − 905,000 − 250,000
> > Net amount raised = $130,045,000
>
> Next, we can calculate the direct costs. Part of the direct costs are given in the problem, but the company also had to pay the underwriters. The stock was offered at $34.40 per share, and the company received $32 per share. The difference, which is the underwriters' spread, is also a direct cost. The total direct costs were:
>
> > Total direct costs = $905,000 + ($34.40 − 32)(4,100,000 shares)
> > Total direct costs = $10,745,000
>
> We are given part of the indirect costs, but the underpricing is another indirect cost. The total indirect costs were:
>
> > Total indirect costs = $250,000 + ($41 − 34.40)(4,100,000 shares)
> > Total indirect costs = $27,310,000
>
> The total costs are:
>
> > Total costs = $10,745,000 + 27,310,000
> > Total costs = $38,055,000
>
> The flotation costs as a percentage of the amount raised is the total cost divided by the amount raised, or:
>
> > Flotation cost percentage = $38,055,000/$130,045,000
> > Flotation cost percentage = .2926, or 29.26%

CONCEPT QUESTIONS

15.7a What are the different costs associated with security offerings?

15.7b What lessons do we learn from studying issue costs?

15.8 ISSUING LONG-TERM DEBT

The general procedures followed in a public issue of bonds are the same as those for stocks. The issue must be registered with the SEC, there must be a prospectus, and so on. The registration statement for a public issue of bonds, however, is different from the one for common stock. For bonds, the registration statement must indicate an indenture.

Another important difference is that more than 50 percent of all debt is issued privately. There are two basic forms of direct private long-term financing: term loans and private placement.

Term loans are direct business loans. These loans have maturities of between one year and five years. Most term loans are repayable during the life of the loan. The lenders include commercial banks, insurance companies, and other lenders that specialize in corporate finance. **Private placements** are very similar to term loans except that the maturities are longer.

The important differences between direct private long-term financing and public issues of debt are

1. A direct long-term loan avoids the cost of Securities and Exchange Commission registration.
2. Direct placement is likely to have more restrictive covenants.
3. It is easier to renegotiate a term loan or a private placement in the event of a default. It is harder to renegotiate a public issue because hundreds of holders are usually involved.
4. Life insurance companies and pension funds dominate the private-placement segment of the bond market. Commercial banks are significant participants in the term-loan market.
5. The costs of distributing bonds are lower in the private market.

The interest rates on term loans and private placements are often higher than those on an equivalent public issue. This difference may reflect the trade-off between a higher interest rate and more flexible arrangements in the event of financial distress, as well as the lower costs associated with private placements.

An additional, and very important, consideration is that the flotation costs associated with selling debt are much less than the comparable costs associated with selling equity.

term loans
Direct business loans of, typically, one to five years.

private placements
Loans, usually long-term in nature, provided directly by a limited number of investors.

CONCEPT QUESTIONS

15.8a What is the difference between private and public bond issues?
15.8b A private placement is likely to have a higher interest rate than a public issue. Why?

15.9 SHELF REGISTRATION

To simplify the procedures for issuing securities, in March 1982, the SEC adopted Rule 415 on a temporary basis, and it was made permanent in November 1983. Rule 415 allows shelf registration. Both debt and equity securities can be shelf registered.

Shelf registration permits a corporation to register an offering that it reasonably expects to sell within the next two years and then sell the issue whenever it wants during that two-year period. In July 2018, information technology company Helios & Matheson announced a shelf registration to sell up to $1.2 billion of debt and equity. According to the registration documents filed by the company, the proceeds were to be used for future acquisitions of other businesses, assets, or securities.

Not all companies can use Rule 415. The primary qualifications are

1. The company must be rated investment grade.
2. The firm cannot have defaulted on its debt in the past three years.

shelf registration
Registration permitted by SEC Rule 415, which allows a company to register all issues it expects to sell within two years at one time, with subsequent sales at any time within those two years.

3. The aggregate market value of the firm's outstanding stock must be more than $150 million.

4. The firm must not have had a violation of the Securities Act of 1934 in the past three years.

The rule has been controversial. Arguments have been constructed against shelf registration:

1. The costs of new issues might go up because underwriters might not be able to provide as much current information to potential investors as they would otherwise, so investors would pay less. The expense of selling the issue piece by piece therefore might be higher than that of selling it all at once.

2. Some investment bankers have argued that shelf registration will cause a "market overhang" that will depress market prices. In other words, the possibility that the company could increase the supply of stock at any time will have a negative impact on the current stock price. There is little evidence to support this position, however.

In addition to shelf registrations, companies also sell stock through continuous equity offerings, or "dribble" programs. In a dribble program, the company registers the stock with the SEC through a variety of different methods and sells the shares in dribbles as it sees fit. In other words, the company sells the stock on the secondary market like any other investor would.

CONCEPT QUESTIONS

15.9a What is shelf registration?

15.9b What are the arguments against shelf registration?

SUMMARY AND CONCLUSIONS

This chapter has looked at how corporate securities are issued. The following are the main points:

1. The venture capital market is a primary source of financing for new high-risk companies.

2. The costs of issuing securities can be quite large. They are much lower (as a percentage) for larger issues.

3. Firm commitment underwriting is far more prevalent for large issues than best efforts underwriting. This is probably connected to the uncertainty of smaller issues. For a given size offering, the direct expenses of best efforts underwriting and firm commitment underwriting are of the same magnitude.

4. The direct and indirect costs of going public can be substantial. However, once a firm is public, it can raise additional capital with much greater ease.

connect POP QUIZ!

Can you answer the following questions? If your class is using *Connect,* log on to SmartBook to see if you know the answers to these and other questions, check out the study tools, and find out what topics require additional practice!

Section 15.1 What are some important considerations when choosing between venture capitalists?

Section 15.2 When is a new issue usually priced?

Section 15.3 What are the differences between general cash offers and rights offers?

Section 15.4 What grants an underwriter the ability to purchase additional shares of stock at the offer price?

Section 15.5 What occurs if IPO shares are sold at an offering price that is too low? Assume the offering is a firm commitment offering.

Section 15.6 What has been presented as a reason why stock prices tend to decline when a new equity issue is announced?

Section 15.7 What are the costs associated with issuing new securities?

Section 15.8 What reasons are given as potential explanations why interest rates on private debt are higher than the interest rates paid on comparable public debt?

Section 15.9 What is offered as the primary argument against shelf registration?

CHAPTER REVIEW AND SELF-TEST PROBLEMS

15.1 Flotation Costs   The L5 Corporation is considering an equity issue to finance a new space station. A total of $10 million in new equity is needed. If the direct costs are estimated at 6 percent of the amount raised, how large does the issue need to be? What is the dollar amount of the flotation cost? (See Problem 2.)

■ Answer to Chapter Review and Self-Test Problem

15.1   The firm needs to net $10 million after paying the 6 percent flotation costs. So, the amount raised is given by:

Amount raised × (1 − .06) = $10 million
Amount raised = $10,000,000/.94 = $10.638 million

The total flotation cost is thus $638,000.

CRITICAL THINKING AND CONCEPTS REVIEW

LO 2   **15.1   Debt versus Equity Offering Size**   In the aggregate, debt offerings are much more common than equity offerings and typically much larger as well. Why?

LO 2   **15.2   Debt versus Equity Flotation Costs**   Why are the costs of selling equity so much larger than the costs of selling debt?

LO 2 **15.3 Bond Ratings and Flotation Costs**   Why do noninvestment-grade bonds have much higher direct costs than investment-grade issues?

LO 2 **15.4 Underpricing in Debt Offerings**   Why is underpricing not a great concern with bond offerings?

Use the following information to answer the next three questions. Zipcar, the car-sharing company, went public in April of 2011. Assisted by the investment bank Goldman, Sachs & Co., Zipcar sold 9.68 million shares at $18 each, thereby raising a total of $174.24 million. By the end of the first day of trading, the stock had zipped to $28 per share, down from a high of $31.50. On the basis of the end-of-day numbers, Zipcar shares were apparently underpriced by about $10 each, meaning that the company missed out on an additional $96.8 million.

LO 3 **15.5 IPO Pricing**   The Zipcar IPO was underpriced by about 56 percent. Should Zipcar be upset at Goldman over the underpricing?

LO 3 **15.6 IPO Pricing**   In the previous question, how would it affect your thinking to know that the company was incorporated about 10 years earlier, had only $186 million in revenues in 2010, and had never earned a profit? Additionally, the viability of the company's business model was still unproven.

LO 3 **15.7 IPO Pricing**   In the previous two questions, how would it affect your thinking to know that in addition to the 9.68 million shares offered in the IPO, Zipcar had an additional 30 million shares outstanding? Of those 30 million shares, 14.1 million shares were owned by four venture capital firms, and 15.5 million shares were owned by the 12 directors and executive officers.

LO 3 **15.8 IPO Underpricing**   In 1980, a certain assistant professor of finance bought 12 initial public offerings of common stock. He held each of these for approximately one month and then sold. The investment rule he followed was to submit a purchase order for every firm commitment initial public offering of oil and gas exploration companies. There were 22 of these offerings, and he submitted a purchase order for approximately $1,000 in stock for each of the companies. With 10 of these, no shares were allocated to this assistant professor. With 5 of the 12 offerings that were purchased, fewer than the requested number of shares were allocated.The year 1980 was very good for oil and gas exploration company owners: On average, for the 22 companies that went public, the stocks were selling for 80 percent above the offering price a month after the initial offering date. The assistant professor looked at his performance record and found that the $8,400 invested in the 12 companies had grown to $10,000, representing a return of only about 20 percent (commissions were negligible). Did he have bad luck, or should he have expected to do worse than the average initial public offering investor? Explain.

LO 1 **15.9 Venture Capital**   In the chapter, we mentioned that venture capital is very expensive. Why do you think this is true?

LO 3 **15.10 IPO Pricing**   The following material represents the cover page and summary of the prospectus for the initial public offering of the Pest

Investigation Control Corporation (PICC), which is going public tomorrow with a firm commitment initial public offering managed by the investment banking firm of Erlanger and Ritter. Answer the following questions:

a. Assume that you know nothing about PICC other than the information contained in the prospectus. Based on your knowledge of finance, what is your prediction for the price of PICC tomorrow? Provide a short explanation of why you think this will occur.

b. Assume that you have several thousand dollars to invest. When you get home from class tonight, you find that your stockbroker, whom you have not talked to for weeks, has called. She has left a message that PICC is going public tomorrow and that she can get you several hundred shares at the offering price if you call her back first thing in the morning. Discuss the merits of this opportunity.

PROSPECTUS	PICC

200,000 shares
PEST INVESTIGATION CONTROL CORPORATION

Of the shares being offered hereby, all 200,000 are being sold by the Pest Investigation Control Corporation, Inc. ("the Company"). Before the offering, there has been no public market for the shares of PICC, and no guarantee can be given that any such market will develop.

These securities have not been approved or disapproved by the SEC nor has the commission passed upon the accuracy or adequacy of this prospectus. Any representation to the contrary is a criminal offense.

	Price to Public	Underwriting Discount	Proceeds to Company*
Per share	$11.00	$1.10	$9.90
Total	$2,200,000	$220,000	$1,980,000

*Before deducting expenses estimated at $27,000 and payable by the Company.

This is an initial public offering. The common shares are being offered, subject to prior sale, when, as, and if delivered to and accepted by the Underwriters and subject to approval of certain legal matters by their Counsel and by Counsel for the Company. The Underwriters reserve the right to withdraw, cancel, or modify such offer and to reject offers in whole or in part.

Erlanger and Ritter, Investment Bankers
July 12, 2019
Prospectus Summary

The Company	The Pest Investigation Control Corporation (PICC) breeds and markets toads and tree frogs as ecologically safe insect-control mechanisms.
The Offering	200,000 shares of common stock, no par value.
Listing	The Company will seek listing on NASDAQ and will trade over the counter.
Shares Outstanding	As of June 30, 2019, 400,000 shares of common stock were outstanding. After the offering, 600,000 shares of common stock will be outstanding.
Use of Proceeds	To finance expansion of inventory and receivables and general working capital, and to pay for country club memberships for certain finance professors.

Selected Financial Information (amounts in thousands except per-share data)			
	Fiscal Year Ended June 30		
	2017	2018	2019
Revenues	$60.00	$120.00	$240.00
Net earnings	3.80	15.90	36.10
Earnings per share	.01	.04	.09
	As of June 30, 2019		
	Actual	As Adjusted for This Offering	
Working capital	$ 8	$ 1,961	
Total assets	511	2,464	
Stockholders' equity	423	2,376	

QUESTIONS AND PROBLEMS

connect   Select problems are available in McGraw-Hill *Connect*. Please see the packaging options section of the Preface for more information.

BASIC (Questions 1–7)

LO 3   **1. IPO Underpricing**   The Koepka Co. and the Johnson Co. both have announced IPOs at $40 per share. One of these is undervalued by $12.25, and the other is overvalued by $5.50, but you have no way of knowing which is which. You plan on buying 1,000 shares of each issue. If an issue is underpriced, it will be rationed, and only half your order will be filled. If you could get 1,000 shares in Koepka and 1,000 shares in Johnson, what would your profit be? What profit do you actually expect? What principle have you illustrated?

LO 3   **2. Calculating Flotation Costs**   The Sullivan Co. needs to raise $78 million to finance its expansion into new markets. The company will sell new shares of equity via a general cash offering to raise the needed funds. If the offer price is $31 per share and the company's underwriters charge a spread of 7 percent, how many shares need to be sold?

LO 3   **3. Calculating Flotation Costs**   In the previous problem, if the SEC filing fee and associated administrative expenses of the offering are $1,425,000, how many shares need to be sold now?

LO 3   **4. Calculating Flotation Costs**   The Sugarland Co. has just gone public. Under a firm commitment agreement, the company received $17.67 for each of the 27 million shares sold. The initial offering price was $19 per share, and the stock rose to $24.80 per share in the first few minutes of trading. The company paid $1,475,000 in legal and other direct costs and $350,000 in indirect costs. What was the flotation cost as a percentage of funds raised?

LO 3   **5. Calculating Flotation Costs**   The Elkmont Corporation needs to raise $63.8 million to finance its expansion into new markets. The company will sell new shares of equity via a general cash offering to raise the needed funds.

If the offer price is $22 per share and the company's underwriters charge a spread of 7.5 percent, how many shares need to be sold?

LO 3 6. **Calculating Flotation Costs** In the previous problem, if the SEC filing fee and associated administrative expenses of the offering are $1,450,000, how many shares need to be sold now?

LO 3 7. **Calculating Flotation Costs** The Wiley Oakley Co. has just gone public. Under a firm commitment agreement, Wiley received $21.39 for each of the 7.75 million shares sold. The initial offering price was $23 per share, and the stock rose to $26.30 per share in the first few minutes of trading. Wiley paid $1,350,000 in legal and other direct costs and $210,000 in indirect costs. What was the flotation cost as a percentage of funds raised?

WHAT'S ON THE WEB?

15.1 IPO Filings Go to www.ipomonitor.com and find the most recent IPO. Now go to the SEC website at www.sec.gov and look up the company's filings with the SEC. What is the name of the filing the company made to sell stock to the public? What does this company do? How does the company propose to use the funds raised by the IPO?

15.2 Secondary Offerings Go to www.ipomonitor.com and find the most recent secondary stock offering. At what price was the stock offered for sale to the public? How does this offer price compare to the market price of the stock on the same day?

15.3 Initial Public Offerings What was the largest IPO? Go to www.ipomonitor.com and find out. In what country was the company located? What was the largest IPO in the United States?

CHAPTER CASE
S&S Air Goes Public

Mark Sexton and Todd Story have been discussing the future of S&S Air. The company has been experiencing fast growth, and the two see only clear skies in the company's future. However, the fast growth can no longer be funded by internal sources, so Mark and Todd have decided the time is right to take the company public. To this end, they have entered into discussions with the investment bank of Crowe & Mallard. The company has a working relationship with Renata Harper, the underwriter who assisted with the company's previous bond offering. Crowe & Mallard have assisted numerous small companies in the IPO process, so Mark and Todd feel confident with this choice.

Renata begins by telling Mark and Todd about the process. Although Crowe & Mallard charged an underwriter fee of 4 percent on the bond offering, the underwriter fee is 7 percent on all initial stock offerings of the size of S&S Air's offering. Renata tells Mark and Todd that the company can expect to pay about $1,800,000 in legal fees and expenses, $13,500 in SEC registration fees, and $15,000 in other filing fees. Additionally, to be listed on the NASDAQ, the company must pay $125,000. There are also transfer agent fees of $6,500 and engraving expenses of $450,000. The company also should expect to pay $75,000 for other expenses associated with the IPO.

Finally, Renata tells Mark and Todd that to file with the SEC, the company must provide three years' audited financial statements. She is unsure about the costs of the audit. Mark tells Renata that the company provides audited financial statements as part of the bond covenant, and the company pays $300,000 per year for the outside auditor.

QUESTIONS

1. At the end of the discussion, Mark asks Renata about the Dutch auction IPO process. What are the differences in the expenses to S&S Air if it uses a Dutch auction IPO versus a traditional IPO? Should the company go public through a Dutch auction or use a traditional underwritten offering?

2. During the discussion of the potential IPO and S&S Air's future, Mark states that he feels the company should raise $90 million. However, Renata points out that if the company needs more cash in the near future, a secondary offering close to the IPO would be problematic. Instead, she suggests that the company should raise $125 million in the IPO. How can we calculate the optimal size of the IPO? What are the advantages and disadvantages of increasing the size of the IPO to $125 million?

3. After deliberation, Mark and Todd have decided that the company should use a firm commitment offering with Crowe & Mallard as the lead underwriter. The IPO will be for $90 million. Ignoring underpricing, how much will the IPO cost the company as a percentage of the funds received?

4. Many employees of S&S Air have shares of stock in the company because of an existing employee stock purchase plan. To sell the stock, the employees can tender their shares to be sold in the IPO at the offering price, or the employees can retain their stock and sell it in the secondary market after S&S Air goes public. Todd asks you to advise the employees about which option is better. What would you suggest to the employees?

16 | Short-Term Financial Planning

Auto inventory is a closely followed number. A high days' sales in inventory can indicate a forthcoming production slowdown, while a low days' sales in inventory can indicate a need for increased production. A 60-day supply of inventory is considered optimal in the industry, but there is a lot of variation. For example, in April 2018, BMW only had a 35-day supply of its 3-series sedan. Of course, other automobile models had higher inventory levels. Mitsubishi had a 243-day supply of the Eclipse crossover, or almost two-thirds of a year in sales!

Short-term financial planning is one activity that concerns everyone in business. As this chapter illustrates, such planning requires, among other things, sales projections from marketing, cost numbers from accounting, and inventory requirements from operations. Perhaps a particularly good reason to study this chapter for many is that short-term planning and management are frequently where new hires start out in a corporation, especially in finance and accounting. Also, such planning is especially important for small businesses, and a lack of adequate short-term financial resources is a frequently cited reason for small business failure.

LEARNING OBJECTIVES

After studying this chapter, you should be able to:

LO 1 Discuss operating and cash cycles and why they are important.

LO 2 Differentiate between the types of short-term financial policies.

LO 3 Identify the essentials of short-term financial planning.

Please visit us at essentialsofcorporatefinance.blogspot.com for the latest developments in the world of corporate finance.

To this point, we have described many of the decisions of long-term finance, including capital budgeting, dividend policy, and financial structure. In this chapter, we begin to discuss short-term finance. Short-term finance is primarily concerned with the analysis of decisions that affect current assets and current liabilities.

Frequently, the term *net working capital* is associated with short-term financial decision making. As we describe in Chapter 2 and elsewhere, net working capital is the difference between current assets and current liabilities. Often, short-term financial management is called *working capital management*. These mean the same thing. Working capital management can be critical for a company. According to a recent survey, if an average company with $10 billion in sales could match the best working capital management company, it could reduce working capital by $1.4 billion, or 14 percent of sales.

521

Interested in a career
in short-term finance?
Visit the Association for
Financial Professionals
website at
www.afponline.org.

There is no universally accepted definition of short-term finance. The most important difference between short-term and long-term finance is the timing of cash flows. Short-term financial decisions typically involve cash inflows and outflows that occur within a year or less. For example, short-term financial decisions are involved when a firm orders raw materials, pays in cash, and anticipates selling finished goods in one year for cash. In contrast, long-term financial decisions are involved when a firm purchases a special machine that will reduce operating costs over, say, the next five years.

What types of questions fall under the general heading of short-term finance? To name a few:

1. What is a reasonable level of cash to keep on hand (in a bank) to pay bills?
2. How much should the firm borrow in the short term?
3. How much credit should be extended to customers?

This chapter introduces the basic elements of short-term financial decisions. First, we discuss the short-term operating activities of the firm. We then identify some alternative short-term financial policies. Finally, we outline the basic elements of a short-term financial plan and describe short-term financing instruments.

16.1 TRACING CASH AND NET WORKING CAPITAL

In this section, we examine the components of cash and net working capital as they change from one year to the next. We have already discussed various aspects of this subject in Chapters 2 and 3. We briefly review some of that discussion as it relates to short-term financing decisions. Our goal is to describe the short-term operating activities of the firm and their impact on cash and working capital.

To begin, recall that *current assets* are cash and other assets that are expected to convert to cash within the year. Current assets are presented on the balance sheet in order of their liquidity—the ease with which they can be converted to cash and the time it takes to convert them. Four of the most important items found in the current asset section of a balance sheet are cash and cash equivalents, marketable securities, accounts receivable, and inventories.

Analogous to their investment in current assets, firms use several kinds of short-term debt, called *current liabilities*. Current liabilities are obligations that are expected to require cash payment within one year. Three major items found as current liabilities are accounts payable; expenses payable, including accrued wages and taxes; and notes payable.

Because we want to focus on changes in cash, we start off by defining cash in terms of the other elements of the balance sheet. This lets us isolate the cash account and explore the impact on cash from the firm's operating and financing decisions. The basic balance sheet identity can be written as:

$$\text{Net working capital} + \text{Fixed assets} = \text{Long-term debt} + \text{Equity} \qquad [16.1]$$

Net working capital is cash plus other current assets, less current liabilities; that is:

$$\text{Net working capital} = (\text{Cash} + \text{Other current assets}) - \text{Current liabilities} \qquad [16.2]$$

If we substitute this for net working capital in the basic balance sheet identity and rearrange things a bit, we see that cash is:

$$\text{Cash} = \text{Long-term debt} + \text{Equity} + \text{Current liabilities}$$
$$- \text{Current assets other than cash} - \text{Fixed assets} \qquad [16.3]$$

This tells us, in general terms, that some activities naturally increase cash and some activities decrease it. We can list these along with an example of each as follows:

Activities That Increase Cash

Increasing long-term debt (borrowing over the long term).

Increasing equity (selling some stock).

Increasing current liabilities (getting a 90-day loan).

Decreasing current assets other than cash (selling some inventory for cash).

Decreasing fixed assets (selling some property).

Activities That Decrease Cash

Decreasing long-term debt (paying off a long-term debt).

Decreasing equity (repurchasing some stock).

Decreasing current liabilities (paying off a 90-day loan).

Increasing current assets other than cash (buying some inventory for cash).

Increasing fixed assets (buying some property).

Notice that our two lists are exact opposites. For example, floating a long-term bond issue increases cash (at least until the money is spent). Paying off a long-term bond issue decreases cash.

Activities that increase cash are called *sources of cash*. Those activities that decrease cash are called *uses of cash*. Looking back at our list, we see that sources of cash always involve increasing a liability (or equity) account or decreasing an asset account. This makes sense because increasing a liability means we have raised money by borrowing it or by selling an ownership interest in the firm. A decrease in an asset means that we have sold or otherwise liquidated an asset. In either case, there is a cash inflow.

Uses of cash are the reverse. A use of cash involves decreasing a liability by paying it off, perhaps, or increasing assets by purchasing something. Both of these activities require that the firm spend some cash.

EXAMPLE 16.1 **Sources and Uses**

Here is a quick check of your understanding of sources and uses: If accounts payable go up by $100, is this a source or a use? If accounts receivable go up by $100, is this a source or a use?

Accounts payable are what we owe our suppliers. This is a short-term debt. If it rises by $100, we have effectively borrowed the money, so this is a *source* of cash. Receivables are what our customers owe to us, so an increase of $100 in accounts receivable means that we have loaned the money; this is a *use* of cash.

CONCEPT QUESTIONS

16.1a What is the difference between net working capital and cash?

16.1b Will net working capital always increase when cash increases?

16.1c List five potential uses of cash.

16.1d List five potential sources of cash.

16.2 THE OPERATING CYCLE AND THE CASH CYCLE

The primary concerns in short-term finance are the firm's short-run operating and financing activities. For a typical manufacturing firm, these short-run activities might consist of the following sequence of events and decisions:

Events	Decisions
1. Buying raw materials	1. How much inventory to order
2. Paying cash	2. Whether to borrow or draw down cash balances
3. Manufacturing the product	3. What choice of production technology to use
4. Selling the product	4. Whether credit should be extended to a particular customer
5. Collecting cash	5. How to collect

These activities create patterns of cash inflows and cash outflows. These cash flows are both unsynchronized and uncertain. They are unsynchronized because, for example, the payment of cash for raw materials does not happen at the same time as the receipt of cash from selling the product. They are uncertain because future sales and costs cannot be precisely predicted.

Defining the Operating and Cash Cycles

We can start with a simple case. One day, call it Day 0, you purchase $1,000 worth of inventory on credit. You pay the bill 30 days later, and, after 30 more days, someone buys the $1,000 in inventory for $1,400. Your buyer does not actually pay for another 45 days. We can summarize these events chronologically as follows:

Day	Activity	Cash Effect
0	Acquire inventory on credit	None
30	Pay for inventory	−$1,000
60	Sell inventory on credit	None
105	Collect on sale	+$1,400

operating cycle
The time period between the acquisition of inventory and the collection of cash from receivables.

The Operating Cycle There are several things to notice in our example. First, the entire cycle, from the time we acquire some inventory to the time we collect the cash, takes 105 days. This is called the **operating cycle**.

As we illustrate, the operating cycle is the length of time it takes to acquire inventory, sell it, and collect for it. This cycle has two distinct components. The first part is the time it takes to acquire and sell the inventory. This period, a 60-day span in our example, is called the **inventory period**. The second part is the time it takes to collect on the sale, 45 days in our example. This is called the **accounts receivable period**, or the receivables period.

inventory period
The time it takes to acquire and sell inventory.

Based on our definitions, the operating cycle is obviously the sum of the inventory and receivables periods:

accounts receivable period
The time between sale of inventory and collection of the receivable.

$$\text{Operating cycle} = \text{Inventory period} + \text{Accounts receivable period} \qquad [16.4]$$
$$\text{105 days} = \text{60 days} + \text{45 days}$$

What the operating cycle describes is how a product moves through the current asset accounts. It begins life as inventory, it is converted to a receivable when it is sold, and it is finally converted to cash when we collect from the sale. Notice that, at each step, the asset is moving closer to cash.

The Cash Cycle   The second thing to notice is that the cash flows and other events that occur are not synchronized. For example, we don't actually pay for the inventory until 30 days after we acquire it. The intervening 30-day period is called the **accounts payable period**. Next, we spend cash on Day 30, but we don't collect until Day 105. Somehow, we have to arrange to finance the $1,000 for $105 - 30 = 75$ days. This period is called the **cash cycle**.

> **accounts payable period**
> The time between receipt of inventory and payment for it.

The cash cycle, therefore, is the number of days that pass until we collect the cash from a sale, measured from when we actually pay for the inventory. Notice that, based on our definitions, the cash cycle is the difference between the operating cycle and the accounts payable period:

> **cash cycle**
> The time between cash disbursement and cash collection.

Cash cycle = Operating cycle − Accounts payable period [16.5]
75 days = 105 days − 30 days

Figure 16.1 depicts the short-term operating activities and cash flows for a typical manufacturing firm by looking at the cash flow time line. As is shown, the **cash flow time line** is made up of the operating cycle and the cash cycle. In Figure 16.1, the need for short-term financial management is suggested by the gap between the cash inflows and the cash outflows. This is related to the length of the operating cycle and the accounts payable period.

> **cash flow time line**
> Graphical representation of the operating cycle and the cash cycle.

The gap between short-term inflows and outflows can be filled either by borrowing or by holding a liquidity reserve in the form of cash or marketable securities. Alternatively, the gap can be shortened by changing the inventory, receivables, and payables periods. These are all managerial options that we discuss later and in a subsequent chapter.

The Operating Cycle and the Firm's Organizational Chart

Before we examine the operating and cash cycles in greater detail, it is useful to take a look at the people involved in managing a firm's current assets and liabilities. As Table 16.1 illustrates, short-term financial management in a large corporation involves a number of different financial and nonfinancial managers. Examining Table 16.1, we see that selling

Cash flow time line and the short-term operating activities of a typical manufacturing firm

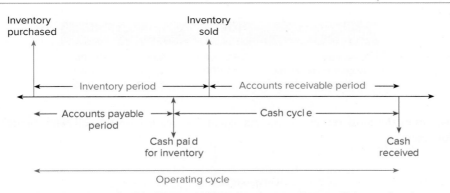

The operating cycle is the time period from inventory purchase until the receipt of cash. The cash cycle is the time period from when cash is paid out to when cash is received.

TABLE 16.1	Title of Manager	Duties Related to Short-Term Financial Management	Assets/Liabilities Influenced
Managers who deal with short-term financial problems	Cash manager	Collection, concentration, disbursement; short-term investments; short-term borrowing; banking relations	Cash, marketable securities, short-term loans
	Credit manager	Monitoring and control of accounts receivable; credit policy decisions	Accounts receivable
	Marketing manager	Credit policy decisions	Accounts receivable
	Purchasing manager	Decisions on purchases, suppliers; may negotiate payment terms	Inventory, accounts payable
	Production manager	Setting of production schedules and materials requirements	Inventory, accounts payable
	Payables manager	Decisions on payment policies and on whether to take discounts	Accounts payable
	Controller	Accounting information on cash flows; reconciliation of accounts payable; application of payments to accounts receivable	Accounts receivable, accounts payable

on credit involves at least three different individuals: the credit manager, the marketing manager, and the controller. Of these three, only two are responsible to the vice president of finance (the marketing function is usually associated with the vice president of marketing). Thus, there is the potential for conflict, particularly if different managers only concentrate on part of the picture. For example, if marketing is trying to land a new account, it may seek more liberal credit terms as an inducement. However, this may increase the firm's investment in receivables or its exposure to bad-debt risk, and conflict can result.

Calculating the Operating and Cash Cycles

In our example, the lengths of time that made up the different periods were obvious. If all we have is financial statement information, we will have to do a little more work. We illustrate these calculations next.

To begin, we need to determine various things such as how long it takes, on average, to sell inventory and how long it takes, on average, to collect. We start by gathering some balance sheet information such as the following (in thousands):

Item	Beginning	Ending	Average
Inventory	$2,000	$3,000	$2,500
Accounts receivable	1,600	2,000	1,800
Accounts payable	750	1,000	875

Also, from the most recent income statement, we might have the following figures (in thousands):

Net sales	$11,500
Cost of goods sold	8,200

We now need to calculate some financial ratios. We discussed these in some detail in Chapter 3; here we define them and use them as needed.

The Operating Cycle   First of all, we need the inventory period. We spent $8.2 million on inventory (our cost of goods sold). Our average inventory was $2.5 million. We thus turned our inventory over $8.2/$2.5 times during the year:[1]

$$\text{Inventory turnover} = \frac{\text{Cost of goods sold}}{\text{Average inventory}}$$

$$= \frac{\$8.2 \text{ million}}{\$2.5 \text{ million}} = 3.28 \text{ times}$$

Loosely speaking, this tells us that we bought and sold off our inventory 3.28 times during the year. This means that, on average, we held our inventory for:

$$\text{Inventory period} = \frac{365 \text{ days}}{\text{Inventory turnover}}$$

$$= \frac{365}{3.28} = 111.3 \text{ days}$$

So, the inventory period is about 111 days. On average, in other words, inventory sat for about 111 days before it was sold.[2]

Similarly, receivables averaged $1.8 million, and sales were $11.5 million. Assuming that all sales were credit sales, the receivables turnover is:[3]

$$\text{Receivables turnover} = \frac{\text{Credit sales}}{\text{Average accounts receivable}}$$

$$= \frac{\$11.5 \text{ million}}{\$1.8 \text{ million}} = 6.4 \text{ times}$$

If we turn over our receivables 6.4 times, then the receivables period is:

$$\text{Receivables period} = \frac{365 \text{ days}}{\text{Receivables turnover}}$$

$$= \frac{365}{6.4} = 57.1 \text{ days}$$

The receivables period also is called the *days' sales in receivables* or the *average collection period*. Whatever it is called, it tells us that our customers took an average of 57 days to pay.

The operating cycle is the sum of the inventory and receivables periods:

$$\text{Operating cycle} = \text{Inventory period} + \text{Accounts receivable period}$$

$$= 111 \text{ days} + 57 \text{ days} = 168 \text{ days}$$

This tells us that, on average, 168 days elapse between the time we acquire inventory and, having sold it, collect for the sale.

The Cash Cycle   We now need the payables period. From the information given above, average payables were $875,000, and cost of goods sold was again $8.2 million. Our payables turnover is:

$$\text{Payables turnover} = \frac{\text{Cost of goods sold}}{\text{Average payables}}$$

$$= \frac{\$8.2 \text{ million}}{\$.875 \text{ million}} = 9.4 \text{ times}$$

---

[1]Notice that in calculating inventory turnover here, we used the average inventory instead of using the ending inventory as we did in Chapter 3. Both approaches are used in the real world. To gain some practice using average figures, we will stick with this approach in calculating various ratios throughout this chapter.

[2]This measure is conceptually identical to the days' sales in inventory we discussed in Chapter 3.

[3]If less than 100 percent of our sales are credit sales, then we need a little more information, namely, credit sales for the year. See Chapter 3 for more discussion of this measure.

The payables period is:

$$\text{Payables period} = \frac{\text{365 days}}{\text{Payables turnover}}$$

$$= \frac{365}{9.4} = 38.9 \text{ days}$$

Thus, we took an average of 39 days to pay our bills.

Finally, the cash cycle is the difference between the operating cycle and the payables period:

$$\text{Cash cycle} = \text{Operating cycle} - \text{Accounts payable period}$$

$$= \text{168 days} - \text{39 days} = \text{129 days}$$

So, on average, there is a 129-day delay from the time we pay for merchandise to the time we collect on the sale.

EXAMPLE 16.2 **The Operating and Cash Cycles**

You have collected the following information for the Slowpay Company:

Item	Beginning	Ending
Inventory	$5,000	$7,000
Accounts receivable	1,600	2,400
Accounts payable	2,700	4,800

Credit sales for the year just ended were $50,000, and cost of goods sold was $30,000. How long does it take Slowpay to collect on its receivables? How long does merchandise stay around before it is sold? How long does Slowpay take to pay its bills?

We can first calculate the three turnover ratios:

Inventory turnover = $30,000/6,000 = 5 times

Receivables turnover = $50,000/2,000 = 25 times

Payables turnover = $30,000/3,750 = 8 times

We use these to get the various periods:

Inventory period = 365/5 = 73 days

Receivables period = 365/25 = 14.6 days

Payables period = 365/8 = 45.6 days

All told, Slowpay collects on a sale in 14.6 days, inventory sits around for 73 days, and bills get paid after about 46 days. The operating cycle here is the sum of the inventory and receivables periods: 73 + 14.6 = 87.6 days. The cash cycle is the difference between the operating cycle and the payables period: 87.6 – 45.6 = 42 days.

Interpreting the Cash Cycle

Our examples show that the cash cycle depends on the inventory, receivables, and payables periods. The cash cycle increases as the inventory and receivables periods get longer. It decreases if the company is able to defer payment of payables and thereby lengthen the payables period.

Most firms have a positive cash cycle, and they thus require financing for inventories and receivables. The longer the cash cycle, the more financing is required. Also, changes in the firm's cash cycle often are monitored as an early-warning measure. A lengthening cycle can indicate that the firm is having trouble moving inventory or collecting on its receivables. Such problems can be masked, at least partially, by an increased payables cycle, so both should be monitored.

Cash Cycle Comparison

In 2017, *CFO* magazine published its annual survey of working capital for various industries. The results of this survey highlight the differences in cash and operating cycles across industries. The table below shows four different industries and the operating and cash cycles for each. Of these, the food products industry has the shortest operating and cash cycles. The auto components industry has the shortest inventory period, a day less than the food products industry. The short inventory period in the auto components industry is due to years of efficiency efforts.

	Receivables Period (days)	Inventory Period (days)	Operating Cycle (days)	Payables Period (days)	Cash Cycle (days)
Auto components	47	36	83	61	22
Chemical services	54	71	125	48	77
Energy services	81	56	137	35	102
Food products	6	37	43	27	16

Compared to the food products industry, the auto components, chemical services, and energy services industries all have a much longer operating cycle. The chemical services and energy services industries have similar operating cycles, but the makeup differs. The chemical services industry has a longer inventory period, while the energy services industry has a longer receivables period. Notice the receivables period is very short for the food products industry as customers tend to pay in cash or use credit cards. As a result, firms in this industry have little or no receivables.

We've seen that operating and cash cycles can vary quite a bit across industries, but these cycles also can be different for companies within the same industry. Below you will find the operating and cash cycles for selected Internet and catalog retail companies. As you can see, there are differences. Wayfair and Amazon both have negative cash cycles. However, the two companies have negative cash cycles for different reasons. Wayfair has both a low receivables period and inventory period, while Amazon's is significantly larger in both cases. But Amazon's payables period is 114 days, or almost three months.

	Receivables Period (days)	Inventory Period (days)	Operating Cycle (days)	Payables Period (days)	Cash Cycle (days)
Wayfair	2	3	5	55	−50
Amazon	16	52	68	114	−46
HSN	34	61	95	46	49
Lands' End	11	156	167	78	89

When you look at the operating and cash cycles, consider that each is really a financial ratio. As with any financial ratio, firm and industry characteristics will have an effect, so take care in your interpretation. For example, in looking at Lands' End, we note it has a long inventory period. Is that a bad thing? Maybe not. Lands' End has a different business model compared to the other three companies shown, and, as a result, it has different inventory management strategies.

We easily can see the link between the firm's cash cycle and its profitability by recalling that one of the basic determinants of profitability and growth for a firm is its total asset turnover, which is defined as Sales/Total assets. In Chapter 3, we saw that the higher this ratio is, the greater are the firm's accounting return on assets, ROA, and return on equity, ROE. Thus, all other things being the same, the shorter the cash cycle is, the lower is the firm's investment in inventories and receivables. As a result, the firm's total assets are lower, and total turnover is higher.

To see how important the cash cycle is, consider the consequences of the U.S. Postal Service's decision to increase the standard delivery time from two days to three days. A working capital expert estimated that as a result of this decision, a company with $10 billion in revenue could see an increase in net working capital of $100 million. The nearby *Finance Matters* box discusses the cash cycles and operating cycles for several industries, as well as for some specific companies.

CONCEPT QUESTIONS

16.2a   What does it mean to say that a firm has an inventory turnover ratio of 4?

16.2b   Describe the operating cycle and cash cycle. What are the differences?

16.2c   Explain the connection between a firm's accounting-based profitability and its cash cycle.

16.3 SOME ASPECTS OF SHORT-TERM FINANCIAL POLICY

The short-term financial policy that a firm adopts will be reflected in at least two ways:

1. *The size of the firm's investment in current assets.* This is usually measured relative to the firm's level of total operating revenues. A *flexible*, or accommodative, short-term financial policy would maintain a relatively high ratio of current assets to sales. A *restrictive* short-term financial policy would entail a low ratio of current assets to sales.[4]

2. *The financing of current assets.* This is measured as the proportion of short-term debt (that is, current liabilities) and long-term debt used to finance current assets. A restrictive short-term financial policy means a high proportion of short-term debt relative to long-term financing, and a flexible policy means less short-term debt and more long-term debt.

If we take these two areas together, we see that a firm with a flexible policy would have a relatively large investment in current assets. It would finance this investment with relatively less in short-term debt. The net effect of a flexible policy is thus a relatively high level of net working capital. Put another way, with a flexible policy, the firm maintains a larger overall level of liquidity.

The Size of the Firm's Investment in Current Assets

Flexible short-term financial policies with regard to current assets include such actions as:

1. Keeping large balances of cash and marketable securities.
2. Making large investments in inventory.
3. Granting liberal credit terms, which results in a high level of accounts receivable.

Restrictive short-term financial policies would be just the opposite of the ones above:

1. Keeping low cash balances and little investment in marketable securities.
2. Making small investments in inventory.
3. Allowing few or no credit sales, thereby minimizing accounts receivable.

---

[4]Some people use the term *conservative* in place of *flexible* and the term *aggressive* in place of *restrictive*.

Determining the optimal level of investment in short-term assets requires an identification of the different costs of alternative short-term financing policies. The objective is to trade off the cost of a restrictive policy against the cost of a flexible one to arrive at the best compromise.

Current asset holdings are highest with a flexible short-term financial policy and lowest with a restrictive policy. So, flexible short-term financial policies are costly in that they require a greater investment in cash and marketable securities, inventory, and accounts receivable. However, we expect that future cash inflows will be higher with a flexible policy. For example, sales are stimulated by the use of a credit policy that provides liberal financing to customers. A large amount of finished inventory on hand ("on the shelf") provides a quick delivery service to customers and may increase sales. Similarly, a large inventory of raw materials may result in fewer production stoppages because of inventory shortages.

A more restrictive short-term financial policy probably reduces future sales levels below those that would be achieved under flexible policies. It is also possible that higher prices can be charged to customers under flexible working capital policies. Customers may be willing to pay higher prices for the quick delivery service and more liberal credit terms implicit in flexible policies.

Managing current assets can be thought of as involving a trade-off between costs that rise and costs that fall with the level of investment. Costs that rise with increases in the level of investment in current assets are called **carrying costs**. The larger the investment a firm makes in its current assets, the higher its carrying costs will be. Costs that fall with increases in the level of investment in current assets are called **shortage costs**.

In a general sense, carrying costs are the opportunity costs associated with current assets. The rate of return on current assets is very low when compared to that on other assets. For example, the rate of return on U.S. Treasury bills is usually well below 5 percent. This is very low compared to the rate of return firms would like to achieve overall. (U.S. Treasury bills are an important component of cash and marketable securities.)

Shortage costs are incurred when the investment in current assets is low. If a firm runs out of cash, it will be forced to sell marketable securities. Of course, if a firm runs out of cash and cannot readily sell marketable securities, it may have to borrow or default on an obligation. This situation is called a *cash-out*. A firm may lose customers if it runs out of inventory (a *stock-out*) or if it cannot extend credit to customers.

More generally, there are two kinds of shortage costs:

1. *Trading, or order, costs.* Order costs are the costs of placing an order for more cash (brokerage costs, for example) or more inventory (production setup costs, for example).
2. *Costs related to lack of safety reserves.* These are costs of lost sales, lost customer goodwill, and disruption of production schedules.

The top part of Figure 16.2 illustrates the basic trade-off between carrying costs and shortage costs. On the vertical axis, we have costs measured in dollars, and, on the horizontal axis, we have the amount of current assets. Carrying costs start out at zero when current assets are zero and then climb steadily as current assets grow. Shortage costs start out very high and then decline as we add current assets. The total cost of holding current assets is the sum of the two. Notice how the combined costs reach a minimum at CA*. This is the optimal level of current assets.

Optimal current asset holdings are highest under a flexible policy. This policy is one in which the carrying costs are perceived to be low relative to shortage costs. This is Case A in Figure 16.2. In comparison, under restrictive current asset policies, carrying costs are

carrying costs
Costs that rise with increases in the level of investment in current assets.

shortage costs
Costs that fall with increases in the level of investment in current assets.

FIGURE 16.2

Carrying costs and shortage costs

Short-term financial policy: the optimal investment in current assets

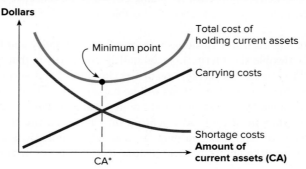

CA* represents the optimal amount of current assets.
Holding this amount minimizes total costs.

Carrying costs increase with the level of investment in current assets. They include
the costs of maintaining economic value and opportunity costs. Shortage costs
decrease with increases in the level of investment in current assets. They include
trading costs and the costs related to being short of the current asset (for example,
being short of cash). The firm's policy can be characterized as flexible or restrictive.

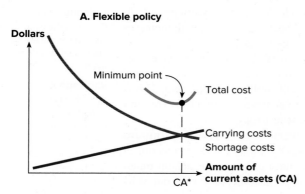

A. Flexible policy

A flexible policy is most appropriate when carrying costs
are low relative to shortage costs.

B. Restrictive policy

A restrictive policy is most appropriate when carrying costs
are high relative to shortage costs.

perceived to be high relative to shortage costs, resulting in lower current asset holdings. This
is Case B in Figure 16.2.

Alternative Financing Policies for Current Assets

In previous sections, we looked at the basic determinants of the level of investment in current assets, and we thus focused on the asset side of the balance sheet. Now we turn to the
financing side of the question. Here we are concerned with the relative amounts of short-
term and long-term debt, assuming the investment in current assets is constant.

A growing firm can be thought of as having a total asset requirement consisting of the
current assets and long-term assets needed to run the business efficiently. The total asset requirement may exhibit change over time for many reasons, including (1) a general growth trend,
(2) seasonal variation around the trend, and (3) unpredictable day-to-day and month-to-month

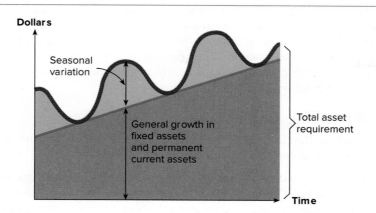

FIGURE **16.3**

The total asset requirement over time

fluctuations. This situation is depicted in Figure 16.3. (We have not tried to show the unpredictable day-to-day and month-to-month variations in the total asset requirement.)

The peaks and valleys in Figure 16.3 represent the firm's total asset needs through time. For example, for a lawn and garden supply firm, the peaks might represent inventory build-ups prior to the spring selling season. The valleys come about because of lower off-season inventories. There are two strategies such a firm might consider to meet its cyclical needs. First, the firm could keep a relatively large pool of marketable securities. As the need for inventory and other current assets begins to rise, the firm sells off marketable securities and uses the cash to purchase whatever is needed. Once the inventory is sold and inventory holdings begin to decline, the firm reinvests in marketable securities. This approach is the flexible policy illustrated in Figure 16.4 as Policy F. Notice that the firm essentially uses a pool of marketable securities as a buffer against changing current asset needs.

At the other extreme, the firm could keep relatively little in marketable securities. As the need for inventory and other assets begins to rise, the firm borrows the needed cash on a short-term basis. The firm repays the loans as the need for assets cycles back down. This approach is the restrictive policy illustrated in Figure 16.4 as Policy R.

FIGURE **16.4**   **Alternative asset financing policies**

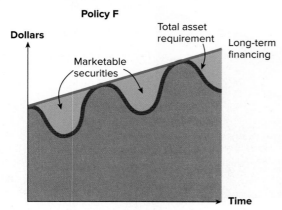

Policy F always implies a short-term cash surplus and a large investment in cash and marketable securities.

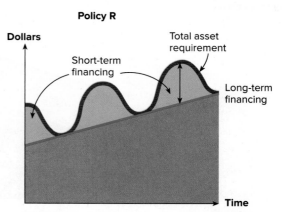

Policy R uses long-term financing for permanent asset requirements only and short-term borrowing for seasonal variations.

In comparing the two strategies illustrated in Figure 16.4, notice that the chief difference is the way in which the seasonal variation in asset needs is financed. In the flexible case, the firm finances internally, using its own cash and marketable securities. In the restrictive case, the firm finances externally, borrowing the needed funds on a short-term basis. As we discussed earlier, all else being the same, a firm with a flexible policy will have a greater investment in net working capital.

Which Financing Policy Is Best?

What is the most appropriate amount of short-term borrowing? There is no definitive answer. Several considerations must be included in a proper analysis:

1. *Cash reserves.* The flexible financing policy implies surplus cash and little short-term borrowing. This policy reduces the probability that a firm will experience financial distress. Firms may not have to worry as much about meeting recurring short-run obligations. However, investments in cash and marketable securities are zero net present value investments at best.

2. *Maturity hedging.* Most firms attempt to match the maturities of assets and liabilities. They finance inventories with short-term bank loans and fixed assets with long-term financing. Firms tend to avoid financing long-lived assets with short-term borrowing. This type of maturity mismatching would necessitate frequent refinancing and is inherently risky because short-term interest rates are more volatile than longer-term rates.

3. *Relative interest rates.* Short-term interest rates are usually lower than long-term rates. This implies that it is, on average, more costly to rely on long-term borrowing as compared to short-term borrowing.

The two policies, F and R, that we discuss above are, of course, extreme cases. With F, the firm never does any short-term borrowing, and, with R, the firm never has a cash reserve (an investment in marketable securities). Figure 16.5 illustrates these two policies along with a compromise, Policy C.

FIGURE 16.5

A compromise financing policy

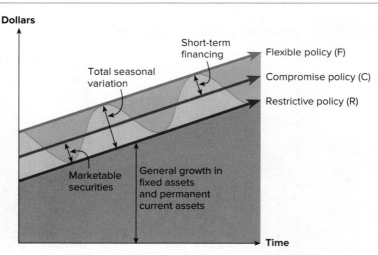

With a compromise policy, the firm keeps a reserve of liquidity that it uses to initially finance seasonal variations in current asset needs. Short-term borrowing is used when the reserve is exhausted.

TABLE 16.2

Current assets and current liabilities as a percentage of total assets for selected companies: 2018

	Amazon	Boeing	Cisco	Walmart
Cash and near cash	13.20%	8.13%	5.89%	3.85%
Marketable securities	6.56	.58	41.85	.00
Accounts receivable	9.52	11.33	8.02	2.23
Inventories	10.95	53.99	1.67	21.13
Other current assets	.00	2.18	1.46	1.70
Total current assets	40.22%	76.22%	58.89%	28.91%
Accounts payable	33.13%	64.77%	4.81%	34.51%
Short-term borrowings	.00	1.74	6.79	4.90
Other short-term liabilities	4.89	.00	13.53	.00
Total current liabilities	38.02%	66.52%	25.12%	39.41%

With this compromise approach, the firm borrows in the short term to cover peak financing needs, but it maintains a cash reserve in the form of marketable securities during slow periods. As current assets build up, the firm draws down this reserve before doing any short-term borrowing. This allows for some run-up in current assets before the firm has to resort to short-term borrowing.

Current Assets and Liabilities in Practice

Short-term assets represent a significant portion of a typical firm's overall assets. For U.S. manufacturing, mining, and trade corporations, current assets were about 50 percent of total assets in the 1960s. Today, this figure is closer to 40 percent. Most of the decline is due to more efficient cash and inventory management. Over this same period, current liabilities rose from about 20 percent of total liabilities and equity to almost 30 percent. The result is that liquidity (as measured by the ratio of net working capital to total assets) has declined, signaling a move to more restrictive short-term policies.

The cash cycle is longer in some industries than in others because of different products and industry practices. Table 16.2 illustrates this point by comparing the current asset and liability percentages for four different companies. Of the four, Boeing has the highest level of inventories. Does this mean Boeing is less efficient? Probably not; instead, the relatively high inventory levels are consistent with the industry. Boeing manufactures airplanes, and manufacturing a jetliner can take one to two years. During this time, the partially completed plane is on Boeing's balance sheet as inventory. Walmart also needs a higher level of inventory on hand to satisfy customers who walk into its stores. In contrast, Cisco is mostly software and information technology, so its inventory levels are lower. Notice also that Walmart has the lowest levels of current assets to total assets, implying that fixed assets are large, as you would expect from such a capital-intensive company. Walmart does have a somewhat unique feature in its working capital. If you notice, current liabilities exceed current assets, which means Walmart has a negative net working capital.

CONCEPT QUESTIONS

16.3a   What considerations determine the optimal size of the firm's investment in current assets?

16.3b   What considerations determine the optimal compromise between flexible and restrictive net working capital policies?

16.4 THE CASH BUDGET

Excel Master
coverage online

cash budget
A forecast of cash receipts and disbursements for the next planning period.

The **cash budget** is a primary tool in short-run financial planning. It allows the financial manager to identify short-term financial needs and opportunities. Importantly, the cash budget will help the manager explore the need for short-term borrowing. The idea of the cash budget is simple: It records estimates of cash receipts (cash in) and disbursements (cash out). The result is an estimate of the cash surplus or deficit.

Sales and Cash Collections

We start with an example for the Fun Toys Corporation. We will prepare a quarterly cash budget. We could just as well use a monthly, weekly, or even daily basis. We choose quarters for convenience and also because a quarter is a common short-term business planning period.

All of Fun Toys' cash inflows come from the sale of toys. Cash budgeting for Fun Toys therefore must start with a sales forecast for the coming year, by quarter:

	Q1	Q2	Q3	Q4
Sales (in millions)	$200	$300	$250	$400

Note that these are predicted sales, so there is forecasting risk here; actual sales could be more or less. Also, Fun Toys started the year with accounts receivable equal to $120.

Fun Toys has a 45-day receivables, or average collection, period. This means that half of the sales in a given quarter will be collected the following quarter. This happens because sales made during the first 45 days of a quarter will be collected in that quarter. Sales made in the second 45 days will be collected in the next quarter. Note that we are assuming that each quarter has 90 days, so the 45-day collection period is the same as a half-quarter collection period.

Based on the sales forecasts, we now need to estimate Fun Toys's projected cash collections. First, any receivables that we have at the beginning of a quarter will be collected within 45 days, so all of them will be collected sometime during the quarter. Second, as we discussed, any sales made in the first half of the quarter will be collected within the quarter, so total cash collections are:

Cash collections = Beginning accounts receivable + ½ × Sales   [16.6]

For example, in the first quarter, cash collections would be the beginning receivables of $120 plus half of sales, ½ × $200 = $100, for a total of $220.

Because beginning receivables all are collected along with half of sales, ending receivables for a particular quarter would be the other half of sales. First-quarter sales are projected at $200, so ending receivables will be $100. This will be the beginning receivables in the second quarter. Cash collections in the second quarter will thus be $100 plus half of the projected $300 in sales, or $250 total.

Continuing this process, we can summarize Fun Toys's projected cash collections in Table 16.3 as the only source of cash. Of course, this might not be the case. Other sources of cash could include asset sales, investment income, and receipts from planned long-term financing.

	Q1	Q2	Q3	Q4
Beginning receivables	$120	→$100	→$150	→$125
Sales	200	300	250	400
Cash collections	−220	−250	−275	−325
Ending receivables	100	150	125	200

TABLE 16.3

Cash collections for Fun Toys (in millions)

Collections = Beginning receivables + ½ × Sales

Ending receivables = Beginning receivables + Sales − Collections

= ½ × Sales

Cash Outflows

Next, we consider the cash disbursements, or payments. These come in four basic categories:

1. *Payments of accounts payable.* These are payments for goods or services rendered by suppliers, such as raw materials. Generally, these payments will be made sometime after purchases.
2. *Wages, taxes, and other expenses.* This category includes all other regular costs of doing business that require actual expenditures. Depreciation, for example, is often thought of as a regular cost of business, but it requires no cash outflow and is not included.
3. *Capital expenditures.* These are payments of cash for long-lived assets.
4. *Long-term financing expenses.* This category, for example, includes interest payments on long-term debt outstanding and dividend payments to shareholders.

Fun Toys's purchases from suppliers (in dollars) in a quarter are equal to 60 percent of the next quarter's predicted sales. Fun Toys's payments to suppliers are equal to the previous quarter's purchases, so the accounts payable period is 90 days. For example, in the quarter just ended, Fun Toys ordered .60 × $200 = $120 in supplies. This will actually be paid in the first quarter (Q1) of the coming year.

Wages, taxes, and other expenses are routinely 20 percent of sales; interest and dividends are currently $20 per quarter. In addition, Fun Toys plans a major plant expansion (a capital expenditure) of $100 in the second quarter. If we put all this information together, the cash outflows are as shown in Table 16.4.

The Cash Balance

The predicted *net cash inflow* is the difference between cash collections and cash disbursements. The net cash inflow for Fun Toys is shown in Table 16.5. What we see immediately is that there is a net cash inflow in the first and third quarters and a net outflow in the second and fourth.

	Q1	Q2	Q3	Q4
Payment of accounts (60% of sales)	$120	$180	$150	$240
Wages, taxes, other expenses	40	60	50	80
Capital expenditures	0	100	0	0
Long-term financing expenses (interest and dividends)	20	20	20	20
Total cash disbursements	$180	$360	$220	$340

TABLE 16.4

Cash disbursements for Fun Toys (in millions)

TABLE 16.5		Q1	Q2	Q3	Q4
Net cash inflow for Fun Toys (in millions)	Total cash collections	$220	$250	$275	$325
	Total cash disbursements	180	360	220	340
	Net cash inflow	$ 40	−$110	$ 55	−$ 15

TABLE 16.6		Q1	Q2	Q3	Q4
Cash balance for Fun Toys (in millions)	Beginning cash balance	$20	$60	−$50	$ 5
	Net cash inflow	40	−110	55	− 15
	Ending cash balance	$60	−$50	$ 5	−$10
	Minimum cash balance	− 10	− 10	− 10	− 10
	Cumulative surplus (deficit)	$50	−$60	−$ 5	−$20

We will assume that Fun Toys starts the year with a $20 cash balance. Furthermore, Fun Toys maintains a $10 minimum cash balance to guard against unforeseen contingencies and forecasting errors. So, we start the first quarter with $20 in cash. This rises by $40 during the quarter, and the ending balance is $60. Of this, $10 is reserved as a minimum, so we subtract it out and find that the first-quarter surplus is $60 − 10 = $50.

Fun Toys starts the second quarter with $60 in cash (the ending balance from the previous quarter). There is a net cash inflow of −$110, so the ending balance is $60 − 110 = −$50. We need another $10 as a buffer, so the total deficit is −$60. These calculations and those for the last two quarters are summarized in Table 16.6.

Beginning in the second quarter, Fun Toys has a cash shortfall of $60. This occurs because of the seasonal pattern of sales (higher toward the end of the second quarter), the delay in collections, and the planned capital expenditure.

The cash situation at Fun Toys is projected to improve to a $5 deficit in the third quarter, but, by year's end, Fun Toys is showing a $20 deficit. Without some sort of financing, this deficit will carry over into the next year. We explore this subject in the next section.

For now, we can make the following general comments on Fun Toys's cash needs:

1. Fun Toys's large outflow in the second quarter is not necessarily a sign of trouble. It results from delayed collections on sales and a planned capital expenditure (presumably a worthwhile one).

2. The figures in our example are based on a forecast. Sales could be much worse (or better) than the forecast figures.

CONCEPT QUESTIONS

16.4a   How would you do a sensitivity analysis (discussed in Chapter 9) for Fun Toys's net cash balance?

16.4b   What could you learn from a sensitivity analysis?

16.5 SHORT-TERM BORROWING

Fun Toys has a short-term financing problem. It cannot meet the forecast cash outflows in the second quarter from internal sources. How it will finance the shortfall depends on its financial policy. With a very flexible policy, Fun Toys might seek up to $60 million in long-term debt financing.

In addition, note that much of the cash deficit comes from the large capital expenditure. Arguably, this is a candidate for long-term financing. Nonetheless, because we have discussed long-term financing elsewhere, we will concentrate here on two short-term borrowing options: (1) unsecured borrowing and (2) secured borrowing.

Unsecured Loans

The most common way to finance a temporary cash deficit is to arrange a short-term, unsecured bank loan. Firms that use short-term bank loans often arrange a line of credit. A **line of credit** is an agreement under which a firm is authorized to borrow up to a specified amount. To ensure that the line is used for short-term purposes, the borrower will sometimes be required to pay the line down to zero and keep it there for some period during the year, typically 60 days (called a *cleanup period*).

Short-term lines of credit are classified as either *committed* or *noncommitted*. The latter is an informal arrangement that allows firms to borrow up to a previously specified limit without going through the normal paperwork (much as you would with a credit card). A *revolving credit arrangement* (or *revolver*) is similar to a line of credit, but it is usually open for two or more years, whereas a line of credit would usually be evaluated on an annual basis.

Committed lines of credit are more formal legal arrangements and often involve a commitment fee paid by the firm to the bank. The interest rate on the line of credit will usually float. A firm that pays a commitment fee for a committed line of credit is essentially buying insurance to guarantee that the bank can't back out of the agreement (absent some material change in the borrower's status).

line of credit
A formal (committed) or informal (noncommitted) prearranged, short-term bank loan.

Secured Loans

Banks and other finance companies often require security for a short-term loan as they do for a long-term loan. Security for short-term loans usually consists of accounts receivable, inventories, or both.

Accounts Receivable Financing   Accounts receivable financing involves either *assigning* receivables or *factoring* receivables. Under assignment, the lender has the receivables as security, but the borrower is still responsible if a receivable can't be collected. With *conventional factoring*, the receivable is discounted and sold to the lender (the factor). Once it is sold, collection is the factor's problem, and the factor assumes the full risk of default on bad accounts. With *maturity factoring*, the factor forwards the money on an agreed-upon future date.

accounts receivable financing
A secured short-term loan that involves either the assignment or factoring of receivables.

EXAMPLE 16.3   **Cost of Factoring**

For the year just ended, LuLu's Pies had an average of $50,000 in accounts receivable. Credit sales were $500,000. LuLu's factors its receivables by discounting them 3 percent, in other words, by selling them for 97 cents on the dollar. What is the effective interest rate on this source of short-term financing?

(continued)

To determine the interest rate, we first have to know the accounts receivable, or average collection, period. During the year, LuLu's turned over its receivables $500,000/$50,000 = 10 times. The average collection period is therefore 365/10 = 36.5 days.

The interest paid here is a form of "discount interest." In this case, LuLu's is paying 3 cents in interest on every 97 cents of financing. The interest rate per 36.5 days is thus .03/.97 = .0309, or 3.09%. The APR is 10 × 3.09% = 30.9%, but the effective annual rate is:

$$EAR = 1.0309^{10} - 1 = .356, \text{ or } 35.6\%$$

The factoring is a relatively expensive source of money in this case.

We should note that if the factor takes on the risk of default by a buyer, then the factor is providing insurance as well as immediate cash. More generally, the factor essentially takes over the firm's credit operations. This can result in a significant saving. The interest rate we calculated is therefore overstated, particularly if default is a significant possibility.

inventory loan
A secured short-term loan to purchase inventory.

Inventory Loans   Inventory loans, short-term loans to purchase inventory, come in three basic forms: blanket inventory liens, trust receipts, and field warehouse financing:

1. *Blanket inventory lien.* A blanket lien gives the lender a lien against all the borrower's inventories (the blanket "covers" everything).
2. *Trust receipt.* A trust receipt is a device by which the borrower holds specific inventory in "trust" for the lender. Automobile dealer financing, for example, is done by use of trust receipts. This type of secured financing also is called *floor planning*, in reference to inventory on the showroom floor. However, it is somewhat cumbersome to use trust receipts for, say, wheat grain.
3. *Field warehouse financing.* In field warehouse financing, a public warehouse company (an independent company that specializes in inventory management) acts as a control agent to supervise the inventory for the lender.

Other Sources

There are a variety of other sources of short-term funds employed by corporations. Two of the most important are *commercial paper* and *trade credit.*

Commercial paper consists of short-term notes issued by large and highly rated firms. Typically, these notes are of short maturity, ranging up to 270 days (beyond that limit, the firm must file a registration statement with the SEC). Because the firm issues these directly, the interest rate the borrowing firm obtains can be significantly below the rate a bank would charge for a direct loan.

Another option available to a firm is to increase the accounts payable period; in other words, it may take longer to pay its bills. This amounts to borrowing from suppliers in the form of trade credit. This is an extremely important form of financing for smaller businesses in particular. As we discuss in Chapter 17, a firm using trade credit may end up paying a much higher price for what it purchases, so this can be a very expensive source of financing.

CONCEPT QUESTIONS

16.5a   What are the two basic forms of short-term financing?

16.5b   Describe two types of secured loans.

16.6 A SHORT-TERM FINANCIAL PLAN

To illustrate a completed short-term financial plan, we will assume that Fun Toys arranges to borrow any needed funds on a short-term basis. The interest rate is 20 percent APR, and it is calculated on a quarterly basis. From Chapter 5, we know that the rate is 20%/4 = 5% per quarter. We will assume that Fun Toys starts the year with no short-term debt.

From Table 16.6, we see that Fun Toys has a second-quarter deficit of $60 million. We will have to borrow this amount. Net cash inflow in the following quarter is $55 million. We now have to pay $60 × .05 = $3 million in interest out of that, leaving $52 million to reduce the borrowing.

We still owe $60 − 52 = $8 million at the end of the third quarter. Interest in the last quarter thus will be $8 × .05 = $.4 million. In addition, net inflows in the last quarter are −$15 million, so we have to borrow a total of $15.4 million, bringing our total borrowing up to $15.4 + 8 = $23.4 million. Table 16.7 extends Table 16.6 to include these calculations.

Notice that the ending short-term debt is equal to the cumulative deficit for the entire year, $20 million, plus the interest paid during the year, $3 + .4 = $3.4 million, for a total of $23.4 million.

Our plan is very simple. For example, we ignored the fact that the interest paid on the short-term debt is tax deductible. We also ignored the fact that the cash surplus in the first quarter would earn some interest (which would be taxable). We could add on a number of refinements. Even so, our plan highlights the fact that in about 90 days Fun Toys will need to borrow $60 million or so on a short-term basis. It's time to start lining up the source of the funds.

Our plan also illustrates that financing the firm's short-term needs will cost about $3.4 million in interest (before taxes) for the year. This is a starting point for Fun Toys to begin evaluating alternatives to reduce this expense. For example, can the $100 million planned expenditure be postponed or spread out? At 5 percent per quarter, short-term credit is expensive.

Also, if Fun Toys's sales are expected to keep growing, then the $20 million plus deficit will probably also keep growing, and the need for additional financing is permanent. Fun Toys may wish to think about raising money on a long-term basis to cover this need.

CONCEPT QUESTIONS

16.6a   In Table 16.7, does Fun Toys have a projected deficit or surplus?

16.6b   In Table 16.7, what would happen to Fun Toys's deficit or surplus if the minimum cash balance was reduced to $5?

	Q1	Q2	Q3	Q4	
					TABLE 16.7
Beginning cash balance	$20	$60	$10	$10.0	**Short-term financial**
Net cash inflow	40	−110	55	− 15.0	**plan for Fun Toys**
New short-term borrowing	—	60	—	15.4	**(in millions)**
Interest on short-term borrowing	—	—	− 3	− .4	
Short-term borrowing repaid	—	—	− 52	—	
Ending cash balance	$60	$10	$10	$10.0	
Minimum cash balance	− 10	− 10	− 10	− 10.0	
Cumulative surplus (deficit)	$50	$ 0	$ 0	$ .0	
Beginning short-term borrowing	0	0	60	8.0	
Change in short-term debt	0	60	− 52	15.4	
Ending short-term debt	$ 0	$60	$ 8	$23.4	

SUMMARY AND CONCLUSIONS

1. This chapter has introduced the management of short-term finance. Short-term finance involves short-lived assets and liabilities. We traced and examined the short-term sources and uses of cash as they appear on the firm's financial statements. We saw how current assets and current liabilities arise in the short-term operating activities and the cash cycle of the firm.

2. Managing short-term cash flows involves the minimizing of costs. The two major costs are carrying costs, the returns foregone by keeping too much invested in short-term assets such as cash, and shortage costs, the costs of running out of short-term assets. The objective of managing short-term finance and doing short-term financial planning is to find the optimal trade-off between these two costs.

3. In an "ideal" economy, the firm could perfectly predict its short-term uses and sources of cash, and net working capital could be kept at zero. In the real world we live in, cash and net working capital provide a buffer that lets the firm meet its ongoing obligations. The financial manager seeks the optimal level of each of the current assets.

4. The financial manager can use the cash budget to identify short-term financial needs. The cash budget tells the manager what borrowing is required or what lending will be possible in the short run. The firm has available to it a number of possible ways of acquiring funds to meet short-term shortfalls, including the use of unsecured and secured loans.

▥ connect POP QUIZ!

Can you answer the following questions? If your class is using *Connect,* log on to SmartBook to see if you know the answers to these and other questions, check out the study tools, and find out what topics require additional practice!

Section 16.1 Will decreasing accounts payable decrease cash?

Section 16.2 If the inventory period is 40 days and the accounts receivable period is 60 days, then how long is the operating cycle?

Section 16.3 What are the opportunity costs of holding current assets called?

Section 16.5 Under what type of loan does the lender have a lien against all of the borrower's inventory?

CHAPTER REVIEW AND SELF-TEST PROBLEMS

16.1   The Operating and Cash Cycles   Consider the following financial statement information for the Glory Road Company:

Item	Beginning		Ending
Inventory	$1,543		$1,669
Accounts receivable	4,418		3,952
Accounts payable	2,551		2,673
Net sales		$11,500	
Cost of goods sold		8,200	

Calculate the operating and cash cycles. (See Problem 6.)

16.2   Cash Balance for Masson Corporation   The Masson Corporation has a 60-day average collection period and wishes to maintain a $5 million minimum cash balance. Based on this and the information below, complete the following cash budget. What conclusions do you draw? (See Problem 16.)

MASSON CORPORATION Cash Budget (in millions)				
	Q1	**Q2**	**Q3**	**Q4**
Beginning receivables	$120			
Sales	90	$120	$150	$120
Cash collections				
Ending receivables				
Total cash collections				
Total cash disbursements	80	160	180	160
Net cash inflow				
Beginning cash balance	$ 5			
Net cash inflow				
Ending cash balance				
Minimum cash balance				
Cumulative surplus (deficit)				

◼ Answers to Chapter Review and Self-Test Problems

16.1   We first need the turnover ratios. Note that we use the average values for all balance sheet items and that we base the inventory and payables turnover measures on cost of goods sold.

$$\text{Inventory turnover} = \$8,200/[(\$1,543 + 1,669)/2]$$
$$= 5.11 \text{ times}$$
$$\text{Receivables turnover} = \$11,500/[(\$4,418 + 3,952)/2]$$
$$= 2.75 \text{ times}$$
$$\text{Payables turnover} = \$8,200/[(\$2,551 + 2,673)/2]$$
$$= 3.14 \text{ times}$$

We can now calculate the various periods:

$$\text{Inventory period} = 365 \text{ days}/5.11 \text{ times} = 71.49 \text{ days}$$
$$\text{Receivables period} = 365 \text{ days}/2.75 \text{ times} = 132.83 \text{ days}$$
$$\text{Payables period} = 365 \text{ days}/3.14 \text{ times} = 116.27 \text{ days}$$

So, the time it takes to acquire inventory and sell it is about 71 days. Collection takes another 133 days, so the operating cycle is thus $71 + 133 = 204$ days. The cash cycle is this 204 days less the payables period, $204 - 116 = 88$ days.

16.2   Since Masson has a 60-day collection period, only those sales made in the first 30 days of the quarter will be collected in the same quarter. Total cash collections in the first quarter will thus equal $30/90 = ⅓$ of sales plus beginning receivables, or $120 + ⅓ × $90 = 150. Ending receivables for the first quarter (and the second-quarter beginning receivables) are the other ⅔ of sales, or ⅔ × $90 = 60. The remaining calculations are straightforward, and the completed budget follows.

MASSON CORPORATION Cash Budget (in millions)				
	Q1	**Q2**	**Q3**	**Q4**
Beginning receivables	$120	$ 60	$ 80	$100
Sales	90	120	150	120
Cash collections	150	100	130	140
Ending receivables	$ 60	$ 80	$100	$ 80
Total cash collections	$150	$100	$130	$140
Total cash disbursements	80	160	180	160
Net cash inflow	$ 70	−$ 60	−$ 50	−$ 20
Beginning cash balance	$ 5	$ 75	$ 15	−$ 35
Net cash inflow	70	− 60	− 50	− 20
Ending cash balance	$ 75	$ 15	−$ 35	−$ 55
Minimum cash balance	−$ 5	−$ 5	−$ 5	−$ 5
Cumulative surplus (deficit)	$ 70	$ 10	−$ 40	−$ 60

The primary conclusion from this schedule is that, beginning in the third quarter, Masson's cash surplus becomes a cash deficit. By the end of the year, Masson will need to arrange for $60 million in cash beyond what will be available.

CRITICAL THINKING AND CONCEPTS REVIEW

LO 1   **16.1 Operating Cycle**   What are some of the characteristics of a firm with a long operating cycle?

LO 1   **16.2 Cash Cycle**   What are some of the characteristics of a firm with a long cash cycle?

LO 3   **16.3 Sources and Uses**   For the year just ended, you have gathered the following information on the Holly Corporation:

   a.   A $200 dividend was paid.

   b.   Accounts payable increased by $500.

   c.   Fixed asset purchases were $900.

   d.   Inventories increased by $625.

   e.   Long-term debt decreased by $1,200.

   Label each item as a source or use of cash and describe its effect on the firm's cash balance.

LO 2   **16.4 Cost of Current Assets**   Kane Manufacturing, Inc., has recently installed a just-in-time (JIT) inventory system. Describe the effect this is likely to have on the company's carrying costs, shortage costs, and operating cycle.

LO 1   **16.5 Cycles**   Is it possible for a firm's cash cycle to be longer than its operating cycle? Explain why or why not.

Use the following information to answer Questions 16.6–16.10. Last month, BlueSky Airline announced that it would stretch out its bill payments to 45 days from 30 days. The reason given was that the company wanted to "control costs and optimize cash flow." The increased payables period will be in effect for all of the company's 4,000 suppliers.

LO 1 **16.6 Operating and Cash Cycles** What impact did this change in payables policy have on BlueSky's operating cycle? Its cash cycle?

LO 1 **16.7 Operating and Cash Cycles** What impact did the announcement have on BlueSky's suppliers?

LO 1 **16.8 Corporate Ethics** Is it ethical for large firms to unilaterally lengthen their payables periods, particularly when dealing with smaller suppliers?

LO 1 **16.9 Payables Period** Why don't all firms increase their payables periods to shorten their cash cycles?

LO 1 **16.10 Payables Period** BlueSky lengthened its payables period to "control costs and optimize cash flow." Exactly what is the cash benefit to BlueSky from this change?

QUESTIONS AND PROBLEMS

connect Select problems are available in McGraw-Hill *Connect*. Please see the packaging options section of the Preface for more information.

BASIC (Questions 1–12)

LO 3 1. **Changes in the Cash Account** Indicate the impact of the following corporate actions on cash, using the letter *I* for an increase, *D* for a decrease, or *N* when no change occurs.

    a. A dividend is paid with funds received from a sale of debt.

    b. Real estate is purchased and paid for with short-term debt.

    c. Inventory is bought on credit.

    d. A short-term bank loan is repaid.

    e. Next year's taxes are prepaid.

    f. Preferred stock is repurchased.

    g. Sales are made on credit.

    h. Interest on long-term debt is paid.

    i. Payments for previous sales are collected.

    j. The accounts payable balance is reduced.

    k. A dividend is paid.

    l. Production supplies are purchased and paid for with a short-term note.

    m. Utility bills are paid.

    n. Cash is paid for raw materials purchased for inventory.

    o. Marketable securities are purchased.

LO 3 2. **Cash Equation** Peeples, Inc., has a book value of equity of $14,325. Long-term debt is $8,200. Net working capital, other than cash, is $2,340. Fixed assets are $19,260. How much cash does the company have? If current liabilities are $1,840, what are current assets?

LO 1 3. **Changes in the Operating Cycle** Indicate the effect that the following will have on the operating cycle. Use the letter *I* to indicate an increase, the letter *D* for a decrease, and the letter *N* for no change.

    a. Average receivables go up.

    b. Credit payment times for customers are increased.

c. Inventory turnover goes from 3 times to 7 times.

d. Payables turnover goes from 6 times to 11 times.

e. Receivables turnover goes from 7 times to 9 times.

f. Payments to suppliers are accelerated.

4. Changes in Cycles Indicate the impact of the following on the cash and operating cycles, respectively. Use the letter *I* to indicate an increase, the letter *D* for a decrease, and the letter *N* for no change.

a. The terms of cash discounts offered to customers are made less favorable.

b. The cash discounts offered by suppliers are increased; thus, payments are made earlier.

c. An increased number of customers begin to pay in cash instead of with credit.

d. Fewer raw materials than usual are purchased.

e. A greater percentage of raw material purchases are paid for with credit.

f. More finished goods are produced for inventory instead of for order.

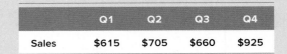

5. Calculating Cash Collections The Geller Company has projected the following quarterly sales amounts for the coming year:

	Q1	Q2	Q3	Q4
Sales	$615	$705	$660	$925

a. Accounts receivable at the beginning of the year are $360. The company has a 45-day collection period. Calculate cash collections in each of the four quarters by completing the following:

	Q1	Q2	Q3	Q4
Beginning receivables				
Sales				
Cash collections				
Ending receivables				

b. Rework part (a) assuming a collection period of 60 days.

c. Rework part (a) assuming a collection period of 30 days.

6. Calculating Cycles Consider the following financial statement information for the Sourstone Corporation:

Item	Beginning	Ending
Inventory	$7,203	$9,041
Accounts receivable	3,069	3,995
Accounts payable	3,617	4,599
Net sales		$95,982
Cost of goods sold		59,814

Assume all sales are on credit. Calculate the operating and cash cycles. How do you interpret your answer?

LO 3 **7. Factoring Receivables**   Your firm has an average collection period of 43 days. Current practice is to factor all receivables immediately at a 2 percent discount. What is the effective cost of borrowing in this case? Assume that default is extremely unlikely.

LO 3 **8. Calculating Payments**   Wentworth Products has projected the following sales for the coming year:

	Q1	Q2	Q3	Q4
Sales	$650	$740	$875	$805

Sales in the year following this one are projected to be 15 percent greater in each quarter.

a. Calculate payments to suppliers assuming that the company places orders during each quarter equal to 30 percent of projected sales for the next quarter. Assume that the company pays immediately. What is the payables period in this case?

	Q1	Q2	Q3	Q4
Payment of accounts				

b. Rework part (a) assuming a 90-day payables period.
c. Rework part (a) assuming a 60-day payables period.

LO 3 **9. Calculating Payments**   The MacDonald Corporation's purchases from suppliers in a quarter are equal to 75 percent of the next quarter's forecast sales. The payables period is 60 days. Wages, taxes, and other expenses are 30 percent of sales, and interest and dividends are $110 per quarter. No capital expenditures are planned. Projected quarterly sales are:

	Q1	Q2	Q3	Q4
Sales	$1,640	$1,920	$2,215	$2,355

Sales for the first quarter of the following year are projected at $2,050. Calculate the company's cash outlays by completing the following:

	Q1	Q2	Q3	Q4
Payment of accounts				
Wages, taxes, other expenses				
Long-term financing expenses (interest and dividends)				
Total				

LO 3 **10. Calculating Cash Collections**   The following is the sales budget for Coore, Inc., for the first quarter of 2019.

	January	February	March
Sales budget	$168,000	$186,000	$199,000

Credit sales are collected as follows:

65 percent in the month of the sale

20 percent in the month after the sale

15 percent in the second month after the sale

The accounts receivable balance at the end of the previous quarter was $107,000 ($78,100 of which was uncollected December sales).

a. Compute the sales for November.

b. Compute the sales for December.

c. Compute the cash collections from sales for each month from January through March.

LO 3 **11. Calculating the Cash Budget** Here are some important figures from the budget of Crenshaw, Inc., for the second quarter of 2019.

	April	May	June
Credit sales	$689,000	$598,000	$751,000
Credit purchases	302,000	282,000	338,000
Cash disbursements			
Wages, taxes, and expenses	137,000	129,000	179,000
Interest	15,600	15,600	15,600
Equipment purchases	53,500	6,600	248,000

The company predicts that 5 percent of its credit sales will never be collected, 35 percent of its sales will be collected in the month of the sale, and the remaining 60 percent will be collected in the following month. Credit purchases will be paid in the month following the purchase.

In March 2019, credit sales were $561,000. Using this information, complete the following cash budget:

	April	May	June
Beginning cash balance	$182,000		
Cash receipts			
Cash collections from credit sales			
Total cash available			
Cash disbursements			
Purchases	289,000		
Wages, taxes, and expenses			
Interest			
Equipment purchases			
Total cash disbursements			
Ending cash balance			

LO 3 **12. Calculating Cash Collections** The Doak Company has projected the following quarterly sales amounts for the coming year:

	Q1	Q2	Q3	Q4
Sales	$3,900	$4,700	$4,300	$3,600

a. Accounts receivable at the beginning of the year are $1,700. The company has a 45-day collection period. Calculate cash collections in each of the four quarters by completing the following:

	Q1	Q2	Q3	Q4
Beginning receivables				
Sales				
Cash collections				
Ending receivables				

b. Rework part (a) assuming a collection period of 60 days.

c. Rework part (a) assuming a collection period of 30 days.

INTERMEDIATE (Questions 13–16)

LO 3   **13. Costs of Borrowing**   You've worked out a line of credit arrangement that allows you to borrow up to $40 million at any time. The interest rate is .527 percent per month. In addition, 4 percent of the amount that you borrow must be deposited in a noninterest-bearing account. Assume that your bank uses compound interest on its line-of-credit loans.

    a. What is the effective annual interest rate on this lending arrangement?

    b. Suppose you need $15 million today and you repay it in six months. How much interest will you pay?

LO 3   **14. Costs of Borrowing**   A bank offers your firm a revolving credit arrangement for up to $75 million at an interest rate of 1.54 percent per quarter. The bank also requires you to maintain a compensating balance of 4 percent against the unused portion of the credit line, to be deposited in a noninterest-bearing account. Assume you have a short-term investment account at the bank that pays .53 percent per quarter, and assume that the bank uses compound interest on its revolving credit loans.

    a. What is your effective annual interest rate (an opportunity cost) on the revolving credit arrangement if your firm does not use it during the year?

    b. What is your effective annual interest rate on the lending arrangement if you borrow $40 million immediately and repay it in one year?

    c. What is your effective annual interest rate if you borrow $75 million immediately and repay it in one year?

LO 3   **15. Cash and Operating Cycles**   Hanse, Inc., has a cash cycle of 38.5 days, an operating cycle of 62.4 days, and an inventory period of 24.4 days. The company reported cost of goods sold in the amount of $445,000, and credit sales were $724,000. What is the company's average balance in accounts payable and accounts receivable?

LO 3   **16. Cash Budget**   Hurzdan, Inc., has a 32-day average collection period and wants to maintain a minimum cash balance of $20 million, which is what the company currently has on hand. The company currently has a receivables balance of $236 million and has developed the following sales and cash disbursement budgets (in millions):

	Q1	Q2	Q3	Q4
Sales	$390	$493	$595	$545
Total cash disbursement	321	432	767	463

Complete the following cash budget for the company. What conclusions do you draw?

HURZDAN, INC.
Cash Budget
(in millions)

	Q1	Q2	Q3	Q4
Beginning receivables				
Sales				
Cash collections				
Ending receivables				
Total cash collections				
Total cash disbursements				
Net cash inflow				
Beginning cash balance				
Net cash inflow				
Ending cash balance				
Minimum cash balance				
Cumulative surplus (deficit)				

CHALLENGE (Questions 17–18)

LO 3 17. **Costs of Borrowing** In exchange for a $400 million fixed commitment line of credit, your firm has agreed to do the following:

1. Pay 1.58 percent per quarter on any funds actually borrowed.
2. Maintain a 5 percent compensating balance on any funds actually borrowed.
3. Pay an up-front commitment fee of .25 percent of the amount of the line.

Based on this information, answer the following:

a. Ignoring the commitment fee, what is the effective annual interest rate on this line of credit?

b. Suppose your firm immediately uses $210 million of the line and pays it off in one year. What is the effective annual interest rate on this $210 million loan?

LO 3 18. **Costs of Borrowing** Come and Go Bank offers your firm a discount interest loan with an interest rate of 7.3 percent for up to $20 million, and in addition requires you to maintain a 4 percent compensating balance against the face amount borrowed. What is the effective annual interest rate on this lending arrangement?

16.1 Cash Cycle   Go to www.reuters.com. You will need to find the most recent annual income statement and the two most recent balance sheets for McKesson (MCK) and Newmont Mining (NEM). McKesson is involved in pharmaceuticals and consumer health care, while Newmont Mining is a leading gold mining company. Calculate the cash cycle for each company and comment on any similarities or differences.

16.2 Operating Cycle   Using the information you gathered in the previous problem, calculate the operating cycle for each company. What are the similarities or differences? Is this what you would expect from companies in each of these industries?

16.3 Sources and Uses of Cash   Find the two most recent balance sheets for 3M at the "Investor Relations" link on the website www.3m.com. For each account in the balance sheet, show the change during the most recent year and note whether this was a source or use of cash. Do your numbers add up and make sense? Explain your answer for total assets as compared to your answer for total liabilities and owners' equity.

WHAT'S ON THE WEB?

EXCEL *MASTER IT!* PROBLEM

Heidi Pedersen, the treasurer for Wood Products, Inc., has just been asked by Justin Wood, the company's president, to prepare a memo detailing the company's ending cash balance for the next three months. Following, you will see the relevant estimates for this period.

Excel Master
coverage online

	July	August	September
Credit sales	$1,275,800	$1,483,500	$1,096,300
Credit purchases	765,480	890,160	657,780
Cash disbursements			
Wages, taxes, and expenses	348,600	395,620	337,150
Interest	29,900	29,900	29,900
Equipment	0	158,900	96,300
Credit sales collections:			
Collected in month of sale	35%		
Collected month after sale	60%		
Never collected	5%		
June credit sales	$1,135,020		
June credit purchases	$ 681,012		
Beginning cash balance	$ 425,000		

All credit purchases are paid in the month after the purchase.

a. Complete the cash budget for Wood Products for the next three months.

b. Heidi knows that the cash budget will become a standard report completed before each quarter. To help reduce the time preparing the report each quarter, she would like a memo with the appropriate information in Excel linked to the memo. Prepare a memo to Justin that will automatically update when the values are changed in Excel.

CHAPTER CASE
Piepkorn Manufacturing Working Capital Management, Part 1

You recently have been hired by Piepkorn Manufacturing to work in its newly established treasury department. Piepkorn Manufacturing is a small company that produces cardboard boxes in a variety of sizes. Gary Piepkorn, the owner of the company, works primarily in the sales and production areas. Currently, the company puts all receivables in one shoe box and all payables in another. Because of the disorganized system, the finance area needs work, and that's what you've been brought in to do.

The company currently has a cash balance of $138,000 and plans to purchase new box-folding machinery in the fourth quarter at a cost of $275,000. The purchase of the machinery will be made with cash because of the discount offered. The company's policy is to maintain a target cash balance of $100,000. All sales are in cash and all purchases are made on credit.

Gary Piepkorn has projected the following gross sales for each of the next four quarters:

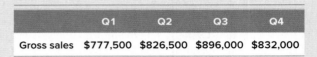

	Q1	Q2	Q3	Q4
Gross sales	$777,500	$826,500	$896,000	$832,000

Gross sales for the first quarter of next year are projected at $815,000.

Piepkorn typically orders 50 percent of next quarter's projected gross sales in the current quarter, and suppliers are typically paid in 53 days. Wages, taxes, and other costs run about 30 percent of gross sales. The company has a quarterly interest payment of $105,000 on its long-term debt.

The company uses a local bank for its short-term financial needs. It pays 1.5 percent per quarter on all short-term borrowing and maintains a money market account that pays 1 percent per quarter on all short-term deposits.

Gary has asked you to prepare a cash budget and short-term financial plan for the company under the current policies. He also has asked you to prepare additional plans based on changes in several inputs.

QUESTIONS

1. Use the numbers given to complete the cash budget and short-term financial plan.

2. Rework the cash budget and short-term financial plan assuming Piepkorn changes to a target balance of $80,000.

PIEPKORN MANUFACTURING Cash Budget				
	Q1	Q2	Q3	Q4
Beginning cash balance				
Net cash inflow				
Ending cash balance				
Minimum cash balance				
Cumulative surplus (deficit)				

PIEPKORN MANUFACTURING Short-Term Financial Plan				
	Q1	Q2	Q3	Q4
Target cash balance				
Net cash inflow				
New short-term investments				
Income from short-term investments				
Short-term investments sold				
New short-term borrowing				
Interest on short-term borrowing				
Short-term borrowing repaid				
Ending cash balance				
Minimum cash balance				
Cumulative surplus (deficit)				
Beginning short-term investments				
Ending short-term investments				
Beginning short-term debt				
Ending short-term debt				

17 | Working Capital Management

Most often, when news breaks about a firm's bank accounts, it's because the company is running low on cash. However, that wasn't the case for many companies in the middle of 2018. For example, Apple had a cash balance of about $285 billion, or $57 per share! Other companies also had large cash balances. For example, Microsoft had a cash hoard of about $147 billion, while Alphabet had about $102 billion. Why would firms such as these hold such large quantities of cash? We examine cash management in this chapter to find out.

This chapter considers various aspects of working capital management. Commonly, responsibility for working capital is spread across several different disciplines. Accounting is frequently responsible for payables and receivables, operations is in charge of inventory, and finance handles cash management. Marketing also plays an important role because sales forecasts are a key determinant of working capital needs. So, an understanding of working capital management is important for just about everyone in the firm.

LEARNING OBJECTIVES

After studying this chapter, you should be able to:

LO 1 Explain how firms manage their cash, and identify some of the collection, concentration, and disbursement techniques used.

LO 2 Analyze how firms manage their receivables and the basic components of a firm's credit policies.

LO 3 Differentiate between the types of inventory and inventory management systems used by firms, and explain what determines the optimal inventory level.

Please visit us at essentialsofcorporatefinance.blogspot.com for the latest developments in the world of corporate finance.

This chapter examines working capital management. Recall from Chapter 1 that working capital management deals with a firm's short-term, or current, assets and liabilities. A firm's current liabilities consist largely of short-term borrowing. We discussed short-term borrowing in our previous chapter, so this chapter mainly focuses on current assets, in particular, cash, accounts receivable, and inventory.

17.1 FLOAT AND CASH MANAGEMENT

We begin our analysis of working capital management by looking at how firms manage cash. The basic objective in cash management is to keep the investment in cash as low as possible while still operating the firm's activities efficiently and effectively. This goal usually reduces to the dictum "Collect early and pay late." Accordingly, we discuss ways of accelerating collections and managing disbursements.

In addition, firms must invest temporarily idle cash in short-term marketable securities. As we discuss in various places, these securities can be bought and sold in the financial markets. As a group, they have very little default risk, and most are highly liquid. There are different types of these so-called money market securities, and we discuss a few of the most important ones a bit later.

Reasons for Holding Cash

John Maynard Keynes, in his great work *The General Theory of Employment, Interest, and Money*, identified three reasons why liquidity is important: the speculative motive, the precautionary motive, and the transaction motive. We discuss these next.

speculative motive
The need to hold cash to take advantage of additional investment opportunities, such as bargain purchases.

The Speculative and Precautionary Motives   The **speculative motive** is the need to hold cash in order to be able to take advantage of, for example, bargain purchase opportunities that might arise, attractive interest rates, and (in the case of international firms) favorable exchange rate fluctuations.

For most firms, reserve borrowing ability and marketable securities can be used to satisfy speculative motives. Thus, for a modern firm, there might be a speculative motive for liquidity, but not necessarily for cash per se. Think of it this way: If you have a credit card with a very large credit limit, then you can probably take advantage of any unusual bargains that come along without carrying any cash.

precautionary motive
The need to hold cash as a safety margin to act as a financial reserve.

This is also true, to a lesser extent, for precautionary motives. The **precautionary motive** is the need for a safety supply to act as a financial reserve. Once again, there probably is a precautionary motive for liquidity. However, given that the value of money market instruments is relatively certain and that instruments such as T-bills are extremely liquid, there is no real need to hold substantial amounts of cash for precautionary purposes.

transaction motive
The need to hold cash to satisfy normal disbursement and collection activities associated with a firm's ongoing operations.

The Transaction Motive   Cash is needed to satisfy the **transaction motive**, the need to have cash on hand to pay bills. Transaction-related needs come from the normal disbursement and collection activities of the firm. The disbursement of cash includes the payment of wages and salaries, trade debts, taxes, and dividends.

Cash is collected from sales, the selling of assets, and new financing. The cash inflows (collections) and outflows (disbursements) are not perfectly synchronized, and some level of cash holdings is necessary to serve as a buffer. Perfect liquidity is the characteristic of cash that allows it to satisfy the transaction motive.

As electronic funds transfers and other high-speed, "paperless" payment mechanisms continue to develop, even the transaction demand for cash may all but disappear. Even if it does, however, there will still be a demand for liquidity and a need to manage it efficiently.

Benefits of Holding Cash   When a firm holds cash in excess of some necessary minimum, it incurs an opportunity cost. The opportunity cost of excess cash (held in currency or bank deposits) is the interest income that could be earned in the next best use, such as investing in marketable securities.

Given the opportunity cost of holding cash, why would a firm hold excess cash? The answer is that a cash balance must be maintained to provide the liquidity necessary for transaction needs—paying bills. If the firm maintains too small a cash balance, it may run out of cash. If this happens, the firm may have to raise cash on a short-term basis. This could involve, for example, selling marketable securities or borrowing.

Activities such as selling marketable securities and borrowing involve various costs. As we've discussed, holding cash has an opportunity cost. To determine the appropriate cash balance, the firm must weigh the benefits of holding cash against these costs. We discuss this subject in more detail in the sections that follow.

Understanding Float

As you no doubt know, the amount of money you have according to your checkbook can be very different from the amount of money that your bank thinks you have. The reason is that some of the checks you have written haven't yet been presented to the bank for payment. The same thing is true for a business. The cash balance that a firm shows on its books is called the firm's *book*, or *ledger, balance.* The balance shown in its bank account as available to spend is called its *available*, or *collected, balance.* The difference between the available balance and the ledger balance is called the **float**, and it represents the net effect of checks in the process of *clearing* (moving through the banking system).

float
The difference between book cash and bank cash, representing the net effect of checks in the process of clearing.

Disbursement Float   Checks written by a firm generate *disbursement float*, causing a decrease in the firm's book balance but no change in its available balance. For example, suppose General Mechanics, Inc. (GMI), currently has $100,000 on deposit with its bank. On June 8, it buys some raw materials and pays with a check for $100,000. The company's book balance is immediately reduced by $100,000 as a result.

GMI's bank, however, will not find out about this check until it is presented to GMI's bank for payment on, say, June 14. Until the check is presented, the firm's available balance is greater than its book balance by $100,000. In other words, before June 8, GMI has a zero float:

Float = Firm's available balance − Firm's book balance
= **$100,000**   **− 100,000**
= **$0**

GMI's position from June 8 to June 14 is:

Disbursement float = Firm's available balance − Firm's book balance
= **$100,000**   **− 0**
= **$100,000**

During this period of time while the check is clearing, GMI has a balance with the bank of $100,000. It can obtain the benefit of this cash while the check is clearing. For example, the available balance could be temporarily invested in marketable securities and thus earn some interest. We will return to this subject a little later.

Collection Float and Net Float   Checks received by the firm create *collection float.* Collection float increases book balances but does not immediately change available balances. Suppose GMI receives a check from a customer for $100,000 on October 8. Assume, as before, that the company has $100,000 deposited at its bank and a zero float. It deposits the check and increases its book balance by $100,000, to $200,000. However, the additional cash is not available to GMI until its bank has presented the check to the customer's bank and received $100,000. This will occur on, say, October 14. In the meantime, the cash position at GMI will reflect a collection float of $100,000. We can summarize these events. Before October 8, GMI's position is:

Float = Firm's available balance − Firm's book balance
$$= \$100,000 \qquad\qquad - 100,000$$
$$= \$0$$

GMI's position from October 8 to October 14 is:

Collection float = Firm's available balance − Firm's book balance
$$= \$100,000 \qquad\qquad - 200,000$$
$$= -\$100,000$$

In general, a firm's payment (disbursement) activities generate disbursement float, and its collection activities generate collection float. The net effect—that is, the sum of the total collection and disbursement floats—is the *net float*. The net float at any point in time is the overall difference between the firm's available balance and its book balance. If the net float is positive, then the firm's disbursement float exceeds its collection float and its available balance exceeds its book balance. If the available balance is less than the book balance, then the firm has a negative net float.

A firm should be concerned with its net float and available balance more than its book balance. If a financial manager knows that a check written by the company will not clear for several days, that manager will be able to keep a lower cash balance at the bank than might be true otherwise. This can generate a great deal of money.

For example, take the case of retail giant Walmart. The average daily sales for Walmart were about $1.37 billion in 2017. If Walmart's collections could have been sped up by a single day, then the company could have freed up $1.37 billion for investing. At a relatively modest .01 percent daily rate, the interest earned would have been on the order of $137,000 *per day.*

EXAMPLE 17.1   Staying Afloat

Suppose you have $5,000 on deposit. One day you write a check for $1,000 to pay for books, and you deposit $2,000. What are your disbursement, collection, and net floats?

After you write the $1,000 check, you show a balance of $4,000 on your books, but the bank shows $5,000 while the check is clearing. This means you have a disbursement float of $1,000.

After you deposit the $2,000 check, you show a balance of $6,000. Your available balance doesn't rise until the check clears. This means you have a collection float of −$2,000. Your net float is the sum of the collection and disbursement floats, or −$1,000.

Overall, you show $6,000 on your books. The bank shows a $7,000 balance, but only $5,000 is available because your deposit has not cleared. The discrepancy between your available balance and your book balance is the net float (−$1,000), and it is bad for you. If you write another check for $5,500, there may not be sufficient available funds to cover it, and it might bounce. This is the reason the financial manager has to be more concerned with available balances than book balances.

Float Management   Float management involves controlling the collection and disbursement of cash. The objective in cash collection is to speed up collections and reduce the lag between the time customers pay their bills and the time the cash becomes available. The objective in cash disbursement is to control payments and minimize the firm's costs associated with making payments.

Total collection or disbursement times can be broken down into three parts: mailing time, processing delay, and availability delay:

1. *Mailing time* is the part of the collection and disbursement process during which checks are trapped in the postal system.

2. *Processing delay* is the time it takes the receiver of a check to process the payment and deposit it in a bank for collection.

3. *Availability delay* refers to the time required to clear a check through the banking system.

Speeding up collections involves reducing one or more of these components. Slowing disbursements involves increasing one or more of them. We describe some procedures for managing collection and disbursement times below.

Ethical and Legal Questions   The cash manager must work with collected bank cash balances and not the firm's book balance (which reflects checks that have been deposited but not collected). If this is not done, a cash manager could be drawing on uncollected cash as a source of funds for short-term investing. Most banks charge a penalty rate for the use of uncollected funds. However, banks may not have good enough accounting and control procedures to be fully aware of the use of uncollected funds. This raises some ethical and legal questions for the firm.

For example, in May 1985, E. F. Hutton (a large investment bank), pleaded guilty to 2,000 charges of mail and wire fraud in connection with a scheme the firm had operated from 1980 to 1982. E. F. Hutton employees wrote checks totaling hundreds of millions of dollars against uncollected cash. The proceeds were then invested in short-term money market assets. This type of systematic overdrafting of accounts (or check *kiting*, as it is sometimes called) is neither legal nor ethical and is apparently not a widespread practice among corporations. Also, the particular inefficiencies in the banking system that Hutton was exploiting have been largely eliminated.

For its part, E. F. Hutton paid a $2 million fine, reimbursed the government (the U.S. Department of Justice) $750,000, and reserved an additional $8 million for restitution to defrauded banks. We should note that the key issue in the case against Hutton was not its float management per se, but, rather, its practice of writing checks for no economic reason other than to exploit float. Unfortunately, check kiting is still not dead. In March 2018, a Nebraska business owner pleaded guilty to a check kiting scheme that involved four different banks. His plea agreement helped avoid a potential 30-year federal prison term, but he faced five years of probation, incurred a $1 million fine, and had to pay about $835,000 in restitution.

Electronic Data Interchange and Check 21: The End of Float?   *Electronic data interchange* (EDI) is a general term that refers to the growing practice of direct, electronic information exchange between all types of businesses. One important use of EDI, often called financial EDI, or FEDI, is to electronically transfer financial information and funds between parties, thereby eliminating paper invoices, paper checks, mailing, and handling. For example, it is possible to arrange to have your checking account directly debited each month to pay many types of bills, and corporations now routinely directly deposit paychecks into employee accounts. More generally, EDI allows a seller to send a bill electronically to a buyer, thereby avoiding the mail. The buyer can then authorize payment, which also occurs electronically. Its bank then transfers the funds to the seller's account at a different bank. The net effect is that the length of time required to initiate and complete a business transaction is shortened considerably, and much of what we normally think of as float is sharply reduced or eliminated. As the use of FEDI increases (which it will), float management will evolve to focus much more on issues surrounding computerized information exchange and funds transfers.

On October 29, 2004, the Check Clearing Act for the 21st Century, also known as Check 21, took effect. Before Check 21, a bank receiving a check was required to send the physical check to the customer's bank before payment could be made. Now a bank can transmit an electronic image of the check to the customer's bank and receive payment immediately. Previously, an out-of-state check might take three days to clear, but with Check 21, the clearing time is typically one day, and often, a check can clear the same day it is written. Thus, Check 21 has significantly reduced float.

CONCEPT QUESTIONS

17.1a   What is the transaction motive for holding cash?

17.1b   What is the cost to the firm of holding excess cash?

17.1c   Which of these would a firm be more interested in reducing: collection float or disbursement float? Why?

17.1d   What is the benefit from reducing or eliminating float?

17.2 CASH MANAGEMENT: COLLECTION, DISBURSEMENT, AND INVESTMENT

As a part of managing its cash, a firm must make arrangements to collect from its customers, pay its suppliers, and invest any excess cash on hand. We begin by examining how firms collect and concentrate cash.

Cash Collection and Concentration

From our previous discussion, we know that collection delays work against the firm. All other things being the same, then, a firm will adopt procedures to speed up collections and thereby decrease collection times. In addition, even after cash is collected, firms need procedures to funnel, or concentrate, that cash where it can be best used. We discuss some common collection and concentration procedures next.

Components of Collection Time   Based on our discussion above, we can depict the basic parts of the cash collection process as follows: The total time in this process is made up of mailing time, check-processing delay, and the bank's availability delay.

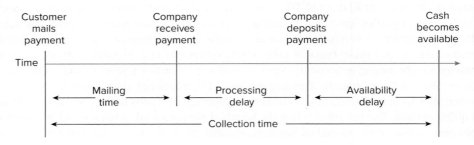

The amount of time that cash spends in each part of the cash collection process depends on where the firm's customers and banks are located and how efficient the firm is at collecting cash.

Cash Collection How a firm collects from its customers depends in large part on the nature of the business. The simplest case would be a business such as a restaurant chain. Most of its customers will pay with cash, check, or credit card at the point of sale (this is called *over-the-counter collection*), so there is no problem with mailing delay. Normally, the funds would be deposited in a local bank, and the firm would have some means (discussed next) of gaining access to the funds.

When some or all of the payments a company receives are checks that arrive through the mail, all three components of collection time become relevant. The firm may choose to have all the checks mailed to one location, or, more commonly, the firm might have a number of different mail collection points to reduce mailing times. Also, the firm may run its collection operation itself or might hire an outside firm that specializes in cash collection. We discuss these issues in more detail later.

Other approaches to cash collection exist. One that is becoming more common is the preauthorized payment system. With this arrangement, the payment amounts and payment dates are fixed in advance. When the agreed-upon date arrives, the amount is automatically transferred from the customer's bank account to the firm's bank account, sharply reducing or even eliminating collection delays. The same approach is used by firms that have online terminals, meaning that when a sale is rung up, the money is immediately transferred to the firm's accounts.

Lockboxes When a firm receives its payments by mail, it must decide where the checks will be mailed and how the checks will be picked up and deposited. Careful selection of the number and locations of collection points can greatly reduce collection times. Many firms use special post office boxes called **lockboxes** to intercept payments and speed cash collection.

lockboxes
Special post office boxes set up to intercept and speed up accounts receivable collections.

Figure 17.1 illustrates a lockbox system. The collection process is started by customers mailing their checks to a post office box instead of sending them to the firm. The lockbox is maintained by a local bank. A large corporation may actually have more than 20 lockboxes around the country.

In the typical lockbox system, the local bank collects the lockbox checks from the post office several times a day. The bank deposits the checks directly to the firm's account. Details of the operation are recorded (in some computer-usable form) and sent to the firm.

A lockbox system reduces mailing time because checks are received at a nearby post office instead of at corporate headquarters. Lockboxes also reduce the processing time because the corporation doesn't have to open the envelopes and deposit checks for collection. In all, a bank lockbox should enable a firm to get its receipts processed, deposited, and cleared faster than if it were to receive checks at its headquarters and deliver them itself to the bank for deposit and clearing.

Cash Concentration As we discussed earlier, a firm will typically have a number of cash collection points, and, as a result, cash collections may end up in many different banks and bank accounts. From here, the firm needs procedures to move the cash into its main accounts. This is called **cash concentration**. By routinely pooling its cash, the firm greatly simplifies its cash management by reducing the number of accounts that must be tracked. Also, by having a larger pool of funds available, a firm may be able to negotiate a better rate on any short-term investments.

cash concentration
The practice of and procedures for moving cash from multiple banks into the firm's main accounts.

FIGURE 17.1

Overview of lockbox processing

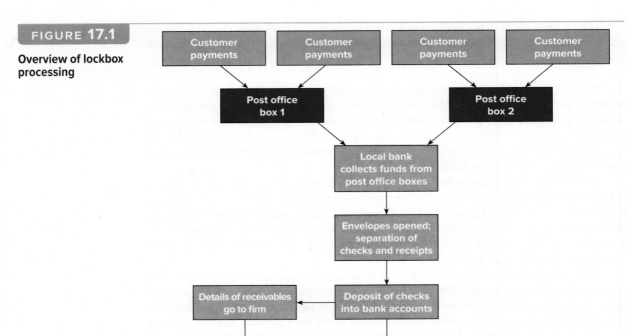

The flow starts when a customer mails remittances to a post office box instead of to the corporation. Several times a day the bank collects the lockbox receipts from the post office. The checks are then put into the company bank accounts.

In setting up a concentration system, firms typically will use one or more *concentration banks*. A concentration bank pools the funds obtained from local banks contained within some geographic region. Concentration systems often are used in conjunction with lockbox systems. Figure 17.2 illustrates how an integrated cash collection and cash concentration system might look.

Managing Cash Disbursements

From the firm's point of view, disbursement float is desirable, so the goal in managing disbursement float is to slow down disbursements as much as possible. To do this, the firm may develop strategies to *increase* mail float, processing float, and availability float on the checks it writes. Beyond this, firms have developed procedures for minimizing cash held for payment purposes. We now discuss the most common of these procedures.

Increasing Disbursement Float   As we have seen, float in terms of slowing down payments comes from the time involved in mail delivery, check processing, and collection of funds. Disbursement float can be increased by writing a check on a geographically distant bank. For example, a New York supplier might be paid with checks drawn on a Los Angeles bank. This will increase the time required for the checks to clear through the banking system. Mailing checks from remote post offices is another way firms slow down disbursement.

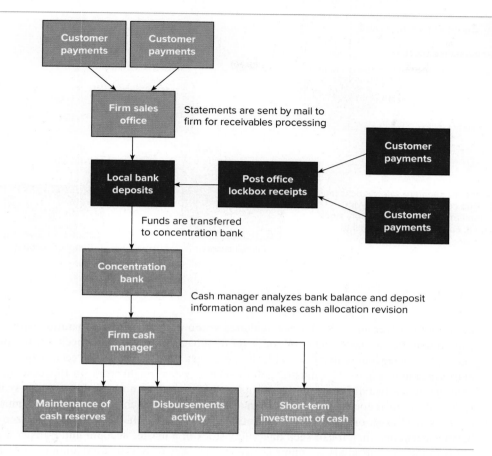

FIGURE **17.2**

Lockboxes and concentration banks in a cash management system

Tactics for maximizing disbursement float are debatable on both ethical and economic grounds. First, as we discuss later, payment terms very frequently offer a substantial discount for early payment. The discount is usually much larger than any possible savings from "playing the float game." In such cases, increasing mailing time will be of no benefit if the recipient dates payments based on the date received (as is common) as opposed to the postmark date.

Beyond this, suppliers are not likely to be fooled by attempts to slow down disbursement. The negative consequences from poor relations with suppliers can be costly. In broader terms, intentionally delaying payments by taking advantage of mailing times or unsophisticated suppliers may amount to avoiding paying bills when they are due, an unethical business procedure.

Controlling Disbursements We have seen that maximizing disbursement float is probably poor business practice. However, a firm still will wish to tie up as little cash as possible in disbursements. Firms therefore have developed systems for efficiently managing the disbursement process. The general idea in such systems is to have no more than the minimum amount necessary to pay bills on deposit in the bank. We discuss some approaches to accomplishing this goal next.

| FIGURE 17.3 | **Zero-balance accounts** |

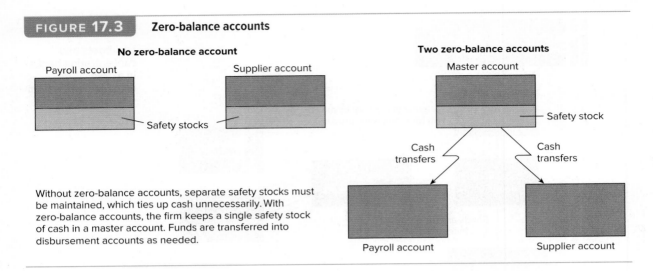

Without zero-balance accounts, separate safety stocks must be maintained, which ties up cash unnecessarily. With zero-balance accounts, the firm keeps a single safety stock of cash in a master account. Funds are transferred into disbursement accounts as needed.

zero-balance account
A disbursement account in which the firm maintains a zero balance, transferring funds in from a master account only as needed to cover checks presented for payment.

Zero-balance accounts   With a **zero-balance account**, the firm, in cooperation with its bank, maintains a master account and a set of subaccounts. When a check written on one of the subaccounts must be paid, the necessary funds are transferred in from the master account. Figure 17.3 illustrates how such a system might work. In this case, the firm maintains two disbursement accounts, one for suppliers and one for payroll. As is shown, if the firm does not use zero-balance accounts, then each of these accounts must have a safety stock of cash to meet unanticipated demands. If the firm does use zero-balance accounts, then it can keep one safety stock in a master account and transfer the funds to the two subsidiary accounts as needed. The key is that the total amount of cash held as a buffer is smaller under the zero-balance arrangement, which frees up cash to be used elsewhere.

controlled disbursement account
A disbursement practice under which the firm transfers an amount to a disbursing account that is sufficient to cover demands for payment.

Controlled disbursement accounts   Almost all payments that must be made in a given day are known in the morning. With a **controlled disbursement account**, the bank informs the firm of the day's total, and the firm transfers (usually by wire) the amount needed.

Investing Idle Cash

If a firm has a temporary cash surplus, it can invest in short-term securities. As we have mentioned at various times, the market for short-term financial assets is called the *money market*. The maturity of short-term financial assets that trade in the money market is one year or less.

Most large firms manage their own short-term financial assets, transacting through banks and dealers. Some large firms and many small firms use money market mutual funds. These are funds that invest in short-term financial assets for a management fee. The management fee is compensation for the professional expertise and diversification provided by the fund manager.

Among the many money market mutual funds, some specialize in corporate customers. In addition, banks offer arrangements in which the bank takes all excess available funds at the close of each business day and invests them for the firm.

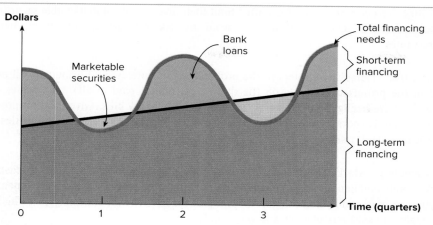

FIGURE **17.4**

Seasonal cash demands

Time 1: A surplus cash position exists. Seasonal demand for current assets is low. The surplus is invested in short-term marketable securities.

Time 2: A deficit cash position exists. Seasonal demand for current assets is high. The financial deficit is financed by selling marketable securities and by bank borrowing.

Temporary Cash Surpluses Firms have temporary cash surpluses for various reasons. Two of the most important are the financing of seasonal or cyclical activities of the firm and the financing of planned or possible expenditures.

Seasonal or cyclical activities Some firms have a predictable cash flow pattern. They have surplus cash flows during part of the year and deficit cash flows the rest of the year. For example, MasterCraft, known for its sport boats, has a seasonal cash flow pattern influenced by summer.

A firm such as MasterCraft may buy marketable securities when surplus cash flows occur and sell marketable securities when deficits occur. Of course, bank loans are another short-term financing device. The use of bank loans and marketable securities to meet temporary financing needs is illustrated in Figure 17.4. In this case, the firm is following a compromise working capital policy in the sense we discussed in the previous chapter.

Planned or possible expenditures Firms frequently accumulate temporary investments in marketable securities to provide the cash for a plant construction program, dividend payment, or other large expenditure. Thus, firms may issue bonds and stocks before the cash is needed, investing the proceeds in short-term marketable securities and then selling the securities to finance the expenditures. Also, firms may face the possibility of having to make a large cash outlay. An obvious example would be the possibility of losing a large lawsuit. Firms may build up cash surpluses against such a contingency.

Characteristics of Short-Term Securities Given that a firm has some temporarily idle cash, there are a variety of short-term securities available for investing. The most important characteristics of these short-term marketable securities are their maturity, default risk, marketability, and taxability.

Maturity Maturity refers to the time period over which interest and principal payments are made. From Chapter 6, we know that for a given change in the level of interest rates, the prices of longer-maturity securities will change more than those of shorter-maturity securities. As a consequence, firms often limit their investments in marketable securities to those maturing in less than 90 days to avoid the risk of losses in value from changing interest rates.

Default risk   Default risk refers to the probability that interest and principal will not be paid in the promised amounts on the due dates (or not paid at all). Of course, some securities have negligible default risk, such as U.S. Treasury bills. Given the purposes of investing idle corporate cash, firms typically avoid investing in marketable securities with significant default risk.

Marketability   Marketability refers to how easy it is to convert an asset to cash; so, marketability and liquidity mean much the same thing. Some money market instruments are much more marketable than others. At the top of the list are U.S. Treasury bills, which can be bought and sold very cheaply and very quickly.

Taxability   Interest earned on money market securities that are not some kind of government obligation (either federal or state) is taxable at the local, state, and federal levels. U.S. Treasury obligations such as T-bills are exempt from state taxation, but other government-backed debt is not. Municipal securities are exempt from federal taxes, but they may be taxed at the state level.

Some Different Types of Money Market Securities

Money market securities are generally highly marketable and short term. They usually have low risk of default. They are issued by the U.S. government (e.g., U.S. Treasury bills), domestic and foreign banks (e.g., certificates of deposit), and business corporations (e.g., commercial paper). There are many types in all, and we only illustrate a few of the most common here.

U.S. Treasury bills are obligations of the U.S. government that mature in 4, 13, 26, or 52 weeks. The 4-, 13-, and 26-week bills are sold by auction every week, and 52-week bills are sold every four weeks.

Short-term tax-exempts are short-term securities issued by states, municipalities, and certain other agencies. Because these are all considered municipal securities, they are exempt from federal taxes. Short-term tax-exempts have more default risk than U.S. Treasury issues and are less marketable. Because the interest is exempt from federal income tax, the pretax yield on tax-exempts is lower than that on comparable securities such as U.S. Treasury bills. Also, corporations face some restrictions on holding tax-exempts as investments.

Commercial paper refers to short-term securities issued by finance companies, banks, and corporations. Typically, commercial paper is unsecured. Maturities range from a few weeks to 270 days.

There is no especially active secondary market in commercial paper. As a consequence, the marketability can be low; however, firms that issue commercial paper often will repurchase it directly before maturity. The default risk of commercial paper depends on the financial strength of the issuer.

Certificates of deposit (CDs) are short-term loans to commercial banks. These are normally jumbo CDs—those in excess of $100,000. There are active markets in CDs of 3-month, 6-month, 9-month, and 12-month maturities.

Because 70 to 80 percent of the dividends received by one corporation from another are exempt from taxation, the relatively high dividend yields on preferred stock provide a strong incentive for investment. The only problem is that the dividend is fixed with ordinary preferred stock, so the price can fluctuate more than is desirable in a short-term investment.

Check out short-term rates online at www.bloomberg.com.

So-called money market preferred stock is a recent innovation featuring a floating dividend. The dividend is reset fairly often (usually every 49 days), so this type of preferred has much less price volatility than ordinary preferred, and it has become a popular short-term investment.

CONCEPT QUESTIONS

17.2a What is a lockbox? What purpose does it serve?

17.2b What is a concentration bank? What purpose does it serve?

17.2c Is maximizing disbursement float a sound business practice?

17.2d What are some types of money market securities?

17.3 CREDIT AND RECEIVABLES

When a firm sells goods and services, it can demand cash on or before the delivery date, or it can extend credit to customers and allow some delay in payment.

Why would firms grant credit? The obvious reason is that offering credit is a way of stimulating sales. The costs associated with granting credit are not trivial. First, there is the chance that the customer will not pay. Second, the firm has to bear the costs of carrying the receivables. The credit policy decision thus involves a trade-off between the benefits of increased sales and the costs of granting credit.

From an accounting perspective, when credit is granted, an account receivable is created. These receivables include credit to other firms, called *trade credit*, and credit granted to consumers, called *consumer credit*, and they represent a major investment of financial resources by U.S. businesses. Furthermore, trade credit is a very important source of financing for corporations. However we look at it, receivables and receivables management are very important aspects of a firm's short-term financial policy.

Components of Credit Policy

If a firm decides to grant credit to its customers, then it must establish procedures for extending credit and collecting. In particular, the firm will have to deal with the following components of credit policy:

1. **Terms of sale:** The terms of sale establish how the firm proposes to sell its goods and services. If the firm grants credit to a customer, the terms of sale will specify (perhaps implicitly) the credit period, the cash discount and discount period, and the type of credit instrument.

2. **Credit analysis:** In granting credit, a firm determines how much effort to expend trying to distinguish between customers who will pay and customers who will not pay. Firms use a number of devices and procedures to determine the probability that customers will not pay, and, put together, these are called credit analysis.

3. **Collection policy:** After credit has been granted, the firm has the potential problem of collecting the cash when it becomes due, for which it must establish a collection policy.

In the next several sections, we will discuss these components of credit policy that collectively make up the decision to grant credit.

terms of sale
Conditions under which a firm sells its goods and services for cash or credit.

credit analysis
The process of determining the probability that customers will or will not pay.

collection policy
Procedures followed by a firm in collecting accounts receivable.

Terms of Sale

As we described earlier, the terms of a sale are made up of three distinct elements:

1. The period for which credit is granted (the credit period).
2. The cash discount and the discount period.
3. The type of credit instrument.

Within a given industry, the terms of sale are usually fairly standard, but these terms vary quite a bit across industries. In many cases, the terms of sale are remarkably archaic and literally date to previous centuries. Organized systems of trade credit that resemble current practice can be traced easily to the great fairs of medieval Europe, and they almost surely existed long before then.

The Basic Form   The easiest way to understand the terms of sale is to consider an example. For bulk candy, terms of 2/10, net 60 might be quoted.[1] This means that customers have 60 days from the invoice date (discussed next) to pay the full amount. However, if payment is made within 10 days, a 2 percent cash discount can be taken.

Consider a buyer who places an order for $1,000, and assume that the terms of the sale are 2/10, net 60. The buyer has the option of paying $1,000 × (1 − .02) = $980 in 10 days or paying the full $1,000 in 60 days. If the terms were stated as net 30, then the customer would have 30 days from the invoice date to pay the entire $1,000, and no discount would be offered for early payment.

In general, credit terms are interpreted in the following way:

(take this discount off the invoice price)/(if you pay in this many days), (else pay the full invoice amount in this many days)

Thus, **5**/10, net 45 means take a 5 percent discount from the full price if you pay within 10 days, or else pay the full amount in 45 days.

credit period
The length of time for which credit is granted.

The Credit Period   The **credit period** is the basic length of time for which credit is granted. The credit period varies widely from industry to industry, but it is almost always between 30 and 120 days. If a cash discount is offered, then the credit period has two components: the net credit period and the cash discount period.

The net credit period is the length of time the customer has to pay. The cash discount period, as the name suggests, is the time during which the discount is available. With 2/10, net 30, for example, the net credit period is 30 days and the cash discount period is 10 days.

invoice
Bill for goods or services provided by the seller to the purchaser.

The invoice date   The invoice date is the beginning of the credit period. An **invoice** is a written account of merchandise shipped to the buyer. For individual items, by convention, the invoice date is usually the shipping date or the billing date, not the date that the buyer receives the goods or the bill.

Length of the credit period   A number of factors influence the length of the credit period. Two of the most important are the *buyer's* inventory period and the operating cycle. All other things being equal, the shorter these are, the shorter the credit period normally will be.

---

[1]The terms of sale cited from specific industries in this section and elsewhere are drawn from Theodore N. Beckman, *Credits and Collections: Management and Theory* (New York: McGraw-Hill, 1962).

Based on our discussion in Chapter 16, the operating cycle has two components: the inventory period and the receivables period. The inventory period is the time it takes the buyer to acquire inventory (from us), process it, and sell it. The receivables period is the time it then takes the buyer to collect on the sale. Note that the credit period that we offer is effectively the buyer's payables period.

By extending credit, we finance a portion of our buyer's operating cycle and thereby shorten the buyer's cash cycle. If our credit period exceeds the buyer's inventory period, then we are financing not only the buyer's inventory purchases, but part of the buyer's receivables as well.

Furthermore, if our credit period exceeds our buyer's operating cycle, then we are effectively providing financing for aspects of our customer's business beyond the immediate purchase and sale of our merchandise. The reason is that the buyer effectively has a loan from us even after the merchandise is resold, and the buyer can use that credit for other purposes. For this reason, the length of the buyer's operating cycle is often cited as an appropriate upper limit to the credit period.

There are a number of other factors that influence the credit period. Many of these also influence our customers' operating cycles; so, once again, these are related subjects. Among the most important are:

For more on the credit process for small businesses, see www.newyorkfed.org /smallbusiness/index.html.

1. *Perishability and collateral value.* Perishable items have relatively rapid turnover and relatively low collateral value. Credit periods are thus shorter for such goods.

2. *Consumer demand.* Products that are well established generally have more rapid turnover. Newer or slow-moving products often will have longer credit periods associated with them to entice buyers.

3. *Cost, profitability, and standardization.* Relatively inexpensive goods tend to have shorter credit periods. The same is true for relatively standardized goods and raw materials. These all tend to have lower markups and higher turnover rates, both of which lead to shorter credit periods.

4. *Credit risk.* The greater the credit risk of the buyer, the shorter the credit period is likely to be (assuming that credit is granted at all).

5. *The size of the account.* If the account is small, the credit period may be shorter because small accounts are more costly to manage and the customers are less important.

6. *Competition.* When the seller is in a highly competitive market, longer credit periods may be offered as a way of attracting customers.

7. *Customer type.* A single seller might offer different credit terms to different buyers. A food wholesaler, for example, might supply groceries, bakeries, and restaurants. Each group would probably have different credit terms. More generally, sellers often have both wholesale and retail customers, and they frequently quote different terms to the two types.

Cash Discounts   As we have seen, **cash discounts** are often part of the terms of sale. The practice of granting discounts for cash purchases in the United States dates to the Civil War and is widespread today. One reason discounts are offered is to speed up the collection of receivables. This will have the effect of reducing the amount of credit being offered, and the firm must trade this off against the cost of the discount.

Notice that when a cash discount is offered, the credit is essentially free during the discount period. The buyer only pays for the credit after the discount expires. With 2/10, net 30, a rational buyer either pays in 10 days to make the greatest possible use of the free credit

cash discount
A discount given to induce prompt payment. Also *sales discount.*

or pays in 30 days to get the longest possible use of the money in exchange for giving up the discount. So, by giving up the discount, the buyer effectively gets $30 - 10 = 20$ days' credit.

Another reason for cash discounts is that they are a way of charging higher prices to customers that have had credit extended to them. In this sense, cash discounts are a convenient way of charging for the credit granted to customers.

Visit the National
Association of Credit
Management at
www.nacm.org.

In our examples, it might seem that the discounts are rather small. With 2/10, net 30, for example, early payment only gets the buyer a 2 percent discount. Does this provide a significant incentive for early payment? The answer is "yes" because the implicit interest rate is extremely high.

To see why the discount is important, we will calculate the cost to the buyer of not paying early. To do this, we will find the interest rate that the buyer is effectively paying for the trade credit. Suppose the order is for $1,000. The buyer can pay $980 in 10 days or wait another 20 days and pay $1,000. It's obvious that the buyer is effectively borrowing $980 for 20 days and that the buyer pays $20 in interest on the "loan." What's the interest rate?

With $20 in interest on $980 borrowed, the rate is $\$20/\$980 = .020408$, or 2.0408%. This is relatively low, but remember that this is the rate per 20-day period. There are $365/20 = 18.25$ such periods in a year, so, by not taking the discount, the buyer is paying an effective annual rate of:

$$EAR = 1.020408^{18.25} - 1 = .446, \text{ or } 44.6\%$$

From the buyer's point of view, this is an expensive source of financing!

Given that the interest rate is so high here, it is unlikely that the seller benefits from early payment. Ignoring the possibility of default by the buyer, the decision by a customer to forgo the discount almost surely works to the seller's advantage.

EXAMPLE 17.2 **What's the Rate?**

Ordinary tiles are often sold with terms of 3/30, net 60. What effective annual rate does a buyer pay by not taking the discount? What would the APR be if one were quoted?

Here we have 3 percent discount interest on $60 - 30 = 30$ days' credit. The rate per 30 days is $.03/.97 = .03093$, or 3.093%. There are $365/30 = 12.17$ such periods in a year, so the effective annual rate is:

$$EAR = 1.03093^{12.17} - 1 = .449, \text{ or } 44.9\%$$

The APR, as always, would be calculated by multiplying the rate per period by the number of periods:

$$APR = .03093 \times 12.17 = .376, \text{ or } 37.6\%$$

An interest rate calculated like this APR is often quoted as the cost of the trade credit, and, as this example illustrates, this seriously can understate the true cost.

---

credit instrument
The evidence of
indebtedness.

Credit Instruments The **credit instrument** is the basic evidence of indebtedness. Most trade credit is offered on *open account*. This means that the only formal instrument of credit is the invoice, which is sent with the shipment of goods and which the customer signs as evidence that the goods have been received. Afterwards, the firm and its customers record the exchange on their books of account.

At times, the firm may require that the customer sign a *promissory note*. This is a basic IOU and might be used when the order is large or when the firm anticipates a problem in collections. Promissory notes are uncommon, but they can eliminate possible controversies later about the existence of debt.

One problem with promissory notes is that they are signed after delivery of the goods. One way to obtain a credit commitment from a customer before the goods are delivered is to arrange a *commercial draft*. Typically, the firm draws up a commercial draft calling for the customer to pay a specific amount by a specified date. The draft is then sent to the customer's bank with the shipping invoices.

If immediate payment on the draft is required, it is called a *sight draft*. If immediate payment is not required, then the draft is a *time draft*. When the draft is presented and the buyer "accepts" it, meaning that the buyer promises to pay it in the future, then it is called a *trade acceptance* and is sent back to the selling firm. The seller then can keep the acceptance or sell it to someone else. If a bank accepts the draft, meaning that the bank is guaranteeing payment, then the draft becomes a *banker's acceptance*. This arrangement is common in international trade.

Optimal Credit Policy

In principle, the optimal amount of credit is determined by the point at which the incremental cash flows from increased sales are exactly equal to the incremental costs of carrying the increased investment in accounts receivable.

The Total Credit Cost Curve   The trade-off between granting credit and not granting credit isn't hard to identify, but it is difficult to quantify precisely. As a result, we only can describe an optimal credit policy.

To begin, the carrying costs associated with granting credit come in three forms:

1. The required return on receivables.
2. The losses from bad debts.
3. The cost of managing credit and credit collections.

We already have discussed the first and second of these. The third cost, the cost of managing credit, is the expense associated with running the credit department. Firms that don't grant credit have no such department and no such expense. These three costs all will increase as credit policy is relaxed.

If a firm has a very restrictive credit policy, then all of the above costs will be low. In this case, the firm will have a "shortage" of credit, so there will be an opportunity cost. This opportunity cost is the extra potential profit from credit sales that is lost because credit is refused. This forgone benefit comes from two sources: the increase in quantity sold and, potentially, a higher price. These costs go down as credit policy is relaxed.

The sum of the carrying costs and the opportunity costs of a particular credit policy is called the total **credit cost curve**. We have drawn such a curve in Figure 17.5. As Figure 17.5 illustrates, there is a point, C^*, where the total credit cost is minimized. This point corresponds to the optimal amount of credit, or, equivalently, the optimal investment in receivables.

credit cost curve
Graphical representation of the sum of the carrying costs and the opportunity costs of a credit policy.

If the firm extends more credit than this amount, the additional net cash flow from new customers will not cover the carrying costs of the investment in receivables. If the level of receivables is below this amount, then the firm is forgoing valuable profit opportunities.

In general, the costs and benefits from extending credit will depend on characteristics of particular firms and industries. All other things being equal, for example, it is likely that firms with (1) excess capacity, (2) low variable operating costs, and (3) repeat customers will extend credit more liberally than other firms. See if you can explain why each of these contributes to a more liberal credit policy.

Organizing the Credit Function   Firms that grant credit have the expense of running a credit department. In practice, firms often choose to contract out all or part of the credit function to a factor, an insurance company, or a captive finance company. Chapter 16 discussed factoring, an arrangement in which the firm sells its receivables. Depending on

The costs of granting credit

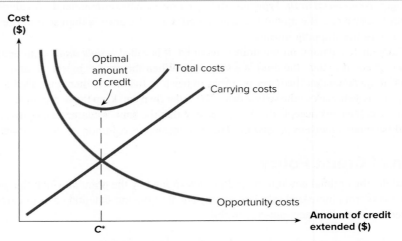

Carrying costs are the cash flows that must be incurred when credit is granted. They are positively related to the amount of credit extended.

Opportunity costs are the lost sales from refusing credit. These costs go down when credit is granted.

the specific arrangement, the factor may have full responsibility for credit checking, authorization, and collection. Smaller firms may find such an arrangement cheaper than running a credit department.

Firms that manage internal credit operations are self-insured against default, meaning that they bear all the risk of nonpayment. An alternative is to buy credit insurance through an insurance company. The insurance company offers coverage up to a preset dollar limit for accounts. As you would expect, accounts with a higher credit rating merit higher insurance limits. This type of insurance is particularly important for exporters, and government insurance is available for certain types of exports.

captive finance company
A partially or wholly owned subsidiary that handles the credit function for the parent company.

Large firms often extend credit through a **captive finance company**, which is a partially or wholly owned subsidiary that handles the credit function for the parent company. Toyota Financial Services, or TFS, is a well-known example. Toyota sells to car dealers, who in turn sell to customers. TFS finances the dealer's inventory of cars and also finances customers who buy the cars.

Credit Analysis

Thus far, we have focused on establishing credit terms. Once a firm decides to grant credit to its customers, it then must establish guidelines for determining who will and who will not be allowed to buy on credit. *Credit analysis* refers to the process of deciding whether or not to extend credit to a particular customer. It usually involves two steps: gathering relevant information and determining creditworthiness.

Credit Information   If a firm does want credit information on customers, there are a number of sources. Information sources commonly used to assess creditworthiness include the following:

1. *Financial statements.* A firm can ask a customer to supply financial statements such as balance sheets and income statements. Minimum standards and rules of thumb based

on financial ratios like the ones we discussed in Chapter 3 then can be used as a basis for extending or refusing credit.

2. *Credit reports on the customer's payment history with other firms.* Quite a few organizations sell information on the credit strength and credit history of business firms. The best-known and largest firm of this type is Dun & Bradstreet, which provides subscribers with a credit reference book and credit reports on individual firms. Experian is another well-known credit-reporting firm. Ratings and information are available for a huge number of firms, including very small ones. Equifax, TransUnion, and Experian are the major suppliers of consumer credit information.

3. *Banks.* Banks generally will provide some assistance to their business customers in acquiring information on the creditworthiness of other firms.

4. *The customer's payment history with the firm.* The most obvious way to obtain information about the likelihood of a customer's not paying is to examine whether they have settled past obligations and how quickly they have met these obligations.

> Web-surfing students should visit the Dun & Bradstreet home page— this major supplier of credit information can be found at www.dnb.com.

Credit Evaluation and Scoring There are no magical formulas for assessing the probability that a customer will not pay. In very general terms, the classic **five Cs of credit** are the basic factors to be evaluated:

> **five Cs of credit**
> The five basic credit factors to be evaluated: character, capacity, capital, collateral, and conditions.

1. *Character.* The customer's willingness to meet credit obligations.
2. *Capacity.* The customer's ability to meet credit obligations out of operating cash flows.
3. *Capital.* The customer's financial reserves.
4. *Collateral.* Assets pledged by the customer for security in case of default.
5. *Conditions.* General economic conditions in the customer's line of business.

Credit scoring refers to the process of calculating a numerical rating for a customer based on information collected; credit is then granted or refused based on the result. For example, a firm might rate a customer on a scale of 1 (very poor) to 10 (very good) on each of the five Cs of credit using all the information available about the customer. A credit score could then be calculated based on the total. From experience, a firm might choose to grant credit only to customers with a score above, say, 30.

> **credit scoring**
> The process of quantifying the probability of default when granting consumer credit.

Firms such as credit card issuers have developed elaborate statistical models for credit scoring. Usually, all of the legally relevant and observable characteristics of a large pool of customers are studied to find their historic relation to default rates. Based on the results, it is possible to determine the variables that best predict whether or not a customer will pay and then calculate a credit score based on those variables.

Because credit-scoring models and procedures determine who is and who is not creditworthy, it is not surprising that they have been the subject of government regulation. In particular, the kinds of background and demographic information that can be used in the credit decision are limited.

Collection Policy

Collection policy is the final element in credit policy. Collection policy involves monitoring receivables to spot trouble and obtaining payment on past-due accounts.

Monitoring Receivables To keep track of payments by customers, most firms will monitor outstanding accounts. First, a firm normally will keep track of its average collection period, ACP, through time. If a firm is in a seasonal business, the ACP will fluctuate during the year, but unexpected increases in the ACP are a cause for concern. Either customers in

aging schedule
A compilation of accounts receivable by the age of each account.

general are taking longer to pay, or some percentage of accounts receivable is seriously overdue.

The **aging schedule** is a second basic tool for monitoring receivables. To prepare one, the credit department classifies accounts by age.[2] Suppose a firm has $100,000 in receivables. Some of these accounts are only a few days old, but others have been outstanding for quite some time. The following is an example of an aging schedule.

Aging Schedule		
Age of Account	**Amount**	**Percentage of Total Value of Accounts Receivable**
0–10 days	$ 50,000	50%
11–60 days	25,000	25
61–80 days	20,000	20
Over 80 days	5,000	5
	$100,000	100%

If this firm has a credit period of 60 days, then 25 percent of its accounts are late. Whether or not this is a serious problem depends on the nature of the firm's collections and customers. It is often the case that accounts beyond a certain age are almost never collected. Monitoring the age of accounts is very important in such cases.

Firms with seasonal sales will find the percentages on the aging schedule changing during the year. For example, if sales in the current month are very high, then total receivables also will increase sharply. This means that the older accounts, as a percentage of total receivables, become smaller and might appear less important. Some firms have refined the aging schedule so that they have an idea of how it should change with peaks and valleys in their sales.

Collection Effort   A firm usually goes through the following sequence of procedures for customers whose payments are overdue:

1. It sends out a delinquency letter informing the customer of the past-due status of the account.
2. It makes a telephone call to the customer.
3. It employs a collection agency.
4. It takes legal action against the customer.

At times, a firm may refuse to grant additional credit to customers until arrearages are cleared up. This may antagonize a normally good customer, and it points to a potential conflict of interest between the collections department and the sales department.

CONCEPT QUESTIONS

17.3a   What are the basic components of credit policy?

17.3b   Explain what terms of "3/45, net 90" mean. What is the effective interest rate?

17.3c   What are the five *C*s of credit?

---

[2]Aging schedules are used elsewhere in business. For example, aging schedules often are prepared for inventory items.

17.4 INVENTORY MANAGEMENT

Like receivables, inventories represent a significant investment for many firms. For a typical manufacturing operation, inventories often will exceed 15 percent of assets. For a retailer, inventories could represent more than 25 percent of assets. From our discussion in Chapter 16, we know that a firm's operating cycle is made up of its inventory period and its receivables period. This is one reason for considering credit and inventory policy in the same chapter. Beyond this, both credit and inventory policies are used to drive sales, and the two must be coordinated to ensure that the process of acquiring inventory, selling it, and collecting on the sale proceeds smoothly. For example, changes in credit policy designed to stimulate sales must be simultaneously accompanied by planning for adequate inventory.

Visit the Society for Inventory Management Benchmarking Analysis at www.simba.org.

The Financial Manager and Inventory Policy

Despite the size of a typical firm's investment in inventories, the financial manager of a firm normally will not have primary control over inventory management. Instead, other functional areas such as purchasing, production, and marketing usually will share decision-making authority. Inventory management has become an increasingly important specialty in its own right, and financial management often only will have input into the decision. However, inventory policy can have dramatic financial effects. We therefore survey some basics of inventory and inventory policy in the sections ahead.

Inventory Types

For a manufacturer, inventory normally is classified into one of three categories. The first category is *raw material*. This is whatever the firm uses as a starting point in its production process. Raw materials might be something as basic as iron ore for a steel manufacturer or something as sophisticated as disk drives for a computer manufacturer.

The second type of inventory is *work-in-progress*, which is what the name suggests—unfinished product. How big this portion of inventory is depends in large part on the length of the production process. For an airframe manufacturer, for example, work-in-progress can be substantial. The third and final type of inventory is *finished goods*, that is, products ready to ship or sell.

There are three things to keep in mind concerning inventory types. First, the names for the different types can be a little misleading because one company's raw materials could be another's finished goods. For example, going back to our steel manufacturer, iron ore would be a raw material, and steel would be the final product. An auto body panel stamping operation will have steel as its raw material and auto body panels as its finished goods, and an automobile assembler will have body panels as raw materials and automobiles as finished products.

The second thing to keep in mind is that the various types of inventory can be quite different in terms of their liquidity. Raw materials that are commodity-like or relatively standardized can be easy to convert to cash. Work-in-progress, on the other hand, can be quite illiquid and have little more than scrap value. As always, the liquidity of finished goods depends on the nature of the product.

Finally, a very important distinction between finished goods and other types of inventories is that the demand for an inventory item that becomes a part of another item usually is termed *derived*, or *dependent*, *demand* because the firm's need for these inventory types depends on its need for finished items. In contrast, the firm's demand for finished goods is not derived from demand for other inventory items, so it is sometimes said to be *independent*.

Inventory Costs

As we discussed in Chapter 16, there are two basic types of costs associated with current assets in general and with inventory in particular. The first of these are *carrying costs*. Here, carrying costs represent all of the direct and opportunity costs of keeping inventory on hand. These include:

1. Storage and tracking costs.
2. Insurance and taxes.
3. Losses due to obsolescence, deterioration, or theft.
4. The opportunity cost of capital for the invested amount.

The sum of these costs can be substantial, roughly ranging from 20 to 40 percent of inventory value per year.

The other types of costs associated with inventory are *shortage costs*. These are costs associated with having inadequate inventory on hand. The two components of shortage costs are restocking costs and costs related to safety reserves. Depending on the firm's business, order, or restocking, costs are either the costs of placing an order with suppliers or the cost of setting up a production run. The costs related to safety reserves are opportunity losses such as lost sales and loss of customer goodwill that result from having inadequate inventory.

A basic trade-off in inventory management exists because carrying costs increase with inventory levels while shortage, or restocking, costs decline with inventory levels. The basic goal of inventory management thus is to minimize the sum of these two costs. We consider ways to reach this goal in the next section.

CONCEPT QUESTIONS

17.4a   What are the different types of inventory?

17.4b   What are three things to remember when examining inventory types?

17.4c   What is the basic goal of inventory management?

17.5 INVENTORY MANAGEMENT TECHNIQUES

As we described earlier, the goal of inventory management is usually framed as cost minimization. Three techniques are discussed in this section, ranging from the relatively simple to the very complex.

The ABC Approach

The ABC approach is a simple approach to inventory management where the basic idea is to divide inventory into three (or more) groups. The underlying rationale is that a small portion of inventory in terms of quantity might represent a large portion in terms of inventory value. For example, this situation would exist for a manufacturer that uses some relatively expensive, high-tech components and some relatively inexpensive basic materials in producing its products.[3]

Figure 17.6 illustrates an ABC comparison of items in terms of the percentage of inventory value represented by each group versus the percentage of items represented. As Figure 17.6 shows, the A Group constitutes only 10 percent of inventory by item count, but it represents

---

[3]The ABC approach to inventory should not be confused with activity-based costing, a common topic in managerial accounting.

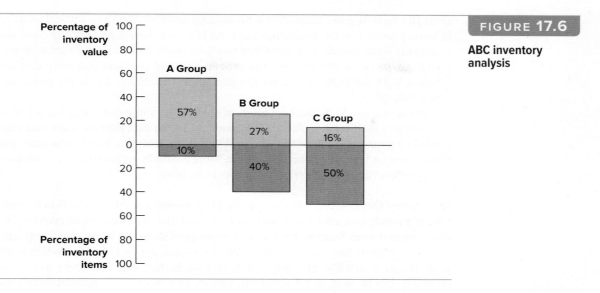

FIGURE **17.6**

ABC inventory analysis

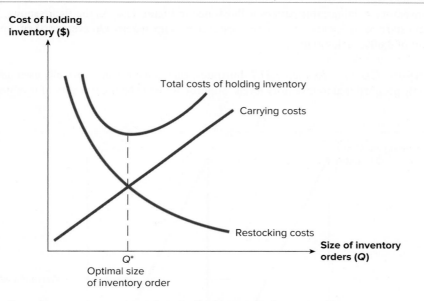

FIGURE **17.7**

Costs of holding inventory

Restocking costs are greatest when the firm holds a small quantity of inventory.
Carrying costs are greatest when there is a large quantity of inventory on hand.
Total costs are the sum of the carrying and restocking costs.

over half of the value of inventory. The A Group items are thus monitored closely, and inventory levels are kept relatively low. At the other end, basic inventory items, such as nuts and bolts, also will exist, but because these are crucial and inexpensive, large quantities are ordered and kept on hand. These would be C Group items. The B Group is made up of in-between items.

The Economic Order Quantity Model

The **economic order quantity,** or **EOQ,** model is the best-known approach to explicitly establishing an optimal inventory level. The basic idea is illustrated in Figure 17.7, which

economic order quantity (EOQ)
The restocking quantity that minimizes the total inventory costs.

plots the various costs associated with holding inventory (on the vertical axis) against inventory levels (on the horizontal axis). As is shown, inventory carrying costs rise and restocking costs decrease as inventory levels increase. From our discussion of the total credit cost curve in this chapter, the general shape of the total inventory cost curve is familiar. With the EOQ model, we will attempt to specifically locate the minimum total cost point, Q^*.

In our discussion below, an important point to keep in mind is that the actual cost of the inventory itself is not included. The reason is that the *total* amount of inventory the firm needs in a given year is dictated by sales. What we are analyzing here is how much the firm should have on hand at any particular time. More precisely, we are trying to determine what order size the firm should use when it restocks its inventory.

Inventory Depletion   To develop the EOQ, we will assume that the firm's inventory is sold at a steady rate until it hits zero. At that point, the firm restocks its inventory back to some optimal level. Suppose the Eyssell Corporation starts out today with 3,600 units of a particular item in inventory. Annual sales of this item are 46,800 units, which is 900 per week. If Eyssell sells 900 units in inventory each week, then, after four weeks, all the available inventory will be sold, and Eyssell will restock by ordering (or manufacturing) another 3,600 and will start over. This selling and restocking process produces a sawtooth pattern for inventory holdings; this pattern is illustrated in Figure 17.8. As the figure shows, Eyssell always starts with 3,600 units in inventory and ends up at zero. On average, then, inventory is half of 3,600, or 1,800 units.

Carrying Costs   As Figure 17.7 illustrates, carrying costs are normally assumed to be directly proportional to inventory levels. Suppose we let Q be the quantity of inventory that

FIGURE 17.8

Inventory holdings for the Eyssell Corporation

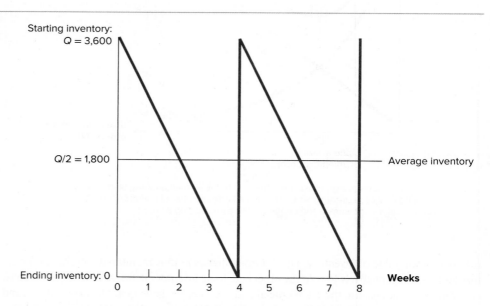

The Eyssell Corporation starts with inventory of 3,600 units. The quantity drops to zero by the end of the fourth week. The average inventory is $Q/2 = 3,600/2 = 1,800$ over the period.

Eyssell orders each time (3,600 units); we will call this the restocking quantity. Average inventory would then be $Q/2$, or 1,800 units. If we let CC be the carrying cost per unit per year, Eyssell's total carrying costs will be:

Total carrying costs = Average inventory × Carrying costs per unit   [17.1]
= (Q/2) × CC

In Eyssell's case, if carrying costs were $.75 per unit per year, then total carrying costs would be the average inventory of 1,800 multiplied by $.75, or $1,350 per year.

Shortage Costs   For now, we will focus only on the restocking costs. In essence, we will assume that the firm never actually runs short on inventory, so that costs relating to safety reserves are not important. We return to this issue later.

Restocking costs are normally assumed to be fixed. In other words, every time we place an order, there are fixed costs associated with that order (remember that the cost of the inventory itself is not considered here). Suppose we let T be the firm's total unit sales per year. If the firm orders Q units each time, then it will need to place a total of T/Q orders. For Eyssell, annual sales were 46,800, and the order size was 3,600. Eyssell thus places a total of $46,800/3,600 = 13$ orders per year. If the fixed cost per order is F, the total restocking cost for the year would be:

Total restocking cost = Fixed cost per order × Number of orders   [17.2]
= F × (T/Q)

For Eyssell, order costs might be $50 per order, so the total restocking cost for 13 orders would be $50 × 13 = $650 per year.

Total Costs   The total costs associated with holding inventory are the sum of the carrying costs and the restocking costs:

Total costs = Carrying costs + Restocking costs   [17.3]
= (Q/2) × CC + F × (T/Q)

Our goal is to find the value of Q, the restocking quantity, that minimizes this cost. To see how we might go about this, we can calculate total costs for some different values of Q. For the Eyssell Corporation, we had carrying costs (CC) of $.75 per unit per year, fixed costs (F) of $50 per order, and total unit sales (T) of 46,800 units. With these numbers, some possible total costs are (check some of these for practice):

Restocking Quantity (Q)	Total Carrying Costs (Q/2 × CC)	+	Restocking Costs (F × T/Q)	=	Total Costs
500	$ 187.5		$4,680.0		$4,867.5
1,000	375.0		2,340.0		2,715.0
1,500	562.5		1,560.0		2,122.5
2,000	750.0		1,170.0		1,920.0
2,500	**937.5**		**936.0**		**1,873.5**
3,000	1,125.0		780.0		1,905.0
3,500	1,312.5		668.6		1,981.1

Inspecting the numbers, we see that total costs start out at almost $5,000, and they decline to just under $1,900. The cost-minimizing quantity appears to be approximately 2,500.

To find the precise cost-minimizing quantity, we can take a look back at Figure 17.7. What we notice is that the minimum point occurs right where the two lines cross. At this point, carrying costs and restocking costs are the same. For the particular types of costs we have assumed here, this always will be true, so we can find the minimum point by setting these costs equal to each other and solving for Q^*:

$$\text{Carrying costs} = \text{Restocking costs} \qquad\qquad\qquad \text{[17.4]}$$
$$(Q^*/2) \times CC = F \times (T/Q^*)$$

With a little algebra, we get:

$$(Q^*)^2 = \frac{2T \times F}{CC} \qquad\qquad\qquad \text{[17.5]}$$

To solve for Q^*, we take the square root of both sides to find:

$$Q^* = \sqrt{\frac{2T \times F}{CC}} \qquad\qquad\qquad \text{[17.6]}$$

This reorder quantity, which minimizes the total inventory cost, is called the economic order quantity. For the Eyssell Corporation, the EOQ is:

$$
\begin{aligned}
Q^* &= \sqrt{\frac{2T \times F}{CC}} \\
&= \sqrt{\frac{(2 \times 46,800) \times \$50}{.75}} \\
&= \sqrt{6,240,000} \\
&= 2,498 \text{ units}
\end{aligned}
$$

Thus, for Eyssell, the economic order quantity is actually 2,498 units. At this level, verify that the restocking costs and carrying costs are identical (they're both $936.75).

EXAMPLE 17.3   **Carrying Costs**

Thiewes Shoes begins each period with 100 pairs of hiking boots in stock. This stock is depleted each period and reordered. If the carrying cost per pair of boots per year is $3, what are the total carrying costs for the hiking boots?

Inventories always start at 100 items and end up at 0, so average inventory is 50 items. At an annual cost of $3 per item, total carrying costs are $150.

EXAMPLE 17.4   **Restocking Costs**

In Example 17.3, suppose Thiewes sells a total of 600 pairs of boots in a year. How many times per year does Thiewes restock? Suppose the restocking cost is $20 per order. What are total restocking costs?

Thiewes orders 100 items each time. Total sales are 600 items per year, so Thiewes restocks six times per year, or about every two months. The restocking costs would be 6 orders × $20 per order = $120.

EXAMPLE 17.5	The EOQ

Based on our previous two examples, what size orders should Thiewes place to minimize costs? How often will Thiewes restock? What are the total carrying and restocking costs? The total costs?

We have that the total number of pairs of boots ordered for the year (T) is 600. The restocking cost (F) is $20 per order, and the carrying cost (CC) is $3. We can calculate the EOQ for Thiewes as follows:

$$EOQ = \sqrt{\frac{2T \times F}{CC}}$$

$$= \sqrt{\frac{(2 \times 600) \times \$20}{\$3}}$$

$$= \sqrt{8,000}$$

$$= 89.44 \text{ units}$$

Because Thiewes sells 600 pairs per year, it will restock $600/89.44 = 6.71$ times. The total restocking costs will be $\$20 \times 6.71 = \$134.16$. Average inventory will be $89.44/2 = 44.72$. The carrying costs will be $\$3 \times 44.72 = \$134.16$, the same as the restocking costs. The total costs are thus $268.33.

Extensions to the EOQ Model

Thus far, we have assumed that a company will let its inventory run down to zero and then reorder. In reality, a company will wish to reorder before its inventory goes to zero for two reasons. First, by always having at least some inventory on hand, the firm minimizes the risk of a stockout and the resulting losses of sales and customers. Second, when a firm does reorder, there will be some time lag before the inventory arrives. Thus, to finish our discussion of the EOQ, we consider two extensions: safety stocks and reorder points.

Safety Stocks   A *safety stock* is the minimum level of inventory that a firm keeps on hand. Inventories are reordered whenever the level of inventory falls to the safety stock level. Part A of Figure 17.9 illustrates how a safety stock can be incorporated into an EOQ model. Notice that adding a safety stock means that the firm does not run its inventory all the way down to zero. Other than this, the situation here is identical to that considered in our earlier discussion of the EOQ.

Reorder Points   To allow for delivery time, a firm will place orders before inventories reach a critical level. The *reorder points* are the times at which the firm will actually place its inventory orders. These points are illustrated in Part B of Figure 17.9. As is shown, the reorder points occur some fixed number of days (or weeks or months) before inventories are projected to reach zero.

One of the reasons that a firm will keep a safety stock is to allow for uncertain delivery times. We therefore can combine our reorder point and safety stock discussions in Part C of Figure 17.9. The result is a generalized EOQ model in which the firm orders in advance of anticipated needs and also keeps a safety stock of inventory to guard against unforeseen fluctuations in demand and delivery times.

Managing Derived-Demand Inventories

A third type of inventory management technique is used to manage derived-demand inventories. As we described previously, demand for some inventory types is derived from, or dependent on, other inventory needs. A good example is given by the auto manufacturing industry, where the demand for finished products derives from consumer demand, marketing programs, and other factors related to projected unit sales. The demand for inventory

FIGURE **17.9**

Safety stocks and reorder points

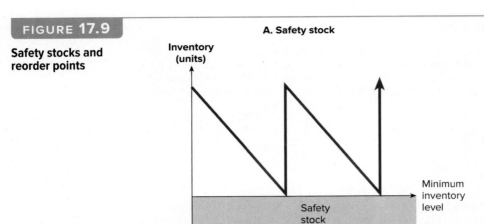

A. Safety stock

With a safety stock, the firm reorders when inventory reaches a minimum level.

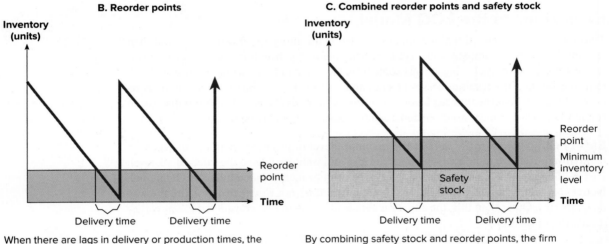

B. Reorder points

When there are lags in delivery or production times, the firm reorders when inventory reaches the reorder point.

C. Combined reorder points and safety stock

By combining safety stock and reorder points, the firm maintains a buffer against unforeseen events.

items such as tires, batteries, headlights, and other components is then completely determined by the number of autos planned. Materials requirements planning and just-in-time inventory management are two methods for managing demand-dependent inventories.

materials requirements planning (MRP)

A set of procedures used to determine inventory levels for demand-dependent inventory types, such as work-in-progress and raw materials.

Materials Requirements Planning Production and inventory specialists have developed computer-based systems for ordering and/or scheduling production of demand-dependent types of inventories. These systems fall under the general heading of **materials requirements planning (MRP)**. The basic idea behind MRP is that, once finished goods inventory levels are set, it is possible to determine what levels of work-in-progress inventories must exist to meet the need for finished goods. From there, it is possible to calculate the quantity of raw materials that must be on hand. This ability to schedule backwards from finished goods inventories stems from the dependent nature of work-in-progress and raw materials inventories. MRP is particularly important for complicated products for which a variety of components are needed to create the finished product.

Supply Chain Management

JIT inventory has been widely adopted because of the potential savings in inventory. And JIT inventory systems have led to the increased importance of supply chain management (SCM). SCM deals with all movement and storage of raw materials, work-in-process inventory, and finished goods from the raw material phase until the point of sale. Because JIT relies on little or no inventory, SCM is critical, especially when there is a disruption in the flow of raw materials necessary for production.

In March 2011, the powerful earthquake and resulting tsunami in Japan caused tremendous damage locally, but the supply chain effects were felt around the world. For example, less than a week after the earthquake, a GM plant in Shreveport, Louisiana, was forced to shut down entirely because of a shortage in a single part that was supplied from a Japanese manufacturer. GM also was forced to slow down production in its Tonawanda, New York, engine plant less than a week later.

Other companies and industries were affected as well. For example, Toyota shut down its 13 U.S. plants temporarily,

and John Deere announced that it was delaying delivery of excavators and mining equipment. Even domestic Japanese companies weren't immune from supply chain problems. Famed camera maker Canon was forced to halt production at its Japanese plants because of parts shortages, not earthquake-related damages.

While natural catastrophes can be one cause of SCM problems, smaller events also can have a dramatic impact. For example, in May 2018, a fire occurred at the Meridian Magnesium Products plant in Eaton Rapids, Michigan. This plant produces die-cast parts for the auto industry. Ford was the hardest hit as the plant made parts for Ford's highly profitable F-150 pickup truck. As a result of the parts shortage caused by the fire, Ford was forced to idle the company's Missouri plant, sending 3,600 workers home. Other auto manufactures also were affected as General Motors shut down production of its full-size van production lines at its Missouri plant and Fiat Chrysler was forced to adjust the production schedule at its Windsor, Ontario, plant.

Just-in-Time Inventory   Just-in-time, or JIT, inventory is a modern approach to managing dependent inventories. The goal of JIT is essentially to minimize such inventories, thereby maximizing turnover. The approach began in Japan, and it is a fundamental part of much of Japanese manufacturing philosophy. As the name suggests, the basic goal of JIT is to have only enough inventory on hand to meet immediate production needs.

The result of the JIT system is that inventories are reordered and restocked frequently. Making such a system work and avoiding shortages require a high degree of cooperation among suppliers. Japanese manufacturers often have a relatively small, tightly integrated group of suppliers with whom they work closely to achieve the needed coordination. These suppliers are a part of a large manufacturer's (such as Toyota's) industrial group, or *keiretsu*. Each large manufacturer tends to have its own *keiretsu*. It also helps to have suppliers located nearby, a situation that is common in Japan.

The *kanban* is an integral part of a JIT inventory system, and JIT systems are sometimes called *kanban systems*. The literal meaning of *kanban* is "card" or "sign," but, broadly speaking, a kanban is a signal to a supplier to send more inventory. For example, a kanban literally could be a card attached to a bin of parts. When a worker pulls that bin, the card is detached and routed back to the supplier, who then supplies a replacement bin.

A JIT inventory system is an important part of a larger production planning process. A full discussion of it would necessarily shift our focus away from finance to production and operations management, so we will leave it here. The nearby *Finance Matters* box discusses some of the potential problems with a JIT inventory system.

just-in-time (JIT) inventory
A system for managing demand-dependent inventories that minimizes inventory holdings.

CONCEPT QUESTIONS

17.5a   What does the EOQ model determine for the firm?

17.5b   Which cost component of the EOQ model does JIT inventory minimize?

SUMMARY AND CONCLUSIONS

This chapter has covered cash, receivables, and inventory management. Along the way, we have touched on a large number of subjects. Some of the more important issues we examined are:

1. Firms seek to manage their cash by keeping no more than is needed on hand. The reason is that holding cash has an opportunity cost, namely, the returns that could be earned by investing the money.

2. Float is an important consideration in cash management, and firms seek to manage collections and disbursements in ways designed to optimize the firm's net float.

3. A firm's credit policy includes the terms of sale, credit analysis, and collection policy. The terms of sale cover three related subjects: credit period, cash discount, and credit instrument.

4. The optimal credit policy for a firm depends on many specific factors, but generally involves trading off the costs of granting credit, such as the carrying costs of receivables and the possibility of nonpayment, against the benefits in terms of increased sales.

5. There are different types of inventories that differ greatly in their liquidity and management. The basic trade-off in inventory management is the cost of carrying inventory versus the cost of restocking. We developed the famous EOQ model, which explicitly balances these costs.

6. Firms use different inventory management techniques; we described a few of the better known, including the ABC approach and just-in-time, or JIT, inventory management.

connect POP QUIZ!

Can you answer the following questions? If your class is using Connect, log on to SmartBook to see if you know the answers to these and other questions, check out the study tools, and find out what topics require additional practice!

Section 17.2 What are the components of total collection time?

Section 17.3 What are the components of credit policy?

Section 17.4 What are shortage costs?

Section 17.5 If the reorder quantity Q equals 4,000 units and carrying costs are $2.00 per unit per year, what will the total annual carrying costs be?

CHAPTER REVIEW AND SELF-TEST PROBLEMS

17.1 **Calculating Float**   You have $10,000 on deposit with no outstanding checks or uncleared deposits. One day you write a check for $4,000 and then deposit a check for $3,000. What are your disbursement, collection, and net floats? (See Problem 3.)

17.2 The EOQ Heusen Computer Manufacturing starts each period with 4,000 central processing units (CPUs) in stock. This stock is depleted each month and reordered. If the carrying cost per CPU is $1 and the fixed order cost is $10, is Heusen following an economically advisable strategy? (See Problem 13.)

■ Answers to Chapter Review and Self-Test Problems

17.1 First, after you write the check for $4,000, you show a balance of $6,000. However, while the check is clearing, your bank shows a balance of $10,000. This is a $4,000 disbursement float, and it is good for you. Next, when you deposit the $3,000, you show a balance of $9,000, but your account will not be credited for the $3,000 until it clears. This is a −$3,000 collection float, and it is bad for you.

The sum of the disbursement float and the collection float is your net float of $1,000. In other words, you show a balance of $9,000, but your bank shows a $10,000 balance, so, in net terms, you are benefiting from the float.

17.2 We can answer by first calculating Heusen's carrying and restocking costs. The average inventory is 2,000 CPUs, and, because the carrying costs are $1 per CPU, total carrying costs are $2,000. Heusen restocks every month at a fixed order cost of $10, so the total restocking costs are $120. What we see is that carrying costs are large relative to reorder costs, so Heusen is carrying too much inventory.

To determine the optimal inventory policy, we can use the EOQ model. Because Heusen orders 4,000 CPUs 12 times per year, total needs (T) are 48,000 CPUs. The fixed order cost is $10, and the carrying cost per unit (CC) is $1. The EOQ is therefore:

$$EOQ = \sqrt{\frac{2T \times F}{CC}}$$
$$= \sqrt{\frac{(2 \times 48,000) \times \$10}{\$1}}$$
$$= \sqrt{960,000}$$
$$= 979.80 \text{ units}$$

We can check this by noting that, at the EOQ, the average inventory is about 490 CPUs, so the carrying cost is $490. Heusen will have to reorder $48,000/979.8 = 49$ times. The fixed order cost is $10, so the total restocking cost is also $490.

CRITICAL THINKING AND CONCEPTS REVIEW

LO 1 **17.1 Cash Management** Is it possible for a firm to have too much cash? Why would shareholders care if a firm accumulates large amounts of cash?

LO 1 **17.2 Cash Management** What options are available to a firm if it believes it has too much cash? How about too little?

LO 1 **17.3 Agency Issues** Are stockholders and creditors likely to agree on how much cash a firm should keep on hand?

LO 1 **17.4 Motivations for Holding Cash** In the chapter opening, we discussed the cash positions of several companies. Automobile manufacturers also have enormous cash reserves. In the middle of 2018, Ford Motor Co. had about $27.5 billion in cash, General Motors had about $17.2 billion, and Toyota had about $53.8 billion. Why would firms such as these hold such large quantities of cash?

LO 1   **17.5**   **Short-Term Investments**   Why is a preferred stock with a dividend tied to short-term interest rates an attractive short-term investment for corporations with excess cash?

LO 2   **17.6**   **Collection and Disbursement Floats**   Which would a firm prefer: a net collection float or a net disbursement float? Why?

LO 1   **17.7**   **Float**   Suppose a firm has a book balance of $2 million. At the automatic teller machine (ATM), the cash manager finds out that the bank balance is $2.5 million. What is the situation here? If this is an ongoing situation, what ethical dilemma arises?

LO 1   **17.8**   **Short-Term Investments**   For each of the short-term marketable securities given here, provide an example of the potential disadvantages the investment has for meeting a corporation's cash management goals.

    a.   U.S. Treasury bills

    b.   Ordinary preferred stock

    c.   Negotiable certificates of deposit (NCDs)

    d.   Commercial paper

LO 1   **17.9**   **Agency Issues**   It is sometimes argued that excess cash held by a firm can aggravate agency problems (discussed in Chapter 1) and, more generally, reduce incentives for shareholder wealth maximization. How would you frame the issue here?

LO 1   **17.10**   **Use of Excess Cash**   One option a firm usually has with any excess cash is to pay its suppliers more quickly. What are the advantages and disadvantages of this use of excess cash?

LO 1   **17.11**   **Use of Excess Cash**   Another option usually available for dealing with excess cash is to reduce the firm's outstanding debt. What are the advantages and disadvantages of this use of excess cash?

LO 1   **17.12**   **Float**   An unfortunately common practice goes like this: (*Warning:* Don't try this at home.) Suppose you are out of money in your checking account; however, your local grocery store, as a convenience to you as a customer, will cash a check for you. So you cash a check for $200. Of course, this check will bounce unless you do something. To prevent this, you go to the grocery the next day and cash another check for $200. You take this $200 and deposit it. You repeat this process every day, and, in doing so, you make sure that no checks bounce. Eventually, manna from heaven arrives (perhaps in the form of money from home) and you are able to cover your outstanding checks.

    To make it interesting, suppose you are absolutely certain that no checks will bounce along the way. Assuming this is true, and ignoring any question of legality (what we have described is probably illegal check kiting), is there anything unethical about this? If you say yes, then why? In particular, who is harmed?

LO 2   **17.13**   **Credit Instruments**   Describe each of the following:

    a.   Sight draft

    b.   Time draft

    c.   Banker's acceptance

    d.   Promissory note

    e.   Trade acceptance

LO 2 **17.14** **Trade Credit Forms**   In what form is trade credit most commonly offered? What is the credit instrument in this case?

LO 2 **17.15** **Receivables Costs**   What are the costs associated with carrying receivables? What are the costs associated with not granting credit? What do we call the sum of the costs for different levels of receivables?

LO 2 **17.16** **Five Cs of Credit**   What are the five Cs of credit? Explain why each is important.

LO 2 **17.17** **Credit Period Length**   What are some of the factors that determine the length of the credit period? Why is the length of the buyer's operating cycle often considered an upper bound on the length of the credit period?

LO 2 **17.18** **Credit Period Length**   In each of the following pairings, indicate which firm would probably have a longer credit period and explain your reasoning.

    a. Firm A sells a miracle cure for baldness; Firm B sells toupees.

    b. Firm A specializes in products for landlords; Firm B specializes in products for renters.

    c. Firm A sells to customers with an inventory turnover of 10 times; Firm B sells to customers with an inventory turnover of 20 times.

    d. Firm A sells fresh fruit; Firm B sells canned fruit.

    e. Firm A sells and installs carpeting; Firm B sells rugs.

LO 3 **17.19** **Inventory Types**   What are the different inventory types? How do the types differ? Why are some types said to have dependent demand whereas other types are said to have independent demand?

LO 3 **17.20** **Just-in-Time Inventory**   If a company moves to a JIT inventory management system, what will happen to inventory turnover? What will happen to total asset turnover? What will happen to return on equity, ROE? (*Hint:* Remember the DuPont equation from Chapter 3.)

QUESTIONS AND PROBLEMS

connect   Select problems are available in McGraw-Hill *Connect*. Please see the packaging options section of the Preface for more information.

BASIC (Questions 1–14)

LO 1 **1.** **Calculating Float**   You have $85,000 on deposit with no outstanding checks or uncleared deposits. One day you write a check for $21,600. Does this create a disbursement float or a collection float? What is your available balance? Book balance?

LO 1 **2.** **Calculating Float**   You have $11,900 on deposit with no outstanding checks or uncleared deposits. If you deposit a check for $2,200, does this create a disbursement float or a collection float? What is your available balance? Book balance?

LO 1 **3.** **Calculating Float**   You have $21,400 on deposit with no outstanding checks or uncleared deposits. One day you write a check for $4,300 and then deposit a check for $4,900. What are your disbursement, collection, and net floats?

LO 2   **4. Cash Discounts**   You place an order for 560 units of Good X at a unit price of $67. The supplier offers terms of 1/10, net 30.

     a.   How long do you have to pay before the account is overdue? If you take the full period, how much should you remit?

     b.   What is the discount being offered? How quickly must you pay to get the discount? If you do take the discount, how much should you remit?

     c.   If you don't take the discount, how much interest are you paying implicitly? How many days' credit are you receiving?

LO 1   **5. Calculating Float**   In a typical month, the Pier Corporation receives 100 checks totaling $57,400. These are delayed three days on average. What is the average daily float? Assume 30 days in a month.

LO 1   **6. Calculating Net Float**   Each business day, on average, a company writes checks totaling $26,700 to pay its suppliers. The usual clearing time for the checks is four days. Meanwhile, the company is receiving payments from its customers each day, in the form of checks, totaling $39,600. The cash from the payments is available to the firm after two days.

     a.   Calculate the company's disbursement float, collection float, and net float.

     b.   How would your answer to part (a) change if the collected funds were available in one day instead of two?

LO 2   **7. Size of Accounts Receivable**   Essence of Skunk Fragrances, Ltd., sells 6,700 units of its perfume collection each year at a price per unit of $215. All sales are on credit with terms of 1/10, net 30. The discount is taken by 60 percent of the customers. What is the amount of the company's accounts receivable? In reaction to sales by its main competitor, Sewage Spray, Essence of Skunk is considering a change in its credit policy to terms of 3/10, net 30 to preserve its market share. How will this change in policy affect accounts receivable?

LO 2   **8. Size of Accounts Receivable**   The Malibu Corporation has annual credit sales of $29.5 million. The average collection period is 34 days. What is the average investment in accounts receivable as shown on the balance sheet?

LO 2   **9. ACP and Accounts Receivable**   Miyagi Data, Inc., sells earnings forecasts for Japanese securities. Its credit terms are 1/10, net 30. Based on experience, 65 percent of all customers will take the discount.

     a.   What is the average collection period?

     b.   If the company sells 1,100 forecasts every month at a price of $1,950 each, what is its average balance sheet amount in accounts receivable?

LO 2   **10. Size of Accounts Receivable**   Four Doors Down, Inc., has weekly credit sales of $36,500, and the average collection period is 31 days. What is the company's average accounts receivable figure?

LO 2   **11. Terms of Sale**   A firm offers terms of 1/10, net 30. What effective annual interest rate does the firm earn when a customer does not take the discount? Without doing any calculations, explain what will happen to this effective rate if:

     a.   The discount is changed to 2 percent.

     b.   The credit period is increased to 40 days.

     c.   The discount period is decreased to 20 days.

     d.   What is the EAR for each scenario?

LO 2 **12. ACP and Receivables Turnover** Rose, Inc., has an average collection period of 29 days. Its average daily investment in receivables is $91,300. What are annual credit sales? What is the receivables turnover?

LO 3 **13. EOQ** Clap Off Manufacturing uses 975 switch assemblies per week and then reorders another 975. If the relevant carrying cost per switch assembly is $6.25 and the fixed order cost is $430, is the company's inventory policy optimal? Why or why not?

LO 3 **14. EOQ** The Trektronics store begins each month with 735 phasers in stock. This stock is depleted each month and reordered. If the carrying cost per phaser is $26 per year and the fixed order cost is $365, what is the total carrying cost? What is the restocking cost? Should the company increase or decrease its order size? Describe an optimal inventory policy for the company in terms of order size and order frequency.

INTERMEDIATE (Question 15)

LO 3 **15. EOQ Derivation** Prove that when carrying costs and restocking costs are as described in the chapter, the EOQ must occur at the point where the carrying costs and restocking costs are equal.

CHALLENGE (Question 16)

LO 3 **16. Safety Stocks and Order Points** Saché, Inc., expects to sell 700 of its designer suits every week. The store is open seven days a week and expects to sell the same number of suits every day. The company has an EOQ of 500 suits and a safety stock of 100 suits. Once an order is placed, it takes three days for Saché to get the suits in. How many orders does the company place per year? Assume that it is Monday morning before the store opens, and a shipment of suits has just arrived. When will Saché place its next order?

17.1 Commercial Paper Chevron sells commercial paper to interested institutional investors. Go to the Chevron website at www.chevron.com to find information on Chevron's commercial paper. What is the credit rating for Chevron's commercial paper? What is the minimum size Chevron will sell? What size does it require for one- to four-day commercial paper?

17.2 Commercial Paper Rates What were the highest and lowest historical interest rates for commercial paper? Go to www.stlouisfed.org, find the "FRED®" data link, then the "Interest Rates" link. What were the highest and lowest interest rates for one-, two-, and three-month AA nonfinancial commercial paper? What about for financial commercial paper? Did these occur at the same time? Why might the nonfinancial and financial commercial paper rates be different?

WHAT'S ON THE WEB?

CHAPTER CASE
Piepkorn Manufacturing Working Capital Management, Part 2

After completing the short-term financial plan for next year (at the end of Chapter 16), Gary Piepkorn approaches you and asks about the company's credit policy. In looking at the competition, most companies in the industry offer credit to customers, so Piepkorn Manufacturing appears to be one of the few companies that does not. Several customers have expressed the possibility of changing to a different supplier because of the lack of credit. Gary is interested in knowing how implementing a credit policy will affect the short-term financial plan for next year. Additionally, he would like you to inquire as to the possibility of getting improved credit terms for the company's purchases.

To analyze the possible switch to the new credit terms, Gary has asked you to investigate industry standard credit terms and rework the short-term financial plan assuming Piepkorn Manufacturing offers credit to its customers. He also would like to investigate how better credit terms from the company's suppliers would affect the short-term financial plan.

QUESTIONS

1. You have looked at the credit policy offered by your competitors and have determined that the industry standard credit policy is 1/10, net 45. The discount will begin to be offered on the first day of the year. You want to examine how this credit policy would affect the cash budget and short-term financial plan. If this credit policy is implemented, you believe that 60 percent of customers will take advantage of the credit offer and the accounts receivable period will be 24 days. Rework the cash budget and short-term financial plan under the new credit policy and a target cash balance of $80,000. What interest rate are you effectively offering customers?

2. You have talked to the company's suppliers about the credit terms Piepkorn receives. Currently, the company receives terms of net 45. Your suppliers have stated that they would offer new credit terms of 2/25, net 40. The discount would begin to be offered on the first day of the year. What interest rate are the suppliers offering the company? Rework your cash budget and short-term financial plan from the previous question assuming you take advantage of the discount offered.

18 | International Aspects of Financial Management

In Chapter 17, we mentioned the cash balances held by several large companies, but we didn't mention that much of that cash was held overseas. For example, Apple led the way with over $250 billion in overseas cash, followed by Microsoft ($130 billion) and Alphabet ($94 billion). Before 2018, companies like Apple had a strong tax incentive to keep huge cash hoards outside the United States. All of that changed with the signing of the Tax Cuts and Jobs Act of 2017, which ushered in big changes in the way U.S. corporations are taxed on their overseas operations. In this chapter, we discuss this topic, along with the important roles played by currencies, exchange rates, and other features of the international finance landscape.

As businesses of all types have increased their reliance on international operations, all areas of business have been strongly affected. Human resources, production, marketing, accounting, and strategy, for example, all become much more complex when nondomestic considerations come into play. This chapter discusses one of the most important aspects of international business: the impact of shifting exchange rates and what companies (and individuals) can do to protect themselves against adverse exchange rate movements.

LEARNING OBJECTIVES

After studying this chapter, you should be able to:

LO 1 Explain how exchange rates are quoted, assess what they mean, and differentiate between spot and forward exchange rates.

LO 2 Discuss purchasing power parity and interest rate parity, and analyze their implications for exchange rate changes.

LO 3 Identify the different types of exchange rate risk and ways firms manage exchange rate risk.

LO 4 Discuss the impact of political risk on international business investing.

Please visit us at essentialsofcorporatefinance.blogspot.com for the latest developments in the world of corporate finance.

Companies with significant foreign operations often are called *international corporations*, or *multinationals*. Such companies must consider many financial factors that do not directly affect purely domestic firms. These include foreign exchange rates, differing interest rates from country to country, complex accounting methods for foreign operations, foreign tax rates, and foreign government intervention.

The basic principles of corporate finance still apply to international corporations; like domestic companies, they seek to invest in projects that create more value for the shareholders (or owners) than they cost and to arrange financing that raises cash at the lowest possible cost. In other words, the net present value principle holds for both foreign and domestic operations, but it is usually more complicated to apply the NPV rule to foreign investments.

We won't have much to say here about the role of cultural and social differences in international business. We also will not be discussing the implications of differing political and economic systems. These factors are of great importance to international businesses, but it would take another book to do them justice. Consequently, we will focus only on some purely financial considerations in international finance and some key aspects of foreign exchange markets.

18.1 TERMINOLOGY

A common buzzword for the student of business finance is *globalization*. The first step in learning about the globalization of financial markets is to conquer the new vocabulary. As with any specialty, international finance is rich in jargon. Accordingly, we get started on the subject with a highly eclectic vocabulary exercise.

See www.adr.com for more.

The terms that follow are presented alphabetically, and they are not all of equal importance. We choose these particular ones because they appear frequently in the financial press or because they illustrate some of the colorful language of international finance.

American Depositary Receipt (ADR)
A security issued in the United States representing shares of a foreign stock and allowing that stock to be traded in the United States.

1. An **American Depositary Receipt**, or **ADR**, is a security issued in the United States that represents shares of a foreign stock, allowing that stock to be traded in the United States. Foreign companies use ADRs, which are issued in U.S. dollars, to expand the pool of potential U.S. investors. ADRs are available in two forms: company sponsored, which are listed on an exchange, and unsponsored, which usually are held by the investment bank that deals in the ADR. Both forms are available to individual investors, but only company-sponsored issues are quoted daily in newspapers.

cross-rate
The implicit exchange rate between two currencies (usually non-U.S.) quoted in some third currency (usually the U.S. dollar).

2. The **cross-rate** is the implicit exchange rate between two currencies (usually non-U.S.) when both are quoted in some third currency, usually the U.S. dollar.

Eurobonds
International bonds issued in multiple countries but denominated in a single currency (usually the issuer's currency).

3. A **Eurobond** is a bond issued in multiple countries but denominated in a single currency, usually the issuer's home currency. Such bonds have become an important way to raise capital for many international companies and governments. Eurobonds are issued outside the restrictions that apply to domestic offerings and are syndicated and traded mostly from London. Trading can and does take place anywhere there is a buyer and a seller.

Eurocurrency
Money deposited in a financial center outside the country whose currency is involved.

4. **Eurocurrency** is money deposited in a financial center outside of the country whose currency is involved. For instance, Eurodollars—the most widely used Eurocurrency—are U.S. dollars deposited in banks outside the U.S. banking system.

foreign bonds
International bonds issued in a single country, usually denominated in that country's currency.

5. **Foreign bonds**, unlike Eurobonds, are issued in a single country and are usually denominated in that country's currency. Often, the country in which these bonds are issued will draw distinctions between them and bonds issued by domestic issuers, including different tax laws, restrictions on the amount issued, and tougher disclosure rules.

Foreign bonds often are nicknamed for the country where they are issued: Yankee bonds (United States), Samurai bonds (Japan), Rembrandt bonds (the Netherlands), Bulldog bonds (Britain), and dim sum bonds (Chinese yuan-denominated bonds issued in Hong Kong). Partly because of tougher regulations and disclosure requirements, the foreign-bond market hasn't grown in past years with the vigor of the Eurobond market. A substantial portion of all foreign bonds are issued in Switzerland.

6. **Gilts**, technically, are British and Irish government securities, although the term also includes issues of local British authorities and some overseas public-sector offerings.

7. The **London Interbank Offered Rate (LIBOR)** is the rate that most international banks charge one another for loans of Eurodollars overnight in the London market. LIBOR is a cornerstone in the pricing of money market issues and other debt issues by both government and corporate borrowers. Interest rates are frequently quoted as some spread over LIBOR, and they then float with the LIBOR rate.

8. There are two basic kinds of **swaps**: interest rate and currency. An interest rate swap occurs when two parties exchange a floating-rate payment for a fixed-rate payment or vice versa. Currency swaps are agreements to deliver one currency in exchange for another. Often, both types of swaps are used in the same transaction when debt denominated in different currencies is swapped.

gilts
British and Irish government securities.

London Interbank Offered Rate (LIBOR)
The rate most international banks charge one another for overnight Eurodollar loans.

swaps
Agreements to exchange two securities or currencies.

For current **LIBOR** rates, see www.global-rates.com.

CONCEPT QUESTIONS

18.1a What are the differences between a Eurobond and a foreign bond?
18.1b What are Eurodollars?

18.2 FOREIGN EXCHANGE MARKETS AND EXCHANGE RATES

The **foreign exchange market** is undoubtedly the world's largest financial market. It is the market where one country's currency is traded for another's. Most of the trading takes place in a few currencies such as the U.S. dollar ($), the British pound sterling (£), the Japanese yen (¥), and the euro (€). Table 18.1 lists some of the more common currencies and their symbols.

The foreign exchange market is an over-the-counter market, so there is no single location where traders get together. Instead, market participants are located in the major commercial and investment banks around the world. They communicate using computer terminals, telephones, and other telecommunications devices. For example, one communications network for foreign transactions is the Society for Worldwide Interbank Financial Telecommunication (SWIFT), a Belgian not-for-profit cooperative. Using data transmission lines, a bank in New York can send messages to a bank in London via SWIFT regional processing centers.

The many different types of participants in the foreign exchange market include the following:

1. Importers who pay for goods in foreign currencies.
2. Exporters who receive foreign currency and may want to convert to their domestic currency.
3. Portfolio managers who buy or sell foreign stocks and bonds.
4. Foreign exchange brokers who match buy and sell orders.
5. Traders who "make a market" in foreign currencies.
6. Speculators who try to profit from changes in exchange rates.

foreign exchange market
The market in which one country's currency is traded for another's.

Excel Master coverage online

Visit SWIFT at www.swift.com.

Information on doing business globally can be found at www.internationalist.com.

For online currency rates, go to www.bloomberg.com/markets/currencies.

Country	Currency	Symbol
Australia	Dollar	A$
Brazil	Real	R$
Canada	Dollar	Can$
China	Yuan (Renminbi)	$\bar{\pi}$
Denmark	Kroner	DKr
EMU (Eurozone)	Euro	€
India	Rupee	Rs
Iran	Rial	RI
Japan	Yen	¥
Kuwait	Dinar	KD
Mexico	Peso	Ps
New Zealand	Dollar	NZ$
Norway	Kroner	NKr
Saudi Arabia	Riyal	SR
Singapore	Dollar	S$
South Africa	Rand	R
South Korea	Won	₩
Sweden	Krona	SKr
Switzerland	Franc	SF
Thailand	Baht	฿
Turkey	Lira	₺
United Kingdom	Pound	£
United States	Dollar	$

Exchange Rates

exchange rate

The price of one country's currency expressed in terms of another country's currency.

An **exchange rate** is the price of one country's currency expressed in terms of another country's currency. In practice, almost all trading of currencies takes place in terms of the U.S. dollar. For example, both the Swiss franc and the Japanese yen are traded with their prices quoted in U.S. dollars. Exchange rates are constantly changing. Our nearby *Work the Web* box shows you how to get up-to-the-minute rates.

W🌐RK THE WEB

You just returned from your dream vacation to Jamaica and feel rich because you have 10,000 Jamaican dollars left over. You now need to convert this to U.S. dollars. How much will you have? You can look up the current exchange rate and do the conversion yourself, or work the web. We went to www.xe.com and used the currency converter on the site. This is is what we found:

10,000 JMD = **77.2170** USD

Jamaican Dollar ↔ US Dollar
1 JMD = 0.00772170 USD   1 USD = 129.505 JMD
2018-07-10 19:35 UTC

Source: xe.com

Looks like you left Jamaica just before you ran out of money.

Exchange Rate Quotations   Table 18.2 reproduces exchange rate quotations from www.wsj.com and www.hsbcnet.com. The first column (labeled "USD equiv") gives the number of dollars it takes to buy one unit of foreign currency. For example, the Australian dollar is quoted at .7467, which means that you can buy one Australian dollar with .7467 U.S. dollar.

The second column shows the amount of foreign currency per U.S. dollar. The Australian dollar is quoted here at 1.3392, so you can get 1.3392 Australian dollars for one U.S. dollar. Naturally, this second exchange rate is just the reciprocal of the first one; $1/1.3392 = .7467$, allowing for a possible rounding error.

Cross-Rates and Triangle Arbitrage   Using the U.S. dollar as the common denominator in quoting exchange rates greatly reduces the number of necessary cross-currency quotes. For example, with five major currencies, there would potentially be 10 exchange rates instead of 4. Also, the fact that the dollar is used throughout cuts down on inconsistencies in the exchange rate quotations.

> Get up-to-the-minute exchange rates at www.xe.com and www.exchangerate.com.
>
> Current and historical foreign exchange data are available at many websites. A particularly good site is maintained by the Federal Reserve Bank of St. Louis. Go to www.stlouisfed.org and find their "FRED®" link for up-to-date exchange rate data.

| TABLE 18.2 | Exchange rates: July 9, 2018 |

Country/Currency	USD equiv	Currency per USD	Country/Currency	USD equiv	Currency per USD
Americas			**Europe**		
Argentina peso	.0358	27.9173	Czech Rep. koruna	.04545	22
Brazil real	.2582	3.8730	Denmark krone	.1577	6.3431
Canada dollar	.7628	1.3110	Euro area euro	1.1733	.8523
Chile peso	.001537	605.6000	Hungary forint	.00363135	275.38
Ecuador US dollar	1	1	Norway krone	.1246	8.0244
Mexico peso	.0521	19.2036	Poland zloty	.2725	3.6701
Uruguay peso	.031870	31.380	Romania leu	.2522	3.9653
Venezuela bolivar	.00000871	114,855.0001	Russia ruble	.01602	62.414
			Sweden krona	.1146	8.7241
Asia-Pacific			Switzerland franc	1.0086	.9915
Australia dollar	.7467	1.3392	1-mo forward	1.0104	.9897
1-mo forward	.7464	1.3397	3-mos forward	1.0156	.9846
3-mos forward	.7464	1.3397	6-mos forward	1.0249	.9757
6-mos forward	.7469	1.3389	Turkey lira	.2112	4.7342
China yuan	.1511	6.6161	UK pound	1.3258	.7543
Hong Kong dollar	.1274	7.8485	1-mo forward	1.3284	.7528
India rupee	.01457	68.6567	3-mos forward	1.3319	.7508
Indonesia rupiah	.0000699	14308	6-mos forward	1.3380	.7474
Japan yen	.00902	110.84			
1-mo forward	.00900	111.06	**Middle East/Africa**		
3-mos forward	.00904	110.58	Bahrain dinar	2.6345	.3796
6-mos forward	.00911	109.73	Egypt pound	.0558	17.918
Malaysia ringgit	.2482	4.0295	Israel shekel	.2754	3.6306
New Zealand dollar	.6838	1.4624	Kuwait dinar	3.3049	.3026
Pakistan rupee	.00821	121.740	Oman sul rial	2.59703	.3900
Philippines peso	.0187	53.393	Qatar rial	.2743	3.6453
Singapore dollar	.7371	1.3566	Saudi Arabia riyal	.2666	3.7506
South Korea won	.0008982	1,113.32	South Africa rand	.0746	13.4128
Taiwan dollar	.03298	30.320			
Thailand baht	.03025	33.060			
Vietnam dong	.0000434	23040			

EXAMPLE 18.1	**A Yen for Euros**

Suppose you have $1,000. Based on the rates in Table 18.2, how many Japanese yen can you get? Alternatively, if a Porsche costs €200,000 (€ is the symbol for the euro), how many dollars will you need to buy it?

The exchange rate in terms of yen per dollar is 110.84. Your $1,000 will thus get you:

$1,000 × 110.84 yen per $1 = 110,840 yen

Because the exchange rate in terms of dollars per euro is 1.1733, you will need:

€200,000 × 1.1733 $ per euro = $234,660

Earlier, we defined the cross-rate as the exchange rate for a non-U.S. currency expressed in terms of another non-U.S. currency. Suppose we observed the following for the Mexican peso (Ps) and the Swiss franc (SF):

Ps per $1 = 10.00
SF per $1 = 2.00

Suppose the cross-rate is quoted as:

Ps per SF = 4.00

What do you think?

The cross-rate here is inconsistent with the exchange rates. To see this, suppose you have $100. If you convert this to Swiss francs, you will receive:

$100 × SF 2 per $1 = SF 200

If you convert this to pesos at the cross-rate, you will have:

SF 200 × Ps 4 per SF 1 = Ps 800

However, if you convert your dollars to pesos without going through francs, you will have:

$100 × Ps 10 per $1 = Ps 1,000

What we see is that the peso has two prices, Ps 10 per $1 and Ps 8 per $1, depending on how we get the pesos.

For international news and events, visit www .ft.com.

To make money, we want to buy low, sell high. The important thing to note is that pesos are cheaper if you buy them with dollars because you get 10 pesos instead of 8. You should proceed as follows:

1. Buy 1,000 pesos for $100.
2. Use the 1,000 pesos to buy Swiss francs at the cross-rate. Because it takes four pesos to buy a franc, you will receive Ps 1,000/4 = SF 250.
3. Use the SF 250 to buy dollars. Because the exchange rate is SF 2 per dollar, you receive SF 250/2 = $125, for a round-trip profit of $25.
4. Repeat Steps 1 through 3.

This particular activity is called *triangle arbitrage* because the arbitrage involves moving through three different exchange rates:

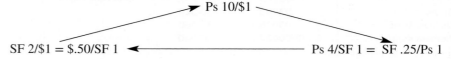

To prevent such opportunities, it is not difficult to see that because a dollar will buy you either 10 pesos or two francs, the cross-rate must be:

(Ps 10/$1)/(SF 2/$1) = Ps 5/SF 1

That is, five pesos per franc. If it were anything else, there would be a triangle arbitrage opportunity.

EXAMPLE 18.2   Shedding Some Pounds

Suppose the exchange rates for the British pound and Swiss franc are:

    Pounds per $1 = .60
       SF per $1 = 2.00

The cross-rate is three francs per pound. Is this consistent? Explain how to go about making some money.

    The cross-rate should be SF 2.00/£.60 = SF 3.33 per pound. You can buy a pound for SF 3 in one market, and you can sell a pound for SF 3.33 in another. So, we want to first get some francs, then use the francs to buy some pounds, and then sell the pounds. Assuming you had $100, you could:

1.   Exchange dollars for francs: $100 × 2 = SF 200.

2.   Exchange francs for pounds: SF 200/3 = £66.67.

3.   Exchange pounds for dollars: £66.67/.60 = $111.11.

This would result in an $11.11 round-trip profit.

Types of Transactions

There are two basic types of trades in the foreign exchange market: spot and forward. A **spot trade** is an agreement to exchange currency "on the spot," which actually means that the transaction will be completed, or settled, within two business days. The exchange rate on a spot trade is called the **spot exchange rate**. Implicitly, all of the exchange rates and transactions we have discussed so far have referred to the spot market.

A **forward trade** is an agreement to exchange currency at some time in the future. The exchange rate that will be used is agreed upon today and is called the **forward exchange rate**. A forward trade will normally be settled sometime in the next 12 months.

If you look back at Table 18.2, you will see forward exchange rates quoted for some of the major currencies. For example, the spot exchange rate for the Swiss franc is SF 1 = $1.0086. The six-month forward exchange rate is SF 1 = $1.0249. This means that you can buy a Swiss franc today for $1.0086, or you can agree to take delivery of a Swiss franc in six months and pay $1.0249 at that time.

Notice that the Swiss franc is more expensive in the forward market ($1.0249 versus $1.0086). Because the Swiss franc is more expensive in the future than it is today, it is said to be selling at a *premium* relative to the dollar. For the same reason, the dollar is said to be selling at a *discount* relative to the Swiss franc.

Why does the forward market exist? One answer is that it allows businesses and individuals to lock in a future exchange rate today, thereby eliminating any risk from unfavorable shifts in the exchange rate.

spot trade
An agreement to trade currencies based on the exchange rate today for settlement within two business days.

spot exchange rate
The exchange rate on a spot trade.

forward trade
Agreement to exchange currency at some time in the future.

forward exchange rate
The agreed-upon exchange rate to be used in a forward trade.

EXAMPLE 18.3 **Looking Forward**

Suppose you are expecting to receive 100 million Japanese yen in one month, and you agree to a forward trade to exchange your yen for dollars. Based on Table 18.2, how many dollars will you get in six months? Is the yen selling at a discount or a premium relative to the dollar?

In Table 18.2, the spot exchange rate and the one-month forward rate in terms of dollars per yen are \$.00902 = ¥1 and \$.00900 = ¥1, respectively. If you expect ¥100 million in six months, then you will get ¥100 million × \$.00900 per ¥ = \$900,000. Because it is less expensive to buy yen in the forward market than in the spot market (\$.00902 versus \$.00900), the yen is selling at a discount relative to the dollar.

As we mentioned earlier, it is standard practice around the world (with a few exceptions, including the euro) to quote exchange rates in terms of the U.S. dollar. This means that rates are quoted as the amount of currency per U.S. dollar. For the remainder of this chapter, we will stick with this form. Things can get extremely confusing if you forget this. Thus, when we say things like "the exchange rate is expected to rise," it is important to remember that we are talking about the exchange rate quoted as units of foreign currency per U.S. dollar.

CONCEPT QUESTIONS

18.2a What is triangle arbitrage?

18.2b What do we mean by the three-month forward exchange rate?

18.2c If we say that the exchange rate is SF 1.12, what do we mean?

18.3 PURCHASING POWER PARITY

Now that we have discussed what exchange rate quotations mean, we can address an obvious question: What determines the level of the spot exchange rate? In addition, we know that exchange rates change through time. A related question is thus: What determines the rate of change in exchange rates? At least part of the answer in both cases goes by the name of **purchasing power parity (PPP)**, and it is the idea that the exchange rate adjusts to keep purchasing power constant among currencies. As we discuss next, there are two forms of PPP: *absolute* and *relative*.

purchasing power parity (PPP)
The idea that the exchange rate adjusts to keep purchasing power constant among currencies.

Absolute Purchasing Power Parity

The basic idea behind *absolute purchasing power parity* is that a commodity costs the same regardless of what currency is used to purchase it or where it is selling. This is a very straightforward concept. If a beer costs £2 in London, and the exchange rate is £.60 per dollar, then a beer costs £2/.60 = \$3.33 in New York. In other words, absolute PPP says that \$1 will buy you the same number of, say, cheeseburgers anywhere in the world.

More formally, let S_0 be the spot exchange rate between the British pound and the U.S. dollar today (Time 0), and remember that we are quoting exchange rates as the amount of foreign currency per dollar. Let P_{US} and P_{UK} be the current U.S. and British prices, respectively, on a particular commodity, say, apples. Absolute PPP says that:

$$P_{UK} = S_0 \times P_{US}$$

This tells us that the British price for something is equal to the U.S. price for that same something, multiplied by the exchange rate.

The rationale behind PPP is similar to that behind triangle arbitrage. If PPP did not hold, arbitrage would be possible (in principle) if apples were moved from one country to another. For example, suppose apples in New York are selling for $4 per bushel, while in London the price is £2.40 per bushel. Absolute PPP implies that:

$$P_{UK} = S_0 \times P_{US}$$
$$£2.40 = S_0 \times \$4$$
$$S_0 = £2.40/\$4 = \$.60$$

That is, the implied spot exchange rate is £.60 per dollar. Equivalently, a pound is worth $1/£.60 = \$1.67$.

Suppose, instead, that the actual exchange rate is £.50. Starting with $4, a trader could buy a bushel of apples in New York, ship it to London, and sell it there for £2.40. Our trader could then convert the £2.40 into dollars at the prevailing exchange rate, $S_0 = £.50$, yielding a total of £2.40/.50 = $4.80. The round-trip gain is 80 cents.

Because of this profit potential, forces are set in motion to change the exchange rate and/or the price of apples. In our example, apples would begin moving from New York to London. The reduced supply of apples in New York would raise the price of apples there, and the increased supply in Britain would lower the price of apples in London.

In addition to moving apples around, apple traders would be busily converting pounds back into dollars to buy more apples. This activity increases the supply of pounds and simultaneously increases the demand for dollars. We would expect the value of a pound to fall. This means that the dollar is getting more valuable, so it will take more pounds to buy one dollar. Because the exchange rate is quoted as pounds per dollar, we would expect the exchange rate to rise from £.50.

For absolute PPP to hold absolutely, several things must be true:

1. The transaction costs of trading apples—shipping, insurance, spoilage, and so on—must be zero.

2. There must be no barriers to trading apples, such as tariffs, taxes, or other political barriers such as VRAs (voluntary restraint agreements).

3. Finally, an apple in New York must be identical to an apple in London. It won't do for you to send red apples to London if the English eat only green apples.

Given the fact that the transaction costs are not zero and that the other conditions are rarely exactly met, it is not surprising that absolute PPP is really applicable only to traded goods, and then only to very uniform ones.

For this reason, absolute PPP does not imply that a Mercedes costs the same as a Ford or that a nuclear power plant in France costs the same as one in New York. In the case of the cars, they are not identical. In the case of the power plants, even if they were identical, they are expensive and very difficult to ship. On the other hand, we would be very surprised to see a significant violation of absolute PPP for gold. See our nearby *Finance Matters* box for an interesting example of PPP violations.

McPricing

As we discussed in the chapter, absolute purchasing power parity (PPP) does not seem to hold in practice. One of the more famous violations of absolute PPP is the Big Mac Index constructed by *The Economist.* To construct the index, prices for a Big Mac in different countries are gathered from McDonald's. We went to www.economist.com to find the January 2018 Big Mac index (we will leave it to you to find the most recent index).

According to the index on that day, absolute PPP does not seem to hold, at least for the Big Mac. In fact, in only 6 of the 42 currencies surveyed by *The Economist* is the exchange rate within 10 percent of that predicted by absolute PPP. The largest disparity was in Ukraine, where the currency was apparently undervalued by 69 percent. And 14 of the 42 currencies were "incorrectly" priced by more than 40 percent. Why?

There are several reasons. First, a Big Mac is not really transportable. Yes, you can load a ship with Big Macs and send it to a country where the currency is supposedly overvalued. But do you really think people would buy your Big Macs? Probably not. Even though it is relatively easy to transport a Big Mac, it would be relatively expensive, and the hamburger would suffer in quality along the way.

Also, if you look in the index, the price of the Big Mac in the United States is the average price from five cities. The reason is that the Big Mac does not sell for the same price in different parts of the United States, where presumably they are all purchased with the dollar. The cost of living and competition are only a few of the factors that will affect the price of a Big Mac in the United States. If Big Macs are not priced the same in the same currency, would we expect absolute PPP to hold across currencies?

Finally, differing tastes can account for the apparent discrepancy. In the United States, hamburgers and fast food have become a staple of the American diet. In other countries, hamburgers have not become as entrenched. We would expect the price of the Big Mac to be lower in the United States because there is more fast-food competition. In fact, when calculating PPP for the Indian rupee/U.S. dollar, the price of the Maharaja Mac, which is made with chicken, is used because beef is not sold at McDonald's in India.

Having examined the Big Mac prices, we should say that absolute PPP should hold more closely for more easily transportable items. For instance, there are many companies with stock listed on both the NYSE and the stock exchange of another country. If you examine the share prices on the two exchanges, you will find that the price of the stock is almost exactly what absolute PPP would predict. The reason is that a share of stock in a particular company is (usually) the same wherever you buy it and whatever currency is used.

Relative Purchasing Power Parity

As a practical matter, a relative version of purchasing power parity has evolved. *Relative purchasing power parity* does not tell us what determines the absolute level of the exchange rate. Instead, it tells what determines the *change* in the exchange rate over time.

The Basic Idea   Suppose the British pound-U.S. dollar exchange rate is currently $S_0 = £.50$. Further suppose that the inflation rate in Britain is predicted to be 10 percent over the coming year and (for the moment) the inflation rate in the United States is predicted to be zero. What do you think the exchange rate will be in a year?

If you think about it, a dollar currently costs .50 pound in Britain. With 10 percent inflation, we expect prices in Britain to generally rise by 10 percent. So we expect that the price of a dollar will go up by 10 percent, and the exchange rate should rise to $£.50 \times 1.1 = £.55$.

If the inflation rate in the United States is not zero, then we need to worry about the *relative* inflation rates in the two countries. Suppose the U.S. inflation rate is predicted to be 4 percent. Relative to prices in the United States, prices in Britain are rising at a rate of $10\% - 4\% = 6\%$ per year. So we expect the price of the dollar to rise by 6 percent, and the predicted exchange rate is $£.50 \times 1.06 = £.53$.

The Result In general, relative PPP says that the change in the exchange rate is determined by the difference in the inflation rates of the two countries. To be more specific, we will use the following notation:

S_0 = Current (Time 0) spot exchange rate (foreign currency per dollar)

$E(S_t)$ = Expected exchange rate in t periods

h_{US} = Inflation rate in the United States

h_{FC} = Foreign country inflation rate

Based on our preceding discussion, relative PPP says that the expected percentage change in the exchange rate over the next year, $[E(S_1) - S_0]/S_0$, is:

$$[E(S_1) - S_0]/S_0 = h_{FC} - h_{US} \qquad [18.1]$$

In words, relative PPP says that the expected percentage change in the exchange rate is equal to the difference in inflation rates. If we rearrange this slightly, we get:

$$E(S_1) = S_0[1 + (h_{FC} - h_{US})] \qquad [18.2]$$

This result makes a certain amount of sense, but care must be used in quoting the exchange rate.

In our example involving Britain and the United States, relative PPP tells us that the exchange rate will rise by $h_{FC} - h_{US} = 10\% - 4\% = 6\%$ per year. Assuming that the difference in inflation rates doesn't change, the expected exchange rate in two years, $E(S_2)$, therefore will be:

$$
\begin{aligned}
E(S_2) &= E(S_1) \times (1 + .06) \\
&= .53 \times 1.06 \\
&= .562
\end{aligned}
$$

Notice that we could have written this as:

$$
\begin{aligned}
E(S_2) &= .53 \times 1.06 \\
&= (.50 \times 1.06) \times 1.06 \\
&= .50 \times 1.06^2
\end{aligned}
$$

In general, relative PPP says that the expected exchange rate at some time in the future, $E(S_t)$, is:

$$E(S_t) = S_0 \times [1 + (h_{FC} - h_{US})]^t \qquad [18.3]$$

Because we don't really expect absolute PPP to hold for most goods, we will focus on relative PPP in any future discussion. Henceforth, when we refer to PPP without further qualification, we mean relative PPP.

EXAMPLE 18.4 **It's All Relative**

Suppose the Japanese exchange rate is currently 105 yen per dollar. The inflation rate in Japan over the next three years will run, say, 2 percent per year, while the U.S. inflation rate will be 6 percent. Based on relative PPP, what will the exchange rate be in three years?

Because the U.S. inflation rate is higher, we expect that a dollar will become less valuable. The exchange rate change will be 2% − 6% = −4% per year. Over three years, the exchange rate will fall to:

$$
\begin{aligned}
E(S_3) &= S_0 \times [1 + (h_{FC} - h_{US})]^3 \\
&= 105 \times [1 + (-.04)]^3 \\
&= 92.90 \text{ yen per dollar}
\end{aligned}
$$

Currency Appreciation and Depreciation   We frequently hear things like "the dollar strengthened (or weakened) in financial markets today" or "the dollar is expected to appreciate (or depreciate) relative to the pound." When we say that the dollar strengthens, or appreciates, we mean that the value of a dollar rises, so it takes more foreign currency to buy a dollar.

What happens to exchange rates as currencies fluctuate in value depends on how exchange rates are quoted. Because we are quoting them as units of foreign currency per dollar, the exchange rate moves in the same direction as the value of the dollar: It rises as the dollar strengthens, and it falls as the dollar weakens.

Relative PPP tells us that the exchange rate will rise if the U.S. inflation rate is lower than the foreign country's. This happens because the foreign currency depreciates in value and therefore weakens relative to the dollar.

CONCEPT QUESTIONS

18.3a What does absolute PPP say? Why might it not hold for many types of goods?

18.3b According to relative PPP, what determines the change in exchange rates?

18.4 EXCHANGE RATES AND INTEREST RATES

The next issue we need to address is the relationship between spot exchange rates, forward exchange rates, and nominal interest rates. To get started, we need some additional notation:

> F_t = Forward exchange rate for settlement at Time t
> R_{US} = U.S. nominal risk-free interest rate
> R_{FC} = Foreign country nominal risk-free interest rate

As before, we will use S_0 to stand for the spot exchange rate. You can take the U.S. nominal risk-free rate, R_{US}, to be the T-bill rate.

Covered Interest Arbitrage

Suppose we observe the following information about U.S. and Swiss currency in the market:

> S_0 = SF 2.00 R_{US} = 10%
> F_1 = SF 1.90 R_S = 5%

where R_S is the nominal risk-free rate in Switzerland. The period is one year, so F_1 is the 360-day forward rate.

Do you see an arbitrage opportunity here? There is one. Suppose you have $1 to invest, and you want a riskless investment. One option you have is to invest the $1 in a riskless U.S. investment such as a 360-day T-bill. We will call this Strategy 1. If you do this, then, in one period, your $1 will be worth:

> $ value in 1 period = $1(1 + R_{US})
> = $1.10

Alternatively, you can invest in the Swiss risk-free investment. To do this, you need to convert your $1 to francs and simultaneously execute a forward trade to convert francs back to dollars in one year. We will call this Strategy 2. The necessary steps would be as follows:

1. Convert your \$1 to \$1 $\times S_0 =$ SF 2.00.
2. At the same time, enter into a forward agreement to convert francs back to dollars in one year. Because the forward rate is SF 1.90, you get \$1 for every SF 1.90 that you have in one year.
3. Invest your SF 2.00 in Switzerland at R_S. In one year, you will have:

For exchange rates and even pictures of non-U.S. currencies, see www .travlang.com/money.

$$\text{SF value in 1 year} = \text{SF } 2.00 \times (1 + R_S)$$
$$= \text{SF } 2.00 \times 1.05$$
$$= \text{SF } 2.10$$

4. Convert your SF 2.10 back to dollars at the agreed-upon rate of SF 1.90 = \$1. You end up with:

$$\$ \text{ value in 1 year} = \text{SF } 2.10/1.90$$
$$= \$1.1053$$

Notice that the value in one year from this strategy can be written as:

$$\$ \text{ value in 1 year} = \$1 \times S_0 \times (1 + R_S)/F_1$$
$$= \$1 \times 2.00 \times 1.05/1.90$$
$$= \$1.1053$$

The return on this investment is apparently 10.53 percent. This is higher than the 10 percent we get from investing in the United States. Because both investments are risk-free, there is an arbitrage opportunity.

To exploit the difference in interest rates, you need to borrow, say, \$5 million at the lower U.S. rate and invest it at the higher Swiss rate. What is the round-trip profit from doing this? To find out, we can work through the preceding steps:

How are the international markets doing? Find out at marketwatch.com.

1. Convert the \$5 million at SF 2.00 = \$1 to get SF 10 million.
2. Agree to exchange francs for dollars in one year at SF 1.90 to the dollar.
3. Invest the SF 10 million for one year at $R_S = 5\%$. You end up with SF 10.5 million.
4. Convert the SF 10.5 million back to dollars to fulfill the forward contract. You receive SF 10.5 million/1.90 = \$5,526,316.
5. Repay the loan with interest. You owe \$5 million plus 10 percent interest, for a total of \$5.5 million. You have \$5,526,316, so your round-trip profit is a risk-free \$26,316.

The activity that we have illustrated here goes by the name of *covered interest arbitrage.* The term *covered* refers to the fact that we are covered in the event of a change in the exchange rate because we lock in the forward exchange rate today.

Interest Rate Parity

If we assume that significant covered interest arbitrage opportunities do not exist, then there must be some relationship between spot exchange rates, forward exchange rates, and relative interest rates. To see what this relationship is, note that, in general, Strategy 1, investing in a riskless U.S. investment, gives us $(1 + R_{US})$ for every dollar we invest. Strategy 2, investing in a foreign risk-free investment, gives us $S_0 \times (1 + R_{FC})/F_1$ for every dollar we invest. Because these have to be equal to prevent arbitrage, it must be the case that:

$$1 + R_{US} = S_0 \times (1 + R_{FC})/F_1$$

interest rate parity (IRP)

The condition stating that the interest rate differential between two countries is equal to the percentage difference between the forward exchange rate and the spot exchange rate.

Rearranging this a bit gets us the famous **interest rate parity (IRP)** condition:

$$F_t/S_0 = (1 + R_{FC})/(1 + R_{US})$$ [18.4]

There is a very useful approximation for IRP that illustrates very clearly what is going on and is not difficult to remember. If we define the percentage forward premium or discount as $(F_1 - S_0)/S_0$, then IRP says that this percentage premium or discount is *approximately* equal to the difference in interest rates:

$$(F_1 - S_0)/S_0 = R_{FC} - R_{US}$$ [18.5]

Very loosely, what IRP says is that any difference in interest rates between two countries for some period is offset by the change in the relative value of the currencies, thereby eliminating any arbitrage possibilities. Notice that we also could write:

$$F_1 = S_0 \times [1 + (R_{FC} - R_{US})]$$ [18.6]

In general, if we have t periods instead of one, the IRP approximation will be written as:

$$F_t = S_0 \times [1 + (R_{FC} - R_{US})]^t$$ [18.7]

EXAMPLE 18.5   **Parity Check**

Suppose the exchange rate for Japanese yen, S_0, is currently ¥120 = $1. If the interest rate in the United States is R_{US} = 10% and the interest rate in Japan is R_J = 5%, then what must the one-year forward rate be to prevent covered interest arbitrage?

$$F_1 = S_0 \times [1 + (R_J - R_{US})]$$
$$= ¥120 \times [1 + (.05 - .10)]$$
$$= ¥120 \times .95$$
$$= ¥114$$

Notice that the yen will sell at a premium relative to the dollar (why?).

CONCEPT QUESTIONS

18.4a   What is interest rate parity?

18.4b   Do you expect that interest rate parity will hold more closely than purchasing power parity? Why?

18.5 EXCHANGE RATE RISK

exchange rate risk

The risk related to having international operations in a world where relative currency values vary.

Exchange rate risk is the natural consequence of international operations in a world where relative currency values move up and down. As we discuss next, there are three different types of exchange rate risk, or exposure: short-run exposure, long-run exposure, and translation exposure.

Short-Run Exposure

The day-to-day fluctuations in exchange rates create short-run risks for international firms. Most such firms have contractual agreements to buy and sell goods in the near future at set prices. When different currencies are involved, such transactions have an extra element of risk.

Imagine that you are importing imitation pasta from Italy and reselling it in the United States under the Impasta brand name. Your largest customer has ordered 10,000 cases of Impasta. You place the order with your supplier today, but you won't pay until the goods arrive in 60 days. Your selling price is $6 per case. Your cost is €4.48 per case, and the exchange rate is currently €.80, so it takes €.80 to buy $1.

At the current exchange rate, your cost in dollars from filling the order is €4.48/€.80 = $5.60 per case, so your pretax profit on the order is 10,000 × ($6 − 5.60) = $4,000. However, the exchange rate in 60 days probably will be different, so your profit will depend on what the exchange rate in the future turns out to be.

For example, if the rate goes to €.85, your cost is €4.48/€.85 = $5.27 per case. Your profit goes to $7,294. If the exchange rate goes to, say, €.747, then your cost is €4.48/€.747 = $6 per case, and your profit is zero.

The short-run exposure in our example can be reduced or eliminated in several ways. The most obvious way is to enter into a forward exchange agreement to lock in an exchange rate. Suppose the 60-day forward rate is €.82. What will your profit be if you hedge?

If you hedge, you lock in an exchange rate of €.82. Your cost in dollars thus will be €4.48/€.82 = $5.46 per case, so your profit will be 10,000 × ($6 − 5.46) = $5,366.

Long-Run Exposure

In the long run, the value of a foreign operation can fluctuate because of unanticipated changes in relative economic conditions. Imagine that we own a labor-intensive assembly operation located in another country to take advantage of lower wages. Through time, unexpected changes in economic conditions can raise the foreign wage levels to the point where the cost advantage is eliminated or even becomes negative.

Hedging long-run exposure is more difficult than hedging short-term risks. For one thing, organized forward markets don't exist for such long-term needs. Instead, the primary option that firms have is to try to match up foreign currency inflows and outflows. The same thing goes for matching foreign currency-denominated assets and liabilities. For example, a firm that sells in a foreign country might try to concentrate its raw material purchases and labor expense in that country. That way, the dollar values of its revenues and costs will move up and down together.

Similarly, a firm can reduce its long-run exchange rate risk by borrowing in the foreign country. Fluctuations in the value of the foreign subsidiary's assets then will be at least partially offset by changes in the value of its liabilities.

One of the more common methods used to reduce long-term exchange rate exposure is to build a plant in the country that imports the products. This method often is used in the automotive industry. Honda, Toyota, and BMW, to name a few, have built plants in the United States. BMW's situation is particularly interesting. It produces about 400,000 cars per year in South Carolina and exports about 280,000 of them. The costs of manufacturing the cars are mostly paid in dollars, and when BMW exports the cars to Europe, it receives euros. So, when the dollar weakens, these vehicles become more profitable for BMW. At the same time, BMW imports about 200,000 more cars to the United States each year. The costs of manufacturing these imported cars are mostly in euros, so they become less profitable when the dollar weakens. Taken together, these gains and losses tend to offset each other and provide BMW with a natural hedge.

Translation Exposure

When a U.S. company calculates its accounting net income and EPS for some period, it must "translate" everything into dollars. This can create some problems for the accountants when there are significant foreign operations. In particular, two issues arise:

1. What is the appropriate exchange rate to use for translating each balance sheet account?

2. How should balance sheet accounting gains and losses from foreign currency translation be handled?

To illustrate the accounting problem, suppose that we started a small foreign subsidiary in Lilliputia a year ago. The local currency is the gulliver, abbreviated GL. At the beginning of the year, the exchange rate was GL 2 = $1, and the balance sheet in gullivers looked like this:

Assets	GL 1,000	Liabilities	GL 500
		Equity	500

At two gullivers to the dollar, the beginning balance sheet in dollars was:

Assets	$500	Liabilities	$250
		Equity	250

Lilliputia is a quiet place, and nothing at all actually happened during the year. As a result, net income was zero (before consideration of exchange rate changes). However, the exchange rate did change to 4 gullivers = $1, perhaps because the Lilliputian inflation rate is much higher than the U.S. inflation rate.

Because nothing happened, the accounting ending balance sheet in gullivers is the same as the beginning one. However, if we convert it to dollars at the new exchange rate, we get:

Assets	$250	Liabilities	$125
		Equity	125

Notice that the value of the equity has gone down by $125, even though net income was exactly zero. Despite the fact that absolutely nothing really happened, there is a $125 accounting loss. How to handle this $125 loss has been a controversial accounting question.

One obvious and consistent way to handle this loss is to report the loss on the parent's income statement. During periods of volatile exchange rates, this kind of treatment can dramatically impact an international company's reported EPS. This is purely an accounting phenomenon, but, even so, such fluctuations are disliked by some financial managers.

The current approach to translation gains and losses is based on rules set out in Financial Accounting Standards Board (FASB) Statement Number 52, issued in December 1981. For the most part, FASB 52 requires that all assets and liabilities be translated from the subsidiary's currency into the parent's currency using the exchange rate that currently prevails.

Any translation gains and losses that occur are accumulated in a special account within the shareholders' equity section of the balance sheet. This account might be labeled something like "unrealized foreign exchange gains (losses)." These gains and losses are not reported on the income statement. As a result, the impact of translation gains and losses will not be recognized explicitly in net income until the underlying assets and liabilities are sold or otherwise liquidated.

Managing Exchange Rate Risk

For a large multinational firm, the management of exchange rate risk is complicated by the fact that there can be many different currencies involved for many different subsidiaries. It is very likely that a change in some exchange rate will benefit some subsidiaries and hurt others. The net effect on the overall firm depends on its net exposure.

Suppose a firm has two divisions. Division A buys goods in the United States for dollars and sells them in Britain for pounds. Division B buys goods in Britain for pounds and sells them in the United States for dollars. If these two divisions are of roughly equal size in terms of their inflows and outflows, then the overall firm obviously has little exchange rate risk.

In our example, the firm's net position in pounds (the amount coming in less the amount going out) is small, so the exchange rate risk is small. However, if one division, acting on its own, were to start hedging its exchange rate risk, then the overall firm's exchange rate risk would go up. The moral of the story is that multinational firms have to be conscious of the overall position that the firm has in a foreign currency. For this reason, management of exchange rate risk is probably best handled on a centralized basis.

CONCEPT QUESTIONS

18.5a What are the different types of exchange rate risk?

18.5b How can a firm hedge short-run exchange rate risk? Long-run exchange rate risk?

18.6 POLITICAL RISK

One final element of risk in international investing is **political risk**. Political risk refers to changes in value that arise as a consequence of political actions. For example, in June 2016, British voters shocked the rest of Europe when they voted in favor of "Brexit," the U.K. exit from the European Union. Although the treaty that tied the U.K. to the rest of Europe required a two-year process to complete the withdrawal, financial markets didn't take that long to react. The British pound dropped 11 percent against the U.S. dollar on the day, and London's FTSE and Stoxx Europe 600 stock market indexes dropped about 8 percent. Preeminent British banks Barclays and Lloyds Banking Group both were hit even harder, as they saw stock price drops of more than 30 percent on the day. Unfortunately (or fortunately, depending on your view), the drop in the British pound wasn't finished. It continued to fall against the U.S. dollar, reaching its lowest level since 1985. Political risk is not a problem faced exclusively by international firms. As we discuss next, for example, changes in U.S. tax

political risk
Risk related to changes in value that arise because of political actions.

laws and regulations may benefit some U.S. firms and hurt others, so political risk exists nationally as well as internationally.

The Tax Cuts and Jobs Act

In our chapter opener, we described the large cash balances held "overseas" by U.S. corporations. As we noted, the reason Apple and other large U.S. corporations held such large balances overseas has to do with U.S. tax law. Tax laws are a form of political risk faced by multinational firms.

Specifically, before the signing of the Tax Cuts and Jobs Act of 2017, the U.S. had corporate tax rates that were among the highest in the developed world. At the same time, the U.S. was somewhat unique in that it taxed corporate profits wherever they were earned, but only after the profits were brought back, or "repatriated," to the U.S. But what does this mean, exactly?

To answer, let's go back to Lilliputia, which has a 20 percent corporate tax rate, compared to what would have been 35 percent in the U.S. If we earned a profit in our Lilliputian subsidiary, that subsidiary would pay taxes to Lilliputia at the 20 percent rate. If we had left the profits in Lilliputia, then no additional taxes were owed. But if we had brought the profits back to the U.S., we would have owed additional taxes of 15 percent, the difference between the U.S. and Lilliputian tax rates. Avoiding this extra tax gave U.S. companies a strong incentive *not* to repatriate profits.

Here is where it gets confusing. In the media, companies like Apple are depicted as having huge piles of cash sitting outside the borders of the U.S., but that's not what is really going on. Apple's cash is actually mostly in dollars, and it is mostly invested in various U.S. financial assets. So, the money isn't really "outside" the U.S.

Instead, because Apple has chosen not to pay the extra tax on its overseas profits, it is prohibited from using that cash inside the U.S. to do things like pay dividends or build new facilities. Note that Apple easily can get around this limitation by, for example, borrowing against its cash and securities portfolio if it chooses to do so.

The Tax Cuts and Jobs Act of 2017 changed things in a number of ways. First, the new flat 21 percent tax rate (down from a maximum of 35 percent) reduced the incentive to leave cash overseas. Second, the law imposed a one-time tax of 15.5 percent on cash, securities, and receivables and a one-time tax of 8 percent on other, less-liquid assets purchased with untaxed overseas dollars (e.g., plant, property, and equipment). Finally, broadly speaking, repatriated earnings are no longer subject to additional U.S. taxes, thereby eliminating the repatriation issue.

Managing Political Risk

Some countries do have more political risk than others, however. When firms have operations in these riskier countries, the extra political risk may lead them to require higher returns on overseas investments to compensate for the risk that funds will be blocked, critical operations interrupted, or contracts abrogated. In the most extreme case, the possibility of outright confiscation may be a concern in countries with relatively unstable political environments.

Political risk also depends on the nature of the business; some businesses are less likely to be confiscated because they are not particularly valuable in the hands of a different owner. An assembly operation supplying subcomponents that only the parent company uses would not be an attractive "takeover" target, for example. Similarly, a manufacturing operation that requires the use of specialized components from the parent is of little value without the parent company's cooperation.

Natural resource developments, such as copper mining or oil drilling, are the opposite. Once the operation is in place, much of the value is in the commodity. The political risk for such investments is much higher for this reason. Also, the issue of exploitation is more pronounced with such investments, again increasing the political risk.

Political risk can be hedged in several ways, particularly when confiscation or nationalization is a concern. The use of local financing, perhaps from the government of the foreign country in question, reduces the possible loss because the company can refuse to pay on the debt in the event of unfavorable political activities. Based on our discussion above, structuring the operation in such a way that it requires significant parent company involvement to function is another way to reduce political risk.

CONCEPT QUESTIONS

18.6a What is political risk?

18.6b What are some ways of hedging political risk?

SUMMARY AND CONCLUSIONS

The international firm has a more complicated life than the purely domestic firm. Management must understand the connection between interest rates, foreign currency exchange rates, and inflation, and it must become aware of a large number of different financial market regulations and tax systems. This chapter was intended to be a concise introduction to some of the financial issues that come up in international investing.

Our coverage was necessarily brief. The main topics we discussed included:

1. Some basic vocabulary. We briefly defined some exotic terms such as *LIBOR* and *Eurocurrency.*

2. The basic mechanics of exchange rate quotations. We discussed the spot and forward markets and how exchange rates are interpreted.

3. The fundamental relationships between international financial variables:

   a. Absolute and relative purchasing power parity, or PPP.

   b. Interest rate parity, or IRP.

   Absolute purchasing power parity states that $1 should have the same purchasing power in each country. This means that an orange costs the same whether you buy it in New York or in Tokyo.

   Relative purchasing power parity means that the expected percentage change in exchange rates between the currencies of two countries is equal to the difference in their inflation rates.

   Interest rate parity implies that the percentage difference between the forward exchange rate and the spot exchange rate is equal to the interest rate differential. We showed how covered interest arbitrage forces this relationship to hold.

4. Exchange rate and political risk. We described the various types of exchange rate risk and discussed some commonly used approaches to managing the effect of fluctuating exchange rates on the cash flows and value of the international firm. We also discussed political risk and some ways of managing exposure to it.

■ connect POP QUIZ!

Can you answer the following questions? If your class is using *Connect,* log on to SmartBook to see if you know the answers to these and other questions, check out the study tools, and find out what topics require additional practice!

Section 18.1 A cross-rate between two currencies is usually quoted in what currency?

Section 18.2 If $1 will buy Can$.99 and A$.95, how many Canadian dollars are needed to buy one Australian dollar?

Section 18.3 What do you call the condition in which a commodity costs the same regardless of the currency used or where it is purchased?

Section 18.4 Suppose the euro currently costs $1.37 and the nominal risk-free interest rate in France is 3 percent while only 2 percent in the United States. What does interest rate parity imply the forward rate for the euro will be?

Section 18.5 What are some strategies for hedging long-term exchange rate risk?

Section 18.6 Is a change in translation exposure a good example of political risk?

CHAPTER REVIEW AND SELF-TEST PROBLEMS

18.1 Relative Purchasing Power Parity   The inflation rate in the United States is projected at 6 percent per year for the next several years. The Australian inflation rate is projected to be 2 percent during that time. The exchange rate is currently A$2.2. Based on relative PPP, what is the expected exchange rate in two years? (See Problem 12.)

18.2 Covered Interest Arbitrage   The spot and 360-day forward rates on the Swiss franc are SF 1.8 and SF 1.7, respectively. The risk-free interest rate in the United States is 8 percent, and the risk-free rate in Switzerland is 5 percent. Is there an arbitrage opportunity here? How would you exploit it? (See Problem 7.)

■ Answers to Chapter Review and Self-Test Problems

18.1   From relative PPP, the expected exchange rate in two years, $E(S_2)$, is:

$$E(S_2) = S_0 \times [1 + (h_A - h_{US})]^2$$

where h_A is the Australian inflation rate. The current exchange rate is A$2.2, so the expected exchange rate is:

$$E(S_2) = A\$\,2.2 \times [1 + (.02 - .06)]^2$$
$$= A\$\,2.2 \times .96^2$$
$$= A\$\,2.03$$

18.2 From interest rate parity, the forward rate should be (approximately):

$$F_1 = S_0 \times [1 + (R_S - R_{US})]$$
$$= 1.8 \times [1 + .05 - .08]$$
$$= 1.75$$

Because the forward rate is actually SF 1.7, there is an arbitrage opportunity.

To exploit the arbitrage opportunity, we first note that dollars are selling for SF 1.7 each in the forward market. From IRP, this is too cheap because they should be selling for SF 1.75. So, we want to arrange to buy dollars with Swiss francs in the forward market. To do this, we can:

1. Today: Borrow, say, $10 million for 360 days. Convert it to SF 18 million in the spot market, and buy a forward contract at SF 1.7 to convert it back to dollars in 360 days. Invest the SF 18 million at 5 percent.
2. In one year: Your investment has grown to SF 18 × 1.05 = SF 18.9 million. Convert this to dollars at the rate of SF 1.7 = $1. You will have SF 18.9 million/1.7 = $11,117,647. Pay off your loan with 8 percent interest at a cost of $10 million × 1.08 = $10,800,000 and pocket the difference of $317,647.

CRITICAL THINKING AND CONCEPTS REVIEW

LO 1   **18.1 Spot and Forward Rates**   Suppose the exchange rate for the Swiss franc is quoted as SF 1.10 in the spot market and SF 1.13 in the 90-day forward market.

    a. Is the dollar selling at a premium or a discount relative to the franc?

    b. Does the financial market expect the franc to strengthen relative to the dollar? Explain.

    c. What do you suspect is true about relative economic conditions in the United States and Switzerland?

LO 2   **18.2 Purchasing Power Parity**   Suppose the rate of inflation in Russia will run about 3 percent higher than the U.S. inflation rate over the next several years. All other things being the same, what will happen to the ruble versus dollar exchange rate? What relationship are you relying on in answering?

LO 2   **18.3 Exchange Rates**   The exchange rate for the Australian dollar is currently A$1.40. This exchange rate is expected to rise by 10 percent over the next year.

    a. Is the Australian dollar expected to get stronger or weaker?

    b. What do you think about the relative inflation rates in the United States and Australia?

    c. What do you think about the relative nominal interest rates in the United States and Australia? Relative real rates?

LO 3   **18.4 Yankee Bonds**   Which of the following most accurately describes a Yankee bond?

    a. A bond issued by General Motors in Japan with the interest payable in U.S. dollars.

   b. A bond issued by General Motors in Japan with the interest payable in yen.

   c. A bond issued by Toyota in the United States with the interest payable in yen.

   d. A bond issued by Toyota in the United States with the interest payable in dollars.

   e. A bond issued by Toyota worldwide with the interest payable in dollars.

LO 1 **18.5 Exchange Rates**   Are exchange rate changes necessarily good or bad for a particular company?

LO 4 **18.6 International Risks**   At one point, Duracell International confirmed that it was planning to open battery-manufacturing plants in China and India. Manufacturing in these countries would allow Duracell to avoid import duties of between 30 and 35 percent that have made alkaline batteries prohibitively expensive for some consumers. What additional advantages might Duracell see in this proposal? What are some of the risks to Duracell?

LO 3 **18.7 Multinational Corporations**   Given that many multinationals based in many countries have much greater sales outside their domestic markets than within them, what is the particular relevance of their domestic currency?

LO 2 **18.8 Exchange Rate Movements**   Are the following statements true or false? Explain why.

   a. If the general price index in Great Britain rises faster than that in the United States, we would expect the pound to appreciate relative to the dollar.

   b. Suppose you are a German machine tool exporter and you invoice all of your sales in foreign currency. Further suppose that the European monetary authorities begin to undertake an expansionary monetary policy. If it is certain that the easy money policy will result in higher inflation rates in "Euroland" relative to those in other countries, then you should use the forward markets to protect yourself against future losses resulting from the deterioration in the value of the euro.

   c. If you could accurately estimate differences in the relative inflation rates of two countries over a long period of time while other market participants were unable to do so, you could successfully speculate in spot currency markets.

LO 2 **18.9 Exchange Rate Movements**   Some countries encourage movements in their exchange rate relative to those of some other country as a short-term means of addressing foreign trade imbalances. For each of the following scenarios, evaluate the impact the announcement would have on an American importer and an American exporter doing business with the foreign country.

   a. Officials in the administration of the U.S. government announce that they are comfortable with a rising Mexican peso relative to the dollar.

b. British monetary authorities announce that they feel the pound has been driven too low by currency speculators relative to the dollar.

c. The Brazilian government announces that it will print billions of new reais and inject them into the economy in an effort to reduce the country's 40 percent unemployment rate.

LO 3 **18.10 International Investment** If financial markets are perfectly competitive and the Eurodollar rate is above that offered in the U.S. loan market, you would immediately want to borrow money in the United States and invest it in Eurodollars. True or false? Explain.

QUESTIONS AND PROBLEMS

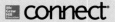 Select problems are available in McGraw-Hill *Connect*. Please see the packaging options section of the Preface for more information.

BASIC (Questions 1–10)

LO 1 **1. Using Exchange Rates** Take a look back at Table 18.2 to answer the following questions:

a. If you have $100, how many Polish zlotys can you get?

b. How much is one euro worth?

c. If you have five million euros, how many dollars do you have?

d. Which is worth more, a New Zealand dollar or a Singapore dollar?

e. Which is worth more, a Mexican peso or a Chilean peso?

f. How many Swiss francs can you get for a euro? What do you call this rate?

g. Per unit, what is the most valuable currency of those listed? The least valuable?

LO 1 **2. Using the Cross-Rate** Use the information in Table 18.2 to answer the following questions:

a. Which would you rather have, $100 or £100? Why?

b. Which would you rather have, $100 Canadian or £100? Why?

c. What is the cross-rate for Canadian dollars in terms of British pounds? For British pounds in terms of Canadian dollars?

LO 1 **3. Forward Exchange Rates** Use the information in Table 18.2 to answer the following questions:

a. What is the six-month forward rate for the Japanese yen in yen per U.S. dollar? Is the yen selling at a premium or a discount? Explain.

b. What is the three-month forward rate for the Australian dollar in U.S. dollars per Australian dollar? Is the dollar selling at a premium or a discount? Explain.

c. What do you think will happen to the value of the dollar relative to the yen and the Australian dollar, based on the information in the table? Explain.

LO 1   **4. Using Spot and Forward Exchange Rates**   Suppose the spot exchange rate for the Canadian dollar is Can$1.12 and the six-month forward rate is Can$1.17.

   a.   Which is worth more, a U.S. dollar or a Canadian dollar?

   b.   Assuming absolute PPP holds, what is the cost in the United States of an Elkhead beer if the price in Canada is Can$2.49? Why might the beer actually sell at a different price in the United States?

   c.   Is the U.S. dollar selling at a premium or a discount relative to the Canadian dollar?

   d.   Which currency is expected to appreciate in value?

   e.   Which country do you think has higher interest rates—the United States or Canada? Explain.

LO 1   **5. Cross-Rates and Arbitrage**   Suppose the Japanese yen exchange rate is ¥119 = $1 and the British pound exchange rate is £1 = $1.39.

   a.   What is the cross-rate in terms of yen per pound?

   b.   Suppose the cross-rate is ¥168 = £1. Is there an arbitrage opportunity here? If there is, explain how to take advantage of the mispricing.

LO 2   **6. Interest Rate Parity**   Use Table 18.2 to answer the following questions. Suppose interest rate parity holds, and the current risk-free rate in the United States is 2.1 percent per six months. What must the six-month risk-free rate be in Australia? In Japan? In Great Britain?

LO 2   **7. Interest Rates and Arbitrage**   The treasurer of a major U.S. firm has $30 million to invest for three months. The interest rate in the United States is .24 percent per month. The interest rate in Great Britain is .31 percent per month. The spot exchange rate is £.73, and the three-month forward rate is £.75. Ignoring transaction costs, in which country would the treasurer want to invest the company's funds? Why?

LO 2   **8. Inflation and Exchange Rates**   Suppose the current exchange rate for the Russian ruble is RUB 64.18. The expected exchange rate in three years is RUB 69.32. What is the difference in the annual inflation rates for the United States and Russia over this period? Assume that the anticipated rate is constant for both countries. What relationship are you relying on in answering?

LO 3   **9. Exchange Rate Risk**   Suppose your company imports computer motherboards from Singapore. The exchange rate is given in Table 18.2. You have just placed an order for 30,000 motherboards at a cost to you of 185.50 Singapore dollars each. You will pay for the shipment when it arrives in 90 days. You can sell the motherboards for $150 each. Calculate your profit if the exchange rate goes up or down by 10 percent over the next 90 days. What is the break-even exchange rate? What percentage rise or fall does this represent in terms of the Singapore dollar versus the U.S. dollar?

LO 2   **10. Exchange Rates and Arbitrage**   Suppose the spot and six-month forward rates on the South Korean won are ₩1,118.33 and ₩1,120.87, respectively. The annual risk-free rate in the United States is 2.5 percent, and the annual risk-free rate in South Korea is 3.1 percent.

   a.   Is there an arbitrage opportunity here? If so, how would you exploit it?

   b.   What must the six-month forward rate be to prevent arbitrage?

INTERMEDIATE (Questions 11–15)

LO 2 **11. Spot versus Forward Rates** Suppose the spot and three-month forward rates for the yen are ¥108.46 and ¥107.13, respectively.

    a. Is the yen expected to get stronger or weaker?

    b. What would you estimate is the difference between the inflation rates of the United States and Japan?

LO 2 **12. Expected Spot Rates** Suppose the spot exchange rate for the Hungarian forint is HUF 287. Interest rates in the United States are 2.7 percent per year. They are 4.8 percent in Hungary.

    a. What do you predict the exchange rate will be in one year?

    b. In two years?

    c. In five years? What relationship are you using?

LO 2 **13. Cross-Rates and Arbitrage** The British pound trades at $1.3679 in London and $1.3668 in New York. How much profit could you earn on each trade with $10,000?

LO 2 **14. Purchasing Power Parity and Exchange Rates** According to purchasing power parity, if a Big Mac sells for $4.89 in the United States and króna 522.50 in Iceland, what is the króna/$ exchange rate?

LO 3 **15. Translation Exposure** Betancourt International has operations in Arrakis. The balance sheet for this division in Arrakeen solaris shows assets of 40,000 solaris, debt in the amount of 12,500 solaris, and equity of 27,500 solaris.

    a. If the current exchange ratio is 1.35 solaris per dollar, what does the balance sheet look like in dollars?

    b. Assume that one year from now the balance sheet in solaris is exactly the same as at the beginning of the year. If the exchange rate is 1.45 solaris per dollar, what does the balance sheet look like in dollars now?

    c. Rework part (b) assuming the exchange rate is 1.26 solaris per dollar.

CHALLENGE (Question 16)

LO 3 **16. Translation Exposure** In the previous problem, assume the equity increases by 2,200 solaris due to retained earnings. If the exchange rate at the end of the year is 1.29 solaris per dollar, what does the balance sheet look like?

18.1 Purchasing Power Parity As we discussed in the chapter, one of the more famous examples of a violation of absolute purchasing power parity is the Big Mac index calculated by *The Economist*. This index calculates the dollar price of a McDonald's Big Mac in different countries. You can find the Big Mac index by going to www.economist.com. Using the most recent index, which country has the most expensive Big Macs? Which country has the cheapest Big Macs? Why is the price of a Big Mac not the same in every country?

18.2 Interest Rate Parity Go to the *Financial Times* site at www.ft.com, and find the current exchange rate between the U.S. dollar and the euro. Next, find the U.S. dollar LIBOR and the euro LIBOR interest rates. What must the one-year forward rate be to prevent arbitrage? What principle are you relying on in your answer?

WHAT'S ON THE WEB?

EXCEL *MASTER IT!* PROBLEM

Excel
Master
coverage online

The Federal Reserve Bank of St. Louis has historical exchange rates on its website, www
.stlouisfed.org. Go to the website and look for the "FRED®" data. Then, download the exchange rate with the U.S. dollar over the past five years for the following currencies: Brazilian real, Canadian dollar, Hong Kong dollar, Japanese yen, Mexican new peso, South
Korean won, Indian rupee, Swiss franc, Australian dollar, and euro. Graph the exchange
rate for each of these currencies in a dashboard that can be printed on one page.

CHAPTER CASE
S&S Air Goes International

Mark Sexton and Todd Story, the owners of S&S Air, have been in discussions with an aircraft dealer in Europe about selling the company's Eagle airplane. The Eagle sells for $98,000 and has a variable cost of $81,000 per airplane. Amalie Diefenbaker, the dealer, wants to add the Eagle to her current retail line. Amalie has told Mark and Todd that she feels she will be able to sell 15 airplanes per month in Europe. All sales will be made in euros, and Amalie will pay the company €78,400 for each plane. Amalie proposes that she order 15 aircraft today for the first month's sales. She will pay for all 15 aircraft in 90 days. This order and payment schedule will continue each month.

Mark and Todd are confident they can handle the extra volume with their existing facilities, but they are unsure about the potential financial risks of selling their aircraft in Europe. In their discussion with Amalie, they found out that the current exchange rate is $1.25/€. This means that they can convert the €78,400 per airplane paid by Amalie to $98,000. Thus, the profit on the international sales is the same as the profit on dollar-denominated sales.

Mark and Todd decided to ask Chris Guthrie, their financial analyst, to prepare an analysis of the proposed international sales. Specifically, they ask Chris to answer the following questions.

QUESTIONS

1. What are the pros and cons of the international sales? What additional risks will the company face?

2. What happens to the company's profits if the dollar strengthens? What if the dollar weakens?

3. Ignoring taxes, what are S&S Air's projected gains or losses from this proposed arrangement at the current exchange rate of $1.25/€? What happens to profits if the exchange rate changes to $1.39/€? At what exchange rate will the company break even?

4. How could the company hedge its exchange rate risk? What are the implications of this approach?

5. Taking all factors into account, should the company pursue the international sales deal further? Why or why not?

Mathematical Tables

| APPENDIX A.1 | Future value of $1 at the end of t periods $= (1 + r)^t$ |

	Interest Rate								
Number of Periods	1%	2%	3%	4%	5%	6%	7%	8%	9%
1	1.0100	1.0200	1.0300	1.0400	1.0500	1.0600	1.0700	1.0800	1.0900
2	1.0201	1.0404	1.0609	1.0816	1.1025	1.1236	1.1449	1.1664	1.1881
3	1.0303	1.0612	1.0927	1.1249	1.1576	1.1910	1.2250	1.2597	1.2950
4	1.0406	1.0824	1.1255	1.1699	1.2155	1.2625	1.3108	1.3605	1.4116
5	1.0510	1.1041	1.1593	1.2167	1.2763	1.3382	1.4026	1.4693	1.5386
6	1.0615	1.1262	1.1941	1.2653	1.3401	1.4185	1.5007	1.5869	1.6771
7	1.0721	1.1487	1.2299	1.3159	1.4071	1.5036	1.6058	1.7138	1.8280
8	1.0829	1.1717	1.2668	1.3686	1.4775	1.5938	1.7182	1.8509	1.9926
9	1.0937	1.1951	1.3048	1.4233	1.5513	1.6895	1.8385	1.9990	2.1719
10	1.1046	1.2190	1.3439	1.4802	1.6289	1.7908	1.9672	2.1589	2.3674
11	1.1157	1.2434	1.3842	1.5395	1.7103	1.8983	2.1049	2.3316	2.5804
12	1.1268	1.2682	1.4258	1.6010	1.7959	2.0122	2.2522	2.5182	2.8127
13	1.1381	1.2936	1.4685	1.6651	1.8856	2.1329	2.4098	2.7196	3.0658
14	1.1495	1.3195	1.5126	1.7317	1.9799	2.2609	2.5785	2.9372	3.3417
15	1.1610	1.3459	1.5580	1.8009	2.0789	2.3966	2.7590	3.1722	3.6425
16	1.1726	1.3728	1.6047	1.8730	2.1829	2.5404	2.9522	3.4259	3.9703
17	1.1843	1.4002	1.6528	1.9479	2.2920	2.6928	3.1588	3.7000	4.3276
18	1.1961	1.4282	1.7024	2.0258	2.4066	2.8543	3.3799	3.9960	4.7171
19	1.2081	1.4568	1.7535	2.1068	2.5270	3.0256	3.6165	4.3157	5.1417
20	1.2202	1.4859	1.8061	2.1911	2.6533	3.2071	3.8697	4.6610	5.6044
21	1.2324	1.5157	1.8603	2.2788	2.7860	3.3996	4.1406	5.0338	6.1088
22	1.2447	1.5460	1.9161	2.3699	2.9253	3.6035	4.4304	5.4365	6.6586
23	1.2572	1.5769	1.9736	2.4647	3.0715	3.8197	4.7405	5.8715	7.2579
24	1.2697	1.6084	2.0328	2.5633	3.2251	4.0489	5.0724	6.3412	7.9111
25	1.2824	1.6406	2.0938	2.6658	3.3864	4.2919	5.4274	6.8485	8.6231
30	1.3478	1.8114	2.4273	3.2434	4.3219	5.7435	7.6123	10.063	13.268
40	1.4889	2.2080	3.2620	4.8010	7.0400	10.286	14.974	21.725	31.409
50	1.6446	2.6916	4.3839	7.1067	11.467	18.420	29.457	46.902	74.358
60	1.8167	3.2810	5.8916	10.520	18.679	32.988	57.946	101.26	176.03

10%	12%	14%	15%	16%	18%	20%	24%	28%	32%	36%
1.1000	1.1200	1.1400	1.1500	1.1600	1.1800	1.2000	1.2400	1.2800	1.3200	1.3600
1.2100	1.2544	1.2996	1.3225	1.3456	1.3924	1.4400	1.5376	1.6384	1.7424	1.8496
1.3310	1.4049	1.4815	1.5209	1.5609	1.6430	1.7280	1.9066	2.0972	2.3000	2.5155
1.4641	1.5735	1.6890	1.7490	1.8106	1.9388	2.0736	2.3642	2.6844	3.0360	3.4210
1.6105	1.7623	1.9254	2.0114	2.1003	2.2878	2.4883	2.9316	3.4360	4.0075	4.6526
1.7716	1.9738	2.1950	2.3131	2.4364	2.6996	2.9860	3.6352	4.3980	5.2899	6.3275
1.9487	2.2107	2.5023	2.6600	2.8262	3.1855	3.5832	4.5077	5.6295	6.9826	8.6054
2.1436	2.4760	2.8526	3.0590	3.2784	3.7589	4.2998	5.5895	7.2058	9.2170	11.703
2.3579	2.7731	3.2519	3.5179	3.8030	4.4355	5.1598	6.9310	9.2234	12.166	15.917
2.5937	3.1058	3.7072	4.0456	4.4114	5.2338	6.1917	8.5944	11.806	16.060	21.647
2.8531	3.4785	4.2262	4.6524	5.1173	6.1759	7.4301	10.657	15.112	21.199	29.439
3.1384	3.8960	4.8179	5.3503	5.9360	7.2876	8.9161	13.215	19.343	27.983	40.037
3.4523	4.3635	5.4924	6.1528	6.8858	8.5994	10.699	16.386	24.759	36.937	54.451
3.7975	4.8871	6.2613	7.0757	7.9875	10.147	12.839	20.319	31.691	48.757	74.053
4.1772	5.4736	7.1379	8.1371	9.2655	11.974	15.407	25.196	40.565	64.359	100.71
4.5950	6.1304	8.1372	9.3576	10.748	14.129	18.488	31.243	51.923	84.954	136.97
5.0545	6.8660	9.2765	10.761	12.468	16.672	22.186	38.741	66.461	112.14	186.28
5.5599	7.6900	10.575	12.375	14.463	19.673	26.623	48.039	85.071	148.02	253.34
6.1159	8.6128	12.056	14.232	16.777	23.214	31.948	59.568	108.89	195.39	344.54
6.7275	9.6463	13.743	16.367	19.461	27.393	38.338	73.864	139.38	257.92	468.57
7.4002	10.804	15.668	18.822	22.574	32.324	46.005	91.592	178.41	340.45	637.26
8.1403	12.100	17.861	21.645	26.186	38.142	55.206	113.57	228.36	449.39	866.67
8.9543	13.552	20.362	24.891	30.376	45.008	66.247	140.83	292.30	593.20	1178.7
9.8497	15.179	23.212	28.625	35.236	53.109	79.497	174.63	374.14	783.02	1603.0
10.835	17.000	26.462	32.919	40.874	62.669	95.396	216.54	478.90	1033.6	2180.1
17.449	29.960	50.950	66.212	85.850	143.37	237.38	634.82	1645.5	4142.1	10143.
45.259	93.051	188.88	267.86	378.72	750.38	1469.8	5455.9	19427.	66521.	*
117.39	289.00	700.23	1083.7	1670.7	3927.4	9100.4	46890.	*	*	*
304.48	897.60	2595.9	4384.0	7370.2	20555.	56348.	*	*	*	*

*The factor is greater than 99,999.

APPENDIX A.2   Present value of $1 to be received after t periods $= 1/(1 + r)^t$

Number of Periods	Interest Rate								
	1%	2%	3%	4%	5%	6%	7%	8%	9%
1	.9901	.9804	.9709	.9615	.9524	.9434	.9346	.9259	.9174
2	.9803	.9612	.9426	.9246	.9070	.8900	.8734	.8573	.8417
3	.9706	.9423	.9151	.8890	.8638	.8396	.8163	.7938	.7722
4	.9610	.9238	.8885	.8548	.8227	.7921	.7629	.7350	.7084
5	.9515	.9057	.8626	.8219	.7835	.7473	.7130	.6806	.6499
6	.9420	.8880	.8375	.7903	.7462	.7050	.6663	.6302	.5963
7	.9327	.8706	.8131	.7599	.7107	.6651	.6227	.5835	.5470
8	.9235	.8535	.7894	.7307	.6768	.6274	.5820	.5403	.5019
9	.9143	.8368	.7664	.7026	.6446	.5919	.5439	.5002	.4604
10	.9053	.8203	.7441	.6756	.6139	.5584	.5083	.4632	.4224
11	.8963	.8043	.7224	.6496	.5847	.5268	.4751	.4289	.3875
12	.8874	.7885	.7014	.6246	.5568	.4970	.4440	.3971	.3555
13	.8787	.7730	.6810	.6006	.5303	.4688	.4150	.3677	.3262
14	.8700	.7579	.6611	.5775	.5051	.4423	.3878	.3405	.2992
15	.8613	.7430	.6419	.5553	.4810	.4173	.3624	.3152	.2745
16	.8528	.7284	.6232	.5339	.4581	.3936	.3387	.2919	.2519
17	.8444	.7142	.6050	.5134	.4363	.3714	.3166	.2703	.2311
18	.8360	.7002	.5874	.4936	.4155	.3503	.2959	.2502	.2120
19	.8277	.6864	.5703	.4746	.3957	.3305	.2765	.2317	.1945
20	.8195	.6730	.5537	.4564	.3769	.3118	.2584	.2145	.1784
21	.8114	.6598	.5375	.4388	.3589	.2942	.2415	.1987	.1637
22	.8034	.6468	.5219	.4220	.3418	.2775	.2257	.1839	.1502
23	.7954	.6342	.5067	.4057	.3256	.2618	.2109	.1703	.1378
24	.7876	.6217	.4919	.3901	.3101	.2470	.1971	.1577	.1264
25	.7798	.6095	.4776	.3751	.2953	.2330	.1842	.1460	.1160
30	.7419	.5521	.4120	.3083	.2314	.1741	.1314	.0994	.0754
40	.6717	.4529	.3066	.2083	.1420	.0972	.0668	.0460	.0318
50	.6080	.3715	.2281	.1407	.0872	.0543	.0339	.0213	.0134

10%	12%	14%	15%	16%	18%	20%	24%	28%	32%	36%
.9091	.8929	.8772	.8696	.8621	.8475	.8333	.8065	.7813	.7576	.7353
.8264	.7972	.7695	.7561	.7432	.7182	.6944	.6504	.6104	.5739	.5407
.7513	.7118	.6750	.6575	.6407	.6086	.5787	.5245	.4768	.4348	.3975
.6830	.6355	.5921	.5718	.5523	.5158	.4823	.4230	.3725	.3294	.2923
.6209	.5674	.5194	.4972	.4761	.4371	.4019	.3411	.2910	.2495	.2149
.5645	.5066	.4556	.4323	.4104	.3704	.3349	.2751	.2274	.1890	.1580
.5132	.4523	.3996	.3759	.3538	.3139	.2791	.2218	.1776	.1432	.1162
.4665	.4039	.3506	.3269	.3050	.2660	.2326	.1789	.1388	.1085	.0854
.4241	.3606	.3075	.2843	.2630	.2255	.1938	.1443	.1084	.0822	.0628
.3855	.3220	.2697	.2472	.2267	.1911	.1615	.1164	.0847	.0623	.0462
.3505	.2875	.2366	.2149	.1954	.1619	.1346	.0938	.0662	.0472	.0340
.3186	.2567	.2076	.1869	.1685	.1372	.1122	.0757	.0517	.0357	.0250
.2897	.2292	.1821	.1625	.1452	.1163	.0935	.0610	.0404	.0271	.0184
.2633	.2046	.1597	.1413	.1252	.0985	.0779	.0492	.0316	.0205	.0135
.2394	.1827	.1401	.1229	.1079	.0835	.0649	.0397	.0247	.0155	.0099
.2176	.1631	.1229	.1069	.0930	.0708	.0541	.0320	.0193	.0118	.0073
.1978	.1456	.1078	.0929	.0802	.0600	.0451	.0258	.0150	.0089	.0054
.1799	.1300	.0946	.0808	.0691	.0508	.0376	.0208	.0118	.0068	.0039
.1635	.1161	.0829	.0703	.0596	.0431	.0313	.0168	.0092	.0051	.0029
.1486	.1037	.0728	.0611	.0514	.0365	.0261	.0135	.0072	.0039	.0021
.1351	.0926	.0638	.0531	.0443	.0309	.0217	.0109	.0056	.0029	.0016
.1228	.0826	.0560	.0462	.0382	.0262	.0181	.0088	.0044	.0022	.0012
.1117	.0738	.0491	.0402	.0329	.0222	.0151	.0071	.0034	.0017	.0008
.1015	.0659	.0431	.0349	.0284	.0188	.0126	.0057	.0027	.0013	.0006
.0923	.0588	.0378	.0304	.0245	.0160	.0105	.0046	.0021	.0010	.0005
.0573	.0334	.0196	.0151	.0116	.0070	.0042	.0016	.0006	.0002	.0001
.0221	.0107	.0053	.0037	.0026	.0013	.0007	.0002	.0001	*	*
.0085	.0035	.0014	.0009	.0006	.0003	.0001	*	*	*	*

*The factor is zero to four decimal places.

APPENDIX A.3   Present value of an annuity of $1 per period for t periods $= [1 - 1/(1 + r)^t]/r$

Number of Periods	Interest Rate								
	1%	2%	3%	4%	5%	6%	7%	8%	9%
1	.9901	.9804	.9709	.9615	.9524	.9434	.9346	.9259	.9174
2	1.9704	1.9416	1.9135	1.8861	1.8594	1.8334	1.8080	1.7833	1.7591
3	2.9410	2.8839	2.8286	2.7751	2.7232	2.6730	2.6243	2.5771	2.5313
4	3.9020	3.8077	3.7171	3.6299	3.5460	3.4651	3.3872	3.3121	3.2397
5	4.8534	4.7135	4.5797	4.4518	4.3295	4.2124	4.1002	3.9927	3.8897
6	5.7955	5.6014	5.4172	5.2421	5.0757	4.9173	4.7665	4.6229	4.4859
7	6.7282	6.4720	6.2303	6.0021	5.7864	5.5824	5.3893	5.2064	5.0330
8	7.6517	7.3255	7.0197	6.7327	6.4632	6.2098	5.9713	5.7466	5.5348
9	8.5660	8.1622	7.7861	7.4353	7.1078	6.8017	6.5152	6.2469	5.9952
10	9.4713	8.9826	8.5302	8.1109	7.7217	7.3601	7.0236	6.7101	6.4177
11	10.3676	9.7868	9.2526	8.7605	8.3064	7.8869	7.4987	7.1390	6.8052
12	11.2551	10.5753	9.9540	9.3851	8.8633	8.3838	7.9427	7.5361	7.1607
13	12.1337	11.3484	10.6350	9.9856	9.3936	8.8527	8.3577	7.9038	7.4869
14	13.0037	12.1062	11.2961	10.5631	9.8986	9.2950	8.7455	8.2442	7.7862
15	13.8651	12.8493	11.9379	11.1184	10.3797	9.7122	9.1079	8.5595	8.0607
16	14.7179	13.5777	12.5611	11.6523	10.8378	10.1059	9.4466	8.8514	8.3126
17	15.5623	14.2919	13.1661	12.1657	11.2741	10.4773	9.7632	9.1216	8.5436
18	16.3983	14.9920	13.7535	12.6593	11.6896	10.8276	10.0591	9.3719	8.7556
19	17.2260	15.6785	14.3238	13.1339	12.0853	11.1581	10.3356	9.6036	8.9501
20	18.0456	16.3514	14.8775	13.5903	12.4622	11.4699	10.5940	9.8181	9.1285
21	18.8570	17.0112	15.4150	14.0292	12.8212	11.7641	10.8355	10.0168	9.2922
22	19.6604	17.6580	15.9369	14.4511	13.1630	12.0416	11.0612	10.2007	9.4424
23	20.4558	18.2922	16.4436	14.8568	13.4886	12.3034	11.2722	10.3741	9.5802
24	21.2434	18.9139	16.9355	15.2470	13.7986	12.5504	11.4693	10.5288	9.7066
25	22.0232	19.5235	17.4131	15.6221	14.0939	12.7834	11.6536	10.6748	9.8226
30	25.8077	22.3965	19.6004	17.2920	15.3725	13.7648	12.4090	11.2578	10.2737
40	32.8347	27.3555	23.1148	19.7928	17.1591	15.0463	13.3317	11.9246	10.7574
50	39.1961	31.4236	25.7298	21.4822	18.2559	15.7619	13.8007	12.2335	10.9617

10%	12%	14%	15%	16%	18%	20%	24%	28%	32%
.9091	.8929	.8772	.8696	.8621	.8475	.8333	.8065	.7813	.7576
1.7355	1.6901	1.6467	1.6257	1.6052	1.5656	1.5278	1.4568	1.3916	1.3315
2.4869	2.4018	2.3216	2.2832	2.2459	2.1743	2.1065	1.9813	1.8684	1.7663
3.1699	3.0373	2.9137	2.8550	2.7982	2.6901	2.5887	2.4043	2.2410	2.0957
3.7908	3.6048	3.4331	3.3522	3.2743	3.1272	2.9906	2.7454	2.5320	2.3452
4.3553	4.1114	3.8887	3.7845	3.6847	3.4976	3.3255	3.0205	2.7594	2.5342
4.8684	4.5638	4.2883	4.1604	4.0386	3.8115	3.6046	3.2423	2.9370	2.6775
5.3349	4.9676	4.6389	4.4873	4.3436	4.0776	3.8372	3.4212	3.0758	2.7860
5.7590	5.3282	4.9464	4.7716	4.6065	4.3030	4.0310	3.5655	3.1842	2.8681
6.1446	5.6502	5.2161	5.0188	4.8332	4.4941	4.1925	3.6819	3.2689	2.9304
6.4951	5.9377	5.4527	5.2337	5.0286	4.6560	4.3271	3.7757	3.3351	2.9776
6.8137	6.1944	5.6603	5.4206	5.1971	4.7932	4.4392	3.8514	3.3868	3.0133
7.1034	6.4235	5.8424	5.5831	5.3423	4.9095	4.5327	3.9124	3.4272	3.0404
7.3667	6.6282	6.0021	5.7245	5.4675	5.0081	4.6106	3.9616	3.4587	3.0609
7.6061	6.8109	6.1422	5.8474	5.5755	5.0916	4.6755	4.0013	3.4834	3.0764
7.8237	6.9740	6.2651	5.9542	5.6685	5.1624	4.7296	4.0333	3.5026	3.0882
8.0216	7.1196	6.3729	6.0472	5.7487	5.2223	4.7746	4.0591	3.5177	3.0971
8.2014	7.2497	6.4674	6.1280	5.8178	5.2732	4.8122	4.0799	3.5294	3.1039
8.3649	7.3658	6.5504	6.1982	5.8775	5.3162	4.8435	4.0967	3.5386	3.1090
8.5136	7.4694	6.6231	6.2593	5.9288	5.3527	4.8696	4.1103	3.5458	3.1129
8.6487	7.5620	6.6870	6.3125	5.9731	5.3837	4.8913	4.1212	3.5514	3.1158
8.7715	7.6446	6.7429	6.3587	6.0113	5.4099	4.9094	4.1300	3.5558	3.1180
8.8832	7.7184	6.7921	6.3988	6.0442	5.4321	4.9245	4.1371	3.5592	3.1197
8.9847	7.7843	6.8351	6.4338	6.0726	5.4509	4.9371	4.1428	3.5619	3.1210
9.0770	7.8431	6.8729	6.4641	6.0971	5.4669	4.9476	4.1474	3.5640	3.1220
9.4269	8.0552	7.0027	6.5660	6.1772	5.5168	4.9789	4.1601	3.5693	3.1242
9.7791	8.2438	7.1050	6.6418	6.2335	5.5482	4.9966	4.1659	3.5712	3.1250
9.9148	8.3045	7.1327	6.6605	6.2463	5.5541	4.9995	4.1666	3.5714	3.1250

APPENDIX A.4 Future value of an annuity of $1 per period for t periods $= [(1 + r)^t - 1]/r$

Number of Periods	Interest Rate								
	1%	2%	3%	4%	5%	6%	7%	8%	9%
1	1.0000	1.0000	1.0000	1.0000	1.0000	1.0000	1.0000	1.0000	1.0000
2	2.0100	2.0200	2.0300	2.0400	2.0500	2.0600	2.0700	2.0800	2.0900
3	3.0301	3.0604	3.0909	3.1216	3.1525	3.1836	3.2149	3.2464	3.2781
4	4.0604	4.1216	4.1836	4.2465	4.3101	4.3746	4.4399	4.5061	4.5731
5	5.1010	5.2040	5.3091	5.4163	5.5256	5.6371	5.7507	5.8666	5.9847
6	6.1520	6.3081	6.4684	6.6330	6.8019	6.9753	7.1533	7.3359	7.5233
7	7.2135	7.4343	7.6625	7.8983	8.1420	8.3938	8.6540	8.9228	9.2004
8	8.2857	8.5830	8.8932	9.2142	9.5491	9.8975	10.260	10.637	11.028
9	9.3685	9.7546	10.159	10.583	11.027	11.491	11.978	12.488	13.021
10	10.462	10.950	11.464	12.006	12.578	13.181	13.816	14.487	15.193
11	11.567	12.169	12.808	13.486	14.207	14.972	15.784	16.645	17.560
12	12.683	13.412	14.192	15.026	15.917	16.870	17.888	18.977	20.141
13	13.809	14.680	15.618	16.627	17.713	18.882	20.141	21.495	22.953
14	14.947	15.974	17.086	18.292	19.599	21.015	22.550	24.215	26.019
15	16.097	17.293	18.599	20.024	21.579	23.276	25.129	27.152	29.361
16	17.258	18.639	20.157	21.825	23.657	25.673	27.888	30.324	33.003
17	18.430	20.012	21.762	23.698	25.840	28.213	30.840	33.750	36.974
18	19.615	21.412	23.414	25.645	28.132	30.906	33.999	37.450	41.301
19	20.811	22.841	25.117	27.671	30.539	33.760	37.379	41.446	46.018
20	22.019	24.297	26.870	29.778	33.066	36.786	40.995	45.762	51.160
21	23.239	25.783	28.676	31.969	35.719	39.993	44.865	50.423	56.765
22	24.472	27.299	30.537	34.248	38.505	43.392	49.006	55.457	62.873
23	25.716	28.845	32.453	36.618	41.430	46.996	53.436	60.893	69.532
24	26.973	30.422	34.426	39.083	44.502	50.816	58.177	66.765	76.790
25	28.243	32.030	36.459	41.646	47.727	54.865	63.249	73.106	84.701
30	34.785	40.568	47.575	56.085	66.439	79.058	94.461	113.28	136.31
40	48.886	60.402	75.401	95.026	120.80	154.76	199.64	259.06	337.88
50	64.463	84.579	112.80	152.67	209.35	290.34	406.53	573.77	815.08
60	81.670	114.05	163.05	237.99	353.58	533.13	813.52	1253.2	1944.8

10%	12%	14%	15%	16%	18%	20%	24%	28%	32%	36%
1.0000	1.0000	1.0000	1.0000	1.0000	1.0000	1.0000	1.0000	1.0000	1.0000	1.0000
2.1000	2.1200	2.1400	2.1500	2.1600	2.1800	2.2000	2.2400	2.2800	2.3200	2.3600
3.3100	3.3744	3.4396	3.4725	3.5056	3.5724	3.6400	3.7776	3.9184	4.0624	4.2096
4.6410	4.7793	4.9211	4.9934	5.0665	5.2154	5.3680	5.6842	6.0156	6.3624	6.7251
6.1051	6.3528	6.6101	6.7424	6.8771	7.1542	7.4416	8.0484	8.6999	9.3983	10.146
7.7156	8.1152	8.5355	8.7537	8.9775	9.4420	9.9299	10.980	12.136	13.406	14.799
9.4872	10.089	10.730	11.067	11.414	12.142	12.916	14.615	16.534	18.696	21.126
11.436	12.300	13.233	13.727	14.240	15.327	16.499	19.123	22.163	25.678	29.732
13.579	14.776	16.085	16.786	17.519	19.086	20.799	24.712	29.369	34.895	41.435
15.937	17.549	19.337	20.304	21.321	23.521	25.959	31.643	38.593	47.062	57.352
18.531	20.655	23.045	24.349	25.733	28.755	32.150	40.238	50.398	63.122	78.998
21.384	24.133	27.271	29.002	30.850	34.931	39.581	50.895	65.510	84.320	108.44
24.523	28.029	32.089	34.352	36.786	42.219	48.497	64.110	84.853	112.30	148.47
27.975	32.393	37.581	40.505	43.672	50.818	59.196	80.496	109.61	149.24	202.93
31.772	37.280	43.842	47.580	51.660	60.965	72.035	100.82	141.30	198.00	276.98
35.950	42.753	50.980	55.717	60.925	72.939	87.442	126.01	181.87	262.36	377.69
40.545	48.884	59.118	65.075	71.673	87.068	105.93	157.25	233.79	347.31	514.66
45.599	55.750	68.394	75.836	84.141	103.74	128.12	195.99	300.25	459.45	700.94
51.159	63.440	78.969	88.212	98.603	123.41	154.74	244.03	385.32	607.47	954.28
57.275	72.052	91.025	102.44	115.38	146.63	186.69	303.60	494.21	802.86	1298.8
64.002	81.699	104.77	118.81	134.84	174.02	225.03	377.46	633.59	1060.8	1767.4
71.403	92.503	120.44	137.63	157.41	206.34	271.03	469.06	812.00	1401.2	2404.7
79.543	104.60	138.30	159.28	183.60	244.49	326.24	582.63	1040.4	1850.6	3271.3
88.497	118.16	158.66	184.17	213.98	289.49	392.48	723.46	1332.7	2443.8	4450.0
98.347	133.33	181.87	212.79	249.21	342.60	471.98	898.09	1706.8	3226.8	6053.0
164.49	241.33	356.79	434.75	530.31	790.95	1181.9	2640.9	5873.2	12941.	28172.3
442.59	767.09	1342.0	1779.1	2360.8	4163.2	7343.9	22729.	69377.	*	*
1163.9	2400.0	4994.5	7217.7	10436.	21813.	45497.	*	*	*	*
3034.8	7471.6	18535.	29220.	46058.	*	*	*	*	*	*

*The factor is greater than 99,999.

B Key Equations

CHAPTER 2

1. The balance sheet identity, or equation:
   Assets = Liabilities + Shareholders' equity [2.1]

2. The income statement equation:
   Revenues − Expenses = Income [2.2]

3. The cash flow identity:
   Cash flow from assets = Cash flow to creditors
   $\qquad\qquad$ + Cash flow to stockholders [2.3]

   where:

   a. Cash flow from assets = Operating cash flow (OCF) − Net capital spending − Change in net working capital (NWC)
      (1) Operating cash flow = Earnings before interest and taxes (EBIT) + Depreciation − Taxes
      (2) Net capital spending = Ending net fixed assets − Beginning net fixed assets + Depreciation
      (3) Change in net working capital = Ending NWC − Beginning NWC
   b. Cash flow to creditors = Interest paid − Net new borrowing
   c. Cash flow to stockholders = Dividend paid − Net new equity raised

CHAPTER 3

1. The current ratio:
   $$\text{Current ratio} = \frac{\text{Current assets}}{\text{Current liabilities}} \quad [3.1]$$

2. The quick, or acid-test, ratio:
   $$\text{Quick ratio} = \frac{\text{Current assets } - \text{ Inventory}}{\text{Current liabilities}} \quad [3.2]$$

3. The cash ratio:
   $$\text{Cash ratio} = \frac{\text{Cash}}{\text{Current liabilities}} \quad [3.3]$$

4. The total debt ratio:
   $$\text{Total debt ratio} = \frac{\text{Total assets} - \text{Total equity}}{\text{Total assets}} \quad [3.4]$$

5. The debt-equity ratio:
   Debt-equity ratio = Total debt/Total equity [3.5]

6. The equity multiplier:
   Equity multiplier = Total assets/Total equity [3.6]

7. The times interest earned (TIE) ratio:
   $$\text{Times interest earned ratio} = \frac{\text{EBIT}}{\text{Interest}} \quad [3.7]$$

8. The cash coverage ratio:
   $$\text{Cash coverage ratio} = \frac{\text{EBIT + Depreciation}}{\text{Interest}} \quad [3.8]$$

9. The inventory turnover ratio:
   $$\text{Inventory turnover} = \frac{\text{Cost of goods sold}}{\text{Inventory}} \quad [3.9]$$

10. The average days' sales in inventory:
    $$\text{Days' sales in inventory} = \frac{365 \text{ days}}{\text{Inventory turnover}} \quad [3.10]$$

11. The receivables turnover ratio:
    $$\text{Receivables turnover} = \frac{\text{Sales}}{\text{Accounts receivable}} \quad [3.11]$$

12. The days' sales in receivables:
    $$\text{Days' sales in receivables} = \frac{365 \text{ days}}{\text{Receivables turnover}} \quad [3.12]$$

13. The total asset turnover ratio:
    $$\text{Total asset turnover} = \frac{\text{Sales}}{\text{Total assets}} \quad [3.13]$$

14. Profit margin:
    $$\text{Profit margin} = \frac{\text{Net income}}{\text{Sales}} \quad [3.14]$$

15. Return on assets (ROA):
    $$\text{Return on assets} = \frac{\text{Net income}}{\text{Total assets}} \quad [3.15]$$

16. Return on equity (ROE):
    $$\text{Return on equity} = \frac{\text{Net income}}{\text{Total equity}} \quad [3.16]$$

17. Earnings per share (EPS):
    $$\text{EPS} = \frac{\text{Net income}}{\text{Shares outstanding}} \quad [3.17]$$

18. The price-earnings (PE) ratio:
    $$\text{PE ratio} = \frac{\text{Price per share}}{\text{Earnings per share}} \quad [3.18]$$

19. The price-sales ratio:
    $$\text{Price-sales ratio} = \frac{\text{Price per share}}{\text{Sales per share}} \quad [3.19]$$

20. The market-to-book ratio:
    $$\text{Market-to-book ratio} = \frac{\text{Market value per share}}{\text{Book value per share}} \quad [3.20]$$

21. The enterprise value:
    Enterprise value = Total market value of the stock
    $\qquad\qquad$ + Book value of all liabilities − Cash [3.21]

22. The EBITDA ratio:
    $$\text{EBITDA ratio} = \frac{\text{Enterprise value}}{\text{EBITDA}} \quad [3.22]$$

23. The DuPont identity:
    $$\text{ROE} = \underbrace{\frac{\text{Net income}}{\text{Sales}} \times \frac{\text{Sales}}{\text{Assets}}}_{\text{Return on assets (ROA)}} \times \frac{\text{Assets}}{\text{Total equity}}$$
    ROE = Profit margin [3.23]
    $\qquad$ × Total asset turnover
    $\qquad$ × Equity multiplier

24. The dividend payout ratio:
    $$\text{Dividend payout ratio} = \frac{\text{Cash dividends}}{\text{Net income}} \quad [3.24]$$

25. The retention ratio:
    $$\text{Retention ratio} = \frac{\text{Addition to retained earnings}}{\text{Net income}} \quad [3.25]$$

26. The internal growth rate:
    $$\text{Internal growth rate} = \frac{\text{ROA} \times b}{1 - \text{ROA} \times b} \quad [3.26]$$

27. The sustainable growth rate:
    $$\text{Sustainable growth rate} = \frac{\text{ROE} \times b}{1 - \text{ROE} \times b} \quad [3.27]$$

CHAPTER 4

1. The future value of $1 invested for t periods at a rate of r per period:
   Future value = $\$1 \times (1 + r)^t$ [4.1]

2. The present value of $1 to be received t periods in the future at a discount rate of r:
   PV = $\$1 \times [1/(1 + r)^t] = \$1/(1 + r)^t$ [4.2]

3. The relationship between future value and present value (the basic present value equation):
$$PV \times (1 + r)^t = FV_t$$
$$PV = FV_t / (1 + r)^t = FV_t \times [1/(1 + r)^t]$$ **[4.3]**

CHAPTER 5

1. The present value of an annuity of C dollars per period for t periods when the rate of return, or interest rate, is r:
$$\text{Annuity present value} = C \times \left(\frac{1 - \text{Present value factor}}{r} \right)$$
$$= C \times \left\{ \frac{1 - [1/(1 + r)^t]}{r} \right\}$$ **[5.1]**

2. The future value factor for an annuity:
$$\text{Annuity FV factor} = (\text{Future value factor} - 1)/r$$
$$= [(1 + r)^t - 1]/r$$ **[5.2]**

3. The present and future factor for an annuity due:
Annuity due value = Ordinary annuity value $\times (1 + r)$ **[5.3]**

4. Present value for a perpetuity:
PV for a perpetuity = $C/r = C \times (1/r)$ **[5.4]**

5. Effective annual rate (EAR), where m is the number of times the interest is compounded during the year:
$$EAR = (1 + \text{Quoted rate}/m)^m - 1$$ **[5.5]**

CHAPTER 6

1. Bond value if bond has (1) a face value of F paid at maturity, (2) a coupon of C paid per period, (3) t periods to maturity, and (4) a yield of r per period:
Bond value = $C \times [1 - 1/(1 + r)^t]/r + F/(1 + r)^t$
$$\text{Bond value} = \frac{\text{Present value of}}{\text{the coupons}} + \frac{\text{Present value of}}{\text{the face amount}}$$ **[6.1]**

2. The Fisher effect:
$$1 + R = (1 + r) \times (1 + h)$$ **[6.2]**
where h is the inflation rate

3. $R = r + h + r \times h$ **[6.3]**

4. $R \approx r + h$ **[6.4]**

CHAPTER 7

1. $P_0 = (D_1 + P_1)/(1 + R)$ **[7.1]**
2. $P_0 = D/R$ **[7.2]**
3. $P_0 = \frac{D_0 \times (1 + g)}{R - g} = \frac{D_1}{R - g}$ **[7.3]**
4. $P_t = \frac{D_t \times (1 + g)}{R - g} = \frac{D_{t+1}}{R - g}$ **[7.4]**
5. $R = D_1/P_0 + g$ **[7.5]**
6. Price at Time t = Benchmark PE ratio $\times$ EPS$_t$ **[7.6]**

CHAPTER 8

1. Net present value (NPV):
NPV = Present value of future cash flows − Investment cost
2. Payback period:
Payback period = Number of years that pass before the sum of an investment's cash flows equals the cost of the investment

3. The average accounting return (AAR):
$$AAR = \frac{\text{Average net income}}{\text{Average book value}}$$

4. Internal rate of return (IRR):
IRR = Discount rate of required return such that the net present value of an investment is zero

5. Profitability index:
$$\text{Profitability index} = \frac{\text{PV of cash flows}}{\text{Cost of investment}}$$

CHAPTER 9

1. Project cash flow = Project operating cash flow
− Project change in net working capital
− Project capital spending
2. Operating cash flow = EBIT + Depreciation − Taxes
3. The tax shield approach to operating cash flow:
OCF = (Sales − Costs) $\times (1 - T_C)$ + Depreciation $\times T_C$
4. Total cash flow = Operating cash flow − Change in NWC
− Capital spending
5. Cash flow = Cash inflow − Cash outflow

CHAPTER 10

1. Total dollar return = Dividend income
+ Capital gain (or loss) **[10.1]**
2. Total cash if stock is sold = Initial investment + Total return **[10.2]**
3. Variance of returns, Var(R), or σ^2:
$$\text{Var}(R) = \frac{1}{T - 1} [(R_1 - \bar{R})^2 + \cdots + (R_T - \bar{R})^2]$$ **[10.3]**
4. Geometric average return = $[(1 + R_1) \times (1 + R_2) \times \cdots \times (1 + R_T)]^{1/T} - 1$ **[10.4]**

CHAPTER 11

1. Risk premium = Expected return − Risk-free rate **[11.1]**
$= E(R) - R_f$
2. Expected return on a portfolio:
$E(R_p) = x_1 \times E(R_1) + x_2 \times E(R_2) + \cdots + x_n \times E(R_n)$ **[11.2]**
3. Total return = Expected return + Unexpected return **[11.3]**
$R = E(R) + U$
4. Announcement = Expected part + Surprise **[11.4]**
5. $R = E(R)$ + Systematic portion + Unsystematic portion **[11.5]**
6. Total risk = Systematic risk + Unsystematic risk **[11.6]**
7. The capital asset pricing model (CAPM): **[11.7]**
$E(R_i) = R_f + [E(R_M) - R_f] \beta_i$

CHAPTER 12

1. $R_E = D_1/P_0 + g$ **[12.1]**
2. $R_E = R_f + \beta_E \times (R_M - R_f)$ **[12.2]**
3. $R_P = D/P_0$ **[12.3]**
4. $V = E + D$ **[12.4]**
5. $100\% = E/V + D/V$ **[12.5]**
6. Weighted average cost of capital (WACC)
$= (E/V) \times R_E + (D/V) \times R_D \times (1 - T_C)$ **[12.6]**

7. $\text{WACC} = (E/V) \times R_E + (P/V) \times R_p + (D/V)$
$\times R_D \times (1 - T_C)$ **[12.7]**

8. $\text{Taxes}^* = \text{EBIT} \times T_C$ **[12.8]**

9. $\text{CFA}^* = \text{EBIT} + \text{Depreciation} - \text{Taxes}^*$
$- \text{Change in NWC} - \text{Capital spending}$
$= \text{EBIT} + \text{Depreciation} - \text{EBIT} \times T_C$
$- \text{Change in NWC} - \text{Capital spending}$ **[12.9]**

10. $\text{CFA}^* = \text{EBIT} \times (1 - T_C) + \text{Depreciation} - \text{Change in NWC}$
$- \text{Capital spending}$ **[12.10]**

11. $V_0 = \dfrac{\text{CFA}_1^*}{1 + \text{WACC}} + \dfrac{\text{CFA}_2^*}{(1 + \text{WACC})^2} + \dfrac{\text{CFA}_3^*}{(1 + \text{WACC})^3} + \cdots$
$+ \dfrac{\text{CFA}_t^* + V_t}{(1 + \text{WACC})^t}$ **[12.11]**

12. $V_t = \dfrac{\text{CFA}_{t+1}^*}{\text{WACC} - g}$ **[12.12]**

CHAPTER 13

1. Modigliani-Miller Proposition II, no taxes:
$R_E = R_A + (R_A - R_D) \times (D/E)$ **[13.1]**

2. Modigliani-Miller propositions, with taxes:
   a. Present value of the interest tax shield:
   $= (T_C \times D \times R_D)/R_D$
   $= T_C \times D$ **[13.2]**

   b. Proposition I:
   $V_L = V_U + T_C \times D$ **[13.3]**

CHAPTER 16

1. Net working capital + Fixed assets
$= \text{Long-term debt} + \text{Equity}$ **[16.1]**

2. Net working capital = (Cash + Other current assets)
$- \text{Current liabilities}$ **[16.2]**

3. Cash = Long-term debt + Equity + Current liabilities
$- \text{Current assets other than cash} - \text{Fixed assets}$ **[16.3]**

4. The operating cycle:
Operating cycle = Inventory period
$+ \text{Accounts receivable period}$ **[16.4]**

5. The cash cycle:
Cash cycle = Operating cycle
$- \text{Accounts payable period}$ **[16.5]**

6. Total cash collections:
Cash collections = Beginning accounts receivable
$+ \frac{1}{2} \times \text{Sales}$ **[16.6]**

CHAPTER 17

1. The economic order quantity (EOQ) model:
Total carrying costs = Average inventory
$\times \text{Carrying costs per unit} = (Q/2) \times \text{CC}$ **[17.1]**

2. Total restocking cost = Fixed cost per order
$\times \text{Number of orders} = F \times (T/Q)$ **[17.2]**

3. Total costs = Carrying costs + Restocking costs
$= (Q/2) \times \text{CC} + F \times (T/Q)$ **[17.3]**

4. Carrying costs = Restocking costs
$(Q^*/2) \times \text{CC} = F \times (T/Q^*)$ **[17.4]**

5. $(Q^*)^2 = \dfrac{2T \times F}{\text{CC}}$ **[17.5]**

6. The optimal order size Q^*:
$Q^* = \sqrt{\dfrac{2T \times F}{\text{CC}}}$ **[17.6]**

CHAPTER 18

1. $[E(S_1) - S_0]/S_0 = h_{\text{FC}} - h_{\text{US}}$ **[18.1]**

2. $E(S_1) = S_0 \times [1 + (h_{\text{FC}} - h_{\text{US}})]$ **[18.2]**

3. Relative purchasing power parity (PPP):
$E(S_t) = S_0 \times [1 + (h_{\text{FC}} - h_{\text{US}})]^t$ **[18.3]**

4. Interest rate parity (IRP), exact, single period:
$F_1/S_0 = (1 + R_{\text{FC}})/(1 + R_{\text{US}})$ **[18.4]**

5. $(F_1 - S_0)/S_0 = R_{\text{FC}} - R_{\text{US}}$ **[18.5]**

6. $F_1 = S_0 \times [1 + (R_{\text{FC}} - R_{\text{US}})]$ **[18.6]**

7. IRP, approximate, multiperiod:
$F_t = S_0 \times [1 + (R_{\text{FC}} - R_{\text{US}})]^t$ **[18.7]**

Answers to Selected End-of-Chapter Problems

CHAPTER 2

1. Owners' equity = $5,690
   NWC = $380
3. $86,050
5. $42,170
7. $21,290.20
9. $105
11. −$146,500
13. Book value = $4,190,000
   Total NWC and market value = $5,550,000
15. $5,911
17. a. $1,200
    b. $0
19. $160,000
21. a. $8,399; $7,543
    b. −$427
    c. $3,468; $14,469
    d. −$28; $1,311

CHAPTER 3

1. Current ratio = 1.40 times
   Quick ratio = .94 time
3. Receivables turnover = 12.88 times
   Days' sales in receivables = 28.35 days
5. Debt-equity ratio = .75
   Equity multiplier = 1.75
7. 14.29%
9. 87.37 days
11. 6.21%
13. 11.63%
17. 18.73%
19. 7.77%
21. 15.53%
23. 10.92%
25. 5.53%
27. $529.76
29. Child profit margin = 4.00%
   Store profit margin = 2.00%
   Store ROE = 10.13%
31. 4.40 times
33. 6.61%

37. PE ratio = 26.40 times
   P/S ratio = 3.18 times
   DPS = $1.60
   Market-to-book = 7.92 times
39. 6.61%
41. 1.23 times
43. 10.98%; $7,466.35; 6.09%

CHAPTER 4

1. $2,110.50
3. $7,036.89; $20,560.31; $90,426.27; $29,645.07
5. 19.48; 4.87; 20.16; 12.22
7. 13.42 years; 26.84 years
9. 56.30 years
11. $1,519.27
13. 8.10%; $22,319,707.83
15. −13.17%
17. $60,532.72
19. $15,433.02
21. $63,176.81; $55,948.50
23. 175.63 months
25. $7,765.45; $82,532.61

CHAPTER 5

1. $2,344.76; $1,937.54; $1,700.16
3. $5,080.91; $5,281.28; $6,232.93
5. $3,545.65; $3,583.81; $16,975.33; $28,334.98
7. $2,282.94; $7,513.71; $7,112.97; $5,936.19
9. $289,647.54; $2,273,988.16
11. 3.88%
13. 14.76%; 8.37%; 8.99%; 13.89%
15. 13.02%
17. $6,008.23; $7,599.74; $12,159.18
19. APR = 145.20%
   EAR = 293.79%
21. 67.03 months
23. .69%; 8.25%; 8.57%
25. $1,598,270.55
27. $3,121.03
29. 5.01%

31. $1,010.81

33. $1.18; $1.39

35. PV: $136,244.11; $138,909.01

37. G: 13.75%
    H: 14.06%

39. 127.52

41. $38,443,284.41

43. APR = 5.04%
    EAR = 5.16%

45. 4.15%

47. $36,317.13

49. $17,234.85

51. $111,497.16

53. APR = 29.52%
    EAR = 33.86%

CHAPTER 6

3. $891.74

5. 6.50%

7. 4.78%

9. 2.80%; 2.75%

11. 2.75%

13. Previous asked = $1,206.015

17. $4,700.15

19. +2%: −8.15%; −21.86%
    −2%: 9.03%; 32.09%

21. 5.88%; 5.95%; 6.03%

23. $1,039.08

25. 8.74%; 8.29%

31. 6.31%

33. 6.12%

CHAPTER 7

1. $P_0 = $40.76
    $P_3 = $45.72
    $P_{15} = $72.36

3. Dividend yield = 6.14%
    Capital gains yield = 4.50%

5. 9.90%

7. $90.69

9. Straight voting = $9,975,038
    Cumulative voting = $3,990,038

11. $71.83

13. $66.24; $77.28

15. $118.49

17. $75.11

19. $136.78

21. 4.95%; 3.88%

23. 2.30%

25. $98.82; 5.61%

27. $90.27

CHAPTER 8

1. 2.68 years

3. 2.32 years; 3.12 years

5. 16.26%

7. $5,626.19; −$466.40; 22.19%

9. $7,220; $2,941.10; −$268.06; −$2,744.56

11. a. 14.58%; 13.94%
    b. 9.25%

13. 1.113; 1.032; .934

15. a. 3.34 years; 1.97 years
    b. $58,136.83; $14,228.22
    c. 20.54%; 27.38%
    d. 1.237; 1.268

17. a. 1.264; 1.180
    b. $12,579.51; $14,564.04

19. 0%; <0%

21. a. 2.13 years; 3.05 years
    b. $116,496.82; $168,215.71

23. Discounting approach = 14.52%
    Reinvestment approach = 10.98%
    Combination approach = 10.98%

25. 7.27%; $3,983.47; −$12,000; $20,896.98

CHAPTER 9

1. $38,410,000

3. $100,100

5. Year 7 allowance = $66,528.50

7. $1,394,459.20

9. $919,433

11. $31,981.29

13. $83,070.88

15. $82,288.43

17. NPV @ $135,000 cost savings = $100,160.15
    NPV @ $95,000 cost savings = −$19,628.71

21. Base-case NPV = $3,020,917.19
    Worst-case NPV = −$2,089,860.22

23. $37,447.31

CHAPTER 10

1. Total return = 15.11%
    Dividend yield = 2.47%
    Capital gains yield = 12.64%

3. $2,917.50

5. 12.10%; 8.83%

7. X: Average return = 7.6%
    X: Variance = .01463
    X: Standard deviation = 12.10%
    Y: Average return = 16.80%
    Y: Variance = .07032
    Y: Standard deviation = 26.52%

9. a. 10.80%
    b. .01797; 13.41%

11. .97%; 6.50%

13. 6.58%

15. 31.91%; 35.93%

17. −1.90% to 14.70%
    −10.20% to 23.00%

19. 18%; 15.72%

21. 10.09%; 9.71%

23. 2.92%

25. .422%; .00000035%

CHAPTER 11

1. A: .6775
   B: .3225

3. 13.05%

5. 10.80%

7. A: 10.55%; 4.25%
   B: 15.35%; 19.94%

9. **a.** 11.67%
   b. .01598

11. 1.08

13. 11.92%

15. 11.80%

17. **a.** 7.45%
    b. Weight of stock = .6087
    c. .801
    d. Weight of stock = 200%

19. Reward-to-risk ratios:
    Market = 7.00%
    Y: 7.42%
    Z: 6.88%

21. 9.25%; 9.95%

23. J: .4103
    E(R) = 11.69%

27. C = $173,035.71
    R_f = $76,964.29

CHAPTER 12

1. 10.61%

3. 11.13%; 11.11%

5. 4.59%; 3.63%

7. $200,000,000; $190,295,000; 3.99%

9. 8.67%

11. **a.** .2732; .7268
    b. .7375; .2625

13. **a.** 4.73%
    b. 10.90%

17. 8.09%

19. 12.16%

21. Cost < $49,263,502.45

23. **a.** 5.41%
    b. 12.31%

CHAPTER 13

1. **a.** $1.24; $1.91; $2.29
   b. $1.15; $1.95; $2.40

3. **a.** 4.39%; 6.75%; 8.10%
   b. 4.08%; 6.89%; 8.50%
   c. 3.47%; 5.33%; 6.40%
      3.22%; 5.44%; 6.71%

5. $28.40; $9,088,000; $9,088,000

7. $47.50; $47.50

9. **a.** $1,846.91
   b. $2,065.88
   c. Sell 85 shares

11. **a.** 10.90%
    b. 12.83%
    c. 17.65%
    d. 10.90%; 10.90%

13. $3,146,000

15. .64; .56

CHAPTER 14

1. $18,314

3. $79.86

5. **a.** New shares = 90,000; Par value = $.50
   b. New shares = 9,000; Par value = $5.00

7. $31.40; $30.25

11. Par value = $.50; Dividend per share last year = $1.22

13. **a.** $51.58
    b. $51.58

CHAPTER 15

1. $6,750; $625

3. 2,754,943 shares

5. 3,135,135 shares

CHAPTER 16

1. **a.** No change
   b. No change
   c. No change
   d. Decrease
   e. Decrease
   f. Decrease
   g. No change
   h. Decrease
   i. Increase
   j. Decrease
   k. Decrease
   l. No change
   m. Decrease
   n. Decrease
   o. Decrease

3. **a.** Increase
   b. Increase
   c. Decrease
   d. No change
   e. Decrease
   f. No change

5. **a.** $668; $660; $683; $793
   b. $565; $645; $690; $748
   c. $770; $675; $675; $837

7. 18.71%

9. $1,902.00; $2,199.75; $2,470.75; $2,506.50

11. $264,650; $434,150; $331,200

13. a. 6.78%
b. $500,617.69

15. Average payables = $29,138.36
Average receivables = $75,375.34

CHAPTER 17

1. $85,000; $63,400

3. $4,300; −$4,900; −$600

5. $5,740

7. $71,038.36

9. a. 17 days
b. $1,198,849.32

11. d. 20.13%; 44.59%; 13.01%; 44.32%

13. 2,641.27

CHAPTER 18

1. a. Z 367.01
b. $1.1733
c. $5,866,500

d. Singapore dollar
e. Mexican peso
f. Fr/€ = $.8596
g. Kuwait dinar; Venezuelan bolivar

3. a. ¥109.73; premium
b. A$1.3397; discount

5. a. ¥/£ = 165.41
b. arbitrage profit per $ = $.0157

7. Invest in U.S. = $30,216,518.81
Invest in Great Britain = $29,472,402.71

9. Current = $397,832.82
+10% = $770,757.11
−10% = −$57,963.54
Break-even = $1.2367; −8.84%

11. −4.82%

13. $8.05

15. a. Equity = $20,370.37
b. Equity = $18,965.52
c. Equity = $21,825.40

Using the HP-10B and TI BA II Plus Financial Calculators

D

This appendix is intended to help you use your Hewlett-Packard HP-10B or Texas Instruments BA II Plus financial calculator to solve problems encountered in the introductory finance course. It describes the various calculator settings and provides keystroke solutions for nine selected problems from this book. Please see your owner's manual for more complete instructions. For more examples and problem-solving techniques, please see *Financial Analysis with an Electronic Calculator*, 6th edition, by Mark A. White (New York: McGraw-Hill, 2007).

CALCULATOR SETTINGS

Most calculator errors in the introductory finance course are the result of inappropriate settings. Before beginning a calculation, you should ask yourself the following questions:

1. Did I clear the financial registers?
2. Is the compounding frequency set to once per period?
3. Is the calculator in END mode?
4. Did I enter negative numbers using the **+/−** key?

Clearing the Registers

All calculators have areas of memory, called registers, where variables and intermediate results are stored. There are two sets of financial registers, the time value of money (TVM) registers and the cash flow (CF) registers. These must be cleared before beginning a new calculation. On the Hewlett-Packard HP-10B, pressing ▇ {CLEAR ALL} clears both the TVM and the CF registers.[1] To clear the TVM registers on the BA II Plus, press **2nd** {CLR TVM}. Press **2nd** {CLR Work} from within the cash flow worksheet to clear the CF registers.

Compounding Frequency

Both the HP-10B and the BA II Plus are hardwired to assume monthly compounding, that is, compounding 12 times per period. Because very few problems in the introductory finance course make this assumption, you should change this default setting to once per period. On the HP-10B, press 1 ▇ {P/YR}. To verify that the default has been changed, press the ▇ key, then press and briefly hold the **INPUT** key.[2] The display should read "1P_Yr".

On the BA II Plus, you can specify both payment frequency and compounding frequency, although they should normally be set to the same number. To set both to once per period, press the key sequence **2nd** {P/Y} 1 **ENTER**, then press ↓ 1 **ENTER**. Pressing **2nd** {QUIT} returns you to standard calculator mode.

---

1 The ▇ key is colored orange and serves as a Shift key for the functions in curly brackets.

2 This is the same keystroke used to clear all registers; pretty handy, eh?

END Mode and Annuities Due

In most problems, payment is made at the end of a period, and this is the default setting (end mode) for both the HP-10B and the BA II Plus. *Annuities due* assume payments are made at the *beginning* of each period (begin mode). On the HP-10B, pressing ▇ {BEG/END} toggles between begin and end mode. Press the key sequence **2nd** {BGN} **2nd** {SET} **2nd** {QUIT} to accomplish the same task on the BA II Plus. Both calculators will indicate on the display that your calculator is set for begin mode.

Sign Changes

Sign changes are used to identify the direction of cash inflows and outflows. Generally, cash inflows are entered as positive numbers and cash outflows are entered as negative numbers. To enter a negative number on either the HP-10B or the BA II Plus, first press the appropriate digit keys and then press the change sign key, **+/−**. Do *not* use the minus sign key, **−**, as its effects are quite unpredictable.

SAMPLE PROBLEMS

This section provides keystroke solutions for selected problems from the text illustrating the nine basic financial calculator skills.

1. Future Value or Present Value of a Single Sum

Compute the future value of $2,250 at a 17 percent annual rate for 30 years.

HP-10B	BA II PLUS
−2,250.00 **PV**	−2,250.00 **PV**
30.00 **N**	30.00 **N**
17.00 **I/YR**	17.00 **I/Y**
FV 249,895.46	**CPT** **FV** 249,895.46

The future value is $249,895.46.

2. Present Value or Future Value of an Ordinary Annuity

Betty's Bank offers you a $20,000, seven-year term loan at 11 percent annual interest. What will your annual loan payment be?

HP-10B	BA II PLUS
−20,000.00 **PV**	−20,000.00 **PV**
7.00 **N**	7.00 **N**
11.00 **I/YR**	11.00 **I/Y**
PMT 4,244.31	**CPT** **PMT** 4,244.31

Your annual loan payment will be $4,244.31.

3. Finding an Unknown Interest Rate

Assume that the total cost of a college education will be $75,000 when your child enters college in 18 years. You presently have $7,000 to invest. What rate of interest must you earn on your investment to cover the cost of your child's college education?

HP-10B	BA II PLUS
−7,000.00 **PV**	−7,000.00 **PV**
18.00 **N**	18.00 **N**
75,000.00 **FV**	75,000.00 **FV**
I/YR 14.08	**CPT** **I/Y** 14.08

You must earn an annual interest rate of at least 14.08 percent to cover the expected future cost of your child's education.

4. Finding an Unknown Number of Periods

One of your customers is delinquent on his accounts payable balance. You've mutually agreed to a repayment schedule of $374 per month. You will charge 1.4 percent per month interest on the overdue balance. If the current balance is $12,000, how long will it take for the account to be paid off?

HP-10B	BA II PLUS
−12,000.00 **PV**	−12,000.00 **PV**
1.40 **I/YR**	1.40 **I/Y**
374.00 **PMT**	374.00 **PMT**
N 42.90	**CPT** **N** 42.90

The loan will be paid off in 42.90 months.

5. Simple Bond Pricing

Mullineaux Co. issued 11-year bonds one year ago at a coupon rate of 8.25 percent. The bonds make semiannual payments. If the YTM on these bonds is 7.10 percent, what is the current bond price?

HP-10B	BA II PLUS
41.25 **PMT**	41.25 **PMT**
1,000.00 **FV**	1,000.00 **FV**
20.00 **N**	20.00 **N**
3.55 **I/YR**	3.55 **I/Y**
PV −1,081.35	**CPT** **PV** −1,081.35

Because the bonds make semiannual payments, we must halve the coupon payment (8.25 ÷ 2 = 4.125 ==> $41.25), halve the YTM (7.10 ÷ 2 ==> 3.55), and double the number of periods (10 years remaining × 2 = 20 periods). Then, the current bond price is $1,081.35.

6. Simple Bond Yields to Maturity

Vasicek Co. has 12.5 percent coupon bonds on the market with eight years left to maturity. The bonds make annual payments.

If one of these bonds currently sells for $1,145.68, what is its YTM?

HP-10B	BA II PLUS
−1,145.68 **PV**	−1,145.68 **PV**
125.00 **PMT**	125.00 **PMT**
1,000.00 **FV**	1,000.00 **FV**
8.00 **N**	8.00 **N**
I/YR 9.79	**CPT** **I/Y** 9.79

The bond has a yield to maturity of 9.79 percent.

7. Cash Flow Analysis

What are the IRR and NPV of the following set of cash flows? Assume a discount rate of 10 percent.

Year	Cash Flow
0	−$1,300
1	400
2	300
3	1,200

HP-10B	BA II PLUS
−1,300.00 **CFj**	**CF**
400.00 **CFj**	**2ND** {CLR Work}
1.00 {Nj}	−1,300.00 **ENTER** ↓
300.00 **CFj**	400.00 **ENTER** ↓
1.00 {Nj}	1.00 **ENTER** ↓
1,200.00 **CFj**	300.00 **ENTER** ↓
1.00 {Nj}	1.00 **ENTER** ↓
{IRR/YR} 17.40	1,200.00 **ENTER** ↓
10.00 **I/YR**	1.00 **ENTER** ↓
{NPV} 213.15	**IRR** **CPT** 17.40
	NPV
	10.00 **ENTER**
	↓ **CPT** 213.15

The project has an IRR of 17.40 percent and an NPV of $213.15.

8. Loan Amortization

Prepare an amortization schedule for a three-year loan of $24,000. The interest rate is 16 percent per year, and the loan calls for equal annual payments. How much interest is paid in the third year? How much total interest is paid over the life of the loan?

To prepare a complete amortization schedule, you must amortize each payment one at a time:

HP-10B	BA II PLUS
−24,000.00 **PV**	−24,000.00 **PV**
16.00 **I/YR**	16.00 **I/Y**
3.00 **N**	3.00 **N**
PMT 10,686.19	**CPT** **PMT** 10,686.19
1.00 **INPUT** {AMORT} = 3,840.00 <== Interest	**2ND** {AMORT} **2ND** {CLR Work}
= 6,846.19 <== Principal	
= −17,153.81 <== Balance	1.00 **ENTER** ↓
2.00 **INPUT** {AMORT} = 2,744.61 <== Interest	1.00 **ENTER** ↓ −17,153.81 <== Balance
= 7,941.58 <== Principal	↓ 6,846.19 <== Principal
= −9,212.23 <== Balance	↓ 3,840.00 <== Interest
3.00 **INPUT** {AMORT} = 1,473.96 <== Interest	↓
= 9,212.23 <== Principal	2.00 **ENTER** ↓
= 0.00 <== Balance	2.00 **ENTER** ↓ −9,212.23 <== Balance
	↓ 7,941.58 <== Principal
	↓ 2,744.61 <== Interest
	↓
	3.00 **ENTER** ↓
	3.00 **ENTER** ↓ 0.00 <== Balance
	↓ 9,212.23 <== Principal
	↓ 1,473.96 <== Interest
	↓

Interest of $1,473.96 is paid in the third year.

Enter both a beginning and an ending period to compute the total amount of interest or principal paid over a particular period of time.

HP-10B	BA II PLUS
−24,000.00 **PV**	−24,000.00 **PV**
16.00 **I/YR**	16.00 **I/Y**
3.00 **N**	3.00 **N**
PMT 10,686.19	**CPT** **PMT** 10,686.19
1.00 **INPUT**	**2ND** {AMORT} **2ND** {CLR Work}
3.00 {AMORT} = 8,058.57 <== Interest	1.00 **ENTER** ↓
= 24,000.00 <== Principal	
= 0.00 <== Balance	3.00 **ENTER** ↓ 0.00 <== Balance
	↓ 24,000.00 <== Principal
	↓ 8,058.57 <== Interest

Total interest of $8,058.57 is paid over the life of the loan.

9. Interest Rate Conversions

Find the effective annual rate, EAR, corresponding to a 7 percent annual percentage rate, APR, compounded quarterly.

HP-10B	BA II PLUS
4.00 {P/YR}	**2ND** {IConv}
7.00 {NOM%}	7.00 **ENTER**
{EFF%} 7.19	↓ ↓
	4.00 **ENTER**
	↑ **CPT** 7.19

The effective annual rate equals 7.19 percent.

Glossary

absolute priority rule (APR) The rule establishing priority of claims in liquidation.

Accelerated Cost Recovery System (ACRS) Depreciation method under U.S. tax law allowing for the accelerated write-off of property under various classifications.

accounts payable period The time between receipt of inventory and payment for it.

accounts receivable financing A secured short-term loan that involves either the assignment or factoring of receivables.

accounts receivable period The time between sale of inventory and collection of the receivable.

agency problem The possibility of conflict of interest between the owners and management of a firm.

aging schedule A compilation of accounts receivable by the age of each account.

alpha The excess return an asset earns based on the level of risk taken.

American Depositary Receipt (ADR) A security issued in the United States representing shares of a foreign stock and allowing that stock to be traded in the United States.

annual percentage rate (APR) The interest rate charged per period multiplied by the number of periods per year.

annuity A level stream of cash flows for a fixed period of time.

annuity due An annuity for which the cash flows occur at the beginning of the period.

arithmetic average return The return earned in an average year over a particular period.

asked price The price a dealer is willing to take for a security.

average accounting return (AAR) An investment's average net income divided by its average book value.

average tax rate Total taxes paid divided by total taxable income.

balance sheet Financial statement showing a firm's accounting value on a particular date.

bankruptcy A legal proceeding for liquidating or reorganizing a business. Also, the transfer of some or all of a firm's assets to its creditors.

bearer form A bond issued without record of the owner's name; payment is made to whomever holds the bond.

best efforts underwriting The underwriter sells as much of the issue as possible but can return any unsold shares to the issuer without financial responsibility.

beta coefficient Amount of systematic risk present in a particular risky asset relative to that in an average risky asset.

bid price The price a dealer is willing to pay for a security.

bid-ask spread The difference between the bid price and the asked price.

broker An agent who arranges security transactions among investors.

business risk The equity risk that comes from the nature of the firm's operating activities.

call premium The amount by which the call price exceeds the par value of the bond.

call protected bond Bond during period in which it cannot be redeemed by the issuer.

call provision Agreement giving the issuer the option to repurchase a bond at a specific price prior to maturity.

capital asset pricing model (CAPM) Equation of the security market line showing the relationship between expected return and beta.

capital budgeting The process of planning and managing a firm's long-term investments.

capital gains yield The dividend growth rate, or the rate at which the value of an investment grows.

capital rationing The situation that exists if a firm has positive net present value projects but cannot obtain the necessary financing.

capital structure The mixture of debt and equity maintained by a firm.

captive finance company A partially or wholly owned subsidiary that handles the credit function for the parent company.

carrying costs   Costs that rise with increases in the level of investment in current assets.

cash budget   A forecast of cash receipts and disbursements for the next planning period.

cash concentration   The practice of and procedures for moving cash from multiple banks into the firm's main accounts.

cash cycle   The time between cash disbursement and cash collection.

cash discount   A discount given to induce prompt payment. Also *sales discount*.

cash flow from assets   The total of cash flow to creditors and cash flow to stockholders, consisting of the following: operating cash flow, capital spending, and change in net working capital.

cash flow time line   Graphical representation of the operating cycle and the cash cycle.

cash flow to creditors   A firm's interest payments to creditors less net new borrowing.

cash flow to stockholders   Dividends paid out by a firm less net new equity raised.

clean price   The price of a bond net of accrued interest; this is the price that is typically quoted.

clientele effect   Argument that stocks attract particular groups based on dividend yield and the resulting tax effects.

collection policy   Procedures followed by a firm in collecting accounts receivable.

common stock   Equity without priority for dividends or in bankruptcy.

common-size statement   A standardized financial statement presenting all items in percentage terms. Balance sheet items are shown as a percentage of assets and income statement items as a percentage of sales.

compound interest   Interest earned on both the initial principal and the interest reinvested from prior periods.

compounding   The process of accumulating interest in an investment over time to earn more interest.

consol   A type of perpetuity.

contingency planning   Taking into account the managerial options implicit in a project.

controlled disbursement account   A disbursement practice under which the firm transfers an amount to a disbursing account that is sufficient to cover demands for payment.

corporation   A business created as a distinct legal entity owned by one or more individuals or entities.

cost of capital   The minimum required return on a new investment.

cost of debt   The return that lenders require on the firm's debt.

cost of equity   The return that equity investors require on their investment in the firm.

coupon   The stated interest payment made on a bond.

coupon rate   The annual coupon divided by the face value of a bond.

credit analysis   The process of determining the probability that customers will or will not pay.

credit cost curve   Graphical representation of the sum of the carrying costs and the opportunity costs of a credit policy.

credit instrument   The evidence of indebtedness.

credit period   The length of time for which credit is granted.

credit scoring   The process of quantifying the probability of default when granting consumer credit.

cross-rate   The implicit exchange rate between two currencies (usually non-U.S.) quoted in some third currency (usually the U.S. dollar).

cumulative voting   A procedure in which a shareholder may cast all votes for one member of the board of directors.

current yield   A bond's coupon payment divided by its closing price.

date of payment   Date that the dividend checks are mailed.

date of record   Date by which holders must be on record to receive a dividend.

dealer   An agent who buys and sells securities from inventory.

debenture   Unsecured debt, usually with a maturity of 10 years or more.

declaration date   Date on which the board of directors passes a resolution to pay a dividend.

default risk premium   The portion of a nominal interest rate or bond yield that represents compensation for the possibility of default.

deferred call provision Bond call provision prohibiting the company from redeeming the bond prior to a certain date.

depreciation tax shield The tax saving that results from the depreciation deduction, calculated as depreciation multiplied by the corporate tax rate.

designated market makers (DMMs) NYSE members who act as dealers in particular stocks. Formerly known as "specialists."

direct bankruptcy costs The costs that are directly associated with bankruptcy, such as legal and administrative expenses.

direct listing A security offering in which the company offers securities directly to investors, bypassing underwriters.

dirty price The price of a bond including accrued interest, also known as the *full* or *invoice price*. This is the price the buyer actually pays.

discount Calculation of the present value of some future amount.

discount rate The rate used to calculate the present value of future cash flows.

discounted cash flow (DCF) valuation (a) Calculating the present value of a future cash flow to determine its value today. (b) The process of valuing an investment by discounting its future cash flows.

distribution Payment made by a firm to its owners from sources other than current or accumulated retained earnings.

dividend Payment made out of a firm's earnings to its owners, in the form of either cash or stock.

dividend Payments by a corporation to shareholders, made in either cash or stock.

dividend growth model A model that determines the current price of a stock as its dividend next period divided by the discount rate less the dividend growth rate.

dividend yield A stock's expected cash dividend divided by its current price.

DMM's post A fixed place on the exchange floor where the DMM operates.

DuPont identity Popular expression breaking ROE into three parts: operating efficiency, asset use efficiency, and financial leverage.

Dutch auction underwriting The type of underwriting in which the offer price is set based on competitive bidding by investors. Also known as a *uniform price auction*.

economic order quantity (EOQ) The restocking quantity that minimizes the total inventory costs.

effective annual rate (EAR) The interest rate expressed as if it were compounded once per year.

efficient capital market Market in which security prices reflect available information.

efficient markets hypothesis (EMH) The hypothesis that actual capital markets, such as the New York Stock Exchange, are efficient.

electronic communications networks (ECNs) Websites that allow investors to trade directly with one another.

erosion The cash flows of a new project that come at the expense of a firm's existing projects.

Eurobonds International bonds issued in multiple countries but denominated in a single currency (usually the issuer's currency).

Eurocurrency Money deposited in a financial center outside the country whose currency is involved.

exchange rate The price of one country's currency expressed in terms of another country's currency.

exchange rate risk The risk related to having international operations in a world where relative currency values vary.

ex-dividend date Date two business days before the date of record, establishing those individuals entitled to a dividend.

expected return Return on a risky asset expected in the future.

face value The principal amount of a bond that is repaid at the end of the term. Also *par value*.

financial distress costs The direct and indirect costs associated with going bankrupt or experiencing financial distress.

financial ratios Relationships determined from a firm's financial information and used for comparison purposes.

financial risk The equity risk that comes from the financial policy (i.e., capital structure) of the firm.

firm commitment underwriting The underwriter buys the entire issue, assuming full financial responsibility for any unsold shares.

Fisher effect The relationship among nominal returns, real returns, and inflation.

five Cs of credit The five basic credit factors to be evaluated: character, capacity, capital, collateral, and conditions.

float The difference between book cash and bank cash, representing the net effect of checks in the process of clearing.

floor brokers NYSE members who execute customer buy and sell orders.

forecasting risk The possibility that errors in projected cash flows will lead to incorrect decisions. Also *estimation risk*.

foreign bonds International bonds issued in a single country, usually denominated in that country's currency.

foreign exchange market The market in which one country's currency is traded for another's.

forward exchange rate The agreed-upon exchange rate to be used in a forward trade.

forward trade Agreement to exchange currency at some time in the future.

free cash flow Another name for cash flow from assets.

future value (FV) The amount an investment is worth after one or more periods. Also *compound value*.

general cash offer An issue of securities offered for sale to the general public on a cash basis.

Generally Accepted Accounting Principles (GAAP) The common set of standards and procedures by which audited financial statements are prepared.

geometric average return The average compound return earned per year over a multiyear period.

gilts British and Irish government securities.

Green Shoe provision A contract provision giving the underwriter the option to purchase additional shares from the issuer at the offering price. Also *overallotment option*.

hard rationing The situation that occurs when a business cannot raise financing for a project under any circumstances.

homemade leverage The use of personal borrowing to change the overall amount of financial leverage to which an individual is exposed.

income statement Financial statement summarizing a firm's performance over a period of time.

incremental cash flows The difference between a firm's future cash flows with a project and those without the project.

indenture The written agreement between the corporation and the lender detailing the terms of the debt issue.

indirect bankruptcy costs The costs of avoiding a bankruptcy filing incurred by a financially distressed firm.

inflation premium The portion of a nominal interest rate that represents compensation for expected future inflation.

initial public offering (IPO) A company's first equity issue made available to the public. Also *unseasoned new issue*.

inside quotes The highest bid quotes and the lowest ask quotes for a security.

interest on interest Interest earned on the reinvestment of previous interest payments.

interest rate parity (IRP) The condition stating that the interest rate differential between two countries is equal to the percentage difference between the forward exchange rate and the spot exchange rate.

interest rate risk premium The compensation investors demand for bearing interest rate risk.

interest tax shield The tax saving attained by a firm from the tax deductibility of interest expense.

internal growth rate The maximum possible growth rate a firm can achieve without external financing of any kind.

internal rate of return (IRR) The discount rate that makes the net present value of an investment zero.

inventory loan A secured short-term loan to purchase inventory.

inventory period The time it takes to acquire and sell inventory.

invoice Bill for goods or services provided by the seller to the purchaser.

just-in-time (JIT) inventory A system for managing demand-dependent inventories that minimizes inventory holdings.

line of credit A formal (committed) or informal (noncommitted) prearranged, short-term bank loan.

liquidation Termination of the firm as a going concern.

liquidity premium The portion of a nominal interest rate or bond yield that represents compensation for lack of liquidity.

lockboxes Special post office boxes set up to intercept and speed up accounts receivable collections.

lockup agreement The part of the underwriting contract that specifies how long insiders must wait after an IPO before they can sell stock.

London Interbank Offered Rate (LIBOR) The rate most international banks charge one another for overnight Eurodollar loans.

M&M Proposition I   The value of a firm is independent of its capital structure.

M&M Proposition II   A firm's cost of equity capital is a positive linear function of its capital structure.

managerial options   Opportunities that managers can exploit if certain things happen in the future. Also known as "real" options.

marginal tax rate   Amount of tax payable on the next dollar earned.

market risk premium   Slope of the security market line; the difference between the expected return on a market portfolio and the risk-free rate.

materials requirements planning (MRP)   A set of procedures used to determine inventory levels for demand-dependent inventory types, such as work-in-progress and raw materials.

maturity   Specified date on which the principal amount of a bond is paid.

member   As of 2006, a member is the owner of a trading license on the NYSE.

multiple rates of return   The possibility that more than one discount rate will make the net present value of an investment zero.

mutually exclusive investment decisions   A situation where taking one investment prevents the taking of another.

net present value (NPV)   The difference between an investment's market value and its cost.

net present value profile   A graphical representation of the relationship between an investment's net present value and various discount rates.

net working capital   Current assets less current liabilities.

nominal rates   Interest rates or rates of return that have not been adjusted for inflation.

noncash items   Expenses charged against revenues that do not directly affect cash flow, such as depreciation.

normal distribution   A symmetric, bell-shaped frequency distribution that is completely defined by its average and standard deviation.

note   Unsecured debt, usually with a maturity of under 10 years.

operating cash flow   Cash generated from a firm's normal business activities.

operating cycle   The time period between the acquisition of inventory and the collection of cash from receivables.

opportunity cost   The most valuable alternative that is given up if a particular investment is undertaken.

order flow   The flow of customer orders to buy and sell securities.

par value   The principal amount of a bond that is repaid at the end of the term. Also *face value*.

partnership   A business formed by two or more individuals or entities.

payback period   The amount of time required for an investment to generate cash flows sufficient to recover its initial cost.

perpetuity   An annuity in which the cash flows continue forever.

political risk   Risk related to changes in value that arise because of political actions.

portfolio   Group of assets such as stocks and bonds held by an investor.

portfolio weight   Percentage of a portfolio's total value in a particular asset.

precautionary motive   The need to hold cash as a safety margin to act as a financial reserve.

preferred stock   Stock with dividend priority over common stock, normally with a fixed dividend rate, sometimes without voting rights.

present value (PV)   The current value of future cash flows discounted at the appropriate discount rate.

primary market   The market in which new securities are originally sold to investors.

principle of diversification   Spreading an investment across a number of assets will eliminate some, but not all, of the risk.

private placements   Loans, usually long-term in nature, provided directly by a limited number of investors.

pro forma financial statements   Financial statements projecting future years' operations.

profitability index (PI)   The present value of an investment's future cash flows divided by its initial cost. Also *benefit-cost ratio*.

prospectus   A legal document describing details of the issuing corporation and the proposed offering to potential investors.

protective covenant   A part of the indenture limiting certain actions that might be taken during the term of the loan, usually to protect the lender's interest.

proxy   A grant of authority by a shareholder allowing another individual to vote his or her shares.

purchasing power parity (PPP) The idea that the exchange rate adjusts to keep purchasing power constant among currencies.

pure play approach Use of a weighted average cost of capital that is unique to a particular project, based on companies in similar lines of business.

quoted interest rate The interest rate expressed in terms of the interest payment made each period. Also *stated interest rate.*

real rates Interest rates or rates of return that have been adjusted for inflation.

red herring A preliminary prospectus distributed to prospective investors in a new issue of securities.

registered form The registrar of a company records who owns each bond, and bond payments are made directly to the owner of record.

registration statement A statement filed with the SEC that discloses all material information concerning the corporation making a public offering.

regular cash dividend Cash payment made by a firm to its owners in the normal course of business, usually quarterly.

reorganization Financial restructuring of a failing firm to attempt to continue operations as a going concern.

repurchase Refers to a firm's purchase of its own stock; an alternative to a cash dividend. Also called *stock repurchase.*

reverse split Stock split under which a firm's number of shares outstanding is reduced.

rights offer A public issue of securities in which securities are first offered to existing shareholders. Also known as *rights offering.*

risk premium The excess return required from an investment in a risky asset over that required from a risk-free investment.

scenario analysis The determination of what happens to net present value estimates when we ask what-if questions.

seasoned equity offering (SEO) A new equity issue of securities by a company that has previously issued securities to the public.

secondary market The market in which previously issued securities are traded among investors.

security market line (SML) Positively sloped straight line displaying the relationship between expected return and beta.

sensitivity analysis Investigation of what happens to net present value when only one variable is changed.

shelf registration Registration permitted by SEC Rule 415, which allows a company to register all issues it expects to sell within two years at one time, with subsequent sales at any time within those two years.

shortage costs Costs that fall with increases in the level of investment in current assets.

simple interest Interest earned only on the original principal amount invested.

sinking fund An account managed by the bond trustee for early bond redemption.

soft rationing The situation that occurs when units in a business are allocated a certain amount of financing for capital budgeting.

sole proprietorship A business owned by a single individual.

speculative motive The need to hold cash to take advantage of additional investment opportunities, such as bargain purchases.

spot exchange rate The exchange rate on a spot trade.

spot trade An agreement to trade currencies based on the exchange rate today for settlement within two business days.

spread Compensation to the underwriter, determined by the difference between the underwriter's buying price and offering price.

stakeholder Someone other than a stockholder or creditor who potentially has a claim on the cash flows of the firm.

stand-alone principle The assumption that evaluation of a project may be based on the project's incremental cash flows.

standard deviation The positive square root of the variance.

Standard Industrial Classification (SIC) code U.S. government code used to classify a firm by its type of business operations.

stated interest rate The interest rate expressed in terms of the interest payment made each period. Also *quoted interest rate.*

static theory of capital structure Theory that a firm borrows up to the point where the tax benefit from an extra dollar in debt is exactly equal to the cost that comes from the increased probability of financial distress.

stock dividend Payment made by a firm to its owners in the form of stock, diluting the value of each share outstanding.

stock split An increase in a firm's shares outstanding without any change in owners' equity.

straight voting A procedure in which a shareholder may cast all votes for each member of the board of directors.

strategic options Options for future, related business products or strategies.

sunk cost A cost that has already been incurred and cannot be recouped and therefore should not be considered in an investment decision.

supplemental liquidity providers (SLPs) Investment firms that are active participants in stocks assigned to them. Their job is to make a one-sided market (i.e., offering to either buy or sell). They trade purely for their own accounts.

sustainable growth rate The maximum possible growth rate a firm can achieve without external equity financing while maintaining a constant debt-equity ratio.

swaps Agreements to exchange two securities or currencies.

syndicate A group of underwriters formed to share the risk and to help sell an issue.

systematic risk A risk that influences a large number of assets. Also *market risk*.

systematic risk principle The expected return on a risky asset depends only on that asset's systematic risk.

taxability premium The portion of a nominal interest rate or bond yield that represents compensation for unfavorable tax status.

term loans Direct business loans of, typically, one to five years.

term structure of interest rates The relationship between nominal interest rates on default-free, pure discount securities and time to maturity; that is, the pure time value of money.

terms of sale Conditions under which a firm sells its goods and services for cash or credit.

tombstone An advertisement announcing a public offering.

trading range Price range between highest and lowest prices at which a stock is typically traded.

transaction motive The need to hold cash to satisfy normal disbursement and collection activities associated with a firm's ongoing operations.

Treasury yield curve A plot of the yields on Treasury notes and bonds relative to maturity.

underwriters Investment firms that act as intermediaries between a company selling securities and the investing public.

unsystematic risk A risk that affects at most a small number of assets. Also *unique* or *asset-specific risk*.

variance The average squared difference between the actual return and the average return.

venture capital (VC) Financing for new, often high-risk, ventures.

weighted average cost of capital (WACC) The WACC is the overall return the firm must earn on its existing assets to maintain the value of its stock.

working capital A firm's short-term assets and liabilities.

yield to maturity (YTM) The rate required in the market on a bond.

zero coupon bond A bond that makes no coupon payments, and thus is initially priced at a deep discount.

zero-balance account A disbursement account in which the firm maintains a zero balance, transferring funds in from a master account only as needed to cover checks presented for payment.

Name Index

Subject Index